PETER LOMBARD

BRILL'S STUDIES IN INTELLECTUAL HISTORY

Ms. 286, Bibliothèque Municipale, Troyes. Incipit of *Sentences* of Peter Lombard (1159), Fol. 1ʳ. Reproduced courtesy of the Bibliothèque Municipale, Troyes.

PETER LOMBARD

BY

MARCIA L. COLISH

VOLUME ONE

E.J. BRILL
LEIDEN · NEW YORK · KÖLN
1994

The paper in this book meets the guidelines for permanence and durability of the Committee on Production Guidelines for Book Longevity of the Council on Library Resources.

Library of Congress Cataloging-in-Publication Data

Colish, Marcia L.
  Peter Lombard / by Marcia L. Colish.
    p.   cm. — (Brill's studies in intellectual history, ISSN 0920-8607 ; v. 41)
  Includes bibliographical references and indexes.
  ISBN 9004098615 (set : alk. paper). — ISBN 9004098593 (v. 1 : alk. paper). — ISBN 9004098607 (v. 2 : alk. paper)
  1. Peter Lombard, Bishop of Paris, ca. 1100-1160.   2. Theology, Doctrinal—History—Middle Ages, 600-1500.   I. Title.   II. Series.
BX1749.P4C64   1993
230'.2'092—dc20   93-8757
                                                                          CIP

Die Deutsche Bibliothek - CIP-Einheitsaufnahme

Colish, Marcia L.:
Peter Lombard / by Marcia L. Colish. – Leiden ; New York ; Köln : Brill.
  (Brill's studies in intellectual history ; Vol. 41)
  ISBN 90–04–09861–5
NE: GT
Vol. 1 (1993)
  ISBN 90–04–09859 3

ISSN   0920-8607
ISBN   90 04 09859 3 (Vol. 1)
ISBN   90 04 09861 5 (Set)

CONTENTS

VOLUME ONE

Author's Note ix
List of Abbreviations xi

Preface 1

1. Peter Lombard's Life and Works 15
   Biography 15
   Works 23
   Reputation 30

2. The Theological Enterprise 33
   Systematic Theology in the Twelfth Century 34
   Monastic Parallels and Contrasts 35
   The Scholastic Sentence Collection as a Genre of
      Theological Literature 42
   The Criticism and Evaluation of Authorities 44
   Peter Abelard and His Followers 47
   Gilbert of Poitiers and His Followers 52
   Hugh of St. Victor and the *Summa sententiarum* 57
   Roland of Bologna, Robert Pullen, Robert of Melun 65
   The Lombard 77

3. The Problem of Theological Language 91
   The Abelardian Challenge 96
   The Lombardian Response 119
   The Porretan Challenge 131
   The Lombardian Response 148

4. *Sacra pagina* 155
   Psalms Exegesis: The Monastic Approach 158
   Pre-Lombardian Scholastic Psalms Exegesis 162
   Peter Lombard on the Psalms 170
   Pauline Exegesis: The Monastic Approach 189
   Pauline Exegesis among the Lombard's
      Scholastic Predecessors and Contemporaries
      and the Lombard's *Collectanea* 192

5. The Doctrine of God 227
      Man's Knowledge of God: Proofs of God's
      Existence, Analogies of the Trinity 229
      Hugh of St. Victor, Robert Pullen, Robert of Melun 230
      The Lombard 238
      Nature and Person in the Trinity 245
        The Critique of Abelard 254
      The Divine Nature in Relation to the Creation 263
        God's Ubiquity 264
        God's Foreknowledge, Providence, and
          Predestination, and Free Will and Contingency 268
        Can God Do Better or Different Than He Does? 290

6. The Creation, Angels, Man, and the Fall 303
      The Doctrine of Creation 303
        The Chartrain Challenge 305
        The Response of the Scholastic Theologians 319
        The Lombard on Creation 336
      Angels among the Lombard's Scholastic
      Predecessors and Contemporaries 342
      The Lombard on Angels 347
      Human Nature before the Fall: The Contemporary
      Debates 353
      The Lombard on Prelapsarian Human Nature 366
      The Fall: The Contemporary Debates 372
      The Lombard on the Fall 377
      The Effects of Original Sin: The Contemporary
      Debates 381
      The Lombard's Position 383
      The Transmission of Original Sin: The
      Contemporary Debates 385
      The Lombard on the Transmission of Original Sin 393

7. Christ, His Nature, and His Saving Work 398
      The Hypostatic Union: Ancient and Current
      Understandings 399
      The Lombard on the Hypostatic Union 417
      The Debates over the Lombard's Christology 427
      Christ's Human Knowledge: Ancient and Current
      Debates 438
      The Lombard on Christ's Human Knowledge 442
      Other Attributes of Christ's Humanity 443

The Atonement: The Contemporary Debates 448
The Lombard's Doctrine of the Atonement 459

VOLUME TWO

8. Ethics, Sacraments, and Last Things 471
    Ethics 471
      Intentionalism in Ethics: The Consensus
        and the Disagreements Within It 473
      The Lombard as an Intentionalist 480
      Vice and Sin 484
      Virtue: Free Will and Grace in Its Attainment 488
      The Theological Virtues 493
      The Cardinal Virtues 504
      The Gifts of the Holy Spirit 507
      The Moral Law of the Old Testament 510
      Conclusion 514
    The Sacraments 516
      The Idea of Sacrament in General 517
      Baptism 532
      Confirmation 548
      The Eucharist 551
      Penance 583
      Unction 609
      Holy Orders 614
      Marriage 628
    Last Things 698
      The Non-Scholastic Challenge 700
      The Scholastic Response 704
      Peter Lombard on Last Things 710

Conclusion 718

Bibliography 779

Index of Names 819

Index of Subjects 859

AUTHOR'S NOTE

I include this author's note in order to clarify some technical stylistic decisions made in this book which entail apparent inconsistencies, inconsistencies which medievalists have long since come to live with, if not to love, but which may trouble readers coming to this book from another part of the landscape.

First, there was no agreement on Latin spelling in the Middle Ages, a fact reflected in the policies of editors of medieval texts and the houses that publish them. Some editors and publishers systematically classicize the spelling of medieval Latin, however the language may be used in the manuscripts on which the texts depend. For example, they substitute "i" for "j" or "u" for "v" on this basis. On the other hand, some editors and publishers retain the spellings found in the manuscripts. I have followed the practice, when quoting from editions of medieval Latin texts, of preserving whichever decision regarding the spelling is followed by the edition in question.

Another discrepancy concerns the Anglicization, or not, of the Latin names of medieval personages, and the titles of well known works. There are names, such as John of Salisbury, Gilbert of Poitiers, and Peter Lombard, whose English form is in common use among Anglophone readers. It would be an affectation to refer to these people in Latin or in another language. On the other hand, there are figures, such as Ordericus Vitalis and Jacques de Vitry, for whom this is not the case. My practice has been to use whichever version of the name has the greatest immediate recognition value, regardless of the lack of symmetry that any result. Similarly, while the titles of works written in Latin will usually be cited in that language in the text, others, such as Abelard's *Ethics* and Augustine's *City of God* or *Eighty-Three Diverse Questions*, will be given in English as more familiar or as less cumbersome than their Latin originals.

I will have occasion to cite repeatedly in this book the works of scholastic theologians and canonists, not only by the page or column number in the texts in which their works are printed, but according to the more specific, and traditional, finding tools indicated by the subdivisions within their texts. This practice, too, is quite standard for medievalists, who will readily recognize abbreviations such as "d" for *distinctio*, "c" for *capitulum* or *causa*, "q" for *quaestio*, and *dictum* for a canonist's summation of a point. This system of abbreviations should serve as a guide for any readers unfamiliar with this standard scheme of citation for medieval texts.

Let me note as well that no effort has been made here to regularize the spelling of "mediaeval" to "medieval" or vice versa. When these adjectives occur in titles or in the house style of publishers, the spelling given by the author or by the publisher is the spelling that will be followed.

I will have occasion to cite female scholars, both in the bibliography and in footnotes organized alphabetically, who began to publish under one surname but who have changed their surnames thanks to a change in their marital status. I will cite their works alphabetized according to the first surnames under which they began to publish, with their subsequent surnames indicated in square brackets following their original names. I trust that this practice will not be confusing to readers who may initially seek citations to the writings of these scholars in locations where they will not be found.

ABBREVIATIONS

AHDLMA	*Archives d'histoire doctrinale et littéraire du moyen âge*
Beiträge	Beiträge zur Geschichte der Philosophie [und Theologie] des Mittelalters
CCCM	Corpus Christianorum, continuatio medievalis
CCSL	Corpus Christianorum, series latina
CIMAGEL	*Cahiers de l'Institut du moyen âge grec et latin de l'Université de Copenhague*
CSEL	Corpus scriptorum ecclesiasticorum latinorum
DTC	*Dictionnaire de théologie catholique*
ETL	*Ephemerides Theologicae Lovanienses*
FS	*Franciscan Studies*
Landgraf, *Dogmengeschichte*	Artur Michael Landgraf, *Dogmengeschichte der Frühscholastik*, 4 vols. (Regensburg: Friedrich Pustet, 1952–56)
MGH, Scriptores	Monumenta Germaniae Historica, Scriptores
Misc. Lomb.	*Miscellanea Lombardiana* (Novara: Istituto Geografico de Agostini, 1957)
PL	*Patrologia latina, cursus completus*, ed. J. P. Migne
RHE	*Revue d'histoire ecclésiastique*
Rolls Series	Rerum Brittanicarum medii aevi, Scriptores
RSPT	*Revue des sciences philosophiques et théologiques*
RSR	*Revue des sciences religieuses*
RTAM	*Recherches de théologie ancienne et médiévale*
ZkT	*Zeitschrift für katholische Theologie*

PREFACE

Like the account of creation in Genesis, this book came into being in two stages, in response to two successive inspirations, although in this case they were purely human. Shortly after he had completed a book on Adam Wodeham, the early fourteenth-century Oxford scholastic, William J. Courtenay happened to remark to me that, in Wodeham's day, university students engaged in getting over the academic hurdle of the commentary on the *Sentences* of Peter Lombard mandated by the theological faculties felt no obligation to gloss all sections of the work in equal detail. Instead, they gave very cursory attention to the parts they found uninteresting and concentrated on those they found stimulating or problematic. A few years later, John Van Dyk noted in print that, in the fifteenth century, scholastics had abandoned that practice and had returned to the systematic commentary on the entire text.[1] Combining these two observations and pushing the common question they raised backward in time, I was struck by the fact that medievalists would be able to survey and map the *terra incognita* that remains in our knowledge of much of the history of speculative thought from the middle of the twelfth century to the end of the period if the *Sentence* commentaries of all the scholastics known to have made them could be studied in chronological order and in a comparative way. Such a study, I ruminated, would enable us to track, and possibly to account for, the shifting interests in different generations, in different geographical centers, in different religious orders or pedagogical cadres—whatever categories such an investigation might reveal as significant.

Hard on the heels of that thought came a sobering reflection. Except for a handful of the best-researched of the scholastics, the *Sentence* commentaries of the high Middle Ages have not been edited and published. To be sure, thanks to the assiduous labors of Friedrich Stegmüller and his continuators, the authorship and present whereabouts of hundreds of manuscripts which preserve

---

[1] John Van Dyk, "The Sentence Commentary: A Vehicle in the Intellectual Transition of the Fifteenth Century," in *Fifteenth-Century Studies*, 8, ed. Guy P. Mermier and Edelgard E. DuBruck (Detroit: Fifteenth-Century Symposium, 1983), pp. 227–38

these commentaries are now known.[2] At the same time, the very
extensiveness of this body of material makes the task of editing, or
even sampling, all these manuscripts too daunting to be undertaken by a single scholar, in a single lifetime. Having been pulled
back to earth by this thought, I was buoyed up again by another
observation. Even if the editing and publishing of all known *Sentence*
commentaries could be done, ideally by a large international
équipe of medievalists with unlimited funding, it would not be
possible to interpret fully what the commentators had said unless
we had, as a base line, a clear idea of what the Lombard himself
had said in the *Sentences*. Do we really know, I asked myself, what
the Lombard's theology actually had been? Preliminary research
into that question revealed an astonishing fact. Peter Lombard
makes an appearance in all manuals and textbook surveys, because
all medievalists acknowledge the formative role that his *Sentences*
played in the education of university theologians and philosophers
in the high Middle Ages. Also, no less than three successive critical
editions of the *Sentences* have been produced within the past
century.[3] Yet, there exists no good modern book-length treatment

---

[2] Friedrich Stegmüller, *Reportorium commentariorum in Sententias Petri Lombardi*,
2 vols. (Würzburg: F. Schöningh, 1947). This ground-breaking survey has been
supplemented by Victorinus Doucet, *Commentaires sur les Sentences: Supplément au
Répertoire de M. F. Stegmüller* (Quaracchi: Collegii S. Bonaventurae ad Claras
Aquas, 1954); J. B. Korolec and R. Palacz, "Commentaires sur les *Sentences*:
Supplément au Répertoire de F. Stegmüller," *Mediaevalia Philosophica Polonorum* 11
(1963): 140–45; J. B. Korolek, A. Póltawski, and Z. Wlodek, "Commentaires sur
les *Sentences*: Supplément au Répertoire de F. Stegmüller," ibid. 1 (1958): 28–30;
Zdzislaw Kuksewicz, "Commentaires sur les *Sentences*: Supplément au Répertoire
de F. Stegmüller," ibid. 5 (1960): 45–49; Jerzy Rebeta, "Commentaires sur les
Sentences: Supplément au Répertoire de F. Stegmüller," ibid. 12 (1967): 135–37;
Josef Tříška, "Sententiarii Pragensis," ibid. 13 (1968): 100–10; Zofia Wlodek,
"Commentaires sur les *Sentences*: Supplément au Répertoire de F. Stegmüller
d'après les MSS. de la Bibliothèque du Grand Séminaire de Pelplin," ibid. 8
(1961): 33–38; "Commentaires sur les *Sentences*: Supplément au Répertoire de F.
Stegmüller," ibid. 5 (1963): 144–46; "Commentaires sur les *Sentences*: Supplément au
Répertoire de F. Stegmüller d'après les MSS. de la Bibliothèque de Wrocław,"
Bulletin de philosophie médiévale 6 (1964): 100–04; "Commentaires sur les *Sentences*:
Supplément au Répertoire de F. Stegmüller d'après les MSS. des bibliothèques de
Prague," ibid. 7 (1965): 91–95; Kazimierz Wójciki, "Commentaires sur les *Sentences*:
Supplément au Répertoire de F. Stegmüller," *Mediaevalia Philosophorum Polonorum* 13
(1968): 111–14; John Van Dyk, "Thirty Years since Stegmüller: A Bibliographical
Guide to the Study of Medieval Sentence Commentaries," *FS* 39 (1979): 255–315;
William J. Courtenay, "Newly Identified 'Sentences' Commentaries in the Stuttgart
Landesbibliothek," *Scriptorium* 41 (1987): 113–15. I am indebted to Professor Courte-
nay for this last reference.
[3] On the editorial history of the *Sentences* in modern times, see Ignatius C.
Brady, "The Three Editions of the 'Liber Sententiarum' of Master Peter Lombard
(1882–1977)," *Archivum Franciscanum Historicum* 70 (1977): 400–11.

of Peter Lombard's thought. The only general monographs on this subject were published at the turn of the twentieth century or earlier; and they are all seriously out of date.[4] The only relatively modern introductions to Lombardian theology are found in brief encyclopedia articles.[5] Once I had made that surprising discovery, the idea of writing the present book came into focus with startling clarity. A full-dress study of the Lombard's theology would be well worth doing in its own right, I concluded, in order to fill this gap in our knowledge of the twelfth century's most renowned and influential theologian, independent of its potential utility for scholars who might want to study successive *Sentence* commentaries as a barometer of later medieval speculative thought.

Confident that I had hit upon the useful project of understanding a thinker who has the distinction of being, at the same time, famous and poorly known, I next sought to assuage my curiosity as to how such a paradoxical situation could have arisen in the first place. This led to the second genesis of the book, whose inspiration was an extremely illuminating historiographical essay on Peter Lombard by Ermenegildo Bertola.[6] Bertola's paper helps to show how and why Peter Lombard has fallen through the cracks, in modern historiography of medieval thought. At the same time, it shows how the disesteem for the Lombard has functioned as an index of the ways in which the received tradition has conceptualized the history of medieval speculative thought, ever since this subject started to be revalued in the nineteenth century. What is involved here is not a series of periodic inflations and deflations of the Lombard's reputation, but rather a succession of unsympathetic appraisals of it. The consistency of this dismissive view is striking, even though it has been informed by a variety of inter-confessional, intra-confessional, philosophical, and other interpretive agendas. What-

---

[4] Otto Baltzer, *Die Sentenzen des Petrus Lombardus: Ihre Quellen und ihre dogmenge-schichtliche Bedeutung* (Leipzig: Dieter'sche Verlags-Buchhandlung, 1902); Joh. Nep. Espenberger, *Die Philosophie des Petrus Lombardus und ihre Stellung im zwölften Jahrhundert*, Beiträge, 3:5 (Münster: Aschendorff, 1901); Julius Kögel, *Petrus Lombardus in seiner Stellung zur Philosophie des Mittelalter* (Greifswald: Julius Abel, 1897); F. Protois, *Pierre Lombard, évêque de Paris dit le maître des Sentences: Son époque, sa vie, ses écrits, son influence* (Paris: Société Générale de Librairie Catholique, 1887).

[5] Joseph de Ghellinck, "Pierre Lombard," in *DTC* (Paris: Letouzey et Ané, 1935), 12 part 2: 1941–2019; now superseded by Martin Anton Schmidt, "Das Sentenzenwerk des Petrus Lombardus und sein Aufstieg zum Muster- und Textbuch der theologischen Ausbildung," in *Handbuch der Dogmen- und Theologiege-schichte* (Göttingen: Vandenhoeck & Ruprecht, 1982), 1: 587–615. I would like to thank Dr. Max Haas for the latter reference.

[6] Ermenegildo Bertola, "Pietro Lombardo nella storiografica filosofica mediocvale," *Pier Lombardo* 4 (1960): 95–113.

ever the reasons, commentators have succeeded in marginalizing the most central theologian of his time, and have created a modern Peter Lombard who is a caricature of his medieval reality, making it all but impossible to appreciate what his contemporaries found worthwhile in him. The line of inquiry opened up by Bertola, therefore, pointed to two other considerations which went into the shaping of this book. First, it suggested that, in rescuing a major figure from undeserved neglect, I might also be able to contribute to a rethinking of the larger issue of how we conceptualize the twelfth century and its place in the history of medieval thought. Second, it suggested the *modus operandi* which I have followed in my attack on this assignment, the reading of Peter Lombard not from an anachronistic or tendentious perspective, but in relation to the schools and masters of theology in the first half of the twelfth century. For, it is only by positioning him in the context of contemporary debates that we will be able to see what the agenda of scholastic theology was at that time, and why the Lombard was held to have succeeded better than his coevals in addressing its needs and concerns.

Given the extensive attention lavished on the thought of the twelfth century in the decades since its status as an age of renaissance was established, the claim that its contours need to be redrawn may require a defense. That claim can be validated, I will argue, if we juxtapose the older assessments of Peter Lombard side by side with the interpretive problems which they fail to solve. Here, we can take Bertola as our starting point, and supplement what he has brought to light.[7] As he has shown, scholars have agreed in finding Peter wanting, for one reason or another, since the sixteenth century. Reformation Protestants objected to him as the progenitor of scholasticism, a movement which, for them, stood for false doctrine, a tortuous and hair-splitting mode of reasoning, and the incorporation of philosophy into theology that had forged the leaden bonds which their own polemic sought to shatter. For them, Peter's problem was that he was too scholastic. At the same time, Counter-Reformation Catholics, especially those supporting the revival of Thomism in their day, rejected him, substituting the *Summa theologiae* of Thomas Aquinas for his *Sentences* as their school text, because they did not find him scholastic enough. The early modern rationalists, who distanced themselves from these controversies, dismissed him for being too theological and not suf-

---

[7] Ibid. Unless otherwise noted, the material in the next three paragraphs depends on Bertola.

ficiently philosophical. Like their Protestant predecessors, Enlight-
enment thinkers equated the Middle Ages with scholasticism,
understood pejoratively. They criticized the Lombard for seeking
to unite Aristotle with the Augustinian tradition, viewing this
union as a mésalliance from the other direction, although in the
eyes of some philosophes, Anselm of Canterbury had to share the
blame with Peter for this misstep.

In the historiography of the nineteenth century, scholars turned
from a Peter Lombard held up as an example of whatever was
deemed worthy of attack to a Peter Lombard seen as irrelevant.
However they may have diverged in their versions of the story line
of medieval intellectual history, they agreed in treating him as all
but invisible, a character with no real part to play, virtually writing
him out of the script. The German school, starting with Heinrich
Ritter and continuing with Bernhard Geyer, Clemens Bauemker,
and Martin Grabmann, saw the high Middle Ages as a period of
philosophical revival. Important as they held the reception of Aristotle to have been, they regarded the influence of Platonism as
equally critical. They tended to subdivide twelfth-century thinkers
into two groups, depending on which of these schools of ancient
philosophy they were deemed to have espoused. For them, Adelard
of Bath, Anselm of Canterbury, and the Chartrains formed the
honor guard of Platonism, with Peter Abelard, Gilbert of Poitiers,
and Honorius Augustodunensis in the vanguard of Aristotelianism.
Since they saw in Peter Lombard a man without commanding
allegiances to either of these traditions, the German school concluded that he was simply not in tune with contemporary intellectual trends. This view is repeated by J. N. Espenberger in one of the
earliest full-length studies of Peter's thought.[8]

The French school, launched by Victor Cousin and followed by
Barthélemy Hauréau, Maurice DeWulf, and Émile Bréhier, also
accented philosophical renewal in the twelfth century, but took a
somewhat different tack from the Germans. Strong proponents of
rationalism, and anxious to defend the view that the Christianity of
medieval thinkers had not prevented them from being real philosophers, they placed particular emphasis on the revival of metaphysics, the reopening of the debate over universals, and the
effort to correlate reason and revelation, concerns destined to receive more attention in the thirteenth century. Judged according to
this proleptic and increasingly neo-Thomist standard, the relevant

---

[8] Espenberger, *Die Philosophie*, passim and esp. pp. 8–15.

groupings among the twelfth-century thinkers were not the Platonists and Aristotelians. Rather, the century took shape, for the
French school, as a conflict between the conservatives, such as
Anselm of Laon, William of Champeaux, Bernard of Clairvaux,
and the Victorines, on the one side, and such harbingers of the
future as Anselm of Canterbury and, above all, the Abelardians
and Porretans, on the other. Now, Peter Lombard borrowed from
both of these groups but was not a card-carrying member of either.
So, once again, he was relegated to the sidelines and seen as having
avoided the great issues of the day. He was held to have lacked an
interest in metaphysics and was described as an enemy of logic
even though he was sometimes constrained to use it, with no
position on universals to defend and with nothing to contribute to
the synthesis of reason and revelation.

In short, for the French as well as the German school, Peter was
regarded as being of no philosophical interest at all, and, therefore,
as being of no interest at all, globally. He simply watched the great
parade go by, and did not march in it himself. So great was Peter's
perceived refusal that F. Protois could devote an entire monograph
to condemning a figure whose attitude toward philosophy he presents as one of avoidance, abstention, indifference, and disdain.[9]
And, as late as 1969, an echo of this position could be found in
David Luscombe. Of Peter, he says, "he expected nothing from
philosophers and he excluded them in favor of an exclusive cultiva-
tion of the theological tradition."[10] A much more influential extension of the French school into the historiography of the twentieth
century was the work of Étienne Gilson. It is instructive to note
that he does not even include Peter Lombard in his *History of
Christian Philosophy in the Middle Ages*, except when he refers to the
commentaries on Peter's work made by scholastics who can be
pressed more easily into the Procrustean bed of the realism-versus-
nominalism or reason-versus-revelation debates.

In the first wave of the revolt of the medievalists, theology took a
decidedly back seat to philosophy as an index of why the twelfth
century should be seen as a period of revival. Such did not invariably remain the case in the historiographical sequel, in which
theology now came to be included in the plot, and in which it could

---

[9] Protois, *Pierre Lombard*, passim and esp. pp. 40–41. This same line is taken by
Kögel, *Petrus Lombardus*.
[10] David E. Luscombe, *The School of Peter Abelard: The Influence of Abelard's
Thought in the Early Scholastic Period* (Cambridge: Cambridge University Press,
1969), p. 279.

be conceded that it was not sufficient to read medieval theologians across their theology for the sake of the philosophy that might thereby be extracted. Welcome as this shift in perspective has been in many quarters, it has not necessarily led to a more generous or less tendentious appraisal of the Lombard. At issue here is not just confessional or philosophical polemics but also hermeneutics. Whether or not they share the views of the neo-Thomists, many of the scholars in this group have basic difficulty reading a sentence collection and understanding how ideas are being put forth in this genre of theological literature, of which Peter's *Sentences* is the salient example. They tend to measure this genre against the norm of a late thirteenth-century *summa*, which it does not resemble formally. By that standard, they find it wanting. At first glance—and, typically, a first glance is all that Peter's *Sentences* receive from them—it looks like a compilation of the opinions of past authorities, pure and simple, rather than as the vehicle for the theologian's own positions. This is the way in which the *Sentences* have been described, all too often.

Otto Baltzer framed the terms of this assessment almost a century ago. He observes that Peter states, in the prologue of the *Sentences*, that his aim is to bring together the views of the church fathers. Baltzer reads this statement literally, as exhausting the Lombard's objectives, and uses it to define the parameters of his own study. He confines his efforts to cataloguing Peter's sources and subjecting them to statistical analysis, in order to see which authorities he relies on the most.[11] It never occurs to Baltzer that Peter's prologue needs to be read as a *captatio benevolentiae*, an expression of the "modest author" topos. Nor does it occur to him to go beyond the noting of Peter's citations to a consideration of the uses to which Peter puts them. This understanding of Peter's relationship to his authorities has remained remarkably durable. In 1960, Enrico Nobile could call the *Sentences* a *cento* lacking in any discernible principle of organization.[12] A year later, Philippe Delhaye could describe it as the mere echo of a tradition.[13] The same view informs Jaroslav Pelikan's recent assessment of the *Sentences* as an exercise in running in place, "the reaffirmation of Augustine,"

---

[11] Baltzer, *Die Sentenzen*, passim and esp. pp. 1–14.

[12] Enrico Nobile, "Appunti sulla teologia dei *Quattro libri delle Sentenze* di Pier Lombardo," *Pier Lombardo* 4 (1960): 49–59.

[13] Philippe Delhaye, *Pierre Lombard, sa vie, ses oeuvres, sa morale* (Montreal: Institut d'Études Médiévales, 1961), p. 27.

and as nothing much else.[14] And it can be found as well in Gillian
Evans's still more recent estimate of the *Sentences* as essentially a
reference book in which Peter's main project is to promote certitude
and orthodoxy by anxiously placing a cordon sanitaire around the
theological boundaries fixed by the church fathers.[15]

Although they come to Peter from the history of theology rather
than from the history of philosophy, these interpreters still produce
the same cumulative effect. They tell the reader that modern scholarship is justified in not taking Peter Lombard seriously. They
report the fact of the scholarly neglect of him with complacency and
satisfaction, not with regret or self-doubt. On the first page of the
book he writes to document the correctness of this state of affairs,
Protois announces, "Pierre Lombard est aujourd'hui plus cité que
lu et plus célèbre que connu."[16] Luscombe agrees, calling the
Sentences "one of the least read of the world's great books," a
circumstance commensurate with his view that its author was "a
cautious, sober, and apparently dull expositor."[17]

This alleged dullness has been traced to Peter's lack of a sufficiently speculative mind as a theologian by Antonio Brancaforte.
Brancaforte sees the Lombard as a religious thinker, seeking to find
a middle ground between mysticism and rationalism, of the sort he
thinks Thomas Aquinas later achieved. Unfortunately, because of
his intellectual shortcomings, Peter's reach exceeded his grasp.[18]
Still more dismissive than this criticism of Peter as a failed Thomist
avant la lettre has been the criticism of him as a twelfth-century
humanist manqué. While he acknowledges that Peter could
and did use grammar as a tool of theological analysis, Marie-
Dominique Chenu mentions him only occasionally, and dispar-
agingly, as having failed to promote the speculative grammar that
flowed into the *logica modernorum* and as having contributed nothing
to the discovery of the world and man concurrently taking place in
the school of Chartres, which Chenu sees as the main achievements
of twelfth-century thought.[19] And, Jean Leclercq rejects the Lom-

---

[14] Jaroslav Pelikan, *The Christian Tradition: A History of the Development of Doctrine*
(Chicago: University of Chicago Press, 1978), 3: 270.
[15] Gillian R. Evans, *The Language and Logic of the Bible: The Road to Reformation*
(Cambridge: Cambridge University Press, 1985), pp. 102–04.
[16] Protois, *Pierre Lombard*, p. 1.
[17] Luscombe, *The School of Peter Abelard*, p. 263.
[18] Antonio Brancaforte, "Contributo di Pietro Lombardo all'unità del pensiero
medioevale," *Teoresi* 8 (1953): 230–45.
[19] Marie-Dominique Chenu, *La théologie au douzième siècle* (Paris: J. Vrin, 1957),
pp. 93, 96, 99, 116.

bard, that prototypical sentence collector, as a tiresome florilegist, in his repeated efforts to argue that it was not the scholastics but the monastic theologians who were the true Christian humanists and the true authors of theological renewal in the twelfth century.[20]

To be sure, Leclercq speaks for the monks, especially those in the reformed orders such as the Cistercians, in the effort to win them a hearing, along with the scholastics who have tended to dominate the histories of medieval theology. There are some historians of scholasticism who, while not ceding an inch of their turf, have yet manifested some disquiet over the traditional image of the Lombard as an also-ran or as the negative mirror image of the really important developments in twelfth-century thought. Also, as historians they feel the prick of their professional conscience and an obligation to account for the status Peter attained in the medieval chapter of the story. Some commentators have therefore made an earnest effort to find some merit in Peter's work and to grasp why it caught on. But, the best they have been able to come up with is a mixed review. In the judgment of Artur Michael Landgraf, the scheme of organization of the *Sentences* is a coherent one; it became canonical with good reason. On the other hand, its contents are both impersonal and unoriginal.[21] For Joseph de Ghellinck, the *Sentences* definitely enjoyed more posthumous glory than they deserved. He sees this work as a cold and lifeless résumé lacking in boldness or creativity. At the same time, he concedes that Peter did do his research thoroughly, assembling an impressive dossier of patristic citations but without manifesting any indiscreet curiosity.

---

[20] Jean Leclercq, "The Renewal of Theology," in *Renaissance and Renewal in the Twelfth Century*, ed. Robert L. Benson and Giles Constable (Cambridge, MA: Harvard University Press, 1982), pp. 68–87, reprising his more extended argument for the same position in *The Love of Learning and the Desire for God: A Study of Monastic Culture*, 2nd ed. rev., trans. Catherine Misrahi (New York: Fordham University Press, 1974), passim and esp. pp. 1–7. Leclercq is followed by Stephen C. Ferruolo, *The Origins of the University: The Schools of Paris and Their Critics, 1100–1215* (Stanford: Stanford University Press, 1985), ch. 3. Recently, Brian P. Gaybba, *Aspects of the Mediaeval History of Theology: 12th to 14th Century* (Pretoria: University of South Africa, 1988), pp. 7–65, has noted some of the inconsistencies of Leclercq's view and has suggested that the distinction between monastic and scholastic theology which he draws be replaced by a distinction between "experiential" and "notional" theology; but he does not place Peter Lombard in this scheme.

[21] Artur Michael Landgraf, *Introduction à l'histoire de la littérature théologique de la scolastique naissante*, ed. Albert-M. Landry, trans. Louis-B. Geiger (Montreal: Institut d'Études Médiévales, 1973), pp. 53, 132. This view is shared by Henry Cloes, "La systématisation théologique pendant la première moitié du XIIᵉ siècle," *ETL* 34 (1958): 329, although he paradoxically sees this alleged unoriginality as a virtue.

His organization is cogent and his coverage is well balanced. But these traits are not sufficient to overturn Ghellinck's basic conclusion.[22] Ludwig Ott is rather more generous. Not only does he accept the idea that Peter's sweep of the fathers is wider than that of his contemporaries, but also that he is more accurate than they are in the way he presents them, often correcting thinkers with whom he disagreed by showing that they had misused their sources. Ott has also noticed that Peter uses logic constructively in a number of ways, to order his material lucidly, to harmonize discrepancies among his authorities, and to introduce distinctions that clarify theological topics. Still, on balance, like Landgraf and Ghellinck, he finds Peter impersonal, unoriginal, and uncreative.[23] Jacques Le Goff finds "force, clarity, and a synthetic spirit" in Peter's work but concurs in the view that he made no significant or original contribution.[24] While acknowledging that Peter recognized the initiatives made by other twelfth-century thinkers and incorporated them into the *Sentences*, while noting that he did not shrink from controversy, and while admitting that he did advance the debates at times, Luscombe's final verdict is the harsh one cited above.[25] One of the single most influential historians of scholasticism in modern times, Martin Grabmann, has signaled another positive feature of the *Sentences*. Both the clarity and cogency of its plan and its method for weighing and analyzing authorities, he observes, lent the book a high degree of pedagogical utility. Yet, in the last analysis, it is not the intrinsic merit of the Lombard's work that sealed its fate, he thinks, but the lucky timing of its appearance and the influence of Peter of Poitiers, the disciple of the Lombard who promoted it.[26]

Even with these hesitant steps toward the recognition of Peter Lombard as more than just a nay-sayer to the major intellectual movements of his day and more than a mere compiler, a good, gray florilegist, the historiography to date still fails to explain how he

---

[22] Joseph de Ghellinck, *L'Essor de la littérature latine au XIIe siècle*, 2 vols. (Brussels: L'Édition Universelle, 1946), 1: 70–73; *Le Mouvement théologique du XIIe siècle*, 2nd ed. (Bruges: De Tempel, 1948), pp. 202–49.

[23] Ludwig Ott, "Petrus Lombardus: Persönlichkeit und Werk," *Münchener theologische Zeitschrift* 5 (1954): 105–13; reprised in "Pietro Lombardo: Personalità e opera," *Misc. Lomb.*, pp. 15–21.

[24] Jacques Le Goff, *The Birth of Purgatory*, trans. Arthur Goldhammer (Chicago: University of Chicago Press, 1984), p. 148.

[25] Luscombe, *The School of Peter Abelard*, pp. 262–79.

[26] Martin Grabmann, *Die Geschichte der scholastischen Methode*, 2 vols. (Graz: Akademische Druck- u. Verlagsanstalt, 1957 [repr. of Freiburg im Breisgau, 1911 ed.]), 2: 404–07.

succeeded in seizing the theological initiative and in capturing the imagination of his contemporaries. It also fails to explain why it was he, and not one of his allegedly more exciting compeers, who became the enduring classic, the standard introduction to systematic theology in the medieval university curriculum, starting with Paris in 1215. The book which follows will be an effort to rediscover the medieval scenario in which Peter plays the role of the hero, the scenario obscured by the modern versions of the twelfth century in which he is relegated to the role of a bit player or a chorus character, at least when his lines are not consigned to the cutting room floor altogether. In our view, the best way to place Peter Lombard in his own time is to read him, always, in conjunction with the theologians in the first half of the twelfth century. This is the context within which he worked and the audience to which he spoke.

The body of this book will be divided into two parts, of unequal length. In the first section, after a chapter presenting what is known about Peter's life, works, and medieval reputation, I will offer three chapters which may be regarded, collectively, as an extended essay on method. They will treat, respectively, the emergence in the twelfth century of systematic theology as a sustained pedagogical enterprise, in chapter 2; the problem of theological language in early and mid-century theology, in chapter 3; and biblical exegesis among the scholastics, in chapter 4. In each case my goal will be to target the methodological problems and opportunities arising from these concerns and to explore why the Lombard's address to them was, and was perceived to be, an improvement over the other current options. The second part of the book will treat the substance of Lombardian theology. In four chapters, largely but not entirely taking the four books of Peter's *Sentences* as my organizational guide, I will present his teachings on the divine nature and the Trinity in chapter 5; the creation, man, and the fall in chapter 6; Christology and the redemptive work of Christ in chapter 7; and, in the lengthiest part of the book, ethics, sacraments, and Last Things in chapter 8. In each area I will seek to position Peter's opinions in relation to the debates of his own time. The book will end with a conclusion summing up the findings of this investigation and offering my assessment of Peter's contribution to the development of Christian thought in the twelfth century.

But before moving on to that assignment, it is my welcome duty to acknowledge my appreciation to a number of institutions and individuals whose help and support have been as gratefully received as they have been essential in the research and writing of this book. First, I would like to thank several publishers for permitting me to reuse material first printed in journals or collaborative publications on which they hold the copyrights. These include the Librairie Philosophique J. Vrin for "Another Look at the School of Laon," *Archives d'histoire doctrinale et littéraire du moyen âge* 53 (1986): 7–22; the Bibliopolis Press of Naples for "Gilbert, the Early Porretans, and Peter Lombard," in *Gilbert de Poitiers et ses contemporaines: Aux origines de la logica modernorum*, ed. Jean Jolivet and Alain de Libera (1987): 229–50; the Duke University Press for "Systematic Theology and Theological Renewal in the Twelfth Century," *Journal of Medieval and Renaissance Studies* 18 (1988): 135–56; the Abbaye de Mont-César in Louvain for "Early Porretan Theology," *Recherches de théologie ancienne et médiévale* 56 (1989): 58–79; the Villanova University Press for "*Quae hodie locum non habent*: Scholastic Theologians Reflect on Their Authorities," in *Proceedings of the PMR Conference*, 15, ed. Phillip Pulsiano (Villanova: Augustinian Historical Institute, 1990), pp. 1–17; the Southeastern Medieval Association for "From *sacra pagina* to *theologia*: Peter Lombard as an Exegete of Romans," *Medieval Perspectives* 6 (1991): 1–19; E. J. Brill for "Peter Lombard and Abelard: The *Opinio Nominalium* and Divine Transcendence," *Vivarium* 30 (May 1992): 139–56; to the University of Notre Dame Press for "Peter Lombard as an Exegete of St. Paul," in *Ad litteram: Authoritative Texts and Their Medieval Readers*, ed. Mark D. Jordan and Kent Emery, Jr. (Notre Dame: University of Notre Dame Press, 1992), pp. 71–92; and the Medieval Academy of America for "*Psalterium Scholasticorum*: Peter Lombard and the Development of Scholastic Psalms Exegesis," *Speculum* 67 (July 1992): 531–48. I am much in their debt for their gracious cooperation.

I also owe a considerable debt of gratitude to the institutions whose generosity made possible my research and writing, providing me with time, financial support, and hospitable environments for my work. Foremost among these are Oberlin College, the Institute for Advanced Studies in Princeton, and the John Simon Guggenheim Foundation. Oberlin granted me the leaves in 1982, 1986–87, and 1989–90 essential for my research. My year as a member of the School of Historical Studies at the Institute in 1986–87 enabled me to profit from the support and stimulation of that unparalleled community of scholars. And, a fellowship from the Guggenheim Foundation in 1989–90 enabled me to bring the research and writing of this book to a conclusion. I would also like to record here my lively appreciation to the Weston School of Theology, the Institute of Medieval Canon Law of the University of California, Berkeley, and to the History Departments of Harvard and Yale Universities, for the welcome, the colleagueship, and the facilities which they warmly extended to me. Among the libraries where the research was done whose staffs went well beyond the call of duty in making their collections available to me and in procuring materials difficult of access I would like, in particular, to thank the Biblioteca Municipale of Novara, the Deutsches Historisches Institut of Rome, King's College, Cambridge, the Bibliothèque Municipale of Troyes, and the Sterling Memorial Library at Yale.

There are also many friends and colleagues who have helped me in a host of ways, from extending a cordial welcome on behalf of their institutions to alerting me to important bibliography that I otherwise would have missed, sharing their own knowledge and critical acumen with me, lending and giving me materials that I needed, serving as my sponsors, and offering professional and personal courtesies and kindnesses too numerous to mention. In alphabetical order, they are: Uta-Renate Blumenthal, Eve Borsook, John E. Boswell, the late Ignatius Brady, James A. Brundage, Giles Constable, William J. Courtenay, Karlfried Froelich, Margaret T. Gibson, Penny S. Gold, Theresa Gross-Diaz, Max Haas, the late David Herlihy, Ralph Hexter, William E. Hood, Peter I. Kaufman, Paul Knoll, Stephan Kuttner, Robert E. Lerner, David E. Luscombe, Gary Macy, Laurant Mayali, Harry Miskimin, Karl Morrison, Francis C. Oakley, John O'Malley, Jaroslav Pelikan, Fred C. Robinson, John Van Dyk, John Van Engen, and Grover A. Zinn. In a special category are two other people for whose help I am profoundly grateful, Thelma Roush, for technical assistance that was literally invaluable, and the Rev. Peter Eaton for his keen-eyed and generous contribution to the thankless task of reading proof. To all of them I extend my sincere and heartfelt appreciation. Such merit as this book may have owes much to them; such flaws as it retains are mine alone.

M. L. C.
Oberlin, Ohio

CHAPTER ONE

PETER LOMBARD'S LIFE AND WORKS

For a man of his acknowledged importance, Peter Lombard left behind him a remarkably scanty biographical record. Although he attained swift and enduring fame as an exegete and theologian, as well as high ecclesiastical office in a land far from his own, no contemporary biographer thought of commemorating his life. Nor did Peter himself leave any letters or personal documents that would help us to reconstruct and date his activities and relationships. Large gaps remain in the evidence that we do have concerning his life and works. Legends started to grow up about him as early as the thirteenth century; some of them still remain in circulation. The best of the modern scholars who has labored to establish what can be known for certain about Peter's life and works, who has sifted uncritical hypothesis from likely conjecture, is undoubtedly Ignatius C. Brady.[1] His studies lay the foundation for the material in this chapter, along with such amplifications and corrections as it has been possible to make.

BIOGRAPHY

Peter was born in the region of Novara, in Lombardy, probably between 1095 and 1100. Some scholars continue to give his birthplace as the small town of Lumellogno, although this is a fancy going back to the Renaissance historian Paolo Giovo, who derived

---

[1] The most reliable introductions to this subject, and our chief guides to it in this chapter, are the prolegomena to the two volumes of Peter Lombard, *Sententiae in IV libris distinctae*, 3rd ed. rev., ed. Ignatius C. Brady, 2 vols. (Grottaferrata: Collegii S. Bonaventurae ad Claras Aquas, 1971–81), 1: 8*–129*, 2: 7*–52*, which supersede Brady's own earlier studies of Peter's life and works, "Peter Lombard: Canon of Notre Dame," *RTAM* 32 (1965): 277–95 and "Peter Lombard," in *New Catholic Encyclopedia* (New York: McGraw-Hill Book Company, 1967), 11: 221–22, studies which, in turn, offer correctives to the earlier investigations of Ludwig Ott, "Petrus Lombardus: Persönlichkeit und Werk," *Münchener theologische Zeitschrift* 5 (1954): 99–105; reprised as "Pietro Lombardo: Personalità e opera," in *Misc. Lomb.*, pp. 11–15; and Damien Van den Eynde, "Précisions chronologiques sur quelques ouvrages théologiques du XIIe siècle," *Antonianum* 26 (1951): 223–33; "Nouvelles précisions sur quelques ouvrages théologiques du XIIe siècle," *FS* 13 (1953): 110–18; "Essai chronologique sur l'oeuvre littéraire de Pierre Lombard," in *Misc. Lomb.*, pp. 45–63.

it from a play on the words *lumen omnium* in reference to Peter.[2] Nothing is known for certain about his origins, his social background, or his early education. Indeed, the first thirty-some years of Peter's life remain a complete blank. In the early fourteenth century the chronicler Ricobaldo of Ferrara invented the charming legend that he was the son of an impoverished widow who earned a meager living as a laundress. When news of Peter's election as bishop of Paris reached Novara, the city fathers decided to equip her in splendid style, at public expense, and to send her to Paris to visit her son with an escort of local notables. As the story goes, when the Novarese delegation arrived and made their courtesy call, Peter failed to recognize his mother in this richly attired lady. It was not until she returned, clad in her ordinary humble clothing, and chastised him, that he acknowledged her, embraced her, and did her honor.[3] This legend remained so enduring that it could be invoked in the nineteenth century by the Novarese poet and politician Giuseppe Regaldi. As a defender of the working class, he sought to harness the aura of Novara's most famous citizen, the "son of a laundress," to his own cause.[4] Another now-exploded legend is the "myth of the three brothers," which also derives from a chronicler of the high Middle Ages, Godfrey of Viterbo, and which is grounded on the geographically and chronologically impossible claim that Peter Lombard, his disciple Peter Comestor, and Gratian of Bologna were all siblings.[5]

Our first documented reference to Peter Lombard is found in a letter written by Bernard of Clairvaux to Gilduin, prior of St. Victor in Paris, between 1134 and 1136.[6] Noting that this promis-

---

[2] Antonio Massara, "La leggenda di Pier Lombardo," in *Miscellanea storica Novarese a Raffaele Tarella* (Novara: G. Parzini, 1906), pp. 118–20. His source is Ricobaldo of Ferrara, *Historia imperatorum Romano-Germanicorum a Carolo M. usque ad an. 1298*, ed. L. A. Muratori, Rerum Italicorum Scriptores (Milan, 1726), 9: 124. This legend has died hard; it is retained in the most recent treatments of Peter's biography, Ludwig Hödl, "Petrus Lombardus," in *Gestalten der Kirchengeschichte*, ed. Martin Greschat (Stuttgart: Kohlhammer, 1983), 3 part 1: 205 and Mark A. Zier, "Peter Lombard," in *Dictionary of the Middle Ages*, ed. Joseph R. Strayer (New York: Charles Scribner's Sons, 1987), 9: 516.

[3] Massara, "La leggenda," pp. 121–36.

[4] Mario Nogari, "Giuseppe Regaldi e Pier Lombardo," *Bolletino storico per la provincia de Novara* 68 (1977): 78–94.

[5] Massara, "La leggenda," pp. 122–36. The "three brothers" legend was first rejected by Antoninus of Florence. See *Gallia Christiana, in provincias ecclesiasticas distributa* (Paris: H. Welter, 1899 [repr. of Paris: Ex Typographia Regia, 1744 ed.]), 7: 70; Joseph de Ghellinck, *Le Mouvement théologique du XIIe siècle*, 2nd ed. (Bruges: De Tempel, 1948), p. 285.

[6] Bernard of Clairvaux, *Epistola* 410, in *Opera*, ed. J. Leclercq, C. H. Talbot, and H. M. Rochais (Rome: Editiones Cistercienses, 1957–77), 8: 391.

ing individual had been brought to his attention by Humbert, bishop of Lucca, and that he himself had borne the expenses connected with his education at Rheims for a time, Bernard recommends Peter to Gilduin. He clearly thinks that Paris is where Peter should go to enhance his theological education. Bernard urges Gilduin to support Peter for what he evidently envisions will be a fairly brief period of study.

The cathedral school of Rheims had initially suggested itself as a likely place for Peter to go because of the current presence there of masters who were continuing the tradition of Anselm of Laon, the best known theologian in France in the early years of the twelfth century.[7] The most renowned of these, famous—or notorious—for his opposition to Peter Abelard, was Alberic. Also present was Lotulph of Novara. He had engaged in a public debate on Christology with Gerhoch of Reichersberg in Rome in 1126. His repute in Italy may have been an added draw in the eyes of his fellow-citizen. At Rheims as well Peter could study with Walter of Mortagne, who had also taught at Laon and whose correspondence shows him to have maintained connections with a number of masters at other centers. The pedagogy of these masters, like that of Anselm of Laon, was strong on traditional exegesis and relatively unresponsive to the philosophical concerns animating a number of theologians in this period. This fact, along with Alberic's departure from Rheims to accept the bishopric of Bourges in 1136, may account for the timing of Peter's decision to leave that school. And, the fact that it was Hugh of St. Victor to whom Walter had turned for clarification on the doctrine of the Trinity may have suggested the profitability of studying with Hugh, whose masterpiece, the *De sacramentis*, was now nearing completion.[8]

Peter arrived in Paris in 1136. Nothing can be proved about his exact whereabouts in that city until he emerged in ca. 1142 as an acknowledged writer and teacher. Whether or not he was already teaching at Notre Dame at that point, he most certainly lent luster to that school from at least 1145, when he became a canon of Notre Dame. Peter's means of support before he was able to earn a living as a teacher and before he derived income from his canon's prebend

---

[7] John R. Williams, "The Cathedral School of Reims in the Time of Master Alberic, 1118–1136," *Traditio* 20 (1964): 93–114. See also Carlo Ramponi, "Leutaldo: Scuola teologica di Reims," *Pier Lombardo* 1 (1953): 14–15.

[8] Damien Van den Eynde, *Essai sur la succession et la date des écrits de Hugues de Saint-Victor* (Rome: Pontificium Athenaeum Antonianum, 1960), pp. 39–110, gives a thorough analysis of the date of the *De sacramentis* in relation to Hugh's other works and concludes, p. 110, that it was most likely completed in 1137.

remains a mystery. Did Gilduin respond favorably to Bernard's appeal, offering Peter hospitality at St. Victor and tuition with Hugh? This question has attracted debate. It is true that Peter's work reflects a thorough familiarity with Hugh's *De sacramentis* and with its largely Victorine sequel, the anonymous *Summa sententiarum*. He is deeply influenced by these sources. At the same time, one of the marks of Peter's theology is his grasp of the works of many other contemporary masters. He is thoroughly conversant, for example, with the writings of Peter Abelard, Gilbert of Poitiers and his earliest disciples, Robert Pullen, and Gratian. It was certainly possible in this period to acquaint oneself with the teachings of thinkers with whom one was not bound in a formal master-disciple relationship. An objection has also been raised to the idea that Peter actually studied with Hugh on the antiquated, and sketchy, grounds that the school of St. Victor was already closed to externs by Hugh's day.[9] Thus, William J. Courtenay maintains that the most Gilduin could have offered Peter was "meals and possibly accommodations . . . for at least a few months;" and he adds that "there is no evidence that he received formal instruction there, although he may have profited from personal contacts and possible access to the library."[10] In response to this statement, it is important to distinguish the issue of subvention, on which there is, indeed, no documentation whatever, from the question of whether, as an extern, Peter could have had access to the formal pedagogy of Hugh of St. Victor. For, on the latter point, we have solid evidence that two other contemporary externs did study with Hugh, suggesting that Courtenay's conclusion may be too hasty.

---

[9] Stephen C. Ferruolo, *The Origins of the University: The Schools of Paris and Their Critics, 1100–1215* (Stanford: Stanford University Press, 1985), pp. 27–29; William J. Courtenay, "Schools and Schools of Thought in the Twelfth Century," unpublished. I am indebted to Professor Courtenay for allowing me to use this paper in typescript. On the other hand, it has been pointed out by Philippe Delhaye, "L'organisation scolaire au XII͏e siècle," *Traditio* 5 (1947): 245–50 [repr. in *Enseignement et morale au XII͏e siècle* (Fribourg, Suisse: Éditions Universitaires, 1988, pp. 36–40]; Luc Jocqué, "Les structures de la population claustrale dans l'ordre de Saint-Victor au XII͏e siècle et au début du XIII͏e siècle," in *L'Abbaye parisienne de Saint-Victor au moyen âge*, ed. Jean Longère (Paris: Brepols, 1991), pp. 71–72, 72 n. 50, 91; and Jean Longère, "La fonction pastorale de Saint-Victor à la fin du XII͏e siècle et au début du XIII͏e siècle," in ibid., p. 291 that, unlike monastic houses, St. Victor did not close its doors to externs in this period. Both Jocqué and Longère think that the Lombard did receive hospitality and instruction there, as does Patrice Sicard, intro. to his ed. of *Hugues de Saint-Victor et son école* (Turnhout: Brepols, 1991), p. 17. Hödl, "Petrus Lombardus," p. 206, also thinks that Peter was an extern student at St. Victor.

[10] Courtenay, "Schools," n. 32.

One of these figures is Clarenbald of Arras. In 1142 or after, he wrote a commentary on the *De hebdomadibus* of Boethius, in the preface to which he reflects on his student days at St. Victor. This preface, in the form of a dedicatory epistle, was discovered by Nikolaus M. Häring in a previously unknown St. Omer manuscript and later incorporated by him into his critical edition of Clarenbald's text.[11] Clarenbald offers a justification for the composition of yet another commentary on the *De hebdomadibus*, given the fact that this work had been glossed repeatedly in the first half of the twelfth century. Two of his own masters, he observes, had done so, Thierry of Chartres and Hugh of St. Victor. Now, among twelfth-century authors, Hugh was exceptionally fortunate in the care lavished on his works by his successors. His oeuvre had already been catalogued by the Victorines as early as 1155. But, neither in the first nor in any subsequent inventory of his writings do we find a written commentary on the *De hebdomadibus*.[12] This means, unless there was a written gloss that did not survive, that the only way for Clarenbald to have known about Hugh's interpretation of that work was through his oral teaching. And, indeed, the term Clarenbald uses, *lectiones*, reports that this was the case.

Another contemporary witness to the fact that Hugh provided formal instruction to externs is Lawrence of Westminster. This Englishman began his monastic career at St. Albans and had already risen to the abbacy of Westminster when he decided to interrupt his duties in order to go to France to study with Hugh in the 1130s. After Hugh's death in 1141, he returned to England and moved to the abbey of Durham in 1143. It was here that he met Maurice, a monk of Durham. Maurice left Durham for Rievaulx, whose abbot he became in 1145. It was after that transfer that Lawrence dedicated to Maurice his *Sententiae de divinitate*,[13] whose relationship to the Hugonian canon has received much discussion. The text of the dedicatory epistle was first discovered and printed

---

[11] Nikolaus M. Häring, "A Hitherto Unknown Commentary on Boethius' *de Hebdomadibus* Written by Clarenbaldus of Arras," *MS* 15 (1953): 214–15; Häring, ed., *Life and Works of Clarenbald of Arras, A Twelfth-Century Master of the School of Chartres* (Toronto: Pontifical Institute of Mediaeval Studies, 1965), pp. 19–20, 23. The locus in Clarenbald's text is the dedicatory *Epistola ad Odonem* 3, p. 64.

[12] Rudolf Goy, *Die Überlieferung des Werke Hugos von St. Viktor* (Stuttgart: Hiersemann, 1976).

[13] F. E. Croydon, "Abbot Laurence of Westminster and Hugh of St. Victor," *Mediaeval and Renaissance Studies* 2 (1950): 169–71; Delhaye, "L'organisation scolaire," pp. 245–50 [repr. in *Enseignement et morale*, pp. 36–40]; Sicard, intro. to his ed. of *Hugues de Saint-Victor*, pp. 17, 23–24.

by Bernhard Bischoff;[14] and, more recently, it has been incorporated into his edition of the entire work by Ambrogio Piazzoni.[15] In
it, Lawrence presents the *Sententiae* as a *reportatio* of Hugh's oral
teaching, which Hugh looked over and corrected while Lawrence
was still at St. Victor. The debate over this text has focused on the
question of whether it actually is a *reportatio*, as Lawrence says it is,
and if so, whether the teaching it reports reflects Hugh's opinions
before or after the completion of his *De sacramentis*, or whether, on
the other hand, the *Sententiae* is a work of Lawrence's own authorship, albeit closely dependent on Hugh. These debates, chroni-
cled fully by Piazzoni,[16] do not concern us here. What does concern
us is the fact that Lawrence, as an extern, enjoyed the personal
instruction of Hugh. The fact that master-disciple relations between Hugh and extern students such as Clarenbald and Lawrence
took place in this period suggests that we should not rule out the
lively possibility that such a relationship may have taken place as
well between Hugh and Peter Lombard, between 1136 and the
beginning of Peter's own teaching career, whatever his means of
support may have been during those years.

The Lombard's teaching won rapid recognition; and it is likely
that this is what inspired the canons of Notre Dame to invite him to
join their ranks. Already in 1144, the author of the *Metamorpohosis
Goliae* could confidently add Peter's name as a "celebrated theologian" to the list of prominent Parisian masters whose "mouths
breathe nard and balsam."[17] Such praise recommended Peter to
the canons, whose school had not boasted a theologian of distinction for some time, inspiring them to overcome their ingrained
disinclination to recruit outsiders. The demography of the canons
of Notre Dame in the twelfth century has received detailed and
careful study.[18] They were a highly pre-selected group, tightly knit

---

[14] Bernhard Bischoff, "Aus der Schule Hugos von St. Viktor," in *Aus der
Geisteswelt des Mittelalters: Studien und Texte Martin Grabmann zur Vollendung des 60.
Lebensjahres von Freunden und Schülern gewidmet*, ed. Albert Lang, Joseph Lechner, and
Michael Schmaus, Beiträge, Supplementband 3:1 (Münster: Aschendorff, 1935),
1: 346–50.

[15] Ambrogio M. Piazzoni, "Ugo di San Vittore 'auctor' delle 'Sententiae de
divinitate'," *Studi medievali* 23:2 (1982): 912.

[16] Ibid., pp. 861–911.

[17] R. B. C. Huygens, ed., "Metamorphosis Goliae," *Studi medievali* 3:2 (1962):
771: "Celebrum theologum vidimus Lumbardum,/ cum Yvone Helyam Petrum et
Bernardum,/ quorum opobalsamum spiratos et nardum."

[18] Marcel Pacaut, *Louis VII et les élections épiscopales dans le royaume de France*
(Paris: J. Vrin, 1957), pp. 106–46; *Louis VII et son royaume* (Paris: SEVPEN, 1964),
pp. 109–17. See also Robert-Henri Bautier, "Paris en temps d'Abélard," in *Abélard
en son temps*, ed. Jean Jolivet (Paris: Les Belles Lettres, 1981), pp. 53–77; Jacques

in their social status and relationships. To a man—and this can be said, in essence, of the bishops of regalian France as well—they were members of the Capetian house, relatives of families closely linked to the Capetians by blood or marriage, scions of the Ile-de-France or eastern Loire valley nobility, or relatives of royal officials. This situation was especially pronounced at Notre Dame, where the fortunes of the canons and those of their secular relatives in the royal service went hand in hand. Networking, nepotism, and favor-itism were the standard means of ecclesiastical advancement, promoted not only by the families of such men in order to enhance the power and influence of their lineages, but also as a calculated strategy of the monarch, in the effort to bind the prominent noble families in the royal domain to the royal cause, to reward their loyalty with promotion, and to block the advancement of those who were out of favor. For his part, Peter Lombard had no relatives, no ecclesiastical connections, and no political patrons or associates in France. He thus appears to have been recruited and welcomed by the canons of Notre Dame on the basis of scholarly merit alone. He was the one, and the only, member of that body who lacked its typical social profile. Also, unlike some prominent canons of Notre Dame—Robert of Garland leaps to mind—he was no pluralist. He cannot be identified with the Peter named as a canon of St. Mary's, Chartres, who in any case is described as a physician to King Louis VII, a profession he never practiced. Nor is he the master Peter whom Pope Eugenius III recommends in a letter to Henry, bishop of Beauvais, in 1151, asking him to provide that individual with a prebend. Peter Lombard was a beneficed cleric of Notre Dame of Paris only.[19]

Once a member of the chapter, Peter continued to advance. It is not known at what point he was ordained to the priesthood. He became a subdeacon in 1147. He participated as a theological expert at the council of Rheims, presided over by Eugenius III in 1148, and possibly at the consistory of Paris that prepared the way for it in the preceding year.[20] At some time after 1150 he became a

Boussard, *Nouvelle histoire de Paris: De la fin du siège de 885–886 à la mort de Philippe Auguste* (Paris: Hachette, 1976), pp. 197–225; Elizabeth M. Hallam, *Capetian France, 987–1328* (London: Longman, 1980), pp. 193–95.

[19] Brady, Prolegomenon to *Sent.* 1: 18*–19*.

[20] Ibid., pp. 27*–30*. Brady notes that not all the contemporary sources mention Peter's attendance at this consistory and council. For the most recent analysis of the pertinent sources, see Laura Cioni, "Il concilio di Reims nelle fonti contemporanee," *Aevum* 53 (1979): 273–300. For additional bibliography, see Marcia L. Colish, "Gilbert, the Early Porretans, and Peter Lombard: Semantics

deacon, and an archdeacon by 1156, if not as early as 1152.
Between the middle of July, 1153 and the beginning of December,
1154, his bishop, Theobald, was in Rome on ecclesiastical business.
It is extremely likely that Peter was in his suite. He was certainly of
appropriate rank to accompany his bishop; and, of course, he was
the only member of the chapter who spoke Italian. It is generally
agreed that it was Peter's presence in Rome at this time that
afforded him the opportunity to discover the *De fide orthodoxa* of the
eighth-century Byzantine theologian, John Damascene. Translation
of John's work into Latin had just been completed by Burgundio of
Pisa as a papal commission. Peter was the first Latin theologian to
make use of John's work, and he did so to crucial effect in his own
theology from 1155 onward.

Most striking of all as an index of how this outsider became an
insider is Peter's election as bishop of Paris, a post to which he was
consecrated on about the feast of SS. Peter and Paul, July 28, 1159.
Describing him as "a man of great learning and admirable above
all the other Parisian doctors,"[21] the chronicler who reports this
event leaves no doubt that it was scholarly attainment that won
Peter this honor. The outcome is the more extraordinary given the
fact that learning scarcely ranked high on the list of qualifications
for high ecclesiastical office in the France of Louis VII. Indeed, of
the some 300 men Louis raised to the rank of bishop within the
royal domain, or in sees outside of it where he held regalian rights,
one can number on the fingers of one hand those who were authors
or notable masters. Besides Peter, the only one who was a foreigner
was John of Salisbury. John's elevation to the bishopric of Chartres
later in the century inspired astonishment in the eyes of many
French clerics, notwithstanding his wide-ranging political connections, both in England and on the continent. Unlike Peter and
John, the other exceptions to Louis' episcopal policy had long-
standing ecclesiastical or social ties in the dioceses to which they
were appointed.[22] Moreover, the first name reputed to have been
put forth in the Parisian election of 1159 was not Peter's, but that of
Philip, also an archdeacon of Paris, but, unlike Peter, the king's
younger brother. Philip looked to be the obvious choice. But, when

---

and Theology," in *Gilbert de Poitiers et ses contemporains: Aux origines de la logica
modernorum*, ed. Jean Jolivet and Alain de Libera (Naples: Bibliopolis, 1987), p. 229
n. 1.
    [21] *Continuatio Beccensis*, ed. Richard Howlett, Rolls Series (London: H. M.
Stationer's Office, 1889), 81 part 4: 323: "Magister Petrus Longobardus, vir
magnae scientie et super Parisiensium doctores admirabilis."
    [22] Pacaut, *Louis VII et les élections*, pp. 106–09; Hallam, *Capetian France*, p. 195.

Peter's name was placed in nomination, Philip stepped down, in deference to the man who had been his teacher. Louis may have been surprised initially when the canons presented Peter as their candidate; but he ratified the election without demur or delay.[23] Peter's reign as bishop was as brief as his attainment of the office was remarkable. He died on either July 21 or 22, 1160. His surviving episcopal *acta* are too few and unsubstantial to enable us to infer anything about his administrative style or priorities. His epitaph, which, like his tomb, lay in the church of St. Marcellus in Paris prior to its destruction during the French Revolution, speaks rather to his fame as the author of the *Four Books of Sentences*, and his glosses on the Psalms and the Pauline epistles.[24]

WORKS

These are the works of Peter's that have come down to us, although the assiduous investigation of modern scholarship has shown that they were not his only writings. The commentary on the Psalms is Peter's earliest known work. It was completed before 1138. An English pupil of the Lombard's, Herbert of Bosham, states that it was composed for his own edification and reflection, and not as a text for classroom instruction.[25] There is no evidence that he taught Psalms exegesis formally until 1158–59, although Brady's careful labors as the editor of the *Sentences* reveal the fact that he made significant use of the material in the Psalms gloss in his teaching as a systematic theologian. The next surviving work is his commentary on the Pauline epistles, entitled the *Collectanea*. This work underwent two redactions, the first composed between 1139 and 1141,[26] and the second, which revised some but not all parts of the

---

[23] Robert of Torigni, *Chronica*, ed. Richard Howlett, Rolls Series (London: H. M. Stationer's Office, 1889), 82 part 4: 204 even describes Peter's election as having been promoted "connivente Philippo." See also *Gallia Christiana*, 7: 68. The story of Philip's withdrawal is doubted by Brady, Prolegomonon to *Sent.* 1: 33*–34*. But it is accepted by Pacaut, *Louis VII et les élections*, pp. 119, 139, whose analysis Brady does not consider.

[24] *Gallia Christiana*, 7: 69.

[25] The text is printed by Joseph de Ghellinck, "La carrière de Pierre Lombard: Nouvelle précision chronologique," *RHE* 30 (1934): 98. Peter's glosses on the Psalms are printed in *PL* 191. Herbert's work on these glosses is discussed by H. H. Glunz, *History of the Vulgate in England from Alcuin to Roger Bacon: Being an Inquiry into the Text of Some English Manuscripts of the Vulgate Gospels* (Cambridge: Cambridge University Press, 1933), pp. 219–24.

[26] Recently, Zier, "Peter Lombard," p. 517, has followed Brady in arguing for a date of ca. 1147–48 for the first recension because of Peter's familiarity with the ideas of Gilbert of Poitiers, which gained wide publicity at that time. But he

work, between 1155 and 1158. Finishing touches on both glosses
were added by Herbert, our first external witness to the double
redaction of the *Collectanea*.[27] Internal evidence supporting the double redaction has also been found in the material from the *Sentences*
which Peter incorporates into the second version, reflecting the
development of his thought particularly in cases where he uses
John Damascene.[28] Herbert does not indicate whether Peter's
Pauline exegesis was initially intended for classroom instruction.[29]
That this was the case is highly likely on both substantive and
methodological grounds. There are clear, and reciprocal, borrow-
ings of subject matter between the *Collectanea* and the *Sentences*. Just
as he imported material he was developing for the final edition of
the *Sentences* into the second redaction of the *Collectanea*, so he
assigned large chunks of the *Collectanea* to their appropriate subject
matter categories within the *Sentences*. Here, Brady's careful annotations of Peter's exegetical sources in the *Sentences* document one side
of the transaction, while his discovery and publication of several of
Peter's interim revisions of the first redactions of his commentaries
on Romans and 1 Corinthians, which do not yet reflect his most
mature treatment of the topics involved, illuminate the process of
exegetical revision.[30] This evidence aside, it is difficult to see why
Peter would have gone to the trouble of updating the *Collectanea*
unless he was planning to use it as a teaching text, side by side with
the *Sentences*. According to Brady, he lectured on St. Paul from these
revised glosses in his final year of teaching,[31] an opinion that makes
eminent sense. For, it was in his Pauline exegesis that Peter first
worked out the method for handling conflicting authorities, both in

---

ignores the fact that Gilbert taught in Paris for several years prior to his elevation
to the see of Poitiers in 1142, and the fact that Peter was informed on Porretan
teachings well before the end of the decade. For the chronology of Gilbert's career
as a teacher, see H. C. van Elswijk, *Gilbert Porreta: Sa vie, son oeuvre, sa pensée*
(Louvain: Spicilegium Sacrum Lovaniense, 1966), p. 25; Lauge Olaf Nielsen,
*Theology and Philosophy in the Twelfth Century: A Study of Gilbert Porreta's Thinking and
the Theological Exposition of the Doctrine of the Incarnation during the Period 1130–1180*,
Acta theologica danica, 15 (Leiden: E. J. Brill, 1982), pp. 27–29. The text of the
Collectanea is printed in *PL* 191–192.
   [27] Ghellinck, "La carrière," pp. 95–100.
   [28] Modern scholars who have tracked the internal evidence for the second
redaction of the *Collectanea* include Jean Leclercq, "Les deux redactions du prologue de Pierre Lombard sur les Épîtres de S. Paul," in *Misc. Lomb.*, pp. 109–12;
Ermenegildo Bertola, "I commentari paolini di Pietro Lombardo e loro duplice
redazione," *Pier Lombardo* 3: 2–3 (1959): 75–90. The text of the *Collectanea* printed
in *PL* 191–192 is based on the second redaction.
   [29] Ghellinck, "La carrière," pp. 95–100.
   [30] Brady, Appendices 1–3, in Prolegomenon to *Sent.* 2: 53*–87*.
   [31] Brady, Prolegomenon to *Sent.* 2: 19*.

establishing the correct reading of Paul's text and in addressing the doctrinal questions that flow from it, a method visible in a more full-blown form in the *Sentences*. Methodologically too, then, the organic connections between his exegesis and his systematic theology suggest why he would have treated the *Collectanea* as a school text and as a natural pedagogical companion piece to the *Sentences*.

The *Sentences* constitute the Lombardian *summa* that emerged out of the course in systematic theology which Peter taught for well-nigh two decades. He is thought to have begun this approach to pedagogy soon after the completion of the first version of his glosses on Paul. He continued to revise his treatment of particular topics over the years, sometimes entertaining his students in class by citing, as a position to be refuted, one he had held himself only recently.[32] The development of Peter's ideas in the *Sentences* benefited from his deep, independent, and discriminating research into the thought of earlier authorities and from his wide familiarity with the work of contemporary masters, which sometimes alerted him to the need to take a stand on issues that were otherwise of little interest to him and sometimes led him to abandon, or, alternatively, to emphasize more sharply, opinions he had stated in his own earlier writings. The major turning point in his theological development in the writing of the *Sentences*, which enables us to date its final edition to the years 1155–57, was his encounter with the works of John Damascene in 1154. This author gave Peter the tools with which to reformulate his position on Trinitarian theology and Christology and to develop new arguments against views he rejected. The revised edition of the *Sentences* was probably what he taught in the academic year 1157–58, since, at the instance of his pupils, the following year was given over to the teaching of exegesis. The final version of the *Sentences* went into circulation immediately. And, it was read in circles that went well beyond those of the scholastic classrooms of Paris and environs where one would expect to find it, as is witnessed by the fact that the provenance of the first extant manuscript of the *Sentences*, dated to 1158 in the hand of the same scribe who copied it, now Troyes Bibliothèque Municipal MS. 286, formerly 960, was the monastery of Clairvaux.[33]

---

[32] Ignatius C. Brady, "Peter Manducator and the Oral Teachings of Peter Lombard," *Antonianum* 41 (1966): 454–90.

[33] This manuscript was first noted and described by Joseph de Ghellinck, "Le traité de Pierre Lombard sur les sept ordres ecclésiastiques: Ses sources, ses copistes," *RHE* 10 (1909): 17 n. 2; and Martin Grabmann, *Die Geschichte der scholastischen Methode* (Graz: Akademische Druck- u. Verlagsanstalt, 1957 [repr. of Freiburg im Breisgau, 1911 ed.], 2: 362.

As a member of the cathedral chapter of Notre Dame, Peter Lombard served as a preacher as well as a teacher of theology at the school. Some thirty of his sermons have survived, twenty-six of which are printed among the sermons of Hildebert of Lavardin in Migne's *Patrologia latina*, while the other four, discovered recently, have been edited and published elsewhere.[34] The vast majority were composed for delivery in connection with specific liturgical feast days or seasons, particularly Advent, Lent, and Easter, and very occasionally for saints' days falling within these parts of the liturgical calendar. They adhere closely to the themes of the day, without digressing. Rather than making his point of departure the gospel or another biblical reading assigned to the mass of the day, Peter takes as his text some other biblical passage that relates to it or that sheds light on it. His objective is not to preach on a particular text, but on the significance of the event in the life of Christ commemorated in the liturgy. His goal is less an exegetical one than a dogmatic one, the illumination of doctrinal truths and ethical values, which he always seeks to place in a larger theological framework. He sometimes weaves additional biblical material into the fabric of the sermon to promote these ends.

In handling the Bible in his sermons, Peter displays a firm grasp of the principles of typological exegesis, using them cogently, and in moderation, to show the connection between the revelation of the Old Testament and that of the New. He is not interested in the multiplication of allegorical examples, or in repeating himself. Copiousness is not one of his stylistic ideals. His sermons are lean and have a clear beginning, middle, and end. He evidently expects his audience to be able to follow the structure of his sermons, without the need for him to highlight their organization or to summarize the points made at the end of each section. Peter shows himself to be in command of the standard rhetorical devices used in homiletic oratory. He uses parallel sentence structures, parallel rhythms, and pariform word endings to reinforce his points, as well as the frequent citation of examples in threes. But he is not an orator who speaks because he enjoys the sound of his own voice, in order to overwhelm his audience emotionally, or to impress them with a display of rhetorical pyrotechnics. Both his voice, and his presentation of doctrine, are straightforward. They appeal to the

---

[34] See the analysis in Brady, Prolegomenon to *Sent.* 2: 99*–112*. The sermons belonging to Peter in *PL* 171 are those numbered 4, 7–8, 12–13, 21, 23–25, 32, 35–36, 43, 45, 55, 67–68, 72, 78, 80, 99, 111–112, and 115. See also Damien Van den Eyade, ed., "Deux sermons inédits de Pierre Lombard," in *Misc. Lomb.*, pp. 75–87.

intellect more than to the heart. He deals with essential truths of the faith, grounding them mainly on the birth, life, teaching career, miracles, passion, and resurrection of Christ. The doctrines aired are sometimes ones that were matters of great controversy in the period; but Peter presents them concisely and without polemics. Those sermons dealing with the Trinity and with the co-inherence of the divine and human natures in the incarnate Christ were clearly written in the 1140s or early 1150s, for they do not manifest the more pointed doctrine and the crisper theological vocabulary found in the final edition of the *Sentences* on those subjects. Likewise, the sermons in which Peter discusses the cardinal virtues do not yet reflect the mature doctrine of grace found in his later work. The few scholars who have commented on Peter Lombard's sermons have agreed in finding them clear, instructive, impersonal, grave, and cool in their tone of voice. They are not sermons designed to reveal anything about the inner life of the author. They were probably composed for delivery not to the wider urban congregation of the cathedral of Notre Dame but to the canons and the students at the school.[35] Peter was not a master of the spiritual life and does not seek to present himself as one in his sermons. Rather, he resembles a school chaplain, who wants his educated hearers to apply their intelligence to their experience of the liturgy and to the nodal mysteries of the Christian faith that it commemorates.

As late as 1971, when Brady published the first volume of his edition of the *Sentences*, most scholarly considerations of Peter's works, having disposed of the *dubia* and *spuria*,[36] were inclined to stop right here. More recently, however, and triggered by the pioneering work of Beryl Smalley and George Lacombe,[37] which he

---

[35] Brady, Prolegomenon to *Sent.* 2: 33* n. 2, 34*; Joseph de Ghellinck, "Pierre Lombard," in *DTC* (Paris: Letouzey et Ané, 1935), 12 part 2: 1960; Jean Longère, *Oeuvres oratoires des maîtres parisiens au XIIᵉ siècle: Étude historique et doctrinale* (Paris: Études Augustiniennes, 1975), 1: 87–88.

[36] On this, see Joseph de Ghellinck, "Les 'opera dubia vel spuria' attribués à Pierre Lombard," *RHE* 28 (1932), 829–45; Ludwig Ott, *Untersuchung zur theologischen Briefliteratur der Frühscholastik*, Beiträge, 34 (Münster: Aschendorff, 1937), pp. 80–82; Brady, Prolegomenon to *Sent.* 1: 113*–17*. These include three letters from an unidentified Peter of Paris, two of which are written to a non-existent Philip, archbishop of Rheims, an *apologia* defending Peter against the attack made on his Christology by John of Cornwall after his death, a *Practicae theologiae methodus*, an *In concordiam evangelicam*, and a *Glossa ordinaria*. Brady, Prolegomenon to *Sent.* 2: 112*, later judged that Sermons 31 and 32, printed in *PL* 171 among other of the Lombard's sermons, are dubious and spurious, respectively.

[37] Beryl Smalley and George Lacombe were the first to suggest an expansion of the Lombard's exegetical canon in their "The Lombard's Commentary on Isaias and Other Fragments," *New Scholasticism* 5 (1931): 123–62; followed by Smalley, "Some Gospel Commentaries of the Early Twelfth Century," *RTAM* 45 (1978):

confirmed in his latest research into the Lombardian canon, Brady has pressed forward to the investigation of the other writings that can be attributed to Peter although they are no longer extant. These writings are all exegetical and suggest that the Lombard glossed not only the Psalms and St. Paul, but virtually the entire Bible. Since these works have not survived, it is impossible to date them and to discover why they failed to inspire the interest which the Psalms commentary and the *Collectanea* clearly attracted. And, by the same token, the evidence supporting the composition of these other glosses is, necessarily, indirect. Three main lines of inquiry have been pursued in establishing that they existed, and what they were. In the first place, and following Smalley's lead, Brady has found references to additional glosses of Peter's in the works of contemporaries who were his pupils, such as Peter Comestor, William of Tyre, and Peter the Chanter, and in other figures, such as Stephen Langton, whose exegesis is closely dependent on Peter's.[38] Another of Brady's tactics has been to detect the work of Peter the exegete in citations found in his other writings that cannot be traced to the glosses of the other exegetes on whom he drew.[39]

A third approach of Brady's has been to appeal to external evidence, especially the cartulary of Notre Dame and related documents.[40] The cartulary records Peter's obituary, and with it the bequest he made to the chapter in his last will and testament. This will indicates that he owned a house, next to St. Christopher's church on the Ile-de-la-Cité. This he gave to the chapter along with an "entire chapel" containing a gold chalice, liturgical vestments, two silver basins, and two vessels used in the administration of the water and wine in the Eucharistic service, a breviary in two volumes, and a pallium or altar cloth. In addition, and carefully inventoried, he bequeathed his library. The titles include the entire New Testament, with glosses on all the books. The books of the Old Testament accompanied by glosses are the Psalms, the five books of Moses, the four major prophets, the twelve minor prophets, the Song of Songs, and the books of Job, Esther, Tobias, Judith, Wisdom, and Ecclesiastes. Also listed are Peter's own copy of his *Sentences* and the *Decretum* of Gratian.[41] Since this is Peter's official

---

153–56, 175; "Peter Comestor on the Gospels and His Sources," *RTAM* 46 (1979): 113. This position receives the support of Hödl, "Petrus Lombardus," p. 208.

[38] Brady, Prolegomenon to *Sent.* 2: 19*, 23*–28*, 44*–52*.

[39] Ibid., pp. 29*–33*.

[40] Ibid., p. 21*.

[41] M. Guérard, ed., *Cartulaire de l'église Notre-Dame de Paris*, Collection des cartulaires de France, 4 (Paris: Crapelet, 1850), 1: 60.

and documented bequest, it deserves to be taken seriously. Brady also refers to a library catalogue of Notre Dame which, among other exegetical works, mentions glosses on the books of Esdra and Proverbs. He argues that these glosses, as well, are works of the Lombard's.[42] This document, however, is far more problematic than Peter's last will and testament. The latter can be dated to the year of his death and it specifically refers to the glossed books of the Bible as his own. On the other hand, the library catalogue is not itself dated. It is located in the cartulary between two items that are dated, but their dates are from the late twelfth to early thirteenth century. Nothing is stated about the authorship of any of the exegetical works listed. Included in this catalogue are the *Quaestiones* of Peter of Poitiers, a disciple of the Lombard's whose writings date to the next generation.[43] It may well be, therefore, that Peter of Poitiers, Peter Comestor, or some other Notre Dame master of the second half of the twelfth century is the author of these glosses.

Finally, Brady has stated that none of the manuscripts ascribable to the Lombard in either of these documents were retained by the chapter of Notre Dame. He speculates that they were sold by his successor to the see of Paris, Maurice of Sully,[44] a known critic of some of Peter's teachings and, equally important, an avid fundraiser whose chief administrative objective was to finance the raising of the new, high Gothic cathedral of Notre Dame, whose construction he initiated. Such may have been the case. Brady mentions a copy of the *Sentences* listed in 1271 among the books possessed by Notre Dame for the use of poor scholars, described as *originale Lombardi*. He suggests that the term "original" here means "integral," and that this codex was not Peter's autograph copy.[45] This judgment is plausible, because the same language occurs in another document not noticed by Brady, which can scarcely refer to the selfsame manuscript. In 1296, Peter of St. Audemars, chancellor of Notre Dame, made a donation of his own, a collection of theology books to be kept in the charge of subsequent chancellors of Notre Dame, also for the use of poor scholars who could not afford their own copies. The inventory includes "the *Four Books of Sentences. Item,* the original of the *Sentences* of Master Peter Lombard," and goes on to describe the binding of the codex, its leather now somewhat the

---

[42] Brady, Prolegomenon to *Sent.* 2: 21*–22*.
[43] *Cartulaire de Notre-Dame*, 1: 462, item 39.
[44] Brady, Prolegomenon to *Sent.* 2: 22*–23*.
[45] Brady, Prolegomenon to *Sent.* 1: 129*–30*.

worse for wear.[46] From the standpoint of the physical wanderings
and vicissitudes of medieval codices, the ultimate fate of Peter's
own personal copy of his masterpiece is unknown. But the academic
survival of Peter's *Sentences* was never very much in doubt.

REPUTATION

How far do the biographical facts that can be gleaned, inferred,
or plausibly conjectured about him go in putting a human face on
Peter Lombard? While he remains tantalizingly elusive as a personality, some few glimpses of what he was like do emerge from the
externals of his life. He was clearly a man who made a deep and
lasting impression on his contemporaries, a man who inspired
admiration and respect. As a foreigner without resources and connections, he succeeded in swimming against the current of French
church history in his day, winning reception as a canon of Notre
Dame, advancement in the chapter, and a stunning election to the
bishopric of Paris. Strictly on the basis of talent, he rose to the top
of the academic ladder and thereby captured for Notre Dame a
commanding lead in the teaching of school theology, which was to
flow directly into the theological faculty of the University of Paris in
the immediate sequel. As a career intellectual, he managed to turn
his outsider status in France into an asset. He was open to learning
from a wide number of masters and found decided affinities with
some of them; but he never sacrificed his independence on the altar
of discipleship. In a period when personal animosities and professional jealousies often poisoned the exchanges between thinkers,
embittering the lives of some masters and hindering their work,
Peter appears to have made no enemies, but rather to have won the
esteem of those who knew him, even though he did not shrink from
espousing controversial opinions.

Peter's students quite naturally lauded him. As with William of
Tyre, who was his pupil for six years, the Lombard's outstanding
knowledge, the "sane doctrine commended by all," and the veneration his teaching inspired[47] could be invoked retrospectively as a

---

[46] *Excerpta ex Libro nigro*, 2, Appendix to *Cartulaire de Notre-Dame*, 3: 353: "Quat-
tuor libri Sententiarum. Item, originale Sententiarum magistri Petri Lombardi, in
quodam libro coperto corio vitulino, jam quasi depilato, cum clavis rotundis
cupro."

[47] This fragment from William of Tyre's *Historia* was discovered and first
published by R. B. C. Huygens, ed., "Guillaume de Tyr étudiant: Un chapitre
(XIX, 12) de son 'Histoire' retrouvé," *Latomus* 21 (1962): 823: "In theologia
autem virum in ea scientia singularem, cuius opera que exstant prudentum chorus

measure of his own good fortune and of the solidity of his own academic training. The praises of the author of the *Metamorphosis Goliae* and of the continuator of Bec, cited earlier, came from men who had no such personal stake in his reputation. Even a critic, like Gerhoch of Reichersberg, could refer honestly and gracefully to Peter's distinguished research as the author of the *Sentences*, bringing together as it did "the opinions of many and diverse churchmen and scholastics both old and new,"[48] in the same work where he took exception to Peter's Christology, as he understood it.

Later in the twelfth and thirteenth century, chroniclers from various parts of Europe echo the impression of Peter's decisive seizure of the theological initiative which the inner history of scholasticism reveals. At the very least, with Jacques de Vitry, they hold his work to be useful.[49] More typically, as with Alberic of Trois Fontaines, they describe his *Sentences* as "a most excellent work" and his exegesis as now the acknowledged "greater gloss,"[50] while the Sanblasian continuator characterizes his teaching as brilliant and illustrious.[51] A few thirteenth-century chroniclers repeat these views, sometimes almost verbatim; by then, they had acquired an air of complimentary boiler plate.[52] But Vincent of Beauvais goes on to observe that Peter's works, "all of which are publicly taught

---

cum veneratione amplectitur et colit cum reverentia, virum sana doctrina per omnia commendabilem, magistrum videlicet Petrum Lonbardum, qui postea fuit Parisienssis episcopus, annis sex continuis audivimus."

[48] Gerhoch of Reichersberg, *Liber de gloria et honore Filii hominis* 19, *PL* 194: 1143D.

[49] Jacques de Vitry, *Chronicon Legendae aurae inserto*, MGH, Scriptores (Hannover, 1879). 24: 171: "Floruit magister Petrus Lombardus episcopus Parisiensis, qui Librum Sententiarum, glosas Psalterii, et epistolarum Pauli utiliter compilavit."

[50] Alberic of Trois Fontaines, *Chronaca*, MGH, Scriptores (Hannover, 1874), 23: 843: "Circa hoc tempus magister Petrus Lombardus fuit Parisiensibus episcopus . . . Qui tria fecit opuscula egregia, videlicet Librum Sententiarum, quod est opus excellentissimum, Glossaturam continuam super beati Pauli epistolas, et opus satis grande super Psalterium. Et hec est in scholis illa quae dicitur maior Glossatura."

[51] *Continuatio Sanblasiana*, MGH, Scriptores (Hannover, 1868), 20: 308: "His diebus Petrus Lombardus et Petrus Manducator apud Parisiensium magistri insigni claruerunt . . . Preter hec in Apostolum nec non Psalterium continuas glosas luculenter admodum exposuit."

[52] For instance, *Chronica Pontificium et Imperatorum Mantuana*, MGH, Scriptores (Hannover, 1879), 24: 218: "Eo etiam tempore floruit Petrus Lombardus, episcopus Parisiensis, qui Librum Sententiarum, glosas Psalterii et Epistolarum Pauli utiliter compilavit;" William Andrensus, *Chronica*, MGH, Scriptores (Hannover, 1879), 24: 725: "Et cum eisdem donariis Psalterium glossatum, epistolas Pauli glossatas, sententias magistri Petri."

in the schools," had attained the status of academic classics.[53] It is certainly true that, by the late thirteenth century, scholastics had concurred in dismissing some of Peter's opinions.[54] None the less, Dante Alighieri was on the mark in placing him in the Heaven of the Sun, the heaven of the theologians, along side of some of his most famous commentators.[55] These witnesses testify to the rapid acceptance which Peter's work received and to its continuing impact on both systematic theology and exegesis. But there is one of them, the same Ricobaldo of Ferrara responsible for launching some of the Lombardian apocrypha with which this chapter opened, who goes farther than anyone else in underscoring the particular qualities of mind and character that emerge from the nude facts of Peter's biography, the qualities that informed his writings and gave them their immediate excitement and durable appeal. Peter was recognized, Ricobaldo says, for the "shining intelligence" (*clarus ingenio*) irradiating his *Sentences*; he was "a learned and a humble man" (*vir peritus et humilis*).[56] In the chapters that follow, it will be our task to uncover the teachings that flowered from the stock of these inborn and acquired virtues.

---

[53] Vincent of Beauvais, *Memoriale omnium temporum*, MGH, Scriptores (Hannover, 1879), 24: 157–58: "Sub Ludovico Francorum rege, patre Philippi, magister Petrus Lombardus Parisiensis episcopus claruit, qui Libri Sententiarum et glosas psalteri et epistularum Pauli, que omnia nunc in scholis publice leguntur, ex multis catholicorum patrum dictis utiliter compilavit et ordinavit."

[54] Edward A. Synan, "Brother Thomas, the Master, and the Masters," in *St. Thomas Aquinas, 1274–1974: Commemorative Studies*, 2 vols., ed. Armand A. Maurer et al. (Toronto: Pontifical Institute of Mediaeval Studies, 1974), 2: 227–42.

[55] Dante Alighieri, *Paradiso* 10.107–08: "quel Pietro fu che con la poverella/offerse a Santa Chiesa suo tesoro." Massara, "La leggenda," pp. 135–36, thinks that the legend of Peter as the son of a poor laundress is the source for this image of the widow's mite. But, it derives from Peter's allusion to Mark 12:42–43 and to Luke 21:1–2 in his "modest author" description of his work in the *incipit* to *Sent.* 1 prologus 1, 1: 3.

[56] Ricobaldo, *Historia*, Rerum Italicorum Scriptores, 9: 124.

CHAPTER TWO

THE THEOLOGICAL ENTERPRISE

The most central and enduring contribution to the history of Christian thought made in the time of Peter Lombard was a thoroughgoing reconsideration of the nature of the theological enterprise. As contributing members of the renaissance of learning that swept through the twelfth-century schools in all fields of learning, the theologians in his milieu were eager to amplify and to improve on the quality of instruction in their own subject. And, as with other contemporary masters, they were concerned with turning their subject into a professional discipline, one with a clear intellectual profile and a conscious sense of what pertained to it and where it stood in relation to other forms of intellectual endeavor. Theologians in the schools committed themselves, as never before, to the task of ensuring that their students possessed both the range and depth of knowledge and the technical skills required not only to solve practical problems within the church but also the skills required to train other professional theologians as masters in their own turn. As a consequence, a massive pedagogical assignment now confronted the school theologians. They were required to design a curriculum for the education of professional theologians. In constructing their syllabus, they had to decide what topics to include and the order in which to present them. They needed to supply, as well, a convincing rationale for their particular selection and ordering of the material. In addition, the theologians needed to devise pedagogical strategies for teaching their students how to think theologically. Students would have to learn how to appraise and to analyze the legacy of the Christian tradition and the positions of rival contemporary masters. They would need guidance in the fruitful application of ideas and principles drawn from sister disciplines. And, they would have to master the use of these tools and materials critically and constructively in addressing the theological problems of the day, both the hardy perennials and the questions being newly agitated.

SYSTEMATIC THEOLOGY IN THE TWELFTH CENTURY

The response of the twelfth-century theologians to these perceived educational needs was to invent systematic theology[1] and the sentence collection as a means of doing it. It must be stressed here that both systematic theology and the sentence collection were inventions of the twelfth century. To be sure, a huge amount of theology had been written before this time. Latin theologians from the patristic period onward had produced a large number of genres of theological literature. They had written exegesis, polemics, hortatory, consolatory, and homiletic literature. They had reflected and debated on a host of individual themes and questions, whether dogmatic, sacramental, ethical, or publicistic. They had held up models of excellence in saints' lives and had catalogued heresies to be avoided. They had also, at times, collected debated issues and offered their solutions; they had commented on the creeds of the church; and they had drafted concise summaries of the main points of Christian doctrine for the instruction of neophytes. But, before the twelfth century, no Latin theologian had developed a full-scale theological system, with a place for everything and everything in its place, in a work that went well beyond the bare essentials, that treated theology as a wholesale and coherent intellectual activity, and that, at the same time, imparted the principles of theological reasoning and theological research to professionals in the making.[2] The genre of theological literature which proved to be the twelfth century's most innovative response to the pedagogical challenge presented by the teaching of systematic theology was the scholastic sentence collection. As we know, it was Peter Lombard's *Sentences*

---

[1] A useful introductory overview is provided by Henri Cloes, "La systématisation théologique pendant la première moitié du XIIe siècle," *ETL* 34 (1958): 277–329.

[2] For the contrast between the patristic and the twelfth-century handling of *quaestiones* and the relation of the latter to theological system-building, see Coloman Viola, "Manières personnelles et impersonnelles d'aborder un problème: Saint Augustin et le XIIe siècle. Contribution à l'histoire de la 'quaestio'," in *Les Genres littéraires dans les sources théologiques et philosophiques médiévales: Définition, critique et exploitation* (Louvain-la-Neuve: Institut d'Études Médiévales, 1982), pp. 25–30. Aloys Grillmeier, "Fulgentius von Ruspe, De fide ad Petrum und die Summa Sententiarum: Eine Studie zum Werden der frühscholastischen Systematik," *Scholastik* 34 (1959): 526–65 seeks to show that patristic works such as Fulgentius, *De fide ad Petrum* and Gennadius, *Liber sive definitio ecclesiasticorum dogmatum* should be seen as schematic models for sentence collections such as the *Summa sententiarum*, and not merely as sources for individual opinions; but the effect of his analysis is to show the differences rather than the parallels between these kinds of works.

that was regarded by medieval scholastics as having met the educational objectives involved in this enterprise better than the sentence collections of his competitors. In order to see how and why this was the case, this chapter will consider the *Sentences* in comparison with the work of the actual or would-be systematic theologians of the first half of the twelfth century, not only among the scholastics who made use of the sentence collection as a medium but also among the non-scholastic theologians who wrote systematic theology, tackling parallel assignments but with quite different aims.

MONASTIC PARALLELS AND CONTRASTS

It is important to recognize that systematic theology was not a monopoly of the scholastics, and that not all scholastic theologians at the time were interested in writing it, or equally adequate to the task when they did essay it. There were a number of monastic authors who wrote systematic theology in the first half of the twelfth century. It is not their lack of an esprit de système that differentiates them from contemporary scholastics, but rather the educational agendas with which they associated it. At the same time, not all early twelfth-century scholastics were involved in system-building to the same degree. Some were, but went only part of the distance, while others did not set out on this itinerary at all. The activity was far from being monolithic; it does not always provide an automatic or infallible way of distinguishing one sub-set of theologians from another in this period. In order to illustrate that point, and to heighten our appreciation of what Peter aimed at and achieved, it will be helpful to approach him by way of the theologians of the generation before and during his own, with whom he may be usefully compared.

The earliest systematic theologians of the twelfth century were not scholastics at all but monks, German Benedictines deeply committed to the Gregorian reform movement in general and to monastic reform in particular. Some proponents of monastic reform at this time thought that the best way to achieve it was to found new monastic orders. But Rupert of Deutz and Honorius Augustodunensis, the figures who will serve as our cases in point here, sought to reinvigorate the Benedictine order from within. The energy which they applied to this task and the long term success of the systematic theologies which they wrote for that purpose do much to support John Van Engen's claim that the crisis deemed to have been afflicting Benedictine monasticism at this time has been somewhat exaggerated.[3] While Rupert and Honorius have much in common, a close look at their systematic theologies shows that they are as different from each other as each is from his scholastic counterparts.

Rupert's *On the Trinity and Its Works*, written between 1112 and 1116, is one of the first systematic theologies of the century.[4] It displays many similarities with contemporary and later scholastic sentence collections. As with many current scholastics, Rupert is sensitive to the problem of theological language, particularly as it affects the treatment of Trinitarian theology and Christology. He has an up-to-date command of the terminology of Aristotle and Boethius, now receiving sustained attention in the schools. He is familiar and comfortable with the technical issues in logic and theology embedded in the contemporary debates over the teachings of Roscellinus of Compiègne. Rupert also reflects a preference for a literal account of creation, showing a responsiveness to the new interest in cosmology fashionable in some scholastic centers west of the Rhine. As well, in discussing marriage, he forecasts Hugh of St. Victor's critique of the anti-Pelagian Augustine on that subject, emphasizing the point that marriage is a sacrament instituted in Eden before the fall and that, in man's postlapsarian state, it is not merely a remedy for sin. Even more striking, the organization and coverage of *On the Trinity* has notable parallels with the works of the sentence collectors. Rupert deals with many of the same topics, and in much the same order, starting with God, then moving to creatures, and then treating the fall of man and its consequences, and God's reparation of the situation through Christ's redemption.

Yet, if we move beyond Rupert's vocabulary and schema to his actual handling of the topics he takes up, *On the Trinity* emerges as a *summa* decidedly monastic in character, both with respect to its appeal to the Christian tradition, its intended audience, and the mode of theological reflection it demands and promotes. As is typical with monastic theologians, Rupert is not so much interested

---

[3] John Van Engen, "The 'Crisis of Cenobitism' Reconsidered: Benedictine Monasticism between the Years 1050–1150," *Speculum* 61 (1986): 269–304; *Rupert of Deutz* (Berkeley: University of California Press, 1983), pp. 365–68. For another reappraisal of the openness of twelfth-century monasticism to currents of thought that some scholars would confine only to scholastic circles, see Marjorie Chibnall, *The World of Ordericus Vitalis* (Oxford: Clarendon Press, 1984), pp. 58–85, 90, 99.

[4] For a more extended discussion, see Marcia L. Colish, "Systematic Theology and Theological Renewal in the Twelfth Century," *Journal of Medieval and Renaissance Studies* 18 (1988): 138–41. Rupert's *De sancta Trinitate et operibus eius* has been edited by Rabanus Haacke in CCCM 21–24 (Turnhout: Brepols, 1971–72). On Rupert, see Van Engen, *Rupert of Deutz*, esp. pp. 74–94 for this work.

in debating with authorities he disagrees with as with choosing the
ones he finds illuminating, and weaving them seamlessly into his
own discourse. He is not concerned with helping his readers reconstruct the history of doctrine on any of the points he discusses, but
rather seeks to extract profit from his preferred sources and to
direct the reader's attention to the intellectual sustenance he can
gain from them. The model, and rationale, that Rupert adopts as
his overall strategy is that of salvation history. As he sees it, in this
life the triune God can best be known, short of mysticism, not
primarily as the first cause though His effects in the natural world
or through the analogies of the Trinity in the human soul, but
through the work of divine creation, redemption, and renovation
recounted in Holy Scripture. Rupert takes the standard relational
terms used to describe the Trinitarian persons vis-à-vis each
other—unbegotten, begotten, and proceeding—and applies them
to the work of each Trinitarian person, manifested to man, as it is
revealed in Scripture. This tactic is designed to support the idea
that meditation on God, as He reveals himself in Scripture, will
lead the mind to a knowledge of the eternal, unmanifested Trinity
in itself. Thus, Rupert's whole enterprise yokes systematic theology
to the kind of meditative, reflective *lectio divina* specific to the
monastic calling, although with a stress on fundamental doctrine
rather than on ethical edification.

Our second monastic systematic theologian, Honorius, provides
an even more instructive comparison for our purposes. The particular aspect of the contemporary reform movement on which he
took a stand was the debate over whether the Benedictines should
continue to minister to lay congregations, as they had been doing
for centuries. Contemporary critics opposed the idea, whether out
of a desire to distinguish more clearly between the roles of the
secular clergy and the monks in principle, or because they thought
that the monks were inadequately trained for the ministry, or
because they eyed greedily the tithes which the monks collected
from their parishioners.[5] Honorius was a vigorous defender of the
rights of the Benedictines to serve lay congregations and, not
incidentally, to receive their tithes. His response to the critics was
forthright and practical. In the first year or two of the twelfth
century, and most likely on his return to his native Germany from a

---

[5] A good account of this debate is provided by M. Peuchmaurd, "Le prêtre
ministre de la parole dans la théologie du XIIe siècle: Canonistes, moines, et
chanoines," *RTAM* 29 (1962): 52–76.

course of study in England with Anselm and Eadmer of Canterbury,[6] he wrote the *Elucidarium*, a work of systematic theology aimed at instructing his Benedictine confrères who served in the pastoral ministry, upgrading their theological knowledge, and equipping them to meet the perceived needs of their parishioners.[7] While Honorius's immediate audience was thus a monastic one, his ultimate goal was to instruct the laity. He does not write to stimulate monastic meditation or to encourage theological speculation. He touches firmly, and lightly, on basic doctrines, emphasizing instead their practical consequences in ethics, the sacramental life, and the life to come. He presents a summary overview, sparked by vivid imagery, designed to hold an audience whose theological attention span was likely to be short and whose interest in the subject was anything but professional.

At the same time, the schema laid out in the *Elucidarium* is both inclusive, coherent, and sophisticated. Although some commentators have seen the work as lacking in logical consistency,[8] it can hold its own in this respect, in comparison with the schemata of some of the scholastic systematizers later in the century. Honorius subdivides his work into three books. In the first, he takes up God, the creation of angels and their fall, the creation of man and his fall,

---

[6] On Honorius's biography, his education, and the dating of this work, see Valerie I. J. Flint, ed. "Honorius Augustodunensis, *Imago mundi*," *AHDLMA* 49 (1982): 7–8; "The Career of Honorius Augustodunensis: Some Fresh Evidence," *R. bén.* 82 (1972): 63–86; "The Chronology of the Works of Honorius Augustodunensis" *R. bén.* 82 (1972): 215–42. See also Marie-Odile Garrigues, "Quelques recherches sur l'oeuvre d'Honorius Augustodunensis," *RHE* 70 (1975): 388–425; Eva Matthews Sanford, "Honorius *Presbyter* and *Scholasticus*," *Speculum* 23 (1948): 397–404. Flint's dating of the *Elucidarium* is supported by Robert D. Crouse, "Honorius Augustodunensis: Disciple of Anselm?" in *Analecta Anselmiana*, ed. Helmut Kohlenberger (Frankfurt: Minerva, 1975), 4 part 2: 131–39; Crouse challenges the view that Honorius studied with Anselm of Canterbury, although he admits that it is otherwise difficult to account for his familiarity with the *Cur deus homo*, which had just been completed when he wrote the *Elucidarium*. Janice L. Schultz, "Honorius Augustodunensis," in *Dictionary of the Middle Ages*, ed. Joseph R. Strayer (New York: Charles Scribner's Sons, 1985), 6: 285–86, reports this difference of opinion without taking sides.

[7] Honorius, *Elucidarium*, ed. Yves Lefèvre in *L'Elucidarium et les lucidaires: Contribution par l'histoire d'un texte à l'histoire des croyances religieuses en France au moyen âge* (Paris: É. de Boccard, 1954). On the context in which this work was written, see Valerie I. J. Flint, "The 'Elucidarius' of Honorius Augustodunensis and Reform in Late Eleventh-Century England," *R. bén.* 85 (1975): 179–89; "The Place and Purpose of the Works of Honorius Augustodunensis," *R. bén.* 87 (1977): 97–118. See also Josef A. Endres, *Honorius Augustodunensis: Beitrag zur Geschichte der geistigen Lebens im 12. Jahrhundert* (Kempten: Kösel'schen Buchhandlung, 1906), pp. 16–21.

[8] Endres, *Honorius*, p. 197 n. 1; Joseph de Ghellinck, *Le Mouvement théologique du XIIe siècle*, 2nd ed. (Bruges: De Tempel, 1948), p. 119; Lefèvre, *L'Elucidarium*, pp. 201–05.

the need for redemption, the incarnation, and the earthly life of Christ. Under the latter heading, he considers not only Christ's nature as a God-man and its necessity or propriety as a means of man's redemption, but also offers a historical reprise of His life from the nativity to the ascension. Next, Honorius discusses the earthly survival and extension of Christ's saving work in the church, founded at Pentecost, and understood as Christ's mystical body. This body is manifested and made available most perfectly in the dispensation and ministry of the church by the Eucharist, which Honorius then takes up, adding, as a pendant to this topic, the problem of immoral priests and the efficacy of their Eucharistic ministry.

The ecclesiology developed near the end of Book 1 provides the conceptual foundation for the rest of the material Honorius treats in the next two books. Book 2 addresses, as its central concern, the ethical and sacramental life of the church in this world. Honorius leads off with a brief consideration of the nature of sin, which he sees as rooted in man's intentional use of his free will, and with a discussion of God's omnipotence, providence, and predestination as the basis for an understanding of the interaction of God's grace and man's freedom in the Christian life. Man's soul and the transmission and consequences of original sin are next considered, followed by baptism as the necessary corrective to the fall. After an abbreviated treatment of marriage, Honorius moves on to illustrate the various professions men exercise in Christian society. These are presented not so much as Christian callings but as conditions that bear with them specific moral responsibilities and temptations. Masculine activities alone are considered, from cleric to monk to ruler to soldier to merchant to jongleur to farmer. Honorius assesses the practitioner's chances of salvation in each case, with farmers leading the field and jongleurs all but condemned to perdition *ex officio*. While he ignores women, their social roles and their varying states of life, Honorius does take up the ethical problems and opportunities of different age groups. Refreshingly, he thinks young people are more likely to be saved than the old, since they are more flexible and open to change.[9] Clearly, this presentation and analysis of ethical examples, drawn largely from lay professional life, is something Honorius finds more important than the psychogenesis of ethical acts and the intractable problem of free will and grace, to which he gives such perfunctory treatment. He rounds out Book 2 with the modes by which man has been ethically

---

[9] Honorius, *Elucidarium* 2.52–66, pp. 427–31.

governed. Penance is the means available for moral correction and
progress in the present dispensation, he notes; it was preceded in
the Old Testament by the Mosaic law and the exhortation of the
prophets. Throughout, guardian angels have been on hand to assist
men against diabolical temptation. Honorius concludes this book
with the sacrament of unction, which typically comes at the end of
the earthly life of the individual Christian.

Fully one third of the *Elucidarium* is devoted to Last Things, a
subject which Honorius takes up as a sequel and conclusion to the
life of the church on earth, in the permanent assignments of its
members in the life to come. Last Things is a topic which he embraces enthusiastically. All aspects of the eschatological scenario,
from the condition of souls before the coming of Antichrist, the
arrival and reign of Antichrist, the general resurrection, the second
coming of Christ, the last judgment, Hell, Purgatory, and Heaven,
are described in painstaking detail and in glorious technicolor.
Honorius relies on such sources as the final chapters of Augustine's
City of God and on the most imaginative passages of Julian of
Toledo's *Prognosticon futuri saeculi*. He paints a synaesthetic and
multi-media picture both of the torments of the damned[10] and of
the joys of the saved.[11]

There are, to be sure, some problems in Honorius's coverage and
organization. But it is also quite clear that his emphasis is dictated
by his canny estimate of the intellectual needs, tolerances, and
interests of his intended audience. Honorius's handling of the
sacraments is intermingled with other subjects, whether dogmatic,
as in the case of the Eucharist, or ethical, as in the case of the other
sacraments. He omits confirmation and takes up holy orders only
obliquely, in connection with the sacramental ministry of bad
priests in Book 1 and the moral duties of clerics in Book 2. In his
account of creation, he mentions angels, men, and animals, but not
plants and other inanimate beings. His analysis, and his often
harsh judgments, of the chances for salvation of various occupa-
tional groups on the basis of profession alone in Book 2 does not
square entirely with his stress on intentionality in the moral life
elsewhere in the same book. None the less, in comparison with
many of the systematic theologians who wrote later in the century,
Honorius is remarkably inclusive and his inconsistencies are relatively minor. Within the terms of his project, as he has envisioned

---

[10] Ibid., 3.12–18, pp. 447–49.
[11] Ibid., 3.38–49, 3.79–120, pp. 454–57, 463–77.

it, his schema is cogent and easy to follow. It reflects his idea that the average Christian has both the need, and the capacity, to understand how individual doctrines hang together. And, the *Elucidarium* shows Honorius's willingness to give pride of place to the subjects his audience cares most about, the subjects on which their attention can be caught and directed to the theological reasons undergirding the norms ruling their daily lives and the faith that is the foundation of their hopes, fears, and expectations.

This elaborate and carefully orchestrated schema is combined with another feature of the *Elucidarium* which serves as an equally clear index of its intended function as a systematic theology for the common man, an utterly simplistic and catechetical presentation of the material it contains. In no sense does Honorius seek to alert his readers to the theological controversies of the day. Nor does he want to inform them of the fact that the authorities sometimes disagree and, if so, what to do about it. Honorius himself is prodigiously learned. The *Elucidarium* is based on thorough and up-to-date research. From his own rich command of the relevant theological literature, he makes his choices but without flaunting his knowledge. Since his aim is not to provoke inquiry but to lay questions to rest, what he does is simply to state clearly and firmly in his own words the best answers he can find to the questions he raises. He does not indicate by name or work the particular authorities he uses for this purpose and he does not explain why he prefers their conclusions. As Valerie Flint has aptly noted, in the *Elucidarium* the author's intention is "to reduce the most complex to the most simple, to substitute the answers for the learning process, and so supposedly to render that process unnecessary by the deft finding of answers."[12]

As the first systematic theologians of the twelfth century, Honorius and Rupert both bring a keen and judicious sense of audience to their tasks. Both hit the marks at which they aimed. Their works were immensely popular, as the numerous manuscripts preserving them over the next several hundred years attest.[13] Together, they suggest how shortsighted it is to locate the revival of monastic theology in this period exclusively in those authors who took their cue from Bernard of Clairvaux. When *On the Holy Trinity* and the

---

[12] Valerie I. J. Flint, "Henricus of Augsburg and Honorius Augustodunensis: Are They the Same Person?" *R. bén.* 92 (1982): 150–51.

[13] For Rupert, see Haacke's preface to the *De sancta Trinitate*, CCCM 22; for Honorius, see Lefèvre, *L'Elucidarium*, pp. 334–57; Flint, "Place and Purpose," pp. 119–27.

Elucidarium were written, they were quite original. Neither Rupert nor Honorius had either monastic or scholastic models to follow. Honorius's likely master, Anselm of Canterbury, the towering theological mind of the day, had moved theology a major step forward by his rigorous insistence on rational argument as a means of clarifying the faith. But his own oeuvre continued to reflect the earlier tendency of theologians to take on specific and limited problems in individual works rather than to provide a synthetic theological curriculum. And, the leading scholastics at the turn of the twelfth century, Anselm of Laon and his followers, while they made notable advances in one area of scholastic pedagogy, the analysis and criticism of authorities, did not see the construction of a systematic approach to theology as part of their project.

THE SCHOLASTIC SENTENCE COLLECTION AS A GENRE OF THEOLOGICAL LITERATURE

This last statement may still require emphasis, given the fact that some of the most influential medievalists of our century have seen in Anselm of Laon and his disciples the inventors of the systematic sentence collection. This notion was popularized by Martin Grabmann, who saw their work as both dialectical and architectonic, and as heralding not only the elaborate sentence collections of the mid-century but also the *summae* of the thirteenth century to come.[14] While he plays down their appeal to logic, Joseph de Ghellinck joins Grabmann in describing the works of the Laon masters as mini-*summae*, which present theological topics under a series of specific and highly coherent dogmatic headings.[15] This view has been perpetuated by a number of other scholars.[16] But its most enthusiastic supporter has been Franz Bliemetzrieder, one of the earliest editors of the Laon school manuscripts, who

---

[14] Martin Grabmann, *Die Geschichte der scholastischen Methode*, 2 vols. (Graz: Akademische Druck- u. Verlagsanstalt, 1957 [repr. of Freiburg im Breisgau, 1911 ed.]), 2: 157–68.

[15] Joseph de Ghellinck, *L'Essor de la littérature latine au XIIᵉ siècle*, 2 vols. (Brussels: L'Édition Universelle, 1946), 1: 41–45; *Le Mouvement théologique*, pp. 138–48.

[16] See, for example, Francesco Carpino, "Una difficoltà contro la confessione nella scolastica primitiva: Anselmo di Laon e la sua scuola," *Divus Thomas*, 3ª ser. 16 (1939): 39; Cloes, "La systématisation de théologie," pp. 277 ff.; Artur Michael Landgraf, "Zum Werden der Theologie des 12. Jarhhunderts," *ZkT* 79 (1957): 425, 428; Ludwig Ott, "Petrus Lombardus: Persönlichkeit und Werk," *Münchener theologische Zeitschrift* 5 (1954): 105; "Pietro Lombardo: Personalità e opera," in *Misc. Lomb.*, p. 15; René Silvain, "La tradition des Sentences d'Anselme de Laon," *AHDLMA* 22–23 (1947–48): 1–52.

depicts Anselm of Laon as the century's most creative theologian in this respect and as the model for all subsequent systematic theologians up through Peter Lombard.[17]

The very wave of editorial activity unleashed by Bliemetzrieder has provided the corrective to this interpretation, by showing that the attribution of a systematic character to the writings of the Laon masters rests on a very shaky foundation, a far-too sketchy examination of the manuscripts in which they are preserved. More recent editors, in addition to bringing new texts to light, and proposing connections among them, have undermined the earlier view. Thus, Heinrich Weisweiler has proposed that Anselm set his face against the dialectical theologians of the age and that he did not create a new structure or model for theological education, preferring an approach embedded in biblical exegesis. As Weisweiler has observed, both Anselm's own works and those of his disciples only received schematic form later on, a form often imposed on the materials by the redactors who compiled their individual opinions.[18] The most recent editor, Odon Lottin, agrees that both the literary form and the ordering of the doctrinal content found in the Laon school manuscripts is a function of *ex post facto* editorial arrangement and that they cannot be taken as an index of the school of Laon's own view of theological education. While there are identifiable family relations among the authors in this group, and while many of their individual opinions received respectful attention from other theologians during the first half of the century, he concludes, it cannot be shown that either Anselm or his followers created the systematic sentence collection, or that they organized their teaching along the lines of a later *summa*.[19]

---

[17] Franz Bliemetzrieder, "Autour de l'oeuvre d'Anselme de Laon," *RTAM* 1 (1929): 436.

[18] Heinrich Weisweiler, "L'École d'Anselme de Laon et de Guillaume de Champeaux: Nouveaux documents," *RTAM* 4 (1932): 237–69, 371–91; Weisweiler, ed., *Das Schrifttum der Schule Anselms von Laon und Wilhelms von Champeaux in deutschen Bibliotheken*, Beiträge, 33:1–2 (Münster: Aschendorff, 1936), pp. 3–6, 27–257. For the most recent review of the literature dealing with the filiation of these texts, see Heinrich J. F. Reinhardt, "Literaturkritische und theologiegeschichtliche Studie zu den *Sententiae Magistri A.* und deren Prolog 'Ad iustitiam credens debemus'," *AHDLMA* 36 (1969): 23–29.

[19] Odon Lottin, *Psychologie et morale aux XIIe et XIIIe siècles*, vols. 1–5 (Louvain: Abbaye de Mont-César, 1948–59), 5: 7–10, 178–83, 229–30, 444–47; Lottin, ed., "Quatre sommes fragmentaires de l'école d'Anselme de Laon," in *Mélanges August Pelzer: Études d'histoire littéraire et doctrinale de la scolastique médiévale offerts à Monseigneur August Pelzer à l'occasion de son soixante-dixième anniversaire* (Louvain: Bibliothèque de l'Université, 1947), pp. 81–108. This judgment has been supported by

THE CRITICISM AND EVALUATION OF AUTHORITIES

While the Laon masters can no longer be viewed as the creators of the systematic sentence collection, their opinions do reflect another dimension of the approach to theological education taken up by later scholastics who did use that genre, and one which distinguishes their work sharply from that of the monastic systematizers just discussed. It also distinguishes the work of the scholastic theologians of this period from that of the canonists, even though the boundaries between these two disciplines in the early twelfth century were far less distinct and more permeable than they became later in the Middle Ages. Well before Peter Abelard had formulated his famous rules for the analysis and evaluation of authorities in his *Sic et non*,[20] the Laon masters indicate that they had already grasped and had learned how to apply the principles of authorial intention and historical criticism. The fact that this development was occurring, before Abelard's time, and that theologians such as the Laon masters as well as the canonists were contributing to it, has received a certain amount of scholarly appreciation.[21] It has also been recognized that both canonists and

---

Ermenegildo Bertola, "Le critiche di Abelardo ad Anselmo di Laon ed a Guglielmo di Champeaux," *Rivista di filosofia neo-scolastica* 52 (1960): 503–04; Bernard Merlette, "Écoles et bibliothèques à Laon, du déclin de l'antiquité au développement de l'Université," in *Enseignement et vie intellectuelle, IXe–XVIe siècle*, Actes du 95e congrès national des sociétés savantes, Reims, 1970 (Paris: Bibliothèque Nationale, 1975), 1: 43. For more on this subject, see Marcia L. Colish, "Another Look at the School of Laon," *AHDLMA* 53 (1986): 7–11.

[20] Peter Abelard, *Sic et non* prologus, ed. Blanche B. Boyer and Richard McKeon (Chicago: University of Chicago Press, 1976), p. 96. Good discussions of Abelard's essay on method here, which do not speculate on his sources for it, are Jean Jolivet, "Le traitement des autorités contraires selon le *Sic et non* d'Abélard," in *Aspects de la pensée médiévale: Abélard. Doctrines du langage* (Paris: J. Vrin, 1987), pp. 79–92; G. Paré, A. Brunet, and P. Tremblay, *La renaissance du XIIe siècle: Les écoles et l'enseignement* (Paris: J. Vrin. 1933), pp. 290–91. Scholars who have recognized Abelard's methodological dependence on the school of Laon as well as on the canonists, at least in part, include Ermenegildo Bertola, "I precedenti storici del metodo del 'Sic et non' di Abelardo," *Rivista di filosofia neo-scolastica* 53 (1961): 266–76 and Mary M. McLaughlin, "Abelard as Autobiographer: The Motives and Meaning of His 'Story of Calamities'," *Speculum* 42 (1967): 478.

[21] Franz Bliemetzrieder, "Gratian und die Schule Anselms von Laon," *Archiv für katholische Kirchenrecht* 112 (1932): 37–63; Nikolaus M. Häring, "The Interaction between Canon Law and Sacramental Theology in the Twelfth Century," in *Proceedings of the Fourth International Congress of Medieval Canon Law*, ed. Stephan G. Kuttner (Vatican City: Biblioteca Apostolica Vaticana, 1976), pp. 483–93; "The Sententiae Magistri A. (Vat. *Ms. lat.* 4361) and the School of Laon," *MS* 17 (1955): 1–45; Stephan G. Kuttner, "Zur Frage der theologischen Vorlagen Gratians," *Zeitschrift der Savigny-Stiftung für Rechtsgeschichte*, kanonistische Abteilung 23 (1934): 243–68. Still, the exclusion of the school of Laon from the group of

theologians freely invoked ancient authorities as a rationale for the departures from existing norms and practices that they might wish to advocate.[22] Yet, typical of the theologians in this respect, the Laon masters reveal a bolder and more independent reading of authorities than what we find in contemporary canonists. While certainly defending their own positions, the canonists tried to find ways of adjusting the authorities who disagreed with their views with the authorities who supported them. In Stephan Kuttner's words, they strove to bring "harmony from dissonance." They felt a constitutional disinclination to abandon any of the authorities. Like thrifty housewives, they disliked waste. They wanted to save everything, and somehow find a place for it in the ragoût. On the other hand, the Laon, masters are an early witness to the theologians' recognition of the fact that, in choosing some authorities as more cogent or relevant to contemporary needs and sensibilities, they might well have to exclude others. The theologians were able to accept the fact that the conflicts among authorities were sometimes real, and not merely apparent, and that when this was the case, they could be reconciled only at the price of being fudged. With their fellow theologians, the Laon masters felt free to make principled choices among the authorities. They did not feel as bound by precedent as the canonists and were perfectly willing to reject those authorities who failed to meet their critical standards.[23]

---

theologians in this current dies hard, as is seen in the work of Ghellinck, *Le Mouvement*, pp. 164–66; Grabmann, *Die Geschichte*, 1: 236–46; Stephan G. Kuttner, *Harmony from Dissonance: An Interpretation of Medieval Canon Law* (Latrobe, PA: Archabbey Press, 1960), pp. 13, 25, 30; David E. Luscombe, *The School of Peter Abelard: The Influence of Abelard's Thought in the Early Scholastic Period* (Cambridge: Cambridge University Press, 1969), pp. 214–16, 218–22; George Makdisi, "The Scholastic Method in Medieval Education: An Inquiry into Its Origins in Law and Theology," *Speculum* 49 (1974): 640–61; Paré, Brunet, and Tremblay, *La renaissance du XIIᵉ siècle*, pp. 284–92; J. G. Sikes, *Peter Abailard* (Cambridge: Cambridge University Press, 1932), pp. 76–87, 239–47.

[22] Karl F. Morrison, *Tradition and Authority in the Western Church, 300–1140* (Princeton: Princeton University Press, 1969), p. 345. Morrison provides a good introduction to the previous scholarship on this subject, pp. vii–xi, 3–8, 15–33, 37–110.

[23] For this characterization of the canonical enterprise, see Kuttner, *Harmony from Dissonance*. The greater flexibility of the theologians in their approach to authorities and in their willingness to take an innovative line in using them has been noted by Paul Fournier and Gabriel Le Bras, *Historie des collections canoniques en occident depuis les fausses décrétales jusqu'au Décret de Gratien*, 2 vols. (Paris: Sirey, 1932), 2: 314–52; Häring, "The Interaction between Canon Law and Sacramental Theology," pp. 483–93. Cf. on the other hand Artur Michael Landgraf, "Diritto canonico e teologia nel secolo XII," *Studia Gratiana* 1 (1953): 371–413, who sees theologians as more conservative than canonists in this period, and Alfons M.

This tendency will be visible in a more wholesale fashion in the generation after 1130, by which point Anselm of Laon and his followers had either died or had passed from teaching to administrative positions in the church. But the method can be illustrated quite easily from the opinions of members of this school. Let us consider two examples, which are of interest because they both invoke the authority of Pope Leo I, in one case to approve it against the countervailing authority of Augustine and in the other case to reject it on the basis of historical criticism. As historical critics, these theologians handle the idea of the primitive church in a manner quite different from that of the canonists.[24] Rather than appealing to antiquity as a guarantee for a practice they want to retain, or reinstitute, or institute for the first time, these masters feel free to treat it as an index of obsolescence, invoking it in order to relativize and dismiss practices that may have made sense centuries ago but which fail to speak to present needs and conditions. This attitude is clearly visible in the Laon masters' consideration of the time of baptism. Leo had laid down the rule that persons to be baptized should be received by the church only on Easter or Pentecost Sunday, unless they were in danger of death. This ruling had established the canonical practice in the early church. The Laon masters reject this tradition on grounds of pastoral utility; for it does not regard the needs of the infants who now make up the vast majority of baptizands and who are incapable of articulating the fact if they are in danger of death. In addition to the welfare of these infants, the church must minister to the legitimate anxieties of their parents. The Laon masters anchor this pastoral agenda with a historical argument. In the time of the *ecclesia primitiva*, they observe, most new Christians were adults, who were capable of alerting their ministers if their health was at risk. Their collective reception in baptism on the great feasts of the resurrection liturgy served not only as an important form of public witness to the largely pagan society in which they lived, but also as a potent source of group reinforcement. But, none of these conditions now

---

Stickler, "Teologia e diritto canonico nella storia," *Salesianum* 47 (1985): 695, who sees the influences running as a one-way street from the canonists to the theologians.

[24] Glenn Olsen, "The Idea of the *Ecclesia Primitiva* in the Writings of the Twelfth-Century Canonists," *Traditio* 25 (1969): 61–86. For the theologians' countervailing use of this idea, see Colish, "Another Look at the School of Laon," pp. 12–14; "*Quae hodie locum non habent*: Scholastic Theologians Reflect on Their Authorities," *Proceedings of the PMR Conference*, 15, ed. Phillip Pulsiano (Villanova: Augustinian Historical Institute, 1990), pp. 1–17.

obtain, the Laon masters conclude. Therefore, Leo's rule is no longer appropriate and may be disregarded.[25]

In the case of our second example, taken from a Leonine ruling on marriage, historical relevance is not the issue, but rather the judgment that Leo offers better reasons for supporting his conclusions than Augustine does, on general principles. One of the standard questions raised in the twelfth century, under the heading of impediments to marriage, was whether a prior adulterous affair should be viewed as an impediment if the lovers later find themselves free to marry each other. The two authorities invariably cited by thinkers who take up this question, however they resolve it, are Leo, who maintains that the affair is an impediment, and Augustine, who holds that it is not. In explaining why they agree with Leo, the Laon masters argue that he has sounder reasons on his side. Leo had imposed the ban, they note, because he feared that the lovers, if permitted to marry, would be tempted to plot the murder of the obstructive spouse, an outcome they join him in wishing to discourage. Augustine's permission of the union of former adulterers, they continue, might give rise to scandal, making it seem as if the church were condoning their earlier misbehavior. On their own account, our authors add that the marriage of the former adulterers might also lead to the confusion of inheritance rights. For all these reasons, they find Leo's argument more compelling than Augustine's, and his conclusions more acceptable.[26]

PETER ABELARD AND HIS FOLLOWERS

This kind of weighing of authorities, which was to become a central ingredient in the enterprise of systematic theology among the scholastic sentence collectors, was never credited to Anselm of Laon by his erstwhile pupil, Peter Abelard, who is frequently regarded as its inventor, rather than merely its codifier. In the event, and despite his innovative spirit in other respects, neither Abelard nor any of his own disciples emerges as the best example of this method in practice in the generation after Anselm. Nor do the Abelardians fare very well as exemplars of systematic curriculum

---

[25] *Sentences of the School of Laon*, no. 371; *Sententiae Atrebatenses*, ed. Lottin in *Psych. et morale*, 5: 275–76, 431.

[26] Franz Bliemetzrieder, ed., *Anselms von Laon systematische Sentenzen*, Beiträge, 18:2–3 (Münster: Aschendorff, 1919), pp. 148–49; *Sentences of Anselm of Laon from the Liber Pancrisis*, no. 66–67; *Sentences of the School of Laon*, no. 409, ed. Lottin, *Psych. et morale*, 5: 57–58, 288.

building, either. This judgment may be a startling one, given the
fact that Abelard has been hailed as the father of scholasticism
in innumerable textbooks. Yet, the legacy he left to systematic
theology in the twelfth century is a rather scanty one. Abelard's
basic weakness as a guide here is that he left no complete work of
systematic theology of his own. He was one of those academics
constitutionally incapable of finishing anything he started. Abelard
essayed three general treatises, each entitled a *theologia* and each
existing only in several fragmentary versions. His *Theologia "summi
boni"*, *Theologia christiana*, and *Theologia "scholarium"* all announce
the same agenda in their prologues, but none follows that agenda
through to completion. Indeed, the sorting out and dating of these
disiecta membra has become something of a growth industry in recent
Abelard scholarship.[27] Taken together, the Abelardian fragments
as collected by their modern editors state the author's intention to
subdivide Christian theology into three parts—faith, charity, and
sacraments. Under the heading of faith, Abelard limits himself to
what he thinks readers need to know about the definition of faith as
a cognitive state and the doctrine of the Trinity and Christology.
Other things that Christians might need to know in order to be
saved, and that professional theologians need to consider he either
ignores or relegates to separate treatises composed late in his
career, which he evidently sees as lying outside the project of
systematic theology. Thus, his treatment of creation is found in his
Hexaemeron,[28] while his handling of original sin and the redemption
receives full attention only in his commentary on Paul's Epistle to
the Romans.[29] The topic of Last Things does not appear in any of
Abelard's theological treatises.

---

[27] Peter Abelard, *Theologia "summi boni"*, ed. Constant J. Mews, CCCM 13;
Theologia christiana, ed. Eligius M. Buytaert, CCCM 12; *Theologia "scholarium"*, ed.
Constant J. Mews, CCCM 13 in Peter Abelard, *Opera theologica* (Turnhout:
Brepols, 1969–87). For the debates about the sequence and dating of the various
fragmentary versions and redactions of these works, see Constant J. Mews, "On
Dating the Writings of Peter Abelard," *AHDLMA* 52 (1985): 73–134; "Peter
Abelard's (*Theologia christiana*) and (*Theologia 'scholarium'*) Re-examined," *RTAM*
52 (1985): 109–58; and his preface to Peter Abelard, *Opera theologica*, CCCM 13:
20–23.
[28] Mary Foster Romig, ed., "A Critical Edition of Peter Abelard's 'Expositio in
Hexameron'," University of Southern California Ph.D. diss., 1981. The text is also
found in *PL* 178. An edition incorporating Romig's work and including additional
manuscripts is forthcoming from CCCM.
[29] Peter Abelard, *In Epistolam Pauli ad Romanos* 3:26, 5:19, ed. Eligius M.
Buytaert, CCCM 11: 114–18, 164–66, 170–72; original sin is also taken up in Peter
Abelard, *Ethics*, ed. and trans. David E. Luscombe (Oxford: Clarendon Press,
1971), pp. 20–22, 58–62.

The second part of Abelard's project addresses ethics. In practice, what he mainly has to say on that subject is that ethical acts can be reduced to ethical intentionalities. He reserves to his *Ethics* his fullest consideration of this claim, but he does not develop his analysis of the psychogenesis of ethical acts into a full-scale treatise on the Christian life.[30] Since sacraments constitute the last part of Abelard's table of contents and he rarely gets that far in his *theologiae*, his treatment of this topic is extremely sketchy, confined to the very small selection of sacraments that he was interested in, for personal reasons or because they could be used to illustrate some of his other concerns. Thus, he brings in baptism in the context of his objections to the traditional doctrine of the transmission of original sin and his handling of it reflects his fascination with circumcision as its Old Testament parallel.[31] Penance is treated as a corollary of the idea that ethical intentionality is paramount in the ethical life.[32] Marriage he gives extremely short shrift, taking it up primarily to dispraise it,[33] while the Eucharist interests him mainly because the doctrine of the real presence affords him the opportunity to explore the suitability of philosophical terminology to describe the change in the elements brought about by the consecration.[34]

Abelard's handling of the sacraments and ethics also points to another deficiency of his work as a model for systematic theology, an occasional logical inconsistency that is startling in a thinker hailed as the paramount dialectician of his time. Abelard offers as his definition of sacrament in general the standard Augustinian statement that a sacrament is a visible sign of invisible grace.[35] He regards marriage as a sacrament. Yet, he finds nothing in the relations between spouses that signifies grace.[36] Equally problematic

---

[30] Peter Abelard, *Ethics*, pp. 4–36, 53–56; also *In Ep. Pauli ad Romanos* 1:16–17, CCCM 11: 65.

[31] Peter Abelard, *Ethics*, pp. 20, 58–62; *In Ep. Pauli ad Romanos* 2:25, CCCM 11: 94; *Theologia christiana* 2.22, CCCM 12: 142.

[32] Peter Abelard, *Ethics*, pp. 76–126. This point has been noted by Richard E. Weingart, "Peter Abailard's Contribution to Medieval Sacramentology," *RTAM* 34 (1967): 173–77.

[33] Peter Abelard, *In Hexaemeron*, ed. Romig, pp. 133–35; *PL* 178: 463C–464C; *In Ep. Pauli ad Romanos* 4:18–19, CCCM 11: 148; *Sermo* 3, *PL* 178: 407C. This point receives judicious treatment from Richard E. Weingart, *The Logic of Divine Love: A Critical Analysis of the Soteriology of Abailard* (Oxford: Clarendon Press, 1970), pp. 195–96; "Peter Abailard's Contribution," pp. 172–73.

[34] Weingart, "Peter Abailard's Contribution," pp. 170–72.

[35] Peter Abelard, *Theologia "scholarium"* 16, CCCM 12: 406. This text, ed. by Eligius M. Buytaert, is the shorter version of the work; the version edited by Mews in CCCM 13 is the longer one that was used more widely in the twelfth century.

[36] See above, n. 33.

is Abelard's handling of penance. Consistent with his intentionalist ethics, it is not surprising that he comes down squarely on
the side of contritionism, in the contemporary debate on whether
the penitent's sins were remitted in the contrition or in the confession stage of the sacrament. The penitent's inner contrition gains
him pardon for sin, Abelard holds, whether or not he goes on to
confess his sin to a priest. None the less, and despite the difficulty of
finding a priest who is upright and discreet, Abelard maintains that
confession must not be omitted. His efforts to defend this notion
find him getting more and more hopelessly entangled in the contradictions he spins.[37] The inconsistency between Abelard's ethical
intentionalism and his actual advice can also be seen in his judgment as a moralist. In documenting his own basic principle that
unknowing or accidental behavior is not morally culpable, he gives
three cases in point. There are the people who put Christ to death,
who, in their estimation, were not doing anything wrong but rather
punishing a criminal and blasphemer. There is the man who sleeps
with a woman not his wife under the misapprehension that she is
his wife. These people, he argues, commit no sin. Then Abelard
turns to his third example, a poor mother who lacks the wherewithal to provide bedding for her baby, who takes him into her own bed
to keep him warm, and who accidentally smothers him while
asleep. Notwithstanding the accidental character of the event and
the woman's loving, maternal intention, he rules that she is deserv-
ing of punishment.[38]

If logical consistency is sometimes a problem in Abelard's theology, despite his prominence in that field of endeavor, one can also
find numerous soft spots in his handling of his authorities in practice, despite the excellent theoretical guidelines he provides in his
Sic et non. Abelard does not hesitate to cite the anti-Pelagian Augustine, scarcely an apposite choice in this context, in support of his
own effort to reduce original sin to actual sin.[39] His sense of the
pertinence of a particular authority to the case he wants to build is
equally if not more questionable in his handling of secular authorities. Abelard's quest for Trinitarian analogies in pagan literature

---

[37] Peter Abelard, *Ethics*, pp. 76–126. The contradictions in this argument have
been noted by Amédée de Zedelghem, "L'Attritionisme d'Abélard," *Estudis Fran-
ciscans* 35 (1925): 333–45; "Doctrine d'Abélard au sujet de la valeur morale de la
crainte des peines," ibid. 36 (1926): 108–25.

[38] Peter Abelard, *Ethics*, pp. 38–48.

[39] Peter Abelard, *In Ep. Pauli ad Romanos* 2:5–6, CCCM 11: 77–78. On this
point, see Julius Gross, "Abälards Umdeutung des Erbsündendogmas," *Zeitschrift
für Religions- und Geistesgeschichte* 15 (1963): 14–33.

raised legitimate doubts in the minds of his contemporaries as to whether he grasped the difference between the orthodox doctrine of the Trinity, with its coequal persons, and the subordinationism implicit in the Platonic doctrine of the World Soul, to which he compared the Holy Spirit.[40] Examples of passages where Abelard fails to take into account the theological or philosophical perspectives informing the views of the authorities he cites, or where he misapplies them, could easily be multiplied.

The followers of Abelard, like their master, drew heavily on philosophical as well as patristic evidence and they reveal a pronounced taste for logic, a dialectical handling of the topics they treat, and a sensitivity to the problem of theological language. They also take as their cue the master's tripartite subdivision of the subject matter. But, rather than trying to fill the gaps he left, thus developing his ideas into a full-blown *summa*, they see their primary task as the defense of the positions that had gotten Abelard into trouble, and even the repetition of some of his least lucid and most regrettable examples.[41] They preserve his inapposite equation of the World Soul with the Holy Spirit, repeating his earlier and less nuanced position in the *Theologia "summi boni"* rather than the somewhat modified version of this idea which he provided in his later works.[42] They also repeat his illogical treatment of marriage as a sacrament but which none the less neither signifies nor imparts any gift of grace.[43] In addition, the organizational skills of some of

---

[40] Peter Abelard, *Theologia "summi boni"* 1.5.36–38, 1.5.41–6.49, 3.4.94–99, CCCM 13: 95–99, 100–13, 198–200; he modifies his position slightly in *Theologia christiana* 1.71–78, 1.96, 1.123, CCCM 12: 101–04, 112, 124. On this point see, in particular, Tullio Gregory, "Abélard et Platon," in *Peter Abelard*, ed. Eligius M. Buytaert (Leuven: Leuven University Press, 1974), pp. 42–46, 51; "L'*anima mundi* nella filosofia del XII secolo," *Giornale critico della filosofia italiana* 30 (1951): 494–508. See also Ludwig Ott, "Die platonische Weltseele in der Theologie der Frühscholastik," in *Parusia: Studien zur Philosophie Platons und zur Problemgeschichte des Platonismus. Festgabe für Johannes Hirschberger*, ed. Kurt Flasch (Frankfurt: Minerva, 1965), pp. 307–15; Mariateresa Beonio-Brocchieri [Fumagalli] and Massimo Parodi, *Storia della filosofia medievale da Boezio a Wyclif* (Bari: Laterza, 1989), pp. 214–15, 226.

[41] These developments are recounted clearly by Luscombe, *The School of Peter Abelard*.

[42] Ott, "Die platonische Weltseele," pp. 315–18.

[43] This teaching is preserved most fully in Hermannus, *Sententie magistri Petri Abelardi* 28, 31, ed. Sandro Buzzetti, Pubblicazioni della facoltà di lettere e filosofia dell'Università di Milano, 101, sezione a cura di storia della filosofia, 31 (Florence: La Nuova Italia, 1983), pp. 120, 135. The status of this text, framed as a *reportatio* of Abelard's teaching, has been contested. Luscombe, *The School of Peter Abelard*, pp. 158–64, makes what we find to be a convincing case for Hermannus as an Abelardian author in his own right, because of his response to criticisms of the master's doctrine of the Trinity, which Abelard himself did not take to heart in his

the Abelardians are questionable. The author of the *Ysagoge in theologiam*, for instance, starts with man, continues with Christology and the redemption, ethics and the sacraments, and places angels and God at the end.[44] His treatment of baptism reflects Abelard's interest in comparing this sacrament, and not others, with its Old Testament precursor. But the author is so taken with the utility of the circumcision-baptism comparison in aid of Jewish-Christian polemic that he blows it up all out of proportion in his sacramental theology as a whole.[45] All of the Abelardians, like their master, ignore Last Things. In addition, they all omit major topics that were heavily debated at the time, omissions that are sometimes stunning. Thus, the authors of the two *Sententiae Parisiensis* leave out penance, a sacrament which no other contemporary theologian ignores; and Hermannus omits, of all things, original sin. The apparent reason for these strategic omissions on the part of Abelard's disciples is their evident inability to find arguments against Abelard's critics on these points. As a technique of theological education, this tactic, like the truncated *theologiae* of Abelard himself, left, and was perceived to leave, a great deal to be desired, in twelfth-century scholastic circles.

GILBERT OF POITIERS AND HIS FOLLOWERS

Another master in this period who is given almost as much praise and attention as Abelard in the scholarly literature for his role as an intellectual innovator is Gilbert of Poitiers, whose trial at Rheims in 1148 as a philosophical and theological radical was the intellectual cause célèbre of the mid-century. Well before Gilbert's ideas had attained their fullest notoriety, he and his disciples had developed a general course in systematic theology, which can be found in two Porretan sentence collections dating to the early 1140s. The doc-

---

latest version of that doctrine, and in his more "Pelagian" handling of grace. Constant J. Mews, in the intro. to his ed. of *Theologia "scholarium"*, CCCM 13: 23–24 and in "The *Sententiae* of Peter Abelard," *RTAM* 53 (1986): 130–84, argues that this work is only a *reportatio* of Abelard's teaching and that its redaction by Hermannus, and not by some other student of Abelard's, is not certain. His main concern is to place this text in relation to other Abelardian works on the points which they have in common, without considering the areas in which the author departs from Abelard's position.

[44] *Ysagoge in theologiam*, ed. Artur Michael Landgraf in *Écrits théologiques de l'école d'Abélard* (Louvain: Spicilegium Sacrum Lovaniense, 1934).

[45] *Ysagoge in theologiam* 2, pp. 181–89, This anti-Jewish agenda has been noted by Landgraf, intro. to his ed., pp. xlvi–xlix; David E. Luscombe, "The Authorship of the *Ysagoge in theologiam*," *AHDLMA* 43 (1968): 7–16.

trine in these works summarizes Gilbert's teaching on the Mont
Ste. Geneviève after his departure from Chartres in ca. 1137 and
before his acceptance of the bishopric of Poitiers in 1142, with
additions and corrections reflecting the opinions of these two
pupils.[46] Together, they indicate how Gilbert and the early Porretans envisioned the theological enterprise. The authors divide their
sentence collections into fourteen books. The first book is devoted
to the problem of theological language, in general, with Books 2
and 3, on the Trinity and Christology, as specific applications of
that problem. Given the amount of controversy that Gilbert had
inflamed on precisely those questions, this represents a relatively
modest allocation of space to the topic.

The vast bulk of the Porretan sentence collections, Books 4
through 11, is devoted to the sacraments, to which the authors now
repair, before the universe has been created, and before man has
fallen and found himself in need of them. In this period, the two
most prevalent ways of organizing sacramental theology, on the
part of authors offering a systematic account of that subject, were in
the order of their institution or in the order of their reception.
Another prominent scheme was to subdivide the sacraments into
two groups, those received by all Christians and those, such as holy
orders and marriage, received only by some Christians. Still
another way of organizing this subject was to distinguish baptism
and the Eucharist, or baptism alone, as necessary for salvation,
from the rest of the sacraments, which might be omitted, in some
circumstances, without jeopardizing one's salvation. The Porretans
depart from all of these models and propose an original four-part
model of their own, which they then, however, immediately
abandon.[47] Sacraments, they state, can be divided into rites of
initiation, rites of strengthening, rites of return, and rites of

---

[46] Nikolaus M. Häring, ed., "Die *Sententie magistri Gisleberti Pictavensis episcopi* I,"
AHDLMA 45 (1978): 83–180; "Die *Sententie magistri Gisleberti Pictavensis episcopi* II:
Die Version der florentiner Handschrift," *AHDLMA* 46 (1979): 45–105. The
dating of these texts derives from Häring's analysis of the paleographical evidence
in the manuscripts on which his edition depends. For the dating of Gilbert's period
of teaching in Paris, see H. C. van Elswijk, *Gilbert Porreta: Se vie, son oeuvre, sa pensée*
(Louvain: Spicilegium Sacrum Lovaniense, 1966), pp. 25–32; Lauge Olaf Neilsen,
*Theology and Philosophy in the Twelfth Century: A Study of Gilbert Porreta's Thinking and
the Theological Exposition of the Doctrine of the Incarnation during the Period 1130–1180*,
Acta theologica danica, 15 (Leiden: E. J. Brill, 1982), p. 29. John Marenbon, "A
Note on the Porretani," in *A History of Twelfth-Century Western Philosophy*, ed. Peter
Dronke (Cambridge: Cambridge University Press, 1988), p. 353 n. 2 notes the
existence of these works but does not discuss their contents.
[47] *Sent. mag. Gisleberti* I 4.61, p. 144; *Sent. mag. Gisleberti* II 4.61, p. 67.

perfection. This scheme suggests that the logical place to begin
their exposition would be with baptism. But, they lead off with the
Eucharist, even though they define it as a sacrament of perfection.
Also, they omit holy orders, even though they repeatedly mention
the clergy as administrators of the other sacraments. And, while
they regard marriage as a sacrament, they cannot decide in which
of their four categories it belongs. In Book 10, while discussing
penance, they belatedly take up the question of original sin, vice,
and virtue, thus presenting the fall of man well before his creation
and well after the incarnation of Christ, ordained to remedy it. The
creation itself is almost an afterthought for the Porretans. We find
it, along with a brief reprise on original sin and an even briefer
allusion to Last Things, in Book 13, sandwiched inexplicably in
between two books devoted to the liturgy of Advent and Lent,
respectively.

This last peculiarity, the inclusion of a lengthy analysis of the
symbolic importance of the liturgy of these two seasons of the
church year, is particularly striking, for it is a total anomaly as a
topic in a scholastic sentence collection in this period. Its presence
here calls attention to the other odd features of the Porretan
scheme, with its heavy imbalance away from dogmatic theology, its
lack of logical and chronological coherence, and its inconsistencies
in the treatment of the sacraments which functions as the principal
theme of these works. The inclusion of the liturgy also points up
what the Porretans exclude. They have not the slightest interest in
cosmology; their account of creation treats of angels and men only.
Nor do they have any interest in discussing faith as a cognitive
state, or, for that matter, as a virtue; ethics, as a topic, is omitted.
Their most remarkable omission, however, is the atonement, a
subject central to any Christian theology and one that was vigorously debated at the time. Yet, on the question of how Christ
accomplishes His saving work the Porretans have nothing at all to
say.

If this schema helps to explain why Porretan theology failed to
capture the imagination of contemporaries as an approach to systematic theological education, much the same can be said for their
handling of authorities. They do, to be sure, display occasional
flashes of real insight, a thorough command of contemporary dialectic, and an acute sensitivity to source criticism. As with most
theologians in this period, they object to Abelard's claim that God
cannot do better or different than He does. In criticizing it, the
Porretans astutely note that a basic flaw in Abelard's argument is
his treatment of God's nature as if it could be compassed by a

logical analysis of possibility, necessity, and contingency, even though Abelard himself insists that, since logic is a formal art, it cannot take us beyond logic to ontology.[48] The Porretans' awareness of the technical features of Abelard's logic and the nature of its claims thus enable them to hoist Abelard on his own petard, and not merely to argue that his position is unacceptable because it is not congruent with God as He is believed to be. The most impressive example of the Porretan critique of patristic authority occurs in their argument against the practice of triple immersion in the administration of baptism. Going back to a point earlier than the fifth century, when Pope Leo I instituted that rule, they note that Cyprian ordained single immersion. In reporting Cyprian's rule, they note, Augustine garbled Cyprian's text and substituted triple immersion, which Leo then followed. Given the fact that the practice of the church since Leo's day has been based on a textual corruption, the Porretans argue that it can be safely dismissed.[49]

These examples, while they certainly are impressive indices of the Porretans' ability to think in precise logical terms and to analyze their sources, are, however, exceptions that prove the rule. In the vast majority of cases, they simply state their own position without offering any particular rationale for it, even when the issue is a debated one. On the occasions when they feel a need to bolster their positions with authorities, whether biblical, patristic, or contemporary, their approach is simply to cite the authority by name, without quoting or paraphrasing his text or considering why he

---

[48] *Sent. mag. Gisleberti* I 2.38–39, p. 119; *Sent. mag. Gisleberti* II 2.38–42, p. 54. This is an understanding of Abelard's logic that is borne out in the studies of modern scholars. The best statements of this position are by Mariateresa Beonio-Brocchieri [Fumagalli], "La relation entre logique, physique et théologie chez Abélard," in *Peter Abelard*, ed. Eligius M. Buytaert (Leuven: Leuven University Press, 1974), pp. 153–63; *The Logic of Abelard*, trans. Simon Pleasance (Dordrecht: D. Reidel, 1969), pp. 13–23, 28–36; Mario Dal Pra, intro. to his ed. of Peter Abelard, *Scritti di logica*, 2nd ed., Pubblicazioni della facoltà di lettere e filosofia dell'Università di Milano, 34, sezione a cura dell'Istituto di storia della filosofia, 3 (Florence: La Nuova Italia, 1964), pp. xxi–xxiii, xxvi–xxviii; Bernhard Geyer, in his ed. of Peter Abelard, *Philosophischen Schriften*, Beiträge, 20:1–4 (Münster: Aschendorff, 1919–33), 4: 621–22, 624–33; Jean Jolivet, *Arts du langage et théologie chez Abélard*, 2nd ed. (Paris: J. Vrin, 1982), pp. 19–22, 117; Martin M. Tweedale, *Abailard on Universals* (Amsterdam: North-Holland Publishing Company, 1976), pp. 93–95, 130–32, 210. The chief dissenters are Lambert M. DeRijk, intro. to his ed. of Peter Abelard, *Dialectica*, 2nd ed. (Assen: Van Gorcum & Comp. N.V., 1970), pp. xxiii–xxviii, xl, lv–lix, xcv, xcviii, and Lucia Urbani Ulivi, *La psicologia di Abelardo e il "Tractatus de intellectibus"* (Rome: Storia e Letteratura, 1976), pp. 85–93, 95–100, not in the sense of Abelard's goals in this connection, but more in his actual achievement of them.

[49] *Sent. mag. Gisleberti* I 7.13–14, p. 140.

takes the stand he takes, and without indicating very systematically the countervailing opinions and why they are objectionable. Despite the fact that they themselves clearly had mastered the necessary techniques, as pedagogues the Porretans are not very concerned with passing their methodology of theological reasoning on to their students.

The next mid-century systematic theologian of discernibly Porretan filiation, the author of the *Sententiae divinitatis*, is notably more eclectic than the earliest Porretans and much more erratic in his handling of authorities.[50] In one area, the creation, he offers a full catalogue of conflicting interpretations and adduces a particularly strong authority in support of each of them. After canvassing the disputes, and distinguishing carefully between those that can be settled with certainty and those on which our knowledge can only remain probable, he gives his own analysis and response at the end of each question. In other areas, however, he tends to ignore current debates. He does not consistently mention the names of authorities he calls on to anchor his own position. Nor does he refer very expressly or frequently to contemporary or recent masters. This unevenness in his treatment of authorities is coupled with an organizational framework that is equally problematic. His work is divided into six parts. He begins with the creation, set forth according to the hexaemeral account in Genesis, up to but not including man. Part 2 deals with man, free will and grace. In Part 3 the author treats original sin and its consequences. In Parts 4 and 5 he considers the incarnation and the sacraments, respectively, positioning the divine nature and the Trinity at the end of the sixth part. This placement of God at the end of the schema is unquestionably the most bizarre feature of the *Sententiae divinitatis*. It does not occur to the author that this topic is both logically, theologically, and chronologically prior to the other dogmatic issues he treats earlier in the work. Aside from this decided peculiarity, there are some notable omissions. The author departs from the early Porretan treatment of the sacraments, dividing them into those received by all Christians and those received only by some Christians. Having made this distinction, the only sacraments he actually discusses are those that fall into the first group, although it has to be said that, with respect to unction, he mentions it only and does not discuss it. Marriage and holy orders receive no attention. As with the early Porretans, he omits soteriology. But the gaps in this

---

[50] *Die Sententiae divinitatis: Ein Sentenzenbuch der Gilbertischen Schule*, ed. Bernhard Geyer, Beiträge, 7: 2–3 (Münster: Aschendorff, 1909).

work are even more extensive, including angels, the devil, vice and virtue, the sacerdotal power of the keys in connection with penance, and Last Things.

HUGH OF ST. VICTOR AND THE *SUMMA SENTENTIARUM*

Far more influential than either the Porretans or the Abelardians was the systematic theology of Hugh of St. Victor, the *De sacramentis fidei christianae*, completed in 1137. In striking contrast to the sentence collections of both of these groups, Hugh produced a work that is both highly inclusive and that is informed by a clear rationale accounting for its organization and coverage, one which also places systematic theology as such along a trajectory of the modes of human knowledge.[51] This rationale is located in Hugh's celebrated distinction between God's work of institution and His work of restitution. Hugh entitles the work *De sacramentis* because he views as sacramental all the modes by which God reveals Himself to man and all the modes by which He redeems man. In describing both of these processes, he follows a largely chronological, not logical, order, subordinating many topics to the larger question of how man comes to a knowledge of God, both as creator and as redeemer. Hugh takes pains to place the exercise of systematic theology very clearly in the context of this broader epistemological concern. It is, he states at the outset, a second-order mode of knowledge. In the first stage is a historical reading of Holy Scripture. Next comes an allegorical understanding of the historical sense. From that allegorical understanding he now proposes to compress the main points of doctrine, that must be known for man's salvation, and that need, therefore, to be included in a theological summary. It is also important, for Hugh, to distill from secular writers what can be known about God's work of institution in the natural world. This material supplements the information which Scripture supplies about creation. But the Scriptural matter, he notes, has a different slant. Its aim is less to tell man about nature as such than to explain how man arrived at his present dilemma and his need for salvation. Reprising a point he had discussed at length in his *Didascalicon*, Hugh completes these introductory remarks by commenting on the utility of the liberal arts for

---

[51] Hugh of St. Victor, *De sacramentis fidei christianae*, PL 176. Good general appreciations include Christian Schütz, *Deus absconditus, Deus manifestus: Die Lehre Hugos von St. Viktor über die Offenbarung Gottes* (Rome: Herder, 1967), pp. 22–89; Roger Baron, *Science et sagesse chez Hugues de Saint-Victor* (Paris: P. Lethielleux, 1957), passim and esp. p. 139; Luscombe, *The School of Peter Abelard*, pp. 185–97.

the theologian, not only for the interpretation of the Bible but also
for the light they shed on the work of institution. He also lists and
describes briefly the books of the Bible, adding the church fathers
as an appendix to the New Testament.[52]

This elaborate essay on method in place, Hugh accordingly
divides the *De sacramentis* into two books, devoted to God's work of
institution and His work of restitution, respectively. The schema he
proposes would, indeed, have provided a very cogent approach to
systematic theology, at least if Hugh had adhered to the plan he
sets forth and if he had defined his key terms more clearly than he
does. One problem immediately apparent in the first book is that
Hugh is not always sure of whether the best way to order the
material is a chronological or a logical one, or according to the way
in which man comes to a knowledge of the subject in question.
Faced with having to make a decision on this question, he seeks to
avoid the issue by trying to do all three things at once. At times, the
results are rather confusing. Thus, at the beginning of Book 1,
Hugh leads off with the creation, rather than with the creator. But,
rather than starting with the work of the six days, he prefaces it
with an account of form and matter and the question of whether
primordial matter is preexistent. He then turns to the creation
proper. But here, he displays a lack of certainty as to whether to
present creatures in a hierarchical order, from primordial or exemplary causes, to invisible creatures, to visible creatures, or whether
to follow the hexaemeral account in Genesis. His decision is to
combine these two approaches, following neither consistently.
Thus, having ushered man onto the stage as the last created being,
Hugh backs up to discuss primordial causes and the question of
why the world was created at all. Hugh also tries to come to grips
with two other problems at this juncture. One is the question of
whether, and how, the primordial causes can be differentiated from
God. The other is the question of the sequence of creation followed
in the Genesis account, which leaves unanswered how certain
beings were capable of existing if they were created prior to the
natural forces or resources needed for their survival. Augustine and
Bede, Hugh's major sources on these issues, had come up with their
own answers, of which Hugh does not make full use. He leaves
the question of primordial causes dangling, although he accepts the
view that God actually created the entire universe *simul*, at the
same time, despite the six-day account related in Genesis. The

---

[52] Hugh of St. Victor, *De sac.* 1, prologus 1.1.1, *PL* 176: 183A–187A.

question of why Genesis is written the way it is he answers by
stating that this decision reflects the author's awareness of the way
man comes to know the creation.[53]

The subject of God, which Hugh takes up initially in the effort to
explain how He differs from primordial causes, leads Hugh to
develop a mini-treatise on the Trinity at that point, followed by
three brief proofs of God's existence, after he has been discussing
the Trinity for some time. But he does not continue with the Trinity
or the divine attributes here because there is still some unfinished
business remaining with respect to the creation, namely, angels.
Angels represent an organizational problem for him since he has
largely opted for a hexaemeral treatment of creation, and the
creation of angels is not included in the work of the six days in
Genesis. To be sure, Hugh could have inserted angels after his
discussion of primordial causes. But he does not make that choice.
He has, as noted, already opted for the creation *simul* theory. But he
still tries to see how angels fit into the hexaemeron, with understandably inconclusive results. Abandoning this unresolved problem, Hugh returns to man, next considering man prior to the fall,
the fall itself, and the consequences and transmission of original
sin. He acknowledges the fact that what we can know about man in
his prelapsarian state is largely conjectural. His tactic for addressing this subject is an interesting one. Rather than invoking a
philosophical "state of nature" analysis, he works backward from
the negative consequences of sin as described in the Bible to the
positive conditions they replaced. In man's fallen state, he needs
redemption, a thought that leads Hugh to remark briefly at this
point on Hell, as the destination he faces without it, and on Purgatory and Heaven as the possibilities open to him with it. Still within
Book 1, although, as he had indicated in his preface, it is the proper
subject matter for Book 2, Hugh then introduces, hard on the heels
of man's need for redemption, the incarnation of Christ. He regards
Christ as the supreme sacrament. This idea leads him to offer a
definition of sacrament itself, which he does, for the first time, in
Book 1, chapter 9, almost at the end of the first book, although the
idea of sacrament is the overall theme of the work, and despite the

---

[53] A good account of this problem, which accents the inconsistencies that result
in Hugh's treatment of the creation, is Charlotte Gross, "Twelfth-Century Concepts of Time: Three Reinterpretations of Augustine's Doctrine of Creation
Simul," *Journal of the History of Philosophy* 23 (1985): 325–34. See also A. Mignon, *Les
origines de la scolastique et Hugues de Saint-Victor*, 2 vols. (Paris: P. Lethielleux, 1895),
1: 321–28; Jakob Kilgenstein, *Die Gotteslehre des Hugo von St. Viktor* (Würzburg:
Andreas Göbel, 1897), pp. 37–57.

fact that he has been using the term, with a variety of denotations, in Book 1, as he plans to do as well in Book 2. For Hugh, sacraments, in any of the senses intended, bring salvation only when joined with faith and good works. And so, still in Book 1, he considers faith and the Ten Commandments.

Even thus far, it is clear that the first book of the *De sacramentis* is both redundant and disorganized. Its schematic problems stem both from delay and anticipation in his positioning of material, as well as from his trying to do too many things at once in his handling of creation. Book 2 has its own schematic difficulties. Hugh opens Book 2 with Christ's incarnation, which he had already introduced in Book 1. He then proceeds to restate his views on the Trinity. It is at this point that he first raises the vexed question of theological language, the meaning of terms such as person, nature, and substance with respect to the deity, although, it must be noted, he has already been using them, and without benefit of any lexical clarifications, in this same connection repeatedly, in both books. Hugh wrestles manfully with the contemporary debates on theological language, criticizing some of the more technically minded theologians of the day for being too abstruse or for turning the issue into a word game. He himself neither appreciates the technical problems involved nor the need for terminological precision in this context. He fails to come up with alternatives to the formulae to which he objects that are both clear and comprehensible and that convey with accuracy and specificity the doctrine he wants to support. Abandoning rather than resolving that subject, he moves on to the church and its sacramental rites, as an extension of the incarnation into the present age. It is possible that Hugh has picked up this idea from Honorius. In any event, he is the first scholastic theologian to include a discussion of ecclesiology in a systematic work.

Hugh's treatment of the sacraments, in the narrow sense of the specific rites of the church, is confined to sensible signs that signify, resemble, and contain grace. Unlike many of his predecessors, he presents a treatise on the sacraments in Book 2 that yokes them all to his general definition, that seeks a parallel treatment of all of them, and that does not weave them into or subordinate them to other topics. Hugh is a proponent of the septiform principle on the grounds he lays down in his definition of sacrament in general. He does not merely take up individual sacraments that interest him, ignoring those that he does not find truly sacramental. Instead, he explains why all seven are sacraments, in contrast with other rituals such as the sign of the cross, which are sacred signs but which lack the capacity to convey grace. If Hugh is clear on that

point, his treatment of sacraments shares with his treatment of
creation in Book 1 a confusing tendency to approach his subject
from several perspectives at once. He begins his account with holy
orders because the priesthood is necessary for the administration of
the other sacraments and because the different grades of holy
orders reflect the ministry of Christ which the church now extends
to the world. Marriage is taken up next because it was the first
sacrament, instituted by God in Eden before the fall. Here we can
see Hugh trying to combine a chronological model, based on the
order in which the sacraments were instituted, with a logical model,
based on the existence in place of the men needed to perform
them. At the same time, Hugh presents baptism, confirmation, the
Eucharist, penance, and unction in the order of reception. And,
also at the same time, he distinguishes these sacraments, as received by all Christians, from the sacraments that some Christians
receive, a thought that impels him to return to marriage, which he
places after the Eucharist and reprises. In between the Eucharist
and matrimony, and for reasons apparent to Hugh alone, he inserts
a discussion of simony. One sometimes does find this topic included
in a treatise on the sacraments within a larger systematic work. But
when this is the case, it is typically presented after holy orders, as a
perversion of that sacrament. Hugh offers no explanation for his
inclusion of simony or for his location of it at the point where he
places it. It is the only sin he treats in this particular context; for his
more extended consideration of sin in general he introduces, more
logically, as a preface to the sacrament of penance. Hugh concludes
with a fairly detailed discussion of Last Things, expanding on what
he had said about Heaven and Hell in Book 1 but not reiterating
his earlier remarks on Purgatory.

While the sentence collections of contemporary and earlier scholastics often suffer from omissions, this is scarcely the problem with
Hugh's *De sacramentis*. His difficulties lie more in the realm of
redundancy and in his unwillingness to adhere to his announced
schema, which would have yielded a more coherent organization
than the one with which he actually emerges. Three other salient
weaknesses are also visible in Hugh's attack on his assignment.
One is the multiple points of view he brings to such subjects as the
sacraments and the creation. Far from illuminating these topics by
shedding light from different angles on them, this tactic leads to
intellectual disjunction and confusion. A second difficulty lies in
Hugh's vagueness about terms that he needs to define and to use
clearly if he is going to succeed in refuting thinkers whom he
opposes, or even if he is going to carry forward his own larger

project. Here, his inconclusive handling of theological language is an obstruction to his argument. Even more serious is his polyvalent use of the term "sacrament." Even after having produced a general definition that applies to the rites of the church which medieval Christians associated with that term, he continues to use it to refer to their Old Testament precursors, without qualifying the word in such a way as to clarify why God deemed it necessary to supplant these usages in the New Testament. Hugh even uses the phrase "sacraments of the devil."[54] From the context, it can be ascertained that what he means by this locution is probably the means by which the devil binds sinners to himself. None the less, it is an electrifying and anomalous formula in the light of Hugh's understandings of "sacrament" elsewhere in the work. Third, Hugh is not always alive to the resources made available by his sources. A good case in point, noted above, is the question of primordial causes. Although Hugh draws heavily here on Augustine's Genesis commentaries, he ignores the fact that Augustine had come to grips with the same problem and had resolved it in a manner that would have been perfectly sensible for Hugh to have adopted, given his doctrinal desiderata on that subject.

This last observation leads us to a consideration of Hugh as a guide to the handling of authorities more generally. Here, although he has a wide knowledge of patristic sources, and one that indicates a personal reading of them that goes beyond the materials available in *catenae* or anthologies, he is less a model for the critical evaluation of authorities than he is, at least potentially, as a guide to systematic theology.[55] In the first place, except in the contexts of Christology and Trinitarian theology, he does not give the names of the authorities to whom he refers. It was typical, in this period, for scholastic theologians to indicate the positions of contemporaries by the conventional use of *quidam* or *alii dicunt*, "as some say" or "as others say;" Hugh extends this usage to the fathers as well. Whether in the rare instances where he mentions them by name or in the more usual cases where he does not, he declines to indicate which of the author's specific works he is drawing upon. He does not quote from them, contenting himself with summarizing their conclusions. This practice does not make it easy for a reader to ascertain why Hugh prefers one position over another. While Hugh, as noted, presents the fathers as an appendix to Holy

---

[54] Hugh of St. Victor, *De sac.* 1.8.11, *PL* 176: 312B.
[55] Ludwig Ott, "Hugo von St. Viktor und die Kirchenväter," *Divus Thomas*, 3rd ser. 27 (1949): 293–95.

Scripture, this does not mean, in practice, that he is unwilling to criticize or to reject patristic authority. When he does so, his tactic is to take his own line, based on the theological considerations he thinks are important at that juncture, but without systematically comparing or analyzing the authorities in question, sifting out their differences through the use of logic or preferring some to others on historical grounds. If he can find concord among the authorities he is pleased. But he is not interested in a sustained exercise in reconciling conflicts; and he does not multiply citations as an illustration of how to do so. He does treat, and take a stand on, some of the leading controversies of the day. But Hugh's disinclination to rationalize his own positions and to explain his reasons for preferring certain authorities to others and for his departures from tradition make him less helpful than he might be as a model for how to replicate the thought processes that have brought him to the conclusions he reaches.

It cannot be said that any of Hugh's immediate followers achieved dramatic rectifications of these Victorine deficiencies. The most important of these is undoubtedly the anonymous author of the *Summa sententiarum*, composed shortly after the completion of Hugh's *De sacramentis*. David Luscombe has aptly described the *Summa sententiarum* as "the Place de l'Étoile of early twelfth-century theological literature, the point of arrival and of departure and the center of circulation for many other writings and teachings."[56] This judgment is eminently sound when it comes to the way in which the author poses the questions he takes up and the positions he takes on them. He certainly tightens up the arguments against contemporary theologians whom Hugh had opposed, borrowing some of their ideas in the process, while avoiding some of Hugh's organizational problems. At the same time, he perpetuates some of the difficulties in Hugh's schema and omits some of the topics that Hugh had included. The *Summa sententiarum* is divided into seven parts. The author first takes up the theological virtues. Then he discusses the Trinity, the incarnation, angels, man, the fall, the nature and transmission of original sin, and the sacraments. For him, the sacraments include the precepts of the Old Law and six of the rites of the New, concluding with marriage.

---

[56] Luscombe, *The School of Peter Abelard*, p. 198. Luscombe gives a fine overall summary of the place of this work in contemporary theology and provides the most cogent analysis of its dating and its possible authorship, reviewing the previous literature, pp. 199–213. We concur with his view that the best date is ca. 1138–42 and that efforts to assign the work to any one author have been inconclusive. The text of the *Summa sententiarum* is printed in *PL* 176.

In comparing this author's schema with Hugh's, we note the omission of a hexaemeral account of creation. Only two creatures, angels and men, are considered. The rest of the cosmos, including the vexed question of primordial causes, goes by the board. Other salient omissions are holy orders, the church, and Last Things, as well as a number of issues hotly debated at this time, on which Hugh had not failed to state his opinions. Good examples can be found in the author's treatment of the sacraments. Under the heading of baptism, he does not take up the validity of baptism by desire or baptism by blood. With respect to penance, he states that contrition, confession, and satisfaction are all required, but indicates neither the fact that contemporaries were arguing about when, in that sequence of events, the penitent's sin is remitted, nor his own felt need to take a stand on this question. The author, like Hugh, offers a general definition of sacrament that is apposite to the rites of the church. But it does not apply, in his view, to the Old Testament practices which he none the less describes as sacraments. Undoubtedly, the most striking organizational peculiarity of the *Summa sententiarum* is the author's decision to discuss the incarnation before the creation and fall of man. This being the case, it is initially quite difficult for the reader to see why the incarnation occurred at all. It also points to another deficiency of this work, an extremely laconic and hasty treatment of soteriology.

The *Summa sententiarum* is much less redundant than Hugh's *De sacramentis*. But the author does repeat himself in the treatment of ethics. He defines sin in general in Book 3, the section of the work where he places the fall of man, introducing that definition, however, after he has already been discussing original sin and its difference from actual sin for some paragraphs. He then moves on to virtue, understood not in its own right but merely as the opposite of vice. Virtue also comes up in two other locations. Faith, hope, and charity form the author's subject in Book 1; and charity reappears as the fulfillment of the law following his consideration of the Ten Commandments in Book 4. In none of these places does he treat the psychogenesis of moral acts or the relation between grace and human effort in man's moral life.

As noted, the author does not address all the debated issues of the day. But he does seek to cover the major bases, whether controversial or not. Unless he is treating controversial questions, he is inclined simply to state his own opinions, without giving reasons for them. In handling some controversial points, he glosses over the fact that they are, indeed, controversial, and proceeds in the same manner. In cases where he does set forth a controversy as controversial, he presents the conflicting views and the authorities on whom the contestants base them. He then tells the reader which position he supports, although he is not terribly skillful or forthcoming in explaining why. He sometimes contents himself with the nude citation of countervailing authorities, as if they were self-explanatory and intrinsically persuasive. While the author sometimes succeeds in selecting extremely pertinent advocates for the positions taken in these debates, his handling of his authorities does not help the reader to see what, in their reasoning or in the context of their arguments, makes them authoritative or not, in the author's eyes. In handling the Trinitarian and Christological debates of the day, the author is more inclined than Hugh to use the technical vocabulary imported into this area by the more avant-garde theologians, although he often uses these terms imprecisely, suggesting that he has not fully grasped the semantic construction which their coiners had placed upon them or the implications flowing from their use. These traits may help to suggest why the *Summa sententiarum* did not become a standard textbook in the teaching of systematic theology despite its strong substantive influence on contemporary scholasticism.

ROLAND OF BOLOGNA, ROBERT PULLEN, ROBERT OF MELUN

As we move deeper into the generation of the 1140s and 1150s, the tendency toward eclecticism, already visible to some degree in the *Summa sententiarum* and the *Sententiae divinitatis*, becomes more pronounced. This is certainly the case with Roland of Bologna, Robert Pullen, and Robert of Melun, Peter Lombard's chief competitors at that time. The first of these figures, Roland of Bologna, is an interesting witness to the fact that books travelled widely in this period, no less than pupils and masters, and that systematic theology was practiced beyond the Alps as well as across the Rhine, and among authors whose primary affiliation might be with a calling other than that of scholastic theology. For Roland was a master at Bologna not known ever to have left his native country, a master equally if not better known as a canonist and as one of the earliest commentators on Gratian's *Decretum*.[57] He produced a

---

[57] On this account, Roland in the past was sometimes confused with the Bolognese canonist Roland Bandinelli, who later became Pope Alexander III. This identification has been disproved by James A. Brundage, "Marriage and Sexuality in the Decretals of Pope Alexander III," in *Miscellanea Rolando Bandinelli, Papa Alessandro III*, ed. Filippo Liotta (Siena: Accademia senese degli Intronati,

summa of canon law, as well as a theological sentence collection written in ca. 1150.[58] Roland's theology bears the imprint of a canonical mentality at some points, no less than the marked influence of Abelard and, to a lesser extent, Hugh of St. Victor. Roland's organization shows the influence of both of these masters. His affinities with the Abelardians can be seen in his tripartite subdivision of his *Sentences* into faith, sacraments, and charity, although he reverses the order of the second and third subdivisions usual in that school. Also typical of the Abelardian approach is Roland's omission of Last Things and holy orders. The only feature of the priesthood on which he comments is the power of the keys. But, unlike the Abelardians, with their deep interest in the theme of free will, he does not discuss the angels' possession of that faculty or the psychogenesis of their fall. He gives un-Abelardian short shrift to these ethical questions in man's case as well.

After an Abelardian curtain-raiser on faith and its nature as a cognitive state, Roland offers a table of contents in his first book that can be seen as an improved version of Hugh's agenda in the *De sacramentis*. Although he does raise some cosmological questions only to leave them dangling, Roland has clearly solved some of the organizational problems that had plagued Hugh in that connection. Roland begins with the divine nature, treating God's attributes as such before moving to the Trinity. Next, he introduces the creation, and finds a far more cogent way of blending logic and chronology here than Hugh does. While he omits primordial causes, he begins with the creation of primordial matter, continuing with angels, the work of the six days, and man. This topic is followed by the fall and the transmission of original sin. Roland concludes Book 1 with a consideration of the Old Law, ordained to govern man. He goes into more detail on this subject than the Abelardians do but he keeps it more firmly under control as a superseded dispensation than Hugh does. Agreeing with Hugh that Christ is the supreme sacrament, Roland begins Book 2 with the incarnation, and treats the sacraments of the church in the order in

---

1986), pp. 59–83; *Law, Sex, and Christian Society in Medieval Europe* (Chicago: University of Chicago Press, 1987), p. 257 n. 3; John T. Noonan, "Who Was Rolandus?" in *Law, Church, and Society: Essays in Honor of Stephan Kuttner*, ed. Kenneth Pennington and Robert Somerville (Philadelphia: University of Pennsylvania Press, 1977), pp. 21–48. I would like to thank Professor Brundage for bringing this matter to my attention.

[58] Roland of Bologna, *Die Sentenzen Rolands*, ed. Ambrosius Gietl (Amsterdam: Editions Rodopi, 1969 [repr. of Freiburg in Breisgau: Herder, 1891 ed.]), pp. xvii–xviii for the dating; *Summa magistri Rolandi*, ed. Friedrich Thaner (Aalen: Scientia Verlag, 1962 [repr. of Innsbruck, 1874 ed.]), p. xli for the dating.

which they are received, as an extension of Christ's saving work in the world.

The weakest point in Roland's organizational scheme is his handling of ethics. Ostensibly, this subject belongs in book 3, under the heading of charity or the moral life of the Christian. He does talk about charity in that book, albeit in a cursory way. But his chief discussion of vice and virtue is placed in Book 2, as an addendum to the sacrament of penance. Another difficulty is Roland's placement of the topic of predestination. He locates it in Book 3 as a means of raising, under the heading of ethics, the question of the relation of free will to grace in the moral life. Both Hugh and Abelard had treated predestination under the heading of God's attributes and powers, perhaps a more logical setting for that topic. The chief debt that Roland the sentence collector owes to Roland the canonist lies in his treatment of the sacraments. As with other canonists, he tends to view the sacraments more from the standpoint of their administration than from the standpoint of their reception, and he assesses their validity largely in that light. In treating marriage, for instance, the aspect of the sacrament that brings a real sparkle to Roland's eyes is the impediments created by consanguinity and affinity, to which he devotes most of his attention and which he discusses with relish. He reflects none of the concern for the internalizing of the sacraments by the recipient and their role in his sanctification that are hallmarks of sacramental reflection on the part of contemporary theologians. Roland's canonical inclinations are also reflected in his tendency to handle legalistically the ethical questions debated the most ardently by current theologians, when he takes them up at all.

If Hugh shares the honors with Abelard in Roland's schema, Roland's methodology places him squarely in the camp of the Abelardians. Indeed, he is a better exponent of the approach Abelard advocated than the master himself in practice. Roland is extremely analytical and rigorous. He gives clear definitions of his terms and presents his material in a highly formal, question-oriented manner. In particular, he is interested in addressing issues that possess a philosophical content. He produces many authorities for and against each position he treats and explains clearly why he supports or rejects them. He seeks to reconcile them systematically when he can, typically citing the various opinions at the beginning of each question and then discussing their merits and demerits as he works toward his personal solution. Roland shows a keen awareness of the importance of historical criticism. A good example can be found in his treatment of confirmation. Roland notes that, in the *ecclesia primitiva*, some authorities had agreed to waive the rule that a bishop is the only proper minister of confirmation, in cases where the Christian population was thin on the ground and a bishop might not be easily available. But, such a dispensation, he observes, is no longer needed in the present.[59] This kind of analysis is less typical of Roland's treatment of authorities than is his tendency to reformulate what they have to say in philosophical terms. In general, he is interested less in the context in which they had written than in the logical or metaphysical implications of their opinions. It is these implications that he is most eager to use, framing them, as well as the questions he addresses, in syllogistic form, whether inductive, deductive, or hypothetical. While Roland also adduces and applies the norm of theological appropriateness, his chief methodological trait is the systematic way in which he applies reason both to the questions he raises and to the authorities he cites.

The effort to refine Hugh of St. Victor's schema and to give more sustained attention to the weighing of authorities also characterize the sentence collections of Robert Pullen and Robert of Melun, both of whom were English theologians teaching in Paris during Peter Lombard's time. Since they lack the canonical outlook informing Roland's work, which is likely to have limited the latter's appeal among theologians, these two figures need to be considered carefully as real contemporary alternatives to Peter. Robert Pullen's efforts to improve on Hugh, on whom he is closely dependent, are more apparent than real. He produced the lengthiest sentence collection of the century, between 1142 and 1144,[60] before being called to Rome and made a cardinal. His *Sentences* occupy eight books. In the first, he begins with a brief proof of God's existence and then considers the divine attributes in general before proceeding to the Trinity. Book 2 covers the creation, angels, man, and the fall, and the nature and transmission of original sin. The theme of the third book is the redemption. Beginning with the Old Law in relation to the New, Robert continues with the incarnation and nature of Christ. Christ's human nature, and, in particular,

---

[59] Roland of Bologna, *Sent.*, p. 24. His methodological affinities to Abelard have been treated well by Gietl, intro. to his ed. of *Sentences*, pp. xxi–lxi; Luscombe, *The School of Peter Abelard*, pp. 244–53.

[60] Robert Pullen, *Sententiarum libri octo, PL* 186. For the dating of this work, see Franz Pelster, "Einege Angaben über Leben und Schriften des Robert Pullus, Kardinal und Kanzler der römischen Kirche (d. 1146)," *Scholastik* 12 (1937): 239–47; F. Courtney, *Cardinal Robert Pullen: An English Theologian of the Twelfth Century* (Rome: Universitas Gregoriana, 1954), p. 23.

Christ's human knowledge, receives more attention than any other dogmatic issue in Robert's *Sentences*. It occupies approximately half of Book 3 and the whole of Book 4. Book 5 continues with a historical account of the life of Christ, culminating with His sending of the Holy Spirit and His entrusting of His disciples with their evangelical mission at Pentecost.

In the remainder of this book and in the books that follow, Robert's concern is with how this evangelical mission is accomplished. He initiates that theme with a consideration of faith and justification, and then moves on to the ethical and sacramental lives of Christians. There is no distinct treatise either on ethics or on the sacraments in this work. Like Honorius, Robert tends to intermingle these subjects. Still in Book 5, and following justification, he takes up baptism and penance. He then backpedals to consider concupiscence as a consequence of original sin and the nature of sin in general, to which these two sacraments speak as a remedy. Sin in general is followed by the theological virtues, with another flashback, following that topic, to sins that are mortal. Ethics continues to concern Robert in Book 6, where he raises the question of the degree to which negligence, ignorance, and diabolical temptation affect man's culpability for sin. He then returns to the types of sin, distinguishing between original and post-baptismal sin. Having mentioned diabolical temptation earlier in Book 6, he picks up that thread again, now discussing the theme in connection with the assistance of the good angels in man's moral life. He ranks both the angels and the demons according to the Pseudo-Dionysian hierarchy. He then returns to penance, in connection with which he discusses the priestly power of the keys and excommunication.

Book 7 begins with another reprise on penance, focusing on the satisfaction stage of the sacrament. Next, Robert inserts a brief treatise on the church. As we can see, he does not position it, as Hugh and Honorius do, after his treatment of Christ's earthly life as the extension of His saving work in sacramental sanctification, even thought he had alluded to the foundation of the church at Pentecost. Rather, Robert takes up the church under the heading of ethics. Making a brief pass at the two-swords theory, unusual among contemporary systematic theologians, who generally conceded this topic to the canonists and publicists in their division of labor, he moves to the various callings within the church. He discusses the grades of holy orders and then treats a series of lay professions, from ruler, to soldier, to civil servant; he then turns to virginity and marriage, and the active and contemplative lives. Returning to marriage, Robert now considers it not as a calling but as a sacrament. In Book 8, Robert leads off with the Eucharist. But the bulk of this book is devoted to Last Things, which he covers in detail, drawing heavily on Augustine's *City of God*, as had Hugh. Antichrist and his reign, the second coming of Christ, the resurrection, the last judgment, and Heaven, Purgatory, and Hell are all described vividly and with much celestial fireworks, completing Robert's *summa*.

Even this bare report on his coverage and organization suggests the problems embedded in Robert Pullen's work as a systematic theologian. It is true that there are some omissions in his *Sentences*. Notably, he does not provide a general definition of sacrament, a discussion or a principled rejection of confirmation and unction as sacraments, or any notice of the confessionist-contritionist debate currently raging in his analysis of penance. Robert, like the author of the *Summa sententiarum*, confines his account of creation to angels and men alone. But it is less his omissions than his other difficulties that make Robert's work unwieldy and intellectually indigestible. There is a marked lack of logic in his handling of many topics. On one level, for example, his inclusion of holy orders and marriage under the heading of the church makes sense, but it does not enable him to distinguish these vocations from other Christian callings that he does not regard as sacraments. Given Robert's scheme for treating the sacraments, the Eucharist is presented almost as an afterthought. He frequently puts the cart before the horse. This tendency in turn results in his *Sentences'* most serious weakness from an organizational standpoint, acute redundancy. Stemming from Robert's inability to decide where to discuss a host of topics, this deficiency leads him to return to them over and over again. He takes up angels three times, once in the creation, next in man's moral life, and finally in the last judgment. Penance also receives three separate treatments, in association with baptism, in man's moral struggle as assisted by angels and as impeded by demons, and in connection with the authority of priests to impose satisfaction. The bits and pieces of what might have been a full-scale consideration of ethics are scattered among five different locations. "Haphazard" is the term used to describe Robert's schema by F. Courtney, and one can only agree.[61]

There are still other problems. A mid-twelfth-century reader picking up this work would gain no sense from it what was important and what was not from the amount of space Robert assigns to

---

[61] Courtney, *Cardinal Robert Pullen*, p. 22.

particular subjects. Robert lacks a sense of proportion. He is also extremely longwinded. He also frequently digresses, including material from biblical history at some points that is not essential to the forwarding of his argument and which is quite irrelevant to the contexts in which it is placed. Not to put too fine a point on it, this tendency reflects Robert's marked propensity for padding. Digression is also one of his ways of beating a strategic retreat from problems he has trouble resolving. Another tactic he uses for the same purpose is the posing of substantive questions in the form of rhetorical questions, which, being unanswered, leave the reader up in the air. There are quite a few topics which he seeks to dispose of in one or another of these ways, the most glaring example being Christ's human knowledge.[62] The reason why Robert leaves so many questions open is not because his sources, patristic and more recent, do not provide clear guidance on how definite conclusions might be drawn, but because he simply cannot make up his mind. He presents many controversial questions at otiose length, providing the alternative solutions, side by side, and then moving on without giving the reader any indication of what he personally finds useful or problematic in any of the opinions cited or what prevents him from choosing among them. As to what, in principle, would be needed in order to make a clear determination, he leaves the reader in the dark. Nor does he give the reader much help in deciding whether conflicting authorities are compatible or not. Often, as well, Robert repeats himself, multiplying long chains of authorities for each and every point, whether controversial or not, piling these citations on top of each other to no useful end, since they are basically saying the same thing, or are quoting each other, without adding any fresh perspective to the debate.

In citing authorities, outside of encumbering his text with superfluous references, Robert's technique is to give the authority's view, and then to offer a view drawn from reason, on the point under review. But he does not integrate reason with authority by investigating the authority's rationale for the position he takes. Robert does refer frequently, and positively, to philosophical sources. He is sensitive to the utility of grammar and logic as analytical tools. At the same time, he does not use logic as a structural principle in his schema, since he does not discriminate between topics that are controversial and need to be settled and topics that are not. Nor

---

[62] A point noted despairingly by Horacio Santiago-Otero, *El conocimiento de Cristo en cuanto hombre en la teología de la primera mitad del siglo XII* (Pamplona: Ediciones Universidad de Navarra, 1970), p. 204.

does he always grasp the difference between assertion, citation of authority, explanation, and proof. Despite his appeal to the verbal disciplines, he does not develop and use a consistent theological vocabulary, or define key terms before he puts them to work. And, despite his exhaustive, and reduplicative, catalogue of patristic witnesses, he appeals to the Bible more than to any other authority. Altogether, it is perhaps not surprising that Robert Pullen did not succeed in attracting disciples and that his influence largely evaporated from the scholastic scene following his removal to Rome.

Working a decade later, Robert of Melun at first glance looks to be a self-conscious critic of many of the weaknesses in the *Sentences* of Robert Pullen. His own *Sentences* were composed from the mid-1150s through 1160, undergoing a double redaction.[63] Robert of Melun's stated goal was to attack Gilbert of Poitiers and to synthesize the theologies of Abelard and Hugh of St. Victor.[64] From Hugh he takes the conceptual model of God's institution and restitution as the basis of his schema, and the broadgauged language of "sacrament" as applied to both of these processes.[65] This appropriation entails, for Robert, as it does for Hugh, an interest in treating God as He manifests Himself to man, rather than God in and of Himself. In comparison with Hugh, Robert devotes more attention to topics such as predestination and original sin, which he feels the Victorines had given too abbreviated a treatment. From Abelard Robert derives his confidence in and command of logic as a tool in theological reasoning. While he does not always agree with Abelard's substantive conclusions, he often follows his lead in deciding what topics ought to be posed and what manner of address should be taken to them.[66] Another feature of the Abelardian legacy absorbed by Robert which sometimes goes by the board among the Abelardians themselves, and which is ignored by many other theologians at this time, is a concern with accuracy in

---

[63] For the dating of the work and the evidence of the two redactions, see Raymond-M. Martin, "L'Oeuvre théologique de Robert de Melun," *RHE* 15 (1914): 485; "Un texte intéressant de Robert de Melun," *RHE* 28 (1932): 313–15.

[64] Robert of Melun, *Sententie* prologus, ed. Raymond-M. Martin, 2 vols. in 3 (Louvain: Spicilegium Sacrum Lovaniense, 1947–52), 3 part 1: 44–49. See, in general, Martin's discussion in his intro., pp. xi–xiv and his annotations to pp. 45–46; Ulrich Horst, *Die Trinitäts- und Gotteslehre des Robert von Melun* (Mainz: Matthias-Grünewald Verlag, 1964), pp. 328–30.

[65] This side of Robert's work is well developed by Ulrich Horst, *Gesetz und Evangelium: Das Alte Testament in der Theologie des Robert von Melun* (Munich: Ferdinand Schöningh, 1971), pp. 3–5.

[66] Ulrich Horst, "Beiträge zum Einfluss Abaelards auf Robert von Melun," *RTAM* 26 (1959): 214–26.

the citation of sources. All too often, Robert complains, writers give a mangled version of a text they are citing, or mis-attribute their sources, or misrepresent the views they are reporting, out of sloppiness or prejudice or ignorance. For this reason, he insists, it is important to give the author's name, the title of his work being cited, and a verbatim quotation rather than a paraphrase of his words.[67] He also criticizes people who are too wordy, who fling about Greek terms so as to flaunt their erudition and who get sidetracked into making inappropriate applications of the liberal arts to theology.[68]

Another feature of Robert's *Sentences* which suggests that he is a serious pedagogue who means business is his careful subdivision of his text into titles, distinctions, and chapters, in order to highlight the intellectual itinerary through which he conducts the student and to facilitate reference. He outlines these subdivisions clearly and explains their purpose.[69] Robert is one of the earliest of twelfth-century scholastic theologians to do so, and his subdivisions are much more detailed than those found in any other such author in his time. Quite apart from the merits of his positions, the thorough-going professionalism which Robert's work projects in all these respects has inclined his editor, Raymond-M. Martin, to aver that he came closer than anyone else in the 1150s to giving Peter Lombard a run for his money. The reason why he did not, in Martin's opinion, is that Robert's *Sentences* remained incomplete.[70] In 1160, he was recalled to England to accept ecclesiastical preferment, ending his life as bishop of Hereford. His work as we have it omits the last three sections of the second part of his *Sentences*, which would have dealt with sacraments, ethics, and Last Things.

But is Martin's judgment accurate, or does it spring from misplaced editorial enthusiasm? A closer look at Robert's schema and his methodology in practice will help us to see whether he lives up to the project he announces in his no-nonsense prologue. As noted, Robert borrows from Hugh the notion of sacrament as his organizing principle. The two parts of his *Sentences*, accordingly, are entitled the sacraments of the Old Law and the sacraments of the New Law, respectively. Omitting the issue of what God reveals of Himself in nature, each section considers only what the Old and New Testaments reveal about Him. Accordingly, Robert prefaces his

---

[67] Robert of Melun, *Sent.* prologus, *Oeuvres*, 3 part 1: 44–49.
[68] Ibid., pp. 4–19, 25–44.
[69] Ibid., pp. 49–56, 59–156.
[70] Martin, "L'Oeuvre théologique," p. 489.

consideration of the divine nature, his first topic in part 1, with a discussion of the relationship of the Old Testament revelation itself to the revelation of the New Testament, as *figura* to *veritas*. He offers suggestions on the ways of reading the Bible, noting that theological language is sometimes used literally and sometimes figuratively in Holy Scripture. Here he recapitulates Augustine's *De doctrina christiana* by way of Hugh's *Didascalicon*. After commenting on the relationship of philosophy to revelation, which expands on the observations he makes on the utility of the *artes* in his prologue, he repeats Hugh's listing of the books of the Bible, adding to it a treatment of the ages of the world. To this he appends a consideration of the six days of creation. For Robert, creation includes unformed matter, formed matter, and man. He omits angels and other cosmological problems. At this point in part 1, having already ushered the world and man onto the stage, he returns to God, taking up the Trinity and how it may be known. This subject leads to another disquisition on theological language. Robert then moves to the divine attributes in general, which leads him to yet another consideration of theological language. Having ignored angels in the context of creation, Robert now introduces them. Judging from the point in his account at which he positions them, they would appear to have been created after the creation of man. Robert discusses their hierarchy, and their duties, including their role in the last judgment. He then returns to man and his composition and, in particular, his soul. After a digression on the so-called World Soul, he continues with the human soul and its similarities to and differences from the souls of animals and plants. A major faculty of the human soul is free will. This thought moves Robert to a comparison between charity and sin, to man's nature before the fall, to the fall itself, and to the character of original sin. The second part of Robert's *Sentences*, designed to cover the sacraments of the New Law, leads off with another reprise of the differences between the Old and New Testaments, this time by contrasting the Mosaic laws and rituals with the Christian sacraments. That task completed, the second section of part 2 treats the incarnation and nature of Christ, the redemption, Christ's conception, His condition in the tomb, and His harrowing of Hell. The text breaks off here, but, judging from the detailed table of contents Robert supplies, he planned to move directly from the harrowing of Hell to the sacraments, ethics, and Last Things in sections 3 through 5 of part 2.

A consideration of this schema reveals that Robert has not been entirely successful in eliminating the illogical order and redundancy that plague the *De sacramentis* and other works influenced by it. In some respects he perpetuates the existing problems of the Victorine model and in other respects he substitutes his own version of repetition and inconsistency. Robert's decision to insert the creation in part 1 of his *Sentences* ahead of the creator reflects the Hugonian idea that man comes to a knowledge of God through His works. At the same time, Robert tries to structure the creation itself, or as much of it as he includes, in a more exclusively hexaemeral order than Hugh does, although without advancing the argument that the sequence of beings created according to the Genesis account is a reflection of the steps in human cognition. His placement of the topic of angels, detached from the creation account, is *sui generis* and has little to recommend it. Robert treats man both under the heading of creation and later on, after a consideration of the role of the angels in the last judgment that appears to jump the gun. The World Soul and the debates surrounding it would seem to belong more appropriately in the section of part 1 dealing with the creation. In part 2 of the *Sentences*, Robert brings up the conception of Christ by the Virgin Mary after His incarnation, nature, and redemption of man have already been discussed. This item is both logically, chronologically, and theologically out of place. We cannot know what Robert was planning to say in the ethical treatise that would have been the fourth section of part 2, and how much it would have reiterated or made use of his analysis of charity and sin in part 1. The most notable redundancy in Robert's *Sentences*, and it is one he is responsible for introducing into the Victorine tradition, lies in his handling of the topic of theological language. He sees, more clearly than Hugh, that this is an important subject, and he does make some notable steps toward attaining a clear and consistent vocabulary. But, the extensive, and repeated, attention paid by Robert to this issue is less an index of his success at resolving it than a reflection of his need to return to it, like a dog worrying a bone, in quest of a full resolution that remains elusive. In these respects, while Robert can be read as having purged his *Sentences* of some of the organizational problems of the *De sacramentis* and the *Summa sententiarum*, not to mention the *Sentences* of Robert Pullen, serious difficulties remain in his schema quite apart from its lack of completion.

On another level, Robert imports a fresh conceptual complication into his schema that is not found in previous works that stand under Hugh's shadow. He defines the material he treats in part 1 as the Old Testament *figurae*, which only shadow forth the New Testament *veritates*. In so doing, Robert compounds an unsolved dilemma concerning the status of the fundamental dogmas he addresses in this part of the *Sentences*. He makes many points about basic and substantive metaphysical and anthropological realities in his treatment of divine and human nature. Thus, he is talking here about what truly is, not about partial and precursory events that merely adumbrate the fullness of revealed truth to come. Robert never comes to grips with the question of how, or whether, these dogmatic topics can truly be understood as typological foreshadowings of reality and not as essential truths of the Christian faith in their own right, truths that will never be superseded.

Turning to Robert's method of argument and his use of authorities, we can measure him here against his stated objectives and his criticisms of practices that he finds objectionable. He certainly does give careful and extended treatment to many of the issues that call for it the most urgently. Unlike the work of Robert Pullen, one can see at a glance in Robert of Melun's *Sentences* which topics are important, which topics are problematic, and which topics are not, in terms of the amount of attention he gives to them. Following Hugh, Robert tends to make little distinction between the Bible and the church fathers as authorities. He draws on a wide range of authorities, and they are authorities who are distinctly apposite to the points debated. He also calls on his own rational analysis. The method he employs reflects a technique which he had already developed as a master of logic, a field which, like Abelard, he had pursued before becoming a theologian. We have as a witness John of Salisbury, who studied with him at that time and who observes that Robert's teaching method typically juxtaposed pros and cons, in order to show that the same terms could bear different meanings and that there was more than one approach or answer. John adds that, although thorough in his exposition and analysis of the alternatives, Robert's own solutions were concise and to the point.[71]

While the first part of Robert's technique carried over into his work as a theologian, concision often goes by the board in his *Sentences*, and for two reasons. Like Robert Pullen, Robert of Melun can be extremely longwinded and repetitious at times. This is particularly the case when he has a weak argument, or no argument at all, and is using loquaciousness as a means of trying to obscure that fact. A second reason for this characteristic is Robert's very skill as a logician and his enjoyment of the use of this art, to a degree that sometimes oversteps the bounds of utility. Despite his own strictures on this very subject, and his praise of brevity, he sometimes ignores the good short answers that exist to the prob-

---

[71] John of Salisbury, *Metalogicon* 2.10, trans. Daniel D. McGarry (Berkeley: University of California Press, 1955), pp. 96–97.

lems he discusses at length in the very works of the authorities he cites on the point, suggesting either poor research, lack of imagination, or an enjoyment of debate for its own sake. This latter possibility is stressed by Luscombe in his appraisal of Robert's style of argument. He describes Robert as a "difficult author to read who often becomes weighted down with the effort of his own reasoning and with the fineness of his own distinctions."[72] There is the undeniable air of a runaway logician in Robert of Melun. If he is analytical, he is primarily interested in analyzing concepts, not authorities, a trait he shares with Roland of Bologna. He does not, typically, concern himself with showing how the authorities have arrived at their conclusions; nor is he interested in contextualizing them. He is more likely to use an authority as the source of a substantive opinion, and then to supply his own logical reflections on that opinion. But he gives the reader little feel for the authority as a working theologian himself. While he demands accuracy in the citation of authorities, he sometimes garbles the authorities he cites, especially Augustine. This practice suggests that Robert was using his sources indirectly, and that he did not take the trouble to verify them. And, despite his objections to the use of Greek terms, he has recourse to them himself, for the simple reason that they are helpful in the clarification of certain doctrines.[73] Whether in his schema, or in his method, or in his doctrinal contributions more widely, it cannot truly be said that Robert of Melun advances the state of systematic theology as an intellectual enterprise very much. His failure to attract a following after his departure from the schools appears to have been a function not so much of the *lacunae* in his *Sentences* as of the fact that students of theology in the mid-twelfth-century came to much the same judgment on Robert's *Sentences* as have most modern scholars.[74]

THE LOMBARD

Let us now, in an act of imagination, place ourselves in the position of a young scholar who arrives in Paris in the 1140s or 1150s, seeking the instruction that would enable him to become a

---

[72] Luscombe, *The School of Peter Abelard*, p. 288.

[73] Milton V. Anastos, "Some Aspects of Byzantine Influence on Latin Thought," in *Twelfth-Century Europe and the Foundations of Modern Society*, ed. Marshall Claggett, Gaines Post, and Robert Reynolds (Madison: University of Wisconsin Press, 1961), pp. 132–34.

[74] Anastos, "Some Aspects," pp. 132–34; Franz Bliemetzrieder, "Robert von Melun und die Schule Anselms von Laon," *Zeitschrift für Kirchengeschichte* 53 (1934): 17–70; Horst, *Die Trinitäts- und Gotteslehre*, pp. 328–30.

master of theology in his own right. Let us assume that he is eager and committed, interested in obtaining the very best education he can find in exchange for the outlay of time, money, and effort which he is prepared to invest in schooling himself for a career as a professional theologian. Let us further suppose that he is also a careful and prudent person, willing to canvas the available options before choosing a master. He takes the trouble to hear Robert of Melun, and, if he arrives at Paris early enough, Robert Pullen, the author of the *Summa sententiarum*, and the Porretans and Abelardians as well. Hearing good reports about Peter Lombard, he attends his lectures too, and decides—as did so many auditors—that Peter is the master for him. In the light of the other alternatives, which we have now examined, and in comparison with them, what does he find in Peter's *Sentences* that sets the Lombard's teaching apart, in his eyes, as so clearly superior?

Having acquainted himself with Robert of Melun's teaching, our hypothetical student would have been pleased to note that Peter shares with Robert a concern for ready reference within his *Sentences* and that he likewise equips his work with the helpful numbering of chapters as a finding tool.[75] He would also have noticed that, like the Victorines, Peter offers a coherent overall rationale for his schema. Unlike the Victorine rationale, however, Peter's is not based on a biblical or historical plan. While he treats many topics in much the same order, and while he retains the Bible as a major theological source, he does not subordinate his material to the history of salvation. He offers, instead, a wider and more inclusive view of the theological enterprise, one that makes room for concerns that are also noetic, anthropological, moral, and metaphysical.[76] In outlining his own conceptual model at the outset of his *Sentences*, Peter calls on a familiar Augustinian principle, while assigning it a new role. The thematic orientation that Peter gives to his work is the distinction between signs and things, use and enjoyment, found in Augustine's *De doctrina christiana* and applied

---

[75] Ignatius C. Brady, "The Rubrics of Peter Lombard's *Sentences*," *Pier Lombardo* 6 (1962): 5–25. The distinctions which supplement this numbering of chapters were added in the early thirteenth century, probably by Alexander of Hales, and the original divisions were not always made in the same places as they were given by later thirteenth-century commentators on the *Sentences*. On this point, see Ignatius C. Brady, "The Distinctions of Lombard's Book of Sentences and Alexander of Hales," *FS* 25 (1965): 90–116.

[76] Cloes, "La systématisation," *ETL* 34 (1958): 327–29; Gillian R. Evans, *Old Arts and New Theology: The Beginnings of Theology as an Academic Discipline* (Oxford: Clarendon Press, 1980), p. 42.

by that author to biblical hermeneutics. Peter takes these distinctions and applies them in turn to his own subject matter, using them to explain to the reader the relative value to be assigned to the topics covered in a work of systematic theology.[77] He agrees with Augustine that God Himself is the supreme *res*, the only being and the only object of knowledge and goodness Who warrants enjoyment in and of Himself. The created universe, the virtues, and the sacraments are *signa*, signs to be used in attaining the enjoyment of God. As for human beings, they are to be enjoyed as well as used. They deserve to be treated as moral ends; and, indeed, the created universe is ordered to their needs. At the same time, human beings ought to enjoy and serve each other with ultimate reference to God and their own salvation. Peter's reassignment of this Augustinian theme to its new task in the *Sentences* has the effect of reappropriating something known, but with a fresh eye and a fresh insight into the uses to which it may be put. This initial impression, gained from a reading of Peter's prologue, would have been reinforced for the student, as it can be reinforced for the modern reader, by a closer inspection of the Lombard's schematic curriculum and methodology.

One very striking feature of the disposition of material in the *Sentences* which sets it apart from its competitors is the fact that Peter combines a remarkably full coverage of the topics discussed by scholastics in this period with a highly personal allocation of space, one that gives the highest priority to the most speculative doctrines of the Christian faith. Fully one half of the four books of his *Sentences* is devoted to the divine nature and the nature of Christ. And, while Peter is concerned with how man comes to a knowledge of God and how God has manifested Himself to man, he also finds it important to consider God as the supreme reality in His own right. This emphasis can be seen immediately at the beginning of Book 1. After some brief remarks on the testimonies of the Trinity in the Old and New Testaments, Peter offers a series of more extended reflections on how God may be known through His similarities to other beings, and, equally, by His dissimilarities from them. An inspection of the universe will lead to the conclusion that the mutable world must have an immutable first cause. Metaphysical analysis will yield the conclusion that beings made up of parts and subject to modification by accidents must be grounded in

---

[77] Peter Lombard, *Sententiae in IV libris distinctae* 1. d. 1. c. 1-c. 3, 3rd ed. rev., ed. Ignatius C. Brady, 2 vols. (Grottaferrata: Collegii S. Bonaventurae ad Claras Aquas, 1971–81), 1: 55–61.

a simple essence that transcends them. Likewise, the triune nature
of God can be appreciated by a comparison between it and created
beings, to which the deity has both similarities and dissimilarities.
Adverting here to Augustine's famous analogy of the Trinity in
man's memory, intellect, and will, Peter finds this comparison
helpful, and for two reasons. It points to the coinherence of the
divine essence in three Trinitarian persons, while at the same time,
the limits of this same analogy, which he is just as concerned with
underlining, permit him to emphasize God's transcendence.[78]

Having laid this foundation, Peter proceeds to a consideration of
the Trinity first, next turning to the attributes which the Trinitarian persons equally share. His accent throughout this discussion
remains squarely on God in and of Himself, as the supreme being,
rather than on God as He has chosen to reveal Himself to man. In
treating the attributes of the deity as a whole, in which all the
Trinitarian persons are coequal, he continues to view the subject
from the standpoint of God as a metaphysical reality. Peter is
deeply interested in the terminology appropriate to the description
of the attributes of the individual members of the unmanifested
Trinity as well as in the terms apposite to the general divine
attributes which They share. He is sensitive to the need for terminological distinctions in this connection, and is far more successful
than his contemporaries and immediate predecessors in making the
lexical specifications which he needs here and in applying his
chosen vocabulary consistently. Other than that, another notable
feature of his treatment of the deity in Book 1 is that Peter, without
getting bogged down in the debates about the World Soul, devotes
much more attention to the Holy Spirit and His mission than is
typical of other scholastic theologians at this time.

Book 2 is devoted to the creation. Starting with the businesslike
observation that God created the universe out of nothing, and that
God was the only cause of the creation, Peter firmly shunts to the
side the issue of exemplary causation. He next raises the question of
why God created the universe at all. Reminding the reader of the
principle that the universe exists for man's sake, which he had
articulated in his prologue under the heading of use and enjoyment,
he finds here a key to the organization of his material which had
eluded compeers who had wrestled with the disjunctions in Hugh

---

[78] Peter Lombard, *Sent* 1. d. 3, 1: 68–77. Giuseppi Lorenzi, "La filosofia di Pier
Lombardo nei *Quattro libri delle Sentenze,*" *Pier Lombardo* 4 (1960): 24–26, may be
reading Peter somewhat proleptically in treating him as a defender of natural
theology.

of St. Victor's account of creation. Beings, Peter notes, are both spiritual and material; and these two modes of being are combined in man. In each case, including man's own, the structure of being has been ordained by God for man's sake. With that principle in mind, he begins at the top of the created hierarchy of being with the angels, and then proceeds to the work of the six days. He feels no need to agonize over the cosmological problems embedded in the hexaemeral account in Genesis because they have nothing to do with the question of the final cause of creation, which is his major concern here. So, while he comments on all the creatures in the account, his treatment of creation is comparatively streamlined. Peter then arrives at the centerpiece of Book 2, the creation of man and his arrival at his present situation. Topics that interest him in this connection are how man was made, what he was like before the fall, and what would have been possible for him had the fall not occurred. Like Hugh of St. Victor, he is perfectly willing to speculate on what might be called the contrary-to-fact condition of man. In so doing, he opens up a wider horizon on the subject of man's natural attributes and aptitudes than Hugh does, before moving on to the exercise of free will that brought about the fall and its effects, particularly on man's capacity to exercise free will, in relation to grace, in his fallen state. The transmission of original sin, the difference between original and actual sin, and the psychogenesis of sin round out the topics covered in Book 2.

Peter then devotes Book 3 to Christology. Here, the theological terminology which he had developed in Book 1 in his analysis of the Trinity and the divine nature comes into play and is used to clear and cogent effect. Peter devotes most of this book to the nature of the incarnate Christ. He offers a full discussion of the debates current at this time concerning the ways in which the divine and human natures can be understood as coinhering in the incarnate Christ. He outlines the support the proponents of the three leading positions of the day could marshal from the Bible and the church fathers. He indicates the difficulties that he finds in all of them, proposing that, since they are all orthodox, yet all problematic, the matter should remain an open question. Peter shows a keen interest in Christ's human nature, and whether He was like us in all but sin. He also raises the question of whether the human Christ should receive worship, or only veneration. More important, however, is the nature of Christ's saving work, to which he devotes extended and finely nuanced attention. Concluding this section of Book 3 with the point that Christ's atonement motivates and empowers men to imitate Him, Peter next takes up the virtues, moving from

the theological to the cardinal virtues and then to the gifts of the
Holy Spirit. While he initially presents these virtues and gifts as
they function in the psychology of the human Christ, a person Who
is unique, Peter's aim in this part of Book 3 is to explore the
operation of virtue in the moral lives of ordinary human beings. He
is content largely to state general principles and to analyze the
overall character of ethical acts. While he does take up the Ten
Commandments one by one, and gives a fair amount of attention to
usury and lying as breaches of the rules against theft and the
bearing of false witness, he is not interested in developing a tax-
onomy of moral conditions and activities as illustrated by particular professions or states of life.

At the beginning of Book 4, the Lombard introduces the sacraments, which, he reminds the reader, are signs intended to be used,
rather than the things intended to be used as well as enjoyed,
which he had been discussing in the two previous books. He also
launches his treatment of the sacraments with a crisp definition of
sacraments in general, and one which distinguishes them clearly
from other devout practices or Christian callings which do not
conform to his definition and which can thus be set to one side here.
Peter also uses his analysis of what a sacrament is, why the sacraments were instituted, and what sacraments consist of as a means
of discriminating sharply between the rites of the Old Law, and
those of the New. This same analysis enables him to explain why he
thinks that all seven of the Christian rites ventilated in this connection by some contemporaries are entitled to the name of sacrament.
He then organizes his own consideration of the sacraments under
the headings of the sacraments received by all Christians, in the
order in which they are received, and those received only by some
Christians, holy orders and marriage. In considering the grades of
holy orders, he combines Hugh of St. Victor's reflections on how
they illustrate different aspects of Christ's personal ministry with
indications of how they are congruent with the gifts of the Holy
Spirit. Unlike either Hugh or Robert Pullen, however, he does not
locate this topic, or the theme of sacraments more widely, within
the context of an overt ecclesiology. His treatment of marriage and
penance, in particular, reflects the benefit Peter derives from his
familiarity with the work of Gratian. But he borrows what he wants
from that master without departing from the strongly pastoral and
moral interest in these subjects typical of the scholastics, concerned, as he is, with the way that these sacraments, and others, are
internalized in the spiritual lives of the people who receive them.

Book 4 concludes with a discussion of Last Things. On this

subject, Peter is much fuller than the Porretans but much less detailed than the Victorines. What is most striking about Peter's handling of this subject is that he is far less interested in the manner in which the end of the world will come about, and where and when, than he is in the state of souls after the last judgment has taken place. The Lombard offers an extremely abbreviated treatment of Christ's second coming. Most notable of all, he omits the Antichrist altogether from his *Sentences*. This is not because he lacks a theology of the Antichrist. For, as we will see below in chapter 4, he developed a full-scale personal position on that subject in his exegesis of 1 and 2 Thessalonians. His goal, in the *Sentences*, appears to be to repress wild-eyed millenarian speculation, as inappropriate to the education of professional theologians. Likewise, while he draws on Julian of Toledo's *Prognosticon futuri saeculi*, Augustine's *City of God*, and Gregory the Great's *Moralia* for his treatment of Hell, Purgatory, and Heaven, as is typical in this period, he avoids the more flamboyant descriptive passages in which other theologians of the time revel. As authorities go, he prefers the more pared-down and sober account in Augustine's *Enchiridion*. Peter's aim in his treatise on Last Things is not to paint a vivid sensory image of the torments of the damned or the joys of the saints. Rather, it is to comment on these moral conditions as outcomes of the ethical and sacramental lives that Christians have led in this world, and as expressions of God's justice and mercy.

In looking at this schema as a whole, one is impressed immediately by two things. In the first place, Peter's *Sentences* make a clear, and personal, statement not only about the importance of the topics to which he gives extended consideration but also about the angle of vision that he thinks is appropriate or illuminating in connection with them. The agenda which he sets for himself in his prologue is carried through systematically in the body of the work. It informs his handling of both the most highly speculative doctrines of the faith and of the intellectual, moral, and spiritual means by which the Christian life may bring individuals to a grasp of the sublime realities which these dogmatic truths articulate. Second, Peter does a remarkable job of slicing through the redundancies, evasions, and confusions found in the other systematic theologians of his time. To be sure, there remain some areas of overlap in his work and his organization does reveal some imperfections. For example, since both angels and men possess free will, Peter offers a discussion of the relations between grace and free will in three different locations, under the heading of the attributes of angels and à propos of man, both before and after the fall. Also, he offers a twofold consideration of Purgatory, once as a pendant to penance and again in his treatise on Last Things. The most serious organizational problem which Peter does not solve is what to do with ethics. He defines virtue, in relation to the ethical intentionality of the moral subject, in Book 1. Also in that book he considers whether virtue is to be used or enjoyed, and virtue as a natural good. Virtue surfaces again under the heading of Christ's human nature in Book 3, along with an analysis of its psychogenesis. But, Peter's analysis of sin, and his consideration of vice in general, is developed in connection with the fall of man and its consequences in Book 2. The positions Peter takes on these ethical questions are logically consistent with each other, wherever he locates the material. But, even though this is the case, ethics as a topic in its own right fails to receive a systematic treatise in Peter's *Sentences*. He tends to find this subject of interest primarily for the light it sheds on human nature and on the nature of the human Christ. Still, even acknowledging these flaws, Peter's *Sentences* goes a long way toward eliminating the deficiencies found in the schemata of his competitors. And, however much he may have learned from them about how to construct a curriculum for the teaching of systematic theology, the schema he produces is by far the most coherent of the day, and is one that bears the stamp of his own personal outlook.

Aside from the merits of his schema, our hypothetical student would readily have judged that Peter's instruction provided a better grounding in the techniques of theological reasoning required by the incipient professional than did the work of other masters of the time. The student would have been impressed both by Peter's sagacious and discriminating use of philosophy and the verbal *artes* and by his command of the Christian tradition. As some modern observers have not, he would have recognized Peter's prefatory criticism of philosophizing as a vain display of erudition and his assertion that reasoning should play a merely ancillary role in theology for what they really were, a *captatio benevolentiae* and not a description of the Lombard's actual practice.[79] Like other occupants of Peter's classroom he would have appreciated, in Peter's oral teaching, his use of syllogistic forms to structure arguments in a positive sense, as well as the appeal to logic to explode the tautologies in positions he sought to demolish. Whether or not the Lombard always imported these pedagogical tactics into the text of

---

[79] Peter Lombard, *Sent.* 1. prologus 3–4, 1: 3–4. See, on the other hand, Émile Lesne, *Histoire de la propriété ecclésiastique en France: Les écoles de la fin du VIII* siècle à la

the *Sentences*, he certainly drew on philosophy in the handling of substantive debates and in the clarification of terms and propositions.[80] As with the Porretans, Peter was able to meet a renowned logician, such as Abelard, on his own terrain, and to undercut him with his own weapons, as is visible in the two-part strategy which he develops to refute Abelard's claim that God cannot do better than He does. On the one hand, Peter shifts the debate from the category of the logic of necessity and possibility. He places it instead under the heading of another philosophical principle, the distinction between God's absolute and ordained power.[81] And, on the other hand, he recasts it in the form of a grammatical argument, one based ultimately on the same Boethian and Aristotelian sources as Abelard had drawn on for his analysis of future contingents. This argument makes its point of departure the signification of a verb in a proposition. As Peter observes, there are two modes of signification in the verb. It denotes an action. And, it also denotes the time, whether past, present, or future, in which the action takes place. But, he continues, time is purely circumstantial with respect to the first mode of signification, the signification of an action. Time does not condition the reality of the action denoted by the verb. If, with respect to this action, the proposition is true at any time, it is true independent of a particular time. And, since God is eternal, the fact of His eternity is not altered even though the Bible may employ the grammatical convention of referring to some of His actions in the past tense of the verb. Thus, Peter concludes, we can rule out the idea of a future time in which God can improve on His creation, as Abelard claims.[82] It is the same familiarity with Boethius, and the same sensitivity to the Aristotelian and Platonic roots of his polyvalent vocabulary, that enabled Peter to grasp what was problematic in the theological lexicons of some of his contemporaries and to discard definitions that were being used by them as inadequate to the

---

fin du XIIe siècle (Lille: Facultés Catholiques, 1940), 5: 656; Lorenzi, "La filosofia di Pier Lombardo," pp. 22–24.

[80] Ludwig Hödl, "Die dialektische Theologie des 12. Jahrhunderts," in *Arts libéraux et philosophie au moyen âge* (Montreal: Institut d'Études Médiévales/ Paris: J. Vrin, 1969), pp. 70–71; "Die theologische Auseinandersetzung zwischen Petrus Lombardus und Odo von Ourscamp nach dem Zeugnis der frühen Quästionen- und Glossenliteratur," *Scholastik* 33 (1958): 137–47.

[81] Beonio-Brocchieri [Fumagalli] and Parodi, *Storia della filosofia medievale*, pp. 254–55.

[82] Marie-Dominique Chenu, *La théologie au douzième siècle* (Paris: J. Vrin, 1957), pp. 93, 96, 99.

theological assignments they were being called upon to shoulder.[83]

It was not just philosophy and the *artes* that provided means for the clarification of ideas and terms and for the criticism of positions to which Peter took exception, as well as for the provision of alternative arguments, but also the church fathers and more recent Christian authorities. The Lombard's handling of his Christian sources reveals a deep and broad education, an acute and discriminating analysis of his authorities, both logically and contextually, in the light of the author's intentions, an appreciation of the importance of citing them accurately and using them appositely, and a willingness to criticize and reject authorities who, in his estimation, lacked cogency or who failed to support his own personal positions. Along with other scholastic theologians of the day, Peter sometimes made use of the *catenae* or chains of patristic citations assembled by earlier writers, such as the Augustinian *catena* put together by the Carolingian Florus of Lyon. In comparison with his contemporaries, however, his recourse to authorities relies less on indirect research of this sort and is based more thoroughly on his own independent reading of his sources, whom he cites more fully and accurately and whom he considers more thoroughly and analytically than anyone else. At times Peter imports into his discussion authors ignored by other contemporary scholastics, or not known to them. The most famous case in point is John Damascene, whose work Peter was the first Latin theologian to bring to bear on Trinitarian and Christological debate.[84] But there are other, less dramatic, examples. Peter has a more circumspect and thoroughgoing grasp of Augustine than his contemporaries. He draws on works, such as the *Eighty-Three Diverse Questions*, not cited by other theologians at the time. He is also fully aware of the fact that there is an anti-Manichean, an anti-Pelagian, and an anti-Donatist Augustine, and that this author's utility on certain topics varies with his particular polemical agenda.

Peter also displays a systematic interest in the reasoning that has led his authorities to the conclusions they reach. He makes it clear

---

[83] Angiolo Gambaro, "Il valore dell'opera di Pier Lombardo," in *Misc. Lomb.*, p. 5; Beonio-Brocchieri [Fumagalli] and Parodi, *Storia della filosofia medievale*, p. 255.

[84] Anastos, "Byzantine Influence," pp. 151–63; Ermenegildo Bertola, "Le 'Sententiae' e le 'Summae' tra il XII e il XIII secolo," *Pier Lombardo* 2 (1953): 25–41; Eligius M. Buytaert, "St. John Damascene, Peter Lombard, and Gerhoh of Reichersberg," *FS* 10 (1950): 323–43; Jacqueline Hamesse, "Le traitement automatique du Livre des Sentences de Pierre Lombard," *Studies in Honour of Roberto Busa* = *Computazionale* 4–5 (1987): 74.

that this consideration is just as important as the author's substantive position in deciding whether to agree with him or not. To mention just one example, which also came up in our discussion of the school of Laon, Peter likewise contrasts the opinions of Leo I and Augustine on whether or not a prior adulterous affair is an impediment to marriage. Peter supports Augustine, because Augustine emphasizes the couple's desire to repent of their sin and to regularize their relationship when events make this possible. The accent on repentance and reparation, and the spiritual healing of the couple, is, in Peter's view, the correct one, and it is consistent with his wider view of the sacraments as having been instituted for the sanctification of Christians. And so, he prefers Augustine's view over Leo's more legalistic and punitive ruling.[85] At the same time, Peter disagrees sharply with Augustine on a host of other questions. In many of the locations where his Augustinian citations are the densest, Peter has brought Augustine forward in order to modify or to disagree with him. The accuracy of his Augustinian citations, whether he agrees with him or not, enabled later readers to use the *Sentences* to correct pseudo-Augustinian attributions or erroneous reports of his views.[86] In order to facilitate his analysis of the authorities, Peter, in agreement with Robert of Melun, insists on quoting them in full and on supplying the name of the author and the title of his work. He does this more consistently than Robert does, however, and the problem of mis-attributions or the corruption of the texts is sharply reduced, in the Lombard's work. As with Robert, Peter is not interested in supplying long chains of authorities to bolster each and every point. On topics that are not controversial, he is usually content to anchor his solution with a single pertinent authority. Where topics are in dispute, he does supply the foundations in authority for the various positions taken. Yet, while seeking to do justice to all sides, he does not multiply citations that merely repeat the same argument. Instead, he selects the strongest and most cogently put of the authorities without unnecessary redu-plications. As with other theologians of the time, he typically refers

---

[85] Peter Lombard, *Sent.* 4. d. 35. c. 4, 2: 471–72.

[86] Artur Michael Landgraf, "Der hl. Augustinus und der Bereich des Petrus Lombardus," *Scholastik* 29 (1954): 321–44; "Die Stellungsnahme der Frühscholastik zur wissenschaftlichen Methode des Petrus Lombardus," *Collectanea Franciscana* 4 (1934): 513–21. This position should stand as a corrective to the views of J. Annat, "Pierre Lombard et ses sources patristiques," *Bulletin de littérature ecclésiastique*, ser. 3:8 (1906): 84–95; Ferdinand Cavallera, "Saint Augustin et le Livre des Sentences de Pierre Lombard," in *Études sur Saint Augustin*, by Régis Jolivet et al. = *Archives de philosophie* 7:2 (Paris: Gabriel Beauchesne, 1930), pp. 186 99.

to contemporary masters as *quidam* or *alii*, recognizing the fact that the students and colleagues in his circle will know to whom he is referring. He even cites himself at times as *quidam*, both to refer to his own exegetical works, or even, in his oral teaching, to distance himself from a view that he had once espoused but that, as he and his students know, he no longer supports.[87]

Equally noteworthy is the independent line that Peter often takes on the authorities he uses, even in cases where he draws on them indirectly. The major area in which he makes use of *catenae* and in which he does not quote his authorities or cite their works by title is in his discussion of creation in Book 2 of the *Sentences*. The ultimate source for most of his material is the series of commentaries on Genesis written by Augustine against the Manichees, made available through the agency of Florus of Lyon. As noted above, the cosmological concern with the discrepancies in the biblical account of creation, which bedevils masters such as Hugh of St. Victor and which can be traced to the attention given to the problem by Augustine himself, is suppressed by Peter, regardless of the fact that this is the way that the Augustinian heritage on this topic had been transmitted. Peter does so because he regards these concerns as not pertinent to the perspective on creation that he wants to take. Similarly, Peter feels free to use Julian of Toledo and Augustine's *City of God* very selectively in treating Last Things, in the service of the theological restraint which he thinks is needed in the field of eschatology.

Selectivity, and the freedom to offer his own way of framing the questions he takes up, are also visible in Peter's use of more recent sources. It has been argued that he draws heavily on the Abelardian dossier of authorities in the *Sic et non*, and in the same order, merely providing the solutions that Abelard omits.[88] But a closer study of his use of these materials has shown that Peter makes extensive use of the *Sic et non* only on some subjects, such as the divine attributes, the Trinity, and Christology, areas where he stood at odds with Abelard and areas in which he was able to draw on materials not available to Abelard, or available to him but ignored by him. Aside from a reference or two to the Eucharist and penance, Peter's appeal to the *Sic et non* in other respects is sketchy.[89] Similarly, it has been known for some time that Peter is

---

[87] Artur Michael Landgraf, "Schwankungen in der Lehre des Petrus Lombardus," *Scholastik* 31 (1956): 533–34.

[88] Luscombe, *The School of Peter Abelard*, pp. 94–95.

[89] Boyer and McKeon, comm. on their ed. of Peter Abelard, *Sic et non*, pp. 635–45.

heavily dependent on the *Summa sententiarum*, on a range of subjects from the doctrine of God, to the sacraments, to the definition of faith, to angelology, and to anthropology, a point which recent scholarship has expanded and consolidated.[90] Yet, while Peter certainly draws frequently from the *Summa sententiarum* both for the manner in which he poses questions and as a guide to the patristic authorities who may be pertinent to their solution, the positions with which he emerges and his rationale for supporting them often take an independent line. To cite one example, on a topic given yet another resolution by the Porretans, Peter, following the author of the *Summa sententiarum*, raises the question of whether baptism should be administered by means of single or triple immersion. With that master, he brings to bear on this question the authority of Gregory the Great, who had indicated that both modes of baptism are practiced in the church and that both convey an edifying liturgical symbolism. Gregory had concluded that the unity of faith would not be prejudiced by diversity of custom in this respect, and had left the matter open. While the author of the *Summa sententiarum* indicates a personal preference for triple immersion, he places as his highest priority the following of local custom. This solution is consistent with the position he takes on other sacraments, in cases where regional practices vary.[91] While the Lombard takes account of the desirability of decorum, in advocating the support of local custom, he finds more compelling than his source the symbolic value of triple immersion, paralleling as it does the neophyte's death to sin and rebirth into new life with the three days Christ's body lay in the tomb between His own death and resurrection.[92] Similarly, Peter goes a long way toward incorporating the work of Gratian into his sacramental theology. He draws heavily on the dossier of authorities assembled pro and con in the *Decretum*. But, Peter does not hesitate to edit Gratian's citations, to contextualize or to relativize them historically, or to subject them to theological criteria not advanced by Gratian himself, as a means of dismissing positions which Gratian cites, or supports, with which Peter disagrees. In the manner typical of his theological compeers, he has a pastoral and moral outlook on the sacraments, not a legalistic one, and he feels free to emphasize aspects of the sacraments not of interest to Gratian and to dismiss considerations high

---

[90] Mignon, *Les origines de la scolastique*, 1: 180–93, although his analysis is flawed by his attribution of the *Summa sent.* to Hugh of St. Victor; the best guide to the current scholarship is found in Brady's annotations throughout the *Sentences* at the pertinent *loci*.

[91] *Summa sent.* 5.4, *PL* 176: 130A-B.

[92] Peter Lombard, *Sent.* 4. d. 3. c. 7, 2: 249–50.

on Gratian's agenda as unimportant. And, in areas where he takes a position diametrically opposed to Gratian's, Peter does not hesitate to stand him, and his catalogue of sources, on their heads when it suits his purpose. Further, since he does not rely exclusively on Gratian's research, he is able to correct some textual corruptions cited by Gratian as well as some apocryphal attributions which he makes.[93]

In short, Peter's use of authorities reveals a well-informed, knowledgeable, and critical spirit, as well as great skill in the application of the materials he adduces to the solution of contemporary problems and to the articulation and defense of his own personal theology. The Lombard's handling of his authorities frequently involves unexpected juxtapositions which have the effect of posing issues in a new way.[94] He makes sustained and consistent use of the principles stated in theory but abandoned in practice by some of the more idiosyncratic theologians of the day, who often harnessed them to theological agendas that proved to be deeply flawed and not very serviceable.[95] In a wider sense, Peter's approach to his authorities suggests why it is a mistake to regard the sentence collection as a mere anthology, and the theologians who worked in this genre as mere compilers. Once one learns how to read it, the sentence collection can be appreciated as the main vehicle that advanced the teaching of systematic theology in the twelfth century, both with respect to the methodology it could convey and to the larger understanding of the theological enterprise it could envision. In both of these respects, Peter Lombard's *Sentences* were deemed to have provided the best response to the pedagogical demands made in the education of professional theologians in the mid-twelfth century because, quite simply, he produced the best version of this new genre of theological literature available at that time.

---

[93] Fournier and Le Bras, *Histoire des collections canoniques*, 2: 314–52; Häring, "The Interaction between Canon Law and Sacramental Theology," *Proceedings of the Fourth International Congress of Medieval Canon Law*, pp. 483–93; Landgraf, "Diritto canonico e teologia," *Studia Gratiana* 1 (1953): 371–413; Gabriel Le Bras, "Pierre Lombard, prince du droit canon," in *Misc. Lomb.*, pp. 247–52.

[94] Bertola, "Le 'Sententiae' e le 'Summae'," pp. 25–41.

[95] Abelard is a good case in point. See Beryl Smalley, "*Prima clavis sapientiae*: Augustine and Abelard," in *Studies in Medieval Thought and Learning from Abelard to Wyclif* (London: Hambledon Press, 1981), pp. 1–8.

CHAPTER THREE

THE PROBLEM OF THEOLOGICAL LANGUAGE

As the previous chapter has made clear, one of the important indices of the perceived capacity of a scholastic theologian to impart a serviceable methodology to his students in the first half of the twelfth century was his ability to develop and to use consistently a lucid theological vocabulary, one that could explain with precision what he meant and why the views of opposing masters were unacceptable to him. To be sure, the problem of theological language is endemic to this discipline. The general question of how human language, with its terms and analogies derived from created beings and experiences, can convey the divine reality had been, and would remain, a concern of theologians, preachers, and writers of religious literature across the centuries. But, more specifically, the professionalizing of theology in the first half of the twelfth century heightened the demand for terminological exactitude, especially in addressing the speculative doctrines of Christianity. A sensitivity to these needs can also be found in writers of monastic theology, as is the case with Rupert of Deutz. It is clearly visible in the works of Anselm of Canterbury.[1] But it was largely the scholastic theologians who made a systematic effort to address the need for terminological precision. Sometimes it was their familiarity with the verbal *artes* which sharpened their perception of this need. Sometimes the very originality of the response made by some scholastics to the problem brought new complications in its train and invited criticism, and the reformulation of the issue by their colleagues. The difficulties under which theologians labored in this period were made much more acute by the fact that, given the current state of philosophical knowledge, they lacked a lexicon that was both technical enough to shoulder the burdens it had to carry, and common to all the thinkers engaged in dogmatic speculation.[2] This lack of

---

[1] Marcia L. Colish, "St. Anselm's Philosophy of Language Reconsidered," in *Anselm Studies*, ed. Gillian R. Evans (London: Kraus International, 1983), 1: 113-23.

[2] Marie-Dominique Chenu, *La théologie au douzième siècle* (Paris: J. Vrin, 1957), pp. 90-107; Gillian R. Evans, *Old Arts and New Theology: The Beginnings of Theology as an Academic Discipline* (Oxford: Clarendon Press, 1980), p. 203; Landgraf, *Dogmengeschichte*, 1 part 1: 20-21.

precision and univocity plagued all the theologians who recognized
it as a problem. Over the course of two generations, there are some
notable efforts to come to grips with it. Yet, here too, as with his
schema for systematic theology and his technique of handling
authorities, it is Peter Lombard who wins the palm. In tackling the
recalcitrant problem of theological language, and in clarifying his
terms and using them with rigor and consistency, he goes farther
toward the development of a practicable vocabulary than was
ahieved by any European thinker prior to the reception of Aristotle, which was to alter fundamentally the terms of the debate in the
sequel.

Outside of the general desire for clarity, there were three main
difficulties specific to the intellectual history of the early twelfth
century that triggered the debates over theological language in that
period. Two of them stem from the fact that contemporary thinkers
were heavily dependent on Boethius as their schoolmaster in the
field of the Aristotelian *logica vetus* and as a philosophical theologian. Both his translations and commentaries on Aristotle's early
logical works and his own theological *opuscula*, aimed at defending
orthodox Christology and Trinitarian doctrine, received an attentive reading in the schools. These works were commented on repeatedly. Yet, the terminology of Boethius was a confusing guide to
the theological language needed for the conduct of doctrinal debate
in the very areas where he applied it, because he himself uses key
terms essential to that debate, such as substance, essence, nature,
and person, in diverse and incompatible ways. Four different definitions of nature are found in his writings[3] and six different
definitions of person.[4] In the former case, he defines nature as that
which can act and be acted upon; as the principle of motion *per se*
and not accidentally; as the special property of a thing or the
specific difference from other things that gives it form; and, more
generally, as that which exists, in whatever mode, and, because it
exists, is capable of being apprehended by the mind in one way or
another. In the latter case, leaving aside *persona* as a theatrical mask
or as a character in a work of drama or fiction, his definitions

---

[3] Karl Bruder, *Die philosophische Elemente in dem Opuscula sacra des Boethius: Ein
Beitrag zur Quellengeschichte der Philosophie der Scholastik* (Leipzig: Felix Meiner,
1928), pp. 64–80; Claudio Micaelli, "'Natura' e 'persona' nel *contra Eutychen et
Nestorium* di Boezio: Osservazioni su alcuni problemi filosofici e linguistici," in *Atti
del congresso internazionale di studi Boeziani*, ed. Luca Obertello (Rome: Herder,
1981), pp. 327–36.

[4] Maurice Nédoncelle, "Les variations de Boèce sur la personne," *RSR* 29
(1955): 201–38; Micaelli, "'Natura' e 'persona'," pp. 327–36.

include an accident or group of accidents in a man that make him different from other members of the human race; a determination of substance itself; a calling to the divine life through reason, love, and freedom; in the incarnate Christ, "the individual substance of a rational nature;" as applied to the Trinity, the eternal emanations of the divine supra-substance; and as a category of relation, according to the sense of the Aristotelian categories. This array of ambiguous definitions reflects the fact that Boethius sometimes uses his terms in a Platonic sense and sometimes places an Aristotelian construction on them. He does this partly because his argument, at any given point in his theological works, is polemical, and he tailors it to the *ad hoc* needs of the moment. He does so partly because of his conviction that these two schools of philosophy are ultimately compatible. The Boethian legacy leaves open two central questions, to which his works offer no clear solution: Given the fact that the creed uses the terms substance and person with reference to the deity, what do these terms mean in this connection, in comparison with what they may mean with respect to created beings? And, given the fact that the standard Trinitarian formula views the persons of the Trinity as joined together by the reciprocal relations of paternity, filiation, and procession, how apposite is the language of relation, or the language of any Aristotelian accident, to the deity?

The third problem relative to theological language confronted by early twelfth-century thinkers stems from the differences in approach taken by the Latin and Greek traditions to the theology of the Trinity, and a corresponding difference in the ways theologians in these churches had used the same terminology or the equivalent terms in each language.[5] The Greeks emphasized the economic Trinity, that is, the persons of the Trinity as They manifest Themselves to man. The Greeks viewed the persons as three hypostases, accenting Their different functions. For them, the difficulty lay in showing how these hypostases possess a unity of nature. To the notion of divine hypostasis they attached the idea of a being possessing a nature, Who gives of that nature to another hypostasis. In each of the persons, nature is a content within a container. The

---

[5] A good account of the contrast between Greeks and Latins and of the problems posed for medieval thinkers by Augustine and Boethius is found in M. Bergeron, "La structure du concept latin de personne: Comment, chez les Latins, 'persona' en est venu à signifier 'relatio'," in *Études d'histoire littéraire et doctrinale du XIIIe siècle*, 2nd ser., Publications de l'Institut d'Études Médiévales d'Ottawa, 2 (Paris: J. Vrin, 1932), pp. 121–61, although he does not address the twelfth-century efforts to cope with the difficulties.

person's transference of that nature can be understood without the need to posit an underlying common nature as an intermediary in the process. Each of the persons is Himself the intermediary. Thus, the unity of nature in the three persons is seen as consecutive. On the other hand, the Latins, as illustrated most typically by Augustine, were concerned with how we can understand the relations of the Trinitarian persons among themselves, quite apart from anything They may choose to manifest of Themselves to man. The Latins based their position on the unity of the divine nature, seen as an ontological or logical substratum, with the Trinitarian persons seen as expressions of that nature, which coinheres in Them equally. With this principle in mind, it was necessary to distinguish between terms that refer properly to the divine nature which the persons equally share, on the one hand, and terms that signify the attributes that distinguish one Trinitarian person from the others, the terms that are specific and unique to each of the persons vis-à-vis the others. The Latins concluded that the best way to arrive at a valid conception of a person in this context was to understand the Trinitarian persons as relations. Unbegotten, begotten, and proceeding could thus serve as proper names of the Father, Son, and Holy Spirit, for they are terms referring to each of these persons alone. To this Augustine added his famous analogy of the Trinity in the human soul, whereby the persons are compared to the psychological functions of memory, intellect, and will. There is a division of labor here; but, Augustine emphasizes, it coincides with a functional interrelation among these faculties, each of which is an activity of the same subsistent soul.

But, given the Latin approach to the Trinity, how was it possible to maintain this position in the light of the Aristotelian understanding of relation, which, if applied to the definition of the Trinitarian persons, would treat Their personhood as accidental? The idea that the deity is a substance subject to modification by accidents made Latin theologians in our period acutely uncomfortable, and with good reason, for it suggested that the divine nature is subject to change and that, as accidents, the persons of the Trinity may inhere in that nature, or not, as the case may be. Further, did an acceptance of the Aristotelian understanding of relation as an accident extend to an Aristotelian understanding of substance as well? If so, the prime significance of substance would be its reference to created beings made up of matter and form. Such an idea would scarcely be apposite to the deity, whether to the divine nature in general or to any one of the Trinitarian persons in particular. And, if these Aristotelian understandings of relation and substance were rejected, what comprehensible understandings could be found to replace them, and would they be adequate to bear the dogmatic weight which the theologians would have to place upon them?

Both the intractability of these questions and the theological centrality of the doctrines whose understanding they affected help to explain why Trinitarian theology and Christology were the controversies par excellence among early twelfth-century theologians. One could, to be sure, ignore that fact. This was the case with Anselm of Laon and his followers, who continued to use the language of the creeds and the fathers as if it were self-explanatory, self-consistent, and non-problematic. They simply repeat the traditional Latin terms, without defining them; one would never be aware of the fact that theological language was such a burning contemporary issue from reading their works.[6] Another approach was to suggest an evasion of the problem by appealing to the *via negativa* in theological language, along the lines of the Pseudo-Dionysius and John Scottus Eriugena. Indeed, this tactic was advocated by thinkers connected with the school of Chartres, well known for its responsiveness to other aspects of the Neoplatonic heritage as well.[7] According to this view, we cannot properly signify

---

[6] See, for example, *Sentences of William of Champeaux*, no. 236; *Sentences of the School of Laon*, no. 282, 521, ed. Odon Lottin, *Psychologie et morale aux XIIe et XIIIe siècles* (Louvain: Abbaye de Mont-César, 1959), 5: 190–94, 230, 333; Heinrich Weisweiler, ed. "Le recueil des sentences 'Deus de cuius principio et fine tacetur' et son remaniement," *RTAM* 5 (1933): 252–53; Friedrich Stegmüller, ed., "Sententiae Berolinensis: Eine neugefundene Sentenzensammlung aus der Schule des Anselms von Laon," *RTAM* 11 (1939): 40; *Sententie divine pagine*, ed. Franz Bliemetzrieder in *Anselms von Laon systematische Sentenzen*, Beiträge, 18:2–3 (Münster: Aschendorff, 1919), pp. 5, 8–9.

[7] Richard W. Southern, "Humanism and the School of Chartres," in *Medieval Humanism and Other Studies* (New York: Harper & Row, 1970), pp. 61–85; *Platonism, Scholastic Method, and the School of Chartres* (Reading: University of Reading, 1979); and "The Schools of Paris and the School of Chartres," in *Renaissance and Renewal in the Twelfth Century*, ed. Robert L. Benson and Giles Constable (Cambridge, MA: Harvard University Press, 1982), pp. 113–37 has argued that this school, as such, never existed. Both on the basis of institutional associations among the thinkers in this group and their demonstrable family connections intellectually, this position has been refuted, effectively in our estimation, by Peter Dronke, "New Approaches to the School of Chartres," *Anuario de estudios medievales* 6 (1969): 117–40; Nikolaus M. Häring, "Paris and Chartres Revisited," in *Essays in Honour of Anton Charles Pegis*, ed. Reginald O'Donnell (Toronto: Pontifical Institute of Mediaeval Studies, 1974), pp. 268–317, 329; Hans Liebeschütz, "Kosmologische Motive in der Bildungswelt des Frühscholastik," *Vorträge der Bibliothek Warburg*, 1923–24, pp. 83–148; Olga Weijers, "The Chronology of John of Salisbury's Studies in France (Metalogicon II. 10)," in *The World of John of Salisbury*, ed. Michael Wilks, Studies in Church History, Subsidia 3 (Oxford: Basil Blackwell, 1989), pp. 114–16.

the deity with theological language framed in positive statements. On the other hand, negative statements yield names of God which are more accurate, or at any rate, less inaccurate. God as He is remains basically inexpressible. Human language cannot compass Him. His nature is so transcendent that any attributes men may give Him, attributes drawn necessarily from their knowledge of created beings, must inevitably fall short of the divine reality, and so constitute an improper use of language. In one way or another, various members of this group of thinkers posit a sharp distinction between man's modes of speech (*forma loquendi*) and God's mode of being (*forma essendi*), and urge that positive statements about God, whatever grammatical form they take, cannot be literally true of God but are, at best, to be understood metaphorically, with a transferred meaning (*translative*).[8]

Despite their willingness to advocate this Dionysian position on the poverty of theological language, the Chartrains, in practice, joined with other scholastic theologians in this period in the effort to work through the difficulties bequeathed by Boethius, Augustine, and the Greeks. They did make the effort to come up with cogent definitions of the all-important terms for describing God positively. In the event, it was not the Chartrains themselves but Peter Abelard and Gilbert of Poitiers who provoked the most intense disputes on theological language at this time.

THE ABELARDIAN CHALLENGE

Despite his keen interest in semantics as a professional logician, Abelard proved surprisingly unsuccessful in arriving at definitions of the key terms needed for Christology and Trinitarian theology. His handling of *natura, substantia, essentia,* and *persona* is polyvalent in the case of each of these terms. In the fields of logic and mathematics, for Abelard, *natura* and its adverbial and adjectival forms mean or imply a necessary order, according to which things have to be as they are. As applied to phenomena, nature means a habit (*habitus*) or disposition (*dispositio*), denoting the phenomenon's concrete mode of being, which endures and serves as that being's cause or continuing principle of activity and which is not exhausted by its ingredients or by the way the being acts. In this sense, nature in act

---

[8] Nikolaus M. Häring, "Die theologische Sprachlogik der Schule von Chartres im zwölften Jahrhundert," in *Sprache und Erkenntnis im Mittelalter*, Miscellanea mediaevalia, ed. Albert Zimmerman, 13:2 (Berlin: Walter de Gruyter, 1981), pp. 930–36.

can be distinguished from nature as the ground of a creature's being. Also, the nature of a genus can be distinguished, on this basis, from the nature of any of its individual members. The idea of nature, in the created order, as a force the creator grants to creatures enabling them to function, to reproduce, and to act as secondary causes underlies Abelard's understanding of nature in the sense of natural law, both as a moral norm and as a mode by which man can come to a knowledge of God through the creation. At the same time, Abelard the ethicist uses the term *natura* both to refer to the human condition as corrupted by sin and to the pristine state of man which was thereby corrupted. At no point in his works does he offer a definition of nature that is self-consistent or that can be understood with respect to the divine nature.[9]

Abelard's definitions of *essentia* are also polyvalent. Sometimes he means by this term essence as contrasted with existence, existence in this context referring to the state in which a being can be modified by accidents. At other times, however, he means by essence a being's mode of being more generally, which would include, not exclude, its actual mode of being as conditioned by accidents. Essence, for Abelard, can also mean a thing's intrinsic nature, as in the phrase *natura rerum*, the law of nature as it applies to the being's created endowment. In this sense, essence cannot be separated from the being's existence. On the other hand, Abelard also uses *essentia* to denote an entity's ground of being, which in turn he understands both as its formal cause and as its material cause. Despite these discrepancies, it is clear that the need to define this term arises in the first instance, for Abelard, as a means of grasping the nature of created beings. What essence may denote as applied to uncreated being is a matter which he never systematically discusses, notwithstanding his attribution of this term to the deity. Further, he sometimes equates essence and substance, using these terms interchangeably with respect to God, while at other times, he distinguishes substance, understood as essence, from *essentia*, understood as existence. When he equates *essentia* with existence, in the context of Trinitarian theology, he also equates *persona*, or Trinitarian person, with this *essentia*-as-existence. This practice is quite confusing, because Abelard also stresses, in the same context, that the persons of the Trinity share the same essence and substance, in passages where he treats *essentia* and *substantia* as

---

[9] Jean Jolivet, "Éléments du concept de nature chez Abélard," in *La filosofia della natura nel medioevo* (Milan: Vita e Pensiero, 1966), pp. 297–304; David E. Luscombe, "Nature in the Thought of Peter Abelard," in ibid., pp. 314–19.

synonymous.[10] To compound his difficulties still further, he also borrows the Boethian definition of person as the individual substance of a rational nature,[11] thus annexing *substantia* both to the attributes that distinguish each Trinitarian person from the others and to the common Godhead which They share. And, at the same time, he insists that, in applying the term substance to God, in either of these senses, we cannot use it in the normal Aristotelian sense of an entity capable of modification by accidents.[12] While explaining what *substantia* does not mean, with reference to God, Abelard never truly clarifies what he thinks it does mean in that connection.

Confusing terminology is only one of Abelard's problems in the development of a semantics adequate to the tasks of theology. Abelard is frequently depicted as having been attacked, for personal reasons, by monastic critics who failed to understand him, who garbled what he had said, or who attributed to him positions not his own.[13] There are, however, technical features of his logic and semantics which his scholastic confrères at the time were perfectly capable of grasping,[14] and which modern critics have also noticed, which raise serious questions about its utility as a tool in theological discussion. Abelard's larger goal is to show that revealed statements about God and the data they convey can be presented in such a way as to display their conformity with the laws of predication. At the same time, his semantics is not basically geared to an epistemology that connects the human psychology of knowledge with the realities that exist outside of the human mind.[15]

---

[10] Jean Jolivet, "Notes de lexicographie abélardienne," in *Aspects de la pensée médiévale: Abélard. Doctrines du language* (Paris: J. Vrin, 1987), pp. 132–37; *Arts du langage et théologie chez Abélard*, 2nd ed. (Paris: J. Vrin, 1982), pp. 41, 296–320; Jolivet, intro. to his trans. of Peter Abelard, *Du bien suprême* (Montreal: Bellarmin, 1978), p. 15.

[11] Peter Abelard, *Theologia "scholarium"* 2.105, ed. Constant J. Mews in Peter Abelard, *Opera theologica*, CCCM 11–13 (Turnhout: Brepols, 1969–87), 13: 459.

[12] J. G. Sikes, *Peter Abailard* (Cambridge: Cambridge University Press, 1932), pp. 119–20, 145–67.

[13] For a good summary of the literature on this point, see Jean Jolivet, "Sur quelques critiques de la théologie d'Abélard," *AHDLMA* 38 (1963): 7–51; Edward Filene Little, "The Heresies of Peter Abelard," University of Montreal Ph.D. diss., 1969, pp. 136–85.

[14] On this point, see above, ch. 2, pp. 54–55, 85.

[15] On this point, see above, ch. 2, p. 55 n. 48, to which may be added Jean Jolivet, "Abélard entre chien et loup," *Cahiers de civilisation médiévale* 20 (1977): 319; *Arts du langage*, pp. 44–45, 67–72, 74–77, 95–104, 229–335; Bruno Maioli, *Gilbert Porretano: Dalla grammatica speculativa alla metafisica del concreto* (Rome: Bulzoni, 1979), pp. 33–36; Sikes, *Peter Abailard*, pp. 119–20; Richard E. Weingart, *The Logic of Divine Love: A Critical Analysis of the Soteriology of Peter Abailard* (Oxford: Clarendon Press, 1970), pp. 11–31.

Rather, he is moving toward a formal logic whose goal is an analysis of intramental concepts and an intramental validation or invalidation of the propositions and arguments made up of the words that signify these concepts. While at an initial remove, many concepts derive from extramental realities, this is not the prime signification which they possess. For, these extramental realities may come into being and pass away. Once we have obtained our concepts of them from them, they are no longer needed for the work of the logician. Also, some nouns, such as indefinite nouns, can refer meaningfully to things that have no existence. The meanings words acquire are conventional, imposed on them by the speakers who use them; they do not signify naturally. This signification by imposition exists at two levels, for Abelard. There is the denomination or appellation, the significance of the actual thing (*significatio rerum*). There is also the signification of the concept derived from the thing (*significatio intellectum*). The perfection of the signification lies in the latter mode of signification, since it is only at this level that the sign can be used in a logical proposition and hence understood.

This theory has an advantage, in Abelard's estimation. For, left to a system of purely real signification, we would be confined to verbal signs that might refer to non-significant things. But, with logical signification, in his sense, we can find meaning in all the parts of speech in whatever propositional contexts they may be used, parts of speech, moreover, which not only manifest meaning but which also can engender it. In one respect, Abelard's logic and semantics may be regarded as post-Aristotelian avant la lettre, for he expands the range of logic and does not subordinate it to modes of verification lying outside its own formal scope. In another respect, however, this logic and semantics restrict their own utility, since the question of how words may correspond with the things they originally signified, the question of how the logician's *intellectus* may correspond with realities outside his own mind, is not the point of Abelard's analysis of signification at all. And, if logic thus makes no claims about ontology in the sense of the world of created nature, the same can be said *a fortiori* in the case of theological statements. Ultimately, Abelard is forced to concede that statements about the Trinity must be understood figuratively,[16] and that the norm governing their use is theological appropriateness.[17] Yet,

---

[16] Jolivet, "Abélard entre chien et loup," p. 319; Sikes, *Peter Abailard*, pp. 119–20.

[17] Jolivet, *Arts du langage*, pp. 280–81.

as in the notorious case of his analogy of bronze, a seal made of bronze, and the impression made by the seal in wax for a Trinity composed of persons Who are coeternal and consubstantial,[18] he is often unequal to the task of providing cogent analogies in the event, a fact noted not only by his monastic critics[19] but also by contemporaries who had frequented the schools[20] as well as by modern scholars.[21] In sum, Abelard never comes to grips with the basic lack of aptitude of a logic and semantics of the type he develops for the work of theological clarification and defense to which he assigns it.

Yet, for all these problems, there was one particular application of theological language made by Abelard that engendered more controversy than any other, his attribution of the nouns power, wisdom, and goodness to the persons of the Trinity as proper names. Abelard is sensitive to the idea that there are some divine properties, such as eternity, that inhere in the Godhead in general, while others can be used to distinguish the personal traits of the Father, Son, and Holy Spirit. In his view, power, wisdom, and goodness are perfectly adequate to the latter task. He supports this claim by multiplying citations to the text of the Bible in which the Trinitarian persons are referred to by his preferred names.[22] This position provoked acute irritation in Abelard's critics, and with excellent reason. For, they noted, if we apply to the Father, Son, and Holy Spirit the terms power, wisdom, and goodness as Abelard urges, then it is impossible to make sense out of all the other biblical passages where these terms are used to refer to more than

---

[18] Peter Abelard, *Theologia christiana* 4.90–93, 4.102, 4.106, ed. Eligius M. Buytaert, CCCM 12: 308–10, 315–16, 317–18; *Theologia "scholarium"* 2.112–18, CCCM 13: 462–66; *In Epistolam Pauli ad Romanos* 1:20, ed. Eligius M. Buytaert, CCCM 11: 70.

[19] The *capitula* drawn up against Abelard at the council of Sens in 1140 describe this bronze seal analogy as a "horrienda similitudo." The text is ed. by Eligius M. Buytaert, CCCM 12: 473.

[20] Thus, Otto of Freising observes à propos of Abelard, "The analogies he used were not good." *Deeds of Frederick Barbarossa* 1.48 (46). trans. Christopher C. Mierow (New York: Columbia University Press, 1953), p. 83.

[21] Jolivet, *Arts du langage*, pp. 308–20; Sikes, *Peter Abailard*, p. 115; Walter Simonis, *Trinität und Vernunft: Untersuchung zur Möglichkeit einer rationalen Trinitätslehre bei Anselm, Abaelard, den Viktorinern, A. Günther und J. Froschammer* (Frankfurt: Josef Knecht, 1972), pp. 54–57.

[22] Peter Abelard, *Theologia "summi boni"* 1.2.5, 3.1.1–51, ed. Constant J. Mews, CCCM 13: 88, 157–59; *Theologia christiana* 1.1–4, 1.7–35, 3.112, 4.47–50, 4.118–19, 4.154–56, 4.161–5.3, CCCM 12: 72–87, 236, 286–87, 324–25, 342–47; *Theologia "scholarium"* 1.30–93, 2.135–36, CCCM 13: 330–56, 475. The best analysis is by Eligius M. Buytaert, "Abelard's Trinitarian Doctrine," in *Peter Abelard*, ed. Eligius M. Buytaert (Leuven: Leuven University Press, 1974), pp. 127–52.

one of the Trinitarian persons, or to a person other than the one to Whom Abelard assigns the name, or to God in general. Abelard does not deny that all the Trinitarian persons possess all of these attributes. He is also aware of some of the theological problems that arise from his insistence that they are, none the less, proper names of the Trinitarian persons. Thus, he notes, all three attributes are involved in the incarnation of Christ, since that event manifests God's power, wisdom, and goodness equally to man. Given this position, it is hard to see why it was the second person of the Trinity Who was incarnated, and not the first or the third.[23] Similarly, it is hard to explain why power should beget wisdom, and why goodness should proceed from power and wisdom, and not vice versa.[24] Still, even having ventilated these questions, questions which he cannot answer, Abelard continues to argue for the propriety of these terms as personal names.[25]

Contemporaries such as Hugh of St. Victor, Gilbert of Poitiers, William of Conches, Thierry of Chartres, Clarenbald of Arras, Robert Pullen, and Robert of Melun were convinced that Abelard was wrong but were unable to pinpoint just how he had erred and how he might effectively be refuted. Hugh agrees that the terms power, wisdom, and goodness apply both to the persons of the Trinity individually and to God in general. But he does not succeed in explaining clearly the semantics of how this would work and he can scarcely repress his feeling that the contestants are engaged in meaningless word games.[26] Gilbert charges Abelard with tritheism for his effort to confine the three attributes preclusively to the three Trinitarian persons. In turn, he himself stresses the unity of God so heavily as to state that the persons of the Trinity can be distinguished from each other only numerically,[27] a point that raised doubts about his own orthodoxy, or at least about the propriety of his own numerical argument. For their part, the Chartrains find

---

[23] Peter Abelard, *Theologia christiana* 4.68, CCCM 12: 296.
[24] Ibid., 4.118–19, CCCM 12: 324–25.
[25] Ibid., 4.47–50, CCCM 12: 286–87.
[26] Hugh of St. Victor, *De sacramentis fidei christianae* 1.2.5–12, 1.3.26–31, *PL* 176: 208A–211A, 227C–234C. The best analysis is by Johann Hofmeier, *Die Trinitätslehre des Hugo von St. Viktor dargestellt im Zussamenhang mit den Strömungen seiner Zeit* (Munich: Max Hueber Verlag, 1963), pp. 188–91, 193–95, 197–268. See also Edmund J. Fortman, *The Triune God: A Historical Study of the Doctrine of the Trinity* (Philadelphia: Westminster Press, 1972), p. 190; Jakob Kilgenstein, *Die Gotteslehre des Hugo von St. Viktor* (Würzburg: Andreas Göbel, 1897), p. 127; Jørgen Pedersen, "La recherche de la sagesse d'après Hugues de Saint-Victor," *Classica et mediaevalia* 16 (1955): 91–133. All these authors note the inconclusiveness of Hugh's critique of Abelard.

Gilbert's critique of Abelard fully as unacceptable as they find
Abelard's position itself. William of Conches observes that power,
wisdom, and goodness are names that are not exclusive to the
Trinitarian persons. But, given his own interest in distinguishing
the cosmological functions of these persons and in analogizing them
with the Platonic One, Nous, and World Soul, he sees the division
of labor here as acceptable and can find no way of distinguishing
between his own cosmological approach and Abelard's salvific and
charismatic treatment of the Trinity.[28] An anonymous writer of the
mid-twelfth century with palpable connections to the Chartrain
tradition agrees that the entire Trinity is involved in any action of
power, wisdom, and goodness undertaken by God and that these
names cannot be applied to the Father, Son, and Holy Spirit
exclusively. None the less, he holds that there are still grounds for
assigning them primarily to these respective persons. While conceding at least this much of the Abelardian argument, he seeks to
analogize these terms to the human soul's faculties of willing,
knowing, and capacity. In both cases, he notes, these activities
operate in and through each other.[29]

   This argument, while it mitigates the exclusivity of the Abelardian attribution of power, wisdom, and goodness to the Trinitarian
persons, raises the question of whether the author has thereby
succumbed to another Abelardian claim which the Chartrains
vigorously disputed, the conflation of an Augustinian-style view of
the Trinitarian persons as distinguishable by Their relations to
each other with an economic view of these persons as distinguishable in their manifestation of Themselves to man, whether in the
order of the cosmos or in the order of grace. Abelard himself fails to
see the difference between these two perspectives. He repeatedly
juxtaposes his power-wisdom-goodness argument with the description of the Trinitarian persons as distinguished by paternity, filiation, and procession. He even calls the former model a distinction
based on relation (*relative*).[30] In general, the Chartrains draw a

---

[27] Gilbert of Poitiers, *In Boethius de Trinitate* 1.3.53–54, 1.5.39, 2.2.72–80; *In
Boethius contra Eutychen et Nestorium* 3.65–74, ed. Nikolaus M. Häring in *The Commen-
taries on Boethius by Gilbert of Poitiers* (Toronto: Pontifical Institute of Mediaeval
Studies, 1966), pp. 113, 145, 178–80, 285–87.
   [28] William of Conches, *Philosophia mundi* 1.6–12, ed. Gregor Maurach (Pretoria:
University of South Africa, 1974), pp. 10–14. On this point, see Heinrich Flatten,
Die Philosophie des Wilhelm von Conches (Koblenz: Görres-Druckerei, 1929), pp.
180–84.
   [29] Haijo Jan Westra, ed., *The Commentary on Martianus Capella's De Nuptiis
Philologiae et Mercurii Attributed to Bernardus Silvestris* 5.424–54, 11.1–63 (Toronto:
Pontifical Institute of Mediaeval Studies, 1986), pp. 107–08, 245–47.

sharp distinction between these approaches and reject out of hand
the idea that the category of relation can be applied to the deity. As
Thierry of Chartres and Clarenbald of Arras see it, relations are
nothing but Aristotelian accidents, which can inhere only in substances subject to these predicaments. God cannot be viewed as a
substance in this sense, they maintain. He is beyond substance.[31]
Promising as is this combination of Aristotelianism and Neoplatonism, Thierry at once compromises it, by attributing substance to
the deity anyway, and by stating that the divine substance is the
common essence which the Trinitarian persons share.[32] And, despite his zealous effort to rule out relations and accidents of all
kinds as apposite to the Trinity, he admits that the distinction
among paternity, filiation, and procession does work and that it is
acceptable, even though it is based on the intratrinitarian relations
of the persons.[33] The chief problem of the Chartrains in coming to
grips with Abelard is that their vocabulary is almost equally impre-
cise. Their arguments have a way of canceling each other out. As
well, Clarenbald adheres to the Boethian definition of person as
the individual substance of a rational nature cited by Abelard,
although it means that there would be three substances in the
Trinity. This idea is compatible neither with the notion of substance as a supra-substantial divine essence, on the one hand, nor
with substance as created being subject to modification by accidents,

---

[30] Peter Abelard, *Theologia christiana* 3.174, 4.50, 4.154–56, CCCM 12: 260, 287,
342–43; *Theologia "scholarium"* 1.21–27, 1.30–68, CCCM 13: 327–30, 330–45. This
point has been noted by Buytaert, intro. to his ed. of *Theologia christiana*, CCCM
12: 415–51; Sikes, *Peter Abailard*, p. 161.
[31] Thierry of Chartres, *Commentum super Boethii librum De trinitate* 1.8–9, 2.67–
4.21, 4.29, 5.1–12; *Lectiones in Boethii librum De trinitate* 1.28–29, 1.35–38, 1.45, 2.1,
2.35–37, 4.13–18, 4.32, 5.15–16, ed. Nicholas M. Häring in *Commentaries on Boethius
by Thierry of Chartres and His School* (Toronto: Pontifical Institute of Mediaeval
Studies, 1971), pp. 64–65, 89–95, 101, 103, 110–13, 140–41, 143–44, 147, 154,
166–67, 190–92, 197, 217–18. On these points, see Enzo Maccagnolo, *Rerum
universitatis: Saggio sulla filosofia di Teodorico di Chartres* (Florence: Le Monnier, 1976),
pp. 54–56, 74, 171–72. Clarenbald of Arras, *Tractatus super librum Boethii De trinitate*
praefatio 20, 1.9–12, 1.24, 1.51–54, 2.42–43, 3.1, 3.14, 3.16–17, 3.31, 3.35–36, 3.38,
3.41, 3.44–92, 5.1–11, 5.17, 6.2, 6.5–12, in Nikolaus M. Häring, ed., *Life and Work
of Clarenbald of Arras, a Twelfth-Century Master of the School of Chartres* (Toronto:
Pontifical Institute of Mediaeval Studies, 1965), pp. 73, 89–90, 95, 97, 104–06,
124, 132, 144–45, 146, 151–52, 156, 159, 159–76, 176–79, 181, 182, 183–84. On
these points, see Wilhelm Jansen, *Der Kommentar des Clarenbaldus von Arras zu
Boethius De trinitate: Ein Werk aus der Schule von Chartres im 12. Jahrhundert* (Breslau:
Müller & Sieffert, 1928), pp. 119–34.
[32] Thierry of Chartres, *Comm. super Boethii De trin.* prologus 10, 5.4, pp. 60, 114.
[33] Ibid., 4.3, p. 96.

on the other, the two definitions of substance which he joins Thierry in defending.[34]

The stern rejection of relation as applicable to God, even though it is brought in through the back door in their acceptance of the relational formula for the Trinity, may be read as an anti-Abelardian tactic on the part of the Chartrains. But they cite it primarily as a means of attacking Gilbert's numerical argument. Among the relations or accidents that Thierry and Clarenbald mention, they single out the accident of number for special attention. Aside from the fact that number is an accident, they note, the sheer addition of one integer to another integer which has no difference from the other integers to which it is added does not provide a clear enough distinction among the Trinitarian persons. In addition, Gilbert's argument raises the question of why we should stop at three persons, or why there needs to be more than one person in the Godhead at all. Thierry and Clarenbald respond with a Trinitarian argument of their own, which tries to address these concerns. It is also based on mathematics and tries to yoke mathematics to a recognition of the relatedness of the Trinitarian persons to each other, which they find lacking in Gilbert's teaching. This argument is grounded on the principle that unity can serve as the mathematical foundation of equality-in-difference. The formula they adopt is: $1 \times 1 = 1$. As Thierry and Clarenbald interpret this formula, in engendering the Son, the Father produces a being fully equal to Himself. The same is the case in the joint procession of the Holy Spirit from the Father and the Son. The whole point of this analysis is summarized under the heading of the names of the Trinitarian persons which Thierry and Clarenbald borrow from Augustine: unity, equality, and connection (*unitas, aequalitas, conexio*).[35] While it stands as a vigorous attempt to reinsert reciproc-

---

[34] Thierry of Chartres, *Commentarius in Boethii librum contra Eutychen et Nestorium* 2.11, 2.14, 3.68, ed. Nikolaus M. Häring in *Commentaries on Boethius by Thierry of Chartres and His School* (Toronto: Pontifical Institute of Mediaeval Studies, 1971), pp. 235, 248; Clarenbald of Arras, *Tractatus super librum Boethii De trin.* 1.8, 5.12–14, pp. 89, 179–80. Another member of this group, William of Conches, *Dragmaticon* 1, trans. Maccagnolo in *Rerum universitatis*, pp. 246–63, adds another definition of substance, namely, being without any specifications, which he thinks is applicable to God.

[35] Thierry of Chartres, *Lectiones* 3.10, 7.5–7, pp. 179, 224–25; Clarenbald of Arras, *Tractatus* 2.34–40, pp. 120–23. On this mathematical argument, see Gillian R. Evans, "*Alteritas*: Sources for the Notion of Otherness in Twelfth-Century Commentaries on Boethius' *Opuscula sacra*," *Bulletin Du Cange* 40 (1975–76): 103–13; Nikolaus M. Häring, "The Creation and Creator of the World according to Thierry of Chartres and Clarenbaldus of Arras," *AHDLMA* 22 (1958): 157–69;

ity into the understanding of the Trinitarian persons, this argument has the demerit of failing to square with the Chartrains' own announced rules. Having rejected relation, in general, and the accident of number, in particular, as apposite to the deity, they then reimport mathematics into the discussion, as well as relation, but without succeeding in justifying these departures from their stated principles.

It was not only the bolder thinkers, like Gilbert and the Chartrains, but also those who were more conservative or who sought to accommodate more than one contemporary viewpoint, like Robert Pullen and Robert of Melun, who grappled valiantly but unsuccessfully with the problem of names apposite to the deity as it had been posed by Abelard. Of the two, Robert Pullen is certainly the less circumspect and the more contradictory. At the beginning of his *Sentences*, Robert Pullen raises the question of whether the term *substantia* can be applied to God, and also, what significance the very term *deus* has. If we follow Aristotle, he says—the only option he canvasses—neither the terms substance nor accident can be attributed to God. Accidents are conferred upon beings by something or someone else. But God receives nothing from any being outside of Himself. Further, substance refers to beings subject to modification by accidents. Since God is immutable, He cannot be altered by accidents and hence He cannot be called a substance. Having banished both of these terms from the lexicon of theology, Robert goes on to note that the noun *deus* can have no meaning at all. Here he shifts from the Aristotelian understanding of created substances as his base line to the definition of a noun as a part of speech given by the ancient grammarians. As Donatus and Priscian have said, a noun is a part of speech that signifies a thing in its substance and its quality. But, as Robert has already indicated, both substance and accidental qualifications are equally inapposite to the deity. The conclusion which follows from Robert's conflation of Aristotle and the grammarians is that it is impossible to speak about God at all.[36]

It would seem that, if a theologian comes to this conclusion and if, like Robert, he is either uninformed about the possibility of negative theology or not interested in pursuing it, his only responsible course of action would be to close up shop and go in for some other line of work. Since, as we know, these disquisitions on

---

Édouard Jeauneau, *"Lectio philosophorum"*: *Recherches sur l'École de Chartres* (Amsterdam: Adolf M. Hakkert, 1973), pp. 10–11, 81–82, 93–97.

[36] Robert Pullen, *Sententiarum libri octo* 1.1, 1.4, *PL* 186: 675A–B, 600C, 682A.

theological language occur at the beginning of the lengthiest sentence collection written in this period, Robert Pullen clearly did not take this logical next step, which his semantics would appear to make unavoidable. Having taken the pains to raise the question of the significance of theological language in the manner just indicated, he proceeds to drop it with a dull thud, and goes on as if he had never taken it up. He goes right ahead and uses the key, and problematic, terms in Trinitarian and Christological discourse, although without ever defining them or indicating the sense in which they apply to the deity. Thus, notwithstanding his earlier remarks on substance, he states that there is a divine substance which is the single essence shared by the Trinitarian persons. The term essence remains undefined. In any event, and this is Robert's critique of Abelard, the divine substance is reflected in God's immensity, beauty, and omnipotence, and also in His power, wisdom, and goodness. These three latter terms are not to be identified with particular Trinitarian persons. Rather, these persons are identified and distinguished from each other by the attributes of paternity, filiation, and procession. These are traits which the Father, Son, and Holy Spirit possess from all eternity. Thus far, what Robert has accomplished can be compared with the practice of the school of Laon on this subject. He has merely stated the standard Latin formula but without explaining why it is apposite and why Abelard's terminology is not. Robert wraps up this portion of his counter-assertion—for it is a counter-assertion and not a counter-argument—by remarking, confusingly, that the filiation of the Son and the procession of the Spirit occur according to substance (*secundum substantiam*), even though he had initially placed substance, whatever he means by it, on the side of the Godhead in general and not on the side of the proper names of the Trinitarian persons.[37] He may simply be trying to affirm here the consubstantiality of the persons, and no more. But his location of this point at the juncture where he places it does not make it clear that this is what is intended.

Robert makes only one passing attempt to indicate what his theological terms mean, in an effort that has the sole effect of telling the reader what these terms do not mean. The divine substance, he notes, is different from substance as the term applies to human beings. In the latter context, each person is a single substance. This is not the case with the Trinity. Abandoning the problem of how

[37] Ibid., 1.3–7, *PL* 186: 676C–689C.

substance and person differ in the Trinity, Robert goes on to argue for the definition of human substance he has proposed, against dialecticians who think that substance should refer to the human race in general and not to its individual members.[38] Robert wraps up these considerations by observing that language is sometimes used properly and sometimes improperly. Without exploring that point any farther, he adds that the properties of the Trinitarian persons are not affects (*affectae*) and know nothing of predicaments. Having stated what a divine person is not, or what He lacks here, Robert concludes that these ideas are matters of faith which transcend the capacity of the human mind to understand in any way,[39] a statement which says more about Robert's visible lack of adeptness in handling the assignment than about the efforts that had been made, and were being made currently, to do so.

In the light of Robert's handling of the Trinity, it may not be surprising to find that his attack on the terms needed to explain Christology is equally self-defeating. According to Robert, both the divinity and the humanity of the incarnate Christ may be described as substances, each of which is an essence.[40] As with his treatment of the divine substance in Book 1 of his *Sentences*, here he makes no effort to endow Christ's divine substance with any positive meaning. Its relationship to His divine person is not clarified, something that must be done if a theologian is to succeed in explaining why it was the Word, and not one of the other Trinitarian persons, Who took on human nature in the incarnation. All that Robert gives us here is the repeated statement that there are two substances in the incarnate Christ, humanity and divinity, or, alternatively, three substances, a human body, a human soul, and the Word.[41] This three-substance theory is one that Robert inherited from the school of Laon.[42] We will also find it cropping up in the work of some of Robert's contemporaries, where it is equally confusing. Aside from Robert's inability to decide how many substances there are in the incarnate Christ, a fact that does not enhance his positive exposition of Christology, the three-substance model has two other disadvantages. It treats the Word, as a divine person, as the equivalent of the divine substance, neither of which terms is explained. And, with respect to the human Christ, it departs from Robert's earlier

---

[38] Ibid., 1.3, *PL* 186: 676C.
[39] Ibid., 1.3, *PL* 186: 679C–D.
[40] Ibid., 3.15, *PL* 186: 784A–B.
[41] Ibid., 2.10, 3.18, 3.20, *PL* 186: 734B–C, 787A–789C, 792C–D.
[42] *Sentences of the School of Laon*, no. 182, ed. Lottin in *Psych. et morale*, 5: 128.

announced definition of the human substance as a human individual who is also a person. In neither his earlier nor his later use of substance, as applied to human nature, and in neither his twin-substance nor his three-substance version of Christ's incarnate nature does Robert indicate how, or if, his language can rule out the heresy of Adoptionism. All in all, Robert Pullen's handling of theological language is seriously defective and his application of his inconsistent or unspecific language to the themes to which he assigns it has nothing to recommend it. While he is less oblivious to the problem, as a problem, than the Laon masters, he does not advance an inch toward the goal of explaining what is wrong with Abelard's semantics and what is better about his own counter-proposals.

In comparison with Robert Pullen, Robert of Melun makes some notable headway in addressing these intractable problems. He devotes extended and repeated attention to the question of theological language, which he takes up at no less than three points in his *Sentences*. Yet, while he strives to use his key terms consistently, and succeeds in doing so to a fair degree, he leaves a number of them undefined and he sometimes contradicts himself or misses the opportunity to capitalize on some of his most valuable arguments. Robert is a critic of Abelard to some degree. But he is reluctant to discard the Abelardian legacy altogether. His simultaneous loyalty to Hugh of St. Victor, and to Hugh's essentially economic view of the Trinity in creation and redemption, also impedes Robert from making the fullest use of some of his most helpful findings.

Robert begins his consideration of theological language in general at the start of the first book of his *Sentences*, under the heading of the understanding of the language of the Bible. Here, he notes, words are to be understood both literally and with the three traditional spiritual senses used by exegetes. He continues by listing six conditions which need to be taken into account in assigning these spiritual meanings.[43] At the same time, he asserts in these prefatory remarks that all theological language is metaphorical, not literal, and that negative theology is more accurate at times than positive theology, in principle.[44] Without entirely clarifying where he stands amid this range of possibilities, Robert goes on to note that some terms, such as "to be" and "good" have a different

---

[43] Robert of Melun, *Sententie* 1.1.6, ed. Raymond-M. Martin in Robert of Melun, *Oeuvres*, 4 vols. (Louvain: Spicilegium Sacrum Lovaniense, 1932–52), 3 part 1: 170–79.

[44] Ibid., 1.3.3, *Oeuvres*, 3 part 2: 19, 21, 26–30.

denotation as applied to God and to creatures.[45] The same might well be said of terms such as essence, substance, and nature, which Robert needs to use in some detail in his theology. While he tries to use them as clearly and consistently as he can, he does not provide any definitions of their meaning with respect either to the deity or to created beings.

None the less, Robert firmly yokes substance to essence and nature, and applies these terms, synonymously, to the single divine being possessed equally by the three Trinitarian persons.[46] Some of the names that refer properly to this divine substance they share, such as justice, or goodness, or the name of creator, are terms that reflect God's manifestation of Himself in His creation. Other terms denoting the divine substance, such as simplicity or immutability, refer to His nature as such. In both of these cases, Robert argues, the attributes denoted are shared fully by all the Trinitarian persons. In the case of the first group, the economic names that describe God's relationship to creatures, the relations involved are not accidental. For, while the universe itself is mutable and full of phenomena subject to modification by predicables, God Himself is changeless.[47] Now, as for the notorious power-wisdom-goodness formula of Abelard, Robert asserts that these attributes are essential properties of God. They pertain to the substance of the God-head, in the sense he has just indicated. They are not proper names of the Trinitarian persons. For, if they were the proper names of these persons, they would yield three different essences. The result would be tritheism. Further, and here rejecting Abelard again, Robert argues that power, wisdom, and goodness are not relative terms. They are, rather, convertible and equal. They are not parts that make up a whole, or individual members of the genus to which they belong. At the same time, they are useful terms because they are analogous to human qualities, which facilitates their comprehension, and they are more fitting than any other divine attributes in the category they inhabit in describing the manifestations of the Trinity to man.[48]

---

[45] Ibid., 1.5.45–46, *Oeuvres*, 3 part 2: 258–76. This point has been studied carefully by Peter W. Nash, "The Meaning of *Est* in the *Sentences* (1152–1160) of Robert of Melun," *MS* 14 (1952): 129–42, who concludes, we think accurately, that Robert tends to confuse *esse* as such with *esse a se*, leading him to treat creatures as passing shadows of the divine being.

[46] Robert of Melun, *Sent.* 1.2.2, 1.3.3–7, 1.5.44, *Oeuvres*, 3 part 1: 268; 3 part 2: 31–46, 254–55.

[47] Ibid., 1.3.3, *Ouevres*, 3 part 2: 31–39.

[48] Ibid., 1.2.5–7, 1.3.2, 1.5.39–40, *Oeuvres*, 3 part 1: 274–92; 3 part 2: 10–18,

Robert, however, cannot let Abelard go completely. Like Hugh, he wants to argue for the acceptability of the power-wisdom-goodness model as a set of proper names for the Trinitarian persons in some way. His proposal is to argue that the Father, Son, and Holy Spirit do possess these properties, respectively, in a special, preeminent, way, even though each of these persons participates, to a lesser degree, in the attributes exemplified in that special way by the other two persons.[49] Valiant as it is as an effort to salvage the least defensible features of the Victorine and Abelardian legacies on power, wisdom, and goodness, Robert's reasoning at this point fails to persuade the reader that his position does not stand in contradiction to his assignment of these properties to the Godhead as such, despite the huge amount of space he devotes to the effort to make this case.[50]

The force of this contradiction is to leave in abeyance the sense Robert assigns to the idea of person, as it is applied to the Trinity. Confusion is not allayed by his other inconsistencies on that subject. In his introductory remarks concerning the conditions affecting the reading of the biblical text in its spiritual senses, he includes *persona* as one of them, defining it à la Boethius as the individual substance of a rational nature.[51] But, he also states that, in Trinitarian discourse, none of the Boethian definitions of person are helpful or apposite and that the specific problem with the particular definition earlier cited is that it yields three substances, that is, three deities.[52] His own preferred definition of person in the Trinitarian context is a fairly content-free one, the differences men can discern among the three persons (*discretum discernens*), a formula which leads him to slide away from what those differences actually are to the modes by which men may know them and may signify what they know.[53] And, in the Christological section of his *Sentences*,

241–46. These points are well developed by Ulrich Horst, *Die Trinitäts- und Gotteslehre des Robert von Melun* (Mainz: Matthias-Grünewald Verlag, 1964), pp. 85–93, 119–38.

[49] Robert of Melun, *Sent.* 1.3.19–30, *Oeuvres*, 3 part 2: 67–97. Raymond-M. Martin, "Pro Petro Abaelardo: Un plaidoyer de Robert de Melun contre S. Bernard," *RSPT* 12 (1923): 308–33 makes Robert more of a supporter of Abelard here than he was.

[50] Robert of Melun, *Sent.* 1.6.1–20, *Oeuvres*, 3 part 2: 285–314; Ulrich Horst, "Beiträge zum Einfluss Abaelards auf Robert von Melun," *RTAM* 26 (1959): 314–26; *Die Trinitäts- und Gotteslehre*, pp. 111–18.

[51] Robert of Melun, *Sent.* 1.1.6, *Oeuvres*, 3 part 1: 176; Horst, "Beiträge," pp. 314–21.

[52] Robert of Melun, *Sent.* 1.3.11–13, *Oeuvres*, 3 part 2: 51–57.

[53] Ibid., 1.3.14, 1.3.16, *Oeuvres*, 3 part 2: 57, 64–65.

which remains unedited, the manuscript evidence indicates that he reverts to the Boethian "individual substance of a rational nature" despite its acknowledged difficulties.[54]

There is still the problem of whether the traditional formula of unbegotten-begotten-proceeding can offer a cogent solution to the question of how the Trinitarian persons are different from each other, despite the difficulties associated with the Aristotelian conception of relation as an accident, which the Chartrains emphasize so heavily. Robert is one of a few theologians of his time to find a way out of this dilemma in Augustine's *De trinitate* 5.16, which he cites specifically, and with great pertinence, to this point. There, as he notes, Augustine had pointed out that we can think about the concept of relation in more than one way. We can, to be sure, view it as an Aristotelian accident. As such, Augustine agrees, it is not and cannot be an attribute of the deity. But Aristotelian logic is not our only resource here. There is also the notion of relative nouns, as discussed by the classical grammarians. In defining and illustrating the concept of relative nouns, Donatus and Priscian include examples such as father-son and master-slave. Such examples have their limits as analogies of the relations among the Trinitarian persons in that they are drawn from human relations that involve priority and posteriority, cause and effect, or circumstance. Augustine prefers pairs of relative nouns such as left-right, or light-dark, because they can be understood relatively (*ad aliud*) while also lacking a temporal or causal dimension. As Robert points out, this type of reasoning allows us to appreciate relations among the Trinitarian persons that are permanent and that never change, a point which enables him to supply a rationale for his support of the traditional Latin formula not found in Robert Pullen.[55] He concludes, therefore, that it is proper to apply the names unbegotten, begotten, and proceeding to the Trinitarian persons, in a manner that would not be apposite if they were applied to the divine essence.[56]

Having attained, at this juncture, a position of decided advantage, Robert at once proceeds to abandon it. Having established that paternity, filiation, and procession do provide adequate proper names for the Trinitarian persons and having appreciated the value of Augustine's grammatical rescue mission for the concept of relation, his argument now reflects the fact that his main concern is not

---

[54] Martin, *Oeuvres*, 3 part 2: 57–58 n.
[55] Robert of Melun, *Sent.* 1.3.3, *Oeuvres*, 3 part 2: 37–39.
[56] Ibid., 1.3.8–9, 1.4.23–24, *Oeuvres*, 3 part 2: 47–49. 150–51. On this point, see Horst, *Die Trinitäts- und Gotteslehre*, pp 140–72.

the understanding of how these interrelations work. Rather, he wants to consider why we use the terms denoting the divine essence in the singular form of the noun, even though they refer to attributes possessed by all three Trinitarian persons, unlike the relational terms, which are used in the singular because they denote the individual properties of the persons. Robert reasserts the point that the persons can be described in terms of their properties. But then, notwithstanding the grammatical argument he has appropriated from Augustine, he returns to the idea that relations cannot be enduring properties, on the basis of the Aristotelian notion of relation as an accident. Robert does not explain why he has withdrawn from the beachhead which Augustine had helped him to win. Nor does he resolve the self-contradiction on the idea of relation in his own argument.[57]

And, for all the help that Augustine is able to provide for the resolution of the vexing questions with which Robert wrestles so inconclusively, his larger reading of the *De trinitate* works at cross purposes to Robert's goal. He takes up one of the analogies Augustine had noted in the human soul, not the memory-intellect-will example but the *mens-notitia-amor* one developed at an earlier point in Augustine's argument. Instead of seeing the parallels with the relational terms which he accepts—and then rejects—as appropriate proper names of the Trinitarian persons, he presents the Augustinian analogy as unacceptable because it conflicts with his own notion that each of the Trinitarian persons possesses His personal attributes in a special and preeminent way. He fails to see that here, and even more so in the case of the memory-intellect-will model, Augustine might not be as hard to accommodate to that claim as Robert thinks. Robert also maintains that Augustine's argument does not differentiate the persons sufficiently. Another objection is that Robert wants to treat one of the three analogous terms, the human intellect alone, as the image of God in man. He ignores the fact that Augustine regards the three terms in his analogies as functions inhering in a single subsistent mind which indeed is viewed as the image of God in man. All in all, Robert makes rather heavy weather of Augustine's *De trinitate*, misunderstanding and garbling this text although he could have put it to more constructive use here.[58]

---

[57] Robert of Melun, *Sent.* 1.5.1–41, 1.6.21–25, 1.6.28–30, 1.6.40–42, *Oeuvres*, 3 part 2: 163–246, 316–24, 327–31, 348–55.
[58] Ibid., 1.4.9–14, 1.6.43–49, *Oeuvres*, 3 part 2: 110–28, 367–68; Horst, *Die Trinitäts- und Gotteslehre*, pp. 172–80, 181–84.

A central blind spot in Robert's treatment of theological language with respect to the Trinity is his inability to grasp the fact that Augustine is not talking about the economic Trinity at all in *De trinitate*. This same problem helps to account for his backing and filling on the subject of relation, which prevents him from seeing that it is the relations associating the persons with each other and distinguishing Them from each other in Their unmanifested state that is the focus of the Augustinian argument concerning relative nouns. Aside from this economic bias, reinforced by his adherance to both Abelard and Hugh of St. Victor, Robert's theology suffers here from his contradictions on the definition of person and his inconsistencies in the handling of the power-wisdom-goodness problem. If he is a mitigated Abelardian on both of these points, he gives full credence to the utility of Abelard's bronze seal analogy,[59] despite its incompatibility with a Trinity viewed as consubstantial and coeternal. He does achieve a clear yoking of the terms essence, substance, and nature and a consistent assignment of them to the shared attributes of the Godhead. He also targets effectively the problem implicit in the Boethian definition of person as the individual substance of a rational nature, even if he remains unwilling to disembarrass himself of it systematically. He does recognize the fact that there is more than one way to think about relation, and that one can use this concept meaningfully in Trinitarian theology, having noted the limitations of Aristotelian logic in that context. This, too, is an insight which he does not exploit as fully and positively as he might have done.

Several of the more constructive features of Robert of Melun's treatment of theological language—at least potentially—can also be found in the two theologians of the period who contributed most heavily to the eventual argument against Abelard's semantics developed by Peter Lombard, Walter of Mortagne and the author of the *Summa sententiarum*. The *Summa sententiarum* has generally been regarded as Peter's most immediate source in this connection,[60] with Walter seen as a source for that work.[61] This may well have

---

[59] Robert of Melun, *Sent.* 1.4.3–9, *Oeuvres*, 3 part 2: 101–10.

[60] Ludwig Ott, "Die Trinitätslehre der *Summa sententiarum* als Quelle des Petrus Lombardus," *Divus Thomas* 21 (1943): 159–86.

[61] Marcel Chossat, *La Somme des Sentences: Oeuvre de Hugues de Mortagne vers 1155* (Louvain: Spicilegium Sacrum Lovaniense, 1923), pp. 83–89; Ludwig Ott, "Die Trinitätslehre Walters von Mortagne als Quelle der *Summa sententiarum*," *Scholastik* 18 (1943): 79–90, 219–39; "Walter von Mortagne und Petrus Lombardus in ihren Verhältnis zueinander," in *Mélanges Joseph de Ghellinck, S.J.*, 2 vols. (Gembloux: J. Duculot, 1951), 2: 646–97. Kilgenstein, *Die Gotteslehre des Hugo von St. Viktor,*

been the line of filiation, although it is worth remembering that Walter's teaching was directly available to Peter, aside from its textual accessibility; and, in some respects, he prefers Walter's treatment to that of the *Summa sententiarum*.

Walter expressly states that he has framed his *De trinitate* as a refutation of the view that power, wisdom, and goodness can be used as proper names of the Trinitarian persons.[62] These attributes, along with attributes such as justice, refer to the single divine essence or substance. They do not signify diverse properties in God Himself, but the diversity of His effects as He operates in creatures.[63] The persons Who exist in this unity of the divine substance are what the Greeks call *hypostases*, or subsistent manifestations of the Godhead.[64] This being the case, for Walter, he raises the question of whether, since the operations of God are carried out by the entire Trinity, we have to say that the Son engenders Himself. Walter answers in the negative. The operations of the Trinity, he observes, are understood in the relation of the Trinity to creatures. Although the actions of the Trinitarian persons are inseparable, some are more appropriate to one person than to another.[65] Walter accepts the application of relative terms to the Trinity, although not in the connection of the Trinity to the creation, since created things are mutable and God is not. Despite his statement that the Trinitarian operations are understood in their relation to the creation, Walter accents the unique appositeness of the terms unbegotten, begotten, and proceeding, which refer to the relations of the Trinitarian persons to each other and which must be distinguished from terms, such as love or charity, which apply substantially to all the persons.[66] As another example of this last point, Walter cites the Augustinian analogy of *mens-notitia-amor*, which he sees as a clear parallel of the intratrinitarian relations of paternity, filiation, and procession. These relations, in either example, are functional correlatives, not relations that are accidental, as they may inhere in creatures.[67] When it comes to the definition of Trinitarian person as the "individual substance of a rational nature," Walter holds that Boethius is just plain wrong. His definition

---

pp. 224–25, sees Hugh as Peter's source here, but that is because he writes before scholars had determined that Hugh was not the author of the *Summa sententiarum*.

[62] Walter of Mortagne, *De trinitate* 13, *PL* 209: 588D–590B.

[63] Ibid., 1, *PL* 209: 577B–C.

[64] Ibid., 2–3, *PL* 209: 577C–578B.

[65] Ibid., 5, *PL* 209: 560A–581A.

[66] Ibid., 7–8, *PL* 209: 583A–584C.

[67] Ibid., 9, 11, *PL* 209: 584D–586A, 586C–587C.

leads to three substances, that is, three deities. Despite its formulation six centuries earlier, Walter dismisses it as a "profane innovation."[68] As to what a person really is, Boethius having been rejected, a *persona*, for Walter, is the name of the properties (*nominum proprietates*) that distinguish the Father, Son, and Holy Spirit from each other.[69]

There is much that Walter does not attempt here. He does not discuss the grammatical rationale for the relational terms that he sees as appropriate proper names of the Trinitarian persons. He has not factored eternity into the nature of those relations. He has therefore not explained fully what distinguishes intratrinitarian relations from relations as the accidents inhering in creatures. He has not defined substance or essence. None the less, he uses these latter terms consistently and applies them clearly to the attributes of the Godhead in general. He makes it clear why power, wisdom, and goodness belong in the latter category. If he claims that the functions of the Trinity are understood in relation to creatures, he also takes a notable step in the direction of reappropriating the Augustinian, and Latin, accent on the understanding of the relations of the Trinitarian persons vis-à-vis each other as the foundation for a set of relational proper names that are truly unique to the Father, Son, and Holy Spirit respectively. He also is crisp, cogent, and unhesitating in his willingness to jettison a Boethian definition of person that simply does not work. In short, Walter makes some important contributions to the resolution of the anti-Abelard debate.

In some respects the author of the *Summa sententiarum* consolidates these gains and in others he takes a step backwards. As with Walter, he does not define the terms substance and essence. He tends to use them consistently, but is less wholehearted than Walter in this respect. He agrees that the divine essence and substance are the same thing, adding that the unity of the divine essence and substance is not changed or infringed upon by God's action in the mutable created universe through His governance or disposition (*dispositio*). While the author also defines the divine substance as God's effects in nature,[70] he more typically equates substance, essence, and nature with the Godhead as such, in contrast with the Trinitarian persons Who share in it. He agrees with Walter in

---

[68] Ibid., 6, *PL* 209: 581A–582A.
[69] Ibid., 12, *PL* 209: 588A–C.
[70] *Summa sententiarum* 1.4, *PL* 176: 48C–49A.

upholding the appositeness of the analogy of *mens-notitia-amor* as relations among the Trinitarian persons, expanding it to include Augustine's point that these relations are eternal and unchanging.[71] With Walter, however, he has missed Augustine's grammatical rationale for the admissibility of relation, so understood, to Trinitarian theology.

In any event, having laid this foundation, the author notes that we must distinguish the terms that signify the unity of substance and nature in the deity, such as omniscience or eternity, which are predicated of God substantially (*dicuntur secundum substantiam*) from those that apply properly to the persons of the Trinity, such as unbegotten, begotten, and proceeding, which signify the properties that distinguish the persons (*significant proprietates quibus personae distinguuntur*) vis-à-vis each other. These latter terms, he adds, are predicated of the persons appropriately because the attributes in question inhere only in the individual persons which they denote.[72] They are used relatively (*relative*), with respect to each other. They do not refer to anything accidental, since the intratrinitarian relations are permanent.[73] As for power, wisdom, and goodness, they belong clearly under the heading of the terms denoting the attributes of the deity as such. They are not acceptable as proper names of the persons.[74]

The main area in which the author of the *Summa sententiarum* backtracks, in comparison with Walter of Mortagne, is in his handling of the problematic Boethian definition of person. He is well aware of the objection that can be leveled against it, and which had been so leveled by Walter and others, namely, that it entails three substances, that is, three deities. But he is too timid to junk this definition entirely. His proposal is to redefine it, so that its semantic force is limited (*restringitur significatio*). According to his own redefinition, Boethius's formula denotes persons who are distinct with respect to their properties but not distinct substantially.[75] The effect of this new definition is to leach the meaning out of Boethius's formula by changing it so much that it stops saying what he intended it to mean. For, the author's own positive definition of a person is that a person is a property (*proprietas*). This claim he anchors by the citation of authority in the phrase "in essence unity

---

[71] Ibid., 1.6, *PL* 176: 51A–52D.
[72] Ibid., 1.7, *PL* 176: 53A–B.
[73] Ibid., 1.9, *PL* 176: 55C–D.
[74] Ibid., 1.10, *PL* 176: 56D–58D.
[75] Ibid., 1.9, *PL* 176: 56C–D.

and in the persons property" (*in essentia unitas, et in personis proprietas*). He adds that the Greeks use the term *hypostasis* to denote the Trinitarian persons and that the Latins translate *hypostasis* as *substantia*. This is an application of the idea of substance which he rejects. The properties in God, he insists, are the relations in God, which are not the same thing as the divine substance, a point on which he concludes his analysis of theological language as applied to the Trinity, with a reprise on the unique appropriateness of the unbegotten-begotten-proceeding formula for the definition of the personhood of the Father, Son, and Holy Spirit.[76]

Although the author of the *Summa sententiarum* waffles on the Boethian definition of person, retaining it while at the same time emptying it of its original meaning, and although he does not attempt to define his other key terms, he does make an energetic if imperfectly realized effort to use them consistently. He clearly assigns substance, essence, and nature to the side of the Godhead while squarely situating person on the side of the intratrinitarian relations, seen as eternal. He uses Augustine effectively, if not exhaustively. And, he shows some awareness of the terminological discrepancies between the Greek and Latin Trinitarian formulae, displaying an understanding of how these discrepancies had helped to muddy the waters. At the same time as he makes significant gains in these respects, however, he dissipates many of them when he turns to the application of the lexicon he has developed for Trinitarian discourse to the task of explaining the constitution of the incarnate Christ.

The author's biggest semantic problem, in the context of Christology, is the term *substantia*. In the incarnation, he notes, the Word, Who is both a divine person and a possessor of the divine nature, took on a human nature. We recall here that, in speaking of the divine essence and nature above, he had rigorously equated these two terms with the divine substance. Exactly what the relationship between Christ's divine substance and His divine personhood may be is not spelled out in this analysis. The author moves on to observe that there are two natures in the incarnate Christ, divine and human. Whether the terms essence and substance have a human denotation, and whether they are univocal with the way these terms are to be understood of the divine nature, or whether they are to be understood equivocally, or analogously, is a question he likewise bypasses, proceeding to the statement that there are

---

[76] Ibid., 1 11, *PL* 176: 59B–61C.

three substances in the incarnate Christ, a human body, a human soul, and the Word.[77] We recognize the formula found in the school of Laon, which has also cropped up in the Christology of Robert Pullen. Its difficulties are manifest, especially in the light of the lexicon which the author of the *Summa sententiarum* has been trying to develop. For, the Word is understood as a person, the second person of the Trinity. It is this person and not one of the other two persons, and not the divine substance in general, that undergoes incarnation. How Christians are to grasp the force of that belief, given the three-substance formula, is indeed difficult to see. It is likewise difficult to know what to make of this formula as it applies to human nature, at least if one wants to adhere to the hylemorphic notion of the human *substantia* inherited from Aristotle.

The author's problems are intensified when he raises the next question, of whether Boethius's "individual substance of a rational nature" is useful in understanding the humanity of Christ. As we have noted, he was unsettled as to its applicability to divine persons. In this context, he rejects Boethius's definition of person because it would confine personhood to Christ's human soul alone. Two difficulties would flow from that position. First, the definition would conflict with the author's own Aristotelian presupposition that human beings are composed of bodies as well as souls. Equally serious, if the soul alone could be equated with the human person, then, in the incarnation, the Word would take on a human person, whether or not that human soul had already been united with a human body. The result would be an individual containing two persons, an idea difficult to sustain conceptually and also an index of the heresy of Adoptionism. This heresy is a doctrine that the author plainly rejects. And so, along with it, he dismisses the Boethian definition as meaningful for human beings. He concludes that it would be pertinent only to spiritual beings, such as angels, that lack bodies.[78]

It is clear that the author's main concern in these passages is to rule out heresies attached to Christ's nature. But, in expressing that concern, he confuses the terminology which he had used for the Trinity. He offers no advice on whether the term *substantia* can be used in the same sense both for God and for creatures, and, if not, how it should be understood in each case. He is equally ambivalent in his application of substance to human nature, contradicting the

---

[77] Ibid., 1.15, *PL* 176: 70C–D.
[78] Ibid., 1.15, *PL* 176: 71A–B.

idea that substance stands for the union of body and soul in man with the notion that substance can be applied to the infra-substantial physical and spiritual components that combine to constitute a human being.

THE LOMBARDIAN RESPONSE

While we can certainly trace the influence of both Walter of Mortagne and the *Summa sententiarum* in Peter Lombard's handling of theological language, Peter takes on a much wider assignment in this connection than any of the predecessors and contemporaries whom we have already considered. As we will see below, he felt a serious need to take stock of the semantics of Gilbert of Poitiers, no less than the terminology of Abelard. Of concern here was not only Gilbert's numerical distinction among the Trinitarian persons but his semantics more generally, as they applied to other aspects of the divine nature and to Christology. Peter also joins with many theologians of his time in seeking a definitive means of banishing the Abelardian power-wisdom-goodness argument from theological discussion. In some respects he employs the same tactics in dealing with the teachings of both of these masters. Most succinctly stated, his ability to bring John Damascene's *De fide orthodoxa* to bear on Trinitarian theology enables him to pinpoint exactly the differences between the Greek and Latin approaches to the Trinity that underlay, and beclouded, much of the debate, both in Abelard's formulation of his teaching and in the arguments of his would-be opponents. On the Latin side, Peter takes the tack of focusing on Augustine and of mining his *De trinitate* more exhaustively than any of the theologians of his time. In the effort to re-Latinize the doctrine of the Trinity he is thus better equipped than other thinkers who had dismissed, or garbled, or misunderstood their Augustine. In appealing to the resources of the two most philosophical of the theologians representing the Greek and Latin traditions, respectively, Peter seeks to find, and to clarify, a vocabulary adequate to bear the speculative weight of the doctrines it would be called upon to bear. He reflects a strong confidence in the ability of theologians, even with the limited philosophical resources currently available, to develop and to use with precision and consistency just such a vocabulary. And, many of the arguments he works out in response to Abelard, whom he regards as the Trinitarian theologian of the day most in need of refutation, also proved to be of great utility when he turned his attention to Gilbert.

Peter grounds his case against Abelard in the Trinitarian theolo-

gies of Augustine and John Damascene because, by comparing
these two prototypical exponents of Latin and Greek theology, he is
able to show, clearly and convincingly, just what had led Abelard
astray.[79] Abelard, he notes, had confused the Latin and Greek
understandings of the Trinity. Damascene made it clear to the
Lombard that Abelard had identified himself primarily with the
Greek effort to understand the economic Trinity, the Trinitarian
persons as They manifest Themselves to man, both cosmologically
and charismatically. At the same time, Abelard had seen the need
to distinguish between the attributes that we can assign to the
single simple divine essence and those we can apply to the Trinitarian persons. Augustine focused Peter's attention on the fact that,
in addressing the second part of that assignment, the Latin tradition insisted on a point that Abelard has not taken with sufficient
seriousness, the need to understand the relations of the Trinitarian
persons among Themselves, quite apart from anything They might
choose to manifest of Themselves to man. With this distinction
between the Latin and Greek approaches clearly laid out, Peter is
able to show that Abelard's doctrine of the Trinity is inadequate to
the explanation of the Trinity in either of these modes. Abelard, he
agrees, had been correct in seeing that some terms apply to God as
such, while other terms apply properly to the Trinitarian persons
individually. Now, the names power, wisdom, and goodness are not
proper names as applied to the persons of the Trinity. For they do
not display what is unique to each of these persons in the internal
family relationship which He enjoys with the other two persons.
Nor do these terms apply properly or exclusively to the ways in
which one, and only one, of the Trinitarian persons manifests
Himself to man, since they denote attributes common to the divine
essence which they share.

Peter's strategy in developing this argument against Abelard can
be seen, first of all, in the way in which he organizes his material in
the first book of his *Sentences*. As we have seen, in considering the
schemata of contemporary systematic theologians in chapter 2
above, many of those who lead off with the deity begin with the

---

[79] Peter Lombard, *Sententiae in IV libris distinctae* 1. d. 3. c. 1.5, d. 8. c. 4–c. 8.1–3,
d. 19. c. 2, d. 22. c. 5, d. 24. c. 6–d. 25. c. 3.4, d. 26. c. 3, c. 8, d. 27. c. 2.3, d. 30. c.
1.1–7, d. 33. c. 1.1–10, d. 34. c. 1.1–9, c. 4.2, 3rd ed. rev., ed. Ignatius C. Brady,
2 vols., (Grottaferrata: Collegii S. Bonaventurae ad Claras Aquas, 1971–81), 1: 70,
98–101, 101–03, 160, 179–80, 189, 195, 203, 204–05, 220–22, 240–43, 245–46,
246–50, 253. On this whole question, see Ermenegildo Bertola, "Il problema di
Dio in Pier Lombardo," *Rivista di filosofia neo-scolastica* 48 (1956): 135–50; Johannes
Schneider, *Die Lehre vom dreieinigen Gott in der Schule des Petrus Lombardus* (Munich:
Max Hueber Verlag, 1961), pp. 145–48, 181–82, 226.

divine nature and then treat the Trinity. Peter does the reverse. In discussing the Trinity first, he gets his basic vocabulary in place and indicates the particular content he is going to give to the troublesome key terms at issue. This done, he next takes up the unity of the Godhead which the Trinitarian persons share, and the various ways in which different subsets of divine names under this heading can be understood. As noted, power, wisdom, and goodness are included in this particular subdivision of Peter's theological lexicon. The are treated as such, before he continues with the modes by which the deity governs the universe, a topic which then leads directly into the subject of the creation, which he addresses in Book 2.

At the outset, and repeatedly in Book 1, Peter emphasizes the point that the reason for writing about the Trinity is to show that God is one in essence and plural in His persons. With Walter of Mortagne, the author of the *Summa sententiarum*, and Robert of Melun, he firmly annexes substance and nature to essence as ways of speaking about the Godhead. Unlike any of these masters, however, he endows these terms with a solid content. For him, essence means absolute being, the fullness of being. Insofar as essence can be compared with anything else, it is not to be contrasted with existence but with non-existence. Peter's reading of Augustine and John Damascene points him to the understanding that, in Latin, essence and its synonyms are the equivalent of the Greek *ousia*. Essence, in his view, is actually a better term than substance in this connection, although substance may be used with this sense, à propos of the Godhead. The chief features of the divine essence are characteristics of God in and of Himself. He is eternal, incommutable, immutable, and simple. He is being as such, and alone may be so called (*Deus ergo solus dicitur essentia vel esse*). Being is not an attribute of God, for Peter, but a statement about His very nature. This divine nature is utterly transcendent of created beings, which have a beginning, even in the case of those that have immortal souls, and which are changeable, subject to modification by accidents. Even when created beings are spiritual, they too lack simplicity and immutability. The term *substantia* must thus be applied to created beings in a manner different from the way it is applied to God. Peter acknowledges that substance refers properly (*proprie*) to created beings subject to change. The term, thus, can be applied to the deity only with caveats and restrictions, of the type he has indicated. But, with that understanding, *substantia* can be equated with the divine *essentia*.[80]

---

[80] Peter Lombard, *Sent.* 1. d. 2. c. 1–c. 2.3, d. 8. c. 1–8, 1: 61–63, 95–103. The quotation is at d. 8. c. 1.7, 1: 96. Peter's accent on *essentia* as the key to his doctrine

Having made this point, Peter indicates that, along with *substantia*, *natura* is to be yoked with essence, on the side of the Godhead; it is not to be used to denote the Trinitarian persons.[81] The term *natura* also refers to the created universe, since it describes the character of concrete individual beings, whatever that character may happen to be, so long as it is intrinsic to the being in question.[82] The consideration of how God's existence and nature may be known from an inspection of created nature which prefaces immediately Peter's discussion of the Trinity is designed to do three things at once. Outside of validating St. Paul's claim that the invisible things of God may be seen through the things that He has made, the proofs give Peter an opportunity to lay a foundation for his anti-Abelardian argument by contrasting the composite and changeable beings in creation with the omnipotent, omniscient, and supremely good creator. This argument goes beyond the offering of physical and metaphysical proofs of God's existence to the annexation of the attributes of power, wisdom, and goodness to the divine simplicity, from the outset.[83] A second anti-Abelardian tactic built into Peter's proofs is his next move to the vestiges of the Trinity in creation. He begins by emphasizing that these are similitudes, not substantial participations of creatures in the incommutable and simple substance of the Trinity. Further, the analogies found in the philosophers are mere pointers which fall short of imparting a real knowledge of the Trinity. The best created analogy of the Trinity is the mind of man, as Augustine had developed that theme in his *De trinitate*.

Peter gives a more comprehensive and more finely nuanced treatment of the Augustinian argument in this section of his *Sentences* than we find in the work of any of the contemporary masters who invoke it. There are three features of his handling of this subject which make it stand out from other current accounts. In the first place, he considers both sets of Augustinian analogies, *memoria-intellectus-voluntas* and *mens-notitia-amor*. Secondly, he takes careful account of the problem of how relation may be understood, and goes farther than anyone else in exploring both the advantages of

---

of the names of God has been aptly noted by Cornelio Fabro, "Teologia dei nomi divini nel Lombardo e in S. Tommaso," *Pier Lombardo* 4 (1960): 79–81; Étienne Gilson, "Pierre Lombard et les théologies d'essence," *Revue du moyen âge latin* 1 (1945): 61–64; Schneider, *Die Lehre*, pp. 25–30, 224–26.

[81] Peter Lombard, *Sent.* 1. d. 2. c. 4.2, d. 34. c. 1, 1: 64, 246–50.

[82] Ibid., 1. d. 3. c. 1.1, 1: 68–69. On *natura* here, see Johann Schupp, *Die Gnadenlehre des Petrus Lombardus* (Freiburg im Breisgau: Herder, 1932), pp. 15–23.

[83] Peter Lombard, *Sent.* 1. d. 3. c. 1.1–6, 1: 68–70.

the grammatical reformulation of this idea by Augustine and the limits as well as the powers of relative nouns in the Trinitarian context. Finally, he brings Damascene to bear on the definition of *persona* with which he emerges and on the ways in which it is appropriate as applied to the Trinitarian persons.

Peter begins with the analogy of memory, intellect, and will. This serves as a useful analogy in that these three functions are not three lives, three minds, three essences but are mental operations that are distinct, as well as being functional correlatives of each other. They coinhere in a single subsistent mind. With Augustine, he accents the point that analogy is not identity. The human mind remains unequal (*licet impar*) to the Trinity. The mind is a rational spirit attached to a body, while God is spiritual and incorporeal. A human being possesses these three faculties, but together they do not comprise the sum total of his being, while the Trinitatian persons do constitute God's whole being. The human being exercising these three mental functions is a single person, while the Trinity is three persons. Still, a powerful source of comparability lies in the fact that in both the divine and human analogates the three functions are understood with reference to each other. In the human no less than in the divine case, the interrelations involved are sharply distinguishable from those pertaining to Aristotlian accidents: "These three may be called one substance, and that is because they exist substantially in the same mind or soul, not as accidents in a subject, which can come and go" (*Haec tria dicantur una substantia: ideo scilicet quia in ipsa anima vel mente substantialiter existunt, non sicut accidentia in subiecto, quae possunt adesse et abesse*).[84]

In support of this point Peter cites Augustine's *De trinitate* 9.4, which no one else at the time who appealed to Augustine's argument had thought of using. He does so because he finds the discussion of relative nouns in *De trinitate* 5.16 too weak for his purposes. For, relatives such as left and right or light and dark involve spatiality and sensory perception, neither of which pertains to the mental faculties of man on which the Trinitarian analogy is based. A *fortiori*, neither spatiality nor sense perception applies to the Trinity itself. As Peter stands alone in recognizing, Augustine himself had indicated the limits of his own grammatical argument. He had arrived here at an argument based instead on man's mental faculties, faculties seen as structured intrinsically into man's very being, and not as accidents that may or may not be attached to it.

---

[84] Ibid., 1. d. 3. c. 1.7–c. 3.2, 1: 70–75. The quotation is at d. 3. c. 2.8, 1: 74.

This argument addresses the critique of the concept of relation made on the side of Aristotelian logic as well as the critique that could be made on the side of grammar, and provides an analogy on which the interrelations of the Trinitiarian persons, structured not only intrinsically but also eternally into their divine being, can be solidly grounded.

With this powerful argument in place, it may not seem immediately apparent why Peter thinks it desirable to advert as well to the *mens-notitia-amor* analogy, especially since, in Augustine's *De trinitate*, it is treated as an argument less finally persuasive than the one Augustine builds on the foundation of *memoria-intellectus-voluntas*. For Peter, the chief limitation of the *mens-notitia-amor* analogy is that it is impossible to make the same case, on the human side, for relations that are intrinsic to the beings that possess them as can be made for memory, intellect, and will. He prudently does not try to extend that analysis of relation to this analogy. What appeals to him about the *mens-notitia-amor* model is that it conjures up the image of a parent and a child as the analogates of the noticing mind and the object of knowledge and love of which it takes cognizance, and of the love passing between them, while asserting their equality and consubstiantiality and the complementarily of their joint interactions. In some respects, Augustine's analogy of the lover, the beloved, and the love that unites them might have served Peter's purpose equally well. But he prefers the *mens-notitia-amor* model, at least with the reading he gives to it, because it points to the ways in which the Trinitarian persons, in their eternal relations to each other, can be distinguished by the particular roles they play vis-à-vis each other.[85]

Having found a way to include the concept of relation within his analysis of the Trinitarian persons, while excluding the limits attaching to relative nouns and to Aristotelian accidents alike, Peter is now well positioned to clarify the meaning of the term *persona* as applied to the Trinity. In general, this task is going to require a set of names that are both proper to each person and which can signify the divine essence, but in such a way as to display "what pertains properly to the individual persons, and which is attributed relatively to each of them" (*illa quae proprie ad singulas pertinet personas, relative ad invicem dicuntur*).[86] Insofar as the names attached to the Godhead signify the divine essence, they signify the divine substance, and may be attributed *substantialiter* to the per-

---

[85] Ibid., 1. d. 3. c. 3.3–c. 4, 1: 74–77.

sons when, but only when, it is the divinity each person shares with the other persons that the speaker wants to denote. In coming to grips with the problem of how substantial attribution of divine names would work in this connection, Peter notes that this is a linguistic problem that occurs both in Greek and Latin. Where the Latins speak of three persons in the Trinity, the Greeks speak of three *hypostases*, which the Latins have translated as *substantiae*. He freely indicates that Boethius is the villian of the piece here. But, he continues, such an understanding of substance is inapposite. Substance, as he has already pointed out, belongs properly to the divine essence, the Godhead, and not to the Trinitarian persons; the Boethian translation of the Greek has confused the issue and should be discarded, lest we emerge with Sabellianism or some other tritheistic heresy.[87] Since we Latins, unlike the Greeks, use substance to refer to the divine essence, it may not be used to refer to the things that the Trinitarian persons do not have in common. By contrast, the names of the persons must refer to properties unique to each person (*nomine proprietas personae intellegatur*). These properties are paternity, filiation, and procession. *Proprietas* as a definition of *persona*, he adds, is clearer than *substantia* and less confusing than *hypostasis*. He expatiates on the dangers connected with *hypostasis* in particular, observing that "poison lurks under this noun" (*sub hoc nomine venenum latere*). To illustrate the latter point, he brings forward a citation from Jerome where that authority tries to argue against the Arians using the language of *hypostasis*. The unedifying spectacle of Jerome unsuccessfully wrestling with this problem is an argument for purging such terminology from the lexicon of Latin theology.[88] On the other hand, the personal properties of paternity, filiation, and procession are clearly understandable as the names denoting the relations among the persons, names which can indeed be used properly of one, and of only one, of the persons. Reminding the reader that these are eternal relations, and not predicables, Peter shows that even Damascene, the source for the Greek alternative to Latin Trinitarian theology on whom he relies, can be used as a positive support for the position he is defending. Quoting Damascene, he report him as stating that "the *hypostases* do not differ from each other according to substance, but according to their charac-

---

[86] Ibid., 1. d. 22. c. 5.1, 1: 179. The same point is made at *Sent.* 1. d. 21. c. 1, 1: 174–75.

[87] Ibid., 1. d. 23. c. 1–c. 5, 1: 181–86.

[88] Ibid., 1. d. 25. c. 2.1–d. 26. c. 1.1, 1: 192–97. The quotation is at d. 26. c. 1.1, 1: 197. On this point, see Schneider, *Die Lehre*, pp. 61–64, 93–96, 98–99.

teristic idioms, that is, their determinative properties" (*Non differunt
ab invicem hypostases secundum substantiam, sed secundum characteristica
idioma, id est determinativas proprietates*).[89] With this argument, and the
joint authority of Augustine and Damascene anchoring it, Peter
rests his case on the significance of the term *persona* as applied to the
Trinity and decisively rules out Trinitarian names that do not
display relationships among the persons which are unique to each
person alone and which do not speak to the eternal structure of the
Trinitarian family in and of itself.

This argument clearly obviates the ascription of power, wisdom,
and goodness as personal names of the Trinitatian persons. But
Peter has more to say on the side of the names given to the divine
unity which they share. Here, he accents the total equality of the
persons. None of the persons surpasses the others in His greatness,
His eternity, His wisdom, His power, His goodness, or in any of the
other attributes of the simple divine essence. Peter uses Damascene
to hammer in the point that the fullness of divine perfections is
found entirely in each of the Trinitarian persons.[90] This line of
argument is leveled as much against Robert of Melun as against
Abelard and his more intransigent defenders. But Peter also shares
with Robert a concern with several other dimensions of that question, which he raises in order to rule out the debate over universals
as relevant to a consideration of the divine nature. He agrees, with
Robert, that the Trinitarian persons cannot be called "parts" of a
"whole" called the Trinity. Nor can They be described as items
that belong to the same genus, possessing a subordinate status with
respect to the larger collective entity of which they are members.
Nor can the divine essence be regarded as a material cause or a
metaphysical substratum of what is common to the three persons, a
point inspiring Peter to take issue with Augustine.[91] Nor is the

---

[89] Peter Lombard, *Sent.* 1. d. 26. c. 2–d. 29. c. 4, 1: 197–219. The quotation from
Damascene is at d. 27. c. 3.1, 1: 205. Peter repeats the same quotation at *Sent.* 1. d.
33. c. 1.8, 1: 243, resuming the larger argument at that point in d. 33. c. 1–d. 34. c.
17, 1: 240–50. Similar language occurs in his *Sermo* 21, where he applies the
argument about persons as properties to the analogy of memory, intellect, and
will, *PL* 171: 435B–436B; this would enable us to date that sermon to the period
following his reading of Damascene in the early 1150s. Schneider, *Die Lehre*, pp.
118–23, 144–48, 166, 181–82, while positioning Peter's definition of person well in
relation to most theologians of his time, omits the material he derives from
Damascene.
[90] Peter Lombard, *Sent.* 1. d. 19. c. 1–6, d. 20, d. 31–32, d. 34. c. 3–4, 1: 159–63,
172–74, 233–39, 251–53. A similar point is made about God's goodness in *Sermo* 4,
PL 171: 357C.
[91] Peter Lombard, *Sent.* 1. d. 19. c. 8, 1: 166.

divine essence a generalization derived from the similarities among the persons, as with men who may share the same sex or physical complexion. Peter uses Damascene here to show that these ways of conceiving of the deity import the debate over universals into theology in an incorrect way, thereby indicating his familiarity with the terms of that debate even as he relegates it to philosophy. While the divine essence cannot be regarded as an abstraction derived from the Trinitarian persons, or as existing on a higher plane of reality, Peter recognizes the grammatical aptness of nouns, such as *homo*, which can refer both to mankind in general and to individual members of the human race. But the capacity of nouns to signify both in general and in particular in the case of created beings which are both individuals and participants in larger conceptual entities must be denied of the deity, since He is not that kind of being.[92] Peter's handling of these issues is both fuller, more pointed, and more streamlined than Robert's.

Having spelled out these particulars as they affect Trinitarian theology specifically, Peter is interested in placing his theory of theological language on a wider canvas. Since his lexicon is now in place, the sense that he gives to the terminology he uses here is unambiguous. He outlines three subdivisions within theological language. The first includes the terms which he had addressed first, the names applying to the Trinitarian persons individually, properly, and exclusively, the names which signify Their interpersonal relations, along the lines of the Augustinian analogies and the relations of paternity, filiation, and procession.[93] Next, there are the names that denote the divine essence in its unity. In addition to terms such as eternal, immutable, and simple, which refer to God in and of Himself, there are other terms that belong in this category, because they can be predicated of the single divine substance, but which also refer to God as He manifests Himself to man. Peter places power, wisdom, and goodness in this group, along with justice and the like.[94] Here, he raises two other questions, both of which are also aired by other contemporary theologians but not so systematically. One is the matter of terms applied to God in the singular or in the plural, a matter also taken up by Robert of Melun. There is, to begin with, the noun "Trinity." It is grammatically singular. Yet, it applies to none of the persons of the Trinity as

---

[92] Ibid., 1. d. 19. c. 5–c. 9, 1: 163–69.
[93] Ibid., 1. d. 22. c. 1.1, c. 5.1, d. 23. c. 2–c. 5, d. 25. c. 1–d. 27. c. 3.1, 1: 178, 179, 182–86, 190–205.
[94] Ibid., 1. d. 22. c. 3, c. 5, d. 31–32, d. 34. c. 3–c. 4, 1: 179, 223–39, 251–53.

individuals but to all of them simultaneously. Further, it is attributed to Them as a collective noun but not to any of Them
substantially.[95] All names, Peter continues, that are applied to God
substantially are used in the singular. Names referring to that
single *substantia* can also be applied in the singular to the Trinitarian persons, but only when one is referring to the attributes that
each person shares with the others. This usage is not proper with
reference to the attributes denoting each member of the Trinity's
personal singularity.[96]

This line of analysis concerning singular and plural or collective
nouns leads Peter to his final question within his second subdivision, the appropriateness of mathematical language as applied to
the deity. As we recall, Gilbert of Poitiers had advanced the view,
against Abelard, that the persons of the Trinity could be distinguished only numerically. The Chartrains had attacked this argument, using against it the weapons forged by Aristotelian logic.
Asserting that accidents cannot be attributed to God and that
number is an accident, Thierry of Chartres and Clarenbald of
Arras had rejected Gilbert's position, while at the same time substituting for it a mathematical argument of their own, the $1 \times 1 = 1$
model by which unity engenders equality and the two engender
connection. This Chartrain formula appears to be just as numerical
a claim as Gilbert's. Now Peter likewise rejects the idea that God is
conditioned by accidents or that He is understandable in terms of
them, although, as we have seen, he succeeds in finding a way of
including relation, detached from its understanding as an accident,
within his Trinitarian theology. His concern with the propriety of
mathematical language in connection with the Trinity derives
partly from the felt need to respond to Gilbert and the Chartrains
on this point. It also arises from the fact that Damascene had
offered a numerical analysis of the Trinity which Peter also finds
problematic and in need of interpretation.

In addressing the point that the Trinitarian persons share an
identity of substance, Peter is, initially, drawn up short by a line he
quotes from Damascene, "the *hypostases* are said to differ by number, and not by nature" (*numero enim, et non natura, differre dicuntur
hypostases*).[97] The problem, as Peter sees it, is either that Damascene
seems to support the Porretan and Chartrain mathematical argu-

---

[95] Ibid., 1. d. 22. c. 3, 1: 179.
[96] Ibid., 1. d. 23. c. 1.1–3, 1: 181–82.
[97] Ibid., 1. d. 19. c. 9.3, 1: 168.

ments, which Peter rejects, or that he seems to support the idea that the divine nature is a universal, while the *hypostases* are particulars, which Peter also rejects. After wrestling with this issue, he concludes that the overall tenor of Damascene's Trinitarian theology is such that he cannot be thought of as a realist in this context; rather, he is merely saying that the divine essence can be attributed to all the Trinitarian person in the same way, and at the same time, and that the divine essence is the same thing whether this term is used to refer to the persons together or individually.[98] As to the matter of differentiating the Trinitarian persons by number, Peter advises caution about how we understand this idea. One way of viewing number is the listing of items—this, that, and the other—because each one is different from the others. An example, which Peter does not use but which would illustrate his point, is an apple, a pear, and a banana in the same fruit basket. This notion of number clearly will not do for the Trinity. Another way of viewing number is as it is used in enumeration or computation, when we are talking about more than one instance of the same type of thing, and we want to indicate how many of them there are, or which particular item in the assortment we are discussing. Using our fruit example, we might enumerate one, two, or three apples in a basket of apples in this way. Now Damascene, according to Peter, means this latter type of numerical thinking. But still, the argument can be accepted only with strict caveats. For one thing, as Peter has already noted, the individual items in this numerical illustration do exist as individual members of a genus, in our example, the genus of "appleness." And, as he has explained above, the persons of the Trinity cannot be viewed as members of a genus called "deity." Further, the numerical argument must also be qualified—and this is a point which Peter makes against both Gilbert, Thierry, and Clarenbald—in that the distinction it posits is insufficient, for it does not include the personal properties that differentiate the Trinitarian persons from each other. The same qualification, he notes, should extend to our appropriation of the Augustinian notion of unity, equality, and connection or concord as Trinitarian names.[99] In addition, this type of numerical distinction does not mean that there is quantitatively "more God," more truth, more power, more of any aspect of the divine essence, when two or three of the persons are considered together than when a single divine person is being

---

[98] Ibid., 1. d. 19. c. 9.3–6, 1: 167–69.
[99] Ibid., 1. d. 19. c. 10.1–3, 1: 169.

regarded alone. We are not talking, here, about quantitative additions to the qualities possessed by any of the divine persons when
we think of them in terms of number, Peter stresses. Nor are we
thinking or speaking of a differentiation in number that is reducible
to the monad which is the conceptual substratum of all numbers.
For the threefold character of the structure of the deity is not
reducible in any way. Nor is the perfection of any of the Trinitarian
persons enlarged by our adding in the others.[100]

Ultimately, the value of using numerical language in speaking
about the divine nature and the Trinity, for Peter, is not that it can
substitute for a discussion of the essence of the Godhead or the
personal properties of the Father, Son, and Holy Spirit. Rather,
and with the restrictions he indicates, it can supplement our understanding of the other divine names. In speaking of God as one, or as
three, Peter essentially treats number in a privative, not in a
positive sense. The idea of God's oneness is designed to exclude any
notion of polytheism, or any thought that there is more than one
Father, one Son, and one Holy Spirit. As for the notion of plurality
as applied to the Trinitarian persons, it does not refer to quantitative diversity, addition, or multiplication, but is designed to rule
out singularity or solitude.[101] Here, Peter is making an effort to
detach the unity of God from the sense that the deity, in and of
Himself, is alone. In God's capacity as being as such, rather, the
deity exists as a consortium, a society. And so, when we say that the
Trinitarian persons are distinct with respect to Their personal
properties we do not posit diversity of Them in the sense of
alienation.[102] The utility of Peter's reflections on number as a
source for the divine names is that it serves as a vehicle for his
understanding of the ultimate metaphysical reality as a state of
intimate, loving, relatedness. One can have a transcendent deity,
he concludes, without having a deity Who is cold, detached, and
aloof.

Having treated the names attributable to the Trinitarian persons
vis-à-vis each other and the names attributable to the divine essence in its transcendent state, Peter next turns to the third general
subdivision under which he considers theological language, moving
to the terms which we can apply to God with respect to time (*ex
tempore*) and in relation to creatures (*relative ad creaturam*).[103] Tem-

---

[100] Ibid., 1. d. 19. c. 11–c. 12, d. 31. c. 2.9–c. 6, 1: 170–71, 228–32.
[101] This point has been discussed with sensitivity by Brady, at *Sent.* 1: 187 n.
[102] Peter Lombard, *Sent.* 1. d. 24, 1: 187–89.
[103] Ibid., 1. d. 22. c. 3, 1: 179.

porality is involved here not because God Himself changes, but because He interacts with creatures which themselves come into being and pass away, and undergo modifications. Divine names expressing such interactions include terms such as creator, lord, refuge, and the like. These terms indicate God's impact on a world which is altered by His governance both in the cosmological and the charismatic orders, in events which do not alter God Himself.[104] Peter assents to the view that individual Trinitarian persons may take on particular functions in Their relations with the creation and that some divine names under this heading, such as redeemer or gift, may apply specifically to the person entrusted with these missions.[105] But his emphasis in his handling of theological language in this subdivision is that the names of God we use here are used of the deity as such. He concludes the third part of his general analysis of this subject with a consideration of those names of God used with reference to creatures that are to be understood metaphorically (*translative, per similitudinem*), such as mirror, splendor, character, and figure.[106] It is clear from the relative weight that he assigns to other aspects of the problem of theological language that Peter does not think we need to enlarge on the theme of metaphor and to qualify the force of positive names of God and, by extension, the force of affirmative statements about God.

THE PORRETAN CHALLENGE

Much of the emphasis in the foregoing pages has reflected Peter's desire to attack Abelard, as the Trinitarian theologian of the day most in need of refutation. It can certainly be said that Peter goes farther than anyone else at the time to expose the inadequacies of Abelard's power-wisdom-goodness model and the more basic confusion between the deity as transcendent and as manifested on which it rests, offering a clearer and more cogent rationale for his critique and for the positive doctrine he puts forward than is true of other actual or would-be anti-Abelardians. To the extent that Abelard's mode of denominating the Trinitarian persons falls off the theological agenda in the sequel, we can give Peter much of the credit for that outcome. But Abelard was not the only major

---

[104] Ibid., 1. d. 30. c. 1–c. 2, 1: 220–23.

[105] Ibid., 1. d. 22. c. 3, 1: 179. On this point, see Ludwig Ott, *Untersuchung zur theologischen Briefliteratur der Frühscholastik*, Beiträge, 34 (Münster: Aschendorff, 1937), p. 266; Schneider, *Die Lehre*, p. 111.

[106] Peter Lombard, *Sent.* 1. d. 34. c. 5.2, 1: 254.

contender in the field. Even more problematic, in many ways, was
Gilbert of Poitiers. As we have seen, in his own attempt to refute
Abelard, Gilbert offered a mathematical understanding of the distinctions among the Trinitarian persons which some contemporaries, including Peter, found wanting. But Gilbert threw an even
greater and more intractable challenge into the arena of theological
language thanks to his development of a semantic theory so original
as to be positively idiosyncratic and very difficult for contemporaries to understand. Quite apart from a vocabulary that is rebarbative, that invents new terms, and that uses existing terms in
standard Latin with Gilbert's own meanings attached to them,
Gilbert's semantics created severe problems when his lexicon was
applied to theology. To some extent, Gilbert himself was aware of
these difficulties and sought to address them. The disciples he
attracted during his own lifetime also saw some problems with his
vocabulary and made notable efforts to disentangle the substance of
his teaching from the lexical company in which it travelled. With
respect to Gilbert's theology and semantic theory, Peter has sometimes been seen as a critic, pure and simple, and even as the *peritus*
responsible for drafting the charges leveled against Gilbert at the
Consistory of Paris in 1147 and the Council of Rheims in 1148.[107]
This view is a distortion of the facts. In some areas, to be sure,
Peter follows the lead of the early Porretans in criticizing Gilbert's
theological terminology. But, in others, he finds Gilbert's definitions

---

[107] See, for example, H. C. van Elswijk, *Gilbert Porreta: Sa vie, son oeuvre, sa pensée*
(Louvain: Spicilegium Sacrum Lovaniense, 1966), p. 95; Fabro, "Teologia dei
nomi divini," pp. 77–93; Nikolaus M. Häring, "Petrus Lombardus und die
Sprachlogik in der Porretanerschule," in *Misc. Lomb.*, pp. 113–27; "San Bernardo
e Gilberto vescovo di Poitiers," in *Studi su S. Bernardo di Chiaravalle nell'ottavo
centenario della canonizzazione* (Rome: Editiones Cistercienses, 1975), pp. 87–88;
"The Porretans and the Greek Fathers," *MS* 24 (1966): 190; Jean Leclercq,
"Textes sur Saint Bernard et Gilbert de la Porrée," *MS* 14 (1952): 107; Lauge Olaf
Nielsen, *Theology and Philosophy in the Twelfth Century: A Study of Gilbert Porreta's
Thinking and the Theological Expositions of the Doctrine of the Incarnation during the Period
1130–1180*, Acta theologica danica, 15 (Leiden: E. J. Brill, 1982), p. 33; Ludwig
Ott, "Petrus Lombardus: Persönlichkeit und Werk," *Münchener theologische Zeit-
schrift* 5 (1954): 110; reprised as "Pietro Lombardo: Personalità e opera," *Misc.
Lomb.*, pp. 11–12; Schneider, *Die Lehre*, pp. 121–23, 145–48, 181–82, 226. On
Peter's purported role in helping to draw up the charges against Gilbert, see Franz
Pelster, "Petrus Lombardus und die Verhandlungen über die Streitfrage des
Gilbertus Porreta in Paris (1147) und Reims (1148)," in *Misc. Lomb.*, pp. 68–69,
72. This latter point has been convincingly refuted and the primary role of
Godescalc of St. Martin in that connection has been emphasized by Gillian R.
Evans, "Godescalc of St. Martin and the Trial of Gilbert of Poitiers," *Analecta
Praemonstratensia* 57 (1981): 209 and Häring, "San Bernardo e Gilberto," pp.
77–78.

of terms accurate and helpful, and makes use of them himself.[108] Peter's relationship to Gilbert of Poitiers on this whole subject is a much more nuanced one than has usually been appreciated.

Gilbert produced both a metaphysics and a semantic theory in the commentaries on the theological *opuscula* of Boethius which he composed between 1135 and 1142,[109] a period during which he taught both at Chartres and Paris. In his account of beings, Gilbert distinguishes their formal aspect, which he calls their *quo est* or *subsistentia*, from their concrete individuality, which he calls their *quod est* or *subsistens*.[110] In his consideration of the *quo est* of beings, Gilbert expressly distances himself from the doctrine of universals. We cannot extrapolate the *subsistentia* of a being from that individual being, he argues, combining it with similar extrapolations from other individual beings, to produce an abstract idea that refers to an abstract being, or even meaningfully to the individual beings from which it has been derived. What other contemporary thinkers, whether realists or nominalists, called universals, he regards as useless concepts, inapposite in metaphysics and logic alike.[111] For Gilbert it is a waste of time to compare the *subsistentia* of

---

[108] For a fuller discussion of this issue, see Marcia L. Colish, "Gilbert, the Early Porretans, and Peter Lombard: Semantics and Theology," in *Gilbert de Poitiers et ses contemporains: Aux origines de la logica modernorum*, ed. Jean Jolivet and Alain de Libera (Naples: Bibliopolis, 1987), pp. 229–50; "Early Porretan Theology," *RTAM* 56 (1989): 58–79. To the accounts of the council of Rheims cited there, now add Marjorie Chibnall, intro. to her ed. and trans. of John of Salisbury, *Historia pontificalis* (Oxford: Clarendon Press, 1986), pp. xl–xli.

[109] For the dates, see Elswijk, *Gilbert Porreta*, p. 63.

[110] Gilbert of Poitiers, *In Boethius de Trinitate* prologus secundus 6–7, 1.2.1–2, 1.3.38; *In Boethius de Hebdomadibus* 1.27–29, 1.32–35, 1.37, 1.53, ed. Nikolaus M. Häring in *The Commentaries on Boethius of Gilbert of Poitiers* (Toronto: Pontifical Institute of Mediaeval Studies, 1966), pp. 58–59, 78, 109, 193–95, 199. For the literature assisting an understanding of Gilbert's metaphysics and semantics, see Colish, "Gilbert," p. 231 n. 8. To these references may be added Lambert M. DeRijk, "De quelques difficultés de nature linguistique dans le vocabulaire de Gilbert de la Porrée," in *Actes du colloque Terminologie de la vie intellectuelle au moyen âge*, ed. Olga Weijers (Turnhout: Brepols, 1988), pp. 19–25.

[111] This point has been interpreted correctly by Evans, "Godescalc of St. Martin," p. 205; *The Mind of St. Bernard of Clairvaux* (Oxford: Clarendon Press, 1983), p. 185; Bruno Maioli, *Gilberto Porretano: Dalla grammatica speculativa alla metafisica del concreto* (Rome: Bulzoni, 1979), pp. 341–61; Christopher J. Martin, intro. to "The *Compendium Logicae Porretanum ex codici Oxoniensi Collegii Corporis Christi 205*: A Manual of Porretan Doctrine by a Pupil of Gilbert's," ed. Sten Ebbesen et al., *CIMAGEL* 46 (1983): xvii–xxiii, 6; Lauge Olaf Nielsen, "On the Doctrine of Logic and Language of Gilbert Porreta and His Followers," *CIMAGEL* 17 (1976): 45–46; *Theology and Philosophy*, p. 51; Sofia Vanni Rovighi, "La filosofia di Gilberto Porretano," in *Studi di filosofia medioevale*, 2 vols. (Milan: Vita e Pensiero, 1978), 1: 229–36. This position supersedes the view of Gilbert as a realist maintained by Ermenegildo Bertola, "La scuola di Gilberto de la Porrée,"

one being with the *subsistentia* of another being, for each *subsistentia* inheres in the being to which it belongs in a radically singular way. The thrust of Gilbert's teaching as a metaphysician is to emphasize the utter individuality of each being, at the level of its *quo est* as well as its *quod est*. For Gilbert, in both aspects, beings possess a uniqueness that is irreducible, a uniqueness of a sort that other thinkers might be inclined to grant only to beings that are persons.

Having laid out this highly original doctrine of being, Gilbert is also concerned with using language precisely, naming the two levels of being with nouns that parallel their respective abstractness and concreteness.[112] Thus, he holds, an abstract noun such as *humanitas* is properly applied to the *subsistentia* of a particular man, while a concrete noun such as *homo* is properly applied to his concrete *subsistens*, the level of his being which can be modified by accidents. It is not proper to say *"homo est humanitas"* because such a statement confuses and conflates the two distinct aspects of being to which the two nouns refer. Even with respect to created beings, this semantic theory has its weaknesses. Gilbert is forced to use abstract nouns to signify the *subsistentia* of these beings, even though he holds that the *subsistentia* is not susceptible of abstraction from them. Also, most created beings are composite. For instance, the body and soul, the ingredients that make up the concrete *subsistens* of a human being, are thus sub-concrete, infra-subsistent on the level of being. Yet, *corpus* and *anima*, the only nouns available for denoting them in Gilbert's lexicon, are nouns no less concrete than the noun *homo*, which applies properly to the fully subsistent being which they compose. Thus, despite Gilbert's concerted effort to use language so that the abstractness and concreteness of terms reflect the metaphysical status of the aspect of being which they denote, he is not entirely successful in enforcing the strict parallelism between language and reality that he seeks. Gilbert has available to him two kinds of nouns, abstract and concrete, with which to denote three levels of being, the *subsistentia*, the *subsistens*, and the infra-subsistent components in a composite *subsistens*.

---

in *Saggi e studi di filosofia medioevale* (Padua: CEDAM, 1951), pp. 19–34; Aimé Forest, "Gilbert de la Porrée et les écoles du XIIᵉ siècle," *Revue néo-scolastique de philosophie* 36 (1934): 101–10; A. Hayen, "Le concile de Reims et l'erreur théologique de Gilbert de la Porrée," *AHDMLA* 11 (1936): 39–102; and Richard J. Westley, "A Philosophy of the Concreted and the Concrete: The Constitution of Creatures according to Gilbert de la Porrée," *Modern Schoolman* 37 (1960): 270–71.
[112] Gilbert of Poitiers, *In Boeth. de Trin.* prologus secundus 12, 1.1.10–34, 1.3.16, 1.3.26–27, 1.3.30, 1.3.36, 1.3.38, 1.3.45–48, 2.1.21; *In Boeth. de Hebd.* 1.32–35, 1.57–69, pp. 60, 72–78, 106, 107–08, 109, 111–12, 167, 194, 199–202.

This is not a problem which Gilbert addresses forthrightly in his semantic theory. Nor does he come to grips with the need to explain how abstract nouns referring to collective objects of knowledge signify, a difficulty he leaves to his disciples.[113] But he does take into account some of the problems involved in his wish to make nouns correspond rigorously to the aspect of being they denote in philosophy and, even more so, in theology. Gilbert is sensitive to the semantic limits of speech in the various scholarly disciplines, and in no sense seeks to be a grammatical reductionist in his application of these disciplines to theological questions. There are gaps, he notes, between things, the concepts we form of them, and the words in which we express those concepts; the words are like images reflected in a mirror.[114] Moreover, language itself is far from univocal. The same terms have different meanings in grammar, logic, and natural philosophy.[115] Our language labors under still greater difficulties in theology. Gilbert asserts repeatedly that theological statements involve a transferred meaning (*dictio translata, proportionali transsumptione, ratione proportione*) and that they are paradoxes (*paradoxa*) and symbolic indicators (*emblemata*).[116] He criticizes heretics for a too-literal application of human language to the deity,[117] and recommends intellectual humility, affirming that faith precedes knowledge and that understanding depends on divine grace.[118] Yet, if Gilbert acknowledges that theological statements are analogous and not exhaustive signs of what they signify, he does not state

---

[113] Ebbesen et al., ed., "*Compendium Logicae Porretanum*," *CIMAGEL* 46 (1983); Martin, intro. to "*Compendium*," pp. xviii–xlvi; Nielsen, "On the Doctrine of Logic and Language," pp. 40–69.

[114] Gilbert of Poitiers, *In Boeth. de Trin.* prologus primus 2, prologus secundus 1.3.21–24, pp. 52, 65–68; the image of the mirror is at 1.3.26, p. 69.

[115] Ibid., 1.3.47, 2.1.1–2, 2.1.5, 2.1.34; *In Boeth. de Hebd.* prologus 8–9; *In Boethius contra Eutychen et Nestorium* 1.1.2, 1.58–61, ed. Nikolaus M. Häring in *The Commentaries on Boethius of Gilbert of Poitiers* (Toronto: Pontifical Institute of Mediaeval Studies, 1966), pp. 111, 163, 164, 170, 184–85, 243, 254–55.

[116] Gilbert of Poitiers, *In Boeth. de Trin.* 1.1.11, 1.2.36–46, 1.2.89, 1.4.28, 1.5.20–21, 1.5.39, 2.1.1–2, 2.1.5, 2.1.34, 2.2.2, 2.4.6; *In Boeth. de Hebd.* 1.58–64, pp. 72, 85–88, 98, 119, 120, 143, 147, 161–64, 170, 200–01. Good discussions of this point are found in Elswijk, *Gilbert Porreta*, pp. 33, 35, 38–39; Häring, "Petrus Lombardus," pp. 113–27; Maioli, *Gilberto Porretano*, pp. xxvi–xxxi, 3–24, 36–46, 73–75, 179–240; Nielsen, *Theology and Philosophy*, pp. 103–27, 130–36; Martin Anton Schmidt, *Gottheit und Trinitaet nach dem Kommentar des Gilbert Porreta zu Boethius, De Trinitate, Studia Philosophica*, supplementum 7 (Basel: Verlag für Recht and Gesellschaft, 1956), passim and esp. pp. 6–10, 11–14; Michael B. Williams, *The Teaching of Gilbert Porreta on the Trinity as Found in His Commentaries on Boethius* (Rome: Universitas Gregoriana, 1951), pp. 77, 78, 128.

[117] Gilbert of Poitiers, *In Boeth. de Trin.* prologus secundus 8, 20, pp. 59, 62.

[118] Ibid., 1.1.1, 1.1.3, 2.1.9, pp. 70, 71, 164.

precisely where and how the analogies they contain fall short. In
practice, notwithstanding his conventional disclaimers, he goes
right ahead and invokes the semantic rules he had developed for
discussing creatures in speaking about the creator, even though
they are not truly apposite to Him. The most notorious case in
point, and parallel with his assertion that it is proper to say "*homo
non est humanitas*" is his statement that "*Deus non est divinitas*,"
although he repeatedly avers that God is a radically simple being
Whose *quo est* is identical with His *quod est*. Unlike created beings,
God has one, and only one, level of being. God's divinity inheres
essentially in God; He is all His qualities.[119] Thus, in applying the
distinction between *deus* and *divinitas* to the deity, Gilbert implies a
parallelism between God and creatures and a distinction between
the *quo est* and the *quod est* in God which he flatly rejects. Similar
difficulties are found in his handling of the key theological terms
substance, nature, and person.

Gilbert would have been happy to dispense with *substantia*
altogether, since it is not equivalent either to *subsistentia* or to
subsistens in his own lexicon.[120] Since the term substance is in the
creed, however, he cannot avoid it. He is aware of the fact that, in
Aristotelian natural philosophy, substance comes closer to his own
subsistens than it does to his *subsistentia*. For, like Aristotle's substance, Gilbert's *subsistens* refers to the level at which beings can be
modified by accidents.[121] Now God, he agrees, cannot be modified
by accidents. None the less, he sometimes calls God an *essens sive
subsistens*.[122] But elsewhere, in an equally inapposite way, he sometimes equates the divine substance with *divinitas* or *deitas*, abstract
terms that point to the divine *subsistentia*.[123]

Despite these ambiguities, Gilbert uses the equation between
substantia and *divinitas* to attack the Trinitarian theologies of Abe-

---

[119] Ibid., 1.2.96, p. 99.
[120] Ibid., 1.4.6, p. 119.
[121] Ibid., 1.4.99, p. 135.
[122] Ibid., 2.1.17–19, 2.1.45–46, pp. 166, 172.
[123] Ibid., 2.1.18–20, 2.1.24, 2.1.45, 2.1.54, 2.1.73, pp. 116, 166, 168, 172, 174,
179. This confusion is perpetuated by students of Gilbert purely on the level of
philosophy. Unsure of whether *substantia* refers properly to the *quo est* or the *quod est*
of beings, they seek to extend its significance to both, according to the intentions of
the speaker and the propositional context in which he uses the term. Yet, they
regard the reference of nouns to the qualities inhering in the *subsistens* as improper.
On this point, see Irène Rosier, "Les acceptions du terms 'substantia' chez
Pierre Hélie," in *Gilbert de Poitiers et ses contemporains: Aux origines de la logica
modernorum*, ed. Jean Jolivet and Alain de Libera (Naples: Bibliopolis, 1987), pp.
315–16.

lard and Augustine alike. Against Abelard, he argues that power, wisdom, and goodness, like other abstract nouns, should be attributed to the single divine substance and essence of the deity. If viewed as properties of the individual Trinitarian persons, these traits would be reduced to accidents inhering in three different beings at the level of *subsistens*. The differences among the Father, Son, and Holy Spirit, he insists, are not substantial or essential but numerical only; They all possess power, wisdom, and goodness in the same way. In Gilbert's terms, the problem with Abelard's Trinitarian theology is that he has collapsed the divine *quo est* into the divine *quod est*, emerging with three deities. In Gilbert's estimation, Augustine has done exactly the reverse, collapsing the divine *quod est* into the divine *quo est* in his analogies of the Trinity in the human soul. As he sees it, if we view the Trinity as parallel with the *mens, notitia*, and *amor* in the human soul, we would reduce God to a monad and blur the distinctions among the Trinitarian persons.[124] But, if this line of reasoning provides a language in which Gilbert can criticize Trinitarian theologies he dislikes, it does not enable him to develop a positive Trinitarian theology that is comprehensible, one that does not lay him equally open to the charge that he has failed to distinguish the persons of the Trinity adequately from each other, and one that does not violate his own philosophical rules.

If Gilbert's handling of substance is problematic, the same can be said for his treatment of nature and person. His difficulties are compounded here by the Boethian point of departure he takes. In one of his definitions of nature, Boethius includes substance as one of the concepts that nature embraces. Gilbert rejects this idea. He wants to be able to apply *natura* to God as a simple, immutable, and purely spiritual being. He thinks, correctly, that it would confuse matters if he also applied *natura* to substances made up of matter and form, which can be modified by accidents.[125] On the other hand, in speaking about created beings that are composite and that are subject to accidents, Gilbert thinks that *natura* is appropriate as well, and that it is attributed properly to these beings at the level of

---

[124] Gilbert of Poitiers, *In Boeth. de Trin.* prologus secundus 14, 1.3.45–48, 1.3.53–54, 2.1.51, 2.2.71, pp. 60, 111–12, 113, 173, 178. Stephan Otto, "Augustinus und Boethius im 12. Jahrhundert," *Wissenschaft und Weisheit* 26 (1963): 18–21, 24–26 has argued that the motive for Gilbert's critique of Augustine was the desire to substitute a metaphysically based understanding of the Trinity for one drawn from the inspection of creatures. He ignores the semantic issues in Gilbert's analysis.

[125] Gilbert of Poitiers, *In Boeth. contra Eut.* 1.1–36, 1.56–61, 1.92–100, pp. 242–49, 254–55, 261–63.

subsistens.[126] In speaking about the incarnate Christ, Gilbert concludes that one must use *natura* in both senses of the word, understanding His divine nature as His pure and simple divine essence while understanding His human nature as His concrete composite phenomenal humanity.[127] Yet, on the level of Christ's human nature, how can a nature that happens to be a human being be distinguished from a human person? And, can the term *persona* be applied comprehensibly both to Christ as God and to Christ as man? Gilbert wrestles with these questions,[128] but does not fully answer them.

Gilbert begins by rejecting the Boethian definition of a person as the individual substance of a rational nature, as did some other theologians of the time, largely as a way of criticizing Abelard's anthropology.[129] Gilbert finds unacceptable the equation of the human person with the human soul which this Boethian formula entails. For him, a human person is a human *subsistens*, a combination of body and soul in man that is neither a casual nor a separable assemblage of parts nor a new amalgam, a *tertium quid* whose ingredients each lose their own properties while uniting to inhere in an individual human being. Although it is a composite, a human person is, for Gilbert, a single being that is a *res per se una*.[130]

Vigorous as is this defense of the human person as a psychosomatic unit, it brings various difficulties in its train, which Gilbert does not dispel. First, given his definition of nature on the human level, it is hard to see how a man's human nature can be different from his human person, since Gilbert equates both the nature and the person with the man as a concrete *subsistens*. Second, it is hard to see how a man's human nature can be part of a wider human community, except mathematically. Finally, having proposed his own definition of the human person, Gilbert states that it does not apply to theological persons (*non convenit theologicis personis*).[131] To be

---

[126] Ibid., 1.83–91, 2.2, pp. 260–61, 265.
[127] Ibid., 1.100–03, pp. 263–64.
[128] Ibid., 2.9–10, 2.18–19, pp. 266–68. As Nielsen, *Theology and Philosophy*, p. 163, has aptly noted, "The nature of the distinction between nature and person remains an unclarified problem with Gilbert."
[129] This point is rightly stressed by Landgraf, *Dogmengeschichte*, 2 part 1: 102–04. Abelard's position on the human soul, its separability from the body, and its introduction into the body after the body is created, is brought out clearly by Thaddeus Kucia, "Die Anthropologie bei Peter Abelard," in *Petrus Abaelardus (1079–1142): Person, Werk, Wirkung*, ed. Rudolf Thomas (Trier: Paulinus-Verlag, 1980), pp. 224–27.
[130] Gilbert of Poitiers, *In Boeth. de Trin.* prologus secundus 12; *In Boeth. contra Eut.* 2.20–3.18, pp. 60, 268–75.

sure, Gilbert makes this assertion because, in his view, a person is not necessarily simple or purely spiritual. A person can be modified by accidents. It is a *subsistens* in a way that the deity is not. Yet, having stated that the persons of the Trinity are not substances, properties, or relations, he insists on the idea that they are distinct as persons,[132] although without having endowed the idea of theological person with any comprehensible positive content.

If Gilbert does not offer a cogent positive exposition of Trinitarian theology, the confusion entailed by his vocabulary is at its most acute in his treatment of the hypostatic union. In this area there are two polemical agendas at work in Gilbert's thought. On the one hand, he wants to attack Abelard for a Christology which Gilbert sees as involving a too-divisible and too-adventitious view of the communication of idioms in the incarnate Christ.[133] On the other, he wants to detach the *assumptus homo* formula for describing the incarnation from the Adoptionist idea that the *homo* assumed by Christ was a man already in existence.[134] But Gilbert's semantic criteria make these tasks intractable indeed. Gilbert argues that the incarnate Christ has a single divine *persona*, here equated with the divine essence and distinguished from that essence as found in the Father and the Holy Spirit only numerically. This divine essence unites with a human *subsistens*. At this juncture Gilbert stresses three main points. First, the human aspect of the incarnate Christ contains all the properties of a human body and a human soul. Once united to the Word, it remains united to the Word. It is the subsistent *homo* that Christ assumes, Gilbert stresses, not *humanitas* since *humanitas* would lack the specific individuality of the man Jesus. Second, the composite being resulting from the hypostatic union is not a *tertium quid*. It retains all the properties of both man and God, neither of which is changed by the union. Third, in taking

---

[131] Gilbert of Poitiers, *In Boeth. de Trin.* 1.5.39, p. 147.

[132] Ibid., 2.2.72–80; *In Boeth. contra Eut.* 3.65–74, pp. 178–80, 285–87.

[133] Good treatments of this point are found in Elswijk, *Gilbert Porreta*, p. 448; Landgraf, *Dogmengeschichte*, 2 part 1: 102–04; Nielsen, *Theology and Philosophy*, pp. 163–89; Robert F. Studeny, *John of Cornwall, an Opponent of Nihilianism: A Study of the Christological Controversy of the Twelfth Century* (Vienna: St. Gabriel's Mission Press, 1939), pp. 89–91.

[134] Good treatments of this point are found in Elswijk, *Gilbert Porreta*, pp. 404–44; Nikolaus M. Häring, "Sprachlogik und philosophische Voraussetzungen zum Verständnis der Christologie Gilberts von Poitiers," *Scholastik* 32 (1957): 373–98; "San Bernardo e Gilberto," pp. 78–87; Nielsen, *Theology and Philosophy*, pp. 163–89. For the patristic developments that encouraged such a view, see Auguste Gaudel, "La théologie de l''Assumptus Homo': Histoire et valeur doctrinale," *RSR* 17 (1937): 64–90.

on manhood, Christ does not take on a preexisting human *persona*, and this, for two reasons. First, a *persona* is, by definition, a *res per se una*. No person can be duplex. Both before and after the incarnation, then, Christ can have one *persona* only, His divine *persona*. Second, and since this is the case, what Christ assumes in the incarnation is, simultaneously, a human body and a human soul, the ingredients that make up a human *subsistens* (*ea quae sunt hominis*), neither of which existed either separately or conjointly prior to the moment of the incarnation.[135]

As Gilbert sums things up, a person cannot take on a person in the incarnation, since no person can be duplex. Nor can a nature take on a nature. For, if it was the divine nature that was incarnated, it would be impossible to explain why it was Christ Who became man and not the Father or the Holy Spirit, since They share the same nature. Nor could Christ have assumed a general human nature, otherwise the man Jesus would not have been an individual human being. Nor can a nature take on a person, for here the lack of differentiation among the Trinitarian persons would be combined with the Adoptionist heresy. So, Gilbert concludes, in the incarnation, a divine person took on a human nature.[136] But, his vocabulary makes it difficult to grasp exactly what he means by this formula. As we have seen, on the human level, the difference between a person and a nature is all but invisible, as Gilbert defines these terms. In stating that the Word assumes *homo*, not *humanitas*, he wants to stress the individuality of the human Christ. But this makes it hard to see how the human Christ is consubstantial with other human beings. And, if He is not, the universality of His saving work is severely compromised. On another level, Gilbert says that the Word assumes *homo* when what he really means to say is that the Word assumes an infra-human and as yet unattached body and soul. In this latter connection, he is as far from Christological nihilianism as he is free from Adoptionism. But, at the same time, he uses his terms inconsistently, and in ways that allow them to be wielded against him.

While Gilbert's modern defenders have vindicated his orthodoxy,[137] it is certainly the case that he left a tangled legacy to

---

[135] Gilbert of Poitiers, *In Boeth. contra Eut.* 4.21–127, pp. 292–314.

[136] Ibid., 4.108, p. 310. The best analysis of Gilbert's Christology and its problems is found in Häring, "Sprachlogik," pp. 373–98 and Nielsen, *Theology and Philosophy*, pp. 163–89.

[137] See, in particular, Elswijk, *Gilbert Porreta*, pp. 77, 318–64; Margaret T. Gibson, "The *Opuscula Sacra* in the Middle Ages," in *Boethius: His Life, Thought and*

his successors. The fact that this was so gave Gilbert's disciples pause, and inspired his earliest pupils, those working within Gilbert's own lifetime, to reassess the utility of his semantics as applied to theology. Adaptation of Gilbert's views, on the part of the early Porretans, begins almost immediately, and can be traced in disciples of Gilbert active in the Paris region in the 1140s.

We may mention in passing a commentary on the Pseudo-Athanasian creed dating to the early 1140s which, aside from finding problems in Gilbert's notorious phrase "*Deus non est divinitas*,"[138] preserves his reasoning and his terminology, even when it is contradictory,[139] because there is no consensus as to whether it was written by an early Porretan or by Gilbert himself.[140] Certainly not from the hand of Gilbert is the *Sententiae divinitatis*, written shortly after 1148. While more correctly defined as a theological eclectic, the author is an identifiable adherent of the Porretan tradition on the issues that concern us here. There are several noteworthy points at which he backs off from Gilbert's language. As with Gilbert, he has an anti-Abelardian brief, and for the same reasons. He agrees with Gilbert's distinction between abstract and concrete nouns as applied to God, and with the principle that the divine properties are in the divine persons essentially. But he departs decisively from the *deus non est divinitas* formula, in the following words:

> For is not divinity God and nothing other than God? I answer that divinity is God and nothing other than God, by an act of reason but not by the form of speaking, by reason of faith, not by reason of human philosophy.[141]

Influence, ed. Margaret T. Gibson (Oxford: Basil Blackwell, 1981), p. 223; Nikolaus M. Häring, "Notes on the Council and Consistory of Rheims (1148)," *MS* 28 (1966): 39–59; "Petrus Lombardus," pp. 113–27; "Sprachlogik," pp. 373–98; "The Case of Gilbert de la Porrée, Bishop of Poitiers (1142–54)," *MS* 13 (1951): 1–40; "The Porretans and the Greek Fathers," *MS* 24 (1966): 181–209.

[138] Nikolaus M. Häring, ed., "A Commentary on the Pseudo-Athanasian Creed by Gilbert of Poitiers," c. 33–39, 47–48, *MS* 27 (1965): 35–37, 38–39.

[139] "Commentary," c. 14–16, 45–47, 108–16, pp. 32–33, 38–39, 48–50.

[140] Häring, "Commentary," pp. 23–31, ascribes the work to Gilbert, while Nielsen, *Theology and Philosophy*, p. 44, thinks that it was written by an early follower of his.

[141] Bernhard Geyer, ed., *Die Sententiae divinitatis: Ein Sentenzenbuch der Gilbertischen Schule* 4.5, Beiträge, 7:2–3 (Münster: Aschendorff, 1909), pp. 68*–69*: "Nonne divinitas est Deus et non aliud a Deo? Respondeo, quod divinitas est Deus et non aliud a Deo, actu rationis, sed non forma loquendi, ratione fidei, non ratione humanae philosophiae." More on this point can be found at 6.1.4, 6.25, pp. 160*–63*, 170*–71*.

The author treats *natura* as referring to *subsistentia*.[142] He does not, however, discuss the specific sense in which substance, essence, person, and properties apply to the deity. In his Christology, he opposes the idea that the incarnate Christ is composed of separable parts,[143] and he repeats Gilbert's assertion that "*non persona personam, nec natura personam, nec natura naturam, sed persona naturam assumpsit.*"[144] At the same time, he retains the Boethian definition of person as the individual substance of a rational nature, which Gilbert rejects, and he abandons Gilbert's distinction between *homo* and *humanitas* in considering Christ's assumption of a human body and a human soul. He states, although without explaining why, that in this context the two terms mean the same thing, and that they obviate equally Christ's assumption of a preexistent human person.[145]

Much more thoroughgoing reassessments of Gilbert's theological language were made by other early disciples of his. The author of a treatise entitled *Invisibilia dei*, dating to ca. 1150, makes his own swift response to the semantic and dogmatic controversies to which Gilbert's views had recently led at Rheims. Our author has an extremely lively awareness of both the philosophical and the theological issues which these views had raised. His treatise leads off with the Pauline idea that the invisible things of God are known through the creation, which yields information about God to man through his reason and his senses.[146] This observation is a curtain-raiser for the author's main theme, the correct grammatical and logical ways of expressing that knowledge. With Gilbert, he argues that composite created beings can best be denoted by distinguishing their durable and informing features, expressed by abstract nouns, from their concrete manifestations, susceptible to accidents, expressed by concrete nouns.[147] What is striking, in his formulation of this point, is the author's rejection of the Gilbertian terms *subsistentia* and *subsistens*. He has evidently come to the conclusion that they are a losing proposition, so he kisses them goodbye and moves on without a backward look. He agrees with Gilbert that every subject (*res*) is singular and that no subject is universal.[148]

---

[142] *Sent. div.* 4.5, pp. 69*–70*.
[143] Ibid., p. 69*.
[144] Ibid., 4.1, 4.2, pp. 53*, 57*.
[145] Ibid., 4.2, 6.2.1, pp. 55*, 163*–64*.
[146] Nikolaus M. Häring, ed., "The Treatise 'Invisibilia dei' in MS. Arras, Bibl. mun. 981 (399)," *RTAM* 40 (1973): 118.
[147] Ibid., 40, 49–50, pp. 124, 126–27.
[148] Ibid., 59–60, 62, pp. 128–29.

Yet, here too, he departs from Gilbert in admitting the cogency and utility of universal concepts, such as the idea of genus. He defines the universal as a substantial likeness among things that differ by their species, citing the *Topica* of Boethius as his authority.[149] Since he agrees with Gilbert that no *res* is a universal, how does he interpret the Boethian universal which he admits? The author's solution is to distinguish between the predication of an abstract noun properly (*per se*) and its predication with reference to something else (*per aliud*). If, for example, one refers to the *humanitas* that inheres in Peter as an individual human being, one predicates *humanitas per se*; if one refers to the *humanitas* that links Peter with other human beings, one predicates *humanitas per aliud*. *Per aliud* predication is also a way of handling Peter's sub-personal attributes, such as the accidents that may modify his body, although in this case the nouns used may be concrete.[150]

This argument provides an ingenious way of supporting the overall tenor of Gilbertian semantics while remedying some of its literal limitations. The author also thinks that one needs a still more precise and exclusive way of denoting the radical uniqueness of individual beings than Gilbert had provided, one that goes beyond a person's proper name. After all, the terms *humanitas* and *homo* can be applied properly to more than one human being. The name Peter has likewise been given to more than one man. None of these nouns denotes precisely what makes a particular man named Peter a *res per se una*. The term that does the job, in the author's view, is his *Petritas*, his "Peterness,"[151] an interesting and perhaps pregnant formula, and one that reveals the author's willingness to coin neologisms and to break the enforced parallelism between abstract and concrete nouns and the things they represent that marks Gilbert's thought as well.

The author of *Invisibilia dei* is willing to depart even farther from Gilbert in his theological language and method. He takes more closely to heart than Gilbert the announced limits of a vocabulary framed to describe composite created beings as adequate for speaking about an utterly simple deity. His solution, and it is one not envisaged by Gilbert, is to draw on the Pseudo-Areopagite's analysis of the *via affirmativa* and *via negativa*.[152] When it comes to the affirmative way, he notes, the created order tells us that there is a

---

[149] Ibid., 62–65, pp. 129–30.
[150] Ibid., 66–68, pp. 131–32.
[151] Ibid., 74, p. 132.
[152] Ibid., 40–43, pp. 124–25.

gap between nature and the human intellect, since the mind can separate by abstraction things that are conjoined in nature. This thought provides him with an analogy for the transference of our human way of thinking and speaking to the deity, and one which accents its limits. Affirmative statements about God, the author stresses, should not be understood literally. Thus, instead of trying to enforce a rigid grammatical parity between theological and non-theological language which simply does not work, he underscores instead the disparities between these two vocabularies and the necessarily partial, or metaphorical, significance of anything positive we say about God. This argument, as well as his case for the *via negativa*,[153] relies heavily on Dionysius. It reflects the author's marked alteration of Gilbert's semantics, although it is a change made in aid of Gilbert's metaphysics.

The author is also responsive to critics who had held that Gilbert's merely numerical distinction among the persons of the Trinity was not satisfactory. He abandons Gilbert on this point, in favor of a position that Gilbert had opposed, the idea that the Trinitarian persons manifest distinct properties which can be viewed as relations, especially paternity, filiation, and procession. Had the author stopped there, he would have been able to marshal powerful support from Augustine. But, throwing away that advantage, he compares these relations with accidents inhering extrinsically in a subject without changing its basic nature.[154] In this way, then, while the author seizes correctly on a weak feature of Gilbert's Trinitarian doctrine, his substitute position creates as many problems as it solves.

One final, and important, departure from Gilbert in *Invisibilia dei* can be seen in the sources on which the author relies. As noted, he draws on Dionysius in a thoroughly un-Gilbertian way. Equally striking is his total omission of Hilary of Poitiers, one of Gilbert's favorite authors. The source the author mines the most heavily is Boethius, also a favorite of Gilbert's, but he draws a more authentically Aristotelian logic from Boethius than Gilbert does. At the same time, there is an obvious point of connection between the author and Gilbert in the heavy stress on grammatical and logical analysis, of a specifically Gilbertian type, visible throughout the treatise. None the less, this dependence is coupled with the author's desire to jettison confusing Gilbertian terminology, to abandon Gilbertian

---

[153] Ibid., 44–45, pp. 125–26.
[154] Ibid., 124, 127–29, pp. 144–45.

positions that are hard to defend, and to find less controversial ways of carrying forward some of the essentials of Gilbert's project, in the teeth of criticism.

Still more noteworthy, in these respects, since they were written before the Council of Rheims had given Gilbert's theology its fullest notoriety, are the two early Porretan sentence collections composed in Paris shortly after the Parisian chapter of Gilbert's teaching career was ended by his move to the bishopric of Poitiers in 1142. We have encountered these sentence collections, framed as *reportationes* of Gilbert's teaching, in chapter 2 above, since they outline a full-blown course in systematic theology. As we have noted, the authors devote full and specific attention to the problem of theological language in their schemata, assigning the first of their fourteen books to that topic in general and considering its particular application to Trinitarian and Christological language in Books 2 and 3. Like the author of the *Invisibilia dei*, these early Porretan sentence collectors show how Gilbert's earliest pupils accepted, or altered, his semantics and its theological ramifications. Both of these authors are sensitive to the need to define the capacities and limits of theological language more clearly than Gilbert does. Both of them move away from a strict adherence to his terminology in favor of a more traditional vocabulary. They tend to agree with the substance of Gilbert's theology on the Trinity and on Christology, but think that the language in which he had advanced it is counterproductive, a fact indicating that these problems troubled Gilbert's followers no less than his critics, and that this was the case well before matters came to a head at Rheims. The authors' strategy is to replace Gilbert's lexicon with a more familiar one, a move which they justify in theory before they apply it in practice. In their prefatory remarks, they observe that theological language must be both true and apposite. Appositeness is to be found in words that derive from the authority of the saints (*ex aliqua auctoritate sanctorum*).[155] Newfangled, idiosyncratic terms (*novitates sermonum*) are to be shunned.[156] The authors follow this guideline by pointedly ignoring the vexed question of whether *deus* is *divinitas*, by avoiding

---

[155] Nikolaus M. Häring, ed., "Die *Sententie magistri Gisleberti Pictavensis episcopi* I" 1.1–2, *AHDLMA* 45 (1978): 108; "Die *Sententie magistri Gisleberti episcopi Pictavensis* II: Die Version der florentiner Handschrift" 1.1–4, *AHDLMA* 46 (1979): 46–47. John Marenbon, "A Note on the Porretani," in *A History of Twelfth-Century Western Philosophy*, ed. Peter Dronke (Cambridge: Cambridge University Press, 1988), p. 353 n. 2 does not discuss the content of these works.
[156] *Sent.* I 1.4, p. 108; *Sent.* II 2.35–36, pp. 53–54.

Gilbertian terms such as *subsistentia* and *subsistens*, and by employing language consistent with patristic usage. They also try valiantly, if not always successfully, to define clearly and to use consistently the terms they substitute for Gilbert's.

The authors observe that *substantia* has been applied both to the Trinitarian persons and to the divine essence They share. They are aware of the fact that, in Latin theology, substance has been used as a translation and synonym of *hypostasis* or person in Greek. But, in Greek theology, they note, substance means *ousia*, the single essence shared by the divine persons.[157] These authors go farther than any Latin theologians of the time before Peter Lombard in grasping this critical distinction. They decide, furthermore, to follow the Greek usage systematically, applying *substantia* to the unity of the divine essence exclusively. They can thus explain how the Greek term *homoousion* may be rendered by the Latin *consubstantialis*,[158] without getting bogged down in the different semantic functions of abstract and concrete nouns, or in the question of whether the properties of the Trinitarian persons are attributes comparable to those that modify created beings, which bedevils Gilbert's handling of this issue.

The early Porretans capitalize on this notable clarification of the idea of substance, but then, in their treatment of nature and person, they abandon the high ground they have won. Ignoring Gilbert's *subsistentia* and *subsistens* in connection with the two latter terms, they retain only his definition of a person as a *res per se una*. As to the semantic content of that formula, they state that personal properties are simply whatever properties distinguish one person from another. This argument shows that they, like Gilbert, are dissatisfied with Boethius's definition of a person as the individual substance of a rational nature. But, compared with Gilbert's floundering about on *persona* and his emergence with a formula which, as he frankly admits, is useless with respect to the Trinitarian persons, their own definition marks a salient improvement, since it places no restrictions on what the properties may be in different kinds of persons. The authors thus provide a term capable of being used appositely for divine and human persons alike.[159]

In contrast with Gilbert, who allies nature with person, our authors transfer *natura* decisively into the camp of *substantia* as essence, as they have already defined it. With these tools in hand,

---

[157] *Sent.* I 2.14, 2.36, pp. 110–11; *Sent.* II 2.1–4, pp. 47–48.
[158] *Sent.* I 2.6, p. 110; *Sent.* II 2.4, 2.6, p. 48.
[159] *Sent.* I 2.9, p. 112; *Sent.* II 2.9, p. 49.

one would expect them to arrive at a less ambiguous explanation of the hypostatic union than the one they in fact provide. With Gilbert, they argue that the incarnation did not produce a new *tertium quid*,[160] that the Word assumed simultaneously a human body and a human soul and not a preexisting human person,[161] and that, once the union had taken place, the divine and human components were not partible.[162] They also quote Gilbert's maxim, *"nec natura naturam nec persona personam nec natura personam sed persona naturam assumpsit."*[163] But, in support of this formula, they get ensnared in the reasoning which they offer in place of Gilbert's. Although they reiterate Gilbert's definition of a person as a *res per se una*, they fail to see why it provides the most economical answer to the question of why one person cannot assume another person. Instead of simply saying, as Gilbert does, that a duplex person is a contradiction in terms, the early Porretan response, which is not really explained, is that Christ's divinity would be diminished in the incarnation if one person had assumed another person.[164] Also, having annexed substance to nature, the authors find it hard to defend the idea that a nature did not take on another nature. Indeed, they argue at cross purposes against the principle they are trying to support at this juncture, by stating that there are two substances in the incarnate Christ, the divine *substantia* and the human *substantia vel natura*, equating the latter term with Christ's *humanitas* composed of body and soul.[165]

On the divine side, the difficulty with this vocabulary is apparent. It makes it impossible to explain why it was the Son Who was incarnated, rather than the Father or the Holy Spirit, since all three possess the same divine nature, substance, and essence. If this were not problematic enough, the early Porretans also appeal to the language of the school of Laon by saying that there are three substances in the incarnate Christ, the Word, a human body, and a human soul.[166] Aside from contradicting their own two-substance position, this claim muddies the distinction between nature and

---

[160] *Sent.* I 3.6, p. 123; *Sent.* II 3.6, p. 56.
[161] *Sent.* I 3.5, 3.10, p. 123; *Sent.* II 3.5, p. 56.
[162] *Sent.* I 3.16, p. 136; *Sent.* II 3.8–16, pp. 57–58.
[163] *Sent.* I 3.3, p. 122; *Sent.* II 3.3–5, p. 56.
[164] *Sent.* I 3.3, pp. 122–23.
[165] *Sent.* I 3.7, 3.10, pp. 123, 124; *Sent.* II 3.5, p. 56.
[166] *Sent.* I 3.16, p. 126. The author of *Sent.* II 3.7, p. 56, confines himself to the three-substance theory, thus regarding the body and soul of the human Christ as substances before they were united with each other and with the Word; he refers to them indifferently as substances and as natures.

person in the deity, a distinction on which the defense of the Gilbertian formula depends, while at the same time, it confuses the sense of *substantia* as that term applies to the infra-substantial physical and spiritual ingredients making up the man Jesus. To complicate matters still farther, one of the sentence collectors uses, indifferently, three phrases to describe the hypostatic union. The first is "a person assumes a nature" (*persona assumpsit naturam*), or, sometimes, "a person assumes human nature" (*persona assumpsit naturam humanam*). The second is "God was made man" (*deus homo factus est*). The third describes the union as "the conjunction of divinity and humanity" (*coniunctio divinitatis et humanitatis*).[167] The author quite evidently fails to see that, both in Gilbertian terms and in ordinary Latin, these propositions make different, and incompatible, claims. In addition, the third formula comes close to stating the principle, which both authors join Gilbert in rejecting, that, in the incarnation, a nature takes on a nature. So, while the goal of the early Porretans' handling of theological language is clearly to disembarrass Gilbert's teachings of Gilbert's terminology, they do not manage to attain this objective entirely.

THE LOMBARDIAN RESPONSE

Peter Lombard's position with respect to Gilbert and his early disciples is a twofold one. In his view, Gilbert, even more than Abelard, has locked himself into a vocabulary which, aside from being idiosyncratic and confusing, does not permit the kind of clear distinctions between God and creatures which Trinitarian and Christological theology demands. At the same time, Peter is perfectly willing to take a leaf from the book of the early Porretans, and to unshackle the Gilbertian doctrines of which he approves both from Gilbert's own terminology and from the lexical ambiguities still remaining in the language of his early disciples. Peter finds that the combined assistance of Augustine and Damascene is just as helpful in addressing this part of his agenda in the area of theological language as it is in refuting Abelard. He is deeply conscious of the need for a consistent, precise, and comprehensible language, whose semantic aptitudes and limits are clearly delineated and systematically applied. In positioning himself vis-à-vis Gilbert and the early Porretans, he rejects a view of the poverty of language so acute as to reduce all theological statements to metaphor or to

---

[167] *Sent.* I 3.16, 3.28, pp. 126, 128.

gibberish, or to the *via negativa*. On the other side, he rejects as arrogant and sophistic the claim that human linguistic conventions, new or old, can encompass the divine reality.[168] Peter's response is to use the traditional language of the creeds, under the guidance of patristic writers whose own approach to theological language is a speculative one, and who are able to explain what they mean by their terms in ways both wide and specific enough to enable language to function as it must function in theology, without forcing it into any one, preemptive, philosophical mold. In this connection, the criteria Peter invokes in making his choices are lucidity, consistency, and theological utility.

There are certain areas in which Peter follows Gilbert's lead. He agrees with Gilbert that God is a radically simple being, in contrast with creatures that may be composite, physical, and modified by accidents. Following the Porretan sentence collectors, but with more rigor, he annexes the terms substance, nature, and essence, as the Latin parallels of the Greek *ousia*, to the divine nature viewed in its absolute unity and simplicity, making use of Damascene to clarify and to expand on a point which they had not been able to elaborate in such detail.[169] Peter also explains the advantages of a doctrine of God that includes His operations as well as His essence, which had inspired the author of the *Invisibilia dei* to reimport Augustine into the discussion. But, drawing on Damascene here as well, Peter takes the argument much farther. He grounds it on two complementary contrasts. The first is the contrast between God's immutability and the changeable world of nature. The second is the contrast between the enduring, unconditioned, differentiation and coinherence of the unmanifested Trinity and the ways in which God manifests Himself, as the Godhead primarily, in the economy of His creation and redemption.[170] Both of these contrasts are based on eternity as a central attribute of God, a principle that allows Peter to dispose of Gilbert's objections to Augustine and to specify

---

[168] Peter Lombard, *Sent.* 1. d. 23. c. 1.3, 1: 182; *Tractatus de Incarnatione* 1.6, 1.8, 1.9.1–2, ed. Ignatius C. Brady in *Sent.* 2: 59*, 60*, 61*–63*. This latter text incorporates parts of Peter's commentary on St. Paul that were subjected to revision in the light of his later teaching in the *Sentences*.

[169] Peter Lombard, *Sent.* 1. d. 2. c. 1–c. 3, d. 3. c. 4, d. 4. c. 2.1–4, d. 8. c. 8.31, d. 19. c. 7–c. 10, d. 23 c. 3.1, c. 4.2, d. 25. c. 1.1, c. 2.2–5, d. 27. c. 3.1, d. 33. c. 1.3, 1: 60–63, 67, 77, 79–80, 103, 165–69, 182, 185, 190, 192–94, 205, 241.

[170] Ibid., 1. d. 3. c. 1.5, d. 8. c. 4–c. 7, c. 8.1–3, d. 19. c. 2, d. 34. c. 4.2, 1: 70, 98–101, 101–03, 160, 253. The issue, as Peter sees it, involves more than a stress on God's immutability as a means of mediating between Bernard of Clairvaux and Gilbert. Cf. Bertola, "Il problema di Dio," pp. 135–50.

the limits, as well as the powers, of Augustine's psychological analogies. The relations among the persons of the Trinity, he shows, are not passing accidents but are personal properties structured permanently into the eternal inner life of the Trinity.[171] And, man's way of knowing willing, remembering, and loving, to which the functions of the Trinitarian persons can be compared, is time-bound, sequential, and rooted in a body. Between the conception, the desire, and the consummation falls the shadow, for man, but not for the timeless Trinity.[172] Peter thus emerges with a stable lexicon with which he can articulate and address metaphysical issues in Trinitarian theology ignored by the shriller critics of Gilbert, and one which enables him to explain the differences between God and creatures and the distinctions in the personal properties of the Father, Son, and Holy Spirit better than Gilbert and his followers.

Peter also eliminates some of the problems in the language which Gilbert and the early Porretans had used in the field of Christology. His substantive position is much closer to Gilbert's in this area than it is in his Trinitarian theology. With Gilbert, Peter maintains that Christ did not assume a preexistent human person but a human body and a human soul, "the soul and body in which man subsists" (*anima et caro in quibus subsistit homo*), which were not conjoined prior to their union with the Word, which were assumed by Christ at the same time, and which remained united to Him thereafter.[173] With Gilbert and the Porretan sentence collectors, as well as Walter of Mortagne and Robert of Melun, he rejects the Boethian definition of person as the individual substance of a rational nature, both as objectionable in and of itself and as a way of criticizing Abelard, maintaining that neither man's soul nor his body can denominate his whole person. Peter uses this same argument to support a claim which the earlier Porretans and the author of the *Sententiae divinitatis* had made, but had not defended, the idea that we may use either *homo, humana natura* or *humanitas* to denote the infra-personal human components assumed by Christ. As Peter

---

[171] Peter Lombard, *Sent.* 1. d. 22. c. 5, d. 24. c. 8, d. 25. c. 3.3–4, d. 26. c. 3.1, c. 8, d. 27. c. 2.3, d. 30. c. 1.1–7, d. 33. c. 1.1–10, c. 3.3–5, d. 34. c. 1.1–9, 1: 179–80, 189, 195, 203, 204–05, 220–22, 240–43, 245–46, 246–50.

[172] Ibid., 1. d. 3. c. 2–c. 3.8, d. 19. c. 3–c. 4, 1: 72–76, 161–63.

[173] *Tract. de Inc.* 1.31, 2: 75*; see also *Sent.* 3. d. 2. c. 1.1–c. 3.1, d. 3. c. 4.2–4, d. 5. c. 1.1, c. 2.1, c. 3.1, 2: 28–29, 30–31, 36–37, 41, 46, 47. This point has been brought out well by Landgraf, *Dogmengeschichte*, 2 part 1; 84–89, 136–37; Jean Longère, *Oeuvres oratoires des maîtres parisiens au XIIe siècle: Étude historique et doctrinale*, 2 vols. (Paris, Études Augustiniennes, 1975), 1:83–85.

sees it, in this particular context, it would be as mistaken to restrict the appositeness of any of these terms as it would be to deny that the incarnate Christ possessed a human soul. He links this semantic directive to an economic argument derived from Damascene, which permits him to expand on an important corollary of the hypostatic union to which the Porretans gave short shrift. Just as Christ assumed both a body and a soul, in order that both body and soul might be redeemed, so the consubstantiality of the incarnate Christ with other human beings denoted by the terms *humana natura* and *humanitas* serves as a bridge between His own identity as a human being and His redemption of mankind. Looked at as a phenomenon of created nature, that is to say, the human Christ is both a unique individual man and a member of the human race. Thus, it is appropriate to use both *homo* and *humanitas* to refer to His *humana natura*.[174]

Peter gives thorough consideration to Gilbert's view that a person assumes a nature in the incarnation, which he supports. But he rings several changes on this theme, on the basis of the distinction he draws between a divine *persona* and a human *persona*. For Peter, a divine person enjoys consubstantiality with the divine nature or essence as such. On the other hand, a human person cannot be equated with or exhausted by his *humanitas*. Peter's contrast between a Trinity in which the addition of another person to a person already there does not yield "more God," and the quantitative enlargement that occurs when one item is added to another member of the same genus already present, is to be remembered here. Aside from this basic difference between divine persons and human persons, the incarnate Christ does not possess a human *persona* for Peter any more than He does for Gilbert. Thus, it is correct to say that a person assumes a nature in the incarnation. Peter, like Gilbert, rejects Adoptionism. But, since he gives a clearer and fuller content to *natura* on the human side of Christ's constitution, he has a better defense against the charge of Christological nihilianism, in that it is *aliquid natura*,[175] and on two human levels, individual and generic, that the Word took on humanity in the incarnation.

---

[174] Peter Lombard, *Tract. de Inc.* 1.4, 2: 58*; *Sent*, 3. d. 2. c. 1.4, c. 2, d. 5. c. 3.2–4, 2: 28–29, 47–49. Cf. Schneider, *Die Lehre*, pp. 118–23, who argues incorrectly that Peter departs from Gilbert in supporting this Boethian definition of *persona*.

[175] Peter Lombard, *Sent.* 3. d. 10. c. 1–c. 2, 2: 72–76. This point has been noted correctly by Brady, *ad loc.*, p. 73 n. 1 and in his "Peter Manducator and the Oral Teachings of Peter Lombard," *Antonianum* 41 (1966): 454–79; Elswijk, *Gilbert Porreta*, p. 417; Nielsen, *Theology and Philosophy*, pp. 261–74.

Peter also agrees that the divine nature cannot take on a person, since what Christ assumed was infra-personal. Nor can a person be a composite. At the same time, Peter accepts the idea, which Gilbert rejects, that the divine nature can take on a human nature. As Peter understands this idea, he associates it with a principle he shares with Gilbert, the notion that no *tertium quid* results from the hypostatic union; the properties of the two natures are not blended or confused. He offers two arguments in support of this idea. First, in the case of the divine Christ, the fullness of the divine nature dwells in His divine person. And second, in the case of the human Christ, *natura* denotes adequately the infra-personal components that are united to the Word as well as the human Christ's more general connection with the rest of mankind. Peter's preferred formula for describing the hypostatic union is to say that "the person of the Son assumed human nature, and that the divine nature was joined with a human nature united in the Son" (*et personam Filii assumpsisse naturam humanam, et naturam divinam humanae naturae in Filio unitam*).[176] Given the care with which Peter defines and uses his terms, the meaning of this language to him, and to the reader, is perfectly clear. Adding to his elucidation of the hypostatic union his clarification of the term *persona* and a soteriological concern not found in Gilbert, Peter joins him in rejecting any notion of the communication of idioms in the incarnate Christ that would denature the divine and human components or treat them as partible or as accidental.

There is one other major area in which Peter's familiarity with the language of both Gilbert and the early Porretans enables him to clarify and to correct a confusing pair of opinions which he himself had shared with the latter masters, along with Robert Pullen in one case and along with the school of Laon, Robert, and the *Summa sententiarum* in the other, but which he rejects decisively in his *Sentences*. One is the view that the incarnate Christ can be understood as possessing three substances, the Word, a human body, and a human soul.[177] The other is the idea that the incarnate Christ has two substances, divinity and humanity.[178] The encounter with Gilbert and his disciples made Peter realize that the twin-substance

---

[176] Peter Lombard, *Sent.* 3. d. 5. c. 1.10, 2: 45. For the whole passage, see *Tract. de Inc.* 1.4, 1.14–21; *Sent.* 3. d. 5. c. 1.2–12, 2: 57*–58*, 64*–68*, 42–46.
[177] Peter Lombard, *Sermo* 43, *PL* 171: 559B–C.
[178] Peter Lombard, *Sermo* 7, 9, 12, 55, 99, *PL* 171: 371C, 382A, 396A, 605D–606B, 806B. The same *gemina substantia* language occurs in Peter Lombard, *In Epistolam Pauli ad Romanos* 1:3, *PL* 191: 1307C.

language, despite its Augustinian roots, was not acceptable, because it might imply that there was no difference between the person of the Son and the divine substance which He shares with the Father and the Holy Spirit. At the same time, it might suggest that the human Christ was a human substance, that is, a human person already in existence when He was joined to the Word.[179] As for the three-substance theory, Peter concludes that it too must be abandoned, because it involves an improper attribution of *substantia* to the infra-substantial body and soul that the Word assumes.[180]

In these several ways, Peter Lombard reflects a certain dependence upon Gilbert and the Porretans, even as he seeks to criticize their use of theological language. In substance, Peter's Christology has more in common with Gilbert's than it does with the Christology of any of his other contemporaries. He is a critic of Gilbert's Trinitarian theology. Peter joins Robert of Melun in going beyond the narrow Aristotelian understanding of the idea of relation, taught by Gilbert and others, expanding on and refining this point in comparison with Robert. In specifying the positive content of the properties of the Trinitarian persons, he makes far more pointed the application of the Augustinian argument based on the analysis of relative nouns. Peter also does more than any of his contemporaries to expose the limits of Gilbert's numerical handling of that subject, as well as the treatment given to it by his would-be critics in the school of Chartres. Even in those areas where he disagrees with Gilbert and his disciples, however, he has learned from them how to pose many of the issues which they raise concerning the language appropriate to the speculative doctrines of the Christian faith, where theological terminology is so crucial. The very difficulties embedded in Gilbert's own lexicon, which provoked the clarifications and retrenchments made by his pupils, were also an indirect inspiration to the Lombard in his own quest for alternative language that was understandable and that was adequate to the assignments that theologians needed to impose upon it. In this respect, the questions raised by Gilbert and the Porretans were fully as important as those raised by Abelard, in setting the agenda to which Peter responded in developing his own constructive address to the problem of theological language. Thanks to his efforts, to the extent that twelfth century scholastics attained a

---

[179] Peter Lombard, *Sent.* 3. d. 6. c. 3.5, d. 7. c. 1.13–17, 2: 54, 63–64.
[180] Ibid., 3. d. 2. c. 2.4, d. 6. c. 2.5, c. 3.1, c. 3.6, d. 7. c. 1.4–9, 2: 29, 51, 52–53, 54, 60–62.

common theological vocabulary capable of performing its doctrinal tasks prior to the reception of Aristotle, that outcome was a consequence of the Lombard's ability to meet the challenges made by Gilbert and Abelard more successfully than anyone else at the time.

CHAPTER FOUR

SACRA PAGINA

There is no doubt that medieval Christian thinkers saw the Bible as the book of books and its study as the discipline of disciplines. Nor is there any question of the privileged position which exegetes in the twelfth century, as in previous centuries, gave to certain portions of the biblical text. In the Old Testament, their favorite section was the Book of Psalms, and in the New Testament, it was the Epistles of St. Paul. The Psalms were seen as a guide to the Christian life, while St. Paul was appreciated for the doctrinal richness of his teachings and was revered as a model theologian. In the first half of the twelfth century, these two subdivisions of the Bible received more sustained attention than did any other parts of the Old and New Testaments. They now did so, however, from more than one quarter. The twelfth century continued to witness interest in both the Psalms and St. Paul on the part of monastic exegetes. As had always been the case, their goal remained to excite unction and compunction in the minds of their monastic audience, and their treatment of these texts drew on the meditative and homiletic techniques embedded in monastic *lectio divina*. At the same time, the emergence of scholastic theology in the first half of the century created a new demand for a different kind of biblical exegesis, a more systematic and detached study of the text geared to the needs of doctrinal debate, and to the training of professional theologians. The scholastics seized on the Psalms and St. Paul for these purposes. For them, these portions of the Bible were not only key sources of Christian doctrine, whether moral or dogmatic, but also complex and composite segments of Holy Scripture whose interpretation often required the help of other resources. Further, the relation of the parts to each other, and to the whole, demanded investigation. Hence, the exegesis of the Psalms and the Pauline epistles were a test case for the developing hermeneutic principles which the professionalizing of the liberal arts, no less than the professionalizing of theology itself, brought to the fore in the reading of the biblical text.[1]

---

[1] The best introduction to this subject is Jean Châtillon, "La Bible dans les écoles du XII⁰ siècle," in *Le moyen âge et la Bible*, ed. Pierre Riché and Guy

Among these scholastic exegetes of the Psalms and St. Paul in the first half of the twelfth century, Peter Lombard holds pride of place. Like his *Sentences*, Peter's commentary on the Psalms, composed before 1138, and his *Collectanea*, or commentary on Paul, written between 1139 and 1141, became instant classics in their own sphere. In the schools of theology they at once became the most frequently cited, copied, and studied exegetical works produced in the twelfth century. Peter's exegesis was swiftly dubbed the *Magna glossatura*, outpacing both the earlier *Glossa ordinaria* of the school of Laon and the *Media glossatura* of Gilbert of Poitiers, as well as contemporary and immediately subsequent Pauline glosses, whether of Abelardian, Porretan, or Victorine provenance.[2] Peter's commentary on the Psalms likewise decisively replaced the Psalms gloss of Gilbert of Poitiers and that of the *Glossa ordinaria* as the

---

Lobrichon (Paris: Beauchesne, 1984), pp. 163–97. See also Heinrich Denifle, "Quel livre servait de base à l'enseignement des maîtres en théologie dans l'Université de Paris?" *Revue thomiste* 2 (1898): 149–61; Artur Michael Landgraf, *Introduction à l'histoire de la littérature théologique de la scolastique naissante*, ed. Albert-M. Landry, trans. Louis-B. Geiger (Montreal: Institut d'Études Médiévales, 1973), p. 47; Beryl Smalley, *The Study of the Bible in the Middle Ages*, 2nd ed. rev. (New York: Philosophical Library, 1952), ch. 1–4; "L'Exégèse biblique du 12ᵉ siècle," in *Entretiens sur la renaissance du 12ᵉ siècle*, ed. Maurice de Gandillac and Édouard Jeauneau (Paris: Mouton, 1968), pp. 273–83; "The Bible in the Medieval Schools," in *Cambridge History of the Bible: The West from the Fathers to the Reformation*, ed. G. W. H. Lampe (Cambridge: Cambridge University Press, 1969), 2: 197–220; Gillian R. Evans, *The Language and Logic of the Bible: The Earlier Middle Ages* (Cambridge: Cambridge University Press, 1984); Wilfried Hartmann, "Psalmenkommentare aus den Zeit der Reform und Frühscholastik," *Studi Gregoriani* 9 (1972): 313–66. A good summary of monastic exegesis is provided by Jean Leclercq, "Écrits monastiques sur la Bible aux IXᵉ–XII³ siècle," *MS* 15 (1953): 95–106. Older but still useful guides include Artur Michael Landgraf, "Zur Methode der biblischen Textkritik im 12. Jahrhundert," *Biblica* 10 (1929): 445–74; "Familienbildung bei Paulinenkommentaren des 12. Jahrhunderts," *Biblica* 13 (1932): 61–72, 164–93; "Untersuchungen zu den Paulinenkommentaren des 12. Jahrhunderts," *RTAM* 8 (1936): 345–68.

  [2] H. H. Glunz, *History of the Vulgate in England from Alcuin to Roger Bacon: Being an Inquiry into the Text of Some English Manuscripts of the Vulgate Gospels* (Cambridge: Cambridge University Press, 1933), pp. 219–24; Châtillon, "La Bible dans les écoles," pp. 192–93; Jacques-Guy Bougerol, *La théologie de l'espérance aux XIIᵉ et XIIIᵉ siècles* (Paris: Études Augustiniennes, 1985), 1; 9; Werner Affeldt, *Die weltliche Gewalt in der Paulus-Exegese: Röm. 13, 1–7 in den Römerbriefkommentaren der lateinischen Kirche bis zum Ende des 13. Jahrhunderts* (Göttingen: Vandenhoeck & Ruprecht, 1969), p. 138; Z. Alszeghy, *Nova creatura: La nozione della grazia nei commentari medievali di S. Paolo* (Rome: Universitas Gregoriana, 1956), pp. 8–11, 23–24; Guy Lobrichon, "Une nouveauté: Les gloses de la Bible," in *Le moyen âge et la Bible*, ed. Pierre Riché and Guy Lobrichon (Paris: Beauchesne, 1984), pp. 109–10. These authors correct the position, stated by Smalley, *Study*, pp. 51, 64–65 and Margaret T. Gibson, *Lanfranc of Bec* (Oxford: Clarendon Press, 1978), pp. 54–61, who stress the continuities between the *Glossa ordinaria* and Peter Lombard's exegesis to the point of obscuring his differences from his predecessors.

scholastic commentary of choice, in a field marked by fewer competitors, for this portion of the Old Testament. While all the medieval testimonials to the Lombard's fame mention these two works side by side with the *Sentences* as his chief contributions to learning, he was known in some quarters, even beyond the schools, as an exegete primarily. The anonymous author of a book list compiled by a monk in the diocese of Arras in the last third of the twelfth century, who attaches comments to the titles he catalogues, has this to say about him:

> Peter Lombard, the Parisian scholastic, later bishop of the same city, is judged to be preferred most greatly over all the masters of his time and expositors of the Scriptures because, thanks to the sharpness of his intellect and the assiduousness of his labor, he shed light on so many things in explaining the Scriptures that the teaching of the doctors has become merely the glossing of his readings and the effort to understand his teachings.[3]

In grasping why that outcome was the case, the Lombard's handling of the Psalms and the Pauline epistles, in comparison with the other scholastics of his time who glossed these texts, will reveal what most scholastic readers wanted out of biblical exegesis and why they preferred his work to its alternatives. The scholastic exegetes with whom Peter will be compared are those falling within the period ca. 1115 to ca. 1160. In the case of Psalms exegesis, there are more apparent connections between monastic and scholastic authors than is true for the glosses on St. Paul, and so a swift comparison between these two groups of authors will be made as well, to indicate their similarities and differences.

Of these two segments of the Bible, the Book of Psalms had a far more extensive tradition of commentary from the patristic period up to the twelfth century. Many more commentaries on Psalms were produced by twelfth-century monks than commentaries on St. Paul, for the obvious reason that the glossing of Psalms could be and was seen as an adjunct to the chanting of the Psalter in the monastic liturgy. The Psalms continued to be read, and meditated upon, as a source of moral edification by the monks, as well as being read typologically, pointing ahead to the life and teachings of

---

[3] Nikolaus M. Häring, "Two Catalogues of Medieval Authors," *FS* 26 (1966): 211: "Petrus Langobardus scholasticus Parisiensis, postea eiusdem civitatis episcopus, magistri sui temporis et Scripturarum expositoribus eo maxime preferendus iudicatur quod ingenio sagaci et usu assiduo tanta in exponendis Scripturis luce claruerit ut pene magisterio doctoris non egeat qui glosarum ipsius lectioni animum intendere voluerit." For the date and provenance of this catalogue, see pp. 195–97, 206–08.

Christ in the New Testament. To this older agenda, inherited from patristic times, the twelfth-century scholastics attached a new interest. To be sure, the scholastics retained the practice of reading the Psalms polysemously, with an eye to both ethics and Christology. The new perspective they brought to the Psalms was the desire to understand this book of the Bible in conjunction with systematic theology. They brought to it and read out of it a concern with dogmatic topics and an interest in evaluating the interpretations given to the text by the earlier authorities, Anglo-Saxon and Carolingian as well as patristic, helped in some cases by methods of thought derived from the study of the liberal arts.[4]

PSALMS EXEGESIS: THE MONASTIC APPROACH

The continuities and discontinuities between monastic and scholastic Psalms exegesis in our period can be illustrated clearly by four examples, chosen from a range of monastic authors who wrote both before and after Peter Lombard. The works selected for this comparison are those by Letbert of Lille, Bruno the Carthusian, Pseudo-Bruno of Würzburg, and Gerhoch of Reichersberg. These authors express a variety of forms of contemporary monasticism, ranging from the older Black Monks to a representative of a new, reformed order. The comparison also draws on men who received their education in the convent and on one who taught as a secular master at a leading cathedral school before entering the monastery. Without in any way exhausting the possibilities among monastic expositors of the Psalms in the first half of the twelfth century, these four will give us a representative sampling of them.

Letbert of Lille, whose *In Psalmos LXXV commentarius* was written in ca. 1100–10,[5] clearly addresses his work to his fellow monks, urging them, in his gloss on Psalm 45:11, to use meditation on this text as a means of focusing their attention on their cloistered calling and turning away from worldly concerns.[6] While Letbert addresses Christological and ecclesiological issues, the balance of his exegesis is weighted more toward tropology than toward typology; he centers on the personal moral message which the text holds for the individual monastic reader. Letbert offers no *accessus* to the Book of

---

[4] Hartmann, "Psalmenkommentare," pp. 313–66.

[5] For Letbert's biography and the date of his work, see A. Wilmart, "Le commentaire sur les Psaumes imprimé sous le nom de Rufin," *R. bén.* 31 (1914–19): 258–76.

[6] Letbert of Lille, *In Psalmos LXXV commentarius* 45:11, *PL* 21: 830C–D. This text is printed among the works of Rufinus of Aquileia.

Psalms as a whole and gives a brief introduction only to a few individual Psalms. He glosses each verse of the text, frequently bringing in other books of the Bible to help explicate it. Letbert does not mention overtly any of the many patristic authorities on whom he draws. In this sense, his commentary is a veritable catena of unacknowledged patristic readings. Augustine is a favorite of his. He never discusses the readings of these authorities and sometimes ignores the fact that they may provide alternative interpretations of the same biblical passage.[7] Occasionally he garbles his patristic citations. But, principally, they are used as *scholia* to clear up confusing references in the text, or as theological authorities who answer questions and who thus close off discussion of them.

Another monastic exegete of the Psalms, but one who displays a familiarity with some of the developments occurring beyond the walls of the convent, is Bruno the Carthusian. His *Expositio in Psalmos* was probably written between 1141 and 1154,[8] after he had become a Carthusian. It has a decidedly monastic flavor, although Bruno's concern with current events and the range of his reading may reflect a carryover of the mentality of the secular master he had earlier been at the cathedral school of Rheims.[9] An index of his scholastic background is a mode of handling authorities that is rather more sophisticated than that of Letbert. Bruno brings in non-Christian as well as patristic sources.[10] He does note occasions when authorities disagree or when a single authority gives more than one reading of the same line, and makes his own selection. But, in such passages, he does not explain the reasons informing these choices.[11] Bruno tends to cite authorities very sparingly and in an essentially decorative way, at times to provide *scholia* on difficult words or phrases but largely to sum up aptly a point he wants to make. He also takes pains to criticize unnamed "philosophers" who draw Plato into their disputes about the Trinity, although without indicating why he thinks this is inappropriate. He praises, instead, ecclesiastical leaders who take pedagogical initiatives by travelling about to share their teachings. The example of

---

[7] A good example is at Ps. 70:15, *PL* 21: 934C, where the alternative readings are ignored.

[8] Damien Van den Eynde, "Complementary Note on the Early Scholastic Commentarii in Psalmos," *FS* 17 (1957): 149–72. Van den Eynde's dating has been contested by Valerie I. J. Flint, "Some Notes on the Early Twelfth-Century Commentaries on the Psalms," *RTAM* 38 (1971): 80–88.

[9] Châtillon, "La Bible," pp. 173–75.

[10] Bruno the Carthusian, *Expositio in Psalmos* 73, *PL* 152: 1009B. Here, his authority is Josephus.

[11] Bruno the Carthusian, *In Ps.* 77, 91, *PL* 152: 1045D–1049A, 1130A–C.

Dionysius the Areopagite in France, which he gives to illustrate this latter group, suggests a veiled attack on Peter Abelard.[12] More central to Bruno than these sallies is the monastic focus of his commentary. His style is hortatory. He sometimes poses rhetorical questions as if speaking aloud, suggesting that the text was written for, or redacted from, an oral exposition. He refers to his readers as hearers, *auditores*.[13] Further, in his prologue, he compares the Psalms with musical instruments, with which man sings God's praises, treating the text as an adjunct to the liturgical chanting of the Psalms in the monastic *opus dei*.[14] He does not comment on every passage of every Psalm but freely refers to lines that he does not gloss, reflecting his assumption that the entire Psalter is in the minds and ears of his audience. Bruno indicates that the text bears several levels of meaning, the historical, the typological, the moral, and the mystical.[15] In practice, he gives scant attention to the historical sense and to the typological. The role of such events in the life of Christ to which the Psalms may point is to teach the reader how to act and how to pray, to incite his piety and devotion.[16] In this case, then, the author, despite his scholastic background, gives pride of place to his monastic orientation.

The contrast between monastic and scholastic Psalms exegesis can be seen even more clearly in the next two examples. Pseudo-Bruno of Würzburg wrote his *Expositio Psalmorum* in ca. 1150, well after the glosses of Peter Lombard and of other scholastic commentators. He draws on their work, selecting what he wants from them and ignoring what he finds uninteresting or irrelevant. In that latter category he includes the identification of the authorities they cite and the analysis which they apply to these citations. What he does, instead, is to content himself with their conclusions, incorporating them into his own largely moral exegesis. The place the author accords to the Psalms in the context of the monastic life is vividly indicated in his offering of a prayer, reflecting on the message of the Psalm just discussed, at the end of each of his glosses, as well as by his prayerful ejaculations inserted here and there in the body of the gloss itself. The same focus is also reflected in the conclusions he draws and in the allusions he makes. In glossing Psalm 86:4 on the subject of vigils, he reads the text as a criticism of

---

[12] Ibid., 106, *PL* 152: 1205B–C, 1211D.
[13] Ibid., 105, *PL* 152: 1198B.
[14] Ibid., prologus, *PL* 152: 637B–638B.
[15] Ibid., *PL* 152: 638B–639A.
[16] A good example is ibid., 21, *PL* 152: 723C.

monks who fail to maintain their alertness at the night services;[17] and he repeatedly praises monastic *simplicitas* over secular learning, seen as the secular folly which monks should leave behind them.[18] Likewise, he thinks that the swallows mentioned in Psalm 103:18 signify "*monachorum parvitatem*," the deliberately chosen powerlessness of monks who have rejected the inheritance of the mighty, while the swallows' nest signifies the monastery itself, built so that its inhabitants can sing God's praises.[19] Clearly, the Pseudo-Bruno's aim is to draw on and to simplify the work of his predecessors, while applying it to the stimulation of collective and individual monastic devotion.

Another monastic example who was familiar with the scholastic as well as the monastic glosses on the Psalms and who produced the lengthiest commentary of the century on this Old Testament book is Gerhoch of Reichersberg. His *Expositiones in Psalmorum*, dating to between 1144 and 1167/68, is likewise aimed at the edification of monks and canons and the enrichment of their prayer life. But it also tackles another aspect of the monastic agenda, the improvement of the quality of religious life in the cloisters of the older monastic orders. Hence, Gerhoch seeks to harness Psalms exegesis to the reform of moral and institutional problems within the contemporary church.[20] While he pays some attention to the typological reading of the Psalms, his accent is ethical and his style is homiletic. He cites both recent and contemporary authors, in large chunks, scholastic and monastic alike, as well as patristic and classical authors. Sometimes the authorship of these citations is mis-attributed; sometimes the citations are to the point and at other times not. The most noticeable stylistic feature of Gerhoch's exposition is extensive digression. These digressions are not scholastic-type *quaestiones* inspired by the biblical text but examples of the author's tendency toward free association. Subjects on which he expatiates, which may or may not be connected with the themes in the Psalms being glossed, include the liturgy, ethics, ecclesiastical and monastic discipline, canon law, history sacred and profane, legends, anecdotes, current events, and dogma. In the latter case, Gerhoch takes up some dogmatic points controverted at the time

---

[17] Pseudo-Bruno of Würzburg, *Expositio Psalmorum* 86:4, *PL* 142: 287C.

[18] Ibid., 70:17, 91:6, 93:8, *PL* 142: 268A, 341C, 345C.

[19] Ibid., 103:18, *PL* 142: 373D.

[20] Good general orientations on this work are provided by Peter Classen, *Gerhoch von Reichersberg: Eine Biographie* (Wiesbaden: Franz Steiner Verlag, 1960), pp. 114–21 and Damien Van den Eynde, *L'Oeuvre littéraire de Géroch de Reichersberg* (Rome: Antonianum, 1957), pp. 291–329.

on which he takes a stand, such as the contritionist-confessionist debate concerning penance. Here, he clearly sides with the confessionists, attacking contritionism as a Greek heresy.[21] Sometimes his doctrinal observations reinforce the current consensus, as in his remarks on the need for human collaboration with God's grace in man's justification and in the remission of his sins.[22] But doctrinal excurses of this sort do not reflect an effort on Gerhoch's part to develop a theology out of Psalms or to work out the relationship between the content of any one of the Psalms and the theology of the Psalter more generally. Rather, they reflect the fact that, as an exegete, he has a mind like a grab-bag. He has a tendency to get sidetracked all too easily. This digressive trait is more evident in the earlier sections of his commentary, which are much fuller in all respects than are the later sections. By the time he reaches the end of the gloss, Gerhoch appears to have run out of steam, and contents himself with citing authorities, whether acknowledged or not, one after the other, without even writing any continuity between them.

PRE-LOMBARDIAN SCHOLASTIC PSALMS EXEGESIS

The scholastic glosses on the Psalms dating to our target period have a decidedly different appearance, as can be seen by a consideration of the three most important precursors of Peter Lombard in this connection, the Pseudo-Bede, the *Glossa ordinaria*, and Gilbert of Poitiers. The identity of the Pseudo-Bede is not known, but internal references in his work to contemporary events, such as the investiture controversy, enable us to date it to the turn of the twelfth century. The fact that the author is a school theologian is visible in the technicality of the doctrinal issues he discusses, whether as central points in his exegesis or as excursuses on the Psalms. He displays a notable tendency to make logical distinctions and to use grammatical analysis, as well as to draw widely on patristic and classical authors.[23] One striking feature of the Pseudo-

---

[21] Gerhoch of Reichersberg, *Expositionis in Psalmarum* 31:5, in *Opera inedita*, 2 vols in 3, ed. Damien and Odulph Van den Eynde and Angelinus Rijmensdael, with Peter Classen (Rome: Antonianum 1955–56), 2 part 1: 52–56.

[22] Ibid., 31:1, 2 part 1: 6.

[23] A good general description is provided by G. Morin, "Le pseudo-Bède sur les Psaumes et l'*Opus super Psaltarium* de maître Manegold de Lautenbach," *R. bén* 28 (1911): 331–40. See also Bernhard Bischoff, "Zur Kritik der Heerwagenschen Ausgabe von Bedas Werken (Basel, 1563)," in *Mittalterliche Studien: Ausgewählte Aufsätze zur Schriftkunde und Literaturgeschichte* (Stuttgart: Anton Hiersemann, 1966), 1:112–17. I would like to thank Dr. Margaret T. Gibson for this last reference.

Bede that sets him apart from the monastic exegetes and that also reveals his scholastic colors is his interest in the Book of Psalms as a part of the Bible and in the question of authorship connected to it. Is the Book of Psalms a single book, as Cassiodorus says, or five books brought together under one heading, as Jerome maintains? The author holds that this is a single book, although one written, as Hilary of Poitiers states, by several different authors, as is clear from the headings to each individual Psalm.[24] This conclusion reveals an exegete who does not hesitate to engage in controversy, for the more typical view of the authorship of the Psalms, Jerome and Hilary excepted, from the rest of the church fathers up through the scholastic exegetes of the early twelfth century, was that David had written them all.[25]

After a lengthy introduction to the Book of Psalms as a whole, the Pseudo-Bede gives a brief explanation of each Psalm before commenting on it. His exegesis accents overall themes. He considers each Psalm as a whole, and, once he has indicated what it is saying in general, he confines himself to lemmatizing the few phrases in each that may present difficulties. He agrees that the Psalms bear a historical, moral, and mystical meaning. But it is the typological significance of the text, especially its Christological dimensions, that attract his primary attention. The breadth of his reading is visible in the range of authorities he cites, as is his attitude. He urges that philosophers have much of value to say on the immortality of the soul,[26] and cites *scholia* from Horace, Lucan, and Macrobius.[27] His patristic authorities, however, are infrequently cited by name and are treated as scholiasts more than as theologians. Pseudo-Bede does not systematically adduce authorities and investigate the reasoning behind their conflicting readings or interpretations. He tends to offer the opinions he takes from them without analysis, as his own position. Sometimes he presents an alternative reading but without indicating where it comes from and whether it is compatible with the other reading or readings he has given, and, if not, what reasons exist for choosing among them. There are other areas in which the Pseudo-Bede, for all his evident contributions, would be found wanting by a scholastic reader. In a substantial number of cases, Psalms 94 through 100 and Psalms

---

[24] Pseudo-Bede, *De Psalmorum libro exegesis* prologus, *PL* 93: 477B–D.

[25] I am indebted to Theresa Gross-Diaz, in a personal communication of April 5, 1990, for this information.

[26] Pseudo Bede, *In Ps.* 87, *PL* 93: 960B.

[27] Ibid., 9, 34, 89, 103, *PL* 93: 541C–D, 655D, 966C, 1005B.

112 through 150, the author gives no commentary at all apart from his introductory summary of the Psalm. And, in making theological excurses from the text, his position is as noncommittal as it is unexceptional. He does not take sides on the doctrines expounded.

Another important precursor of Peter Lombard's commentary on the Psalms, and one that had an impressive shelf-life in the twelfth century and after among readers whose needs were often less professionally oriented than those of the scholastic theologians, is the *Glossa ordinaria*, composed by Anselm of Laon and his associates between ca. 1080 and ca. 1130.[28] It is not known when, during that period, the gloss on the Psalms was produced, or who the glossator responsible for it was. In its appearance, the *Glossa ordinaria* offers a marked contrast both with the work of the Pseudo-Bede and with that of Gilbert of Poitiers and that of the Lombard, in that it does not take the form of a continuous commentary. Rather, it is a text of the Bible supplied with interlinear and marginal glosses. The glossator opens his commentary with a flourish, giving Jerome's preface to the Book of Psalms. He then quotes Jerome, Cassiodorus, Augustine, and Remigius of Auxerre on the nature of the Psalms, what the number of Psalms signifies, their sequence, and the idea, taken from Augustine, that they should be read with a Christological reference, or with reference to the church and the kinds of people who comprise it. For these various categories of people, the Psalms offer moral guidance on what is required for penance, justice, and eternal life.[29]

The glossator neither comments on each verse, nor does he give

---

[28] On the authorship of the *Glossa ordinaria*, the seminal work was done by Beryl Smalley, *Study*, pp. 46–66 and more recently confirmed by Ermenegildo Bertola, "La 'Glossa ordinaria' biblica ed i suoi problemi," *RTAM* 45 (1978): 34–78; R. Wielockx, "Autour de la *Glossa ordinaria*," *RTAM* 49 (1982): 222–28; Lobrichon, "Une nouveauté," pp. 105–07; Margaret T. Gibson, "The Place of the *Glossa ordinaria* in Medieval Exegesis," in *Ad litteram: Authoritative Texts and Their Medieval Readers*, ed. Mark D. Jordan and Kent Emery, Jr. (Notre Dame: University of Notre Dame Press, 1992), pp. 5–27; "The Glossed Bible," intro. to the facsimile reprint of the editio princeps of *Biblia latina cum Glossa ordinaria*, Adolph Rusch of Strassburg, 1480/81 (Turnhout: Brepols, 1992), 1: vii–xi; A brief description of the main features of the *Glossa ordinaria* is provided by Evans, *Language and Logic*, pp. 41–47.

[29] *Biblia latina cum Glossa ordinaria* prologus, editio princeps, 4 vols. (Strassburg: Adolph Rusch?, c. 1481), 1: unpaginated. Also found in *PL* 113: 841A–844C. Princeton University Library, Ex 1.5168.1480. An anastatic reprint with introduction by Karlfried Froelich and Margaret T. Gibson has been published (Turnhout: Brepols, 1992), as noted in note 28 above. I will also give references to the *PL* edition, although its weaknesses are acknowledged, for the convenience of readers lacking access to the first edition or its reprint. I would like to thank Dr. Gibson for her assistance in locating the copy of the *Glossa ordinaria* in the Princeton collection.

the reader a sense of the overall message of each Psalm. What he does do is to single out particular words and passages that he wants to discuss, leaving to the reader the task of contextualizing them. His explanations are of two types. Either they are *scholia* clarifying difficult phrases, or they are restatements of what the Psalmist has said, in the glossator's own words, or in the words, or in the paraphrased sense, of a chosen authority. The author occasionally supports or elaborates on the point by referring to other biblical texts. The authorities on whom he draws the most heavily, usually one for each passage lemmatized, are Augustine and Cassiodorus. Other patristic authors to whom he appeals are Basil, Gregory the Great, Theodore, and Jerome. Among the post-patristic writers, his favorites are Bede and Remigius. Most of the time his citations of these authorities paraphrase their opinions. But at times the glossator offers a fragmented quotation, of a type that makes his references a mere finding tool. Following the example of the Carolingian exegete, Florus of Lyon,[30] he gives the first few words of the quotation and the last few words, with the phrase *"usque ad"* in between to indicate his omission of the main body of the quotation.

As for the content of his exegesis, the glossator adheres to both the Christological and the moral reading of the Psalms as prescribed by Augustine. The ethical and dogmatic conclusions he draws from the text are, for the most part, theologically unexceptional, and rarely touch on the debated issues of the day. He shows no interest in moving beyond the simple statement of a theological point into a fuller exploration or a speculative analysis of it. His tendency to gloss individual words or phrases militates against a commentary on the overall meaning of a given Psalm, as a text that has a beginning, middle, and end and that conveys a specific message. It also militates against the understanding of the Psalmist's mode of argument or rhetorical strategy. These traits lead to a treatment of the Psalms that is considerably more banal than what can be found in many of the patristic exegetes on whom the glossator relies. There is only one point at which a current theological concern surfaces. In his gloss on Psalm 44, the author offers a liturgical, ecclesiological, and Mariological observation reflecting the contemporary effort to bind Mariology more closely to reflection on the church. This Psalm, he notes, is sung on the feast of the Virgin, in the liturgy for the induction of virgins into the monastic life, on feasts of the apostles and on Christmas day. While it speaks

---

[30] Florus of Lyons, *Expositio in Epistolas beati Pauli, PL* 119.

of the church in general, he adds, it refers to Mary in particular, as the type of the church wedded to Christ at His incarnation.[31] This passage is the exception that proves the rule. Nowhere else in this gloss can one read it as an index of theological interests specific to the twelfth century.

Although the glossator, in his prologue, notes the existence of diverse patristic opinions, he is basically not interested in dealing with conflicting views in the body of his gloss. He is far more likely to accent the concord of opinions when he can, as is the case, for instance, with Psalm 105 and whether the phrase *"alleluia, alleluia"* in the first verse belongs there. As he points out, Cassiodorus, following Jerome, says it does and explains that *alleluia* here is repeated for emphasis, on the analogy of the phrase "Amen, amen I say unto you," found in the gospels. Augustine, he observes, agrees with this point, and adds that the *alleluias* belong at the beginning of this Psalm and not at the end of the previous one, because none of the Greek codices of Psalms that he has consulted places these words after Psalm 104.[32] This is one of the few passages in the *Glossa ordinaria* on the Psalms reflecting any interest in the active comparison of different authorities on the same passage, or in the consideration of the reasoning that lies behind their opinions, or in suggesting the scholarly criteria to bear in mind in deciding which view to follow.

Aside from this particular instance, there is little evidence on the glossator's part of a real interest in offering any advice on how to read the text. Rather, the *Glossa ordinaria* on Psalms can be described less as a pedagogical tool for the training of scholastic theologians than as a catena of the individual patristic and later opinions which the author finds most helpful for each of the words or phrases he chooses to lemmatize. In citing his authorities, he is typically more interested in the conclusions they reach, especially if they are expressed in a concise, maxim-like form, than in the reasoning that has led the authority to his conclusion. In cases where the glossator uses the *usque ad* formula for abbreviating his quotations, it is impossible for the reader, in the absence of additional research on his own part, to see how the authority has gotten to his destination. The glossator never refers to the context in which the authority had written. He tends to overlook the theological and philosophical issues which his authorities had often addressed in

---

[31] *Biblia latina cum Glossa ordinaria*, 2: *In Ps.* 44; *PL* 113: 911B–C.
[32] Ibid., 2: *In Ps.* 105; *PL* 113: 1022A–B.

their Psalms commentaries. He adheres instead to the task of offering his own moral and typological exegesis in a spare, economical manner, without giving his own or his authorities' reflections on the significance of the ethical, Christological, or ecclesiological points which he extracts from their works and presents in a condensed and lapidary fashion.

The Psalms commentary of Gilbert of Poitiers, written between 1110/11 and 1117, was initiated while Gilbert was studying with Anselm of Laon. It incorporates and expands on the *Glossa ordinaria*, emphasizing the same authorities. It preserves the balance between ethics and Christology found in that gloss on the Psalms. Gilbert does not display here the interest in dialectic and semantics that surfaces so forcefully in his later commentaries on Boethius. In his glosses on the Psalms, he is less inclined than the *Glossa ordinaria* to indicate by name the authorities whose views he summarizes. Still, the earlier scholarship on Gilbert's as yet unedited Psalms commentary accents the continuities between it and the *Glossa ordinaria*, except for the fact that it is a continuous commentary and not a set of marginal and interlinear glosses on the Biblical text.[33] However, the recent work of Theresa Gross-Diaz has shown that Gilbert can truly lay claim to being the first seriously scholastic commentator on the Psalms. In this respect, he is the single most important precursor of Peter Lombard. Not only does Gilbert eschew the devotional and hortatory approach to the Psalms typical of the monastic exegetes, as do the Pseudo-Bede and the *Glossa ordinaria*, he also systematically targets specific scholastic concerns not emphasized by these two authors, which will be developed more fully by the Lombard in the sequel.

One place where the winds of change can be felt immediately is in Gilbert's *accessus* to the Book of Psalms. He agrees with the Pseudo-Bede, Jerome, and Hilary, against the prevailing opinion, that the book is an anthology, but he goes much farther than they do. Not only is the Book of Psalms a composite book, he argues, it is also an anthology composed of different types of Psalms.[34] Some, for

---

[33] H. C. van Elswijk, "Gilbert Porreta als glossator van het Psalterium," in *Jubileumbundel voor Prof. Mag. Dr. G. P. Kreling O.P.* (Nijmegen: Dekker & Van de Vegt N.V., 1953), pp. 292–303; *Gilbert Porreta: Sa vie, son oeuvre, sa pensée* (Louvain: Spicilegium Sacrum Lovaniense, 1966), pp. 46–47; Bruno Maioli, *Gilberto Porretano: Dalla grammatica speculativa alla metafisica del concreto* (Rome: Bulzoni, 1979), p. xxiii.

[34] Theresa Gross-Diaz, personal communication, April 5, 1990; "Information Management in the Twelfth Century Schools: The Psalm Commentary of Gilbert of Poitiers or, 'Gilbert, We Hardly Knew Ye'," unpublished paper delivered in

example, are penitential Psalms; others praise and celebrate the deity; still others invoke God's aid against the speaker's enemies; still others pray for comfort in times of tribulation. The Psalms of these diverse types, Gilbert notes, are not placed together in the Book of Psalms according to their thematic character, but are scattered throughout the book. As a composite text, he points out, the Book of Psalms has a rather haphazard scheme of organization, both from the standpoint of the list of putative authors given and from the standpoint of the subject matter of the Psalms themselves. As an exegete, he recognizes that some readers may wish to pursue a study of the different groups of Psalms thematically, tracing the development of the theme from one Psalm to another within the group. In order to facilitate investigations of this sort, Gilbert supplies both a verbal and a visual key for indexing and cross-referencing the different subdivisions that can be made within the larger body of the text. In his prologue, he explains what the categories are and which Psalms pertain to each of them, and he reinforces these verbal finding tools with visual markers in the early manuscript versions of his commentary.

At the same time, Gilbert is really the first scholastic exegete of the Psalms to develop theological *quaestiones* out of the text, in the context of his prevailingly Christological and moral emphasis. Further, he consistently yokes these two exegetical agendas to each other in a coherent manner, both in terms of form and content. These features of his exegesis are found in both of the two redactions of his gloss. The earlier of these gives very abbreviated lemmata, to which it then appends a running commentary combined with *quaestiones*. In the second version, dating to Gilbert's years of teaching at Paris, each page offers, in a double column format, the entire text of each Psalm and, next to it, Gilbert's commentary and *quaestiones*, with the authorities he cites flagged in the margins. In addressing the content, Gilbert begins by noting that the Psalms speak of Christ, and that they refer to Him both in the head and the

---

briefer form at the 24th International Congress of Medieval Studies, Kalamazoo, MI, May 6 1989; "The Psalms Commentary of Gilbert of Poitiers: From *lectio divina* to the Lecture Room," Northwestern University Ph.D. diss., 1992, pp. 63–115, 116–68, 211–55 for the treatment of this commentary's mise-en-page, its *accessus* with the issues of authorship and order of the Psalms, and the independence of Gilbert from the *Glossa ordinaria*, respectively; "From *lectio divina* to the Lecture Room: The Psalms Commentary of Gilbert of Poitiers," in *The Place of the Psalms in the Intellectual Culture of the Middle Ages*, ed. Nancy van Deusen (Binghamton: Center for Medieval and Early Renaissance Studies, forthcoming). I am indebted to Dr. Gross-Diaz for allowing me to consult these papers and her dissertation prior to publication.

members. So, the Psalms must be read not only with reference to the life of Christ in the New Testament, which they forecast, but with reference to the moral lives of the Christians who make up the church, His body. Now, these Christians are both perfect and imperfect. The latter group is the audience to which the Psalms are aimed, in order to draw them from imperfection to perfection.[35]

This general observation sets the stage for Gilbert's actual exegesis of each individual Psalm. In handling Psalm 1, he speaks of conforming oneself to the new man, possible only through Christ. This injunction prompts an analytical excursus into the nature of vice and virtue. Gilbert shares in the contemporary consensus, in which temptation was distinguished from sin and sin was located in the voluntary consent of the moral subject. His three-part formula, embracing thought, delectation, and consent (*cogitatio, delectatio, consensus*) reprises one of the standard vocabularies for these stages used by scholastics of the day.[36] In considering the choice of virtue, he accents not only the rejection of evil that it entails but also the acceptance of God's law as the law of one's own being, as well as perdurance in the good, while seeking goodness not with a sense of sadness, fear, or duress, nor with an eye to its fruits, but for itself alone. The proper motivation is the desire for the *honestum*, not the *utile*. If one acts for this reason, according to Gilbert, one will be enriched by the grace of Christ and bear good spiritual fruit, as well as receive remission of sins and eternal life.[37] The moral subject's judgment and counsel, his conscious and voluntary choice and inner motivation are central, in this mini-treatise on the psychology of the ethical life which Gilbert extracts from the description of the virtuous man in the first Psalm. It is clear that he is not content just to sum up the content of each Psalm and to anchor his points with the well-turned phrase of one authority or another.

Gilbert's handling of Psalm 2 accents Christ's spiritual power in vanquishing His enemies and the enemies of Christians striving for virtue today, in a reading that softens the military imagery in this text. In this Psalm, Christ is held up not only as a protector but as a model. It is His patience and confidence that arm Him, which virtues the Christian should imitate.[38] Another moral lesson that hinges on Christ emerges in Gilbert's account of Psalm 3. The

---

[35] Maria Fontana, ed., "Il commento ai Salmi di Gilberto de la Porrée," *Logos* 13 (1930): 284.
[36] Ibid., pp. 286–87.
[37] Ibid., pp. 288–90.
[38] Ibid., pp. 290–94.

David and Absalom story referred to here is to be read as a type of
Christ and Judas. At the same time, it is an appeal to humility;
those cast down will be raised up and glorified. One can also derive
insight into human psychology from this Psalm, Gilbert notes.
Each person possesses, within his soul, the conflicting drives of
David and Christ, on the one side, and of Absalom and Judas, on
the other, manifested in man's rational and irrational impulses,
respectively. The contest between these drives can be seen as a
battle between the angels and the devils over man's soul, Gilbert
concludes, but it is clear that he prefers the more psychological
account of this psychomachia.[39] These brief glimpses, all that the
present state of Gilbert's Psalms gloss research allows to readers
dependent on the printed texts, make it clear that he is decidedly
interested in developing a real theology out of his exegesis of the
Psalms and that he is concerned with making both the text of
Psalms itself and his own gloss easy to use for students interested in
a more analytical approach to this book of the Bible than characterizes the *Glossa ordinaria*.

PETER LOMBARD ON THE PSALMS

Peter Lombard's commentary on the Psalms has typically been
seen as standing in the tradition of the *Glossa ordinaria*, so firmly
that it can be regarded as a mere re-elaboration of it.[40] If such were
the case, it would be difficult to grasp why his commentary on
Psalms was the scholastic gloss of choice for this part of the Bible.
In understanding why such was the case, we need to highlight his
differences from the *Glossa ordinaria*, even though he certainly makes
extensive use of it. We also need to show how he capitalizes on
some of the concerns and techniques of Gilbert's Psalms commentary and expands on them. To begin with, like Gilbert, Peter
provides his commentary with an elaborate *accessus*, designed to do
several things at once.[41] Heading his agenda is the desire to reassert

---

[39] Ibid., pp. 294–300.
[40] Evans, *Language and Logic*, pp. 44–45; Joseph de Ghellinck, "Pierre Lombard," in *DTC* (Paris: Letouzy et Ané, 1935), 12 part 2: 1953.
[41] A. J. Minnis, *Medieval Theory of Authorship: Scholastic Literary Attitudes in the
Later Middle Ages* (London: Scolar Press, 1984), pp. 47–48, 54; A. J. Minnis and A.
B. Scott, ed., *Medieval Literary Theory and Criticism, c. 1100–c. 1375* (Oxford:
Clarendon Press, 1988), pp. 69–71, although the latter misdates Peter's exegetical
works. See, most recently, Marcia L. Colish, "*Psalterium Scholasticorum*: Peter
Lombard and the Emergence of Scholastic Psalms Exegesis," *Speculum* 67 (July
1992): 531–48.

the claim that David was the sole author of all of the Psalms.[42] This opinion contradicts what the Pseudo-Bede had said, in the name of a more prevalent tradition. Its defense is going to require some fancy footwork indeed in the body of the commentary, as Peter tries to explain away the authorship of Asaph, Heman, Ethan, and the other names attached to the titles of some of the Psalms. So, it demands a clear rationale. Peter seeks to provide one by way of addressing other points he makes in his *accessus*. The objective or intention of the author, he states, is to teach the reader how to behave well, and so to attain eternal life. Duties vary at different points in a person's life. The number of the Psalms is therefore coordinated with the six ages of man, followed by the seventh age, that of the resurrection.[43] The book can also be subdivided into three units of fifty Psalms apiece, corresponding with the Augustinian themes of penance, justice, and eternal life. He gives examples of each type of Psalm, with the incipits of Psalm 50, Psalm 100, and Psalm 150 respectively. As a *summa* of the ethical life, the Psalms, Peter says, were fittingly written by David, who was both a prophet and an evangelist, inspired by the Holy Spirit, who spoke of the coming of Christ and the church, and a sinner who himself experienced God's forgiveness and learned humility when he repented.[44] Peter thus yokes the issues of the author's intention, the subject matter of the Psalms, and their number, to the purported authorship of David.

As to the nature of the book itself, he disagrees with Jerome, thinking it should be called a single book and not an assemblage of books. To clarify this point he compares the Psalms with the Acts of the Apostles and with the Epistles of Paul. All three of these parts of the Bible are composites, but Psalms and Acts have a unified theme. For this reason, Peter sides with Cassiodorus's ruling that the Book of Psalms should be referred to in the singular.[45] Here, Peter goes beyond other exegetes who followed the lead of Cassiodorus by importing his own textual analysis into the question. Having discussed the author and his intention, Peter moves on to the *materia* and *modus tractandi* aspects of his *accessus*. On the first point, he agrees entirely with Augustine and previous commentators that the subject matter is Christ and that

---

[42] Peter Lombard, *Commentarium in Psalmos Davidicos* prologus, *PL* 191: 55A, 57C–D, 59B–C.

[43] Ibid., *PL* 191: 56A–B.

[44] Ibid., *PL* 191: 57C–D.

[45] Ibid., *PL* 191: 58A–B.

the Psalms should be read typologically as well as morally, in that
Christ is the new Adam, the source of the new man who replaces
fallen man. But he adds his own twist to this tradition. In referring to Christ as the head of the body which is the church, he
observes that the Psalms speak sometimes of Christ according to
His divinity, sometimes according to His humanity, and sometimes metaphorically (*per transumptione*); he gives examples of
each mode, citing Psalm 109, Psalm 3, and Psalm 21 as respective illustrations of each of them. Similarly, the Psalms speak of
the church in three ways, referring to the perfect, the imperfect,
and those evildoers who are merely nominal members of the
fold.[46] Peter thus expands the range of ethical categories of
Christians to whom the Psalms are addressed or of whom they
speak; and he associates this theme with the issue of theological
language.

Moving to the *modus tractandi*, Peter agrees with Gilbert that the
order of the Psalms in the book reflects a mode of organization at
odds with the order in which they were written. He follows Gilbert's notion that the Psalms naturally fall into subdivisions
according to their themes, and that they could be regrouped in
sequences which show their interrelations with the other Psalms in
the sub-group of which they are a part, logically or chronologically.
In addition to offering the same kind of key as Gilbert provides in
his preface, as well as in his introduction to the individual Psalms,[47]
Peter offers an explanation of how the Psalms lost the more cogent
arrangement which he thinks they originally had. The prophet
Esdra, he states, faced with salvaging the Psalms when the library
at Babylon burned down, put them together in their current order.
Still, by flagging the cogent sub-groups and by cross-referencing
the Psalms within them, wherever they are presently located in the
text, Peter, like Gilbert, hopes to aid the reader keen on following
the development of ideas in the Psalms in each unit. In addition, for
Peter, this provision of a key is a means of conceptually reconstitut-
ing the original format of the book as it is believed to have been.[48]

Peter thinks that the first Psalm is a compendium of all the main
themes in the Psalms more generally, and he therefore gives it
extended consideration. A glance at this commentary of Psalm 1
will be useful in situating his approach in relation to that of the

---

[46] Ibid., *PL* 191: 59C–D.
[47] E.g. *In Ps.* 21, 129, *PL* 191: 225B–266C, 1167B.
[48] Ibid., prologus, *PL* 191: 59D–60B; Minnis, *Medieval Theory*, pp. 54, 140,
although Minnis does not note Peter's dependence on Gilbert here.

Glossa ordinaria and Gilbert. The first Psalm, Peter affirms, states the central ideas found in the Book of Psalms as a whole, with respect to the author's intention, his subject matter, and his *modus tractandi*. The Lombard observes that the Psalm is divided into two parts, the first speaking about the *beatus vir* and drawing the reader to his happy state by describing it in an appealing way; while the second part speaks of the punishment of the wicked, frightening the reader away from his behavior. Further, the author contrasts the virtuous man with Adam, reminding the reader of the loss of Eden and of his own inability to rid himself of sin without God's grace. Once he has been put on the road to salvation by God, he can exult, even though he faces difficulties along the way. The Psalm, Peter continues, refers to the three forms of resuscitation from the death brought about by sin which the Lord provides, "in the house, at the gateway, in the tomb" (*in domo, in porta, in sepulchro*).[49] Next, the Psalmist describes the seat of the wicked, by which he means the giving of bad example, the teaching and the practice of sin. The first man sinned three ways, in thought, word, and deed. And so, what was brought about by the first man, Adam, must be removed by the new Adam, Christ.[50] This thought leads Peter, at the end of his preface to Psalm 1, to give, in germ, a summary of the analysis of the psychogenesis of ethical acts which he, like Gilbert, develops in the body of his gloss. Adam, he notes, sinned in thought, in intention, and in act; in word, doctrine, and custom (*cogitatione, voluntate et actu, verbi, doctrina vel consuetudo*).[51] First, he embraced temptation in thought, in the initial motion of the soul (*primus motus animae*), which is venial. Then, he embraced the delectation and consent (*delectatio et consensus*), which are mortal. The sin resides in the mind's voluntary consent to temptation; and this sin is then what Adam expressed in deeds, words, and habits.[52]

Here, in the preface, Peter offers not only a detailed analysis of the psychology of ethical choice consistent with but fuller than that of Gilbert, he also combines it integrally with his description of the Psalmist's *modus tractandi*, providing a rhetorical as well as a thematic analysis of Psalm 1 that can serve as a model for the *accessus* he gives to the Psalms, both individually and collectively. In so doing, he draws on most of the same sources used by the *Glossa ordinaria* and Gilbert, adding only Alcuin to the citations from Jerome,

---

[49] Peter Lombard, *In Ps.* 1 prologus, *PL* 191: 60A.
[50] Ibid., *PL* 191: 62A.
[51] Ibid., *PL* 191: 60C.
[52] Ibid., *PL* 191: 60D.

Cassiodorus, Augustine, Bede, and Remigius on which they call. But he has put the entire question of what the exegesis of the Psalms is out to accomplish on a much more solid and clearly articulated foundation.

Moving from the preface to the text of Psalm 1 itself, Peter does something else that sets his exegesis apart, and that he repeats in his handling of all the Psalms. Rather than giving the gist of the Psalm and then merely lemmatizing individual words or phrases, without showing how they occur in the text, he quotes each verse in full, and then discusses the meaning of each verse. In that connection he addresses the significance of the individual words or phrases that he thinks merit attention, or expands on the theological issues which he thinks warrant more extended treatment. Thus, for example, in Psalm 1:1, he observes that the *beatus vir* who does not respond to the counsels of the impious is a man who does not live in a condition of estrangement from God (*regio dissimilitudinis*). In analyzing that state, he takes pains to make it clear that man's occupancy of this zone does not result from an involuntary, cosmic, Neoplatonic "fall of the soul" but that it is the consequence of man's exercise of moral choice.[53] Or, another example, at Psalm 1:2, he explains that the law which the virtuous man meditates on day and night is Christ.[54]

In deriving these explanations, Peter draws on other passages of the Bible and on the authorities cited by the *Glossa ordinaria* and Gilbert, especially Cassiodorus and Augustine. But he uses these sources more integrally and less telegraphically. Rather than being cited to close off discussion, they are brought into the gloss to trigger their own, and Peter's, more extended reflections on the meaning of the Psalm. The whole tenor of Peter's gloss is to seek, and to find in his authorities, ways of opening up the text, ways of dilating on its theological content, and ways of making connections

---

[53] Peter Lombard, *In Ps.* 1:1, *PL* 191: 61B. One finds a similar understanding of *regio dissimilitudinis*, as the generic state of sinful man, stated repeatedly in the Lombard's sermons. See *Sermo* 4, 12, 13, 21, 23, 36, 55, 99, 111, 112, *PL* 171: 357A–B, 397A, 404D, 435D–436A, 445C, 525C, 601C, 850D, 857C. It also occurs in Peter's *In Epistolam Pauli ad Galatas* 2:23, *PL* 192: 126C–129A. For the evolution of this theme from its Neoplatonic beginnings to this very generic Christian sense in the twelfth century, see J. C. Didier, "Pour la fiche *Regio dissimilitudinis*," *Mélanges de science religieuse* 8 (1951): 205–10; Étienne Gilson, "*Regio dissimilitudinis* de Platon à Saint Bernard de Clairvaux," *MS* 9 (1947): 108–30; Margot Schmidt, "*Regio dissimilitudinis*: Ein Grundbegriff mittelhochdeutscher Prosa im Lichte seiner lateinischen Bedeutungsgeschichte," *Freiburger Zeitschrift für Theologie und Philosophie* 15 (1968): 63–108.

[54] Peter Lombard, *In Ps.* 1:2, *PL* 191: 62B.

between it and other parts of the Bible where similar moral teachings are presented, especially the Pauline Epistles. His strategy is the antithesis of that of the *Glossa ordinaria*, which seeks to explicate disconnected lemmata as concisely as possible. Instead, Peter always relates the points he makes on each passage to the central theme of the Psalm, as he has spelled it out in his *accessus*. He also clearly leads the reader along the itinerary that he had mapped out in that *accessus*, indicating when his comment on the first part of the Psalm, on the virtuous, has been completed, and he is ready to pass on to the second part, on the iniquity of the wicked.[55] The relation of the parts of the Psalm, and of his gloss on it, to the whole, is always kept firmly before the reader's eyes.

The features of Peter's exegesis of Psalm 1 which we have just examined are standard for his treatment of all the other Psalms. At the same time, here and elsewhere in this work Peter elaborates a method and a theological content that are specific to this commentary on the Psalms and that set it apart from preceding glosses. He goes farther in developing theological *quaestiones* out of the text of Psalms than any other exegete of his time. Sometimes he presents an early version of a doctrine which he develops or changes later in his career, and sometimes he offers a position that already articulates a basic teaching that he retains and that appears in much the same shape in his *Sentences*. A good example of the first type is his handling of penance in his gloss on Psalm 4:6. Here, he describes penance as involving the three Augustinian stages of contrition, confession, and satisfaction, which he calls *poenitentia, lamentum*, and *satisfactio* or *opera justa*, the third stage involving the decision to abandon the life of sin and to change one's inner attitude.[56] He does not, however, raise the burning question, which made penance a richly disputed topic in this period, of when, in this sequence of events, the penitent receives God's forgiveness, although Peter was later to come down squarely on the side of contritionism. His analysis of the same subject in his gloss on Psalm 33 likewise reflects no differentiation, as yet, among the stages in the sacrament, in Peter's current thinking.[57] Another case in which Peter's Psalms commentary serves as a trial run for an argument which he later changes is the question of whether Christ's human nature should receive worship (*latria*) or only veneration (*dulia*), which arises in his gloss on Psalm 98:5. There, he asserts that our adora-

---

[55] Ibid., *PL* 191: 64A.
[56] Peter Lombard, *In Ps.* 4:6, *PL* 191: 87B–C.
[57] Peter Lombard, *In Ps.* 33, *PL* 191: 319C–321A.

tion of the human Christ should properly be *dulia*,[58] a view he reverses in the *Sentences*,[59] thanks largely to the fact that he was later sensitized to this issue by his reading of John Damascene, who had not been available to him when he wrote the Psalms gloss, as well as by a fuller consideration of Augustine on the subject.

Also striking are the passages where the exegesis of the Psalms affords Peter the opportunity to work out fully developed theological positions which he continued to teach. One noteworthy case in point is the nature of the four moral states in which mankind will be resurrected at the end of time, which recurs in his discussion of Last Things in the *Sentences*.[60] At Psalm 1:6, commenting on the statement that the impious will not rise up in the judgment, he begins by observing that there are two resurrections, the resurrection of the soul, when we rise up from sin, and the resurrection of the body, in the next life. There will be four orders of people in the latter state, he affirms, drawing on Jerome and Augustine. Some, like the apostles and other saints, will judge but will not be judged themselves. Others, like the infidels and those who have persevered in sin up to the end, do not judge and are not themselves judged either. The reason why neither of these groups will be subjected to judgment at the end of time is that they have already been judged. The saints have already won Heaven, thanks to their supererogatory virtue, while the infidels and obdurate sinners have already condemned themselves to perdition. Finer discriminations are needed, however, for the other two groups of people. One of these orders contains people who are judged and saved, as middling good (*mediocriter boni*). The other contains people who are judged and condemned, as middling evil (*mediocriter mali*). So, he concludes, among both the damned and the saved there are two registers of souls, one of which contains people whose posthumous fate is sealed before they die, and the other of which contains people with grayer areas in their moral lives, whose ultimate destinations in the hereafter are not decided immediately but which are determined eventually, after further evaluation or purgation.[61]

In explaining this doctrine, Peter goes beyond his sources, adding an analogy of his own devising to clarify the status of the

---

[58] Peter Lombard, *In Ps.* 98:5, *PL* 191: 895B.

[59] Peter Lombard, *Sententiae in IV libris distinctae* 3. d. 9. c. 1-c. 6, 3rd ed. rev., ed. Ignatius C. Brady, 2 vols. (Grottaferrata: Collegii S. Bonaventurae ad Claras Aquas, 1971–81), 2: 68–71.

[60] Peter Lombard, *Sent.* 4. d. 47. c. 3, 2: 538–40.

[61] Peter Lombard, *In Ps.* 1:6, *PL* 191: 64C–65C.

two classes of the damned and saved. The former may be compared with two kinds of criminals within a principality. One is the criminal who breaks the law of the land, on some particular point. The other is the rebel who, rejecting the authority of the law and the government as such, seeks to overthrow it. The prince, Peter notes, fitly punishes the second type of criminal in a different way than he punishes the first, and more harshly. Since the rebel, in effect, has committed an act of war against the prince, he is put down by force of arms; for he has rejected the jurisdiction of the law and its processes over himself in the very act of rebelling. On the other hand, the first kind of criminal is proved to be a lawbreaker and is sentenced in the context of judicial deliberation.[62] As for the two classes of the saved, the perfected saints do not need judgment, since they have already gone beyond the requirements of the Gospel. They have demonstrated their commitment and their irreproachable virtue and fidelity by their deeds and sufferings. Those who are middling good have died in a state of repentance but their record is mixed. They require further reparation and purgation before being received into Heaven.[63]

The foregoing account is certainly the most elaborate example of a doctrine developed out of Psalms exegesis that Peter carries over into his mature theology. Other examples that might be cited, which he treats with greater concision, are his handling of the hypostatic union, the idea of substance, and the modes of fear in the moral life. At Psalm 64:5, he crisply states that the Word assumed human nature in a unity of person (*unitas personae*). Christ, he observes, did not assume a human person; rather, He assumed the nature of man (*naturam quippe hominis assumpsit*).[64] As for *substantia*, at Psalm 68:2 Peter sets forth a definition that avoids a specifically Aristotelian understanding of the term and that makes it available for proper attribution both to creatures and to the Deity. All kinds of substances, he asserts, can be viewed as beings that possess the qualities intrinsic to themselves (*eo ipso quo sunt*). Thus, not only are men, animals, the earth, and the heavens substances, so is the divine nature shared by the persons of the Trinity. In short, Peter here equates a being's substance with its inborn nature, whatever kind of nature that may be.[65] Although examples could be multiplied, a third, and final illustration under this heading is Peter's

---

[62] Ibid., *PL* 191: 65C–D.
[63] Ibid., *PL* 191: 66B–67B.
[64] Peter Lombard, *In Ps.* 64:5, *PL* 191: 584B.
[65] Peter Lombard, *In Ps.* 68:2, *PL* 191. 627D–D.

doctrine of the four kinds of fear in the moral life, one which was widely held in this period, and which he extracts from the line in Psalm 127 where those who fear the Lord are called blessed. The four kinds of fear are worldly or human, servile, initial, and chaste or filial. The first involves fear of bodily harm or loss of worldly goods, and is an unworthy motive for moral action. Servile fear involves actions undertaken so as to avoid punishment. It may provide negative reasons for doing good, but its motivation is not sufficient to win blessedness. Initial fear, the fear of the Lord that is the beginning of wisdom, begins to exclude servile fear from the soul and to substitute for it the motive of charity. For its part, chaste or filial fear is motivated by love alone. It inspires us not only to flee from evil but also to walk in faith. Only those who possess this fourth type of fear, Peter concludes, are united to Christ.[66] In all these cases, and in others that might be cited, Peter uses his exegesis of the Psalms to articulate in brief theological positions to which he gives more extended elaboration, along the same lines, later in his career.

There are three other areas in which Peter's Psalms commentary is a rehearsal for the theological teaching he develops as a systematic theologian, areas in which we can see him working out his theological method as well as the substance of his theology. These dimensions of his Psalms gloss include his querying of the accuracy of the biblical text, his application of the *artes* to its explication, and his handling of the authorities whom he more typically harnesses to that task, especially when he detects real or apparent conflicts among them. In the first case, the accuracy of the text, Peter stands out, among contemporary exegetes of Psalms, in his concern for textual corruptions or the tamperings of previous readers in their very act of transmitting the text. The point may be as minor as the title of a Psalm, as is the case with his gloss on Psalm 40. Here, he claims, Jerome changed the title from *In finem psalmus David* to *In finem intellectus filiis Core*. At the root of his objection is both the desire to insist on David as the author of all the Psalms as well as his concern with Jerome's alteration of this title. Some codices of the Psalms, he notes, contain the information that Jerome effected this change; others do not. Peter also observes that the Hebrew and Septuagint Greek versions of the Psalms lack Jerome's new title, but that Haimo of Auxerre and the *Glossa ordinaria* mistakenly follow Jerome. He himself argues that Jerome's tampering with the

---

[66] Peter Lombard, *In Ps.* 127:11, *PL*: 1161D–1162D.

title constitutes an interpretation of the biblical text, and not just a translation or transmission of it. Jerome, in his view, was providing a historical gloss on the Psalm, since the sons of Core at one point entered David's service. This fact helps us to date the composition of the Psalm. The gloss was then, incorrectly, incorporated into the title proper. In any event, Peter proposes to read this Psalm as pertaining to the life of Christ. From this standpoint, he asserts, what is important about Core is that the name can be interpreted as meaning Calvary, the place of the crucifixion. Now Jerome himself, in his gloss on Psalm 84, is the source of the latter *scholium*, while Augustine, in his comment on Psalm 85, concurs in that view.[67] Three things are of interest in this textual analysis. First, there is Peter's concern with uncovering mistakes in the transmission of the text and in accounting for how they occurred. Second, there is his felt need to criticize his own immediate sources, Haimo and the *Glossa ordinaria*, for their own failure to question Jerome in the light of the information available about his interpolated title. Third, there is his technique of cross-referencing his authorities in their comments on other Psalms to derive the reading he chooses for the problematic reference to Core.

A second example, which likewise displays Peter's interest in comparing alternative texts of the Psalms, is his handling of Psalm 67:9, which refers to Sinai. Peter observes that the Roman Psalter, along with Augustine and Cassiodorus, read Mount Sinai here. On the other hand, the Septuagint, which he is following, omits the word "Mount." To sort out this problem, Peter goes back to the demonstrative pronoun linked to Sinai in the Hebrew text of Psalms, which, he notes, can be understood to refer to the word "Mount." Peter has relied on Jerome for this philological *scholium*.[68] The whole passage reflects his awareness that the text of the Psalms has a history, in both liturgical and strictly biblical forms, and in a variety of languages, as well as his own inclination to rely on pre-Vulgate texts, such as the Septuagint, as closer to the original Hebrew version.

The third instance in which Peter deals with a discrepancy in the text is a far more dramatic one. It involves a passage which one of his authorities, Augustine, flags down and explains in a manner not noted by the *Glossa ordinaria* or by any other Psalms commentator of this period who glossed the line in question. The problematic line is

---

[67] Peter Lombard, *In Ps.* 40 prologus, *PL* 191: 407D–409B.
[68] Peter Lombard, *In Ps.* 67:9, *PL:* 191: 605C.

in Psalm 70:17 "Because I am not acquainted with business deal-
ings, I will enter into the mighty deeds of the Lord" (*Quoniam non
cognovi negotiationes, introibo in potentias Domini*). Now, there was a
tradition of assessing the morality of mercantile activities derived
from Anselm of Laon and his followers, although it arose from their
comments on 1 Thessalonians and not Psalm 70. Anselm sees a flat
contradiction between the mercantile profession and salvation,
arguing that merchants are invariably motivated by greed and that
they practice fraud and deception. Two of his disciples, however,
while taking the point that greed and fraud are vices, soften and
actually reverse Anselm's negative judgment by pointing out that
not all merchants are in fact afflicted by these vices. Lacking such
sinful motivations, which lie in men and not in the professions they
practice, merchants can be virtuous people who perform a useful
social function.[69] While the glossator responsible for the Psalms in
the *Glossa ordinaria*, like the rest of his équipe, was associated with
Anselm of Laon, it does not occur to him to adopt either the
negative or the positive assessment of the morality of commerce
produced by the Laon masters. His solution to this problem is a
non-solution; he simply ignores this line in Psalm 70 and does not
gloss it.

On the other hand, the Lombard is familiar with the handling of
commerce by Anselm and his disciples, and clearly sides with those
who reject Anselm's opinion of merchants. In so doing, he also
reflects a more thorough familiarity with Augustine's *Enarrationes in
Psalmos*, which uncovers and resolves the difficulties in Psalm 70:17
with a textual analysis of Augustine's own. Peter agrees that the
merchant who is inspired by greed alone and who lies about the
value of the goods he buys or sells is a perjurer and a blasphemer,
who cannot truly sing the praises of God and who would be a
hypocrite to try. He also agrees that these vices inhere in men, and
not in the professions they practice, which can indeed be conducted
without these vices. For all professions can be exercised both vir-
tuously and viciously, depending on the intentions of the practitioner. As with all other professions, so with commerce, he
concludes, "for the art knows nothing of vice" (*ars enim nescit
vitium*).[70]

The basic source for the reading of Psalm 70:17 that inspires this
analysis is in certain fourth-century versions of the Psalms which

---

[69] Marcia L. Colish, "Another Look at the School of Laon," *AHDLMA* 53
(1986): 20–21.
    [70] Peter Lombard, *In Ps.* 70:17, *PL* 191: 652A.

provided the text used in the Milanese Psalter,[71] a fact indicated by Augustine. In his own commentary on this Psalm, Augustine notes that, in a number of exemplars familiar to him, the line reads "Because I am not acquainted with literature" (*Quoniam non cognovi litteraturam*) and that others give *numerationem* for *litteraturam*. Augustine concedes that it is difficult to reconcile these discordant textual variations. Having already argued that intentionality conditions the morality of commerce in a gloss on *negotio*, he finds a happy resolution of the dilemma represented by *numeratio* and *litteratura*. These terms, he points out, can also refer to professions, the mathematical and literary disciplines of the liberal arts, which arts, he concludes, even as with mercantile activities, can be practiced honestly or dishonestly.[72]

This information, supplied by Augustine, suggests that Peter is working with a pre-Vulgate text of Psalms, possibly one deriving from one version of the Psalter or another, since the Vulgate restores *litteraturam* for *negotiationem* and transfers the word to verse 15 of the Psalm. It might be noted parenthetically that *litteraturam* turns out to be just as problematic a reading in that locus as is *negotiationem*. Modern Scripture scholars have replaced both words with *numerationem*, to yield the following reading in the English of the Revised Standard Version of the Bible: "My mouth will tell of Thy righteous acts/ Of Thy deeds of salvation all the day/ For their number is past my knowledge./ With the mighty deeds of the Lord God I will come,/ I will praise Thy righteousness, Thine alone" (Psalm 71:15-16). This reading makes altogether more sense than anything that Peter, or Augustine, are able to provide on the basis of the information available to them. None the less, Peter's resolution of the moral issue embedded in the problematic line as he reads it is of considerable interest in twelfth-century terms, for it indicates a familiarity with Augustine on his part that is highly specific and to the point, and one that recognizes his widening of the scope of the professions to which the general ethical principle at stake can be applied. Augustine's witness to the fact that Jerome was capable of introducing what he believed to be corrections, as well as corruptions, into the Vulgate text of the Psalms receives a hearing, in Peter's gloss, which it does not receive in the work of other contemporary exegetes, a fact which points in turn to a thorough and independent study of Augustine's *Enarrationes in*

---

[71] Augustine, *Enarrationes in Psalmos* 70, ed. D. Eligius Dekkers and Joannes Fraipoint, CCSL 39 (Turnhout: Brepols, 1956), editorial note *ad loc.*, p. 956.
[72] Ibid., *Sermo* 1.17–19, CCSL 39: 954–58.

Psalmos on the Lombard's part, and one that goes well beyond the attention which that work received elsewhere in this period.

Not only does Peter use his authorities more independently than is the case with other Psalms commentators, as the above-mentioned example suggests, he also uses a wider range of sources and he approaches them more critically. There are a number of points at which he brings forward his knowledge of the classical authors and of contemporary development in the liberal arts to help unravel difficult passages. Sometimes his glosses betray a reading of the classics to which he does not refer overtly. Such a case is his comment on the injunction in Psalm 36:28 to depart from evil and do good. Cassiodorus here remarks, he notes, that the two-part structure of this line suggests that conversion is a process that takes some time. Peter himself adds the observation "for no one becomes beautiful all at once" (*nemo repente fit pulcher*), an unacknowledged echo of Juvenal's comment, on the obverse of the point, that "no one ever became bad all at once" (*nemo repente fuit turpissime*).[73] In interpreting another double, or two-part statement, the promise in Psalm 71:13-14 that the souls of the poor will be saved, they will be redeemed from their debts; Peter treats the passage as an example of an equipollent argument,[74] a logical technique in the armory of dialecticians since the second half of the eleventh century.

More typically it is the patristic and Carolingian authorities in the Christian tradition on whom he draws. Peter is much more sensitive than the other scholastic glossators of the Psalms to the need to compare alternative interpretations of the biblical text, to assess the reasoning of the authorities, to decide whether their readings are compatible, and, if he judges that they are not, to offer a principled reason for choosing the authority he accepts, while at the same time providing criteria for the reader's own evaluation of sources.[75] There are a number of cases where he finds the alternative views of different authorities compatible. One reason for such compatibility, when Peter sees it, is that different authorities can be read as referring to different aspects of the same phenomena. Thus, at Psalm 10:3, he notes that there are two theories on how the moon gets its light, one saying that the moon possesses its own light and the other saying that it derives its light by reflection from the sun. Since the interpretation Peter gives to this Psalm is ecclesiological, he argues that both of these theories apply to the church. The first

---

[73] Peter Lombard, *In Ps.* 36:28, *PL* 191: 374B; cf. Juvenal, *Sat.* 2.83.

[74] Peter Lombard, *In Ps.* 71:13–14, *PL* 191: 663D.

[75] Glunz, *History of the Vulgate*, pp. 214–15.

theory refers to the spiritual legacy of the church, which enables it to shine as a channel of grace. But the church has a physical dimension as well, which is suggested by the second theory, since, in this respect, it derives its light from Christ, the sun of justice. Thus, both interpretations make sense, allegorically.[76] In the case of another example, the line "your eyes see justice" in Psalm 16:3, Peter observes that Alcuin reads "eyes" here as the divine illumination that enables our physical eyes to see, while Augustine interprets "eyes" as the eyes of the heart. Since man possesses both a physical and a spiritual nature, these opinions are both acceptable as referring to one or another of these natures.[77] It may be noted that the *Glossa ordinaria* also presents these two opinions, but without discussing the differences between them or whether or not they can be reconciled.[78] A third example of compatible readings seen as applying to different aspects of the same reality occurs in Psalm 43:28. As Peter points out, Alcuin and Jerome interpret the line "Rise up, o Lord, and come to our assistance," as a prayer to God to lift us from earthly to heavenly concerns by causing us to recognize that this conversion will occur through His grace and not through our own merit. Augustine and Cassiodorus read the line as a prayer to Christ offered by the martyrs, asking Him to initiate the second coming and the heavenly resurrection of their own tormented bodies, and to end the persecution of those still alive. These two readings, he holds, are perfectly compatible, as applying to Christians in general and to a particular subset of Christians at the same time.[79]

In glossing other passages of the Psalms, Peter offers another mode of reconciling discrepant readings, here referring to a general exegetical principle for interpreting the Psalms which he had outlined in his *accessus* to the book as a whole, the notion that the text yields more than one level of meaning. On one level, the text refers to Christ or the church; on another level, it offers moral lessons. Thus, for instance, the "difficult paths" mentioned in Psalm 16:5 can mean the passion and crucifixion endured by Christ, as Augustine has it, and also the virtues that men acquire with difficulty, as Jerome and Augustine, in another passage, maintain.[80] The same combination of typology and tropology, connected by the idea that

---

[76] Peter Lombard, *In Ps.* 10:3, *PL* 191: 148C–149A.
[77] Peter Lombard, *In Ps.* 16:3, *PL* 191: 179A.
[78] *Biblia latina cum Glossa ordinaria*, 2: *In Ps.* 16:3; *PL* 113: 866B.
[79] Peter Lombard, *In Ps.* 43:28, *PL* 191: 435B–436B.
[80] Peter Lombard, *In Ps.* 16:5, *PL* 191: 180C.

Christ's behavior gives man a model to follow, controls Peter's
reconciliation of Augustine's moral reading of Psalm 54 and the
Christological reading given by Cassiodorus, Jerome, Alcuin, and
the *Glossa ordinaria*, at various points in this Psalm.[81] Along the
same lines, tropology and anagogy can be combined in different but
compatible interpretations. At Psalm 110:10, Peter observes, Cassiodorus, Alcuin, Haimo, and the *Glossa ordinaria* read the praise of
God referred to in the text as man's movement from fear of the
Lord to wisdom in the present life, while Cassiodorus also sees it as
the confession of praise offered to God by the saved in the life to
come, when they are fully liberated from evil and can adore God
eternally. These readings Peter clearly sees as complementary since
they speak to two stages in man's life which the polysemous structure of the text itself is here addressing.[82]

Peter also confronts cases where authorities disagree and where
he finds a need to make choices between positions that cannot be
reconciled. Sometimes his decisions are informed simply by common sense and the need for clarity. Thus, in his prologue to Psalm
104, he points out that, while both Augustine and Cassiodorus
divide this Psalm into six parts, they make the divisions in different
places. As he sees it, Cassiodorus does a better job of following the
logic of the Psalm's argument in his subdivision than Augustine
does, and this is his reason for following the former and rejecting
the latter.[83] The authorities are not necessarily compatible in their
interpretations of difficult lines, either. This is the case with Psalm
72:16. Commenting on the false happiness of the wicked, the Psalmist contrasts it with the afflictions he has undergone as he strives
to follow the path of virtue. The comparison, he notes, is pointed,
and poignant; and in the line in question the Psalmist says that this
subject is one he has tried hard to understand, and that it was too
difficult for him to grasp (*Existimabam ut cognoscerem hoc; labor est ante
me*), at least until he considered the final destiny of the wicked and
virtuous alike. What is the object, the *hoc*, referred to in this
sentence? Peter points out that both Cassiodorus and Alcuin think
that it means more than one thing. One reading is that it is the
truth, and that the Psalmist is indicating that he possessed only the
first grade of wisdom at the point when he applied this statement to
himself. The same authorities, however, say that the line can also

---

[81] Peter Lombard, *In Ps.* 51:1, 51:15, 54:25, *PL* 191: 509A–510A, 512A–513A,
517A.
[82] Peter Lombard, *In Ps.* 110:10, *PL* 191: 1008A–C.
[83] Peter Lombard, *In Ps.* 104 prologus, *PL* 191: 945D.

refer to foolish people who had debated against God and who have now been converted away from that practice. Peter himself is not taken by either of these opinions, finding the second, in particular, inappropriate (*inconveniens*). Instead, he moves to a different view, put forth by Augustine and Alcuin, which says that the Psalmist had vainly sought to understand God's justice and the fact that evil people sometimes enjoy earthly happiness. But now, he has put the matter of earthly requital behind him as a mystery that cannot be resolved in earthly terms, but only in the light of the posthumous outcome.[84] In this case, Peter's preference stems from his own desire to read the line lemmatized in the context of the argument of the Psalm as a whole. The third opinion reflects such a reading, and it thus makes better sense out of verse 16 than the decontextualized or irrelevant interpretations offered in the first two opinions cited. The fact that a single authority, Alcuin, has given all three readings as possible is an index of the fact that authorities are not always working at the top of their form in interpreting the Bible. They may need to be cited against themselves in the effort to discover the sense of the text.

In the examples just considered, Peter engages in a critique of some authoritative readings by showing that other authorities make a more convincing case for the alternative opinions they present. There are also instances in his Psalms commentary where he takes issue with authorities on his own account, disagreeing with them because, in his own view, they are in error. Thus, at Psalm 51:4, which states that God will destroy evil men in the end, remove them from their tabernacles, and root them out, Augustine, Cassiodorus, and the *Glossa ordinaria* understand the tabernacles to mean the secular vainglory of which God will deprive the wicked. Peter disagrees with this reading. In his view, the tabernacles refer to the church, in which the wheat and the tares are mingled in this life. Later on, God will purge the wicked from the church and save the good. Peter offers this interpretation as his own opinion, which he prefers because he thinks it makes better sense of the Psalm, read ecclesiologically, than the opinion of the authorities cited.[85]

In the foregoing example, Peter's preference stems from his exegetical agenda. There are other cases in which his rejection of certain authorities is based on a difference in doctrinal outlook. One of his favorite authorities, Augustine, comes in for this kind of

---

[84] Peter Lombard, *In Ps.* 72:16, *PL* 191: 674A–675A.
[85] Peter Lombard, *In Ps.* 51:4, *PL* 191: 497B–D.

criticism on more than one occasion. In commenting on the Psalmist's hatred of lying at Psalm 5:6, Peter gives a reprise of Augustine's *Contra mendacium*, crisply repeating his definition of a lie, in
that work, as a false statement made with the deliberate intention
to deceive. But, while Augustine goes on to classify eight types of
lies, of increasing seriousness, before ruling out the acceptability of
lying for any reason at all, including, *a fortiori*, pious fraud, Peter
takes a rather different tack. He distinguishes three, not eight, types
of lies, and finds some lies permissible. One type is, precisely, the
pious fraud, of the sort perpetrated by the Hebrew nurses in the
book of Exodus who thereby managed to save the infant Moses
from the wrath of Pharaoh. This deception he praises as prudent
and legitimate, although he modifies this argument in the *Sentences*.
A second type of lie he admits is one that Augustine defines not as a
lie but as a falsehood told without blame, the joke or tall tale told
merely to amuse, which deceives no one. Peter's third type of
acceptable lie, however, is also one that Augustine flatly rejects.
This occurs in a situation where a person remains silent when asked
a question, answering which might cost him his life. This action, or
failure to act, is acceptable, according to Peter, because the provocation is so extreme, and also because the person in question is
not actually making a false statement.[86] For Augustine, on the other
hand, silence can be equated both morally and semantically with
speech. In circumstances when silence conveys an understood message or an understood response to the questioner, one can lie by
remaining silent. Further, for Augustine, no provocation whatever
justifies lying. In this case, then, Peter does not hesitate to take a far
softer line on lying than Augustine does, on the grounds that
Augustine's rigor is unrealistic and unacceptable.

Another area in which Peter joins some contemporary theologians in softening the harshness of Augustine's teaching is the
morality of sexual relations in marriage. He has much more to say
on this topic both in the *Collectanea* and in the *Sentences*, but his
Psalms commentary already indicates the later directions of his
thought. Like every other Christian thinker in his period, Peter was
confronted by the Augustinian account of the transmission of original sin from parents to children through the unavoidable sexual
feelings accompanying the procreation of offspring. In Augustine's
case, this doctrine was linked to the opinion that the experience of
lust itself was a consequence of original sin, which remained a part

---

[86] Peter Lombard, *In Ps.* 5:6, *PL* 191: 98A–D.

of human nature even in the case of Christian spouses redeemed by faith and baptism and joined in holy matrimony, a state in which he listed offspring as one of the goods of marriage which must not be frustrated. None the less, Augustine held that the sexual pleasure experienced by spouses was always tainted and at least venially sinful. Like many of his contemporaries, Peter wrestled with the perceived contradictions in this Augustinian doctrine. In addition, he felt a need to defend marriage, and the sexual relations leading to procreation, against the Catharist heresy. In glossing Psalm 50:6, "I was conceived in sin," he states his agreement with Augustine's account of the transmission of original sin. But, he takes sharp exception to the condemnation of the sexual relations of spouses as inevitably sinful. Not so, says Peter. These relations are exempted from sin because they serve the goods of marriage; and, in marriage, this work is chaste (*Nam hoc opus castum in conjunge*).[87]

In looking at Peter as an exegete of the Psalms more generally, then, one can see in this maiden venture the earmarks of the scholastic theologian he was to become. One can also see his understanding of biblical exegesis as the training ground for the making of professional theologians, even though he did not, apparently, compose this gloss as a teaching text and lectured on the Psalms only at the end of his career in the classroom, at the instance of his pupils. The exegetical method he develops in this, his earliest work, sets him head and shoulders above the other available scholastic commentators on the Psalms in addressing the needs a non-monastic audience. While he stands in the tradition of the *Glossa ordinaria* and Gilbert of Poitiers, using many of their sources and ideas, the degree to which he handles his assignment differently is striking. First and most noticeably, he expands on Gilbert by providing an *accessus* to each Psalm as well as to the Book of Psalms as a whole, analyzing the argument in every Psalm, its rhetorical structure, and its role as an illustration of the overall themes informing the Book of Psalms in general, as well as its function as a unit in the particular subset of Psalms to which it belongs thematically and to which it is keyed. He then quotes and comments on each line of each Psalm, avoiding a hit-or-miss approach or an arbitrary selection of lemmata. His use of authorities goes beyond that of his immediate predecessors, both in depth, range, thoroughness, and pertinence. He is concerned with presenting and citing their views fully, and without ellipsis. He is eager to explore their reasoning, using it to open up

---

[87] Peter Lombard, *In Ps.* 50:6, *PL* 191: 487D–488A.

theological reflection rather than to terminate it with an *ipse dixit*. He notes the areas where the authorities disagree. Sometimes he shows that they can be reconciled, as speaking to the moral or the typological levels which, he agrees, the text possesses, or to different but complementary aspects of a single problem. At the same time, he accepts the fact that some disagreements are not capable of being reconciled. When this is the case, he offers his own reasonable suggestions for why one opinion should be preferred to another. His criterion is generally to prefer the opinion that makes the most sense out of the text. He does not hesitate to reformulate or reject an authority whose views fail to square with Peter's own theological opinions. There are a few places where Peter brings the *artes* to bear on exegesis and where he reflects on the problems deriving from textual variations and corruptions. But his chief goal, consistent with his moral, Christological, and ecclesiological reading of the Psalms, is to work out an ethical and dogmatic theology on such topics as the nature of Christ, on human nature, especially man as the image of God, on virtue, vice, sin, and the sacramental re-medies for it in penance and marriage. These topics link his exeget-ical ruminations on the Psalms with his later work as a systematic theologian, whether he retains his early views or modifies them in the light of his ongoing research and reflection.

In all these respects, Peter's commentary on the Psalms lays a foundation for his commentary on the Pauline Epistles, a work which provides a still more acute index of his achievement as a scholastic exegete, in an area where the competition was more abundant and in which the theological stakes were considerably higher. In this exegetical field, many more of the entrants were scholastic than monastic writers. In this field, as well, the differ-ences in approach between authors in these two professions are even more sharply etched than is the case with the exegesis of Psalms. Briefly put, monastic commentators on St. Paul approach him with precisely the same goals in view as they bring to the Psalms. While they do not fail to note the doctrinal points made by the apostle, their chief concern is Paul's ethical teaching and the inculcation in their monastic readers of the devotional attitudes suitable to their calling. Two such monastic authors, William of St. Thierry and Hervaeus of Bourg-Dieu, illustrate well the range of monastic approaches to Pauline exegesis found in Peter Lombard's day.

PAULINE EXEGESIS: THE MONASTIC APPROACH

William's gloss on Romans 3:27, "piety is the true wisdom" (*pietas est vera sapientia*)[88] is the theme song of his entire commentary. Written between 1138 and 1145, this work takes specific issue with the scholastics, personified for William by Peter Abelard, whom he does not name but whom he clearly identifies with the wisdom of the worldly philosophers, the profane novelties, and the vain presumption which he writes in order to repress. His introduction recognizes that many theological questions have arisen, in his time, out of the text of Romans. His objective, as he puts it, is not to enter into these debates, debates concerning matters that transcend the human mind, but rather to quell them with ammunition drawn from the fathers, above all Augustine. Adhering to the most authoritative sources in the tradition, which he in no sense seeks to put to the test, he plans to rephrase them in his own words, without indicating which source he is citing. William pointedly notes, as well, that he will refrain from decorating his work with references to the poets and the fabulists. He wants merely to write in all humility for the sake of stirring up the reader's piety, reinforcing this aim with a prayer offered up to God as he concludes these prefatory remarks.[89]

Both the style of the commentary which follows and William's exegetical emphasis carry forth this announced project. In a homiletic and repetitive vein, interlarded with pious ejaculations, he passes lightly over the more speculative doctrines of Paul in Romans and lets the weight of his commentary fall on the moral corrolaries which he sees as flowing from Paul's teaching on justification. Given these purposes, William feels that he can dispense with a general introduction providing an *accessus* to Romans, and moves ahead without further ado to the glossing of every line. His emphasis can clearly be seen in his handling of some of this epistle's most famous passages. In glossing Romans 1:19, for instance, where the apostle states that the invisible things of God can be known through the creation, William makes no effort to enter into a positive discussion of the scope and character of natural theology. Indeed, this is a subject that he wants to ventilate as little as possible. The message he wants to convey in his comment on this line is that, given what Paul has said, the gentiles cannot be

---

[88] William of St. Thierry, *Expositio in Epistolam ad Romanos* 3:27, *PL* 180: 579D.
[89] Ibid., praefatio, *PL* 180: 547A–548D.

excused for failing to know and to do what is morally correct.[90] Continuing, he takes sharp issue with the philosophers who claim that they can discover God's eternity, immutability, intelligence, intelligibility, wisdom, and truth through a rational examination of the creation,[91] in a diatribe that completely loses touch with Paul's positive statement in this passage. Unlike Paul, William wants to argue that men can come to a knowledge of God only through grace, and not through an inspection of nature, a position that leads him to skew Paul's own argument. At the same time, William wants to inspire moral conversion in his audience. This goal leads him to focus repeatedly on a constellation of ideas concerning moral choice and moral behavior. He accents the point that inner intention is more important than external ethical action, that sin and virtue lie in consent, that the faith that justifies is the faith that works in love, that God expects man to cooperate with Him in the working out of his salvation.[92] Despite William's heavy reliance on Augustine, the moral theology with which he emerges emphasizes human free will much more that either Paul or Augustine does, in his effort to stress the moral responsibilities of his readers and in his desire to exemplify, in his own person, the teacher's proper role of consolation and exhortation.[93]

It is true that William's place in the theological debates of his time and his zealous attack on Abelard may account for the special pleading that distorts his reading of Romans. Our second monastic example, Hervaeus of Bourg-Dieu (ca. 1080–ca. 1150) was a figure less in the limelight, who had less of a public image to defend. His commentary on Romans may thus be used to gain a sense of what a more standard and less tendentious monastic exegesis of that epistle would convey. The exact date of his work is not known, but it clearly post-dates the Pauline commentaries of Peter Abelard and Peter Lombard, because Hervaeus makes use of their introductory remarks in his own *accessus*. As with these scholastic exegetes, Hervaeus explains why the Epistle to the Romans is the first epistle given in the New Testament, although it was not the first one written by Paul. He observes that Paul wrote it, along with his other epistles, to instruct and remind the newly founded churches about the gospel. Other than that, he does not expatiate on the

---

[90] Ibid., 1:19, *PL* 180: 558C.
[91] Ibid., 1:24, *PL* 180: 558D–560B.
[92] Ibid., 3:20, 3:24–25, 3:38, 7:19, 7:22, 8:27–30, 12:1–2, *PL* 180: 577D, 578D, 581A–B, 621A–C, 622A–B, 640A, 669C–672A.
[93] Ibid., 12:4–7, *PL* 180: 672C–674C.

particular circumstances in the Roman church to which Paul speaks here, unlike both Abelard and the Lombard. While he notices that faith is a main theme of this epistle, this fact is less important to him than the moral consequences of belief. Paul, in his estimation, wrote to teach the Romans "how they should live and believe" (*quomodo vivant et credant*).[94] But faith is only the foundation of the virtues. The final cause of the epistle is morals, the conducing of the contemporary twelfth-century audience to beatitude. For this reason it is less important, for Hervaeus, to try to contextualize Paul's message in his own time, for the community to which he wrote, than it is to extract from the epistle the general features of his ethical teaching, which apply to the present, so that current readers will receive ethical guidance.[95]

Hervaeus is even less forthcoming than William in referring to patristic authorities and, like him, is completely uninterested in indicating that their readings may disagree. He chooses what he wants from the exegetical tradition, without naming his sources, and weaves this material seamlessly into his own commentary, presenting it as his own opinion. His chief stylistic tactic is repetition, hammering in his points over and over again with references drawn from other books of the Bible to aid the reader's reflection. Like William, he shies away from dogmatic speculation and looks primarily for the moral message that can be extracted from the Pauline text. In handling the *invisibilia dei* passage, for instance, Hervaeus acknowledges that natural reason can discern, by means of the creation, that the creator is eternal and omnipotent. God is known best, he adds, through his noblest creation, man, although this knowledge is not sufficient for salvation. The main point he wants to make in glossing this passage is not to specify the relations between reason and revelation. Nor is his main goal to consider either the modes of human knowledge or the analogies of the deity in nature and man. Rather, he wants to stress that, given man's dignity, his fall, and his redemption, man should strive for the highest good.[96] Throughout his commentary, the moral theology developed by Hervaeus is largely unexceptional. Although he tends to read Paul on the flesh and the spirit in a more dualistic manner than the sense of the text might indicate, he offers a generic, and even a banal, exhortation to moral activism that depresses Paul's

---

[94] Hervaeus of Bourg-Dieu, *In Epistolam ad Romanos* praefatio, *PL* 181: 594A.
[95] Ibid., *PL* 181: 595A–596C.
[96] Hervaeus of Bourg-Dieu, *In Ep. ad Romanos* 1:19–24, *PL* 181: 609B–611C.

emphasis on faith and that largely avoids the complexities in his treatment of grace and free will.

PAULINE EXEGESIS AMONG THE LOMBARD'S SCHOLASTIC PREDECESSORS AND CONTEMPORARIES AND THE LOMBARD'S *COLLECTANEA*

In turning from the monastic commentators on Paul to the scholastic predecessors and contemporaries of the Lombard, we find ourselves in an environment where it was seen as necessary to associate Pauline exegesis with a different set of concerns and to approach Paul with a different exegetical method. For, in the eyes of the scholastics, Paul, more than any other New Testament writer, was both a source of Christian doctrine and the first major interpreter of it. In addition to being a model theologian, he was an authority who conveyed the Christian message differently to the different communities to which he had preached. Hence, he had not always written with the same emphasis, and he needed the help of other resources in his interpretation. More than any other biblical author, therefore, Paul was a test case for the development of hermeneutical strategies that could, at the same time, clarify his own theology, sort out the tradition of Pauline commentary and extract what was truly helpful, and use the findings so obtained as a foundation for theological speculation and construction. In grasping why Peter Lombard's *Collectanea* was deemed by other scholastic theologians of his century to have met the challenges posed by Pauline exegesis better than any other, we will need to compare it, as we have done with his Psalms commentary, with other scholastic exegeses of Paul available in his time. Similarly, our target period will be ca. 1115 to ca. 1160. In so doing, we will consider four main areas. First, there is the physical format and presentation of the material in the commentary itself. Next, there is the exegete's address to the text, how he discovers what Paul has said and how he introduces the text to his readers. Thirdly, we will consider the exegete's solution of problems in the text and his handling of authorities in so doing. And, finally, we will assay the way in which Pauline exegesis serves as a means by which the author develops his own theological outlook.

The physical format of the *Collectanea* is, initially, its most noticeable feature, especially if one comes to it after examining other Pauline commentaries of the period. Commentators at this time typically used, in some combination, the continuous or running commentary, the gloss on individual words or phrases, and the theological question drawn from the text for more extended discussion.[97] In most cases the gloss and the question hold pride of place, threatening to usurp the continuous commentary and even to ignore the text of the epistle itself. To make use of such works, the reader has to have a copy of Paul along with the commentary, in order to see how, or whether, the glosses or questions are related to the sense of the epistle. In contrast, Peter gives the reader Paul's entire text, quoted in coherent subdivisions. He begins by offering a running commentary on each of these subdivisions, before lemmatizing individual passages he wants to gloss or developing theological questions. He thus offers a better balance than any exegete of his time between the general need for an understanding of Paul's argument and the more technical requirements of scholastic readers.[98] The only contemporary exegete of Paul who also quotes chunks of the apostle's text before adding his own analysis is Hervaeus of Bourg-Dieu. But, as we have noted, Hervaeus wrote after Peter Lombard and may well have derived this idea from him.

Also, as we have seen above, Hervaeus is not interested in positioning his reading of Paul in the tradition of patristic and more recent commentary. In this respect as well the *Collectanea* has a format that makes it much easier to use than its competitors. From the *Glossa ordinaria* to Robert of Melun's *Quaestiones de epistolis Pauli*, most exegetes use the *"usque ad"* technique of Florus of Lyon to cite their authorities, offering only the first and the last few words of the quotation. Thus, the citation is a mere finding tool. In order to use it, the reader has to have a library as extensive as that of the exegete. On the other hand, Peter gives either a complete quotation of the passage cited, or a detailed paraphrase of it, so that the reader can follow Peter's argument without having to look up references at every turn. In making both Paul and the authorities adduced fully available to the reader, the *Collectanea*, as a commentary, is a one-stop operation. And, from the very earliest manuscripts, the information is displayed visually in the manner just described. Its format alone thus makes the *Collectanea*, physically, the most usable work of Pauline exegesis of the period.[99]

---

[97] Gustave Bardy, "La littérature patristique des '*Quaestiones et responses*' sur l'Écriture sainte," *Revue biblique* 41 (1932): 210–36, 341–69, 515–37; 42 (1934): 14–30; Bernardo C. Bazán, "La *quaestio disputata*," in *Les Genres littéraires dans les sources théologiques et philosophiques médiévales: Défininition, critique et exploitation* (Louvain-la-Neuve: Institut d'Études Médiévales, 1982), pp. 33–34; Lobrichon, "Une nouveauté," pp. 93–114; Smalley, *Study*, pp. 42–86; Ceslaus Spicq, *Esquisse d'une histoire de l'exégèse latine au moyen âge* (Paris: J. Vrin, 1944), pp. 62–108.

[98] Lobrichon, "Une nouveauté," pp. 109–10.

[99] Ibid.

Closely related to Peter's responsiveness to the needs of readers in this respect is his desire to present the epistle as a text, and Paul as an author, whose aims and strategies of argument require explanation if the reader is going to grasp the epistle's sense. Now, all twelfth-century exegetes possessed the brief introductions to the books of the Bible, including the Pauline epistles, provided by Jerome. Many of them, like the authors of the *Glossa ordinaria*, are content merely to repeat these potted introductions. The Lombard aligns himself with another group of exegetes, including Peter Abelard, who instead supply their own elaborate *accessus ad Paulum*, using the same approach as other scholars of the time to the texts they sought to interpret.[100] While Abelard and the Lombard share this taste, and while they indeed cover much of the same ground in their assessment of the circumstances in which Paul had written, the nature of Paul's audience, and the subdivisions of his argument, the Lombard stands out for the degree to which he lets his *accessus* control his actual reading of the text. For his part, Abelard tends to forget his introductory remarks almost at once, rushing off onto a host of peculiarly Abelardian theological tangents in the body of his commentary, many of which have only the most tenuous connection with the agenda of Romans, the one Pauline epistle which he glosses, as he has outlined it. This fact makes it clear that Abelard's real reason for studying Romans is to use Paul *ex post facto* to support some of the idiosyncratic and controversial positions which he had already taken.[101]

This same approach influenced two other mid-century scholastic exegetes, Robert of Melun and the anonymous Abelardian author

---

[100] On this development in general, see Edwin A. Quain, "The Medieval *Accessus ad auctores*," *Traditio* 3 (1945): 215–64, who makes passing reference to exegetes on p. 261 nn. 1 and 2. More recent treatments which include discussions of *accessus* to books of the Bible in the twelfth century include Minnis, *Medieval Theory of Authorship*, ch. 1–2 and Minnis and Scott, ed., *Medieval Literary Theory and Criticism*, pp. 69–71, although both confine themselves to Peter's commentary on the Psalms without discussing his Pauline glosses. For the Lombard on St. Paul, see Marcia L. Colish, "From *sacra pagina* to *theologia*: Peter Lombard as an Exegete of Romans," *Medieval Perspectives* 6 (1991): 1–19; "Peter Lombard as an Exegete of St. Paul," in *Ad litteram: Authoritative Texts and Their Medieval Readers*, ed. Mark D. Jordan and Kent Emery, Jr. (Notre Dame: University of Notre Dame Press, 1992), pp. 71–92.

[101] Peter Abelard, *Commentaria in Epistolam Pauli ad Romanos* prologus 1.1, ed. Eligius M. Buytaert in Peter Abelard, *Opera theologica*, CCCM 11–13 (Turnhout: Brepols, 1969–87), 11: 43–55 for the *accessus* and Abelard's other introductory remarks. His departures from this agenda in the body of the work have been noted by Buytaert, ibid., pp. 17–20; Rolf Peppermüller, *Abaelards Auslegung des Römerbriefes*, Beiträge, n.F. 10 (Münster: Aschendorff, 1972), pp. 10–24.

of the text known as the *Commentarius Cantabridgensis*. Both know, and use, the Abelardian and Lombardian *accessus*. And, both follow Abelard's lead in presenting it and then abandoning it in the pursuit of their own theological excursions, some of which drift perilously far from the Pauline mainland. To be sure, Peter also makes excursuses of his own in his theological questions on the Pauline epistles. But he is careful to root them in Paul's context and to steer the reader firmly back to Paul when he is finished. Peter's treatment of exegesis as a primarily rhetorical assignment in this sense reflects his desire to present Paul to his readers as a working theologian, and not just as a source of theological raw materials.

This commitment also requires, for Peter, an understanding of Paul in his own time and place, and a literal reading of his text. It must be stressed here that it was the scholastic exegetes, such as Peter, who were chiefly concerned with retrieving a literal and historical reading of the text. This point may require some insistence, because the prevailing views on this subject still rely heavily on the work of scholars who have paid it inadequate attention. For instance, Henri DeLubac and Ceslaus Spicq stress the pervasiveness of the taste for a polysemous reading of the Bible in the twelfth century, and ignore or soft-pedal those forms of exegesis which do not fit into this mold.[102] The impulse toward literal exegesis is credited by Beryl Smalley to the Victorines.[103] But, in giving them the credit, she pays insufficient attention to two facts. The first is that the literalism of the Victorines, their quest for the *hebraica veritas*, was confined to the Old Testament; it did not extend systematically to the New Testament. And second, they sought to recover the historical sense of Scripture not for the purpose of doctrinal analysis but in order to build a contemplative superstructure on top of that foundation.[104] A partial corrective to the traditional picture of twelfth-century exegesis has been supplied by Marie-Dominique Chenu and Gillian Evans, who accent the ways in which scholastic exegetes imported into their work the technical contributions of

---

[102] Henri DeLubac, *Exégèse médiévale: Les quatre sens de l'écriture*, 2 parts 1–2 (Paris: Aubier, 1961–64); Spicq, *Esquisse*, pp. 70–71; "Pourquoi le moyen âge n'a-t-il pas davantage pratiqué l'exégèse littérale?" *RSPT* 30 (1941–42): 169–79.

[103] Smalley, *Study*, pp. xvii, xxi, 83–195.

[104] Grover A. Zinn, "*Historia fundamentum est*: The Role of History in the Contemplative Life according to Hugh of St. Victor," in *Contemporary Reflections on the Medieval Christian Tradition: Essays in Honor of Ray C. Petry*, ed. George H. Schriver (Durham: Duke University Press, 1974), pp. 138–44, 146–58. See also Châtillon, "La Bible," pp. 186–88, 194.

their colleagues in the liberal arts.[105] But this style of exegesis might, or might not, associate itself with a primary interest in the literal or historical level of the Pauline text. On the other hand, the scholastics wanted to grasp the literal sense of Paul's teaching because they wanted to use it as a basis, and a model, for dogmatic speculation and construction. Their interest in the historical setting in which Paul had written derived largely from their perception that this background was a help in understanding what he had said, and also from their desire to place Paul in historical perspective as a means of contextualizing his teachings. It was the scholastic exegetes, and above all Peter Lombard, who promoted this idea in its most widespread form, as an adjunct to getting their Pauline theology straight.

In this connection, too, Peter's reading of Paul is striking in comparison with that of his immediate predecessors and contemporaries. The *Glossa ordinaria* offers a no-frills summary of Paul, or, at least, of those lines which the glossator lemmatizes; but he sometimes gives Paul a polysemous reading. The glossator is generally content to rephrase what Paul, or some patristic reader of Paul, has said, in his own words, and rarely goes much farther.[106] Gilbert of Poitiers, whose glosses on Paul date to ca. 1130, is even more consistently interested in connecting the literal and allegorical senses of the text.[107] And, while independent in other respects, Abelard's commentary on Romans, dated provisionally to the years 1135–39, does not depart from the Laon tradition on this point.[108] By contrast, apart from a single passage in 2 Thessalonians on the Antichrist, the Lombard's exposition of Paul pays rigorous attention to the letter and to the historical context of each Pauline epistle.

The most sustained example of the Lombard's contextualization

---

[105] Marie-Dominique Chenu, *La théologie au douzième siècle* (Paris: J. Vrin, 1957), pp. 329–37, 344–45; Evans, *Language and Logic*, passim.

[106] Evans, *Language and Logic*, pp. 41–47.

[107] Vincenzo Miano, "Il Commento alle Lettere di S. Paolo di Gilberto Porretano," in *Scholastica: Ratione historico-critica instauranda* (Rome: Pontificium Athenaeum Antonianum, 1951), pp. 171–78; Maurice Simon, "La Glose de l'épître aux Romains de Gilbert de la Porrée," *RHE* 52 (1957): 68–70. For the date of this work, see Elswijk, *Gilbert Porreta*, pp. 57–58; Maioli, *Gilberto Porreta*, pp. xxxiii. I have not inspected the manuscripts myself.

[108] Damien Van den Eynde, "Les écrits perdus d'Abélard," *Antonianum* 37 (1962): 468; confirmed by Buytaert, CCCM 11: 16; Peppermüller, *Abaelards Auslegung*, p. 10; "Exegetische Traditionen und theologische Neuansätze in Abaelards Kommentar zum Römerbrief," in *Peter Abelard*, ed. Eligius M. Buytaert (Leuven: Leuven University Press, 1974), pp. 117–19. For the date, see Buytaert, CCCM 11: xxii–xv.

of Paul is his commentary on the Epistle to the Hebrews. As with previous scholastic commentators on this text, he reprises Jerome's brief introduction, which observes that Paul wrote to a group of converts from Judaism, that he wrote in Hebrew not in Greek, and that he attacked the vice of pride. The *Glossa ordinaria* stops there, and it is only at verse 7:8, where the apostle refers to Melchisedech and the Levites, that the glossator makes any effort to connect Paul's actual argument to this stated agenda.[109] For his part, Peter takes the argument of Jerome found in the *Glossa ordinaria* as his starting point but goes on from there, with a full and detailed introduction of his own, in which he emphasizes the point that Paul's whole strategy in Hebrews is to remind the Jewish converts of the Old Testament events and prophesies which have been fulfilled in the revelation of Christ. Peter urges that Paul is, indeed, the author of Hebrews even though his salutation in this epistle differs in style from those prefacing his other epistles, notably by omitting reference to his name and his status as an apostle. This tactic, according to Peter, is a deliberate omission on his part. Following Jerome, he observes that Paul was sensitive to the fact that his name was hateful to the Jews. Hence, he does not identify himself, lest this opinion prevent his readers from profiting from his message. Likewise, Paul's omission of his status as apostle is designed to teach a lesson in humility, since the major thrust of the epistle is that faith is sufficient, and that the Jewish converts cannot pride themselves on their former status as the chosen people or on their observance of the ceremonial law. Peter notes as well that Paul has written this epistle in Hebrew, and that it displays a style more eloquent than in his other epistles (*et longe splendidiore et facundiore stylo quam aliae resplendeat*). This fluency is attributable to the fact that Hebrew is his native language. As Peter observes, the apostle's overall strategy in Hebrews is to emphasize the connections between the truths adumbrated in the Old Testament and those perfected in the New, "as if there, as a shadow, and here, as the truth" (*quasi ibi umbra, hic veritas*).[110]

This preface sets the stage for Peter's thoroughly typological analysis of Paul's Old Testament references. Conscious of the fact that this is Paul's own tactic, he amplifies on it himself. At Hebrews 1:8–12 and again at 1:12–14 he weaves additional quotations from

---

[109] *Biblia latina cum Glossa ordinaria*, 4: *Epistola ad Hebraeos* praefatio; *PL* 114: 643A, 655A–B.

[110] Peter Lombard, *In Epistolam ad Hebraeos* argument, 1.1–7, *PL* 192: 399A–401A: The quotations are at 400B and 401A respectively.

the Psalms into the main body of Paul's text, and combines them with other Old Testament passages that bolster the apostle's own technique of argument.[111] At chapters 7 and 8 Peter explores in detail the parallels between Melchisedech and Christ and between the Levitical priesthood and the Christian priesthood, accenting as well the superiority of the latter in that it is not confined to any one tribe or group; further, the sacrifice of Christ is greater than the sacrifices offered by the Old Testament priests in that it is the sacrifice of God's own son for the whole human race, rather than the sacrifice of a purely created being for a limited community.[112] Throughout, and responsive to Paul's intentions, Peter preserves a balance between the continuities linking the old and new covenants and the consummation of the former in the latter. For its part, the *Glossa ordinaria* makes no comment on why Paul interlards his argument with references to the Psalms and other passages from the Old Testament and tends to emphasize the differences between the two covenants while omitting their continuities.

There are two coevals of Peter who, although they paraphrase his introductory remarks, ignore the Pauline agenda which those remarks announce, in their actual handling of the text. The Abelardian author of a commentary on the Pauline epistles called the *Commentarius Cantabridgensis*, produced between 1141 and 1153, alludes to Paul's main theme in passing only twice, in a gloss otherwise notable primarily for the heavy attention it pays to dogmatic matters and for its unusual number of digressions and irrelevancies. Glossing Hebrews 5, he asks how the Old Testament sacrifices remitted sin. On Abelard's authority, he responds that they did so only partially, saving their practitioners from Hell and assigning them to Purgatory instead. What he really wants to talk about are the differences between these two posthumous states. Similarly, he argues, circumcision, even in its own time, was less efficacious than baptism in the Christian dispensation. The author goes on to note that Christ received both rites even though He needed neither. In these passages, the relations between the Old and New Testaments stressed by Paul slip away into discussions of Last Things and Christology which are not germane to Paul's argument in this context.[113] The author's only other effort to re-

---

[111] Ibid., *PL* 192: 410C–414A.

[112] Ibid., *PL* 192: 447B–460C.

[113] *In Epistolam ad Hebraeos*, in *Commentarius Cantabridgensis in Epistolas Pauli e schola Petri Abaelardi*, ed. Artur Michael Landgraf, 4 vols. (Notre Dame: University of Notre Dame Press, 1937–45), 4: 724–25, 734. On the dating of this commentary, see Landgraf's analysis, 1: xv.

spond to Paul's agenda is also found in his gloss on the same chapter. How, he asks, are we to understand the idea that Abraham is our father in faith? The question suggests to him the idea that faith, not circumcision, was salvific in Old Testament times since some men, like Abraham, were saved by their faith before circumcision was instituted. So far, so good. But, from this point he moves to an idea which Paul could not have addressed, a critique of monks who devote their wits to the praise of poverty, from which he segues to a recapitulation of the *aut liberi aut libri* topos as treated by Jerome and Theophrastus. This batch of apparent *non sequiturs* is loosely strung together and connected to Paul by the thought that people should do whatever they do for the right moral reasons, not for reasons that may be externally applauded or condemned, a conclusion which the glossator caps with a quotation from Jerome which is actually a citation of Gregory the Great.[114] As this passage illustrates, Abelard was not always fortunate in his disciples. Nor, in this case, is Paul or the reader seeking to discover his concerns in Hebrews.

Another exegete of Hebrews in our target group is Robert of Melun, whose commentary on Paul dates to ca. 1145–55 and who draws on both the Lombard and on Abelard. Robert's interests stray even farther from Paul's text than do those of the Cambridge commentator. He raises only two questions that even touch on it, the comparison between Melchisedech and Christ and the sense in which Abraham is our father in faith. His treatment of the first question is extremely abbreviated, both as a comparison and as a contrast, while he fails to take Paul's point about the second. Discussing how various *figurae* can be understood as descent from the loins of Abraham, Robert treats the connection between Abraham and the rest of mankind physically, not in terms of faith. Robert's chief concern here is how this connection can be true of Christ since Christ lacked original sin, which is transmitted physically through the loins of the parents.[115] With this problem we drift perilously far both from Paul's subject matter and his meaning. While Robert's commentary is replete with other debates and questions, none of them bears any particular relationship to the text of Hebrews.

The glossing of Paul's Epistle to the Romans also supplies good

---

[114] Ibid., 4: 738–41.

[115] Robert of Melun, *In Epistolam ad Hebraeos*, in *Quaestiones de Epistolis Pauli*, ed. Raymond-M. Martin (Louvain: Spicilegium Sacrum Lovaniense, 1938), pp. 302–04. For the date, see Martin's analysis, pp. lvi–lvii.

examples of Peter's willingness to let a literal and historical reading
of the text, as well as Paul's own theme, direct his theological
reflections on it, in a manner that stands out from that of other
contemporary exegetes. His sense of Paul's agenda in this epistle
enables him to connect passages of Romans often treated as separate items by other commentators. Peter recognizes that they are
related to each other in Paul's argument. Connected passages,
which he reads conjointly in this way, are Paul's injunctions on
obedience to worldly authority in Romans 13:1–6[116] and his criticisms of chambering and wantonness later in that chapter and of
Jewish dietary practices in chapter 14.[117] The *Glossa ordinaria* deals
with Romans 13:1–6 in an extremely perfunctory manner, simply
restating Paul's advice in the form of a deductive syllogism and
adding Augustine's idea that rulers must be obeyed as a punishment for sin.[118] Abelard turns this portion of his commentary into a
mini-treatise on political theory, designed to defend the subject's
right to resist a tyrant, defined as a usurper, who therefore lacks
divine authorization.[119] The fact that Paul is neither advocating nor
even considering the rights of subjects in this passage escapes
Abelard's attention. Robert of Melun focuses his attention on
another non-Pauline concern, the distinction between secular and
ecclesiastical authority.[120] So does the Victorine author of the
Quaestiones et decisiones in Epistolas divi Pauli, dating to the years
1155–65, in raising the question, which he fails to answer, of
whether a ruler should be obeyed if his commands contravene the
will of God.[121]

Apart from introducing issues that had not been on Paul's mind
in Romans, none of these exegetes tries to explain what Paul's
advice on rulership is doing in this particular epistle. The reverse is
the case with the Lombard. He sees Paul's main goal in this
passage as the repression of pride and the inculcation of humility,
which is part of the wider message of Romans.[122] Paul is here

---

[116] Peter Lombard, *In Epistolam Pauli ad Romanos* 13:1–6, *PL* 191: 1503D–1506C.
[117] Ibid., 13:13–14, 14:1–3, *PL* 191: 1510B–1513A.
[118] *Biblia latina cum Glossa ordinaria*, 4: *Epistola ad Romanos* 13:1–6; *PL* 114: 512C.
[119] Peter Abelard, *In Ep. ad Romanos* 13:1. CCCM 11: 286.
[120] Robert of Melun, *In Epistolam ad Romanos* 13:1 in *Quaest. de Ep. Pauli*, pp. 152–54.
[121] *Quaestiones et decisiones in Epistolas divi Pauli* q. 299–301, *PL* 175: 505A–C.
[122] Peter Lombard, *In Ep. ad Romanos* prologus, 13:1–6, *PL* 191: 1300C–1302A,
1503D–1506C. Affeldt, *Die weltliche Gewalt*, pp. 139–46, 153–66, 189–98, does not
distinguish adequately between the Lombard's handling of this text and that of his
immediate predecessors and successors.

addressing the men who wield authority as well as their subjects. Rulers, he notes, are being enjoined by the apostle to acknowledge their dependence on God and their responsibilities to their subjects. They have a divine mandate; and they will be held accountable for the way they exercise it. Subjects are being enjoined to patience and obedience, in recognition of the fact that rulers have to punish evildoers. On both sides, Peter observes, Paul is talking about duties, not rights. In particular, Paul is emphasizing the need for concord within the Roman Christian community, composed as it is of both pagan and Jewish converts. Whatever their origins, the members of the Roman church should live in harmony under their leaders, whichever element happens to be represented more strongly in the leadership; and the leaders should govern without fear or favor toward one group or another in the community.

Peter then goes on to read Paul's advice about feasting and foodstuffs in the next section of Romans as a follow-up of the apostle's more general teaching on community relations. Peter gets the idea that Paul's views on eating in Romans are conditioned by the needs of the pagan and Jewish converts from the *Glossa ordinaria*[123] and goes on from there. *Roma la golosa* was evidently alive and well in the first century A.D., he points out, and the apostle was well aware of that fact. His attack on overindulgence in food and drink is thus aimed specifically at the formerly pagan Romans; he urges them instead to make their natural needs the measure of their intake and, otherwise, to treat food medicinally. For Paul, the Jewish converts also have their own culturally induced blind spot with respect to food, and he directs his remarks about the supersession of the Mosaic dietary laws to them. In commenting on these passages Peter is concise and to the point. He is concerned only with linking Paul's advice to both segments of the Roman community to each other and to the wider theme of Romans. On the other hand, other twelfth-century exegetes of Romans tend to get sidetracked by this part of the epistle. Abelard uses his exegesis of Romans 13:13 to flaunt his knowledge of Ovid as an authority on the connection between feasting, drinking, and sexual excess.[124] On the Jewish dietary laws, he brings forward an irrelevant comparison of authorities who disagree on the propriety of eating the flesh of animals used in pagan sacrifices.[125] Paul does take up that subject, but not in Romans 14. Although the

---

[123] *Biblia latina cum Glossa ordinaria*, 4: *Ep. ad Romanos* 13:13; *PL* 114: 514B.
[124] Peter Abelard, *In Ep. ad Romanos* 13:13, CCCM 11: 295.
[125] Ibid., 14:23, CCCM 11: 307–11.

Cambridge commentator does not gloss that theme in Romans, he does, at length, in his commentary on 1 Timothy. Picking up on the point that food should be used medicinally, he considers how various authorities have classified foods in this respect. He is fascinated and bewildered by the fact that Ambrose listed garlic as a medicine, not as a food. After wrestling with this point for some time, he concludes that Ambrose's bizarre tastes are a consequence of his Lombard origins.[126] This is, no doubt, a fascinating window into the world of medieval gastronomic trivia. But it cannot be said that this commentator, or Abelard either, has shed much light on why Paul is interested in food in Romans, in contrast with Peter Lombard.

Peter's consistent interest in contextualizing Paul and in allowing Paul's goals and rhetorical strategies to control his own interpretation does not mean that Peter regards a literal and historical reconstruction of Paul as his sole obligation. There is another dimension to Peter's handling of Paul which must be appreciated, the application of historical criticism to Paul as a biblical writer. As we have noted above, both canonists and theologians in the early twelfth century were developing historical and other modes of criticism as it attached to patristic and other post-biblical authorities in the effort to ascertain how weighty their authority was, how generally it had been intended, and the degree to which if could be magnified or relativized in aid of contemporary needs and debates. What is less well known is the fact that exegetes such as the Lombard were willing to extend the same kind of criticism to Paul himself. In so doing, they show a keen sense of the changes which the church had undergone over the centuries, changes in its beliefs and doctrinal emphases no less than changes in its institutions. Like others in this group, Peter accepts this phenomenon of change, not necessarily as a sad departure from the apostolic age held up as a timeless norm, but rather as a natural development, and one that permits us to see that what made sense in the *ecclesia primitiva* may not be appropriate in the here and now. Peter's historical criticism of Paul, in this sense, partakes more of the contemporary theologians' "moderns versus ancients" conception of the primitive church than it reflects the canonists' desire to modernize or reinvent the primitive church as an ideal. A few examples will serve to illustrate this point.

To begin with, there are cases in which Peter treats develop-

---

[126] *In primam Epistolam ad Timotheum* 4:34, in *Comm. Cant.*, 3: 579.

ments in church history simply as facts we need to know in order to understand what Paul is saying, in a manner fairly neutral with respect to Paul's authority. Thus, in commenting on the apostle's warning against building doctrine on false foundations in Romans 15:15–22, Peter observes that Paul was referring here to the pseudoapostolic tradition and the apocrypha, which had not yet been weeded out of the biblical tradition, since Paul wrote prior to the establishment of the canon of Scripture.[127] Another comparatively neutral historical *scholium*, but one suggesting the transitoriness of the church's institutional arrangements, is Peter's discussion of the women whom Paul addresses or refers to in his epistles, as exercising a leadership role in the church, and his reaction to Paul's countervailing rule that women remain silent in church. In commenting on this apparent contradiction at 1 Corinthians 14:34–40, he sees the injunction to silence as conditioned, for this particular community, by the apostle's desire to correct moral and doctrinal error which had been spread by the teaching of women immediately before his composition of the epistle. Here, then, Paul's rule is a tactic designed to correct a local abuse and is not a general prohibition. Customs of this type, Peter concludes, are not fixed, in contrast to the substance of the gospels.[128]

The silence of women recurs in 1 Timothy 2:12–15, and here it is a theme which Peter orchestrates rather differently. In this passage, he accounts for Paul's rule as a corollary of the subjection of wives to husbands as a punishment for original sin. But his main point is to criticize Paul, who goes on to say that women can none the less be saved through childbearing. Peter regards this claim as ludicrous. He does not hesitate to explain why. Like men, he observes, women will be saved by their faith, their love, and their persistence in virtue, whether they are married or single, fruitful or barren. Childbearing cannot be regarded as salvific, since it is a natural biological function found in women as such regardless of their beliefs. At 1 Timothy 3:5–6, Peter notes that Paul himself had no objection to the then-current practice of ordaining women as deacons, a fact which Peter then uses to undercut the apostle's apparent relegation of women to purely domestic roles.[129] It might

---

[127] Peter Lombard, *In Ep. ad Romanos*, *PL* 191: 1524C.

[128] Peter Lombard, *In I Epistolam ad Corinthios*, *PL* 191: 1672B–C.

[129] Peter Lombard, *In I Epistolam ad Timotheum* 2:12–15, 3:5–6, *PL* 192: 340A–342C, 345D–346A. The moral equality of the sexes in the Christian life is a point he also makes at *In Epistolam ad Colossenses* 3:6–17, *PL* 192: 282D–283A.

be noted, as a footnote to the Lombard's exegesis of 1 Timothy, that the Cambridge commentator enthusiastically endorses his critique of Paul on women. Yoking it with an opinion of Abelard's, he amplifies Peter's point about female leadership in the church by observing that abbesses nowadays perform functions similar to those of the female deacons of Paul's time; and, furthermore, abbesses fitly exercise the teaching office in the church.[130] This argument, like Peter's, uses historical criticism to point up Paul's apparent inconsistency. The argument underscores the exegete's own preference for one aspect of Paul's teaching, seen as normal to Paul, over another, seen as an aberration from that norm, bringing to bear on the text the fact that institutions and the rules governing women, in this case, do change, and appropriately, over time.

There are two other contexts, marriage and the coming of Antichrist, in which Peter imposes a much more stringent mode of historical criticism upon Paul in the effort to limit the force of his authority. In his commentary on 1 Corinthians, where Paul concedes marriage but urges that those who can remain celibate, like himself, Peter pointedly dismisses the apostle's preference for celibacy and uses the occasion to develop a treatise on marriage that highlights the essentials of the position on marriage which he later develops in the *Sentences*. Peter insists that marriage is a good thing and a sacrament which was instituted in Eden before the fall. Marriage is grounded in the present consent of the spouses. Their sexual relations, when ordered to the ends of marriage, are either not sinful at all or at most minimally sinful and excusable. Customs regarding marriage have changed over time. This being the case, Paul was mistaken in regarding marriage not as a requirement but as an indulgence. In truth, Peter states, the reverse is the case; it is continence that is the indulgence. Marriage, after all, is the calling followed by the many. Theologians and preachers, from Paul to the present, he implies, have a duty to address the realities in the lives of most believers. After all, continence requires a special grace which God concedes to very few, a fact which Paul ought to have kept in mind. Peter hastens to add that marital chastity and fidelity are also charisms and gifts of God, but they are distributed more widely. Given the fact that the apostle is aware of all this, Peter finds Paul both logically and theologically inconsistent in his advocacy of the celibate life.[131]

---

[130] *In primam Ep. ad Timotheum*, in *Comm. Cant.*, 3: 251, 261, 274–76.
[131] Peter Lombard, *In I Ep. ad Corinthios* 7:1–28, *PL* 191: 1585D–1597A.

But how is it, Peter asks, that the apostle has arrived at these misguided conclusions? It is at this point that Peter detonates the exegetical time-bomb that he has dropped. Paul's counsel on all of these matters, he points out, was predicated on his belief that the second coming of Christ was imminent, a belief that encouraged him to advise against marital entanglements for those who were single. Now, this belief about the impending end of the *saeculum* is, to be sure, a historical datum about Paul and his times. But, Peter continues, as we are well aware, this world is very much still with us. Thus, we can and should adjust our perspective on marriage and celibacy accordingly. Not even Paul deprived married people of future glory, he observes, implying that Paul's teaching is not wholly consistent even judged in the light of its now superseded eschatological expectations. But the full force of Peter's historical criticism of Paul on marriage in 1 Corinthians is to use it to qualify Paul's theological authority on this subject to the point of dismissing it and to legitimate his own sharp departures from Paul on the theology of marriage.[132]

In addition to misinforming Paul's views on marriage, his teaching on the imminent end of the age yields some other difficulties which Peter seeks to iron out, with the effect of scaling down Paul's authority, by means of historical criticism. The problem is located in the discrepancies between Paul's handling of the Antichrist in 1 and 2 Thessalonians. In his *accessus* to these epistles, Peter acknowledges the fact that Paul was responding to the Thessalonians' curiosity about Last Things, and the errors they had embraced on that subject. The content of the two epistles, he notes, is quite similar, even redundant. Whence, it remains unclear (*licet obscure*) why Paul felt the need to repeat himself.[133] This is especially obscure given the inconsistent descriptions of Antichrist in these two epistles. The difficulties involved lead Peter to depart from his usual exegetical practice. This is the one place in his commentary on Paul where he adds to a strictly literal reading of the text a spiritual dimension, for reasons which will now be apparent. In 1 Thessalonians, Paul depicts Antichrist as a supernatural being, who will reign for three years before being killed by the Archangel Michael. On the other hand, in 2 Thessalonians, he identifies the

---

[132] Ibid., 7:29–35, *PL* 191: 1597B–1598D. For Peter's fuller views on marriage, see *Sent.* 4. d. 26-d. 42, 2: 416–509.

[133] Peter Lombard, *In Epistolam I ad Thessalonicenses* argument; *In Epistolam II ad Thessalonicenses* argument, *PL* 192: 287D–290A, 311A–312C. The quotation is at 311A.

Antichrist with the Roman Empire of the first century A.D. The fall
of the Antichrist is thus equated with the downfall of the Roman
Empire as a world power. This discrepancy had been noticed in the
Glossa ordinaria. The glossator had amplified on the account in 1
Thessalonians, drawing on Daniel for additional information on
the Antichrist and the Apocalypse, but he had repeated the Roman
imperial version of the story in glossing 2 Thessalonians without
trying to square these two accounts.[134] Peter seconds his strategy on
1 Thessalonians, bringing additional Old Testament prophetic
material to bear on Paul's scenario in that epistle.[135] But he takes a
rather different tack on 2 Thessalonians. Warming to his task, he
advises his readers that Paul was not forecasting the fall of Rome as
an actual historical event. Paul was, no doubt, upset by the
persecution inflicted on Christians by the emperors during his time.
But Peter was aware that the Roman Empire later declared Christianity its official religion and protected the church. Thus, an
understanding of Rome different from the one offered by Paul must
be supplied in order to remedy the limitations of Paul's view read
literally.

Peter's solution is to associate Rome, in 2 Thessalonians, not
with the political imperium of Nero but with the spiritual imperium
of the Roman church, and to turn Paul's argument around by 180º.
The fall of Rome cannot mean the future political collapse of an
empire that has not been in existence for centuries. Rather, it
means the falling away of the churches from the Christian faith and
from obedience to Rome. The sense of Paul in 2 Thessalonians
would thus be that Christ will not return to judge the world until all
Christians have apostasized and all churches have fallen into
schism. Peter has recourse to Augustine and Haimo of Auxerre for
this interpretation. He depoliticizes the 2 Thessalonians account
still further by refusing to identify Antichrist with any human
leader, whether of church or state. The Antichrist, he says, will be
the son of the devil, but by imitation not filiation. He will arise in
Babylon, out of the tribe of Dan, as the Old Testament foretold.
But this notion must be read broadly, to include the Greeks as well
as the Jews. For, just as Christ possesses a fullness of divinity, so the
Antichrist possesses a fullness of malice, and his activities embrace
all the sons of pride of whatever nation. The key point Peter makes
is that the reign of Antichrist represents a negative spiritual condi-

---

[134] *Biblia latina cum Glossa ordinaria*, 4: *Epistola I ad Thessalonicenses* 4:15, 5:3;
Epistola II ad Thessalonicenses 2:3, 2:6–7; *PL* 114: 618D–619B, 622A–D.
[135] Peter Lombard, *In Ep. I ad Thess.* 5:1–11, *PL* 192: 306A–308A.

tion, which mankind will help to bring about by allowing faith to wane and charity to grow cold. In so arguing, Peter reject's Paul's equation between Antichrist and the historical Nero. His spiritualizing of the idea of Antichrist permits Peter to treat Nero not as the literal Antichrist but as a type of the Antichrist to come. To be sure, Nero's activities, like those of the other persecuting emperors, were evil and can be seen as having been inspired by the devil. But, Peter concludes, "Nero and the others are shadows of the future, that is, Antichrist, just as Abel and David were figures of Christ" (*et sunt Nero et alii umbra futuri, scilicet Antichristi, sicut Abel et David fuerunt figurae Christi*).[136] This resolution of the problem of Nero as Antichrist found warm support from Peter's immediate successors.[137]

In developing this theology of Antichrist, Peter does not confine himself to contextualizing and relativizing Paul's belief in the light of superseded apostolic expectations and the warping experience of persecution. He goes on from there to reinterpret the whole subject as pointing to a more general, and a less purely institutional, mystery of evil in which the infidelity of the churches is paralleled by the falling away from faith and charity on the part of individual Christians. He thus finds a way of handling Paul's treatment of Antichrist in 2 Thessalonians that is compatible with the account in 1 Thessalonians while expanding Paul's more historically limited political position into a universal moral doctrine, thus yoking his historical critique of Paul with a constructive theology of Antichrist, and one which draws on other post-biblical authorities and on his own ingenuity in the interest of clarification.

This leads us to another striking feature of Peter's *Collectanea* in comparison with other commentaries on Paul dating to our target period, his use of patristic and more recent authorities, both to provide a running commentary on the text and to assist in the unravelling of problematic passages. His recourse to such authorities for the light they shed on Paul is both deft and apposite. In particular, he is more concerned than are other scholastic exegetes of Paul during his time with confronting the fact that the authorities may not agree in their interpretation of Paul. When this is the case, Peter seizes on the fact as an opportunity to explain, by his

---

[136] Peter Lombard, *In Ep. II ad Thess.* 2:1–16, *PL* 192: 317B–321D. The quotation is at 318C. At 318D–319A Peter refers specifically to Nero and to the Augustinian point that he would have to be kept alive miraculously or resurrected specially in order to serve, literally, as the Antichrist. With Augustine, he finds this idea ridiculous.

[137] *In secundam Epistolam ad Thessalonicenses* 2:1–16, in *Comm. Cant.*, 3: 539–41; Robert of Melun, *De Epistola ad Thessalonicenses prima* 2:7, in *Quuest. de Ep. Pauli*, p. 296.

own word and example, how theological reasoning can be brought to bear on the conflicts among the authorities. In this connection, we see in his work as a Pauline exegete the same kinds of methodological concerns that he displays in his Psalms commentary and that surface even more systematically in his *Sentences*. In Peter's case, there is an organic relationship between his study of the *sacra pagina* and the teaching of systematic theology, from the standpoint of methodology no less than from the standpoint of doctrinal development.[138]

Consistent with his handling of conflicting authorities on all subjects in the *Sentences*, Peter's treatment of this problem in his exegesis of Paul accents two important methodological principles, which were often ignored by his contemporaries. In the first place, he finds it insufficient to resolve conflicts by the tactic of nude countercitation. The inadequacy of that method is plainly visible in the *Glossa ordinaria*. The glossator responsible for the Gospels of Matthew and Mark takes exception to Origen on salvation and on angels, and seeks to neutralize him by citing Augustine or Bede against him. But the commentary does not stop to explain why Origen's position is unacceptable and why Augustine and Bede are preferable.[139] On the other hand, Peter explains the reasoning that leads his authorities to the conclusions they adopt, giving his readers the capacity to judge the merits of those conclusions. At the same time, he is aware of the fact that the same authority sometimes contradicts himself. This circumstance may result from the rhetorical requirements of the arguments made by the authority at various points in his oeuvre. It may result from the fact that he has

---

[138] The most important studies of these interrelations have been made by Ignatius C. Brady, in his prolegomena to Books 3 and 4 of the *Sentences*, 2: 8*–52*, coupled with his edition of three texts reflecting Peter's earlier exegetically derived positions on the incarnation, the Eucharist, and marriage, ibid., pp. 53*–87*, which can be compared with his handling of these themes in his reworking of Rom. and 1 Cor. and in the *Sentences*. This material supplements Brady's earlier discussions of Peter's life and works in "Peter Lombard: Canon of Notre Dame," *RTAM* 32 (1965): 277–95 and "Peter Lombard," in *New Catholic Encyclopedia* (New York: McGraw-Hill Book Company, 1967), 11: 221–22. On the double redaction of the *Collectanea*, see also Jean Leclercq, "Les deux rédactions du prologue de Pierre Lombard sur les Épîtres de S. Paul," in *Misc. Lomb.*, pp. 109–12; Ermenegildo Bertola, "I commentari paolini di Pietro Lombardo e la loro duplice redazione," *Pier Lombardo* 3: 2–3 (1959): 75–90. On the connection between exegesis and theology in the Lombard, see also Glunz, *History of the Vulgate*, pp. 232–58; Gillian R. Evans, *Old Arts and New Theology: The Beginnings of Theology as an Academic Discipline* (Oxford: Clarendon Press, 1980), p. 42. These treatments of the point supersede Smalley, *Study*, p. 75.

[139] *Biblia latina cum Glossa ordinaria*, 4: *In Matthaeum* 25:48, *In Marcum* 1:2, 3:29; *PL* 114: 166D, 179C, 193C.

genuinely changed his mind. But these considerations need to be taken into account in deciding whether the authority's views in one case cancel out his views in another, or whether the problem in Paul's text on which one is seeking help from the authority can be resolved within the framework of that authority's thought more generally. Some examples will illustrate how Peter handles issues of this type.

At Romans 2:3–6, for instance, he grapples with the question of whether the sin against the Holy Spirit can be remitted. Some say, he observes, that this sin cannot be remitted because the souls of such sinners are so hardened by despair that they cannot feel the need or the desire for penance. Others say that the sin cannot be remitted because such sinners do not actually do penance, even thought they are capable of it. Peter adduces Augustine on Matthew in support of the first position and Augustine on Mark in support of the second. Now, Peter has another resolution of the question that he wants to advance and he rests his case on a third argument, made by Augustine on John. There, Peter notes, the sin against the Holy Spirit is held to be irremissible not because the sinner cannot or does not repent; he can indeed repent, but he does so rarely and with great difficulty. This conclusion Peter finds the most persuasive of the three and also compatible with the broader outlines of both Augustinian and Pauline theology. For, to say that this type of sinner could not repent would be to undercut his own freedom to respond to the grace of repentence. Equally, if not more important, it would limit the freedom and power of God to extend mercy in converting the sinner. This example is a nice index of the Lombard's awareness of the fact that Augustine is not a monolithic source, and also of the fact that one can discover, through an analysis of his reasoning in assorted *loci*, which Augustinian position is not only the most Augustinian, on the basis of its theological consistency with his idées maîtresses, but also which Augustinian position sheds the most light on Paul.[140]

Another case of conflicting authorities is one which required far more of a virtuoso turn to resolve, the vexed debate between Augustine and Jerome, arising from the text of Galatians, over whether the apostle Peter had dissimulated his beliefs, as a missionary tactic, and whether Paul had been right in criticizing him on that account. This had been a sticky issue from the patristic period onward, not only because it raised the question of whether apostles

---

[140] Peter Lombard, *In Ep. ad Romanos* 2:3–6, *PL* 191: 1340A D.

can lie, or err, but also because Porphyry had seized on this text, and the clash it provoked, as a means of taxing the Christians with being immoral and inconsistent. Jerome had stated that Peter had dissimulated his faith in participating in Jewish dietary practices, while Augustine had rejected that possibility out of hand. The Lombard's first line of attack is to bring the Acts of the Apostles to bear on Galatians. Acts, as he notes, shows that, on another occasion, Peter ate the flesh of animals used in pagan sacrifices, but without having participated in those sacrifices or having approved of them. This kind of dietary practice, he continues, is permitted elsewhere by Paul if it does not give scandal. By analogy, then, in Galatians Peter was fully aware of the suspension of the Jewish dietary laws by the new dispensation but he followed them in this instance so as not to alienate the people he sought to convert. Peter here was acting out a species of Paul's own advice, to become all things to all men for the sake of winning souls. With this reasoning in mind, Peter argues that we can say that Jerome is literally correct in stating that the apostle Peter behaved like a Jew, when he was a Christian. But Augustine is even more correct in stating that Peter's behavior was not mendacious. In the Lombard's view, Peter's actions were above board (*honesta*) because they were guided by good intentions. For his part, Paul was misinformed. His own intention to preach the gospel vehemently was a good intention, although on this occasion it had prevented him from grasping what Peter was really doing. Therefore, Paul was wrong to attack Peter. Peter's missionary zeal was also good, but it too had prevented him from seeing that, in the new dispensation, Jewish and gentile practices are not matters of indifference and that his missionary tactics might therefore be counterproductive. Thus, the Lombard treats both apostles as well-intentioned, although he does not think that either apostle translated his intention into appropriate action in the case at issue. He also sees the merits of the positions of both Augustine and Jerome, although with a preference for Augustine's.[141]

A comparison between the Lombard and other contemporary exegetes of Galatians shows how much his analysis of the patristic authorities on this passage helped to clear the air. The Cambridge commentator thinks that Peter can be excused because he was not truly lying, and because of the difficulties attached to evangelizing the Jews. His gloss on this text gives no indication that there is a

---

[141] Peter Lombard, *In Epistolam ad Galatas* 2:14, *PL* 192: 109D–114A.

patristic debate on it.[142] But Robert of Melun has clearly profited from the Lombard's exegesis. After reviewing his reasoning, Robert supplies an elegant refinement on it. He concludes that both apostles behaved in ways that can be thought of as wrong, externally. But both can be excused, because they acted in good conscience, and there were mitigating factors in each case.[143] Robert thus retains the balance between correct intention and appropriate action central to the Lombard's analysis but invokes the principle of dispensation and the lesser of the two evils as a way of reconciling Augustine and Jerome. And, like the Lombard, Robert shows how Paul's authority can be weighed and judged, and relativized, in the light of post-biblical authority and the ingenuity of the expositor.

While it is typically the confrontation of conflicting authorities or the effort to extract theological principles from the time-bound perspectives of the apostolic age that engender these displays of ratiocination, there are also cases in which the Lombard draws on the disciplines of the trivium as tools of analysis in his Pauline exegesis. As we have already seen, his *accessus* to each epistle exerts a firm control over his handling of his commentary in each case, suggesting the centrality of the discipline of rhetoric for him as a source of hermeneutical principles. Less pronounced, but also present, are his appeals to logic, although it has to be said that they are sparing in comparison with the Abelardians and Porretans. Both metaphor and logical analysis help Peter to gloss Romans 8:20–23, where Paul describes the entire creation as groaning and travailing as it awaits salvation. Now, the proper subject of salvation is man, not the rest of creation, says Peter. So, what does the phrase "all creation" mean here? It can be regarded, he observes, as a universal *(universale locutione)*. But it is a universal not in the sense that it collects the individual traits of all beings but rather in the sense that it collects all the traits of the singular beings, namely men, who are to be saved; for all aspects of human nature—mind, body, and spirit—are saved. At the same time, since he is composed of mind, body, and spirit, man is a microcosm of the rest of creation, and it is saved, metaphorically, in him.[144] There are two passages in the same epistle where the Lombard rephrases the text at issue in the language of cause-effect relationships. In commenting on the point that one man brought sin into the world and one man redeemed it,

---

[142] *In Epistolam ad Galatas*, in *Comm. Cant.*, 2: 351.
[143] Robert of Melun, *In Epistolam ad Galatas* 2:11, in *Quaest. de Ep. Pauli*, pp. 245–46.
[144] Peter Lombard, *In Ep. ad Romanos* 8:20–23, *PL* 191· 1444C–D.

he argues that the role of Adam and Christ as causes is not isomorphic. While Christ is the sole cause of the redemption He effects, Adam is not the sole cause of damnation when it occurs, since the actual as well as the original sins of Adam's posterity are involved. Also, the potentiality for damnation does not always get actualized, since God's grace can overcome sin and does in some men.[145] Similarly, in glossing the point that the law gives rise to sin because of man's inability to adhere to it, Peter also treats the topic in the language of cause-effects relationships. The law, he notes, is not the efficient cause of sin, but rather the occasion of sin.[146]

The examples discussed thus far have shown some of the ways in which Peter uses the *artes*, the authorities, and his own knowledge and ingenuity to provide a literal and historical understanding of Paul. The *Collectanea* also provides excellent documentation of his use of Paul as a resource for the development of his own theological views, in relation to the scholastic concerns and controversies of the day. One hotly debated topic, already noted above, which was given much publicity by the career of Abelard, was the proper role of philosophy in the theological enterprise. Peter takes a definite stand on this subject in his Romans commentary, quite pointedly against Abelard as well as against critics of Abelard of the stamp of William of St. Thierry. As a sequel to the idea that the *invisibilia dei* can be known though created nature, Peter remarks that some divine attributes are accessible to natural reason (*ratione naturale*), including God's eternity, omnipotence, and goodness. The best of the pagan philosophers, he adds, taught that God was incorporeal, incommutable, and simple. Reprising Plotinus and Porphyry, as transmitted by Marius Victorinus, he continues, the same philosophers held God's happiness to lie in His being, life, and thought (*esse, vivere, intelligere*), three activities which, although distinct, are united in His being.[147] This deft introduction of the earliest Latin Christian Neoplatonist on the Trinity into the debate provides Peter with ammunition against Abelard's own appeal to Neopla-

---

[145] Ibid., 5:15–16, *PL* 191: 1392D–1394B.

[146] Ibid., 7:12–13, *PL* 191: 1420B.

[147] Ibid., 1:19–23, 11:33–36, *PL* 191: 1326B–1329A, 1495A. This substitution of one Neoplatonic triad for another is ignored by Johannes Schneider, *Die Lehre vom dreieinigen Gott in der Schule des Petrus Lombardus* (Munich: Max Hueber Verlag, 1961), pp. 21–22. For the transmission of Victorinus, see David N. Bell, "Esse, Vivere, Intellegere: The Noetic Triad and the Image of God," *RTAM* 52 (1985): 5–43. For the range of contemporary readings of the *invisibilia dei* passage, see Artur Michael Landgraf, "Zur Lehre von der Gotteserkenntnis in der Frühscholastik," *New Scholasticism* 4 (1930): 261–88.

tonism to support the claim that the doctrine of the Trinity is not a mystery of the faith requiring revelation, but a philosophical idea equatable with the One, Nous, and World Soul. The same argument arms Peter for his attack on Abelard's notorious denomination of the Trinitarian persons as power, wisdom, and goodness. This passage reveals a Peter Lombard who is far from unappreciative of the philosophical issues embedded in contemporary dogmatic controversies, and far from being an obscurantist, as he is so often type-cast. At the same time, he makes it clear in his discussion of predestination, at Romans 1:7 and 8:29,[148] that he dissociates himself from Abelard's effort to recast this theme into the logical problem of necessity, possibility, and future contingents. And, he agrees with Paul at Colossians 2:48 that we should not be deluded by the beguiling speech of philosophers, a reading which, as followers of Abelard, the Cambridge commentator and Robert of Melun energetically protest.[149]

If his exegesis of Paul affords Peter the opportunity to cross swords with recent and current antagonists, it also gives him the chance to pilot the reader along the current of the contemporary mainstream. A salient case in point is his interpretation of Paul on justification in the Epistle to the Romans, where he states, firmly and crisply, the contemporary consensus position.[150] In discussing the faith that saves the Romans, whether of pagan or Jewish background, Peter makes three main points about justification. First, nothing man knows or does before God grants him faith can increase his merit. Second, faith can be understood in three ways. There is faith as the intellectual assent to theological propositions. There is faith as the acceptance of someone's word as trustworthy. Neither of these kinds of faith justifies; for the devil possesses faith of this sort. To be salvific, faith must combine assent and trust with the love that informs the good deeds bonding Christians to each other and to God. Justifying faith, then, is the faith that works in love. Peter's third point is that, while good works done before or without faith have no merit, good works done in faith and love do have merit, even if the intention to perform them is frustrated by circumstances that prevent their expression in external deeds. As

---

[148] Peter Lombard, *In Ep. ad Romanos* 1:7, 8:29, *PL* 191: 1310B–1311D, 1449B–1450B.

[149] Peter Lombard, *In Ep. ad Colossenses* 2:48, *PL* 192: 270D–272B; *In Epistolam ad Colossenses*, in *Comm. Cant.*, 3: 490–91; Robert of Melun, *In Epistolam ad Colossenses*, in *Quaest. de Ep. Pauli*, pp. 264–65.

[150] Peter Lombard, *In Ep. ad Romanos* 1:8–10, 3:19–4:8, *PL* 191: 1322D–1325A, 1358D–1367C.

he sums up this analysis at Romans 3:27, Peter states "for the intention makes the deed good, and faith directs the intention," underscoring thereby yet another hallmark position in the mid-twelfth-century theological consensus.[151]

In Romans 6:12–14 and 7:7–8, Peter provides the psychological understanding that undergirds that intentionalist outlook in another statement of the contemporary consensus, this time on the psychogenesis of ethical acts.[152] In an analysis whose substance and language can be found widely in this period, including Peter's own gloss on Psalm 1, as noted above, and one which reappears in the *Sentences*, Peter subdivides the stages of ethical choice into three, labeled temptation (*propassio*), contemplation of the temptation or delectation (*delectatio*), and the conscious decision to succumb to it (*consensus*). While man, after the fall, is inclined to sin, Peter stresses that this inclination is not itself sin; nor is its outcome in sin inevitable. Neither is temptation a sin. For, the desires that lead to temptation arise in the moral subject involuntarily. It does not lie within his power to prevent them from occurring. Where he does exercise judgment and voluntary choice is in the next two stages. At the point of *delectatio*, once he has recognized the fact that the temptation is, indeed, a temptation to sin and not just a feeling whose pursuit is morally good or neutral, he has the option of entertaining it or rejecting and resisting it. The outcome of his choice in the *delectatio* stage is seen in the final, or *consensus* stage. If the subject has voluntarily assented to the *propassio* through *delectatio*, then he commits himself to it at the point of *consensus*. Consent, for Peter, is where the essence of the sin lies, and this, irrespective of whether or not the subject has translated the sinful intention into action.

These are just two examples out of a number of passages in Peter's commentary on Paul where the doctrine stated is not only Peter's own, but an opinion of mid-twelfth-century theology more generally. While he certainly draws on his glosses on the other Pauline epistles in the same way, his mining of his Romans gloss in the construction of his systematic theology is particularly notice-

---

[151] For the contemporary consensus on intentionalism in the moral life, see, in particular, Robert Blomme, *La doctrine du péché dans les écoles théologiques de la première moitié du XIIe siècle* (Louvain: Publications Universitaires de Louvain, 1958), passim and esp. pp. x, 15–87, 165–217, 223–94, 330–35, 343–59; also Artur Michael Landgraf, "Die Bestimmung des Verdienstgrades in der Frühscholastik," *Scholastik* 8 (1933): 1–40; Odon Lottin, *Psychologie et morale aux XIIe et XIIIe siècles*, vols. 1–5 (Louvain: Abbaye de Mont-César, 1948–59), 2: 494–96.

[152] Peter Lombard, *In Ep. ad Romanos* 6:12–14, 7:7–8, *PL* 191: 1407C, 1416D.

able. It has been tracked carefully by Ignatius C. Brady, the most recent editor of the *Sentences*, in his annotations of that text. The Themes from Romans that resurface in the *Sentences* in more or less the same form include Peter's analysis of the sin against the Holy Spirit, justification, and the psychology of ethical choice, which we have already discussed, and also original sin, the nature of actual sin, grace and free will, and Christ's human nature. In some cases Peter expands on what he has said in his Pauline gloss; in other cases he streamlines his treatment of the topic. He may combine the material in his gloss with additional citations and reflections. But he generally relies on the gloss in these areas to provide building blocks for the *Sentences* as well as a guide to how the theological questions should be put, and which authorities to call upon in answering them.[153]

Peter's commentary on Paul, finally, allows us to chart the interplay between his exegesis and his systematic theology in areas where his teaching changed and developed over time. A particularly accessible case in point is the Christology which he propounds in his gloss on Romans, for here we have editions of his earlier and later versions of the Roman commentary as well as his ultimate position in the *Sentences*. Peter's remarks on Christology in Romans 1 in the first redaction of his Romans gloss are straightforward, and show little awareness of the debates on theological language inspired by the contemporary study of Boethius's theological tractates.[154] But the second redaction of the gloss and the final edition of the *Sentences* show that Peter had been sensitized to these issues by his reading of Gilbert of Poitiers and John Damascene in the 1140s and early 1150s. His encounters with these two sources can be dated with certainty within this period.[155] Gilbert was well

---

[153] Ignatius C. Brady, prolegomenon to *Sent.* 2: 12*–13*, 19*.

[154] Peter Lombard, *Tractatus de Incarnatione*, ed. Ignatius C. Brady, in *Sent.* 2: 54*–76*.

[155] Gilbert's work was known to the Lombard not only textually but through the Paris chapter of Gilbert's teaching career, from ca. 1137 until his departure to receive the bishopric of Poitiers in 1142. Peter also knew the work of Gilbert's earliest disciples in the Paris area, as well as being one of the *periti* involved in the consistory of Paris in 1147 and the council of Rheims in 1148, at which Gilbert's views were subjected to official scrutiny. On this, see Marcia L. Colish, "Gilbert, the Early Porretans, and Peter Lombard: Semantics and Theology," in *Gilbert de Poitiers et ses contemporains: Aux origines de la logica modernorum*, ed. Jean Jolivet and Alain de Libera (Naples: Bibliopolis, 1987), pp. 229–50; "Early Porretan Theology," *RTAM* 56 (1989): 58–79. For the dating of Peter's encounter with the work of John Damascene, see Eligius M. Buytaert, "St. John Damascene, Peter Lombard, and Gerhoh of Reichersberg," *FS* 10 (1950): 323–43.

known for the terms *subsistentia* and *subsistens* which he applied, respectively, to the formal aspects of beings and to their concrete, phenomenal aspects. While he asserted that this distinction did not extend to the deity, he none the less attributed these terms to the deity. This was confusing enough. But Gilbert also had to grapple with the term *substantia*, because it was in the creed. He was uncomfortable with it, especially as regards the incarnate Christ, since it did not mean the same thing as either *subsistentia* or *subsistens* in his own lexicon. His solution is really a non-solution, and it is one shared by his earliest disciples—the attribution of *substantia* both to the divine and to the human natures of Christ.[156] This problematic Porretan idea is echoed in the second redaction of Peter's gloss on Romans 1:3 in the phrase "we recognize therefore the twin substance of Christ" (*Agnoscamus igitur geminam substantiam Christi*).[157] As we have noted above, this is language which he shares not only with the Porretans but with a number of other contemporary theologians. Peter does refer to John Damascene in this passage, but he has not yet absorbed all the implications of his position. As we can see in the *Sentences*, however, Peter later realized that the Porretans had taken over the ambiguous vocabulary of Boethius. Damascene clarified for him the fact that the Greeks meant the divine essence by *substantia*, and that, if one accepts that definition, it should be used consistently and exclusively with that denotation. So, in the *Sentences*, he drops the twin-substance language, despite the fact that it goes back to Augustine. He uses *substantia* to refer only to Christ's divinity, and employs the terms *humana natura* or *humanitas* to denote His humanity.[158]

Gilbert had also offered an understanding of the communication of idioms in the incarnate Christ which we have discussed in chapter 3 above and which we can see reflected, in part, in the second rescension of Peter's Romans gloss, and reworked in the *Sentences* under Damascene's influence. As will be recalled, Gilbert's formula runs: "A nature does not take on a nature, nor a person a person, nor a nature a person, but a person takes on a nature" (*Nec natura naturam, nec persona personam, nec natura personam, sed persona*

---

[156] Colish, "Gilbert," pp. 231–38.

[157] Peter Lombard, *In Ep. ad Romanos* 1:3, *PL* 191: 1307C. The same language occurs in sermons of Peter dating to the same period in his career. See Peter Lombard, *Sermo* 7, 9, 12, 55, 99, *PL* 171: 371C, 382A, 396A, 605D–606B, 806B.

[158] Peter Lombard, *Sent.* 1. d. 2. c. 1–c. 3, d. 3. c. 4, d. 4. c. 2.1–4, d. 8. c. 8.31, d. 19. c. 7–c. 16, d. 23. c. 3.1, c. 4.2, d. 25. c. 1.1, c. 2.2–5, d. 27. c. 3.1, d. 33. c. 1.3; *Sent.* 3. d. 2. c. 1.4, c. 2, d. 5. c. 3.2–4, d. 6. c. 3.5, d. 7. c. 1.13–17, 1: 60–63, 67, 77, 79–80, 103, 165–69, 182, 185, 190, 192–94, 205, 241; 2: 28–29, 47–49, 54, 63–64.

naturam assumpsit). For Gilbert, a nature cannot assume a nature in the incarnation. If this were the case, the human Christ would not have been the individual man He was. Also, it would be impossible to explain why it was the Son Who was incarnated and not the Father or the Holy Spirit, since they share the same divine nature. As for why a person cannot take on a person, Gilbert adverts to his definition of a person as a *res per se una*. No person can be duplex, by definition; no being can have more than one person. The *persona* of the incarnate Christ is His single, divine, *persona*. Gilbert's arguments on the first two parts of his formula explain why he thinks a nature cannot take on a person in the incarnation. But he also rejects the third possibility because it would open the door to Adoptionism, by suggesting that the Word assumed a human being already in existence. Thus, Gilbert concludes, a divine person took on a human nature, but it is a nature which he understands as a human *subsistens*, the body and soul which make up this particular man but which were not attached either to each other or to the Word prior to the incarnation.[159]

Peter takes much of this doctrine to heart. In the second redaction of his Romans commentary, he agrees that "God took on a human nature in the unity of His person; . . . for He did not assume the person of a man, but the nature" (*Deus humanam naturam in unitate personae suscepit; . . .non enim accepit personam hominis, sed naturam*).[160] In the *Sentences*, he continues to reflect on this idea and sees a problem in understanding Christ's human nature only as the concrete individual *subsistens* of the man Jesus. His reading of Damascene makes it clear to him that, if Gilbert is followed on this point, the incarnation would have consequences for no one but Jesus. The man Jesus would have no necessary connection with other human beings, and the universality of the Savior's work would be severely compromised. Importing this soteriological dimension of the doctrine into Gilbert's formula, the rest of which he continues to find persuasive, Peter argues, finally, that the *natura* understood in the phrase *persona assumpsit naturam* must refer both to the individual *homo* that results from the union of Christ's human body and soul at the moment of His conception *and* His wider *humana natura* or *humanitas*, in order to ensure both His concrete historicity and His consubstantiality with the rest of the human race.[161]

---

[159] Colish, "Gilbert," pp. 237–39.

[160] Peter Lombard, *In Ep. ad Romanos* 1:3, *PL* 191: 1307B. This language is repeated at 1312A–1313C.

[161] Peter Lombard, *Sent.* 3. d. 2. c. 1.4, c. 2, d. 5. c 3.2-4, 2: 28–29, 47–49.

The commentary on Romans yields another excellent example of
a doctrine whose development we can track in Peter's thought by
comparing it with the *Sentences*, the nature of Christ's saving work in
the atonement. Here, we lack an edition of the relevant section of
the first redaction of his Romans gloss; but the text of the second
redaction shows that, at the time when it was written, Peter was
still a supporter of the "rights of the devil" mode of viewing this
problem,[162] and that he shared some of the views of Anselm of
Canterbury, who had opposed the "rights of the devil" position in
his *Cur deus homo*, although without winning many supporters in the
immediate sequel. At Romans 5:8–10, Peter begins by noting that,
since God is omnipotent, He could have redeemed mankind some
other way than by the incarnation and passion of Christ. He agrees
that the way that God in fact chose was more appropriate (*con-
venientior*) than any of the other possibilities. One reason why this is
the case is that the misery of fallen man lies in his ability to grasp
the hopelessness of his situation and his own full responsibility for
it. This realization leads him to despair over the loss of eternal life,
and to frustration over the fruitless desire to possess it. Since Christ
is the Son of God and hence immortal, He can extend that immortality to man, freeing man not only from mortality itself but also
from despair and frustration. Christ turns man's despair and frustration into hope.

At the same time, according to Peter, Christ is proof against the
devil. He agrees with those theologians who maintain that the
devil's sway over man is not just. The devil wields power, but not
legitimate authority over man, a situation which God tolerates,
even though it constitutes a usurpation of His own authority. Now,
for Peter, Christ overcomes the devil, not by brute force, not by a
military or political exercise of divine omnipotence, but through
His justice. Christ is wholly good, wholly blameless as a man. His
undeserved sacrifice on the cross is a just recompense to God for the
evil man has done, repaying God over and above man's debt. His
action is suitable, because Christ serves as a moral example as well
as a redeemer. God wants man to imitate Christ by following the
path of justice, not force. Christ, for Peter, must be a God-man in

---

[162] Good general accounts of the proponents of this theory are provided by D. E.
de Clerck, "Droits du démon et necessité de la rédemption: Les écoles d'Abélard et
de Pierre Lombard," *RTAM* 14 (1947): 32–64; "Questions de sotériologie
médiévale," *RTAM* 13 (1946): 150–84; Jean Rivière, "Le dogme de la rédemption
au XIIe siècle d'après les derniers publications," *Revue du moyen âge latin* 2 (1946):
101–02; Jeffrey Burton Russell, *Lucifer: The Devil in the Middle Ages* (Ithaca: Cornell
University Press, 1984), pp. 161–81.

order for this justice to be effective. If He were not a man, He could not have been put to death. If He were not God, He would not have had the capacity to offer an infinitely acceptable gift that was certain of reception by the Father, since the Father and Son are already united with each other in the bond of love.[163]

This analysis, in Peter's Romans gloss, shows an Anselmian approach by accenting the idea that justice must be served, not only in the sense that the damage done to God's honor by man's fall must be repaired, but also in the sense that Christ's justice must be imitated by man. As with Anselm, Peter sees Christ as imputing to man a gift which Christ Himself has earned. This imputed gift is something objective, eternal life and freedom from the devil as an external ruler. Christ's saving work also brings a subjective gift to man, the substitution of hope for sinful man's frustration and despair.

Now, if we compare this analysis of the atonement with Peter's treatment of the same topic in his *Sentences*, we will be able to see a striking reformulation of his teaching, marked by two notable features. First, he has been deeply influenced by the more subjective and affective understanding of the atonement found in such contemporary theologians as Bernard of Clairvaux and Peter Abelard. Second, and as a consequence of that fact, while he retains some vestiges of the "rights of the devil" theory, he dramatically reinterprets it.[164] Peter's point of departure in the *Sentences* is that Christ won man's redemption through His ethical merit as a man, a merit reflecting the fact that, at all times in His life, His will was in perfect conformity with the will of God. So important is this point, for Peter, that he adds the claim that the passion of Christ was not itself necessary. It was important, to be sure, but only because it illustrated what every other act and intention of the

---

[163] Peter Lombard, *In Ep. ad Romanos* 5:8–10, *PL* 191: 1384D–1387A. Peter gives the same opinion in *In Ep. ad Hebraeos* 1:11–18, *PL* 192: 420B–424A.

[164] Peter Lombard, *Sent.* 3. d. 18. c. 1–c. 5, 2: 111–29. Good accounts of Peter's teaching on the atonement in the *Sentences* include Fritz Bünger, "Darstellung und Würdigung der Lehre des Petrus Lombardus vom Werke Christi (Sentent. III, dist. 18–20)," *Zeitschrift für wissenschaftliche Theologie* 49 (1902): 92–126; J. Patout Burns, "The Concept of Satisfaction in Medieval Redemption Theory," *Theological Studies* 36 (1975): 285–304; Robert S. Franks, *The Work of Christ: A Historical Study of Christian Doctrine*, 2nd ed. (London: Thomas Nelson and Sons Ltd., 1962), pp. 167–76; J. Gottschick, "Studien zur Versöhnungslehre des Mittelalters," *Zeitschrift für Kirchengeschichte* 22 (1901): 35–67; Landgraf, *Dogmengeschichte*, 2 part 2: 170–253, 338; Jean Rivière, "Le mérite du Christ d'après le magistère ordinaire de l'église, II: Époque médiévale," *RSR* 22 (1948): 234–38. For a more detailed account, see chapter 7 below, pp. 459–70.

incarnate Christ manifested throughout His life, His perfect obedience and perfect humility. While the passion did not increase the
perfect merit that Christ already had, in a qualitative sense, merely
giving Him another occasion to reflect that merit, the drama and
pathos of Christ's sufferings displayed His love for His fellow men
as well as His obedience to God. This love energizes human beings,
empowering them to reorder their own loves, to respond to the
grace of God, to love Him in return, and to extend love to their
human neighbors. Once man's love has been reoriented in this
way, he is able to reject the false loves that lead him into sin. His
bondage to sin is broken; and he is now ready to tread the paths to
glory that lead to beatitude. As Peter sees it, the devil's power is
nothing other than the bondage to sin that lies within the soul of
fallen man. The devil has been radically internalized and made a
function of man's psychology of sin.

This theory of the atonement requires, for Peter, a Christ Who is
a God-man, but for reasons different from those advanced by
Anselm, by the traditional defenders of the "rights of the devil"
position, and by the Peter of the Romans gloss. Christ must be a
man, he argues, otherwise He would not have been able to turn
around the hearts of other men and motivate them to love in
response to His own love. Christ must be God so that He Himself
remains immune from sin. His perfect merit is the merit Christ
earns as a man; but what guarantees it is the special divine grace
that the Word grants to the human Christ thanks to Their intimate
union. This sinlessness is important not because it assuages God's
anger or His wounded dignity, and not because it is needed in order
to change God's mind about man. Rather, Christ's sinlessness is
important because it enables Him to possess, and to display, the
perfect humility that inspires and empowers the change of heart
required for man's liberation.

While Peter's commentary on Romans is thus a rich source for
doctrines which he modifies or abandons in his later work, no less
than for positions that he later retains, other Pauline epistles also
inspired him to articulate ideas which he set aside in the *Sentences*.
With other theologians in his period, Peter is a vigorous defender of
the doctrines of the real presence and concomitence in treating the
Eucharist. He likewise stresses the need for its reception in the
salvation of Christians. While he shares the orthodox consensus
view that the Eucharistic elements are changed into the body and
blood of Christ at the time of the consecration, he is just as hard
pressed as are his compeers in finding adequate language in which
to describe that change. In his exegesis of 1 Corinthians, he is also

concerned with the question of what would be received if the consecrated elements were consumed by a mouse, a topic that had been in the theological literature since the Carolingian age and which had been given a new and polemical currency by the use of the idea, on the part of Berengar of Tours and more recently by the Cathars, that the mouse receives Christ's body and blood. As with other contemporary theologians, Peter, in his Pauline exegesis, feels a need to refute this attack on the real presence doctrine.[165] In glossing 1 Corinthians 11:20–25, Peter tacitly invokes the distinction between the consecrated species, the sacrament alone (*sacramentum tantum*), and the body and blood of Christ, the sacred reality which the sacrament contains (*res sacramenti*). He also articulates the view that only a communicant who possesses faith in the real presence actually receives the *res sacramenti* and not the mere *sacramentum tantum*. While he admits that he cannot explain how the sensible attributes of the consecrated elements can inhere in entities which no longer exist as bread and wine after the consecration, he supports the idea that a mouse which accidentally consumes them receives just the physical attributes of those elements.[166]

By the time he wrote the *Sentences*, however, Peter's thought had changed on this topic, and in two respects. First, he now is certain that the change which the elements undergo is a substantial change, not an accidental or a formal one. The accidents of bread and wine remain. In addressing the problem of how they can do so, he contrasts two opinions. One view states that, by an act of God, these accidents are capable of enduring although the material being that subtends them has now been changed substantially. Partisans of the second view think that a certain amount of the substance of the bread and wine remains after the change instituted by the consecration, sufficient to provide a material substratum in which the accidents can inhere. As Peter notes, this second opinion is contradicted by the authorities who say that the change from bread and wine into the body and blood of Christ is full and complete. Peter does not himself resolve this debate in the *Sentences*,[167] perhaps not surprisingly, given the exiguousness of the philosophical vocabulary pertinent to this task available prior to the reception of

---

[165] On this whole debate, see Landgraf, *Dogmengeschichte*, 3 part 2: 207–22; Gary Macy, "Of Mice and Manna: *Quid mus sumit* as a Pastoral Question," *RTAM*, 58 (1991): 157–66; "Berengar's Legacy as a Heresiarch," in *Auctoritas und Ratio: Studien zu Berengar von Tours*, ed. Peter Ganz et al. (Wiesbaden: Otto Harrassowitz, 1990), pp. 55–67.

[166] Peter Lombard, *In I Ep. ad Cor.* 11:20–25, *PL* 191: 1638C–1645D.

[167] Peter Lombard, *Sent.* 4 d. 11. c. 2.5 10, 2: 290–99.

Aristotle. He has, none the less, clarified the issues to a fair extent, spelling out what the two opinions cited entail and where their problems lie, in comparison with his address to this question in his 1 Corinthians commentary. On the other hand, and despite the continuing interest in it shown by other theologians of the day, he now concludes that the reception of the Eucharist by a mouse is an utterly frivolous subject, which does not even merit discussion. He treats it with peremptory dismissiveness: "What then does a mouse receive? What does it eat? God knows!"[168]

A final example of a doctrine on which Peter's thought underwent change, a change which we can document by comparing his *Collectanea* with his *Sentences*, is the hypostatic union. In this case, he moves from a definite position in his Pauline exegesis to a more circumspect and openended one in his systematic theology. The hypostatic union is a question of considerable importance, both in its own dogmatic right and because Peter's teachings were subjected to criticism on this topic after his death. Opponents taxed him with having advocated Christological nihilianism, or the view that, in His human nature, the incarnate Christ was nothing. This position simply cannot be found in the *Sentences*, where Peter outlines the three leading theories of the hypostatic union taught during his time, the *assumptus homo* theory, the subsistence theory, and the *habitus* theory. He indicates that all three of them are orthodox; all three of them receive support from the authorities; and all three are problematic. He leaves the question open.[169] Recognition of the fact that he had done so was what ended the controversy about his alleged teaching on this subject, leading to the vindication of Peter's orthodoxy at the Fourth Lateran council in 1215. Now, of the three opinions, the one hardest to defend against the charge of Christological nihilianism was the *habitus* theory. In holding that Christ took on a human nature the way a person puts on a habit or garment, its proponents made themselves liable to the charge that the humanity of the incarnate Christ was merely accidental and adventitious, in their teaching.

---

[168] Ibid., d. 13. c. 1.8, 2: 314: "Quid ergo sumit? Quid manducat? Deus novit!" Noted by Macy, "Of Mice and Manna," p. 160 n. 16. For further discussion of this point, see chapter 8 below, p. 581.

[169] Peter Lombard, *Sent.* 3. d. 6–d. 7, 2: 49–66. On this debate, see Horacio Santiago-Otero, "El nihilianismo cristológico y las tres opiniones," *Burgense* 10 (1969): 431–43; Walter H. Principe, *William of Auxerre's Theology of the Hypostatic Union* (Toronto: Pontifical Institute of Mediaeval Studies, 1963), 1: 9–12, 68–70; Landgraf, *Dogmengeschichte* 2 part 1; 84–89, 121, 136–37. For a more detailed

There was, however, a point in Peter's career when he seriously entertained the support of the *habitus* theory, his gloss on Philippians 2:1–8. Drawing here on both Augustine and Boethius, he reviews four modes of change. Change occurs, in the first place, when an accident modifies a subject. Another kind of change occurs, for instance, when food is eaten and is assimilated into the body of the eater, transformed substantially into his flesh and his energy. A third type of change is the kind in which neither substance nor accidents change, as when a ring is placed on a person's finger. Finally, there is change in which accidents change, not in their nature but in their form, in acquiring a different shape or appearance. A change of this last type occurs when a person puts on a garment which then takes on the shape of the wearer's figure. In Peter's view, in the Philippians gloss, this fourth kind of change, the kind of change associated with the *habitus* theory, is an adequate description of the hypostatic union, explaining how the Word could take on the form of a servant without His divinity being diminished thereby.[170] At the same time, Peter emphasizes elsewhere in the same passage that the manhood Christ took on was fully real and that He possessed a fully human body and a fully human soul; further, neither His divine nor His human nature was changed by the fact of His incarnation.[171] This assertion clearly blunts the force of a nihilianistic reading of his espousal of the *habitus* theory in the Philippians gloss. But its presence there, despite his decisive later change of mind in the *Sentences*, may suggest how his critics decided that he was, and had remained, an advocate of that theory.

Peter's *Collectanea* thus shows, even more extensively than his commentary on the Psalms, the centrality of his study of the sacred page as the context in which he first began to work out his theological method and his doctrinal positions, both those he later retained and those he altered during the course of his career, whether in response to continuing reflection and additional research, in reaction to contemporary opinions he found problematic, or in accord with the prevailing consensus. Both his substantive explanations, his handling of authorities, and the accessibility of his

---

account of the three opinions and the Lombard's analysis of them, see chapter 7 below, pp. 417–27.

[170] Peter Lombard, *In Epistolam ad Philippenses* 2:1–8, *PL* 192: 235A–D. Cf. Augustine, *De diversis quaestionibus octoginta tribus* q. 73, ed. Almut Mutzenbecher, CCSL 44A (Turnhout: Brepols, 1975), pp. 209–12; Boethius, *Contra Eutychen et Nestorium* 4–7, in Boethius, *The Theological Tractates*, ed. H. F. Stewart, E. K. Rand, and S. J. Tester (Cambridge, MA: Harvard University Press, 1973), pp. 92–120.

[171] Peter Lombard, *In Ep. ad Philippenses* 2:1–8, *PL* 192: 231D–234C.

ideas to the reader in the format and emphasis of his gloss help to explain the popularity of the Lombard as a scholastic commentator on Paul. In drawing on the disciplines of the *artes*, his terminology is clear, straightforward, and easy to understand. His position on the utility of philosophy and natural reason in theology, on the one hand, and their limits, on the other, is circumspect, knowledgeable, and moderate. Therein lies much of the success of his appeal to non-Christian sources, in an age when other exegetes were using a bizarre or rebarbative lexicon or were invoking philosophy and the *artes* in defense of highly questionable conclusions. There are other features of Peter's exegetical work which also recommended themselves to contemporary readers. There is his rigorous adherence to the *accessus* method, which controls his commentary on each Pauline epistle, giving the reader a clear road map so that he always knows where he is in Paul's itinerary. There is also Peter's balanced combination of the continuous commentary, the glossing of individual words and phrases, and the development of theological *quaestiones* on a more extended basis.[172] Peter gives more attention to questions and to theological speculation than do his immediate predecessors. At the same time, in comparison with his immediate successors, his questions are related more integrally to the continuous commentary, and the reader is never allowed to lose sight of the text from which the questions are derived, as a text. However long an excursus he may make, Peter always guides the reader firmly back to Paul's argument. And, however much he may disagree with Paul's emphasis or take stands on controversial issues in his questions, they never become *non sequiturs* or theological flying Dutchmen. Further, Peter aims systematically at reading the text of Paul literally and historically, and interpreting it *ad mentem Pauli*, whether he subjects it to historical criticism or not. He adduces more authorities in resolving vexed questions than either his predecessors or his successors, taking many cues from his forerunners on where to look for help but engaging in his own wideranging personal research. He chooses his authorities aptly and he analyzes and deploys them perceptively. He is thoroughly committed to the task of showing the reader how to evaluate them when they conflict.

---

[172] The mix among the gloss, the question, and the continuous commentary, and the sources for each, as well as the shift in taste toward the question by the end of the twelfth century, are treated by Smalley, *Study*, pp. 42–86; Lobrichon, "Une nouveauté," pp. 93–114; Bardy, "La littérature patristique des '*Quaestiones et responses*'," *R. biblique* 41: 210–36, 341–69, 515–37; 42: 14–30.

All these traits enabled the Lombard to put his own personal stamp upon his work as a biblical exegete. They helped, as well, to shape his approach, and that of his students, to the wider tasks of theological system-building and doctrinal construction which he takes on later in the *Sentences*. The intimate and organic connection he maintains between these related forms of theological study make it clear why his fellow scholastics received his exegetical work with such enthusiasm. It also helps to clarify how that exegetical work could play the integral role which it certainly did play in his own approach to theological education. His address to the *sacra pagina* thus made it possible for the Lombard to set biblical exegesis and systematic theology alike on a decisive new course.

CHAPTER FIVE

THE DOCTRINE OF GOD

When one comes to Book 1 of the *Sentences* of Peter Lombard from the other systematic theologies of the day, one is struck immediately by three of its features. First is the sheer amount of space that Peter devotes to the doctrine of God. This distribution of effort reflects his desire to give sustained attention to a subject that is of absolute theological primacy, and one that had engendered many current controversies that required careful, thorough, and well-informed analysis. It was necessary to clear a path through these debates so that the theologian, and the readers he served, could fix their gaze on God as the supreme being and the supreme good Who alone is worthy of enjoyment as an end in Himself. A second feature of his treatment of God in the first book of the *Sentences* that sets it apart from the work of his contemporaries is the scheme of organization he uses. As we have noted in chapters 2 and 3 above, Peter solves thereby many of the problems of overlap, redundancy, lexical unclarity, and logical inconsistency that mar the writings of other theologians of the day. Peter begins with man's knowledge of God and proofs of God's existence. He moves next to the distinction between nature and person in the Trinity. He concludes with an extended consideration of the divine nature as such and in its principal attributes, both God as transcendent and as unmanifested, and God as the creator and sustainer of the universe. Aside from being neat and orderly, this division of the material provides Peter with an economical means of highlighting the third, and most important, feature of his doctrine of God, his focus on God as absolute being, inexhaustible and unbounded by His workings in man and nature. The Lombard's goal here is to reclaim, for western Christian thought, a theology of divine transcendence, yet one that, at the same time, radically de-Platonizes the doctrine of God.

Ermenegildo Bertola, the modern scholar who has done more than any other to call attention to this dimension of Peter's theology, sees his achievement as a successful effort to mediate between a too-abstract doctrine of God on the part of Gilbert of Poitiers and a too-concrete doctrine of God on the part of Bernard of Clairvaux.[1]

---

[1] Ermenegildo Bertola, "Il problema di Dio in Pier Lombardo," *Rivista di filosofia neo-scolastica* 48 (1956): 135–50. Bertola is closely seconded by Giuseppe

There is much more to the story than this. Quite apart from the transcendental and Platonizing features of Bernard's theology which Bertola's interpretation ignores,[2] the accent on the divine essence in Peter's thought which he rightly stresses must be seen, more broadly, as a critique of the limitations of the economic view of the deity quite common in western theology at this time, no less than as a critique of an immanental or emanational understanding of God that would confuse the creation with the creator or that would make His actions responses to internal necessities of His own being. In this respect, Peter's doctrine of God needs to be positioned no less firmly vis-à-vis those of Hugh of St. Victor, Peter Abelard, and the Chartrains. Even without these polemics, the focus on the divine essence holds an appeal for Peter on other levels. It permits him to cut directly to the metaphysical implications of the doctrine of God, which he sees as having a profound and enduring interest and importance. This, in turn, enables him to develop a mode of *intellectus fidei* that provides a metaphysical rationale for the donnée of revelation on God. And, while his anti-Platonism anticipates an Aristotelian metaphysics and theology in certain respects, making his doctrine of God in Book 1 of the *Sentences* hospitable to Aristotelianism avant la lettre, Peter's doctrine of God does not sacrifice a living God, a God of agency, on the altar of a God as essence.

Peter's organization of his material in the first book of the *Sentences*, and some of his doctrine of the Trinity, have been discussed already, in chapters 2 and 3 above, under the headings of the theological enterprise and the problem of theological language.[3] There, we emphasized the schematic neatness and clarity of his approach, both in disposing swiftly and definitively of issues he feels a need to treat, but not to expatiate on at length, and in allocating large amounts of space to doctrines and debates that

---

Lorenzi, "La filosofia di Pier Lombardo nei *Quattro libri delle Sentenze*," *Pier Lombardo* 4 (1960): 24–28. Other scholars who have noted this emphasis on the divine essence in Peter's theology include Cornelio Fabro, "Teologia dei nomi divini nel Lombardo e in S. Tommaso," *Pier Lombardo* 4 (1960): 79–81; Étienne Gilson, "Pierre Lombard et les théologies d'essence," *Revue du moyen âge latin* 1 (1945): 61–64; Ludwig Hödl, *Von der Wirklichkeit und Wirksamkeit des dreieinigen Gottes nach der appropriativen Trinitätstheologie des 12. Jahrhunderts* (Munich: Max Hueber Verlag, 1965); Johannes Schneider, *Die Lehre vom dreieinigen Gott in der Schule des Petrus Lombardus* (Munich: Max Hueber Verlag, 1961), pp. 25–30, 224–26.

[2] Good treatments of these aspects of Bernard's doctrine of God are found in Marie-Dominique Chenu, "Platon à Cîteaux," *AHDLMA* 29 (1954): 99–106; F. A. Van den Hout, "Pensées de Saint Bernard sur l'être," *Cîteaux* 6 (1955): 233–40.

[3] See above, pp. 79–80, 119–31.

required extended discussion. We also noted the logic of his handling, at the outset, the connected questions of the powers and
limits of reason and of philosophical argument in establishing the existence of the deity, both as a single supreme being and as three and
one, as a means of refining and correcting Hugh of St. Victor, on
the one side, and Abelard, on the other. His definition of the terms
to be applied to the divine nature as such, and to the Trinitarian
persons in Their relation to each other, and his specification of a
concept of relation for this purpose that avoids the limits of both
relative nouns, in the grammatical tradition, and of relations
understood as accidental modifications of substance, in the tradition of Aristotelian logic, sets the stage, lexically speaking, for his
critique of the theological terminology of both Abelard, Gilbert of
Poitiers, and the Chartrains. It also enables him to reassign functions attributed by theologians of a Neoplatonic or economic bent
to individual Trinitarian persons to the deity as such, without
foregoing a crisp and lucid understanding of the personal distinctions within the Trinity from a strictly intratrinitarian vantage
point. While recalling that schematic considerations and the need
to develop and to use a clear and consistent vocabulary set much of
Peter's agenda here, especially given the state of play when he
entered the field, in the present chapter we need to move beyond
these considerations to the positive doctrine of God which they
undergird.

MAN'S KNOWLEDGE OF GOD: PROOFS OF GOD'S EXISTENCE

The first issue in positive theology which Peter takes up, having
stated at the outset that God is one, in essence, and three, in
persons,[4] is the question of what sort of positive knowledge of God
may be possessed by man. It is notable that Peter never ventilates
the doctrine of the *via negativa*. Positive knowledge is the only kind
of knowledge of God that he considers. He first lays out the evidence of Scripture, and then the evidence available through natural
reason, culminating in proofs for the existence of God and analogies
of the Trinity in created nature, and their limits. This overall mode
of attack is traditional. As Peter himself notes, it is grounded in
Augustine's *De trinitate*. As has been pointed out, many of the same
authorities are cited in support of the same, or similar, epistemolog-

---

[4] Peter Lombard, *Sententiae in IV libris distinctae* 1. d. 2. c. 2.1, 3rd ed. rev., ed.
Ignatius C. Brady, 2 vols. (Grottaferrata: Collegii S. Bonaventurae ad Claras
Aquas, 1971–81), 1: 62.

ical claims by contemporaries such as Hugh of St. Victor, the author of the *Summa sententiarum*, Abelard, and Robert of Melun.[5] Yet, Peter puts his own order on this material and uses this standard topos as a means of taking a stand on the knowability of God that is distinctive, amid the range of current treatments of the subject. Unlike Hugh, Robert, and Abelard, in laying out the Old Testament and New Testament testimonies to God's existence as three and one, he does not multiply citations. His technique, rather, is to streamline this operation, paring it down to those biblical texts that anchor his point most effectively, and then to move on.[6] His treatment of this part of the topos is altogether much leaner than that of other contemporaries who invoke it, and his address to the Old Testament witnesses lacks the air of anti-Jewish polemic sometimes found in writers of the Abelardian school who make use of the same material.

Even more his own is Peter's handling of the proofs of God's existence, and of His nature as three and one, available from a consideration of the created universe. To begin with, this topic was one that not all scholastic theologians in the first half of the twelfth century felt obliged to treat. No member of the school of Laon, for instance, takes it up. Nor do Gilbert of Poitiers or his earliest disciples. While Abelard and his followers are deeply committed to the idea that pagan philosophers, especially the Platonists, are witnesses to the doctrine of the Trinity, the proof of God's existence, as such, does not interest them. Aside from the Lombard, the three theologians of the day who do offer proofs of God's existence are Hugh of St. Victor, Robert Pullen, and Robert of Melun. It is worth comparing the Lombard's approach to theirs.

HUGH OF ST. VICTOR, ROBERT PULLEN, ROBERT OF MELUN

The earliest of these three twelfth-century efforts to prove God's existence, and, in many ways, the least useful, is Hugh's. As was noted above in chapter 2, a large part of the difficulty with Hugh's proofs lies in the location which they occupy in Book 1 of his *De sacramentis*. Concerned as he is with the way God manifests Himself to man in the work of institution and restitution, and the accessibility to man of knowledge of God as so mediated,[7] Hugh launches his

---

[5] Noted by Brady, *ad loc.*, 1: 63; Schneider, *Die Lehre*, pp. 12–13, 15, 21–23.
[6] Peter Lombard, *Sent.* 1. d. 2. c. 4–d. 3. c. 1.1, 1: 63–69.
[7] These tendencies in Hugh's theology have been noted by Roger Baron, *Science et sagesse chez Hugues de Saint-Victor* (Paris: P. Lethielleux, 1957), p. 139; Johann

project in the *De sacramentis* not with God as the ontological ground
of the world and man but with an account of creation in which the
emergence of creatures in the order put forth in Genesis jostles
uncomfortably with the creation as a means of access to a creator
held to have produced all creatures at the same time, despite the
way that this process is described in Genesis. In the effort to explain
how primordial causes differ from God, Hugh backs up to provide a
brief introduction to the Trinity, and how it may be known, thus
waiting until the third part of Book 1 to develop his proofs.[8] He
situates them in the context of the two modes of access man has to
the knowledge of God, revelation and a rational consideration of
the natural world, each of which in turn can be subdivided into two
parts, internal and external. With respect to God's work of institution in the natural order, the physical world serves as an external
and visible source of information about God as the creator, accessible to human reason, although reason cannot go the full distance
here, since the physical world cannot show God to be three and
one. The correlative internal mode of rational investigation which
yields a knowledge of God is the mind's examination of itself, since
the mind of man is made in God's image. These two forms of
rational inquiry, external and internal, provide the basis for Hugh's
proofs of God's existence. Hugh offers three proofs. The first is
addressed to the mind's examination of itself. This examination
shows that the human mind can grasp transcendental ideas and
perfections, and can harbor concepts such as eternity and immutability which it cannot find in its own experience. Thus, a higher
cause possessing these perfections must be posited to exist to
account for the ideas about them which man finds within his own
mind. Two proofs then flow from the mind's examination of the
visible world. Here, Hugh invokes the argument from motion to a
first, incorporeal, and immutable mover and the argument from
design to an intelligent and benevolent orderer. In all these cases,
inductive logic leads to a deity with the attributes required to serve
as the cause of effects ascertainable by reason in the mind of man
and in the created universe.[9]

Hofmeier, *Die Trinitätslehre des Hugo von St. Viktor dargestellt im Zusammenhang mit den
trinitarischen Strömungen seiner Zeit* (Munich: Max Hueber Verlag, 1968), pp. 108–
91, 193–95, 197–268, 297–303; Jakob Kilgenstein, *Die Gotteslehre des Hugo von St.
Viktor* (Würzburg: Andreas Göbel, 1897), pp. 37–39, 47–57; Christian Schütz, *Deus
absconditus, Deus manifestus: Die Lehre Hugos von St. Viktor über die Offenbarung Gottes*
(Rome: Herder, 1967), pp. 22–89.
   [8] See above, pp. 57–60.
   [9] Hugh of St. Victor, *De sacramentis fidei christianae* 1.3.10, *PL* 176: 222A–223B.
Good discussions of these proofs are provided by Kilgenstein, *Die Gotteslehre,*

The deity in question, however, is the deity as such, not a deity at the same time three and one. Bearing in mind that Hugh has inserted these proofs into the *De sacramentis* following his introductory remarks about the Trinity and man's knowledge of it, his conclusions leave the reader wide of that mark. Rallying to the task that still awaits him, Hugh next considers in what respect reason can know that the first cause is also three persons. He appeals to Augustine's *De trinitate* for two arguments designed to tackle this assignment. One of these is far less responsive to the question than the other. Hugh first invokes Augustine's distinction between the Son as the Word eternally generated in the mind of the Father (*verbum occultum*) and the Word as revealed and as physically accessible to man (*verbum manifestum*).[10] In so doing, he fails to note that the Augustinian point is addressed to the consubstantiality and coeternity of the unmanifested Son with the Father, an argument developed by Augustine against the Arians, and that it does not provide a third term, which is needed if he is going to provide a rational argument for, or an analogy of, the Trinity, whether in created nature or in the human mind. Abandoning that tack, and understandably so, Hugh then moves to one of Augustine's three-term analogies of the Trinity in the human mind, the mind, its notice of itself, and its love of itself (*mens, notitia, amor*).[11] While potentially not as useful as the analogy of memory, intellect, and will developed by Augustine further along in his *De trinitate*, the Augustinian analogy that he has chosen points to the inner life of the Trinity. This is a fact which Hugh fails to appreciate. Referring next to the Trinitarian formula *ingenitus-genitus-procedens*, as a parallel to *mens-notitia-amor*, he then treats both relational formulae as comparable to the names power, wisdom, and goodness, as applied to the Trinitarian persons, without seeing that he is conflating and confusing an economic view of the Trinity with a view of the Trinity *in se* in which the attributes of power, wisdom, and goodness do not serve to distinguish any one of the Trinitarian persons from the others.[12] At the same time, Hugh does not indicate how the *ingenitus-genitus-procedens* formula can be grasped by the human

---

pp. 61–77; Kilgenstein as reprised by Urbain Baltus, "Dieu d' après Hugues de St.-Victor," *R. bén.* 15 (1898): 109–23, 200–14.

[10] Hugh of St. Victor, *De sac.* 1.3.20, *PL* 176: 225A–B.

[11] Ibid., 1.3.21, *PL* 176: 225B–D.

[12] Ibid., 1.3.22–24, 1.3.26–31, *PL* 176: 226A–D, 227C–234C. Hugh makes a similar conflation of these two ways of viewing the Trinity in his *Tractatus de trinitate*, ed. Roger Baron in "*Tractatus de trinitate et de reparatione hominis* du MS. Douai 365," *Mélanges de science religieuse* 15 (1961): 112.

mind from an inspection of itself or of created nature, the epistemological framework which he is using as the context for this inquiry.
Nor does he indicate whether wisdom, power, and goodness are
rational data, and, if so, whether they can be classified as internal
or external. Other problems accompany Hugh's analysis. While he
certainly wants to exempt the deity from change and from
accidents,[13] he does not display any sensitivity to the fact that the
idea of relation, which he invokes in discussing both the *mens-notitia-
amor* and the *ingenitus-genitus-procedens* formulae, requires any definition or qualification, despite the current debate this very point was
exciting and despite the fact that Augustine himself treats it specifically in the *De trinitate*, Hugh's major source here. Also, although
he had stated that reason cannot know that God is three and one in
full, he does not follow Augustine's lead in indicating where any of
these Trinitarian arguments or analogies falls short.

Looked at as a whole, then, Hugh's treatment of the proofs of
God's existence, and of His nature as three and one, offers a
scrappy and incomplete initiation into this topic while, at the same
time, it points to the wider organizational and lexical burdens
under which the *De sacramentis* labors. Hugh's most positive contribution lies in the examples of *a posteriori* reasoning from effects to
causes as a means of establishing the deity as the basis for phenomena which the human mind can perceive in itself and in created
nature. He does not succeed in capitalizing on this advantage, or
even in adhering to his announced agenda in dealing with the
Trinitarian part of this self-imposed assignment. He does not make
full use of the patristic and contemporary resources apposite to the
issues he raises. And, insofar as his handling of the Trinitarian
analogies and names is designed to set up his treatment of Trinitarian theology more generally, whether as positive doctrine or as
anti-Abelardian critique, it points to his pervasive terminological
vagueness and to his tendency to confuse the Trinity *in se* with the
Trinity *ad extra* and to emphasize the latter so heavily that the deity
as such, in His transcendent determinations, whether as Godhead
or as Trinity, gets lost in the process.[14]

---

[13] Hugh of St. Victor, *De sac.* 1.3.25, *PL* 176: 227A–C.
[14] A good crisp assessment of this point is provided by Edmund J. Fortman, *The
Triune God: A Historical Study of the Doctrine of the Trinity* (Philadelphia: Westminster
Press, 1972), p. 190. See also Kilgenstein, *Die Gotteslehre*, pp. 114–27; A. Mignon,
Les origines de la scolastique et Hugues de Saint-Victor, 2 vols. (Paris: P. Lethielleux,
1895), 1: 302–05; Jørgen Pedersen, "La recherche de la sagesse d'après Hugues de
Saint-Victor," *Classica et mediaevalia* 16 (1955): 103–04, 106; Jerome Taylor, comm.
on his trans. of Hugh of St. Victor, *Didascalicon* (New York: Columbia University
Press, 1961), pp. 113–14.

If Hugh of St. Victor tries manfully to provide a coherent epistemological framework for his proofs of God's existence, which is only
partially sustained in the execution, Robert Pullen offers the most
laconic of such contemporary proofs, while making no attempt
whatever to explain why he takes the trouble to do so or what
connection, if any, this exercise has with the rest of his doctrine of
God. Unlike Hugh, Robert places his proof at the very beginning of
his *Sentences*. He offers a single and very simple proof. All things that
exist require a cause, he notes; and things that come into being and
pass away require a first cause without beginning or end.[15] This
proof reprises a familiar Augustinian-Platonic emphasis on eternity
as a prime attribute of the deity, in contrast with the transience
marking beings in the temporal order; it is not an argument from
design, as is asserted by F. Courtney.[16] In any event, having offered
this proof, Robert makes no effort to take the Augustinian high road
on the role of reason in eliciting natural or psychological arguments
either for the Trinity or for the doctrine of God more generally. His
proof is followed immediately by a remark on theological language
that challenges the appositeness and semantic coherence of the very
noun *deus*;[17] then, ignoring the lexical obstacle which he has placed
in his own path, he proceeds to talk about the deity, and the
Trinity, as if he had never made this point, and with as slight an
appreciation of the need to define and to use terms clearly and
consistently or to address contemporary debates on this subject as
the members of the school of Laon. His proof thus stands at the
head of his *Sentences*, inert. It is not drawn into any kind of logical,
epistemological, or theological connection with anything else he
has to say about God. Robert Pullen evidently leads off with the
proof because he feels that it is appropriate to include one. But he
offers his readers no insight into why he thinks this is the case, or
what relation, if any, the proof is supposed to have to the rest of his
theology of the divine nature, either substantively or methodologically. On the question of rational *indiciae* of the Trinity he has
nothing to say.

The third mid-twelfth-century theologian to offer a proof of
God's existence, Robert of Melun, combines it with a defense of
philosophy as a source for the doctrine of the Trinity along Abelardian lines. His location of his discussion of these points reflects his

---

[15] Robert Pullen, *Sententiarum libri octo* 1.1, *PL* 186: 674D–675A.
[16] F. Courtney, *Cardinal Robert Pullen: An English Theologian of the Twelfth Century*
(Rome: Universitas Gregorianae, 1954), pp. 55–56.
[17] Robert Pullen, *Sent.* 1.1, 1.4, *PL* 186: 675A–B, 680C, 682A.

modified adherance to the schema of Hugh's *De sacramentis*. Not-withstanding his dependence on Hugh and Abelard, Robert emerges with an approach to the proof of God's existence that is genuinely fresh, in comparison with Hugh and Robert Pullen. As we have noted in considering the schema of Robert of Melun's *Sentences*, he takes over Hugh's broad conception of sacrament as its conceptual foundation, and orders his theology under two head-ings, the sacraments of the Old Testament and the sacraments of the New Testament. Instead of giving separate and express treat-ment to what reason and pagan authorities supply about God's work of institution, Robert assimilates this topic into his treatment of the creation account in Genesis, a topic which he, like Hugh, takes up before he addresses the nature of the creator, whether in His divine nature as such or under the heading of Trinitarian theology.[18] While this mode of address reflects Robert's perpetua-tion of Hugh's overlapping of chronology, cosmology, and episte-mology, Robert does move up his consideration of the role of rational proofs in establishing God's existence and nature to a somewhat earlier point in his first book.

Robert makes a valiant initial attempt to salvage and to combine the basic positions of Hugh and Abelard on the knowability of God by human reason and on the utility of the pagan philosophers in this connection. Given the opposition between those two masters on these subjects, is not surprising to note that Robert's effort here does not meet with full success. In support of Abelard, he tries to yoke Augustine's acknowledgement of the help he received from the books of the Platonists to the claim that, when the philosophers treat the same subjects as the Bible, we can accept this pagan witness as referring to the divine essence.[19] Although he concedes that the philosophers do so imperfectly, and although he ignores the fact that Augustine in the passage cited is referring to the incarnation of Christ and to the limitations of the Platonists in this connection, and not to the existence of God or to the Trinity, he proceeds to affirm that the pagan philosophers, especially the Pla-tonists, support the doctrine of the Trinity. It is this Trinitarian position, as articulated by the Platonists, he asserts, that St. Paul was referring to in the Epistle to the Romans when he spoke of the *invisibilia dei* as knowable through the phenomenal world. Without

---

[18] See above, pp. 72–76.
[19] Robert of Melun, *Sententie* 1.1.5, ed. Raymond-M. Martin, in Robert of Melun, *Oeuvres*, 4 vols. (Louvain: Spicilegium Sacrum Lovainiense, 1932–52), 3 part 1: 168–69.

pausing to ask whether the Platonic triad of the One, Nous, and
World Soul can truly be described as an aspect of the visible
creation, and without taking account of the critics of Abelard's
application of this idea to the Trinity or of Abelard's own softening
of the line he takes on the World Soul in his later works, Robert
concludes that the objections of pagans to the doctrine of the
Trinity are groundless, on their own testimony, as are the objections of the Jews on the basis of the evidence for the Trinity in the
Old Testament.[20] While this effort to vindicate Abelard may satisfy
Robert, the reasoning on which he bases it involves a misappro-
priation of both Paul and Augustine and a reverence for Abelard
that is more enthusiastic than it is circumspect.

   Robert's next move is to try to conflate this alleged textual
evidence of the Platonists' defense of the Trinity with Hugh's
account of man's four ways of knowing God, both through nature
in an interior and exterior sense, and through revelation in an
interior and exterior sense. In so doing, however, he departs from
Hugh's epistemology in three ways. First, as we have just seen, he
accords far more weight to the argument from Platonic theology
and cosmogenesis than Hugh is willing to grant. Second, he argues
that man's interior rational knowledge of God, achieved through
his inspection of ideas in his mind that do not derive from man's
experience of created nature, can be obtained only with the aid of
divine illumination. Hugh himself does not impose this stipulation
on man's rational knowledge, whether internal or external. Finally,
Robert asserts that all the modes of knowledge of God available to
man in this life remain incomplete.[21] Now, if one were to place the
Hugonian analysis of natural reason and revealed knowledge within Hugh's wider framework of the modes of knowledge, adding to
them contemplation and the knowledge of God enjoyed by the
saints in the next life, something which Robert does not do here,
then this claim could be sustained. However, in its own sphere,
Hugh treats the *a posteriori* demonstration of a perfect, eternal
deity, an immutable prime mover, and a benevolent and intelligent
creator as an activity that natural reason can accomplish, and
accomplish on its own.

   Despite the maladroitness of this mélange of Hugh and Abelard
with which it is associated, the proof of God's existence provided by
Robert is a rather original one. The most striking thing about it is

---

[20] Ibid., 1.2.8–9, *Oeuvres*, 3 part 1: 292–307.
[21] Ibid., 1.3.2, *Oeuvres*, 3 part 2: 6–10. For Hugh on this point, see M. L.
Fuehrer, "The Principle of Similitude in Hugh of St. Victor's Theory of Divine
Illumination," *American Benedictine Review* 30 (1979): 80–92.

that Robert situates it within a discussion of causality in general. There are three types of causes, he observes, first, final, and intermediate. First causes are so called because they are the first to have effects; final causes are so called because they are the last to have effects. This way of posing the issue indicates that Robert views causation from a temporal standpoint, not according to the order of being. In this sense, he continues, intermediate causes have more in common with first than with final causes, in that they initiate causation in their own sphere of activity and competence. Quoting Hugh here, Robert describes them as primary causes within their own genera (*in suo genere prime cause*). This statement, however, is accurate of intermediary causes only in an operational sense, for they receive their capacity to function as causes from the first cause. Robert cites the example of parents, who take the initiative in engendering offspring, offspring who are the effects of their parents' causal actions. But the capacity of the parents to undertake these causal actions is derived from the first cause. As causes, the parents are not absolute within their own sphere, since they act "in conjunction with the first cause" (*cum adiuncto prime cause*). Now the first cause, which is absolute, is God alone. No other causes are coeternal with Him. Other causes may work through motion or the transference of their own being to their effects, as is the case with the engendering of offspring by parents. But God, as a cause, remains unchanging, a point Robert anchors with a quotation from Boethius's *Consolation of Philosophy* 3.9. God, Robert concludes, does not transfer His own *esse* to other beings when He creates them, when He exercises His direct causation upon them, or when He empowers them to act as intermediary causes. This being the case, the first cause must have a necessary existence.[22]

Both this analysis of causation and the idea that God can create without distributing His own divine essence to other beings are destined to crop up elsewhere in Robert of Melun's doctrine of God, and we will encounter them again below. With respect to his proof of God's existence, Robert's use of these principles bears comparison with the proofs of Robert Pullen and Hugh of St. Victor. Unlike both of these masters, Robert of Melun looks not at the effects in nature that require causal explanation, but at the behavior, and limitations, of secondary or efficient causes in nature. His intermediate causes need both empowerment and assistance on the part of the first cause. Insofar as he endows this first cause with other attributes that distinguish it from other beings, the attributes

---

[22] Robert of Melun, *Sent.* 1.2.1, *Oeuvres*, 3 part 1: 263–65.

on which he focuses are not eternity, as with Robert Pullen, or supreme intelligence and benevolence, a status as the prime mover, or transcendent perfections, as with Hugh. Rather, he emphasizes the immutability and incommutability of the divine essence in God's activity as a cause. This last point is a link between Robert of Melun and Peter Lombard, as is the fact that Robert develops a proof that has an integral connection with other features of his doctrine of God. At the same time, in moving from Robert to Peter we move to the most elaborate arguments for God's existence to be found in mid-twelfth-century theology.

The Lombard

Peter's positioning of his proofs for God's existence reflects, in the first instance, a rejection of the strategy adopted by Hugh and by Robert of Melun and a willingness to take a leaf from the book of Robert Pullen. From his point of view, it does not make sense to begin with the creation. Rather, after determining what can be known about God and proved about His existence and nature, the first step is to clarify the meaning of theological language as applied to the deity, so that a cogent distinction between the Godhead and the Trinitarian persons can be drawn. Following that, the attributes and activities of the deity as such can be explored, including His role as creator. This plan of attack inspires Peter to place his proofs quite early in Book 1 of his *Sentences*. As noted, he leads off with some lexical clarifications, stating at the outset that *essentia* applies to the divine nature rather than to the Trinitarian persons. He then presents a trim and carefully selected assortment of Old and New Testament testimonies to the Trinity. At this juncture he does not raise the question of the testimony supplied by the pagan philosophers, a topic he takes up later, so his omission of it here must be seen as quite deliberate. Instead, he moves directly from the witness of biblical revelation to a consideration of how God's existence and nature may be known from a rational examination of the created universe.

The warrant Peter offers for the plausibility of rational proofs is a twofold one. Both Augustine and Paul have affirmed that God has left His traces in His visible creation. In particular, Peter draws heavily on the Epistle to the Romans and on his earlier gloss on the *invisibilia dei* passage in the *Collectanea*. This being the case, it may be helpful to recall how Peter handles that text as an exegete. As was noted in chapter 4,[23] Peter's gloss on the *invisibilia dei* passage

---

[23] See above, pp. 212–13.

serves as an occasion for him to attain two interlocking objectives at the same time, the critique of Abelard and the articulation of his own positive position on the utility of pagan philosophy in acquiring a knowledge of God. Peter firmly rejects the association of the One, Nous, and World Soul with the Trinity, and, with it, Abelard's claim that the doctrine of the Trinity is not a mystery of the faith for which revelation is required, but a teaching fully available to reason and found in the Platonists. For his part, Peter does not scorn either the philosophers or the appeal to reason here. Natural reason is an epistemic reality for Peter, and one that affords access to a knowledge of a number of divine attributes. These include God's eternity, omnipotence, goodness, incorporality, simplicity, and incommutability. And, he agrees, the best of the pagan philosophers concur in the idea that reason is capable of establishing these conclusions. As for the Trinitarian claim, Peter deftly shifts to another Neoplatonic triad, that of *esse, vivere, intellegere*, a principle made available by Marius Victorinus. Actually, the triad of being, life, and thought had first been applied to the deity by Candidus, the Arian antagonist whom Victorinus sought to refute. It accorded well with the Arian view that God the Father exists on a higher metaphysical plane than the Son, since *esse* has to be seen as a metaphysical substratum for any of the activities that the being in question may engage in.

Sensitive to that point, Victorinus himself, in the course of his debate with Candidus, changed this initial Neoplatonic triad to another one, the triad of moving, thinking, and acting (*movere, intellegere, agere*).[24] This latter triad was a more serviceable support for an orthodox doctrine of the Trinity in which all three persons are seen as metaphysically equal and in which their activities are mutually coinherent. While Peter, in his Romans gloss, does not reveal a familiarity with this shift in Victorinus's argument, even though his own doctrine of the Trinity would have made him sympathetic to it, his citation even of this first triad, against Abelard's triad, is more than a debater's point and more than a display of his own philosophical erudition. It reflects, as well, a pervasive and underlying concern with the salvaging of a doctrine of the

---

[24] Marius Victorinus, *Ad Candidum Arrianum* 19; *Adversus Arrium* 1.4, 1.43, 1.52–53, 3.4, 3.7–11, 3.17, 4.13–15, 4.21–22; *De Homoousio* 3, in Marius Victorinus, *Opera theologica*, ed. Paul Henry and Pierre Hadot, CSEL 83: 1 (Vienna: Hölder-Pichler-Tempsky, 1971), pp. 36–37, 59–60, 133–34, 148–51, 197–99, 202–11, 222–24, 243–48, 256–59, 281–82. The changed triad also appears in Marius Victorinus, *Commentarium in Epistolam Pauli ad Philippenses* 2:68 in *Opera exegetica*, ed. Franco Gori, CSEL 83:2 (Vienna: Hölder-Pichler-Tempsky, 1986), p. 188.

Trinity that sees the definition and description of the Trinitarian
persons as confined, rigorously, to the traits each person uniquely
possesses vis-à-vis the other two persons. With this, Peter's example here also reflects his thoroughgoing distaste for a treatment of
the Trinity that would ascribe to any of the individual persons
attributes that, in his view, apply properly and exclusively to the
divine nature as such.

- Peter's extended reference to his own commentary on Romans,
as a curtain-raiser to his proofs of God's existence, thus makes a
telling and pointed statement. What he undertakes to prove here is
to be proved about the Godhead, not about individual Trinitarian
persons. What is to be proved about the deity, also, is to be proved
by natural reason from the sensible evidence of the creation, and it
finds corroboration in pagan philosophy. On the other hand, pagan
philosophy does not and cannot provide proof of the doctrine of the
Trinity. At best, it can provide analogies, not demonstrations. This
established, Peter offers four proofs of God's existence, which also
specify some of the deity's prime attributes. The first combines two
of the *a posteriori* proofs offered by Hugh of St. Victor. Observing,
with Robert Pullen, that all created beings must have causes since
they are incapable of causing themselves, he yokes the argument
from effects to a first cause with the argument from design; the
coherent order of nature in which these effects of the first cause are
disposed bespeaks the existence of a first cause that is, at the same
time, an intelligent cause. Peter's second proof could also be described as an *a posteriori* proof, although it subtly moves him from
induction to a more analytical mode of reasoning. Created beings
are mutable, he notes; they must hence derive their being from a
ground of being that is immutable. The analysis of being itself
serves to undergird Peter's third and fourth proofs. The inspection
of being yields the conclusion that it exists in a hierarchical order,
with graduated degrees of excellence. Thus, there must be a supreme being, and one that is not merely the highest being at the top
of the chain of being, but still part of the chain. Rather, a being that
is truly supreme would have to transcend all other beings, whether
corporeal or spiritual. As well as possessing degrees, and this moves
Peter to his fourth proof, created being displays the characteristics
of changeability and compositeness. These traits also point to the
need for a creator that is a single, simple essence, not composed of
diverse parts, not subject to change, and not subject to modification
by accidents. The prime attributes of the deity that have been
elicited by means of these proofs are the deity as first cause, as
intelligent, as immutable, as one, and as simple. The theme of

immutability has received the most attention, playing a key role in both the second and the fourth proofs. With this group of divine attributes in hand, Peter finds that, by analyzing their implications, he can derive the attributes of omnipotence, wisdom, and goodness as well, as traits inhering in the Godhead.[25] This conclusion arms him, from the very beginning, for his more extended later attack on Abelard's ascription of power, wisdom, and goodness as proper names to the Trinitarian persons.

The proofs also require further commentary as an index of Peter's approach to the doctrine of God more generally. Peter evidently takes the examination of created nature as his point of departure. But his proofs are metaphysical as well as physical proofs. He is concerned less with examining the ways in which created beings act than with considering the structure of created being and what it requires as a necessary metaphysical substratum. In treating the deity as that necessary ground of being, he is as interested in delineating the respects in which the divine mode of being is radically different from, and transcendent of, the world of created being as he is in showing the ways in which the world of created being is ontologically dependent upon God and connected to Him. This emphasis points to a sharp contrast in tonality between Peter's proofs and those of Hugh of St. Victor and Robert of Melun. Unlike Hugh, Peter is not presenting himself in these proofs primarily as a natural theologian eager to show how God manifests Himself in the creation. And, unlike Robert, when he thinks about causation he thinks about more than the conditions enabling beings to act in particular events. He thinks as well, and more fundamentally, about the conditions that enable them to exist at all. His analysis of priority and posteriority in the treatment of causation is not based on the notion of temporal sequence. It is based on the order of being, not on the order of time. Peter's proofs thus display more than a deft strategist at work, laying the foundations for the polemics he wants to conduct later in Book 1 of the *Sentences*. More fundamentally, they bespeak Peter's felt need to assert a doctrine of God whose role as the necessary ground of being of everything else that exists in no sense infringes on the unconditioned transcendence of the divine essence. In recapturing divine transcendence, Peter in no sense opts for a God Who is the One beyond being. Rather, his God is pure and untrammeled being, in all its force, being as such. Peter's placement of the

---

[25] Peter Lombard, *Sent.* 1. d. 3. c. 1.1–6, 1: 68–70.

deity on this metaphysical plane is important, in its own right, in reimporting this emphasis, purged of Platonism, into twelfth-century theology. It also lays the groundwork for his approach to Trinitarian theology and for his analysis of the divine attributes which he develops later in Book 1 of the *Sentences*, as well as for his handling of the relations between God and the world throughout his theology.

Having offered his proofs for God's existence and nature, Peter next considers the related questions of whether, and how, the creation offers proofs of the Trinity, through its vestiges in creation. Here, he begins forthrightly by remarking that, in this connection, we cannot treat of proofs, but only of similitudes. He emphasizes that vestiges of the Trinity are to be understood as analogies of the Trinity. They are not to be viewed in any sense as substantial participations of God, whether of the incommutable, simple substance of the Godhead or of the personal characteristics of any of the Trinitarian persons.[26] With respect to the Godhead, the divine essence, by definition, cannot be divided and conveyed to other beings since it is simple, unitary, and incommutable. Any kind of emanationist or participationist understanding of God's relation to the world would contradict that fact, and lead to a quasi-pantheism. As for the Trinitarian persons, Peter has already alluded to this point in his Romans gloss and he develops it *in extenso* below. The determinations of the Trinitarian persons lie in Their relationship to each other, not in Their relations with creatures. As for the vexed question of the alleged testimonies to the Trinity in the pagan philosophers, Peter now pulls the issue out into the open and gives his final opinion on it. While the philosophers, he says, may have noted some of the Trinitarian analogies, "they saw the truth as if through a shadow and from afar, and they were deficient in their grasp of the Trinity" (*quasi per umbram et de longinquo viderunt veritatem, deficientes in contuitu Trinitatis*); and this because the contemplation of creatures is not sufficient to provide knowledge of the Trinity "without the teaching and the revelation of inner inspiration" (*sine doctrinae vel interioris inspirationis revelatione*).[27]

This being the case, Peter follows the lead of Augustine's *De trinitate* in seeking analogies of the Trinity above all in the human mind. In comparison with Hugh of St. Victor, who uses the same tactic, Peter is more authentically Augustinian, and in two ways. In the first place, he gives full weight to the analogy of memory,

---

[26] Ibid., c. 1.7–8, 1: 70–71.
[27] Ibid., c. 1.9, 1: 71.

intellect, and will, as well as bringing in the analogy of *mens, notitia,* and *amor.* Secondly, he pursues, with Augustine, the limits of these analogies as well as their suggestive force as similitudes. Memory, intellect, and will provide a good analogy, Peter observes, because we have here not three lives, three minds, or three essences. Each of these faculties is the function of the same, single, subsistent mind. Each is distinct, although they are functionally interrelated. With Augustine, Peter emphasizes the point that this analogy falls short of the Trinity, for the single human mind in which memory, intellect, and will inhere is a rational spirit attached to a body and conditioned, in its modes of knowledge and action, by that fact, while God is pure spirit and incorporeal. Striking a note which he plans to treat much more fully in the sequel, he adds that these three mental functions are understandable with respect to each other and that, in this connection, their names are relative nouns; the relationships involved are not to be seen as the accidental qualifications of substances, which can come and go. Here, he cites the precise passage of Augustine's *De trinitate* 9.4 where Augustine speaks directly to the problem of relatives from both a logical and a grammatical standpoint.[28]

Peter spells out the limitation of this analogy still farther. A man possesses these three faculties of memory, intellect, and will, but together they do not comprise the sum total of his being. On the other hand, the three Trinitarian persons do comprise the totality of God's being. There are three of them, and no more. On another level, the man who possesses these three mental faculties is a single human person, while there are three persons in the Trinity.[29] In comparing this line of argument with Augustine's own elaboration of the limits of his own analogy in the final book of the *De trinitate,* one can detect a notable difference in emphasis between Peter and his chosen authority here. What fascinates Augustine above all is the analysis of the functional similarities and dissimilarities between the Trinity and the human mind. Indeed, it is in this context that he works out much of his psychology of human knowledge. For Peter, on the other hand, it is the arguments drawn from the structure of being that exert the most powerful attractive force on his imagination. He looks at the human mind and at the Trinity both from the standpoint of their essence, not their modes of operation.

As we have noted, Peter is not content to rest his case on the analogy of memory, intellect, and will. He also adverts to the

---

[28] Ibid., c. 2, 1: 71–74.
[29] Ibid., c. 3.1–2, 1: 74–75.

analogy of *mens, notitia*, and *amor*. Strictly speaking, in the light of
what he has already set forth, Peter does not need this second
analogy in order to complete his argument, at least if he were
content to argue merely by recycling Augustine's *De trinitate*. While
it is true that much of the force of his analysis here derives from the
fact that he has mined that text with more pertinence, point, and
circumspection than Hugh of St. Victor, his introduction of the
mens-notitia-amor analogy at this juncture and the way in which he
handles it indicate that Peter is establishing his own priorities in
the use of his Augustinian materials. This point is a constant
reminder of the fact that, in understanding Peter as a theologian,
we have to pay attention to how his mind works on and with his
authorities. We learn very little about his intellectual temperament
by the mere statistical listing of his citations. With respect to the
mens-notitia-amor analogy, it appeals to Peter as a way of concluding
his treatment of the Trinitarian similitudes because he sees in it the
image of a parent, a child, and the love passing between them. To
be sure, he could have used the analogy of the lover, the beloved,
and the love that unites them, which Augustine also includes in his
De trinitate, for this purpose. But the relation between *mens* and
notitia is preferable, for Peter, because it suggests a more conscious
and intellectualistic mode of regard. At the same time, in this
analogy, we do not have a relationship between two distinct essences, as is the case with the lover and beloved and the parent and
child alike. Rather, we have the mind's own intellectual acknowledgement of itself. In Peter's estimation, this makes the *mens-
notitia-amor* analogy a more fitting similitude of the consubstantial
Trinitarian persons. There is still another reason why Peter prefers
this analogy over the lover, beloved, and love model. In the latter
analogy, it is impossible to envision the love relationship as always
having been in place, rather than as having come into being when
the lover and beloved met. On the other hand, the mind's self-
knowledge and self-love can be seen as continuous and permanent
determinants of the mind itself, and not as having begun at a
particular moment in the mind's history. The *mens-notitia-amor* analogy is thus better able to illustrate the relations of the Trinitarian
persons, which are eternally structured into Their being.[30] And, for
Peter, relatedness, whether seen in the analogy of the mind knowing and loving itself or in the analogy of the love and knowledge
bonding two human persons, is the highest and most perfect reality
of all. It may be significant that while, with Augustine, Peter can

---

[30] Ibid., c. 3–c. 4, 1: 75–77.

find areas where the analogy of memory, intellect, and will falls short, he suggests no limitations at all to the analogy of *mens*, *notitia*, and *amor* with which he brings this part of his argument to a close.

NATURE AND PERSON IN THE TRINITY

As we have already had occasion to observe, Peter next makes a forthright and clearheaded decision as to how to proceed. Instead of moving on to the divine nature as such, followed by the Trinity, and instead of moving back and forth between these two subjects, as do many theologians of the time, and confusingly so, Peter's goal is to clarify how the Trinitarian persons should be understood before turning to the divine essence, considered first in and of itself and next in terms of the ways in which it relates itself to the universe and to man. He proceeds in this fashion because, given his chosen mode of attack on Trinitarian theology, and given his objections to the terminology of Abelard, Gilbert of Poitiers, and of many theologians who sought to criticize these masters, he needs to address the problem of theological language systematically, and at length. This question received extended consideration in chapter 3 above. Here we may reprise the essential points that Peter establishes. First, he rigorously equates the divine substance and nature with the divine essence, which he uses consistently to refer to the Godhead shared by the Trinitarian persons and not to the persons individually. He stresses that this divine essence is immutable, eternal, incommutable, simple, and incomparable, and that, in this respect, "God alone is called essence or being" (*Deus ergo solus dicitur essentia vel esse*).[31] God utterly transcends created beings. Further, Peter treats being not as an attribute of God but as a description of His nature as such. This view of God distinguishes Him from created beings, including spiritual beings possessing immortal souls, since the latter are changeable, they come into existence at a particular point in time, and they are capable of being modified by accidents, of developing vices and virtues, and of acquiring learning and the arts, and are subject to shifting inclinations and passions. In contrast, God is, always and totally, His own qualities. There is nothing in God that is not God, the only conclusion compatible with the radical unity and simplicity of the Godhead.[32]

This doctrine serves not only to differentiate God clearly from creatures, it also provides Peter with the foundation on which he

---

[31] Ibid., d. 8. c. 1.7, 1: 96.
[32] Ibid., c.1–c. 8, 1: 95–105.

builds his distinction between nature and person in the Trinity. He stresses that each of the Trinitarian persons possesses the divine essence fully, and in precisely the same way. His argument here, it will be recalled, undergirds his handling of the mathematical claims about the Trinity put forth by both Gilbert, Thierry of Chartres, and Clarenbald of Arras; he shows thereby that the Trinitarian persons are not numerical parts of a whole, or items of the same type collected together, or quantitative additions to the divinity that any one of Them possesses. This same outlook also inspires Peter to modify Augustine in urging that the divine essence cannot be seen as a metaphysical substratum for the Trinitarian persons, understood as existing on a different level of being from Them, and one more fundamental or abstract.[33] This point is worth emphasizing, for it was misinterpreted later in the twelfth century by Joachim of Fiore, who took Peter to be saying exactly the opposite of what he did say. Joachim claimed that Peter advocated a quaternity composed of the divine essence, as one item, and the persons of the Trinity, as three other items. This charge was formally rejected at the Fourth Lateran council in 1215; and, while Joachim's treatise against the Lombard was suppressed and has not survived, his position can be reconstructed from teachings found elsewhere in his work, from a pseudonymous and intransigent Joachite defender of it writing in the early thirteenth century, and from the documents of the council itself.[34] In sharp contrast with that erroneous reading given to his teaching by the Joachites, Peter insists that the divine essence shared by the Trinitarian persons is the one and identical divine essence, that They each possess it perfectly and in the same way, and that terms predicating that divine essence can be applied substantially to the Trinitarian persons only in Their capacity as co-essential sharers of it and not

---

[33] Ibid., d. 19. c. 8, 1: 166.

[34] See the *Liber contra Lombardum*, ed. Carmelo Ottaviano (Rome: Reale Accademia d'Italia, 1934), pp. 74–76, 78–80, 111–250 and the editor's comm. at pp. 81, 83–86. Other reconstructions supporting the fact that Joachim and his followers radically misinterpreted Peter are Antonio Crocco, *Gioacchino da Fiore: La più singolare ed affascinante figura del medioevo cristiano* (Naples: Edizioni Empirico, 1960), pp. 103–39; E. Randolph Daniel, "The Double Procession of the Holy Spirit in Joachim of Fiore's Understanding of History," *Speculum* 55 (1980): 469–70; Giovanni Di Napoli, "Gioacchino da Fiore e Pietro Lombardo," *Rivista di filosofia neo-scolastica* 71 (1979): 621–63, 675–85; Fortman, *The Triune God*, pp. 196–97; Harold Lee, "The Anti-Lombard Figures of Joachim of Fiore: A Reinterpretation," in *Prophesy and Millenarianism: Essays in Honour of Marjorie Reeves*, ed. Ann Williams (London: Longman, 1980), pp. 129–42; Bernard McGinn, *The Calabrian Abbot: Joachim of Fiore in the History of Western Thought* (New York: Macmillan, 1985), pp. 165–68.

in Their personal determinations.

For Peter, the personal traits that do distinguish the members of the Trinity from each other and that enable us to distinguish between person and nature in the deity are, exclusively, the relations structured eternally into the Trinitarian family that are specific and unique to each person vis-à-vis the other persons. In articulating this dimension of his Trinitarian theology, Peter achieves two goals at the same time. One is to reassert the Latin Christian emphasis on the unmanifested Trinity as the prime metaphysical reality. To this end, it is the relations of the Trinitarian persons to each other, as unbegotten, begotten, and proceeding, which are constitutive, differentiating them and bonding them to each other in a timeless and transcendent way, apart from anything They may reveal of Themselves to man in the cosmological or charismatic orders. Peter's insistence on this point reflects his distaste for an economic view of the Trinity that would limit what we can know about the Trinity or what is interesting about the Trinity to what the Trinity may choose to manifest about Its individual or collective interactions with nature and man. To put the point another way, in recovering the unmanifested Trinity in this manner, Peter is saying that the Trinity, as unmanifested, is none the less not a Trinity that remains entirely hidden from man and unknowable except through negative theology or mysticism. For, as he shows so clearly, one can reflect upon and appreciate the Trinity *in se*, by means of positive theology, particularly if one rejects the translation of *hypostasis* as *substantia* and the Boethian definition of *persona* as applied to the Trinitarian persons, which yields three deities, and if one makes a careful point of spelling out the differences between the relations that are eternal properties of the Trinitarian persons vis-à-vis each other and the concept of relation derived both from Aristotelian logic and the grammar of relative nouns.

Peter's second objective is closely related to this first one. If the properties of the Trinitarian persons are eternal, immutable, and transcendent, they are also properties unique to each of the persons as an individual; they apply to no other person within the Trinity. It is the ability of Trinitarian names to measure up to this criterion that defines their literal admissibility as Trinitarian names, for Peter. Other names, and the aspects of being they denote, cannot distinguish one Trinitarian person from another. Hence, they can apply properly only to the divine nature as a whole. While a large part of Peter's motivation in developing this position is his desire to rule out power, wisdom, and goodness as proper names of the Trinitarian persons, as Abelard and others taught, he anchors the point in a wider discussion of the characteristics of the divine nature that are one in the Trinity, subdividing them into several categories. First, there are the determinations of the deity as a pure and perfect essence, the deity Who is being as such, viewed quite apart from other beings that may come into being and pass away. Immutability, unity, eternity, simplicity, incommutability, and the like provide the concepts and language enabling us to consider the common essence shared by the Trinitarian persons in this radically transcendent sense. Next, there are the determinations of the divine nature that God manifests in His creation and governance of the universe. Omnipotence, wisdom, and goodness, and the traits that can be extrapolated from these principles, are apposite here. Likewise, these traits are forms of agency in which all the Trinitarian persons share jointly and fully whenever they are exercised. On another level, the interaction with human beings in the order of redemption, all three persons of the Trinity are also coactive, although here one or another of Them may act as the delegate of the Godhead. In this category Peter places such forms of agency as are denoted by nouns such as judge, redeemer, sanctifier, and gift. Yet, although particular Trinitarian persons may be entrusted with these roles, when They carry them out, They do so on behalf of the entire Trinity, bestowing divine justice, or divine grace, as such, and not the qualities unique to Themselves as individual Trinitarian persons. For, as Peter has already clarified, the properties unique to each Trinitarian person are not His activities *ad extra*.[35] Finally, there are the figurative ways of appreciating the deity's interactions with the world and man, denoted by terms embodying a transferred meaning, such as splendor, mirror, character, and figure. These require relatively little investigation, for Peter, and they do not impinge that heavily on his Trinitarian theology or on his doctrine of God. Indeed, in addition to accenting the unity of the Trinity in action, at both the transcendent and at the manifested levels of reality on which the deity acts, Peter seeks to avoid collapsing the former into the latter, and he wants to preserve as large a zone of affirmative and literal positive theology as he can.

While much of the subject matter treated by the Lombard under the heading of Trinitarian theology is formulated, in the first instance, under the rubric of the problem of theological language, for

---

[35] Peter Lombard, *Sent.* 1. d. 14. c. 2, d. 22. c. 3, 1: 127–28, 179. This Lombardian position, maintained against the more economic understandings of the Trinity in Peter's day, is treated well by Hödl, *Von der Wirklichkeit und Wirksamkeit der dreieinigen Gottes*.

reasons which we have indicated, the positive doctrine of the deity as three and one that emerges from this consideration provides him with tools for addressing other questions pertinent to Trinitarian theology ·which other scholastics either ignored or to which they provided different answers. In this connection it is remarkable how narrowly some of the leading theologians of the day cast their nets. Gilbert of Poitiers has absolutely nothing to say about the doctrine of God in general, or, indeed, about the Trinity, except to press it into the Procrustean bed of his own idiosyncratic vocabulary. While the author of the *Sententiae divinitatis* modifies some of Gilbert's arguments, he too confines Trinitarian theology to the subject of theological language. The same can be said for Robert Pullen. Aside from the vexed question of the comparison of the Trinity to the Platonic triad of One, Nous, and World Soul and the problems resulting from their attribution of power, wisdom, and goodness specifically and preeminently to the Trinitarian persons, and aside from their persistent application of the inapposite analogy of the bronze seal to the Trinity, Abelard and his disciples have little to add to Trinitarian theology either. In addressing himself to the doctrine of the Trinity more broadly, therefore, Peter finds a need to engage in discussion with other contemporary theologians, and not merely these more highly publicized controversialists.

One of these larger questions to which he devotes attention is the engendering of the divine persons. God the Son, it is agreed, is begotten, God the Father unbegotten. But, can it be said that God engenders Himself? The Abelardian power-wisdom-goodness model provides neither a clear answer to this question, nor an answer to the question of why one of these divine attributes should be envisaged as engendering, or as flowing from, another. Abelard raises this problem more than once, without being able to resolve it.[36] The author of the *Summa sententiarum*, on the other hand, draws a distinction between divine person and nature here. While God can be said to engender God in the sense that the Father, as a Trinitarian person, engenders the Son, as a Trinitarian person, it is erroneous, he maintains, to say that the deity engenders either Himself or another deity, since this would conflict both with God's unity and eternity.[37] Peter is aware of the form in which both theologians put this issue. He is sympathetic to the handling of it given in the *Summa sententiarum* and to the author's indication that Augustine's

---

[36] Peter Abelard, *Theologia christiana* 4.118–19; *Theologia "scholarium"* 2.148–68, ed. Eligius M. Buytaert and Constant J. Mews in Peter Abelard, *Opera theologica*, CCCM 11–13 (Turnhout: Brepols, 1969–87), 12: 324–25, 13: 480–89.
[37] *Summa sententiarum* 1.11, *PL* 176: 59D–61A.

De trinitate can be used helpfully here. He develops this topic in
rather greater detail, however. Agreeing that, if we say that God
engenders Himself, we would be admitting that there is more than
one God and that there is something prior to God, he adds, citing
Augustine, that this claim is unacceptable because no entity engenders itself. This principle is a principle of being, in general. In the
case of created beings, it is valid because all such beings are caused
by other beings. In the case of God, it is valid because He is being
as such, uncaused, existing in and of Himself.[38] Here, Peter shows
his propensity for putting questions pertaining to the doctrine of
God on a metaphysical level. At the same time, he recognizes that
this may not be sufficient to quell those voluble and argumentative
thinkers (*garruli ratiocinatores*) who insist on framing the question in
the form of tricky propositions designed to entrap the unwary. As
they would have it, if God the Father engenders God, then He
engenders a God Who is either God the Father or a God Who is not
God the Father. If the latter, then there is more than one God. If
the former, then He engenders Himself. Peter's solution is to reformulate the first hypothesis by inserting into it a qualifying term,
so that it now asks if God the Father engenders God the Son.
Having done so, he can proceed without being constrained, by the
form of the proposition, to argue either for ditheism or for the
self-generation of the Father, since it can be shown that, although
the Father and Son are distinct as persons, and are related to each
other as persons by their respective paternity and filiation, they are
identical in their divine aseity, with respect to their possession of
the divine nature.[39]

Having shown his colors in the field of logic, Peter makes a point
of reminding the reader of the distinction between the divine substance and essence and the divine persons which he has already
drawn. While the divine substance and essence can be predicated
of all three persons of the Trinity, we cannot predicate a triple
personhood of the divine essence without tritheism. With this point
kept firmly in mind, we can conclude that the Father does not
engender Himself. To do so would be to engender another God.
What He engenders is not another God but another person.[40]
Along the same lines, Peter asks whether the Father engenders the
divine essence, whether the divine essence engenders the Son,
whether the divine essence engenders the divine essence, and

---

[38] Peter Lombard, *Sent.* 1. d. 4. c. 1.1, 1: 77–78.
[39] Ibid., c. 1.4, 1: 78. On this point, see also Fortman, *The Triune God*, pp.
196–97.
[40] Peter Lombard, *Sent.* 1. d. 4. c. 2.1–3, 1: 79–80.

whether the divine essence is neither engendering nor engendered. Having taxed his opponents with confusing the Godhead with the Trinitarian persons and having drawn the clear distinction between them that he draws, Peter proceeds to answer all these questions with a firm "no." The questions, and others like them, are mal posée, because they ignore the fact that engendering, and being engendered, are activities that apply, and can only apply, to the Trinitarian persons, and not to the divine essence or substance. Peter concludes this protracted analysis by making three main points. First, and here following Augustine's *De trinitate* 5.7.8, he reminds the reader that the terms Father and Son are relative terms that do not refer to the divine substance. Next, insofar as one can find other texts in Augustine and other authors on the Trinity, such as Hilary of Poitiers, who are less precise in their use of language, he urges that they be understood in the sense of the first Augustinian citation he has given. Finally, he anchors his conclusion by remarking that, in order to emphasize that substance does not engender substance in the Trinity, we should say that the Son and the Holy Spirit are of the same substance as the Father (*eiusdem substantiae cum eo*), capping this observation with a quotation from Augustine's *Contra Maximinum* not brought to bear on this argument by any of his contemporaries to hammer in the idea that the same argument applies to the Holy Spirit as to the Son.[41]

The foregoing topic is a good example both of Peter's outlook and of his methodology. While he may initially sieze on a point as raised by another recent theologian, he expands on it, connecting it to wider issues and bringing a broader range of authorities and a more penetrating analysis to bear on it. And, while clearly adept at logic, he dislikes the attempt in some quarters to try to collapse metaphysical questions into dialectical ones, especially when the logical propositions used fail to make the proper distinctions in the terms at issue. These same traits inform his handling of a related question, discussed even more widely in the period, as to whether the Father generates the Son by will or necessity. On this point, Augustine had stated that neither was the case, in his *De trinitate*. Some theologians, such as Roland of Bologna and the authors of the *Summa sententiarum* and *Sententiae divinitatis*, are content simply to restate Augustine's conclusion and to let it go at that.[42] Robert of Melun seeks to go beyond this mode of Augustinian *ipse dixit* by

---

[41] Ibid., c. 2.4–d. 5. c. 3, 1: 80–88. The quotation is at d. 5. c. 2.17, 1: 87.

[42] Roland of Bologna, *Die Sentenzen Rolands*, ed. Ambrosius M. Gietl (Amsterdam: Editions Rodopi, 1969 [repr. of Freiburg im Breisgau: Herder, 1891 ed.]),

offering some reasoning in support of the same conclusion. To say
that the Father engenders the Son either by will or necessity, he
notes, would be to imply that there is some cause or constraint
under which the Father operates, which is inadmissible. Engendering by nature, on the other hand, requires no such limitations. This
is not to say, Robert adds, that the Father did not want to engender
the Son. To be sure, He did want to do so; but the conclusion
makes it clear that He did so freely.[43] On the other side of the
debate stood one of the followers of Gilbert of Poitiers, whose
response to the question of whether the Father engenders the Son
by will or necessity was not "neither" but "both;" according to
him, the Father exercises His will here, but in a manner not in
contradiction with His nature, and of necessity, but with a necces-
ity not involving constraint.[44]

Amid this spectrum of views, Peter comes the closest to Robert of
Melun both in his conclusions and in his mode of attack on the
problem, although with a crisper sense of the need to refute the
Porretan position. In comparison with Robert, and others who join
him in supporting Augustine here, he feels a need to put the
question into the framework of the divine nature more fully. He
begins by anchoring the answer "neither" with the same Augustinian text that other contemporaries use, but goes on from there. As
for the claim that God acts of necessity, he agrees that it is inadmissible, since God does nothing under constraint. Nothing at
all, not even His own nature, forces Him to act in any particular
way. As for the claim that the Father engenders the Son by will, the
problem with an affirmation of this statement is that, if the Father
could will to engender the Son, and since His will is unconstrained,
He could also will not to engender the Son. This conclusion cannot
be sustained, for, as Peter has already explained, engendering and
being engendered are eternal and unchanging personal determinations of the Father and Son. In any event, Peter asks, is not God's
will identical with His very being? Yes, he answers, in the sense
that everything that is in God is God. He has no attributes that are
not His, by nature. But one can also answer this question negatively. For, just as God does not will personally everything that happens in the created universe, this particular reality is not one

---

p. 31; Bernhard Geyer, ed., *Die Sententiae divinitatis: Ein Sentenzenbuch der Gilbertischen Schule* 6.B.2.5, Beiträge, 7:2–3 (Münster: Aschendorff, 1909), p. 165*; *Summa
sent.* 1.7, *PL* 176: 53C–54C.
    [43] Rober of Melun, *Sent.* 1.4.17, 1.4.19, *Oeuvres,* 3 part 2: 133–35, 139–90.
    [44] Nikolaus M. Häring, ed., "Die *Sententie magistri Gisleberti Pictavensis episcopi* I"
2.37, *AHDLMA* 45 (1978): 119.

subject to His will. Willing involves making a decision. Decision-making is an activity that occurs in time. There was not and cannot be a prior decision on the part of the Father at some point in time to engender the Son. For, to admit that conclusion would be to grant the Father priority to the Son, in point of time, or in point of power. But, the Father and the Son are equal in power, and equal in eternity, although They manifest these qualities, in Their mutual interrelations, as begetter and begotten.[45] This argument serves to emphasize at the same time God's freedom, in the sense of His exemption from both internal and external constraints, and the idea that the transcendent Trinitarian relationships are eternal and are not occasioned by time and circumstance. At the same time, Peter can reemphasize, against the Abelardians, the point that no Trinitarian person is preeminent in any one of the determinations of the divine essence, even as he thereby criticizes current heretics who deny full divinity to the Son.[46]

In addition to this painstaking consideration of the relation between the Father and the Son, stemming as it does not only from the challenge of Christological heresies in this period but also from the debates among orthodox theologians, Peter displays a deep concern with the theology of the Holy Spirit. Not only does he devote extended attention to the intratrinitarian status of the Spirit but he also has much to say about His mission *ad extra*. The first of these concerns springs both from the ongoing need to defend the western doctrine of the double procession of the Holy Spirit against the Greek church and from Peter's more general interest in finding a purely intratrinitarian way of defining the Holy Spirit as a Trinitarian person, in aid of his larger project of clearly distinguishing divine persons in Their unmanifested state from the divine nature. At the same time, he reflects a contemporary interest in the role of the Holy Spirit in the religious lives of Christians. The attention he pays to this subject stems from a felt need to explore it more fully. But it was also triggered, to a very considerable extent, by the handling of the Holy Spirit by Abelard. Peter's treatment of the Holy Spirit indicates that he has paid careful attention to the dossier of authorities assembled by Abelard on this topic, both in the *Sic et non* and in his successive theological works, and also that the tactic of brute denunciation used by critics of Abelard's position, such as Bernard of Clairvaux and William of St. Thierry, did not constitute an adequate mode of refutation that could still pay

---

[45] Peter Lombard, *Sent.* 1. d. 6. c. 1–d. 7. c. 2.3, 1: 89–94.
[46] Ibid., d. 9. c. 1–c. 5, 1: 103–10.

honor to Abelard's desire to emphasize a feature of Trinitarian theology whose importance Peter freely conceded.

The Critique of Abelard

Because Abelard's teaching on the Holy Spirit supplies such vital background, both positively and negatively, for Peter's own, and because the contemporary polemics surrounding it often sparked more heat than light, it is worth outlining this debate, noting both the constants in Abelard's position and the shifts in his treatment of it over time. To begin with, a large part of the problem lay in the fact that Abelard's doctrine of the Holy Spirit was tied in with his assertion that the doctrine of the Trinity could be known by natural reason, and that Plato's *Timaeus* and other philosophical works in the Platonic tradition served to document that claim. This position is one which Abelard stated with no qualifications in his earliest theology, the *Theologia "summi boni"*.[47] Another complication is that from the outset, Abelard invoked the doctrine of *fabula* or *involucrum*, the exegetical technique of peeling away metaphorical veils to arrive at a core of doctrine that had itself been framed in allegorical terms by its author, to explain his reading of the Platonists. This technique was associated in the contemporary mind with the doctrine of creation, stemming from the *Timaeus*, currently under investigation by thinkers associated with the school of Chartres.

Two points must be made about this association, or lack of it, between Abelard and the Chartrains, especially since it engendered confusion at the time, confusion which is still with us in some quarters. In the first place, there is a detectable family resemblance among the thinkers committed to the Chartrain project, despite their individual differences, and irrespective of whether they themselves studied or taught at Chartres,[48] a family resemblance that distinguishes them from Abelard. The Chartrains have two principal traits in common. First, they are not primarily interested in theology, either Trinitarian theology as such or the charismatic

---

[47] Peter Abelard, *Theologia "summi boni"* praefatio, 1.5.38–39, ed. Constant J. Mews, CCCM 13: 85, 98–99. The preface states plainly, p. 85, "quod fidem trinitatis omnes homines naturaliter habent." Cf. Walter Simonis, *Trinität und Vernunft: Untersuchungen zur Möglichkeit einer rationalen Trinitätslehre bei Anselm, Abaelard, den Viktorinern, A. Günther und J. Froschammer* (Frankfurt: Josef Knecht, 1972), pp. 43–49, who claims that, while Abelard goes farther in this direction than anyone in his time, he is not a total rationalist.

[48] The repeated attempt to torpedo the idea of the school of Chartres by Richard W. Southern, "Humanism and the School of Chartres," in *Medieval Humanism and Other Studies* (New York: Harper & Row, 1970), pp. 61–85; *Platonism,*

activities of the divine persons in the religious lives of Christians. Rather, they are cosmologists. Their chief interest in the Trinity is as a source of cosmic causation. After considering the way the universe was brought into being, the Chartrains stop discussing the deity and turn their attention to their real subject, the structure and function of the phenomenal world. In the second place, in reading the *Timaeus* and related philosophical literature, they are dealing with texts whose authors presented teachings on natural science and cosmogenesis in the form of allegory and myth. Thus, the Chartrains' use of *involucrum* as an exegetical technique is addressed to the task of finding the literal meaning set forth indirectly by these texts.

On the other hand, Abelard is primarily a theologian. He is deeply interested in the Trinity, which constitutes most of what he has to say in his *theologiae* under the heading of faith, the beliefs that Christians have to possess in order to be saved. He is also deeply interested in the charismatic role of the Holy Spirit in the Christian life. While he does address cosmogenesis in his *Hexaemeron* and while he does not hesitate to bring philosophy to bear on that subject, the *Hexaemeron* is a late work of his, undertaken in response to queries from Heloise and her nuns, which situates the subject in the exegetical tradition of Genesis commentary. As a theologian Abelard is not particularly concerned with the structure and function of the physical universe. Unlike many sentence collectors of the period, he does not deal with the creation in his theologies. Secondly, while he invokes the language of *fabula* and *involucrum*, his use of it is quite different from that of the Chartrains. Where they seek to extrapolate literal truths about cosmology from pagan authors who expressed themselves allegorically, Abelard seeks to read literal statements from the Platonic philosophers as assertions of theological truths about the Trinity, found in revelation, which, all other

---

Scholastic Method, and the School of Chartres (Reading: University of Reading, 1979); and "The Schools of Paris and the School of Chartres," in *Renaissance and Renewal in the Twelfth Century*, ed. Robert L. Benson and Giles Constable (Cambridge, MA: Harvard University Press, 1982), pp. 113–37, has, in our view, been refuted successfully by Peter Dronke, "New Approaches to the School of Chartres," *Anuario de estudios medievales* 6 (1969): 117–40; Nikolaus M. Häring, "Paris and Chartres Revisited," in *Essays in Honour of Anton Charles Pegis*, ed. J. Reginald O'Donnell (Toronto: Pontifical Institute of Mediaeval Studies, 1974), pp. 268–329; and Hans Liebeschütz, "Kosmologische Motive in der Bildungswelt der Frühscholastik," *Vorträge der Bibliothek Warburg*, 1923–24, pp. 110–43. The most recent guide to the literature of this debate, which also criticizes Southern's thesis, is Olga Weijers, "The Chronology of John of Salisbury's Studies in France (Metalogicon, II. 10)," in *The World of John of Salisbury*, ed. Michael Wilks, Studies in Church History, Subsidia, 3 (Oxford: Basil Blackwell, 1984), pp. 114–16.

Christians held, were mysteries of the Christian faith. In the twelfth century itself, a double confusion was perpetrated by William of St. Thierry. Reading with more prejudice, haste, and zeal than comprehension, he accused Abelard of reducing Trinitarian theology to physical science, while at the same time he accused William of Conches of teaching a rationalist doctrine of the Trinity.[49] This confusion, on one side or another, has been perpetuated by some modern scholars,[50] although we are indebted to a distinguished host of others for sorting out the differences between Abelard and the Chartrains in this connection.[51] This is not to say that the

---

[49] William of St. Thierry, *De erroribus Guillelmi de Conchis*, PL 180: 333A–D.

[50] See, for instance, Hennig Brinckmann, "Verhüllung ('integumentum') als literarische Darstellung im Mittelalter," in *Der Begriff der Repraesentatio im Mittelalter: Stellvertretung, Symbol, Zeichen, Bild*, ed. Albert Zimmermann (Berlin: Walter de Gruyter, 1971), pp. 321–22, 328–29; Wilfried Hartmann, "Manegold von Lautenbach und die Anfänge der Frühscholastik," *Deutsches Archiv für Erforschung des Mittelalters* 26 (1970): 78–79, 82; Edward Filene Little, "The Heresies of Peter Abelard," University of Montreal Ph.D. diss., 1969, pp. 191–92, 222–30; Enzo Maccagnolo, trans., *Il Divino e il megacosmo: Testi filosofici e scientifici della scuola di Chartres* (Milan: Rusconi, 1980), p. 74; Simonis, *Trinität und Vernunft*, pp. 51–53; Anneliese Stollenwerk, "Der Genesiskommentar Thierrys von Chartres und die Thierry von Chartres zugeschriebenen Kommentare zu Boethius 'De trinitate'," University of Cologne Ph.D. diss., 1971, pp. 5–8, 37.

[51] Among the scholars who have clarified this point may be noted Joseph A. Dane, "*Integumentum* as Interpretation: Note on William of Conches' Commentary on Macrobius (1, 2, 10–11)," *Classical Folia* 32 (1978): 201–15; Peter Dronke, *Fabula: Explorations into the Uses of Myth in Medieval Platonism* (Leiden: E. J. Brill, 1974), pp. 14–67, 100–13, 178; Mariateresa Beonio-Brocchiere [Fumagalli] and Massimo Parodi, *Storia della filosofia medievale da Boezio a Wyclif* (Bari: Laterza, 1989), pp. 214–15, 226; Tullio Gregory, "Abelard et Platon," in *Peter Abelard*, ed. Eligius M. Buytaert (Leuven: Leuven University Press, 1974), pp. 42–46, 51; *Anima mundi: La filosofia di Guglielmo di Conches e la scuola di Chartres* (Florence: G. C. Sansoni, 1955), pp. 126–32; "Il *Timeo* e i problemi del platonismo medievale," in *Platonismo medievale: Studi e ricerche*, Istituto storico italiano per il medio evo, studi storici, 26–27 (Rome: Sede dell'Istituto, 1958), pp. 122–50; "L'*anima mundi* nella filosofia del XII secolo," *Giornale critico della filosofia italiana* 30 (1951): 494–508; Édouard Jeauneau, "L'usage de la notion d'*Integumentum* à travers les gloses de Guillaume de Conches," in "*Lectio philosophorum*": *Recherches sur l'École de Chartres* (Amsterdam: Adolf M. Hakkert, 1973), pp. 127–79; Lawrence Moonan, "Abelard's Use of the *Timaeus*," AHDLMA 56 (1989): 33–41, 55–72; Brian Stock, *Myth and Science in the Twelfth Century: A Study of Bernard Silvester* (Princeton: Princeton University Press, 1972), pp. 43–62; Winthrop Wetherbee, *Platonism and Poetry in the Twelfth Century: The Literary Influence of the School of Chartres* (Princeton: Princeton University Press, 1972), pp. 30–34, 36–48; intro. to his trans. of Bernard Silvestris, *The Cosmographia* (New York, Columbia University Press, 1973), pp. 10–12. See also Eileen Kearney, "Peter Abelard as a Biblical Commentator: A Study of the Expositio in Hexaemeron," in *Petrus Abaelardus (1079–1142): Person, Werk und Wirkung*, ed. Rudolf Thomas (Trier: Paulinus-Verlag, 1980), pp. 199–210; Ludwig Ott, "Die platonische Weltseele in der Theologie der Frühscholastik," in *Parusia: Studien zur Philosophie Platons und zur Problemgeschichte des Platonismus. Festgabe für Johannes Hirschberger*, ed. Kurt Flasch (Frankfurt: Minerva GMBH, 1965), pp. 308–15; J. M. Parent, *La doctrine de la creation dans l'école de Chartres* (Paris/Ottawa:

comparisons between the Father, Son, and Holy Spirit with the Platonic One, Nous, and World Soul are unproblematic, in either of these quarters. But it helps considerably to see that a different set of problems is associated with the Abelardian and with the Chartrain projects.

Considering the reactions to his *Theologia "summi boni"*, Abelard appears to have nuanced his position on the Holy Spirit in his later works. In the *Theologia christiana*, while continuing to argue that the Platonic doctrine of the World Soul is a *fabula* or *involucrum*, in his own sense of the term,[52] he now describes the Holy Spirit more guardedly as endowing the universe with life, as it were (*quasi vitam universitatis posuit*) and emphasizes that the Holy Spirit is not on an ontological level subordinate to that of the Father and the Son but that He is consubstantial with the Father and Son.[53] But if Abelard draws back somewhat in his second *theologia*, he returns to the fray in his third theological work, the *Theologia "scholarium"*, trying to advance his cause with new arguments and expanding his brief to include the Son as the Platonic Nous side by side with the Holy Spirit as the Platonic World Soul. He restates his earlier position on the pagans' rational grasp of the doctrine of the Trinity, which, he states, they foreshadowed fully as much as the doctrine of monotheism. Evidently, however, he is now willing to concede that more than reason was required. The Platonists, he now asserts, were recipients of divine grace, enabling them to perceive and to teach the Trinitarian faith in all its details.[54] This effort to cast Plato as a Christian inspired by grace is bolstered by Abelard with two new and equally shaky arguments. In one section of this work, Abelard seeks to exculpate Plato's theology from the charge of subordinationism by arguing that, for Plato, the Nous and World Soul were coeternal with the One and that they were on the same metaphysical level.[55] This misconstruction of Plato is accompanied by citations from other philosophers whose theology, as Abelard presents it, is compatible with the doctrine of the Trinity. Among these he cites Seneca, who, as a Stoic, was both a monotheist and a monist,

---

J. Vrin/Institut d'Études Médiévales, 1938), pp. 37–58, 70–81; J. G. Sikes, *Peter Abailard* (Cambridge: Cambridge University Press, 1932), pp. 67–68; Stollenwerk, "Der Genesiskommentar," pp. 49–50; Haijo Jan Westra, intro. to his ed. of *The Commentary on Martianus Capella's De Nuptiis Philologiae et Mercurii Attributed to Bernardus Silvestris* (Toronto: Pontifical Institute of Mediaeval Studies, 1986), pp. 23–33.

[52] Peter Abelard, *Theologia christiana* 1.98–107, CCCM 12: 112–17.

[53] Ibid., 1.71–78, 1.96, 1.123, CCCM 12: 101–04, 124.

[54] Peter Abelard, *Theologia "scholarium"* praefatio, 1.94–103, 1.107–09, 1.123–34, CCCM 13: 313–14, 356–58, 360–61, 368–73.

[55] Ibid., 2.174, CCCM 13: 492.

treating as authentic the correspondence between Seneca and St. Paul forged in the fourth century.[56] While Abelard continues to describe the Platonic Nous and World Soul doctrine as an *involucrum*, he also continues to read a literal Platonic teaching as a statement about Christian theology,[57] although he softens this assertion to some extent by stating that all theological statements and all applications of logic to theology need to be understood not literally but metaphorically (*translative*).[58] This disclaimer notwithstanding, however, his conclusion remains "that all men may have faith in the Trinity by nature" (*Quod fidem trinitatis omnes homines naturaliter habeant*).[59] And, the functions which Abelard ascribes to the Son and the Holy Spirit in the *Theologia "scholarium"* are scarcely free from difficulties. As the embodiment of the Platonic Nous, the Son, he says, can be understood as the exemplary forms of created beings in the mind of God, while the Holy Spirit, as the World Soul, is the providential order in which God disposes the creation, as well as the donor of charisms to men.[60]

Now, there was more than one way to handle the idea of exemplary causes in the tradition of Christian Platonism. One could, with Augustine, equate them with the mind of God, making them neither Platonic forms understandable as prior to or independent of the deity nor as primordial causes brought into being by the deity with which He shares the work of creation. Or, with John Scottus Eriugena, one could regard them as created and creative, in the second category of John's divisions of nature. Both of these possibilities were considered by Hugh of St. Victor and by the Chartrains. Abelard does not really indicate where, in this tradition, he wants to position his own view of exemplary causes and whether, or how, he can deal with the problem of making the Son less than coeternal with the Father and as distinct enough from creatures so that He cannot be seen as identical with the forms of individual substances. As for the Holy Spirit as World Soul, Abelard wants to maintain that He is equal with the Father and the Son, and that, in this respect, He proceeds from both of Them. Yet, the Holy Spirit is treated here as an aspect or an effect of creation, and not as a creative force Himself. Since the sole functions Abelard grants to Him have to do with the management of the created universe and

---

[56] Ibid., 1.198, CCCM 13: 403–04.

[57] Ibid., 1.147–48, CCCM 13: 379–80.

[58] Ibid., 2.80–93, CCCM 13: 447–58.

[59] Ibid., 2.182–83, CCCM 13: 497, continuing on this point through 2.184, p. 498.

[60] Ibid., 1.37, 2.172–73, CCCM 13: 333, 491–92.

with the inner lives of Christians, it is not at all clear how the Holy Spirit can be seen as coeternal with the Father and the Son, and not as coming into being in order to undertake these cosmological and charismatic assignments once the world and man have been created. Abelard's Holy Spirit would seem to have had no role at all prior to the creation of the universe and man. His activities seem to depend on the existence of a temporal, phenomenal order.

Abelard does not resolve any of these problems in his *Theologia "scholarium"*, but he does make one final attempt to soften his position in his *Dialectica*, the last work in which he takes up any of these arguments. Here, he does draw a distinction between the Holy Spirit as a member of the Trinitarian family, coeternal, consubstantial, and coequal with the Father and Son, and the Holy Spirit as manifested in the creation. This Trinitarian person can be differentiated, as a being, from His functions in time, with respect to human beings. In the *Dialectica*, Abelard drops entirely the cosmological dimension of the work of the Holy Spirit as described in the *Theologia "scholarium"* and, with equal, if late-blooming prudence, he leaves out the Son or Nous as a provider of exemplary forms. He also now treats the Platonic World Soul as an allegorical reference to the way in which the Holy Spirit spreads His gifts in the souls of believers, rather than describing it as a literal parallel to the third person of the Trinity.[61]

In comparing Abelard's handling of the Holy Spirit, in any of these incarnations, with Peter Lombard's doctrine of the Trinity as manifested, four points are immediately noticeable. In the first place, Peter rejects early on the notion of the manifestations of the Trinity, as known by revelation, as having any anticipations or parallels in the pagan philosophers or as accessible to human reason by nature. Rather, as we have seen, it is the divine nature of the unmanifested Trinity which natural reason and earlier philosophy are able to clarify. When it comes to the manifested Trinity, Peter is an unabashed fideist. In this connection, he expresses the orthodox consensus of his time. Secondly, Peter is not interested in talking about cosmology, in any sense, under the heading of the activities of the individual Trinitarian persons. He deals with the creation in Book 2 of the *Sentences*, and God's governance of the world, later in Book 1, under a different heading altogether, that of the activities of the Godhead as such, in which all the Trinitarian

---

[61] Peter Abelard, *Dialectica* 5.1.4, 2nd ed., ed. L. M. DeRijk (Assen: Van Gorcum, 1970), pp. 558–59. These shifts in Abelard's position are also noted by Dronke, *Fabula*, p. 178.

persons jointly and equally share. Thirdly, he draws heavily on a
point he had made earlier, the incommutability and transcendence
of the Trinitarian persons, in Their divine nature, vis-à-vis other
beings, to strengthen the distinction, hinted at by Abelard in the
Dialectica, between the Holy Spirit as unmanifested and as manifested in His charisms. And, finally, Peter expands considerably on
the mission of the Holy Spirit to man, in comparison both with
Abelard and with other contemporary thinkers who take up this
topic, with the possible exception of Rupert of Deutz.

Peter's opening salvo is the observation that, in His mission to
man as sanctifier in the temporal order, just as in His intratrinitarian role in the eternal order, the Holy Spirit proceeds equally from
the Father and the Son. In both respects, He can be called love
(*amor, caritas, dilectio*) in a special sense. Although, to be sure, we
can say that "God is love," as the apostle John does, with reference
to the divine nature as such, and with reference to all the persons of
the Trinity as well. Yet, in His intratrinitarian role, and this harks
back to Augustine's Trinitarian analogies, the Holy Spirit is the
love bonding the Father and the Son and flowing from both of
Them. In this understanding of the Holy Spirit as love one has a
being fully consubstantial with the persons Whose love He is. And,
in contrast with Abelard's handling of the Holy Spirit, whether as
goodness or as the World Soul, one has, in this determination, a
rock-solid defense against the position of the Greeks. One also has a
way of explaining why the terms begotten and unbegotten do not
refer appropriately to the Holy Spirit in this context, since the flow
of mutual love makes comprehensible another mode of derivation,
namely double procession.[62] While Peter takes from other theologians, notably Abelard and the author of the *Summa sententiarum*, a
number of cues as to which authorities to make use of here, his
argument on the double procession of the Holy Spirit against the
Greeks calls upon an authority he names as Jerome, but who has
been identified by Ignatius Brady as Syagrius, author of the *Regulis
definitionum contra haereticos*, on the point that the unbegotten-
begotten language is not appropriate to the Holy Spirit, and why.
As Peter notes, "Jerome" has a different understanding of these
terms from Augustine, the authority on whom all western theologians rely. Augustine means by *ingenitus* underived from anyone
else. "Jerome," on the other hand, means by *ingenitus non-genitus*,
that is to say, not born, leaving the way open to the idea of
procession. For its part, the term *genitus* has to be ruled out, for the

---

[62] Peter Lombard, *Sent.* 1. d. 10–d. 13, 1: 110–25.

Holy Spirit, otherwise there would be more that one Son in the Trinity. As Brady has noted, the Lombard is the only theologian of his time to have known and to have made use of Syagrius, and his application of this authority makes possible a clearer exposition of the doctrine in question that anyone else achieves.[63]

In His mission to men, as well, Peter argues that there is a double procession of the Holy Spirit from the Father and the Son, and that, although the task of diffusing charity into the hearts of men and enabling them to love both God and their neighbors is the work of the entire Trinity, this mission is entrusted by the entire Trinity to the Holy Spirit. There are two central points Peter wishes to emphasize in developing this position. First, since the Holy Spirit is equal to the Father and the Son, in carrying out His charismatic activities He communicates the grace of the whole Trinity. Secondly, and here he relies heavily on Bede and on his own earlier argument, Peter stresses that what the Holy Spirit gives is divine grace. He gives the gift of grace; He does not communicate Himself or the divine essence as such to the believers who receive His charisms.[64] Here, Peter harks back to the distinction between God's essence, as incommutable, and the personal determinations of the Trinitarian persons vis-à-vis each other, on the one hand, and, on the other, the effects of divine action as manifested in the created world and in the sanctification of Christians. This distinction must be preserved in order to avoid any trace of pantheism or participationism in considering the interactions between God and creatures. In speaking of the Holy Spirit as the love bonding believers to each other, and to God, therefore, Peter means, strictly, the effects of the Holy Spirit, which assist man in developing the virtue of charity and other virtues. The notion of the Holy Spirit as charity in His mission to man was later rejected by Thomas Aquinas and some other thirteenth-century scholastics.[65] In taking that line, they appear to have read Peter as the participationist that he decidedly was not, and either objected to his position on that account or wished to advance a different way of viewing the effects of grace, under the headings of created grace or Aristotelian *habitus*.

Understanding the reception of the Holy Spirit in the sense that Peter gives to that idea, he next raises the question of whether

---

[63] Brady, *Sent.* 1: 125 n. *ad loc.*
[64] Peter Lombard, *Sent.* 1. d. 14. c. 1–c. 2, 1: 126–28.
[65] Noted by Fortman, *The Tribune God*, p. 197; Edward A. Synan, "Brother Thomas, the Master, and the Masters," in *St. Thomas Aquinas, 1274 1974: Com memorative Studies*, 2 vols., ed. Armand A. Maurer et al. (Toronto: Pontifical Institute of Mediaeval Studies, 1974), 2: 227.

believers who receive this gift can transfer it to other men. Peter comes down squarely on the negative side of this debate. People who receive the gifts of the Spirit, he argues, do so according to a purely human capacity. They do not become divinized in the event. Insofar as they accept these gifts in order to minister to other people, the ministers, in that capacity, serve only as instruments through whom God communicates His grace to others. It is always God Who gives the gifts of the Holy Spirit, whether He does so in a direct way or through human agents.[66] Peter's handling of this point illustrates well, and reinforces, his temperamental disinclination to view the Christian's incorporation into the order of grace through the gifts of the Holy Spirit as anything more than his achievement of his full humanity.

Pausing briefly to observe that the Holy Spirit both gives and is given, His temporal procession being both His own *donatio* and an *operatio* of God as such,[67] Peter moves on to the point that this temporal mission is twofold, and this in two respects. First, and in this connection there is a parallel here with the temporal mission of the Son, there is the visible mission of the Holy Spirit, in the form of a dove, as well as His invisible workings in the souls of men. Second, the first stage of His temporal mission, like the Son's, occurs in the historical past, during the earthly life of Christ, while the second, or current stage, takes place in the ecclesiastical dispensation, following Christ's resurrection and sending forth of His apostles.[68] In the case of both the Son and the Holy Spirit, then, there is an eternal process of filiation, or spiration, as the case may be, and a two-stage temporal mission. At the same time, Peter is careful to alert his reader to a point he plans to develop in detail in the third book of the *Sentences*. The temporal missions of the Holy Spirit are not strictly analogous to those of the Son. For in the case of the manifestation of the Son to mankind, we have the union of the Word, as a Trinitarian person, with human nature in the incarnate Christ. This personal union continues to be the mode by which the Word interacts with mankind in the ecclesiastical dispensation.[69] The same is not the case with the Holy Spirit. This contrast has been inserted here to reinforce the observations made by Peter above, concerning the difference between the gifts of the Holy Spirit and the Holy Spirit Himself. In completing his discus-

---

[66] Peter Lombard, *Sent.* 1. d. 14. c. 3, 1: 129–30. For the debate on this issue, see Landgraf, *Dogmengeschichte*, 3 part 1: 169–85.
[67] Peter Lombard, *Sent.* 1. d. 15. c. 1.1–3, 1: 130–31.
[68] Ibid., d. 16. c. 1.1–2, 1: 138–39.
[69] Ibid., d. 15. c. 5–c. 8, d. 16. c. 4–c. 5, 1: 134–37, 139–40.

sion of the invisible mission of the Spirit in the hearts of the faithful, he continues to insist on this distinction. The Holy Spirit does not communicate Himself, as the divine substance. His gifts are not to be understood as pantheistic substitutions of divine virtue for human capacity. Rather, they are to be understood as forms of empowerment, stimuli enabling the believer to develop moral and spiritual potentialities that are strictly human. These gifts are given as He wills, and not to the same degree in all people. When they are received, we cannot say that the Holy Spirit is "in us" in the same way in which our natural created spirit is part of our natural human constitution. Reminding the reader that this whole topic of the temporal mission of the Holy Spirit is one of those areas in which we speak of God in a relative sense with respect to time (*de his quae relative dicuntur de Deo ex tempore*), he concludes his discussion of the Holy Spirit, fuller by far than what we find in other contemporary· theologians, by observing that he plans to treat these gifts further, in another place.[70] This he does, as we will see below in chapter 8, in his consideration of man's moral life.

THE DIVINE NATURE IN RELATION TO THE CREATION

The remaining topics dealing with the doctrine of God which Peter addresses in Book 1 of his *Sentences* all concern features of the deity looked at from the standpoint of the divine nature as such, rather than from the perspective of the Trinity. He has carefully laid the foundation for all the questions he treats here, in his earlier discussion of the total coinherence of all the divine determinations in the divine essence and also in his insistence on the point that the incommutable deity remains transcendent of, and unconsumed by, His manifestations of Himself to other beings or His interactions with them. In one way or another, these principles inform Peter's handling of all the questions remaining under the heading of the deity, questions which are all, in this sense, interconnected in his presentation of them. There are three principal issues which he treats here, all responsive to contemporary debates, and all providing occasions for Peter not only to offer his solutions to these debates but also to put his own distinctive doctrine of God to work in so doing. These issues all involve the way in which the deity interacts with the world and could be taken up in any order. We will consider first the problem of God's ubiquity; then the relation

---

[70] Ibid., d. 17. c. 1–d. 18. c. 5.2, 1: 141–59. The quotation is at d. 18. c. 5.2, 1: 189.

between God's foreknowledge, predestination, and providence and freedom and contingency in the created order; and, finally, the most vexed question of all in this area, the question of whether God could do better, or different, than He does.

God's Ubiquity

While God's ubiquity was not a topic that inspired accusations of heresy in this period, it did draw considerable attention, and it affords an excellent vantage point from which we can view approaches to the divine nature in the early twelfth century, and what Peter thought needed clarification in this area. Early in the century, a number of theologians took a stand on God's ubiquity that made them liable to the charge of an immanentalism so unqualified that is was indistinguishable from pantheism. Anselm of Laon typifies this problem, without being conscious that such is the case. He states that "the divine essence is essentially in all things" (*divina essentia essentialiter sit in omnibus*). At the same time, he contradicts himself later in the same passage by stating that God's presence in creatures "is not to be understood essentially" (*non est intelligendum essentialiter*).[71] Anselm's followers compound the difficulty. Agreeing that God is in all creatures *essentialiter*, they add, without explanation, that this essential divine presence may occur in different ways in different creatures and that this presence may be thought of as well as the divine power and substance (*potentia, substantia*).[72] A similar position is taken by Robert Pullen, who holds that God is ubiquitous "not only potentially but also essentially, not as divided into parts but as completely everywhere" (*non solum potentialiter sed et essentialiter, non per partes divisus, sed ubique totus*), although without His purity being affected or His infinity being circumscribed spatially.[73]

Understandably, some theologians in our period were made more than a little nervous by such claims and sought ways of retaining the idea of God's ubiquity that would not force them to fall into this kind of pantheistic morass. Early in the century, Honorius Augustodunensis offered one sort of solution. God dwells everywhere, *potentialiter*, he argues, although substantially He

---

[71] Anselm of Laon, *Sententie divine pagine* 1, ed. Franz P. Bliemetzrieder in *Anselms von Laon systematische Sentenzen*, Beiträge, 18:2–3 (Münster: Aschendorff, 1919), p. 5.

[72] *Sentences of the School of Laon*, no. 286, 288, 315, ed. Odon Lottin in *Psychologie et morale aux XIIᵉ et XIIIᵉ siècles*, vols. 1–5 (Louvain: Abbaye de Mont-César, 1948–59), 5: 232, 233, 251.

[73] Robert Pullen, *Sent.* 1.9, *PL* 186: 689C–690A. The quotation is at 689C.

dwells in the intellectual heaven.[74] Honorius essays no explanation of what any of these terms mean, which may be the reason why this particular-effort to combine God's ubiquity with His transcendence had no takers later in the century. For his part, Hugh of St. Victor gives a critique of the pantheist reading of God's ubiquity and little else. God, he argues, is not substantially or essentially present in corporeal beings. Since He is infinite, He cannot be physically circumscribed.[75] This treatment of the problem confines the ubiquity issue to creatures that have bodies. And, while it denies the pantheist mode of divine ubiquity, Hugh does not indicate if there is a positive concept of divine ubiquity that he can support. In relation to Hugh, the author of the *Summa sententiarum* takes one step backward and one step ahead. He agrees that God cannot be localized and that God is pervasive in the universe, substantially. He states that what he means by "substantial" in this connection is not the presence of God's essence in creatures, but rather God's effects in the order and disposition of mutable beings, as a cause and *per dispositionem*. Yet, despite this apparent backing away from total immanentalism, he continues to insist that the divine substance is everywhere (*Haec divina substantia ubique tota est, et in ipsa sunt omnia*).[76] If he is serious about the qualifications he makes, one wonders why he retains an idea of substance that leads him to this contradictory conclusion. For his part, the author of the *Sententiae divinitatis*, agreeing that God cannot be bounded spatially and that He is immutable, urges that He is not omnipresent in the world *essentialiter*; rather, He is ubiquitous as the sustainer of the universe, *per sustentationem*.[77] But, on the manner in which God performs this function he remains silent.

The author in Peter's environment who comes the closest to him in offering a positive alternative to an essentialist or substantialist way of understanding divine ubiquity, and who presents an account that bears some relation to the rest of his doctrine of God, is Robert of Melun. He situates this question in the context of God as cause, in relation to created beings as causes, and in the context of God as a being in comparison with the *esse* of other beings. He draws the same kind of distinction here as undergirds his handling

---

[74] Honorius Augustodunensis, *Elucidarium* 1.10, ed. Yves Lefèvre in *L'Elucidarium et les lucidaires: Contribution, par l'histoire d'un texte, à l'histoire des croyances religieuses en France au moyen âge* (Paris: É. de Boccard, 1954), p. 362.

[75] Hugh of St. Victor, *De sac.* 1.3.17, *PL* 176: 224B–D. Noted by Kilgenstein, *Die Gotteslehre*, pp. 91–102.

[76] *Summa sent.* 1.4, *PL* 176: 48B–49A. The quotation is at 48B.

[77] *Sent. div.* 6.A, pp. 156*–158*.

of these related issues in his proof of God's existence. According to
Robert, in understanding God's mode of presence in the universe,
one must differentiate between what is being, simply (*quid sit aliquid
simpliciter esse*) and what is being by derivation from something else
(*aliquid ex aliquibus esse*). Simple, underived being is necessary being
(*ipsum esse necesse est*) and is God. Now, he continues, we can
attribute the word *esse* properly both to God and to creatures,
depending on whether we are using the term to denote simple or
derived being, respectively. Whichever choice we make, we then
have to use *esse* with a transferred meaning (*translatio verborum*) in
applying it to the other kind of being. Robert then offers a lengthy
discussion of the propriety of the similitudes that result, when the
verbal traffic goes in either direction, including a consideration of
the *via negativa*. But his whole line of argument is designed to refute
the claims of those theologians who defend the idea that God shares
His essence with creatures, that He is substantially present in the
creation, or that He serves as the form of created beings. The
differences between simple, underived being and created being
which he has outlined make this kind of arrangement a metaphysical impossibility. As Robert concludes, God is not ubiquitous by
His essence, but by His governance and by His effects in the
creation.[78] An unusual way of posing the question in itself, Robert's
handling of the ubiquity problem is also interesting in that, while
he presents it, in the first instance, as a metaphysical issue, he
resolves it largely by means of a semantic argument.

As we turn from Robert of Melun to Peter Lombard on God's
ubiquity and His mode of presence in creation we note a similar
interest in rejecting an immanental or pantheistic approach to the
subject and a similar concern with avoiding the blurring or mixing
of two different types of being. For his part, however, Peter attacks
the problem in a different way, and positions it on a wider canvas.
He begins by observing that God can be in other things by essence,
power, and presence. As for the first, there is one and only one
non-divine being with which God unites Himself essentially. This is
the man Jesus in the incarnation of Christ. Both the human and the
divine natures of Christ are retained, without being blended into a
tertium quid in the hypostatic union. Just as the incarnate Christ is,
metaphysically speaking, *sui generis*, so this case is the unique
instance of God's essential union with a creature, and is the exception that proves the rule. Peter mentions this exception in order to

---

[78] Robert of Melun, *Sent.* 1.5.46–55, *Oeuvres*, 3 part 2: 258–76. A good treatment
of this point is found in Ulrich Horst, *Die Trinitäts- und Gotteslehre des Robert von
Melun* (Mainz: Matthias-Grünewald Verlag, 1964), pp. 294–317.

get the topic of God's essential union with creatures off the agenda more generally, as a fundamentally inappropriate way of regarding God's presence in the world. With respect to other existing beings, he continues, God is present in them as the ground of their being. He exercises this ontological function without thereby serving as their form or definition. With this analysis of the divine ubiquity, grounded in the structure of being, in place, Peter proceeds to use it to explain how God can be present in all times and places without being conditioned or circumscribed by location or change.

Moving beyond God's presence, in this sense, in the order of creation, Peter also considers His presence in the order of grace. To be sure, the dwelling of the deity in the saints by grace has to be distinguished from His ubiquity in the universe, since all creatures require a ground of being without exception, and in the same way, while not all men are saints and, even among those who are, their charisms differ. The point of contact or carryover between the order of creation and the order of grace, for Peter, is the idea that God exercises His power in these two zones in directly parallel ways. In neither area does He communicate His essence or substance. Rather, what He communicates is His power (*virtus*). And, in both cases, He communicates this *virtus* in such a way as to leave intact the creaturely status of the beings to which, or to whom, He communicates it. Just as there is no blending or merging of the divine nature with the natures of created beings in the world, so His dwelling in the saints through His grace in no sense divinizes them or alters their purely human status. Harking back to the observations he had made on the temporal mission of the Holy Spirit, Peter emphasizes that God's relationships with the world, whether direct or indirect and whether all-inclusive or centered on the elect, do not involve the participation of one kind of being into another kind of being.[79] And, as to Peter's positive understanding of God's presence in the world and in the inner life of man, he offers here, as we have seen, the distinction between essence and *virtus*, a notion he specifies still more clearly by distinguishing, with respect to God's love, its eternity and immutability *secundum essentiam*, and its distribution to different people differently, *secundum efficientiam*.[80] In all these respects, Peter's treatment of the ubiquity question is even more broadly gauged than Robert of Melun's. It provides a corrective to immanentalism that rests on his clear and systematically

---

[79] Peter Lombard, *Sent.* 1. d. 37. c. 1.1–c. 3.5, 1: 263–68. A good discussion is found in Ludwig Ott, *Untersuchung zur theologischen Briefliteratur der Frühscholastik*, Beiträge, 34 (Münster: Aschendorff, 1937), pp. 208–11.
[80] Peter Lombard, *Sent.* 3. d. 32, 2: 184–87. The quotations are on p. 186.

applied distinction between the transcendent deity, incommutable
in His essence, and the effects of His working in nature and grace,
which both grounds all created beings in a metaphysically prior
order of being and empowers those human beings who are called
and chosen to attain the fullness of their human nature.

God's Foreknowledge, Province, and Predestination and Free Will and Contingency

Another constellation of questions concerning the divine nature
in God's relation to the world that received wide attention in the
first half of the twelfth century was the problem of God's foreknowledge, His providence, and His predestination in relation to free
will, the agency of secondary causes, and contingency. In addressing this topic, twelfth-century thinkers had a range of authorities on
whom to draw, authorities who accented different aspects of the
problem and who harnessed it to different agendas. Even within the
same author one could find a different emphasis, at different points
in his oeuvre. Augustine, one of the most important of these resources, had drawn a sharp distinction between God's foreknowledge, as neutral, and His providence, as affording a sizeable space
for the agency of secondary causes, in the effort to place the sole
responsibility for moral evil on the misdirected use of human free
will, in his early and in his anti-Manichean works. Later, faced
with the need to refute the Pelagians, he had retained the notion of
God's foreknowledge as neutral, and, while also retaining the idea
that His providence includes both events He causes directly in the
natural order and those effected by other agents, he had emphasized predestination as God's direct causation in the order of redemption and had decreased the scope of free will. Another important
authority in this area was Boethius. While familiar with Augustine's treatments of this problem, he sought, in his *Consolation of
Philosophy*, to include fate within the scenario, as the bearer of good
and bad fortune but as operating under the ultimate control of the
deity, while emphasizing the rational transcendence of the turmoil and
suffering that misfortune could bring in the light of that broader
understanding of it. Earlier, however, he had treated these issues
in a much more strictly logical manner, in his translation of and
commentary on Aristotle's *De interpretatione*, the *locus classicus* of the
Stagirite's treatment of necessity, possibility, and contingency. Aristotle himself was concerned in this work both with the modes of
causation and contingency that occur in the natural order, which
can be tested empirically, and with possibility and necessity in

the order of logic. For his part, Boethius as a commentator had accented the logical side of Aristotle's analysis, and had not hesitated to reformulate some of the Stagirite's arguments, turning them into propositions verifiable in terms of formal logic and not in terms of their empirical testability.

In examining the approaches taken to these questions by Peter, his contemporaries, and his immediate predecessors, one is struck by the one-sidedness of the address of many of them to the resources provided by both the theological tradition and the school tradition on these matters. A number of authors touch only on a few aspects of the problem and omit much else. Some confine themselves only to the implications of the doctrine for man's moral life or salvation. There is not a clear consensus, across the period, as to which divine attribute this constellation of ideas should be seen as illustrating. In some quarters, a purely logical approach is taken, to the point of excluding the theological dimensions of the topic. Some authors get hopelessly tangled up in formulations of the subject that leave them impacted with the detritus of their own poorly framed questions. In the judgment of Calvin Normore, Peter Lombard's handling of this subject was the most influential of any thinker of the twelfth century, and deservedly so. Not only does Peter display a wide-angle approach to it, a sureness of touch as to how to address it, and solid arguments against the positions with which he disagrees, but his positive treatment of the doctrine grounds it firmly in the principle of God's knowledge.[81] This strategy enables Peter to take account of the idea of possibility in the fields of logic and natural philosophy without confining it to those modes of thought, thus drawing together the Boethian-Aristotelian emphasis of his principal antagonist, Abelard, with a stress on the importance of the subject from the perspective of the divine nature, on the theological side of the debate.

Since Abelard set so much of the agenda here, it is worth beginning with his attack on the problem. The first and most important point to be made is that Abelard viewed this whole issue primarily as a logical, not as a theological, one. He takes it up, initially, in his early logical works, written before he decided to move on to theology. When he did make that transition, he retained the logical mode of handling it. This fact is worth noting, in and of itself. Equally

---

[81] Calvin Normore, "Future Contingents," in *Cambridge History of Later Medieval Philosophy*, ed. Norman Kretzman, Anthony Kenny, and Jan Pinborg (Cambridge: Cambridge University Press, 1982), pp. 363–64. Normore rightly associates this position with Peter's stress on God's freedom.

important is the kind of logic that Abelard draws out of, or applies to, his Boethian-Aristotelian materials. In this connection, his understanding of the scope of logic itself needs to be recalled, since it affects powerfully his overall method and also the kinds of claims he would be able to make for his logical arguments on this subject when he transposes them into his theological works. Notwithstanding the fact that he begins by commenting on the Aristotelian texts available in the Latin school tradition, Abelard takes from Boethius and sharpens a Stoic-Megaritic approach to logic as a formal art. In his earliest works, he confirms that, for him, logic is a science of concepts, not a mode of analysis whose goal is to seek verification of its conclusions in the world of nature or in the ontological order. Concepts may, initially, derive from things. But, once in the mind, they are usable, comprehensible, and meaningful in propositional form apart from things. It is the formal structure and relations of the propositions and the terms that comprise them that determine the truth claims they make. Asserted initially in his commentaries,[82] these same principles are developed by Abelard in his own logical treatises, both in his express statements defining the nature and scope of logic as such[83] and, implicitly, in his reformulations of syllogistic arguments drawn from his authorities, in which arguments that involve priority and posteriority in time, or conditions that are verifiable empirically, are converted into propositions and syllogisms that display exclusively logical relations.[84] The fact that Abelard's logic is not envisioned by him as capable of establishing any truth but the intrapropositional truth of formal logic has received general recognition from modern students of his philosophy.[85] The fact that a logic understood as a science of discourse,

---

[82] See, for example, Peter Abelard, *Editio super Porphyrum*; *Glossae in Categorias*; *Editio super Aristotelem de Interpretatione*, ed. Mario Dal Pra in Peter Abelard, *Scritti di logica*, 2nd ed. (Florence: La Nuova Italia, 1969), pp. 5, 61, 84–85, 105–06, 110–13.

[83] Peter Abelard, *Logica "ingredientibus"*, ed. Bernhard Geyer in Peter Abelard, *Philosophische Schriften*, Beiträge, 21:1–3 (Münster: Aschendorff, 1919–27), 21 part 1: 17, 20–21, 28–29, 60–61; 21 part 2: 112–15; 21 part 3: 307–10, 320–22; *Logica "nostrorum petitioni sociorum"*, ed. Bernhard Geyer in Peter Abelard, *Philosophische Schriften*, Beiträge, 21:4 (Münster: Aschendorff, 1933), p. 585, *Dialectica* 2.1.1.4, 2.28, pp. 153–60, 163–64, 210–13.

[84] Peter Abelard, *Dialectica* 3.1.4, 4.1.2 ff., pp. 270–309, 469–532.

[85] Dal Pra, intro. to his ed. of *Scritti di logica*, pp. xxi–xxiii; Mariateresa Beonio-Brocchieri [Fumagalli], "La relation entre logique, physique et théologie chez Abélard," in *Peter Abelard*, ed. Eligius M. Buytaert (Leuven: Leuven University Press, 1974), pp. 153–63; *The Logic of Abelard*, trans. Simon Pleasance (Dordrecht: D. Reidel, 1969), pp. 13–23, 28–36; Geyer, comm. on his ed. of *Philos. Schriften*, 21 part 4: 621–33; Jean Jolivet, "Abélard entre chien et loup," *Cahiers de civilisation médiévale* 20 (1977): 312–18; *Arts du langage et théologie chez Abélard*, 2nd ed. (Paris: J. Vrin, 1982), pp. 19–22, 44–45, 67–72, 74–77, 96–104, 229–335; Martin M.

not as a science of things, a logic understood as having jurisdiction only within its own realm and as unable to establish truth anywhere else, would make an imperfect instrument of theological analysis, does inspire Abelard at times to argue that theological language is metaphorical, or to invoke arguments from theological appropriateness. But it does not dampen his enthusiasm for the claim that dialectic, "to which the judgment of all truth or falsity is subject" (cui quidem omnis veritatis seu falsitatis discretio ita subiecta est), should be used to demonstrate the teachings of the Catholic faith and to refute heretics.[86]

The first theological topic to which Abelard gives logic this somewhat ambiguous assignment, on his own accounting of it, is God's providence and future contingents. Abelard takes up this issue for the first time in his Logica "ingredientibus", where he indicates, by his very address to it, his desire to treat it as a topic in formal logic. He urges that the subject of future contingents be taken out of a temporal framework altogether. Past, present, and future, to be sure, are conditions that occur in nature. But the problem, he argues, should be treated on a conceptual and not on a natural level.[87] Our concepts, whatever their content, exist as if in the present. This report, from the precincts of logic, is used by Abelard to reinforce the analogy made in Augustine's Confessions between the soul's present memory, attention, and expectation as reducible to the soul's present action and the eternity of God, dwelling in the eternal present. But Abelard's analysis, unlike Augustine's, is based on the workings of propositional logic, not on those of human psychology. One can, he notes, argue against those who think that God's providence is undermined by natural contingency and human free will, equating God's providence with universal divine determinism. This can be done, he shows, as Augustine had done it, by distinguishing between providence and predestination. As he reads this distinction, providence is understood as God's foreknowledge of what will happen, whether good or

---

Tweedale, Abailard on Universals (Amsterdam: North-Holland Publishing Company, 1976), pp. 93–95, 130–37, 185–88, 210; Richard E. Weingart, The Logic of Divine Love: A Critical Analysis of the Soteriology of Peter Abailard (Oxford: Clarendon Press, 1970), pp. 11–31. The principal dissenters are DeRijk, intro. to his ed. of Dialectica, pp. xxiii–xxviii, xl, lv–lix, xcv–xcviii and Lucia Urbani Ulivi, La psicologia di Abelardo e il "Tractatus de intellectibus" (Rome: Storia e Letteratura, 1976), pp. 85–93, 95–100, who follows DeRijk in holding that the achievement of a purely formal logic was Abelard's goal but that he did not actually arrive at that destination.
[86] Peter Abelard, Dialectica 4.1 prologus, p. 470.
[87] Peter Abelard, Logica "ingredientibus", 21 part 1: 26–27.

bad, whether caused by God Himself or by the actions of men or other secondary causes. On the other hand, predestination is confined to God's determination of those things He wills to occur by His own direct agency, specifically the granting of grace to the elect. As with the late Augustine, Abelard holds that this grace has two aspects. It prepares the elect to respond to God's call and it helps them to persevere in it. Strictly speaking, predestination is the grace of preparation, and it can be distinguished from the gift that makes salvation possible once that initial grace has been received. Since predestination has this consequence, we can say that its causative effect is always good. Now God knows from all eternity which men He will endow with grace. He also knows which sins men will commit, although He does not cause them.

This Augustinian attack on the question is in no sense the whole story, for Abelard; nor, in his estimation, is it the most interesting way to address it. He next introduces Boethius's reprise of the key chapter in Aristotle's *De interpretatione*, where a more strictly physical and logical account of necessity, possibility, and contingency is provided. In chapter 9 of that work, Aristotle frames the issue in terms of a sea battle that may or may not be fought tomorrow. There is always the possibility that the captains may cancel the battle because the rulers they represent have settled their differences. Or, hostilities may still prevail, but bad weather may prevent the battle from taking place. The natural or human contingencies involved in these possibilities lie within the structure of natural laws and the nature of man. But whether of not they will be activated so as to prevent or call off the battle is a matter of chance or contingency. With this analysis in mind, Abelard now distinguishes providence from fate. Fate he sees as the natural necessities built into the physical order. Fate is ineluctable in the sense that, once the relevant physical laws of cause and effect are set in motion, the outcomes flowing from them will necessarily follow. God knows that these consequences will occur if these physical laws are activated, since He created the universe with the natural laws in question. At the same time, agreeing with Aristotle and Boethius, Abelard observes that there are areas of contingency and human choice here which determine whether or not these natural laws, and their consequences, will be activated in a particular instance. He adds that there are also physical events which God permits to happen—miracles, for instance—even though they occur outside of the causal nexus of the laws of physics. This observation aside, along with Aristotle and Boethius, he accents the idea that creatures, as they are created, possess certain built-in capacities to do or to refrain from doing what they choose. Giving an Aristotelian example here, he notes that a man, by nature, is capable of sitting down, but whether he will do so at a particular moment is a matter of choice, not necessity, on his part. The same analysis applies to a man's capacity to sin. The fact that God knows how the man will exercise this capacity does not mean that God causes him to sin, just as God does not personally cause the other outcomes that are effects of contingencies.

Thus far, Abelard has shifted an initially Augustinian argument preoccupied with grace and predestination to an Aristotelian argument for possibility and contingency as compatible with a universe in which natural laws impose their own physical necessities. He now proceeds to shift his argument once again. Still another way of handling the problem is to transpose it from the realm of necessity, possibility, and contingency as they operate in the natural order to the realm of modal propositions. This option is even more attractive to Abelard, since, once the subject has been reformulated in these terms, the propositions in which they are framed express the ideas of possibility and necessity and their relationships according to the formal structure of the propositions used. The conclusions flowing from these propositions can be evaluated in terms of whether they follow logically from their antecedents quite independent of times, places, and conditions that may or may not exist in the physical or metaphysical order. From this perspective, Abelard now seeks to expose the logical fallacy of the claim that God errs if it can be shown that anything can happen in a way different from the way in which it does happen. The rule he invokes here is this: if the antecedent is possible, the consequent attaches the judgment "Yes, it is possible" to the proposition itself, not to the subject matter or content stated by the antecedent. His treatment of this rule is a clear articulation of the strictly logical approach to the problem of possibility and necessity he is taking at this juncture, an approach which he also advocates as more elegant and satisfactory than the ones that he had set forth before presenting it.

If one applies this kind of formal logical analysis to the question of foreknowledge and predestination, as defined above, it follows that propositions admitting of possibility and contingency can be constructed from propositions in which foreknowledge is asserted. Also, as Abelard points out, it depends on how the word "differently" (*aliter*) is used in propositions that hypothesize on whether things could have turned out differently from the way they do turn out. *Aliter* can be used as a relative term, and also as a negative term. Its causal force is stronger in the latter usage. In the former case, when *aliter* is used as a relative term, the presence of logical possibility can be entertained without a contradiction with foreknowledge, in stating a contingent claim. The use of hypothetical syllogisms to structure the propositions in question here itself emphasizes the formal quality of the logical analysis involved.[88]

It is perfectly obvious what Abelard is trying to accomplish in this handling of the question of God's foreknowledge and future contingents in the *Logica "ingredientibus"*. In moving from a theological account derived from the late Augustine to a physical account derived from Aristotle to a strictly logical account of the issues, to which he is guided by Boethius, he places his arguments in, what is, for him, an ascending order of importance and persuasiveness. Even though Abelard gives a far more elaborate treatment of the *De interpretatione* formulation of the problem than Boethius does in his commentary on that work, taking it through its paces in great detail, and offering a host of variant syllogistic forms in which the ideas involved can be stated, situating them within the larger context of the logical rules for affirmation, negation, and contradiction, and yoking them to an express discussion of hypothetical syllogisms, equipollent propositions, and their probative force, he ends by reducing the Aristotelian position to the position of formal logic far more systematically than Boethius does. Abelard grants more authority to formal logic than to anything else in his handling of this problem, reading across Aristotle and across Boethius himself to obtain a more consistently post-Aristotelain logic than his sources provide. He shows his instinct for moving away from theological reasoning, in redefining the divine nature, or propositions which refer to it, as part of the subject matter of formal logic. While Abelard does admit that the debate at issue can be approached in other ways, the other alternatives are clearly less compelling and persuasive, for him. Above all, the logical sense of propositions is his point of conclusion, whatever sense they may have in the world of physical or metaphysical reality.

Abelard also takes up these same questions in his *Theologia "scholarium"*. His argument here is similar to that in the *Logica "ingredientibus"* except for the fact that he frames the issue of future contingents here along the lines of Aristotle's account of the sea battle in *De interpretatione* 9, giving attention to the claims made in terms of natural law as well as in terms of formal logic. The main differences between his initial treatment of the subject and this one are that, in the *Theologia "scholarium"*, Abelard wants to accent

---

[88] Ibid., 21 part 3: 426–47.

man's freedom and responsibility in the moral life under the heading of contingency; and he wants to emphasize more strongly the point that God can suspend the natural law when He performs miracles. From a logical standpoint, as well, Abelard here frames the question of the compatibility of God's eternal foreknowledge and contingent events in the light of the nominalist theory of the univocity of the noun in its signification, although its consignification in statements using the past or future tenses of the verb may reflect shifts in our knowledge or our description of what the noun signifies.[89]

Abelard returns to the argument offered in the *Logica "ingredientibus"* for a third time in his most mature logical work, the *Dialectica*, there offering a refinement on it.[90] He reprises the point that past, present, and future are categories irrelevent to God, since He lives in the eternal present. He also repeats the observation that God so ordains things that some events are capable of occurring contingently, and that, when this happens, these contingencies do not conflict with divine providence. Nor do events which, as God ordains them, occur of necessity as consequences of the laws of nature which He put in place. In this work, Abelard moves as well from the Augustinian and Aristotelian arguments to attach the idea of possibility to the logical relations between antecedent and consequent propositions that formulate the alternatives in hypothetical form. At the same time, in the *Dialectica* Abelard admits that the idea of necessity also attaches properly to actual natural outcomes, and that, even propositionally, a future contingent can only be defended as a possibility. This conclusion imparts a rather more Aristotelian coloration to his handling of necessity and possibility than he had given to it in the *Logica "ingredientibus"*. Another shift is that, in the *Dialectica*, he omits the distinction between God's foreknowledge and God's causation in treating divine providence. He collapses these two ideas into a view of providence that takes it to mean God's legislation for, and action in, the natural order, and not merely God's oversight of that order. The theme of predestination and grace likewise departs from Abelard's agenda in this work. These shifts in emphasis notwithstanding, the bottom line for his handling of the entire question, both early and late, remains formal logic, not the divine nature.

---

[89] Peter Abelard, *Theologia "scholarium"* 3.5, 3.87–116, CCCM 13: 526, 536–47. This nominalist feature of Abelard's argument has been brought out by William J. Courtenay, *Capacity and Volition: A History of the Distinction of Absolute and Ordained Power* (Bergamo: Pierluigi Lubrina, 1990), pp. 44–50. I am indebted to Professor Courtenay for this reference.

[90] Peter Abelard, *Dialectica* 2.2.10–11, pp. 217–22.

The vast majority of theologians in the first half of the twelfth century found the Abelardian attack on God's foreknowledge and future contingents unacceptably narrow, and even reductionistic. There are several whose objections are grounded in the logic of Aristotle's *De interpretatione,* and who either fail to take Abelard's point about the advantages of formal logic or who are aware of his claims for it and reject them in favor of a logic that could give equal weight to proofs verifiable in the world of real being. What we should probably describe as a pre-Abelardian approach to the issue is found in one of his erstwhile masters, William of Champeaux. God's providence and predestination are the only questions he is known to have raised concerning the divine nature. His handling of the second topic offers a straightforward summary of the position of the late Augustine, with one very striking exception. William agrees that God, from all eternity, grants to His elect the grace of preparation, justification, and perfection. Where he departs from Augustine, a move that will attract unfavorable notice elsewhere in this period, is in stating that, since God knows ahead of time who will use free will to consent to the good, He chooses these people as His elect.[91] In handling providence, William equates it with causation, understanding it in the Aristotelian sense, as the physical laws of nature. He does not bring foreknowledge to bear on this topic, treating it along the lines of *De interpretatione* 9. He agrees that the natural order contains effects that follow necessarily from their natural causes, and that this same natural order also contains beings capable of exercising free choice or of acting contingently. Since this is the arrangement established by God's providence, it is not in conflict with that providence.[92] Another author in our period, and one who would have had available Abelard's fullest arguments on this point but who reflects a preference for the *De interpretatione* account, is a disciple of Gilbert of Poitiers, working in Paris in the early 1140s. He frames the problem in terms of the distinction between natural events that occur as the result of absolute necessities, stemming from the endowments or limitations of the given natures of the beings involved, and natural events conditioned by the choices of free agents or of other contingencies that can also be seen as a part of the natural range of possibilities which they enjoy. He agrees that God provides for both kinds of events

[91] *Sentences of William of Champeaux,* no. 240, ed. Odon Lottin in *Psychologie et morale aux XIIe et XIIIe siècles,* vols. 1–5 (Louvain: Abbaye de Mont-César, 1948–59), 5: 199–200.
[92] Ibid., no. 237–38, 5: 195–98.

even though He does not cause either kind directly.[93]

Much more typical, among objections to Abelard's teaching, is the idea that God's providence ought to be considered as a theological problem, under the heading of the divine nature. Many theologians of the day seek to reroute this topic and to take it up in the context of their discussion of one divine attribute or another. Until Peter Lombard tackled the question, they arrived at no consensus as to which divine attribute was its natural habitat. In addition, few give sustained or well-rounded attention to the problem and some encumber it with difficulties of their own invention. A good reflection of these traits can be seen in Anselm of Laon and his followers. On predestination, Anselm shares with William of Champeaux the problematic claim that God foresees which of the persons whom He justifies will persevere, and that He grants them election on that account.[94] While not as critical of Augustine on this point as William, Anselm's formulation of it suggests that the deity predestines such people because of their foreseen merits, rather than giving them the grace of preparation that enables them to acquire merit. As for the wider issue of providence, predestination, and human freedom, Anselm treats it under the heading of God's will. Here, he says, we can distinguish the will of God's essence (*voluntas essentie*), as manifested in the order and disposition of the universe, the good will of God (*voluntas dei bona*), operating in His saints and inspiring them to love God and their fellow man, and the will of God through precept (*voluntas dei pro precepto*), that is, the moral rules God lays down for men. Anselm adds that, while man is obliged to obey God's will in all three areas, and while God foresees whether or not a man will do so, He does not constrain human freedom in that foresight.[95] This analysis, scanty as it is, manages to compound two major problems. First, and this reminds us of Anselm's handling of the divine ubiquity, is his equation of the natural order with God's essence. Second, he does not seem to appreciate the fact that, while men can reject God's grace and His moral law, exempting themselves from the laws of nature does not constitute an option for human beings. In any event, Anselm is not particularly interested in God's relation, as a cause, to the natural order. His real interest, so far as it goes on this topic, lies in its moral implications only.

---

[93] *Sent. mag. Gisleberti* I 2.41–45, p. 121.

[94] *Sentences of Anselm of Laon*, no. 11, ed. Odon Lottin in *Psychologie et morale aux XIIe et XIIe siècles*, vols. 1–5 (Louvain: Abbays de Mont-César, 1948–59), 5: 22.

[95] Ibid., no. 31–32, 34, 5: 33–35.

Other masters associated with Anselm of Laon appear to have been sensitive to the difficulties with his teachings here and, at some points, offer rectifications, clarifications, or amplifications of it. One of the things they share with him is the treatment of God, as cause, in relation to created agents, under the heading of God's will. The will of God, they observe, can be understood four ways, as efficient, approving, conceding, and permitting (*efficiens, approbans, concedens, permittens*). God's efficient will constitutes His direct causative action, and also His indirect causation in cases where man is given the capacity to function as an efficient cause in his own sphere. God exercises His approving will when He looks with pleasure on something He finds gratifying, or, at any rate, when He chooses not to prevent or impede something He finds less appealing. God's conceding will comes into play when He gives His express permission for an event caused by a secondary agent, an event of which He approves. God's permitting will can be seen at work when He allows something to occur even though He does not approve of it. In this fourth sense, we can say that God permits evils to occur. And, in the wider sense of this fourfold distinction, we can differentiate God's precepts and prohibitions from His counsels, although they are all species of the unitary will of God which moral agents remain free to disobey.[96] In discussing providence the Laon masters reprise the distinction made in their definition of God's fourfold will, observing that this is simply another way of looking at what God does vis-à-vis the world and that His arrangements include the existence of free agents, capable of functioning as secondary causes in the field of moral action, and that God's foreknowledge does not annul the freedom of such agents or prevent Him from tolerating the unpleasing things He may permit them to do. In contrast, God's predestination is confined to what God causes directly with respect to the salvation of the men He elects. Anselm's followers return here to an authentically Augustinian version of this doctrine of election while affirming that the grace granted by means of it requires man's cooperation.[97] Here, all concern for contingency in the natural order has receded from view

---

[96] *Sentences of the School of Laon*, no. 290, 294, 5: 235–37, 240; *Sententie Anselmi*, ed. Franz P. Bliemetzrieder in *Anselms von Laon systematische Sentenzen*, Beiträge, 18:2–3 (Münster: Aschendorff, 1919), pp. 63–64. The source of this argument is Anselm of Canterbury's *De concordia* and philosophical fragments, as has been noted by Gillian R. Evans, *Anselm and a New Generation* (Oxford: Clarendon Press, 1980), pp. 133–34.

[97] *Sent. Anselmi*, pp. 90–92; *Sentences of Probable Authenticity*, no. 115; *Sentences of the School of Laon*, no. 299, 304, 5: 94, 241, 243.

in favor of a purely moral analysis of the problem. And, while human free will is assumed, it is not really explained. The other salient difficulty with the school of Laon on this subject is the overlaps and redundancies in the fourfold subdivision of the divine will which they outline.

Another set of problems is imported into this topic by Honorius, who takes it up under the heading of God's omniscience. God, he states, has known the past, present, and future from the moment of creation—a confusing point, since it makes it seem as if God's omniscience came into being only when the world did.[98] Honorius adds that the universal plan was always present in God's mind, making it difficult to see in what sense the past of the universe could have been known by God. Honorius makes a conflation here between the idea of creation in the mind of God, an idea known eternally, and its phenomenal reification in time.[99] It is on this decidedly shaky foundation that he proceeds to erect his consideration of foreknowledge and predestination. Honorius is as abrupt as he is straightforward here. He offers a bare-bones summary of Augustine on both points. God knows whatever will happen, he notes, whether by His own direct causation, by His indirect action, or by the contingent actions of free agents. Nothing happens without a cause, although the cause is not always a necessary cause. For its part, predestination involves the direct causation of God and it determines, of necessity, who will be saved.[100] Honorius does not offer any express analysis of providence here. The difficulty in his account lies not so much in its highly abbreviated nature as in the confusion between God's eternal knowledge and the divine knowledge and action in time on which it is grounded.

A similar problem afflicts Hugh of St. Victor's handling of God's foreknowledge, providence, and future contingents, exacerbated, in his case, by the heavily economic view of the deity that he maintains. He begins his discussion of this topic by stating that God's foreknowledge implies the existence of the creation, for, if there had been no created universe, there would have been nothing for God to foreknow. What Hugh fails to notice, initially, is that this position makes the creation necessary to the creator. When this difficulty does come to his attention, he finds that he has painted himself into a corner by his manner of posing the question. It does not occur to Hugh that the content of what God foreknows may be independent

---

[98] Honorius, *Eluc.* 1.13, p. 363.
[99] Ibid., 1.15, p. 363.
[100] Ibid., 1.21–31, pp. 413–16.

of attributes that are intrinsic to His nature or necessary to Him. A related difficulty stemming from Hugh's formulation of the issue is that it constrains him to limit God's foreknowledge to events that are going to take place, or that are going to come into being at a future time, while admitting that God does not foreknow what is not to be, even though it is possible to include the latter under the heading of alternatives which He may have considered and rejected. Along the same lines, Hugh understands a contingency as something that was possible before it came into being, at the point when it had not yet eventuated. His analysis here forces him to exclude from the category of contingency events, or actions, that have the capacity to be, or not to be. It also fails to provide him with an adequate distinction between contingencies that occur through the agency of secondary causes possessing the God-given capacity to choose, and events not yet in being which God will cause directly when He brings them into being. It cannot be said that Hugh has profited very fully from the range of accounts of contingency available during his time, whether they accent ethics, physics, metaphysics, or logic.[101]

One thing clear about Hugh, however, is that he is primarily interested in how this whole question factors into the doctrine of predestination. Although he is not concerned with the cosmological dimensions of the subject, he does draw a clear, and largely Augustinian, distinction between providence and predestination. By providence he means the provision by God of what creatures need and what is good for them, both now and in their future state. While this definition is generic enough to encompass the laws of nature and the moral law, Hugh does not specify whether God's role here is direct or indirect, or what freedom of action remains for the creatures so provided. For Hugh as for Augustine predestination is the preparation of grace. It can be seen as a particular subcategory of providence under which God personally decides whom He is going to elect, and gives these people the necessary grace. The principal contrast Hugh draws here is between predestination, as God's decision to do what He is going to do directly, in the order of grace, and God's foreknowledge of what He is going to permit. While in tune with Augustine here, Hugh gives an analysis of the relevant terms that is rather jejune by Augustine's standards.[102]

Two other mid-century theologians who likewise confine them-

---

[101] Hugh of St. Victor, *De sac.* 1.2.14–18, *PL* 176: 211D-213B.
[102] Ibid., 1.2.19–21, *PL* 176: 213B–D. On this point, see Heinrich Köster, *Die Heilslehre des Hugo von Sankt-Viktor: Grundlagen und Grundzüge* (Emsdetten: Heinr. & J. Lechte, 1940), pp. 120–29.

selves to the implications which this topic has for man's moral activity and salvation are Robert Pullen and the author of the *Summa sententiarum*. Robert offers a treatment of providence and foreknowledge that is uncharacteristically laconic, for him, one that stresses the difference between knowledge and causation. As he notes, God knows, from all eternity, what is happening in the present and what will happen, contingently, in the future, without thereby causing these events, events which Robert presents, exclusively, as the outcomes of man's moral choices. He has nothing to say about causation in the physical order and little to say about either providence or predestination.[103] The *Summa sententiarum* takes up this question under the heading of God's wisdom, treating God's knowledge of what is, of what will be in the future, of His own governance of the universe, and of whom He plans to save. Despite this forthright beginning, the author's analysis meanders into a number of relatively trivial issues and is curiously inconclusive. He follows Augustine and Boethius in saying that divine foreknowledge is neutral, not causative. Having established that point, what he does with it is to argue that God can foreknow unimportant matters without losing sight of major ones. He next moves to the question of whether God can foresee what is not going to happen. Leaving that question open, he moves to predestination, his real subject here. Predestination, he stresses, involves God's direct causation, in contrast with His foreknowledge, which may or may not include matters in which God plans to act directly. The main issue he wants to raise about predestination is to confirm Abelard's opinion that God cannot adjust, upward or downward, the number of people He predestines to salvation.[104]

This view was being challenged, even by masters positively influenced by Abelard in many respects, such as Roland of Bologna. Roland is uncomfortable with the idea that God cannot save more people than He does save, or empower more people to please Him than He does. Roland fails to find a convincing argument that enables him to allay his disquiet on this score, even though he draws a distinction between God as an intrinsic cause and God as an extrinsic cause that might have offered at least a partial solution.[105] Nor does Roland see that his claim that God can foreknow, or permit, more than He does might provide him with a

---

[103] Robert Pullen, *Sent.* 1.13. 1.15, 1.16, *PL* 186: 700B–702C, 708D–710C, 714B–718B.
[104] *Summa sent.* 1.12, *PL* 176: 61C–62C.
[105] Roland of Bologna, *Sent.*, pp. 62–67.

parallel argument.[106] The author of the *Summa sententiarum* offers
better grounds for supporting Abelard here than Roland gives for
rejecting him, grounds with which Roland was evidently not acquainted. He treats the problem as a logical one. God cannot alter
the number of people whom He predestines, he urges, because,
were He to do so, God would be contradicting His own eternal
decree, which is impossible. This conclusion, he observes, can be
seen as one instance of the larger logical point that God can do
anything except what is self-contradictory.[107]

While there was no consensus among theologians in this period
about which divine attribute provided the most cogent context
within which to consider providence, foreknowledge, predestination, and future contingents, Robert of Melun is unique in taking
up this constellation of ideas under a number of different headings
at the same time, namely, God's will, God's knowledge, and God's
power. In the first two of these instances, his treatment of the topic
can be seen as an extension of the analysis of God as cause, in
relation to created causes, which looms so large in Robert's doctrine of God. He first addresses the question from the perspective of
God's will. His argument bears some traces of the teaching of the
school of Laon, but it is far more circumspect and streamlined.
God's will, he begins, can be equated with God's essence and, as
such, regarded as the first cause. Both the world order and the
moral order, which God wills and causes, are orders in which some
creatures function as causes in their own genus or sphere of activity. The latter comprises the realm of contingency and freedom,
and it is compatible with the divine order. In this context Robert
also considers the differences between what God wills directly,
what He wills through intermediaries, and what He permits, using
the distinction among God's operation, precept, prohibition, and
permission that had become the standard replacement for the
subdivisions in God's will offered by the Laon masters.[108]

Robert next takes up the same subject under the rubric of God's
knowledge. Just as is the case with God's will, so His knowledge is
identical with His being; and God's being is eternal. It is also
unchanging, in contrast with the knowledge of other beings, who
can learn and forget. With this foundation laid, Robert supports
the position that God cannot foreknow more than He does fore-

---

[106] Ibid., pp. 67–84.
[107] *Summa sent.* 1.12, *PL* 176: 63A–64D.
[108] Robert of Melun, *Sent.* 1.2.2–3, *Oeuvres*, 3 part 1: 265. On this argument, see
Horst, *Die Trinitäts- und Gotteslehre*, pp. 283–93.

know, by definition, while at the same time he argues that this conclusion does not place limitations on God. The things God foreknows that He will do are things which He none the less disposes freely. Robert agrees that foreknowledge is neutral and not determinative. It includes events which, God knows, will occur contingently, and which He allows to occur contingently. God also foreknows what He will cause directly, such as the predestination of the elect. With Augustine, on this latter point, Robert defines predestination as the grace of preparation, and contrasts it with God's governance of the world order.[109] Abbreviated as it is, this account preserves a good balance between the cosmological and theological dimensions of the subject.

The most elaborate discussion of this topic in Robert's theology is the one he takes up under the heading of God's power. He begins by distinguishing, for purposes of comparison, among the ways in which power is exercised among men. All are indirect. There is the case of a ruler who orders his subject to do something, moving the subject to act on the basis of his authority, although the subject is the person actually performing what has been ordered. Then, there is the case in which one person contributes to an outcome carried out by someone else, by helping to finance it or by making needed materials or conditions available. Thirdly, one person may act as the supervisor of a project, directing the other people who do the actual work. Robert suggests that these indirect modes of exercising power bear some analogy to the ways God exercises His power in human affairs, but he does not pause to offer concrete theological illustrations of the point. Rather, he moves on to discuss two other ways in which the deity exercises His power in the world. First, He creates the universe out of nothing. In this connection, God is the sole author or cause. Second, God puts into place the natural operations and actions proper to man. Robert agrees that it is God alone Who endows man initially with these capacities, and that He conserves man's ability to make voluntary choices as well as to translate those choices into actions. But the collaborative role of God in these processes does not conflict with human free will. Robert draws a useful distinction here between man's exercise of volition in the carrying out of his natural activities, on the one hand, and the function of human free will in the order of grace, on the other. He also distinguishes modes of human behavior in these two orders where direct divine causation is needed and where it is

---

[109] Robert of Melun, *Sent.* 1.6.20, *Oeuvres*, 3 part 2: 315–16. On this argument, see Horst, *Die Trinitäts- und Gotteslehre*, pp. 252–82.

not. He also observes that, whether God acts directly or indirectly in man's moral activity, He is not the subject of that activity and He is not responsible for the use man makes of the deity's own collaboration or empowerment. And, while he concedes that God sometimes enables human beings to go beyond their own strength, Robert's emphasis in this entire account is on the idea that, in both man's spiritual and moral life, God has arranged matters so that man can act with his own powers, just as natural phenomena can act in terms of their natural causative powers.[110] While Robert thus brings a physical dimension into play in this discussion, his emphasis rests on man's moral liberty in relation to God's power, although he does not associate this point, at this particular juncture, with the doctrine of predestination.

Robert's threefold treatment of the question has the merit of enabling him to explore most of the dimensions of the problem of foreknowledge, providence, predestination, and contingency, although it also has a disadvantage. In none of the contexts in which he brings it up does he address all the relevant aspects of the problem. A certain amount of repetition is also, of necessity, involved in his inability to decide whether God's will, God's knowledge, or God's power has a better claim than the others as the most appropriate home for the topic. To a certain extent this redundancy and lack of decisiveness cancel out the breadth of vision which Robert brings to the subject, in comparison with the often quite sketchy treatment it receives at the hands of most other theologians of the period. But, perhaps the most important weakness of Robert's argument, to which he does not advert openly but which has the effect of undermining his whole analysis from the start, is the fact that he supports Abelard's view that wisdom, power, and goodness inhere in the individual persons of the Trinity in a preeminent way, and are appropriate personal names for them. If this claim is taken seriously, in the present connection, then one would have to admit that, in two of Robert's three analyses of foreknowledge, predestination, and contingency, he is really talking about the properties of the first two persons of the Trinity individually, and not about the Godhead in general. Robert never acknowledges the fact that, if he wants to maintain his position on the Trinity, that very position seriously

---

[110] Robert of Melun, *Sent.* 1.7.33–36. This citation derives from a portion of Robert's work that remains unedited. Our account is based on the analysis of the doctrine in the manuscripts provided by Raymond-M. Martin, "El problema del influjo divino sobre las acciones humanas, un siglo antes de Santo Tomás de Aquino," *La Ciencia tomista* 5 (1915): 178–93; Horst, *Die Trinitäts- und Gotteslehre*, pp. 228–44.

compromises his intended handling of these features of the divine nature in its relationship with the creation and with man.

In that very connection, Peter Lombard makes his own attack on this problem perfectly plain. The question of God's foreknowledge and related matters is the first topic he takes up after completing his discussion of the Trinity. He states crisply that this subject, and all the questions that follow in the remainder of Book 1 of the *Sentences*, treat of God with reference to the divine substance possessed in common by the Trinity.[111] He also shows his colors at once by aligning himself with theologians such as Honorius and the author of the *Summa sententiarum* by treating this constellation of ideas under the heading of God's knowledge, recognizing that it is easier to annex to this mode of analysis the related questions concerning God's causation than it would be if one tried to cover the necessary ground under the heading of His will or power. Peter begins, typically, by giving his definitions of the key terms. In so doing, he makes it clear that, in handling this topic, his chief focus is going to be on the divine nature as a theological and metaphysical reality. While God's role as a cause in the physical order is going to receive some attention and while care is going to be paid to the logical consistency of his arguments, and to those of thinkers whom he criticizes, Peter never lets the reader forget that he is writing about God here, and that the subject at issue is not a mere pendant to, or illustration of, the sciences of natural philosophy or logic.

God's knowledge is one and simple, he begins. Yet, it can be thought of, in relation to man and the creation, in terms of foreknowledge, disposition, predestination, and wisdom. Foreknowledge is God's knowledge, from all eternity, of all things that will happen, whether for good or for ill. Disposition can be regarded not only as God's general governance of the universe but also as His foreknowledge of the laws of nature that He will put in place before He creates them. Similarly, predestination covers the preparation of grace which God grants directly to His elect and His salvation and coronation of them with bliss in the next life, as well as His knowledge from all eternity of which human beings they will be. Wisdom, finally, is God's knowledge of all things, whether past, present, or future.[112] Having mentioned the dimension of time in setting forth these definitions, Peter next addresses a set of problems with which Hugh of St. Victor and Honorius had wrestled

---

[111] Peter Lombard, *Sent.* 1. d. 35. c. 1, 1: 254.

[112] Ibid., c. 1–c. 6, 1: 254–58. On predestination as the grace of preparation in the Lombard, see Johann Schupp, *Die Gnadenlehre des Petrus Lombardus* (Freiburg im Breisgau: Herder, 1932), pp. 105–15, 141–58, 204–06.

ineffectively. Supposing that there were no temporal order at all, and hence no future in which events not yet in being might take place, and given that God's knowledge is one with His essence, would this not mean, he asks, that God's very being would be in jeopardy? Peter answers this question in the negative. As he observes, when we speak of God's foreknowledge, disposition, and predestination with respect to the created world and man, we speak in a relative sense (*relative, ad aliquid*), just as we do when we refer to the deity as the creator. Such activities vis-à-vis other, created, beings as these relative terms denote in no sense exhaust or diminish the infinite reservoir of being as such which the divine nature possesses, prior to and apart from the creation. Further, there are two ways of regarding foreknowledge. First, if we consider the subject matter, the future, on which God's foreknowledge is exercised, as capable of being there, or not, then His foreknowledge can be understood as relative to the future. But, secondly, if we think of the knowledge that God possesses, with which He is able to know the future when it eventuates, then we speak of His knowledge with respect to His essence, whether or not the temporal world exists at all, or any particular eventuality that may take place within it. In any event, since He is eternal, God knows all things from eternity. His knowledge is not limited by the temporal order applying to creatures.[113]

This solution responds effectively to the dilemmas propounded by Hugh and Honorius and at the same time addresses the question, raised but not answered by the author of the *Summa sententiarum*, of whether God foreknows those future contingents that are not going to eventuate. For, as Peter continues, he next makes the point that, in the second sense of foreknowledge which he has just indicated, God's knowledge is of His essence; it would be incorrect to say that, because He knows all things, all the things that He knows are God or that they share in His essence. Here, he stresses, we have to distinguish between what God is, and what God has in His presence or has within Him. As an illustration of that point, Peter notes, God knows who the elect are; but the elect are human, not divine. They are in God's presence, not His nature. Similarly, God knows the evils that will occur, without being identified with them, just as He knows the good things that will occur and that He will approve, good outcomes which, in this case, He helps along, to a greater or lesser extent, being partially or wholly an *auctor* as well as a knower. For the creation and the temporal order are from

---

[113] Peter Lombard, *Sent.* 1. d. 35. c. 7–c. 9, 1: 255–58.

God. They are not of God; that is, they are not of the same nature as God. Here, Peter acknowledges the utility of Abelard's distinction between the univocal signification of a noun and the differing consignifications it may have in statements using the past, present, and future tenses of the verb. He also indicates the limitations of this argument, from his own perspective.[114] What is strikingly Lombardian about this whole analysis is Peter's success in finding a cogent substitute for the reduction of this problem to an exercise in formal logic. At the same time, he retains a philosophical no less than a theological perspective on it, by grounding the subject in the metaphysical distinction between God viewed in His transcendent essence and God viewed in those aspects of His being that He displays in His relations with other beings.

Peter moves on, then, to a series of other questions pertinent to God's foreknowledge that had been raised and, in his view, answered unsatisfactorily by other masters. He deals in a swift and streamlined manner with God's foreknowledge and its relationship to causation, relying here on Augustine and other patristic sources and not on Boethius and Aristotle. Foreknowledge, he agrees, is not causative. There are some things that God knows, contemplating them in His own mind before He brings them into phenomenal existence as their one and only cause, as is the case with the created universe. In this example, He causes the things He knows, not vice versa. In the case of contingencies, such as the willed actions of created beings who possess free will, God foresees the consequences of contingent actions but does not cause them. His lack of direct causation here is in no sense a failing or imperfection in the divine

---

[114] Ibid., d. 36. c. 1–c. 5, d. 41. c. 3, 1: 258–63, 293. Peter's use of this Abelardian, or more generally nominalist, idea is noted by Marie-Dominique Chenu, *La théologie au douzième siècle* (Paris: J. Vrin, 1957), pp. 93, 96, 99; Artur Michael Landgraf, "Nominalismus in den theologischen Werken der zweiten Hälfte des zwölften Jahrhunderts," *Traditio* 1 (1943): 192–94, 199; Schneider, *Die Lehre*, pp. 43–44, 53; Courtenay, *Capacity and Volition*, pp. 53–55; "*Nominales* and Nominalism in the Twelfth Century," in *Lectionum varietates: Hommage à Paul Vignaux*, ed. Jean Jolivet et al. (Paris: J. Vrin, 1991), pp. 17–20, 23–29. For more on this topic, see Marcia L. Colish, "Peter Lombard and Abelard: The *Opinio Nominalium* and Divine Transcendence," *Vivarium* 30 (May 1992): 139–56. Stephen F. Brown, "Abelard and the Medieval Origin of the Distinction between God's Absolute and Ordained Power," in *Ad litteram: Authoritative Texts and Their Medieval Readers*, ed. Mark D. Jordan and Kent Emery, Jr. (Notre Dame: University of Notre Dame Press, 1992), pp. 199–215, reprises both Abelard's position and the Lombard's argument against it, treating that argument correctly as one that criticizes Abelard for failing to distinguish between God's power and God's will. On the other hand, Brown does not note either the Lombard's contribution to the ordained/absolute power distinction or the appeal made by both Abelard and the Lombard to the *opinio nominalium*.

nature, or in the divine foreknowledge. For He chose to create
beings with free will and He knows how they will freely exercise
it.[115] This section of Peter's discussion both rebukes authors who
feel that they need five times as much space to treat the same
subject and reminds the reader that the divine nature is the perspective from which he thinks it ought to be examined. The exercise
is designed to enlighten the reader about God, the subject of this
book of the *Sentences*, not about the behavior and constitution of
creatures.

Another feature of God's foreknowledge that requires discussion,
not only in and of itself but because of its bearing on predestination,
is its immutability and its exhaustive coverage. As Peter observes,
God's knowledge, like His essence, cannot change, enlarge, or
diminish. God may direct His attention to this or that subject, or
not, without changing His knowledge. Since He is omniscient and
always has been, He knows things that have not yet occurred in the
temporal order, and beings that have not yet come into existence.
In the case of contingent outcomes, He knows whether or not they
will occur. With respect to such future events, beings, and outcomes,
this does not mean that God knows them better when they do
occur. For, while they are conditioned by time, He is not; He has
always been omniscient. In this respect, God cannot know more
than He knows because that would be a self-contradiction, a point
on which Peter agrees with the author of the *Summa sententiarum*.[116]

As for predestination, Peter notes, reminding the reader of his
definition of terms at the beginning of this section of Book 1 of the
Sentences, predestination is included in what God foreknows but it is
different from foreknowledge. Foreknowledge is not causative,
while predestination is causative, referring specifically to God's
direct decision to extend the grace of preparation and perseverance
to those people He chooses to save.[117] Here Peter summarizes the
standard late Augustinian teaching that was the consensus position
on predestination in this period. At the same time, he uses the
argument just developed on the immutability of God's foreknowledge to criticize versions of that teaching that he finds aberrant or
problematic. In the first place, there is the question raised by
Abelard and debated by the author of the *Summa sententiarum* and by
Roland of Bologna as to whether God can alter the number of the

---

[115] Peter Lombard, *Sent.* 1. d. 38, 1: 275–79.
[116] Ibid., d. 39. c. 1.1–c. 4.3, d. 41. c. 3, 1: 280–83, 292–93. On this point, see
Schneider, *Die Lehre*, pp. 54–55.
[117] Peter Lombard, *Sent.* 1. d. 39. c. 4.3, 1: 283–84. Peter makes the same point
in *Sermo* 112, *PL* 171: 860C. See Schneider, *Die Lehre*, pp. 55, 57–60.

elect. Given the way in which Peter has framed his argument here, he can dispose of the idea that God could make such a change as a non-question, not only from the standpoint of God's will but also in the light of God's immutable omniscience. Just as God does not alter His eternal decree, so, since He knows eternally what that decree will be with regard to His elect and since His knowledge never changes, the alteration of God's arrangements here is a non-possibility.[118] There is also the question of the relation between election and the behavior of the elect. Here, Peter wants to criticize the position of William of Champeaux and Anselm of Laon. For the elect, predestination enables them to be justified, to live uprightly, to resist temptation, to persevere in the good, and to attain beatitude in the next life. God foreknows that the elect will respond appropriately to the grace He extends to them, just as He knows that the reprobate will fall into sin, although in the first case He actively prepares the elect for their salvation while He prepares nothing for the reprobate. But, Peter insists, with Augustine and against Anselm and William, God does not choose the elect because He foresees that they will respond positively to His grace and earn merit. Rather, what He foresees is the fact that His grace will provide the elect with the enabling condition for their acquisition of merit after the fact.[119] Before leaving this topic it should be noted that, while Peter, like the majority of theologians of his time, takes a strongly Augustinian line on predestination, there is one important respect in which they all depart from Augustine here, a point that also will condition their handling of the theme of grace and free will. There is no trace whatever of Augustine's doctrine of the irresistibility of grace to be found in any of these twelfth-century theologians, a calculated omission that deserves to be understood as a criticism of Augustine on their part.

In the case of God's foreknowledge and related matters, as can be seen from the above, Peter demonstrates clearly that this constellation of ideas can be treated in as sweeping a manner as need be from the perspective of God's knowledge. He succeeds in addressing a broad range of substantive questions, raised in a variety of contexts by other theologians, irrespective of whether the masters in question approach them from the standpoint of logic, Aristotelian or Abelardian, causation, or other divine attributes. Throughout, he grounds his support for the compatibility of contingency and free will with divine foreknowledge, and with the existence of

---

[118] Peter Lombard, *Sent.* 1. d. 40. c. 1, 1: 285–86.
[119] Ibid., c. 2.1–d. 41. c. 1, 1: 286–92.

direct divine causation in some areas, not on the relations between
necessity and possibility in natural philosophy or in formal logic
but in the distinction between the transcendent God and the God
Who acts, in a variety of ways, in the world He created, but without
being exhausted or consumed by His economic role. Peter's resolutely metaphysical address to this question enables him to put it
on as philosophical a foundation as is true for Aristotle or for
Abelard, although it is a metaphysical foundation, and one that
also affords a good vantage point from which to consider the
specifically theological dimensions of these problems as well.

Can God Do Better or Different Than He Does?

Much the same can be said for Peter's handling of the single most
controversial question concerning the divine nature to be agitated in
this period, can God do better or different than He does, which
Abelard brought to the fore and which his opponents met with only
mitigated success in attacking before it was seized on by Peter. Organ-
ically related, both in content and style, to his handling of the problem
of necessity and possibility, although not presented in his logical
works, Abelard's defense of the position that God cannot do better
than He does is first stated in his *Theologia christiana*, then developed in
a somewhat modified form in his *Theologia "scholarium"*, and then
reprised with only a modest change in his commentary on Romans.

While Abelard does draw on arguments from theological
appropriateness in addressing this issue, he relies more heavily on a
propositional formulation of the question which, on its own
accounting, appears to have been aimed against the contemporary
master, Joscelin of Soissons. Joscelin argued that, if things happen
otherwise than as God foresees, God would be capable of being
mistaken. In attacking this position, Abelard first takes up and
then abandons a highly useful Augustinian idea, found in the
Enchiridion. There, Augustine argues that God's omnipotence
means God's ability to do whatever He wills. This understanding of
divine omnipotence was known to other contemporary theologians
from the school of Laon to the author of the *Summa sententiarum* and
beyond. Among its advantages, it makes it possible to rule out
actions requiring a physical body, as well as sinning, lying, or other
forms of immoral behavior that would constitute imperfections
were they to be divine options, without thereby limiting God's
power.[120] Abelard first accepts this distinction between God's will

---

[120] *Sent. Anselmi* 2, pp. 63–64; *Summa sent.* 1.13–14, *PL* 176: 64D–70B. On this

and God's power in the *Theologia christiana* but then makes no effort to apply it constructively.[121] He moves, rather, to another distinction. God's power can be viewed in two ways, he observes. There is His providence, through which He establishes the world order, and His counsel, exhortation, admonition, approval, or disapproval, which God directs specifically to human beings as moral agents, to whom He may wish to accord His grace. Now, Abelard continues, human beings are bound by God's arrangements in both respects. They are not exempt from the laws of nature; and they also must abide by God's moral law. Abelard is not concerned, at this juncture, with man's freedom or lack of it within these dispensations. Rather, the question he wants to raise is whether God's arrangements themselves, in either area, are the best possible ones. Could God have enacted a better law of nature or a better moral law? Abelard answers in the negative, offering three reasons. First, he notes, the contemplation of the possibility that God's natural or moral law could have been different, and better, would cause a great deal of anxiety to man, from which God is kind enough to exempt him. Second, it would not be fitting for us to think of God as able to do better, but as none the less not doing so. And third, the specific lack of theological appropriateness attaching to the second point lies in the fact that it would derogate from God's goodness. If God can do better than He does, and fails to do it, then He cannot be regarded as supremely good. Or else, it would mean that He is supremely good but that this goodness is capable of being impeded by an insufficiency of power to act on God's part.

Abelard now moves to supplement this argument from theological appropriateness with an argument from logic, saving the best for last in his own strategy of debate as he had on the subject of necessity and possibility. To do better than God does, he asserts, is a logical impossibility, given the claims made by an antecedent proposition which states that God is good, omnipotent, and benevolent, an antecedent which, in Abelard's view, makes logically necessary a consequent proposition which states that God always makes the best possible use of these qualities. Having started with the Augustinian distinction between God's power and will, which he abandons despite its utility, Abelard now collapses God's power into His will because he thinks that this conclusion follows

---

point, see Ivan Boh, "Divine Omnipotence in the Early Sentences," in *Divine Omniscience and Omnipotence in Medieval Philosophy: Islamic, Jewish and Christian Perspectives*, ed. Tamar Rudavsky (Dordrecht: D. Reidel, 1985), pp. 185–211; Sikes, *Peter Abailard*, pp. 126–32.

[121] Peter Abelard, *Theologia christiana* 5.17–57, CCCM 12: 354–72.

logically, a maneuver that has not been seen as logical by all of his commentators.[122] Perhaps more problematically, Abelard's handling of this question as a logician forces God to act in a certain way, which Abelard deems to be the best possible way, out of an internal necessity of His own nature. As he puts it, "what He wills, He must will necessarily, and what He does, He must do necessarily" (*Quae vult, necessario velit, et quae facit, necessario faciat*). Logical necessity constrains God's behavior, behavior which, he states, takes place inevitably (*inevitabiliter*).[123] Thus, as Abelard would have it, God was constrained to create the universe, to create it the way it is, to share His beatitude with his creatures, and to provide them with the particular moral laws and modes of salvation that He has provided. God's freedom, in this analysis, is sharply circumscribed by God's goodness.

Reactions to Abelard's argument in the *Theologia christiana* were not slow in coming. In some respects the most interesting objection of all came from the early Porretans, who could have used it equally well against Abelard's teaching on necessity, possibility, and future contingents. The Porretans appear to have been the only theologians in this period who were sensitive to the technical features of Abelard's logic, and willing to turn it against him. As they observe, Abelard's logic is a formal logic. Its project is to establish what is logically verifiable within the intramental world of predication, inference, and the interrelations of propositions. It is not a logic that claims it can verify its conclusions in the world outside the mind, and it does not seek to do so. Thus, hoisting Abelard on his own petard, they point to the intrinsic limits of the logic he taught as an instrument of theological research. That megaton bomb having been detonated, the Porretans go on to argue that God could have made things better, not in the sense that He could have exercised greater power or wisdom in making the arrangements that He did make, but in the sense that the creatures which He made are themselves imperfect, and could be better than they are.[124]

No doubt more of a virtuoso turn than the more conservative

---

[122] Sikes, *Peter Abailard*, pp. 120–24, 126–32; Weingart, *Logic of Divine Love*, pp. 32–33. Paul L. Williams, *The Moral Philosophy of Peter Abelard* (Lanham, MD: University Press of America, 1980), pp. 5, 63–84, ignores these logical claims entirely.

[123] Peter Abelard, *Theologia christiana* 5.42, CCCM 12: 366.

[124] *Sent. mag. Gisleberti* I 2.38–39, p. 119; Nikolaus M. Häring, ed., "Die *Sententie magistri Gisleberti Pictavensis episcopi* II: Die Version der florentiner Handschrift" 2.38–42, *AHDLMA* 46 (1979): 54.

theologians of the day could manage, this Porretan line of argument had no notable repercussions. Much more typical of the
reaction against Abelard is the critique of Hugh of St. Victor. Hugh
translates Abelard's argument into an entirely theological one. In
his estimation, Abelard has gone overboard in his defense of God's
unbounded goodness, to the point of failing to do full justice to
God's power and freedom. He urges that these latter two attributes
need more support. Hugh also stresses the point that only the
creator is perfect, without realizing that it is not responsive to
Abelard's claim that the creation and the moral law are the best
possible.[125] Perhaps a more serious weakness in Hugh's analysis is
that he does not clarify why one divine attribute should be
preferred over another, or sacrificed if it is seen to conflict with
another aspect of the divine nature. The desire to accent God's
power or freedom, in his own case, thus seems to be just as much a
matter of the theologian's own arbitrary taste as the exaggerated
emphasis on God's goodness which Hugh ascribes to Abelard.

Another contemporary effort to come to grips with the *Theologia
christiana* argument and also one that is largely unresponsive to
Abelard, even though it seeks a more middle of the road position, is
the one made by Robert Pullen. He agrees that God could have
made a world different from the one He did make. Leaving aside
the claim that the world He made is the best possible one, which
Abelard defends, Robert focuses on the argument that, having
decided to make the world we have, God is not going to abdicate
from His providential rule over it, by destroying it and creating the
different world He could have created. Thus, Robert concludes,
God wills nothing other than what he does, in fact, ordain.[126] This
conclusion, we may note, does not consider the issue of whether
God can will something other than what He does will. It subsumes
the divine attribute of goodness, and even of power, under the
heading of God's *de facto* choices. Robert assumes here, without
making it explicit, the Augustinian idea that God's power can be
understood as His capacity to accomplish what He wills. But, his
emphasis on the point that God will not recede from what He has
accomplished distracts Robert from the task of demonstrating that
there were other choices which God could have made.

The author of the *Summa sententiarum* also appeals to Augustine
here, in a more overt and systematic way. He agrees that God's

---

[125] Hugh of St. Victor, *De sac.* 1.2.22, *PL* 176: 214A–216D. This argument is
noted by Kilgenstein, *Die Gotteslehre*, pp. 212–23.
[126] Robert Pullen, *Sent.* 1.15, *PL* 186: 710C–D, 712D–714B. This argument is
noted by Courtney, *Robert Pullen*, pp. 75–80.

omnipotence should be understood in the light of His ability to do whatever He wills, as well as in the absence of conditions that would impose limitations on the deity. He treats the question of whether God could do better than He does as a pendant of that analysis. The fact that God willed the present arrangements, for this master, does not mean that God's options were limited, or that He was constrained to make the choices that He made. God could not be wiser or better than He is. But He could have created a world with better physical or moral laws.[127] How that conclusion is related to the premise that God is all-wise and supremely good, however, the author does not succeed in establishing. The issue, for him, is less the defense of God's omnipotence as such than the way in which God chooses to display it. But his answer ultimately rests, as Hugh's does, on a personal preference for the idea of God's freedom.

Under the pressure of criticism, particularly from those contemporaries who argued that his accent on God's goodness was incompatible with God's omnipotence, Abelard returned to the fray with another effort to coordinate these divine attributes in the *Theologia "scholarium"* and in his Romans commentary. In responding to other masters cool to his effort to frame the problem in terms of logic, he pays more attention, in the *Theologia "scholarium"* version of his argument, to the question of which divine attribute deserves the most attention.[128] He continues to maintain that God's power and goodness are correlative. If we say that God could do better— or worse—than He does, we deny His goodness. But, if we deny His capacity to do whatever He wills, we deny His omnipotence. In the effort to resolve this dilemma and also to remove the question from the logical context of possibility and necessity, Abelard now appeals to a Platonic argument which he had not used before.[129] Plato, he notes, defended the idea that God could not have made a better world because God is perfect. Hence, He acts perfectly. The perfection of the deity thus entails the perfection of His will and His exercise of that will, which subsumes both God's power and His goodness. These attributes, Abelard continues, along with God's rationality and justice, are hence reflected in everything He does, and in everything He refrains from doing.

In this version of the argument, while Abelard still frames his account in the language of antecedent and consequent proposi-

---

[127] *Summa sent.* 1.14, *PL* 176: 68A–70B.

[128] Peter Abelard, *Theologia "scholarium"* 3.27–64, CCCM 13: 511–27.

[129] Moonan, "Abelard's Use of the *Timaeus*," pp. 30–33, 72–74, gives a good analysis of this point.

tions, he has shifted his emphasis from logic to metaphysics. He also shifts his focus from the world order, as it displays a divine providence that cannot be improved on, to the justice with which God operates in the order of redemption. This latter tactic is designed, presumably, to make it more difficult for critics to object to his conclusions, an *ad hominem* response to contemporaries who concerned themselves only with the theological and not also with the philosophical aspects of the problem. In the event, this strategy leads Abelard to tackle the question in the *Theologia "scholarium"* in a more theological manner than he had in the *Theologia christiana*. The effect of this reformulation of the issue is that Abelard now accents God's control over all things and the absolute justice, as well as the omnipotence, with which He operates. As Abelard poses the question in the *Theologia "scholarium"*, while God can act differently than He does, He does not do so, not because He is logically constrained to act as He acts but because His ordinance stands above any such necessity, flowing as it does from the perfection of His nature. Such, at least, is Abelard's conclusion in this second version of his argument. He rings one final change on it in his Romans gloss, where he shifts the emphasis to yet another divine attribute, while preserving the rest of his account in the *Theologia "scholarium"*. Here, he defends the best of all possible worlds position on the grounds that it is a corollary of God's wisdom.[130]

Despite the fact that several of Abelard's disciples rushed to his support,[131] Abelard's reformulation of his argument in the *Theologia "scholarium"* and the Romans gloss still left some problematic features of it open to criticism. There is the difficulty of claiming that one divine attribute should be given pride of place over the others. And, although Abelard moves to a metaphysical argument based on God's perfection, it is no clearer, in the *Theologia "scholarium"*, that God has been freed from acting under the necessity of His own nature than it is, in the *Theologia christiana*, that He is free from the necessities of propositional logic. Further, the best of all possible worlds position fails to take account of the imperfections in the created order, a reality of which his mentor, Plato, was all too well aware. These problems, and others in Abelard's handling of the question in the *Theologia "scholarium"*, were noticed by one by his

---

[130] Peter Abelard, *Commentaria in Epistolam Pauli ad Romanos* 1:20, ed. Eligius M. Buytaert, CCCM 11 (Turnhout: Brepols, 1969), p. 69.

[131] Thus, Roland of Bologna, *Sent.*, pp. 25, 49–61; *Sententiae Parisiensis* I, ed. Artur Michael Landgraf in *Écrits théologiques de l'école d'Abélard* (Louvain: Spicilegium Sacrum Lovaniense, 1934), pp. 20–26.

most trenchant mid-century critics, Robert of Melun.

Robert takes Abelard's Platonic argument and turns it on its head. As he points out, Plato taught that there was an ontological gap between the perfect deity, and also between the perfect exemplary forms which the deity used in the creation, on the one hand, and the created world of time, matter, and multiplicity, on the other. The split-level universe proposed by Plato means that the phenomenal world can never measure up to its ideal form. This analysis neatly disposes of the claim that we are living in the best of all possible worlds. Robert next directs attention to Abelard's argument from God's perfection to the consummate justice of His ordinances in the moral order. He appeals here to the doctrine of progressive revelation. The moral arrangements which God ordains for His people may be as good as possible, in the sense of being responsive to their needs and capacities at a particular point in time, in the estimation of the deity. But that situation may only hold for the time being. As with the Mosaic law, which provided a new and fuller ordinance in comparison with the rules governing the Jews beforehand, it is capable of being superseded, by a subsequent divine ordinance.[132]

Adept as is Robert's critique of the most recent of Abelard's arguments, so far as it goes, it is also the case that, while capitalizing on it and on the contributions of a number of other recent and current theologians, Peter Lombard provides the period's most elaborate, refined, and knowledgeable defense of the claim that God can do better than He does. Peter clarifies arguments that had been garbled in the work of Abelard's defenders and critics alike. He brings a wider range of authorities to bear on the issues, and discusses a larger number of their implications. He makes a number of helpful new distinctions. He places the question firmly under the heading of divine omnipotence, while making it possible to give other divine attributes their due without collapsing one into another or establishing hierarchies among them inappropriate to a deity Who is simple and Who possesses all His essential determinations in exactly the same way. Above all, Peter finds a way of releasing God from the axiological necessitarianism with which Abelard had encumbered Him, whether logically or metaphysically. His solution to this problem, with which he concludes his consideration of the divine nature in Book 1 of the *Sentences*, is also

---

[132] Robert of Melun, *Sent.* 1.7.1–29. This text comes from the unedited portion of Robert's *Sentences* and our account is dependent on the manuscript evidence as reported by Horst, *Die Trinitäts- und Gotteslehre*, pp. 207–28, 245–46.

one that calls upon and reinforces the liberation of the doctrine of God from an economic theology, a goal that is one of his chief objectives throughout that book.

In launching his discussion of God's omnipotence, Peter refers to the Augustinian distinction between God's power and will as a means both of correcting the treatment given to it by some of his contemporaries and of expanding on it considerably in his own theology.[133] He agrees that God's omnipotence means not that He can do everything, but rather that He can do whatever He wills, except for actions that reflect weakness, imperfection, change, or limitation of any kind. God's omnipotence also means, for Peter, that there is no passive potency in God; God is a fully realized being.[134] In Peter's view, this does not suggest that God can do whatever He wills Himself to be able to do, for that would also be true of men. Nor does it suggest that He makes whatever He wills to make. For He has not made anything outside of the things He did make, so that the gap between power and will implied in posing the issue in these terms does not apply in this case. What this doctrine does mean, according to Peter, is that God can accomplish whatever He wants to accomplish, whether He wills it to occur directly or indirectly. These distinctions which the Lombard has drawn between what the phrase "whatever He wills" means in these different statements make the point that not every kind of willing serves as a correct interpretation of the divine nature. As Ivan Boh has well said, the Lombard here is offering "a further refinement on that notion of omnipotence which is based on the connection between the possibility of action and acts of will."[135]

With this foundation laid, Peter moves next to the refutation of the most recent version of Abelard's argument that God cannot do better than He does. As he describes the position to be attacked, it runs like this: God always acts justly and for the good. If He did anything differently, He would be acting in opposition to these values. With respect to this claim, Peter observes that it is true that what God does do is good and just. But, this fact imposes no constraints on the other things that He might do. Nor does it limit His capacity to have done other things which He has not chosen to do. Nor does God's justice constrain Him. True, He only does do things that are compatible with justice. But He remains free not to

---

[133] The best treatment of this subject is Boh, "Divine Omnipotence," pp. 193–200. See also Schneider, *Die Lehre*, pp. 39–41.

[134] Peter Lombard, *Sent.* 1. d. 42, 1: 294–98.

[135] Boh, "Divine Omnipotence," p. 196.

behave in this way. A similar line of reasoning applies to what God ought to do, although here, too, Peter observes that "ought" is a tricky word to apply to the deity because, strictly speaking, He does not "owe" anybody anything. Throughout this discussion, it is God's freedom to act as He chooses that Peter emphasizes as the proper understanding of divine omnipotence, in opposing the idea that God cannot act differently than the way He does act because His reasons are excellent and because He decided to act in these ways from all eternity. Peter agrees that God's reasons for doing whatever He does are eminently right and reasonable. None the less, God is under no constraint to act in this way.

Peter next takes up the objection that, if God could do no differently than he does, He would be acting against His own foreknowledge. Here he brings to bear on the objection his earlier analysis of foreknowledge, in which he had argued that God's omniscience includes the range of options out of which He selects the actions that He decides to perform. At this juncture, he charges other thinkers with twisting the sense of the Augustinian definition of divine omnipotence. As he shows, what Augustine had in mind was not the reduction of God's power to the scope of whatever it is that He actually wills to do, but rather a distinction between will and power. Peter himself expands on the sense of that distinction. It means, he says, not only that God is capable of doing whatever it is that He wills, but also that whatever He can do always remains more, in principle, than what He actually does do. In short, and this is his most creative accomplishment in entering the lists against Abelard on this whole subject, Peter shows that the thrust of Augustine's definition is not to ground a theodicy argument. Rather, it is to ground, more fundamentally than even Augustine himself recognized, the implied distinction between God's ordained and absolute power. God's radical freedom is to be located under the latter of these two headings.[136] While the Lombard does not actually use the terms *potentia ordinata* and *potentia absoluta*, this is the manifest sense of his text. He has staked a clear claim on this terrain and it is one he proceeds to exploit systematically in the argument that God always remains free to act differently than the way in which He has chosen to act. The point is a special application of the principle, in Peter's doctrine of God, that the transcend-

---

[136] Peter Lombard, *Sent.* 1. d. 43, 1: 298–303. This point has been noted by Courtenay, *Capacity and Volition*, p. 55; Beonio-Brocchieri [Fumagalli] and Parodi, *Storia della filos. medievale*, pp. 254–55.

ent divine essence is never exhausted by the the ways in which the deity has chosen to display Himself in His interactions with His creation.

With this equipment in hand, Peter proceeds to clear away the problems that remain. One Abelardian *quidam* here, whose identity we have not been able to ascertain, had cited a passage from Augustine's *Eighty-Three Different Questions* to defend the claim that God cannot do better than He does, a passage which, as Peter shows, is inapposite. In the citation at issue, Augustine is referring to the Father's generation of the Son, His own equal, as an action incapable of being improved on. This point, Peter notes, is irrelevant to the question of whether God could have improved on created beings that do not share His substance.[137] Now, the beings God created are creatures, with created limits. Peter shows an appreciation of this point, which has its parallel in the argument of Robert of Melun, but he presents it as an amplification of the line taken by the anonymous Porretan and the author of the *Summa sententiarum*, so as not to give backhanded support to the Platonic world view. If the universe were as good as it might be, it would be perfect, he observes. But only God is perfect. If creatures were also perfect, this would infringe on the uniqueness of the attribute of perfection as a divine property, making the creation equal to the creator. Since it does not partake of the divine nature, the created universe cannot enjoy this type of equality with it. Now, among those creatures with created limits, he continues, some are capable of improvement, whether through their own efforts, the assistance of God, or both. Quite apart from that, had God chosen to do so, He could have created beings incapable of sinning. He could have provided arrangements in the natural law that might have afforded better conditions of existence for creatures, just as He could have decreed a mode of redemption different from the one He did select. All these examples refer to the quality of life for creatures, not the wisdom and power of.the creator, or His capacity to have constructed alternative arrangements.[138]

There is one more objection Peter wants to deal with before going on to another dimension of the relations between God's power and His will. Some people say that God cannot now do what He once did, citing as their clinching argument the idea that, since Christ was born, crucified, and resurrected once and for all, He cannot be reincarnated, recrucified, and resurrected again. Against

---

[137] Peter Lombard, *Sent.* 1. d. 44. c. 1.2, 1: 304.
[138] Ibid., c. 1.3–4, 1: 304–05.

this claim, Peter points out that God is eternal and immutable. The fact that God chose to do all these things once only does not mean that He could not do them again. In the defense of this extreme example of his general point about the omnipotence of God, Peter brings forward the nominalist argument concerning the verb, which parallels the nominalist argument concerning the noun to which he appeals in considering God's foreknowledge and contingency. Just as the nominalists held that the noun has a unitary signification, although it can consignify when it is used in propositions in conjunction with verbs in different tenses, voices, or moods, so they held that the verb signifies two things, an action and a time when the action takes place. Irrespective of the time, the verb signifies a single action. The time of the action is a consignification which does not alter the proper signification of the verb. Hence, for the nominalists, with respect to the understanding of nouns and verbs alike, one can say that whatever was true once is true always (*semel est verum, semper est verum*). Peter concurs in this analysis. On the analogy of the action signified by the verb, he points out, God's power is always the same. What He was able to do in the past, He is able to do in the present or the future (*Deus semper posse et quidquid semel potuit id est habere omnem illam potentiam quam semel habuit*).[139] This conclusion, connected as it is to the nominalist understanding of verbs, is used by the Lombard not to advance the claims of logic but rather to undergird the fundamentally metaphysical address he takes to the question of God's power. It is perhaps Peter's most pointed and rigorous application of the principle that God's omnipotence always transcends His actual use of it.

Peter now moves to the consideration of other issues in the relation between God's power and God's will. He has a substantial number of points to make about the divine will in this connection. He begins by observing that God's will is spoken of with respect to the divine essence. For God, to be and to will are one and the same; just as to be and to be good are identical in God. At the same time, God is not exhausted by whatever He wills, just as the fact that He knows everything does not mean that He is everything He knows.

---

[139] Ibid., c. 2, 1: 305–06. The quotation is at c. 2.4, 1:306. His comparison of God's power with the signification of the verb is at c. 2.3, 1:106: "Verba enim diversorum temporum, diversi prolata temporibus et diversis enim adiuncta adverbiis, eundum faciunt sensum, ut modo loquentes dicimus: Iste potest legere hodie; cras autem dicimus: Iste potest legisse, vel potuit legere hieri; ubi unius rei monstratur potentia." For modern scholars who have also noted Peter's use of the nominalist understanding of the verb on this context, see the citations in n. 114 above, p. 287.

Rather, we should understand this point about God's will as saying that, like His knowledge, which is of His essence, His will can be directed to this or that subject, subjects which are distinct from Himself, created, and changeable, and of which His will can be regarded as the first cause.[140]

As with most theologians of his time, Peter also understands the divine will under the headings of precept, prohibition, permission, operation, and counsel. The particular change he rings on this standard teaching, and it is a function of his desire to avoid collapsing the divine will as the divine essence into the divine will as God's chosen exercise of the options He selects vis-à-vis His creation, is to view these distinctions as signs of the divine will, signs that are not to be confused with their *significatum*. These signs are ways in which the simple and unchanging God manifests Himself externally.[141] Here, Peter has called upon the Augustinian distinction between signs and things, from the *De doctrina christiana*, transferring it from a verbal to a theological level. With this semantic support for his theology of divine transcendence in place, Peter states the contemporary consensus position in arguing that God's ability to tolerate the breaking of His moral law and the rejection of His grace by sinners does not conflict with or limit His will. Since this is the arrangement He decided to put in place, the exercise of their free will by intelligent beings cannot be seen as frustrating God's desires. Peter also agrees with the consensus in stating that God's permission of sin does not make Him morally responsible for it.[142] Once more, Peter firmly guides this topic back to the principle that God does everything that He wills, and that this fact places no limits on divine omnipotence. And, while God's will as eternal cannot be resisted, the signs of that will in prohibition, precept, permission, and counsel can be rejected by the free moral agents He has chosen to create.[143]

Peter brings in one final example of this same general point, which has the effect of ending his treatment of God's nature on a moral note, and one that attacks one of Abelard's most notorious teachings in the field of ethics as well. Human free will may be good will, he notes, and it may yet seek something that is against God's plan, as is the case when filial piety urges a child to will the health

---

[140] Peter Lombard, *Sent.* 1. d. 45. c. 1–c. 4, 1: 306–09.
[141] Ibid., c. 5–c. 7, 1: 309–12. On this point, see Schneider, *Die Lehre*, pp. 44–49.
[142] Peter Lombard, *Sent.* 1. d. 46. c. 1–c, 7, 1: 312–21. For other contemporary treatments of this topic, see Landgraf, *Dogmengeschichte*, 1 part 2: 204–81.
[143] Peter Lombard, *Sent.* 1. d. 47, 1: 321–24.

of a parent who is seriously ill and whom God wills to die. Thus, the good will of men may or may not be congruent with the will of God. At the same time, God's will may be served by human bad will. This was so in the case of the people responsible for the crucifixion of Christ, who did, *pace* Abelard, act out of bad intentions. As with his general analysis of permission above, Peter reminds the reader that this does not mean that God caused their bad will. Likewise, men of good will are not gratified by the contemplation of the sufferings of Christ on the cross or the sufferings of the martyrs, although they are able to appreciate the fact that these sufferings are permitted by God for man's redemption and edification.[144] As this final series of questions reflects so clearly, the thoroughgoing aim of restoring the transcendent dimension to the deity which informs so consistently Peter's doctrine of the Trinity and doctrine of God alike also has the effect, as he moves to the doctrine of creation and of man in Book 2 of the *Sentences*, of providing a zone of independence for God's creatures that is fully compatible with God's omnipotence, omniscience, and perfectly realized being.

---

[144] Ibid., d. 48. c. 1–c. 4, 1: 327–38.

CHAPTER SIX

THE CREATION, ANGELS, MAN, AND THE FALL

The topics covered by Book 2 of the Lombard's *Sentences* were all controversial in his day, sometimes massively so. At the same time, the contestants ranged on the different sides of the debates were not always the same ones, for each of these subjects. In the case of angels, man, and the fall, the latter topic including the effects and transmission of original sin, the problems arose from the disagreements found within the traditional authorities and their twelfth-century adherents, and, in some cases, from deep internal inconsistencies within individual authorities, which contemporary theologians sought to reconcile with greater or lesser success. Although Augustine is a weighty presence throughout Book 2, the rest of the cast of characters, both ancient and modern, fluctuates considerably from one part of this book to another. So do the problems Peter Lombard wants to target and the particular thinkers, in each area, whom he wants to criticize, support, or improve on. In this respect, there is no one set of central imperatives, no one overarching theme tying together his treatment of the topics in this book, as there is in the case of his doctrine of God in Book 1. Also, he displays different degrees of conservatism and originality as he moves from one of these topics to another, and different degrees of profundity in his exploitation of his sources. For these reasons, and despite the evident thematic connections that tie them together, these subjects in the Lombard's theology are grasped most comprehensibly when treated one by one.

THE DOCTRINE OF CREATION

With respect to the doctrine of creation, the agenda was set, not only for Peter but also for his mid-century confrères, by the challenge raised to the traditional exegetical account of creation in Genesis commentary and to the more speculative treatment of the subject found in the patristic tradition by the theories of creation presented by thinkers associated with the school of Chartres. Despite their individual variations in handling it, their project was to develop a Platonic or Neoplatonic understanding of the creation, a task no one had essayed since John Scottus Eriugena in the ninth century, and at the same time to see whether, and how far, it could be integrated with the hexaemeral account in Genesis. While the members of this school thus drew upon biblical materials and while more than one of them framed his speculation in the form of Genesis exegesis, they were united with each other, and opposed to other thinkers of the time, in approaching this entire subject from the standpoint of natural philosophy, not of theology.[1] The contemporary response to the Chartrains was a varied one. Some theologians, like Honorius Augustodunensis, Rupert of Deutz, and the members of the school of Laon, worked too early in the century to have been aware of the writings of the Chartrains. Others, like Robert Pullen, were chronologically positioned to have been able to take them into account but failed to do so. Still others, like William of St. Thierry, reacted with rhetorical denunciation but with a highly imperfect grasp of the Chartrain project. Still others, like the Porretans, were well aware of what that project was. Had not their master, Gilbert of Poitiers, taught and studied at Chartres for many years and served as chancellor of its school? But they contented themselves with laconic objections to the Platonizing of creation without proposing a cogent refutation or alternative to that approach. There were also a number of theologians, including Peter Abelard, Hugh of St. Victor, the author of the *Summa sententiarum*, and Robert of Melun, who took serious account of the Chartrain doctrine of creation and serious exception to it, at some points. They sought to delineate the areas in which they found it wanting, and the areas in which they found it useful, while trying to yoke it to a more traditional exegetical or patristic treatment of the subject. Peter Lombard can be placed in this last group. For his

---

[1] This common orientation has been rightly stressed, for the school as a whole, and for its individual members, by A. Clerval, *Les Écoles de Chartres au moyen-âge du Ve au XVIe siècle*, Mémoires de la Société archéologique d'Eure-et-Loir, 11 (Paris: R. Selleret, 1895), pp. 267–68; Nikolaus M. Häring, "The Creation and Creator of the World according to Thierry of Chartres and Clarenbaldus of Arras," *AHDLMA* 22 (1958): 146; Häring, ed., *The Life and Work of Clarenbald of Arras, a Twelfth-Century Master of the School of Chartres* (Toronto: Pontifical Institute of Mediaeval Studies, 1965), p. 50; Helen Rodnite [Lemay], "Platonism in the Twelfth-Century School of Chartres," *Acta* 2 (1975): 42–52; "The Doctrine of the Trinity in Guillaume de Conches' Glosses on Macrobius: Text and Studies," Columbia University Ph.D. diss., 1972, pp. 50–51; Enzo Maccagnolo, *Rerum universitatis: Saggio sulla filosofia di Teodorico di Chartres* (Florence: Le Monnier, 1976), pp. 227–50; Ludwig Ott, "Die platonische Weltseele in der Theologie der Frühscholastik," in *Parusia: Studien zur Philosophie Platons und zur Problemgeschichte des Platonismus. Festgabe für Johannes Hirschberger*, ed. Kurt Flasch (Frankfurt: Minerva GMBH, 1965), pp. 308–26; Anneliese Stollenwerk, "Der Genesiskommentar Thierrys von Chartres und die Thierrys von Chartres zugeschreibenen Kommentar zu Boethius 'De trinitate'," University of Cologne Ph.D. diss., 1971, pp. 34–36.

part, he is less interested in mediating between the traditional and
the Chartrain approaches to creation than are some members of
that group. But, at the same time, he offers a more coherent and
surefooted treatment of creation than any of them do, even when he
is drawing heavily and constructively upon them.[2]

The Chartrain Challenge

Since it was the Chartrains who threw down the gauntlet, it
makes sense to begin with the series of creation accounts which
they provided, mostly between the 1130s and the mid-1150s. A
consideration of their teachings here will remind us of the fact that
there was not only a range of Platonisms abroad in the land in this
period but also of the variety of approaches taken to the Platonic
tradition within this single movement.[3] The master in this school
who appears to have been the first to have supported a Platonic
view of creation was its celebrated head in the early twelfth century,
Bernard of Chartres. In a previously unpublished gloss on Plato's
Timaeus, in the Latin translation of Chalcidius in which it was read
in this century, convincingly attributed to Bernard by its discover-
er, Paul Edward Dutton, he is quoted as stating that the three
principles of creation are God, matter, and the forms (*deus, hile et
ideas*),[4] exactly the view that John of Salisbury ascribes to him in the
Metalogicon.[5] As for the nature of the forms, Bernard holds that they
are eternal, once created, but that they are not coeternal with God.
They exist in His mind before the creation of the phenomenal world
but are His products, posterior to Him. Thus far, Bernard's forms
sound much like the exemplary causes of John Scottus Eriugena.
But, unlike them, they do not participate in creating phenomenal
beings directly. Rather, for Bernard, this role is assigned to the
formae nativae, forms which are images or reflections of these
archetypes and which do the actual work of informing matter.[6] As

---

[2] This position of Peter in the contemporary debates on creation is brought out
well by Ermenegildo Bertola, "La dottrina della creazione nel *Liber Sententiarum* di
Pier Lombardo," *Pier Lombardo* 1:1 (1957): 27–44.

[3] This point is articulated clearly by Peter Dronke, *Fabula: Explorations into the
Uses of Myth in Medieval Platonism* (Leiden: E. J. Brill, 1974), and is stated with
particular crispness on p. 8.

[4] Paul Edward Dutton, "The Uncovering of the *Glosae super Platonem* of Bernard
of Chartres," *MS* 46 (1984): 213.

[5] John of Salisbury, *Metalogicon* 4.35, ed. Clement C. J. Webb (Oxford:
Clarendon Press, 1909), p. 205. John makes the same point in *Met.* 2.20, p. 107,
although he erroneously states that the idea goes back to the Stoics.

[6] Dutton, "The Uncovering," pp. 213–19.

for matter itself, Bernard does not appear to have treated the question of whether it is eternal or created.

On all these matters later Chartrains held definite, and often incompatible, opinions. No doubt the most problematic account of creation produced by anyone in this tradition is that of Bernard Silvestris, in that he offers the most thoroughly Platonic, or Neoplatonic, treatment of creation, not to mention one that includes ideas idiosyncratic to him, combining his ingredients in a rich and syncretic broth. For some kinds of readers, he complicates matters by presenting his ideas not in a treatise or commentary but in an allegorical poetic narrative-cum-dialogue, the *Cosmographia*. In this work, Bernard Silvestris by no means rules out the doctrine of preexistent matter and proposes a God who does not act directly in the work of creation, subcontracting it instead to an assortment of subordinate created emanations or theophanies.[7] In addition to his dependence on Neoplatonism for the notion of creation by subdivine intermediaries and his adherance to the Platonic notion of the preexistence of matter, Bernard Silvestris draws as well on the Stoic idea of a cyclical cosmos undergoing endless cycles of creation, destruction, and recreation. This cyclical idea of the cosmos is an essential foundation for his creation scenario. For, at the point when his story begins, we are not about to witness the first or the only creation that ever will be, but rather the present round of the cycle, now, as it were, at ground zero, or at ground zero plus one, since there are already a few theophanies on the stage of the action when Bernard sweeps open the curtains.[8]

In particular, the two characters who supply the matter and form out of which most creatures are made, Silva and Noys, are present from the very beginning. So are several other theophanies, while yet other theophanies emerge during the course of the story to lend a helping hand. Silva represents matter which, at this stage, is unformed or primordial. In some respects she is the heroine of the

---

[7] Scholars have reached consensus on these traits, for the most part. On this work, see in particular Clerval, *Les Écoles*, pp. 259–61; Heinrich Flatten, "Die 'materia primordialis' in der Schule von Chartres," *Archiv für Geschichte der Philosophie* 40 (1931): 58–65; Étienne Gilson, "La Cosmogonie de Bernard Silvestris," *AHDLMA* 3 (1928): 5–24, although Gilson sees the character Noys as coessential with the deity and, at the same time, as identical with the subordinate Neoplatonic *Nous*, p. 12; Theodore Silverstein, "The Fabulous Cosmogony of Bernardus Silvestris," *Modern Philology* 46 (1948): 92–116; Brian Stock, *Myth and Science in the Twelfth Century: A Study of Bernard Silvester* (Princeton: Princeton University Press, 1972), pp. 15–16.

[8] Bernard Silvestris, *Cosmographia*, ed. Peter Dronke (Leiden: E. J. Brill, 1978); trans. Winthrop Wetherbee (New York: Columbia University Press, 1973). Dronke offers a good summary of the story in his preface, pp. 29–48.

Cosmographia, for it is her desires, her longing to receive the impress of form, that get the action started, triggering the arrival of Noys. She does this through the mediation of Natura, the daughter of Noys, who makes Silva's complaint known to her mother. When Noys arrives she brings with her the exemplary forms of all, or most, created beings. The task of joining them to matter is accomplished by a number of other theophanies, under the guidance of Noys. Just as Natura mediates the complaint of Silva, so she acts as the mediator of the forms to matter. She also orders the four elements to dispose themselves for the reception of form and arranges the elements in their allotted stations with respect to each other. It is a still more indirect level of theophany which is responsible for the actual union of matter and form. Noys gives birth to Endelichia or Anima. She marries Mundus, who is born of Silva. It is this marriage of Anima and Mundus that engenders all created beings except man, although, when they do appear, they issue from the womb of Silva.

This obstetrical anomaly aside, Bernard Silvestris next proceeds to the creation of man, the most interesting of the creatures for him. Man has a mode of genesis unique to him, and in two respects. While the immediate progenitors of other beings are Anima and Mundus, the theophanies that serve the analogous functions in man's case are Urania and Physis. Urania, or heavenly wisdom, supplies the human soul, and Physis, or the laws of physical nature, supplies the human body. This part of the scenario suggests that man's body is special, with respect to other corporeal beings, just as his soul is. Also special is the fact that, in this case alone, the permission of the deity must be obtained for the emergence of this particular creature on the part of the theophanies responsible for engendering him. The deity consents; but neither here nor elsewhere does he play a direct role in creation. The job is done by Physis and Urania in collaboration with Natura.

It is easy to see why a twelfth-century Christian reader might find this account of creation unsettling. The creator God has been all but banished from the action. Creation, according to Bernard Silvestris, is accomplished, rather, by a series of secondary theophanies or by the tertiary theophanies which they engender. Moreover, since the cosmos is eternal and the creation just described is not unique but only one of an endless series of creations which recycle both the matter and the forms used in the preceding creations, the notion of a God Who alone is eternal is impossible to sustain. There was no point, in Bernard Silvestris's account, when God was the only being in existence. In all these respects, it can be

seen that Bernard has made no effort at all to accommodate his
treatment of creation to the account in Genesis. Nor does he raise
the question of whether purely spiritual creatures, such as angels,
exist, what their status is if they do, and when and how they were
brought into being. Nor does he speculate on whether any of the
creative theophanies in the *Cosmographia* are comparable to or
coordinate with the persons of the Trinity. The role he assigns to
Anima makes her rather less prominent a figure than the *anima
mundi* is in Plato's *Timaeus* or in the work of other Chartrains, since
she is only one of several forces which collaborate in the union of
matter and form. Also, Anima here plays no role at all in man's
creation. His soul or mind is derived, rather, from Urania. While
Bernard Silvestris devotes extended attention to man and makes
him a special case among creatures, and while Bernard's accent
throughout his discussion of man is on the pure naturalism of his
origin and constitution, the uniqueness of his genesis makes it as
impossible for man to be viewed as a microcosm of nature in
general as it is for him to be viewed as having a soul created by God
in the divine image and likeness.

Bernard Silvestris has some additional reflections on the World
Soul, the human soul, and the biblical God in his commentary on
Martianus Capella, which both fail to cohere with each other and
with his philosophy in the *Cosmographia*. In glossing the first book of
Martianus, he says that the ancients held that, just as the world is a
vast body from which all corporeal beings derive, so the world has a
soul which animates that body. From it all created souls derive,
and to it they return. Plato, he adds, called this spirit the *anima
mundi*. Vergil agreed with Plato's view. For both Plato and Vergil,
the *anima mundi* is subordinate to God. At the same time, Bernard
states that this same spirit is referred to in both the Old and New
Testaments as the spirit of God. This is the spirit said to have
hovered over the deep in Genesis and this spirit is the one in Whom
St. Paul says we live and move and have our being.[9] Bernard
Silvestris does not spell out whether he thinks that the biblical God,
or the Holy Spirit, can or should be assimilated to the subordinate
Platonic *anima mundi*. He just leaves matters at that. On the other
hand, his account of the functions of the World Soul here would
give it a special responsibility for the souls of men, of a sort that
Anima lacks in the *Cosmographia*.

---

[9] Bernard Silvestris, *Commentarius in Martiani Capellae, De Nuptiis Philologiae et
Mercurii* 1.18, trans. Enzo Maccagnolo in *Il Divino e il megacosmo: Testi filosofici e
scientifici della scuola di Chartres* (Milan: Rusconi, 1980), pp. 564–67.

Not all the Chartrains were willing to go as far in the direction of Platonism, or of originality, as Bernard Silvestris. His confrères in the school were much more interested in trying to coordinate their findings as readers of philosophical texts with their beliefs as Christians and with the creation account in Genesis. This is certainly the case with Thierry of Chartres. He wants to integrate the Trinity, understood economically and with each person performing distinct cosmic functions, into the work of creation. He takes a more creationist than emanationist line. He believes in a single creation, but one occurring in two stages, with God engendering everything at once but then developing it, according to the hexaemeral plan of Genesis, by means of seminal reasons. God, for Thierry, remains the remote cause, the ground of the being and capacities of created beings. He holds the *anima mundi* to be a purely naturalistic force and he does not equate it with the Holy Spirit.[10] Thierry elaborates some of these points in his successive commentaries on the *De trinitate* of Boethius, and also in his treatise on the hexaemeron. The latter work, as might be expected, offers a fuller description of creation, although in it he changes his opinion on one important issue, the eternity of exemplary forms, and his adherance to the Genesis format means that he does not discuss the creation and nature of angels.

In all his commentaries on Boethius, Thierry makes the point, also reiterated in his hexaemeron, that God is the *forma essendi*, meaning by that term not form in the Aristotelian sense of the particular form of any created substance and not in the sense of a divine immanentalism but just the reverse. He means that God is the ground of being of creatures, of both their matter and their form and of the coinherence of that matter and form in each creature. This notion is accompanied by a clear distinction, derived by Thierry from Boethius, between the mode of being possessed by the creator and that possessed by creatures.[11] While, in this respect,

---

[10] Good orientations to Thierry are provided by Clerval, *Les Écoles*, pp. 254–59; Charlotte Gross, "Twelfth-Century Concepts of Time: Three Reinterpretations of Augustine's Doctrine of Creation *Simul*," *Journal of the History of Philosophy* 23 (1985): 328–31; Häring, "The Creation and Creator," pp. 146–53; Édouard Jeauneau, "Un Représentant du platonisme au XIIe siècle: Maître Thierry de Chartres," in *"Lectio philosophorum": Recherches sur l'École de Chartres* (Amsterdam: Adolf M. Hakkert, 1973), pp. 77–86; Maccagnolo, *Rerum universitatis*, pp. 26–28, 30–37, 42–49, 227–50; J. M. Parent, *La doctrine de la creation dans l'école de Chartres* (Paris/Ottawa: J. Vrin/Institut d'Études Médiévales, 1938), pp. 54–58; Stollenwerk, "Der Genesiskommentar," pp. 34–36, 38–46, 49–67.

[11] Thierry of Chartres, *Commentum super Boethii librum De Trinitate* 2.16; *Lectiones in Boethii librum De Trinitate* 2.35–37; *Glosa super Boethii librum De Trinitate* 2.18;

creation is the work of "one God alone" (*uno solo deo*) and while the
entire Trinity creates unformed matter, forms it, and governs it,
each Trinitarian person is assigned a particular role to play in
Thierry's account. In this respect, he argues, one can speak of four
causes of earthly substances, God's power as the efficient cause,
God's wisdom as the formal cause, God's goodness as the final
cause, and the four elements as the material cause.[12] The unformed
matter, according to Thierry, is created all at once, at the first
moment of creation.[13] As for the forms, he wavers. In his commentary on Boethius, he insists that God creates both primordial
matter and the forms, and that those who think "that neither form
nor matter is created depart from the truth" (*quod nec formam nec
materiam creatam esse a veritate devians*).[14] On the other hand, in his
hexaemeron, he states that the forms of all things are engendered
from all eternity.[15] This eternity would be compatible with his
understanding of God's wisdom as the formal cause. But Thierry
does not clarify whether these forms, so understood, are an independent category of being which, like God, is eternal but distinct
from Him or whether they are ideas in His mind, identical with
Him. Nor does he explain whether this eternal engendering of the
forms is to be understood along the lines of the Father's eternal
engendering of the Son in the unmanifested Trinity, or in some
economic sense of the term vis-à-vis creation. In any event, and
leaving aside how or if this next point squares with his view of
God's goodness as the final cause, Thierry presents the *anima mundi*
as the force that brings matter and form together and endows
creatures with the natural capacities they have.[16] He understands
this force in a thoroughly naturalistic sense, and in this respect
scholars who exempt Thierry from Platonic subordinationism here
are on the mark. He does observe, however, and unhelpfully, that
Christians call this force the Holy Spirit.[17]

The creation account of William of Conches has much in com-

Tractatus de sex dierum operibus 32, ed. Nikolaus M. Häring in *Commentaries on Boethius
by Thierry of Chartres and His School* (Toronto: Pontifical Institute of Mediaeval
Studies, 1971), pp. 73, 166–67, 272, 569. This point is noted by Maccagnolo, *Rerum
universitatis*, pp. 26–28; Gangolf Schrimpf, *Die Axiomenschrift des Boethius (De hebdomadibus) als philosophisches Lehrbuch des Mittelalters* (Leiden: E. J. Brill, 1966), pp.
57–62; Stollenwerk, "Der Genesiskommentar," pp. 73–79.
[12] Thierry of Chartres, *Tractatus* 1, 3, pp. 555, 556–57. The quotation is on
p. 555.
[13] Ibid., 5, p. 557.
[14] Thierry of Chartres, *Commentum* 2.28, p. 77.
[15] Thierry of Chartres, *Tractatus* 5, p. 557.
[16] Ibid., 26, p. 566.
[17] Ibid., 27, 29, pp. 566, 567.

mon with that of Thierry of Chartres. His model is even more creationist than emanationist and he draws an even sharper distinction between the creator and the created capacities with which He endows other beings. William finds a clearer and less problematic way of dealing with the forms than Thierry does. While his use of Trinitarian language is even less theological than that of Thierry, since he is interested in the deity only in His role in getting the universe in motion and providing it with its built-in natural aptitudes, his use of the terminology of power, wisdom, and goodness to describe the activities of the Trinitarian persons in this connection made William the brunt of the charge of Abelardianism on the Trinity at the hands of William of St. Thierry, even though he took pains to indicate his differences from Abelard on the question of whether these terms are proper names of the Trinitarian persons.[18]

William develops his ideas across a series of works, growing more nuanced after the attack on his *Philosophia mundi* and very cautious indeed in his final work, the *Dragmaticon*. He first broaches the subject of the creation in his *Glosae super Platonem*. There, along the same lines as Thierry, he announces that there are four causes of creation, the divine essence as the efficient cause, the divine wisdom as the formal cause, the divine goodness as the final cause, and unformed matter as the material cause.[19] With respect to the formal cause, he makes two important distinctions that differentiate his handling of this topic from Thierry's. As God's wisdom, this cause is an archetype of the entire creation, he argues. It is eternal and immutable and has always resided in God's mind. When God

---

[18] Good orientations on William of Conches are provided by Clerval, *Les Écoles*, pp. 264–65; Dronke, *Fabula*, pp. 100–03; Heinrich Flatten, *Die Philosophie des Wilhelm von Conches* (Koblenz: Görres-Druckerei, 1929), esp. pp. 90–96, 126–34, 180–84; Tullio Gregory, *Anima mundi: La filosofia di Guglielmo di Conches e la scuola di Chartres* (Florence: G. C. Sansoni, 1955), pp. 49–58, 72–97; "L'Idea della natura nella scuola di Chartres," *Giornale critico della filosofia italiana* 31 (1952): 433–42; Gross, "Twelfth-Century Concepts," pp. 334–37; "William of Conches: A Curious Grammatical Argument against the Eternity of the World," *Proceedings of the PMR Conference*, 11, ed. Phillip Pulsiano (Villanova: Augustinian Historical Institute, 1986), pp. 127–33; Jeauneau, *"Integumentum,"* in *"Lectio philosophorum"*, pp. 151–61, 171–72; Maccagnolo, intro. to *Il Divino*, pp. 66–68; Gregor Maurach, comm. on his ed. of William of Conches, *Philosophia mundi*, Bk. 1 (Pretoria: University of South Africa, 1974), pp. 55, 58; Joseph Moreau, "'*Opifex, id est Creator*': Remarques sur le platonisme de Chartres," *Archiv für Geschichte der Philosophie* 56 (1974): 35–49; Ott, "Die platonische Weltseele," pp. 318–26; Parent, *La doctrine de la creation*, pp. 37–43, 70–76; Rodnite [Lemay], "The Doctrine of the Trinity," pp. 38, 40–42, 49–54, 56–60, 64–72. William's treatment of power, wisdom, and goodness as Trinitarian names has been erroneously equated with Abelard's by John Newell, "Rationalism at the School of Chartres," *Vivarium* 21 (1983): 21.

[19] William of Conches, *Glosae super Platonem* 1.32, ed. Édouard Jeauneau (Paris: J. Vrin, 1965), p. 98.

decides to engender the creation, two other formal principles arrive
on the scene. The divine archetype serves as the exemplar of the
formae nativae which, in turn, are the informing principles of individual substances. Also, in a similar way, God produces seminal
reasons. William sees these seminal reasons not so much as a
means of accounting for the arrival of new kinds of creatures after
the sixth day of creation but as a means of describing a continuous
creation in which creatures are given the capacity to function as
secondary causes. His distinctions here, with respect to the idea of
form, enable him to retain the notion of an archetypal cause identical with and coeternal with the deity without sacrificing the
notion of created forms that do not partake of the divine essence.[20]
With respect to the material cause, William rejects Plato and
agrees with Thierry that primordial matter is not eternal or
preexistent but created, and created *simul* at the first moment of the
creation.[21] With respect to the final cause, William calls it the *anima
mundi* and treats it exclusively as a force of nature that gives
creatures life and motion and the ability to carry out their natural
physical functions. As to whether it can be called the Holy Spirit,
he observes that some people think so. He himself remains noncommittal, saying that he neither denies nor affirms this claim.[22]
But, in the sequel, he makes it very clear that the *anima mundi* as he
envisions it has to be distinguished sharply from any of the Trinitarian persons and from created beings as well. Unlike the Son or the
Holy Spirit, the *anima mundi* is neither engendered, nor does it
proceed. Unlike the phenomenal world, it is not created. The verb
he uses to describe the presence of the *anima mundi* in the world is
excogitare, meaning produced by thought.[23] While William thus
avoids a confusion between the *anima mundi* and the deity, either as
creator or as the Holy Spirit, it is still not entirely clear what
relationship it bears to the deity. It is not created. But does it share
coeternity with God? Or, is it to be understood as an effect of God
that is given its assignment only when the phenomenal world
comes into being, as the providential law of nature He ordains? On
these matters William remains silent.

Further clarifications are provided by William in his *Philosophia
mundi*. Here, he reiterates the position on unformed matter and on
forms that he had already articulated.[24] But he begins by observing

---

[20] Ibid., 1.32, 1.37, 1.45, pp. 99, 104–05, 113.
[21] Ibid., 1.60, 2.94, pp. 130–31, 260.
[22] Ibid., 1.71, pp. 144–47. The quotation is on p. 147.
[23] Ibid., 1.74, pp. 148–50.
[24] William of Conches, *Philosophia mundi* 1.22, ed. Maurach, pp. 27–33.

that, while we should learn what we can about the creator by investigating the creation, the knowledge we can gain thereby remains imperfect.[25] He holds out analogous limits for theological language. While the Trinitarian persons can be called power, wisdom, and will, these terms, especially the third one, must be understood metaphorically (*translative*), not literally. Moreover, these are not proper names exclusive to each of the persons, since They share equally in the qualities involved and work cooperatively in all Their actions.[26] William of St. Thierry clearly did not take account of these disclaimers in charging that William of Conches was teaching the same Trinitarian doctrine as Abelard. Nor did he read far enough into the *Philosophia mundi*; for he completely misses William's next point.[27] William returns to the question of the *anima mundi* and whether it can be equated with the Holy Spirit. He notes that there are two answers that have been given to this question. Some say that the *anima mundi* is the Holy Spirit, which vivifies everything in the world. Others say that the *anima mundi* is purely natural, and not a supernatural force, implanted in creatures and giving them their natural vigor and aptitudes. He refers readers to his gloss on Plato where, as we have just seen, he refrains from deciding between these two positions and in which his own handling of this force suggests that he has a purely naturalistic understanding of it. In the *Philosophia mundi*, William offers a clarification of that last point. Since God wills to create a world in which creatures can operate as secondary causes and since will, with the caveats and limits noted above, can be ascribed to the Holy Spirit, one can associate the *anima mundi* with the mission of the Holy Spirit. But, he insists, this is not to say that the transcendent Holy Spirit immanentalizes Himself in the work of the *anima mundi*. Rather, William concludes, we have to see the *anima mundi* as an effect of the Holy Spirit.[28]

In the first book of his *Elementorum philosophiae* William repeats and nuances still farther his discussion of the Trinity and the *anima mundi* in his earlier works. He states that God is the sole creator, an activity in which all the Trinitarian persons collaborate equally, and that all the qualities of the Trinity inhere equally in all the persons. He adds that nothing precedes or is coeternal with the deity.[29] This last point sweeps away the possibility that the *anima*

---

[25] Ibid., 1.4, pp. 10–11.
[26] Ibid., 1.10–11, pp. 13–15.
[27] William of St. Thierry, *De erroribus Guillelmi de Conchis*, PL 180: 333A–D.
[28] William of Conches, *Philos. mundi* 1.15, pp. 15–16.
[29] William of Conches, *Elementorum philosophiae* 1, PL 90: 1129A–1130B.

mundi is eternal. In rounding up opinions on the *anima mundi*, William notes once more that some seek to equate it with the Holy Spirit and that others treat it as a purely natural force (*naturalem vigorem*) infused in things by God as part of their natural endowment, enabling them to carry out their functions. Adding a third opinion, he notes that still others see the *anima mundi* as an incorporeal substance which gives animate beings their souls individually. This third opinion, which we have found in Bernard Silvestris's Martianus gloss, he rejects. Once more, he takes no official stand on the other two positions, although what he has said in the *Philosophia mundi* as well as in the present work would appear to favor the second view.[30]

In William's final work, the *Dragmaticon*, abandoning the effort to develop the potentially fruitful distinction between the deity and His effects, whether seen as the natural law He ordains or as the beings He creates, he fights a rear-guard action. He rejects his earlier description of the Trinity as power, wisdom, and will. Using the tactic of many of Abelard's critics prior to the Lombard, he cites biblical passages in which these names are applied to Trinitarian persons other than the Father, Son, and Holy Spirit, respectively.[31] William also abandons all reference to the *anima mundi*. In this sense, his final response to criticism is not to try to refute it definitively but to back off from the project which had inspired it.

There were two other mid-century Chartrains, writing after Bernard Silvestris, Thierry of Chartres, and William of Conches who sought to take account of, and to rectify, the overstatements, misstatements, or unclarities which they found in the writings of these masters. They did so with only partial success. One is an anonymous Chartrain whose commentary on Martianus Capella has been ascribed, by some scholars, to Bernard Silvestris. The internal evidence in this text, however, has enabled its editor to make a convincing refutation of that claim, since, while the author glosses some of the same points as Bernard does in his own commentary on the same work, he does so at different lemmata; and, he certainly moves away from some of the positions taken by Bernard. The author has clearly profited from the controversy provoked, willy-nilly, by William of Conches, for he takes pains to agree with him that power, wisdom, and goodness are not proper names of the

---

[30] Ibid., 1, *PL* 90: 1130B–1131D. The quotation is at 1130C.
[31] William of Conches, *Dragmaticon* prologus, trans. Maccagnolo in *Il Divino*, pp. 244–45.

Trinitarian persons but refer to attributes which they all share.[32]
He glosses the name Endelichia, which, as we have noted, Bernard
Silvestris equates with Anima as the female half of the theophanic
couple who combine form and matter in all creatures except man,
in his *Cosmographia*. Our author allows that Endelichia is the
mother of Psyche, meaning that incorporeals, like the soul, cannot
have material causes. Endelichia, he adds, is not a theophany, not
God, and not a person of the Trinity.[33] After raising and rejecting
the Platonic theory that souls preexist their union with bodies,
proposing instead that souls, like everything else, are created, and
created *simul*,[34] he turns to the problem of the World Soul. The
anima mundi, he argues, is not to be identified with the deity. Nor is
it the substance of created souls. Rather, it is a natural power that
animates the whole world.[35] The author then, confusingly enough,
caps this position, which is largely a reprise of William of Conches',
with a gloss on the World Soul supportive of what Bernard Silvestris says in his Martianus commentary, and one which contradicts
what he himself has already stated. In language very close to
Bernard's, he compares the World Soul to the spirit animating the
world, understood as a vast body, the spirit which is the source of
all souls and to which they return. He equates this spirit with the
divine spirit that governs the creation. As both prophets and philosophers have said, he adds, it endows creatures with the capacity
to perform their natural functions. The author does not raise here
the issue of the Trinity, or the charisms of the Holy Spirit. But,
while he stresses above that the *anima mundi* is neither the deity nor
a theophany of the deity, he now identifies the World Soul with
God. The term *anima mundi*, he concludes, confusingly enough,
"plainly signifies the deity" (*Deum esse aperte significat*).[36] It cannot
be said that this effort to square Bernard Silvestris with William of
Conches is a success.

The last Chartrain writer within our time period, Clarenbald of
Arras, makes a valiant attempt to seize the initiative once again, to
treat the range of issues addressed by other masters in the school
who proposed accounts of creation, and to set his own stamp on
this enterprise by de-Platonizing it somewhat and by adding some

---

[32] Haijo Jan Westra, ed., *The Commentary on Martianus Capella's De Nuptiis
Philologiae et Mercurii Attributed to Bernard Silvestris* 5.424–54, 11.30–62 (Toronto:
Pontifical Institue of Mediaeval Studies, 1986), pp. 107–08, 246–47.

[33] Ibid., 6.420–30, p. 143.

[34] Ibid., 6.508–48, pp. 146–47.

[35] Ibid., 8.311–17, p. 183.

[36] Ibid., 8.991–1025, pp. 205–06. The quotation is at 8.1025, p. 206.

original ideas of his own.[37] Framing his discussion as a commentary
on Genesis, he begins by comparing Genesis with other books of the
Old Testament and analogizes their arrangement with the books of
the Roman law. After discussing prophesy and inspiration as
means of access to the biblical text, Clarenbald offers a proof of
God's existence, as the first cause, and one that might be seen as a
criticism of the *Cosmographia*. Since the universe exists, with its
multiple phenomena, elements, and humors, and since it cannot
have been created by nature itself, or by chance, it requires an
artificer (*artifex*). Since this artificer must be supremely intelligent
and omnipotent, as well as being prior to all else, he cannot have
been a man, or an angel, and must be God.[38] Before going on, it is
worth pointing out that Clarenbald's use of the term *artifex* in no
sense means that he sees creation as the imposition of forms,
whether created or not, on preexistent matter. He is a real creationist and an opponent of theophanic intermediaries. This point will
emerge more clearly below. Second, it is worth noting Clarenbald's
acknowledgement of the existence of angels, and of their status as
intelligent and incorporeal beings. But, having referred to them
here, he proceeds to ignore them in the rest of his commentary.
This is not just because the commentary takes the form of a
hexaemeron and angels are not mentioned in the creation account
in Genesis. It is also a consequence of the fact that none of the
thinkers engaged in the Chartrain project felt a need to discuss
angels or to indicate where beings of this type fit into their understandings of creation. This being the case, Clarenbald's mention of
angels is a teaser for an analysis which he does not provide.

In turning to the creation, after establishing that it derives from
God and from no other power, Clarenbald follows the line of
assigning different parts of the work to different persons of the
Trinity. His argument here resembles Thierry's more than that of
William of Conches, for he omits both William's disclaimers concerning the full collaboration of the persons of the Trinity in
everything They do as well as the power, wisdom and will model
that brought William so much grief. Clarenbald rings two important changes on this theme, in comparison with both of these
masters. He omits reference entirely to the Holy Spirit, confining
himself to the creative activities of the Father and the Son only. As

---

[37] A good introduction is provided by Häring, "The Creation and Creator," pp.
169–81; *Life and Works of Clarenbaldus*, pp. 50–53.

[38] Clarenbald of Arras, *Tractatus super librum Genesis* 9–10, ed. Häring in *Life and
Works*, pp. 229–30.

for the natural functions ascribed by Thierry and William to the *anima mundi*, a force also notable by its absence from Clarenbald's commentary, he retains these functions but reassigns them to the Son and to the seminal reasons. He also re-Augustinizes the seminal reasons, in terms of the scope he grants them. At the same time, he collapses the seminal reasons into the exemplary forms, or vice versa, ignoring the useful distinctions between these two types of formal principles that had been drawn by William of Conches.

In Clarenbald's creation scenario, God the Father retains His role as the creator of primordial matter, which, he agrees, is not coeternal with God, but is created all at once, and which comes into being in a state of pure potentiality (*possibilitas absoluta*).[39] God the Son, for His part, combines in His creative office two functions, both those associated by other members of the school of Chartres with the divine wisdom and those they assign as well to the *anima mundi*. The Son, according to Clarenbald, acts by absolute necessity (*necessitas absoluta*). By this he means that He acts completely alone. The Son is the force that providentially imposes forms on matter, moving it from the state of pure potentiality to the state of fulfillment, in which it can be known by the human mind. In addition, the Son supplies the created substances thereby brought into being with seminal forms. These seminal forms have been present in the mind of God from all eternity.[40] At this point, it would appear that Clarenbald is confusing two ideas which it might be more helpful to consider separately. On the one hand, he regards primordial matter as an entity incapable of being grasped by the human mind because it is lacking in form of any kind. This notion appears to depend on the epistemological assumption that the mind comes to a knowledge of material beings by abstracting their formal components from them. From this point of view, it could be argued that there is a first level of formal determination of matter, when inchoate matter is resolved into the four elements and when these elements are placed in relation to each other, prior to their combination and union with substantial forms, in the creation of individual beings. There is a step in Bernard Silvestris's *Cosmographia* account that addresses this concern. For his part, Clarenbald seems to need such a step in his own scenario, but he does not include one. He moves immediately to the seminal reasons, which are determinations not of primordial matter but of actual creatures.

In identifying the seminal reasons with ideas in the mind of God,

---

[39] Ibid., 17, 38, pp. 233, 242. The quotation is at 17, p. 233.
[40] Ibid., 18–23, pp. 233–36.

Clarenbald follows an Augustinian argument designed to refute the idea that exemplary causes, not seminal causes, are coeternal with God but independent of Him. The same argument is a useful weapon to be wielded against the Eriugenian understanding of exemplary causes as created and creative, posterior to the deity but eternal once brought into being. It is certainly possible to defend the idea that both exemplary causes and seminal reasons are present in the mind of God from all eternity, and that neither of them is put into play until He decides to create the universe. But, if one wants to make this point, it is desirable to do so without ignoring the fact that these two sets of formal principles have two kinds of functions, in Augustine's account. What Clarenbald does, even as he assigns to the Son the task of informing matter, is to impose three duties on the seminal reasons. They take over the *anima mundi*'s task of endowing creatures with their natural aptitudes, enabling them to operate as secondary causes in their own sphere of activity without further recourse to the creator. And, with Augustine, he also sees the seminal reasons as explanations of new kinds of creatures that may arise after the sixth day of creation. Even more so, he agrees with Augustine that the seminal reasons can also explain the capacity of creatures to sustain divine miracles without annulling their natural limits under normal circumstances, and as providing for the supernatural aptitudes of animate beings, in the order of grace.[41] In all these connections, while the Son acts with *necessitas absoluta*, the seminal forms act with a *necessitas complexionis*, that is, they act not completely alone but in conjunction with other beings, natural or supernatural as the case may be.

To sum up, Clarenbald's treatment of creation is, on one level, an effort to avoid snares in which some of his Chartrain brethren became entangled, particularly with reference to the createdness or uncreatedness of the forms, the World Soul, and the Holy Spirit. On another level, it is an effort to go beyond Genesis by showing that the deity, at least in the persons of the Father and the Son, relates Himself to the world in four ways. Prior to and independent of time, He operates formally, in conceiving of the forms of all things, and informally, in the creation of unformed matter. In time, He operates formally, and in two ways, actualizing matter as a state of pure potentiality by informing it, and by endowing the beings so produced, through the seminal reasons, with their capacity to carry out their natural functions. And, also in time, and again through the power of the seminal reasons, He operates so as to

---

[41] Ibid., 28, pp. 338–39.

redeem it, by endowing it with the capacity to function in the supernatural order, as a vehicle of or as a collaborator with divine grace.
Clarenbald's importation of a richer Augustinian understanding of
seminal reasons into his account enables him to provide a more
broadly gauged treatment of God in relation to the creation than is
true of the other Chartrains, even though his elimination of the Holy
Spirit truncates his doctrine of God. He takes a clear stand against
emanationism and created intermediaries as playing any role in the
process of creation. His treatment of the forms accents their uncreated
status and identity with the divine mind, but he is less precise and
helpful than is William of Conches, with his distinction between
archetypal form, on the one hand, and created *formae nativae*, on the
other. Perhaps a larger problem lies in Clarenbald's terminology.
While his distinction between the Son's *necessitas absoluta* and the
neccesitas complexionis of the seminal reasons as causes offers a nice, and
an original, way of differentiating causation at two distinct metaphysical levels, his use of the term *necessitas* in each case bears with it
the disturbing implication that, whichever of these types of causation
is at issue, the causal agent in question acts in response to a
necessity of its own being. This would be to deny to the deity
freedom, and to the creation contingency and free will.

The Response of the Scholastic Theologians

As the theologians of the day confronted the assorted doctrines of
creation issuing from these Chartrain authors, they had good
reason to feel inspired to seek alternatives to them. True, there were
those, such as the Porretans and Roland of Bologna, who may have
been impressed by the intemperate and misinformed outburst of
William of St. Thierry against William of Conches, or who had no
temperamental inclination to explore the alleged compatibilities
between Plato's *Timaeus* and Genesis, or who had no real interest in
creation as a subject or in the debates it had occasioned in the
exegetical and patristic traditions. For the Porretans, it was sufficient to denounce "the philosophers" who say that the three
principles of creation are matter, form, and the demiurge and to
substitute the assertion that the principles of creation are the
Father, Son, and Holy Spirit, and that God creates everything *ex
nihilo*, without offering any explanation or elaboration on that
statement.[42] Roland is not hostile, but merely unenthusiastic.

---

[42] Nikolaus M. Häring, ed., "Die *Sententie magistri Gisleberti Pictavensis episcopi* I"
13.2, *AHDLMA* 45 (1978): 162.

Although he draws on Augustine's Genesis commentaries, he uses them to raise more cosmological question than he has any interest in trying to answer. The only remotely physical issue he addresses is what the term "day" means in the Genesis account. Since it was impossible to have "days" in the literal sense of the word before the heavenly bodies were created, he suggests that it should be read metaphorically.[43] This mild flicker of intellectual curiosity is the exception that proves the rule in a description of creation that is as abbreviated as it is jejune.

But there were other theologians left unsatisfied by the Chartrain project, for other reasons. Some of them were sensitive to the internal contradictions within the Chartrain accounts, both individually and collectively. Some could see the philosophical and theological problems which the Chartrain positions bore in their train. There is also the undeniable fact that there were issues which the theologians regarded as important, or controversial, or necessary to discuss, which did not figure in the Chartrains' writings, or which did so in a deeply problematic way. Angels, for instance, are mentioned in the school of Chartres only by Clarenbald of Arras, and by him only in passing. Angels, however, were a subject which the theologians felt a pressing need to debate. True, their metaphysical status and the question of when they had been created were of interest. But the prime concerns of the theologians here were the fall of the angels and the confirmation in evil and good of those who had rebelled and remained loyal to God, as well as the functions and missions of angels in the economy of salvation. But, before one could proceed to discuss these matters, it was necessary to stake out a terrain in the scheme of creation where the angels could be positioned. The hexaemeral tradition offered no guidance here. Neither did the Chartrains. Even more alarming was the comparative disinterest of the Chartrains in man, the crown of creation, and the hinge on which everything else in a systematic theology would have to turn. The only Chartrain to have devoted extended attention to the creation and nature of man was Bernard Silvestris. To be sure, the allegorical trappings attached to his account might not be pleasing to every taste. But more disquieting and unacceptable still was his relentlessly naturalistic understanding of this subject. Moreover, even among those Chartrains who wrote commentaries on Genesis as a vehicle for their teaching,

---

[43] Roland of Bologna, *Die Sentenzen Rolands*, ed. Ambrosius M. Gietl (Amsterdam: Editions Rodopi, 1969 [repr. of Freiburg im Breisgau: Herder, 1891 ed.]), pp. 104–10.

creation was the whole story. Those Chartrains who took the trouble to usher man onto the stage were not interested in his fall and its consequences, topics which any responsible theologian felt impelled to treat. So, not only did the Chartrains' own works suffer from internal difficulties, their coverage of subjects which the theologians felt a need to address was woefully inadequate. And, the theological tradition, which the Chartrains largely ignored, itself supplied a wealth of debated issues related to the creation which required sorting out as well, a point quite evident from the consideration of those twelfth-century theologians who tackled the creation well before it became necessary to respond, in one way or another, to the Chartrain challenge.

Even in as lapidary, as unspeculative, and as unscholastic an early twelfth-century theologian as Honorius Augustodunensis one catches a sense of the questions which the patristic and more recent theological tradition had posed concerning creation, which mid-century theologians would find a continuing need to consider, and then some. It is not Honorius's technique to display the conflicts of authorities openly, or even to name the authorities he uses to anchor his own opinions. But the questions he takes up, however abruptly he treats them, are the tips of massive theological icebergs in one form or another. He raises seven major points. First, he notes that God had the plan of creation in mind before He reified it phenomenally.[44] Honorius follows Augustine here, although without framing the issue in terms of exemplary forms, which, as we have seen, could be done and had been done by Augustine and others. Next, Honorius notes that God "speaks" to create, an observation derived from the rhetoric of the creation account in Genesis and one that leads Honorius to state that this is the sense in which the Father creates everything in the Word.[45] Here, too, the point suggests a range of amplifications on the Son as the Logos of the creation that invites theological no less than philosophical reflection. Honorius agrees with the idea of creation *simul* although, following Hilary of Poitiers here, he maintains that God organized and assigned creatures to their places during the next six days.[46] Hilary was by no means the only authority to offer an opinion here, and the views of Augustine, Gregory, Isidore of Seville, and Bede

---

[44] Honorius Augustodunensis, *Elucidarium* 1.15, ed. Yves Lefèvre in *L'Elucidarium et les lucidaires: Contribution par l'histoire d'une texte à l'histoire des croyances religieuses en France au moyen âge* (Paris: É. de Boccard, 1954), p. 363.

[45] Ibid., 1.16, p. 364.

[46] Ibid., 1.20, p. 364.

received considerable attention from the theologians as well.

Another question Honorius raises is why God created animals, both as such and also disgusting or pestiferous animals such as insects and worms. In addressing the first part of the question he opines that, foreknowing that man would fall and that fallen man would needs be carnivorous, God created animals, although He intended men to be vegetarian in their prelapsarian state. While perhaps intriguing to those moderns who see eating lower on the food chain as morally virtuous and ecologically responsible, this question bears in its train a host of other reflections in which Honorius does not indulge, but which interested the church fathers, on the physical differences in human nature brought about by the fall. The problem of the insects and worms, on which, as both questioner and respondent, he draws on Ambrose's *Hexaemeron* and Augustine's Genesis commentaries, affords an opportunity for him to indulge in a mini-theodicy and an assertion of the intrinsic goodness of the entire creation,[47] themes orchestrated more fully elsewhere by the ancients and moderns. Honorius is also interested in Eden. He feels quite certain of its location, in Hebron, and also of the propriety of describing it under the classical literary topos of the *locus amoenissimus*.[48] On both counts, the subject was controversial. Winding up with man, Honorius's last two questions raise matters of considerable speculative interest. Why was man created? In Honorius's view, and here he supports Anselm of Canterbury against the authority of Augustine, God did not create human beings to make up the number of the fallen angels.[49] Not all theologians agreed. As his final point, about man, and this is one which, thanks to Isidore of Seville, he develops more elaborately than anyone else in his generation in an argument that fell on attentive ears later in the century, Honorius states that man is the microcosm. He is a combination of matter and spirit. Moreover, his body is made up of the four elements and can be analogized with the physical universe with respect to his organs, senses, and humors. Not only that, man is the microcosm because ADAM is an acronym of the cardinal points on the compass.[50] This, too, is a

---

[47] Ibid., 1.66–67, pp. 372–73.

[48] Ibid., 1.68–69, p. 373.

[49] Ibid., 1.57, p. 371. For the debate on this subject in the twelfth century, see Marie-Dominique Chenu, *La théologie au douzième siècle* (Paris: J. Vrin, 1957), pp. 52–61.

[50] Honorius, *Eluc.* 1.58–64, pp. 371–72. The richness of Honorius's exposition of the microcosm theme, by early twelfth-century standards, has been signaled by Lefèvre, p. 115 n. 1.

subject rich in speculative possibilities on which the theological tradition had much to offer, a tradition which the successors of Honorius in Peter Lombard's generation could legitimately feel had been marginalized or ignored by the Chartrains, however accommodating they might be toward those Chartrain doctrines that they might feel were worth trying to salvage.

A good example of a theologian who was well aware of the Chartrain project and responsive to some of its concerns, while at the same time interested in speaking to a number of the theological issues which the Chartrains failed to address, is Peter Abelard. He is also responsive to some of the debates on creation inherited from the patristic tradition, and from the exegetical tradition as well. While there is passing mention of one or two points relative to creation in his *Theologia "scholarium"*, Abelard addresses this subject most fully not in connection with systematic theology but in his *Hexaemeron*, a work written fairly late in his career and in response to a request from Heloise and her nuns, who sought his help in their understanding of the creation account in Genesis. The audience for which this work was written may perhaps account for the way Abelard approaches his task here. As commentators have noted, he adopts a rather conservative mainstream hermeneutical method, closely modeled on that of Augustine's *De genesi ad litteram*, being, if anything, rather more literal in his reading of the text than Augustine is. And, in considering issues raised by both Augustine and the Chartrains, he tends to follow the former rather than the latter.[51]

Abelard composed the *Hexaemeron* during the same period in which he was making the final or semi-final revisions of the *Theologia "scholarium"*. Yet, on a couple of key points, his doctrine of creation in the exegetical work has to be seen as more fully and circumspectly developed, even though he does not import it into the most mature version of his theology. Abelard holds that there is a two-stage process in the creation. First, God creates the four elements out of nothing. There is no preexisting matter. Then, God imposes order on this matter. In the account given in the *Theologia "scholarium"*, Abelard comes as close as he gets to the Chartrains by

---

[51] Good orientations are provided by Eileen Kearney, "Peter Abelard as Biblical Commentator: A Study of the Expositio in Hexaemeron," in *Petrus Abaelardus (1079–1142): Person, Werk und Wirkung*, ed. Rudolph Thomas (Trier: Paulinus-Verlag, 1980), pp. 199–210; Mary Foster Romig, intro. to her ed., "A Critical Edition of Peter Abelard's 'Expositio in Hexaemeron'," University of Southern California Ph.D. diss., 1981, pp. xvii–xlvii; J. G. Sikes, *Peter Abailard* (Cambridge: Cambridge University Press, 1932), pp. 132–44; Richard F. Weingart, *The Logic of Divine Love: A Critical Analysis of the Soteriology of Peter Abailard* (Oxford: Clarendon Press, 1970), pp. 30–35.

assigning to the Son and the Holy Spirit different functions in this
ordering process. In that work, he describes the Son as equivalent
to the exemplary causes in the mind of God, with which matter is
informed in the creation; he gives to the Holy Spirit the role of
providing the natural laws that endow creatures with their natural
capacities.[52] In the *Theologia "scholarium"*, as in Abelard's earlier
theologies, this account is muddied by his lack of clarity concerning
the equatability of these two persons of the Trinity with the Platonic Nous and World Soul as emanations, and by the question,
which his economic approach to the Trinity raises, of whether these
persons participate in the substance of created beings. In his
Hexaemeron, on the other hand, when Abelard addresses this second
stage of creation in which matter is formed and disposed, he speaks
only of the forms as divine ideas. He backs off from the definition of
them as the Logos, as second person of the Trinity, or as archetypes
whose relationship to the deity's eternity and exclusive creativity
needs to be explained. At the same time, he distinguishes between
the primordial forms in the mind of God and the forms which are
actually united with matter to produce created substances. These
latter forms, as well as matter, are created, he states.[53] In this way,
he preserves the deity's transcendence, but without clarifying the
relationship between the one level of forms and the other. In the
Hexaemeron, as well, Abelard takes another prudent step. The Holy
Spirit and World Soul alike vanish from the scene as the force of
nature endowing created beings with their natural capacities. Nor
does Abelard call upon seminal reasons, in either the Chartrain or
the purely Augustinian sense, to perform this function. Instead, he
assigns it to a power which he simply calls the force of nature (*vis
naturae*), which avoids the problems of possible misunderstanding
evoked by these other two terms. This language appears to have
been original to Abelard.[54]

   If Abelard shows a selective use of Augustine thus far, this trait is
also visible in his handling of other features of his creation account.
He is not interested in the question of creation *simul*, either in the
form in which it was taught by Augustine or any of the other
patristic or later authorities, or in the form which it was given by
some of his contemporaries. It is not that Abelard disagrees with
any of these theories overtly. He simply does not take the question

---

[52] Peter Abelard, *Theologia "scholarium"* 1.37, 2.172–73, ed. Constant J. Mews,
CCCM 13 (Turnhout: Brepols, 1987), pp. 333, 491–92.
[53] Peter Abelard, *Hexaemeron*, ed. Romig, pp. 10–11, 24–25.
[54] Ibid., pp. 14–15, 51–54. For Abelard's originality here, see Romig, intro., pp.
xxiv, xlvii–xlviii.

up at all, proceeding to the organization of creatures according to the hexaemeral plan. Nor is he interested in the question of whether the "days" in Genesis should be understood in anything but the literal sense.[55] At the same time, he is content to let man remain in his traditional biblical location in the creation on the sixth day. Abelard emerges as a strong supporter of Augustine as an opponent of astral determinism in his treatment of the creation of the heavenly bodies, drawing on the *City of God* here as well as on Augustine's Genesis commentaries. With Augustine, he argues that the movements of the heavenly bodies are indeed determined themselves, by the laws of nature that govern them, but that they do not control the fortunes of men or limit the contingencies that occur elsewhere in the universe.[56] The other physical issue of a speculative nature that Abelard raises is whether plants have souls. Here, he introduces a range of opinions on all sides, reviews them carefully, and eventually declares that it is impossible to make a positive determination of the question. While leaving it an open one, he points out that his doctrine of *vis naturae* makes it possible to explain the behavior of plants whether they have souls or not.[57]

While Abelard indicates the theologian's strong interest in devoting a major section of the *Hexaemeron* to the subject of man, most of what he has to say on it is devoted to the fall, and we will take it up under that heading later in the present chapter. He has remarkably little to say on the question of why man was created and what human nature was like before the fall. He contents himself with noting that man was given an immortal soul made in God's image, and that he possessed goodness in the sense that all created things are good.[58] But, and this reflects his major departure from his Augustinian model, his chief goal in explaining the creation in general, and the creation of man in particular, is not to defend the goodness of the physical world or to propose a theodicy. As Abelard sees it, God creates man and makes him the crown of creation out of love for man and in order to manifest His own glory.[59] The entire account of creation that he has provided in the *Hexaemeron* is designed to move the reader to penance for the sin that led to the loss of paradise. Abelard's inquiry here, and this may well refer back to the monastic readers for whom he writes, is ultimately a moral and not a scientific or speculative one.

---

[55] Peter Abelard, *Hex.*, p. 11.
[56] Ibid., pp. 55–60.
[57] Ibid., pp. 51–55.
[58] Ibid., pp. 71, 85.
[59] Ibid., p. 69.

This fact, in addition to the scanting or omitting of topics which theologians wanted to investigate more fully in connection with the creation, and the fact that Abelard's doctrine of creation is dealt with in a separate treatise and not coordinated with the enterprise of systematic theology, may well account for the lack of resonance which Abelard's *Hexaemeron* had among the scholastics of his time. With the exception of Roland of Bologna, none of Abelard's disciples took up the subject of the creation. So, the Abelardian trail ends here. Much more important, as efforts to address both the issues raised by the Chartrains and by the patristic tradition in this period were the works of Hugh of St. Victor, the author of the *Summa sententiarum*, and Robert of Melun. These efforts are massive, if not entirely successful, and they constitute the major models which Peter Lombard used, approved, or weighed in the balance and found wanting.

It has been generally acknowledged that Hugh of St. Victor was familiar with the Platonic doctrine of creation in the *Timaeus* as well as the interpretations being given to it by the Chartrains active up through his time, and that he was basically unsympathetic to this entire proposal. Instead, he posits God alone, not the demiurge, matter, and form as the principle of creation. To the extent that he invokes any Platonic terminology here it is used as a rhetorical embellishment. Decorating the idea that man's soul is spread evenly through his body, Hugh may invoke the notion of the World Soul as ubiquitous in the world. Or, describing Christ as the perfect moral exemplar and chief instigator of man's redemption, he may refer to Him as an archetype. But this does not mean that Hugh is associating himself with the Chartrain project. Quite the reverse is the case. His directionality is a different one. Man's redemption, not cosmology, is his focus.[60] And, while he certainly displays a keen interest in trying to find alternatives to some of the speculation of the Chartrains, reviving, for example, the Augustinian version of the doctrine of creation *simul*, he treats the Genesis account from a narratological perspective in the light of what man can learn about God from it and not as a literal statement of how the world

---

[60] Noted by Gregory, *Anima mundi*, pp. 47–48; Christian Schütz, *Deus absconditus, Deus manifestus: Die Lehre Hugos von St. Viktor über die Offenbarung Gottes* (Rome: Herder, 1967), pp. 130–62; Jerome Taylor, intro. to his trans. of Hugh of St. Victor, *Didascalicon* (New York: Columbia University Press, 1961), pp. 22–29; Winthrop Wetherbee, *Platonism and Poetry in the Twelfth Century: The Literary Influence of the School of Chartres* (Princeton: Princeton University Press, 1972), pp. 32, 49–62.

was created.[61] His emphasis throughout is not scientific but sacramental, in the broad Hugonian sense of that term.

In obtaining the objectives he seeks, Hugh is hampered here by two main problems, terminological and organizational. He uses certain terms necessary for the discussion of creation, attaching several meanings to them, without indicating which sense is to be understood in a particular context. A good example of such a key term is *natura*.[62] Sometimes Hugh means by "nature" the archetype, or the exemplar of all things residing in the mind of God and serving as the model He uses when each created being is informed. There are difficulties in his handling of just this definition itself. Hugh opens his *De sacramentis* with what reads as a reprise of the *Periphyseon* of John Scottus Eriugena, locating the exemplars or primordial causes at John's second level of nature, the created and creative. Hugh makes this point, however, in the same breath in which he states that God alone is the creator.[63] And, in the *Didascalicon*, Hugh calls this primordial pattern the divine idea that creates rational beings without intermediaries, identifying it with Christ as the Logos.[64] Further, shortly after Hugh's first assertion in the *De sacramentis*, he observes that the primordial causes are uncreated.[65] This effort to come to grips with the exemplars fails miserably. The reader is left in the dark as to whether Hugh thinks they are created or uncreated, sharers of God's creative power or not, identical with the divine mind, above it, below it, or equal to it as the second person of the Trinity. "Nature" understood as archetypal causation alone thus spreads confusion in its wake. But Hugh also uses this term in the generic Boethian sense of the characteristics proper to a being of whatever sort, which differentiate it from other beings. He also uses "nature" to mean the creative fire (*ignis artifex*) which, in turn, is the power imparted to created beings enabling them to

---

[61] Gross, "Twelfth-Century Concepts," pp. 325–28; A. Mignon, *Les origines de la scolastique et Hugues de Saint-Victor*, 2 vols. (Paris: P. Lethielleux, 1895), 1: 321–28.

[62] Noted by Erich Barkholt, *Die Ontologie Hugos von St. Viktor*, Inaugural-Dissertation, University of Bonn, 1930, pp. 19–20; Roger Baron, "L'Idée de la nature chez Hugues de Saint-Victor," in *La filosofia della natura nel medioevo* (Milan: Vita e Pensiero, 1966), pp. 260–63; Philippe Delhaye, "La nature dans l'oeuvre de Hugues de Saint-Victor" in ibid., pp. 272–78.

[63] Hugh of St. Victor, *De sacramentis fidei christianae* 1.2.2–3, 1.5.4–5, *PL* 176: 206C–207D, 248C–249B.

[64] Hugh of St. Victor, *Didascalicon: De studio legendi* 1.1, 1.4, 1.5, appendix C, ed. Charles Henry Buttimer (Washington: Catholic University of America, 1939), pp. 4, 11, 12, 134–35.

[65] Hugh of St. Victor, *De sac.* 1.4.26, *PL* 176: 246B–C. Barkholt, *Die Ontologie*, p. 11 sees uncreated primordial causes as the only type of primordial causes to which Hugh refers.

accomplish the generation of other created beings, with a sense
more restricted than, but analogous to, the *vis naturae* of Abelard.

Organizational problems also plague Hugh's account of creation, as we saw above in chapter 2, where the schematic confusion
in the first part of Book 1 of the *De sacramentis* was noted.[66] This
confusion stems from Hugh's uncertainty as to whether to follow
the creation account in Genesis in his own table of contents. He
advocates this idea because he claims that it reflects the way man
comes to a knowledge of the creator through the creation. But, at
the same time, the Genesis account says nothing about exemplary
causes, which he feels a need to treat even if he does so unsuccessfully, and spiritual beings such as angels. Hugh does not choose
between hierarchy and hexaemeron as his organizational principle;
he tries to combine them. And so, he starts with the exemplary
causes. Whether they are uncreated or created, they come first. As
for angels, Hugh states that they were created before the emergence of
the visible world.[67] At the same time, he says that primordial matter
was the first thing to be created,[68] which would put it ahead of angels
and created causes, if any. Hugh devotes a great deal of space to the
repetition of these conflicting claims, more space, indeed, than he
assigns to the phenomenal order next on his agenda. One has the
sense that he has recourse to the doctrine of creation *simul* more as an
effort to vaporize this problem of priority than as a means of resolving
the physical discrepancies in the account of the visible creation in
Genesis, as was the case with Augustine.[69]

If, on the one side, the Chartrain approach to creation serves as
an agenda with which Hugh wants to disagree and for which he
wants to find substitutes, Anselm of Laon and his disciples serve as
the main contemporary theologians with whom he wants to take
issue, on the other. The one and only point on which Hugh agrees
with the Laon masters is the idea that matter is not eternal.[70] In
other respects the Laon masters take a rather different tack in
treating the sequence in which the creation occurred. Rather than
trying to coordinate the idea of creation *simul* with the literal
hexaemeral account in Genesis, they reject both of these principles

---

[66] See above, pp. 57–62.
[67] Hugh of St. Victor, *De sac.* 1.1.2, 1.1.4–11, 1.1.13–30, *PL* 176: 187C–188B,
189C–195C, 197B–206A.
[68] Ibid., 1.5.2–3, 1.5.6, *PL* 176: 247A–248C, 249C.
[69] Ibid., 1.5.4–5, *PL* 176: 249B.
[70] Anselm of Laon, *Sententie divine pagine* 4, ed. Franz P. Bliemetzrieder in *Anselms
von Laon systematische Sentenzen*, Beiträge, 18:2–3 (Münster: Aschendorff, 1919),
p. 11.

in favor of a hierarchical account of creation. While he and his disciples ignore the issue of exemplary causes, Anselm follows Bede in urging that the Genesis account should be read not literally but figuratively (*propter figuram*).[71] Dispensing specifically with the concept of creation *simul* in whatever form it had been advocated, Anselm and his followers think it is logical to hold that spiritual beings were created first, with the hierarchy of creation descending from the more rarefied of them on down to material beings. Hence, angels were created first, emerging in accordance with the Gregorian hierarchy of nine orders, with the seraphim on top. Next, human souls were created by God, and then the lesser beings.[72] Hugh's attempt to salvage both creation *simul* and the six-day account does not fare very well as a critique of this logically and ontologically coherent departure from the patristic exegetical tradition on the part of the Laon masters.

Hugh next moves to the creation of man, more interesting to him in any case than the perplexities attending the physical world. Here, too, he finds himself in opposition to the school of Laon. Just as that school does not hesitate to reject tradition on the sequence of the creation, so too Anselm feels free to jettison the Augustinian opinion that man was created to make up the numbers of the fallen angels. While agreeing here with Honorius and with Anselm of Canterbury against Augustine, he does not cite any of the authorities on the opposite side of the debate and does not indicate his reasons for the position he takes.[73] Hugh stoutly rejects this view and sides with Augustine.[74] While making up the numbers of the fallen angels would presumably be a sufficient reason for the creation of man, in Hugh's estimation it is not the only reason. He agrees with Abelard in stating that God created man to display His benevolence.[75] But the most compelling reason is that, by knowing, serving, and loving God man may attain beatitude.[76] Hugh has two

---

[71] Ibid., 4, p. 12.

[72] Ibid., 4; *Sententie Anselmi* 2, ed. Franz P. Bliemetzrieder in *Anselms von Laon systematische Sentenzen*, pp. 13–14, 49; *Sentences of the School of Laon*, no. 308, ed. Odon Lottin in *Psychologie et morale aux XIIe et XIIIe siècles* vols. 1–5 (Louvain: Abbaye de Mont-César, 1948–59), 5: 244; *Deus de cuius principio et fine tacetur*, ed. Heinrich Weisweiler in "Le recueil des sentences 'Deus de cuius principio et fine tacetur' et son remaniement," *RTAM* 5 (1933): 260.

[73] Anselm of Laon, *Sent. divine pagine* 4, p. 15.

[74] Hugh of St. Victor, *De sac.* 1.5.33–34, *PL* 176: 262A–264A. This view is also followed by Roland of Bologna, *Sent.*, pp. 270–71; *Summa magistri Rolandi* c. 27, ed. Friedrich Thaner (Aalen: Scientia Verlag, 1962 [repr. of Innsbruck, 1874 ed.]), pp. 113–14.

[75] Hugh of St. Victor, *De sac* 1.6.1, *PL* 176: 263B.

[76] Ibid., 1.2.1, *PL* 176: 205B–206C.

other major points to make about the creation of man. Man was given a body as well as a soul in order to show that, in and through man, both aspects of the created universe would be elevated to share God's glory.[77] And, finally, he argues that we cannot know exactly when the human soul was created. All we can know is that it was created after the angels had come into being and after the formation of the human body into which it is infused. The soul is not preexistent and is created *ex nihilo*. At the very moment of its creation, Adam's soul was joined to his body.[78] In claiming that we cannot know when this event takes place, Hugh here seems to be refusing the help which the hexaemeral account, which he is trying to salvage as much as he can, might plainly offer. This last point is an index of the difficulties he gets into by trying to do everything at once.

For his part, the author of the *Summa sententiarum* leads off with a ringing denunciation of Platonism: "As Plato said, there are three principles [of creation], matter, form, and the demiurge. But the Catholic faith believes that there was one principle, one cause of all things, namely God" (*Cum Plato dixerit tria esse principia: materiam, formam, opificem; fides Catholica unum principium credit esse omnium rerum causa fuit, Deus scilicet*).[79] Unlike the Porretans, who hold the same position and decline to expatiate on creation, he follows Hugh's effort to do so. He also recapitulates Hugh's notion that the animate creation was brought into being so that man could know, love, and serve the creator and hence be glorified, and that man's combination of body and soul draws the whole universe into this process.[80] At the same time, he offers a more effective way of combining the hierarchical and hexaemeral principles. Perhaps seeing in Hugh's handling of primordial causes in the *De sacramentis* a cautionary tale, he omits them at this juncture. As his initial topic he takes up primordial matter, yoking it with the creation of angels. The angels and the four elements, he states, were created *ex nihilo* and at the same time.[81] This constitutes the only simultaneity he is willing to concede in the creation. Without arguing the point pro and con, he simply drops the question of creation *simul* after this point. Something he adds, however, and to which he gives sustained and cogent treatment is the question of how angels are different in their nature from the deity, although he takes it up not

---

[77] Ibid., 1.6.2, *PL* 176: 264C–D.
[78] Ibid., 1.6.3, *PL* 176: 264D–265B.
[79] *Summa sententiarum* 2.1, *PL* 176: 79C.
[80] Ibid., *PL* 176: 79C–80C.
[81] Ibid., *PL* 176: 81A–B.

in his treatise on angels in Book 2 of his *Summa* but in Book 1, under the heading of God. The deity, he notes there, is immutable and unconditioned by time and space. Like God, angels are spiritual beings and, like God, they are incorporeal and hence share His inability to be conditioned by space. But, once brought into being, they are conditioned by time, and they are changeable, capable of being moved by affections, such as joy or sadness, and capable of learning what they did not know. Also, while they are able to inhabit bodies in connection with their duties, they lack the divine attribute of ubiquity.[82] Helpful as these remarks are, they would have been even more serviceable had the author included them in his treatise on angels.

Between angels and men, the author presents a very swift summary of the creation, reverting here to the hexaemeral model and displaying little interest in coming to grips with the physical discrepancies presented in the Genesis account. With respect to various creatures he offers a range of opinions, without choosing among them. Or, he urges one opinion as more probable, but without explaining why. He is clearly not inspired by this part of the assignment and disposes of it in two brief chapters, getting it out of the way so that he can concentrate on his real subject, the creation, fall, and restoration of man.[83]

Considering his interest in man, the author has remarkably little to say about man's nature as such, except duly to report that the human soul is made in God's image, as can be seen in the Trinitarian analogies it bears.[84] The main topic that exercises him before he proceeds to the fall is the creation of Eve. Here is where he raises, somewhat belatedly, the subject of primordial causes and seminal reasons, although he does not give the latter this name expressly. After noting that Eve's creation from Adam's rib provides a type of the church born of the blood and water issuing from the side of the crucified Christ, a point he shares with Roland of Bologna[85] which goes beyond the standard Augustinian reason other theologians give concerning the marital companionship symbolized by this mode of engendering Eve, he agrees with Augustine's theory of primordial causes as ideas in the mind of God, not separate from Him or prior or posterior to Him. These causes are not created agencies. They are to be distinguished from the causes

---

[82] Ibid., 1.5, *PL* 176: 50C–51A.
[83] Ibid., 3.1–2, *PL* 176: 89A–91A.
[84] Ibid., 3.2, *PL* 176: 91A–92B.
[85] Roland of Bologna, *Sent.*, pp. 110–16.

inserted by God into individual creatures, enabling them to reproduce naturally and also to be the vehicles of miracles. It is this
latter point, the capacity of created beings to function as the
vehicles of miracles, which serves as the link between this topic and
the creation of Eve and which explains why the author brings up
these causes in that context. Adam's body was endowed with the
capacity to function as the instrument of a miracle, the creation of
Eve's body from his rib. Eve's soul, like all human souls, was
created by God.[86] Now, this understanding of seminal reasons is, to
be sure, helpful here. The project of the author of the *Summa
sententiarum* in handling the creation account would have been
better served, in general, had he introduced this discussion of
primordial and seminal causes earlier on, perhaps just prior to the
creation of the angels in the hierarchical portion of his second book.
Had he done so, he would have laid the foundation for the explanation of Eve's creation, which he provides in Book 3, and which
requires him to backpedal in his exposition of it. If his handling of
the creation of Eve is unusual in that respect, it is also *sui generis* in
that this is the only question concerning Eve that he raises at all.
He omits, for instance, the more basic issue of why Eve was created
in the first place.

A third mid-century theologian who, like the author of the *Summa
sententiarum*, is strongly influenced by Hugh of St. Victor and who,
like both of those masters, seeks to offer a cogent alternative to the
Chartrain approach to creation, which he clearly dislikes, is Robert
of Melun. Robert takes a much more systematically hexaemeral
line than either of these two authors. He is a strong proponent of
the Augustinian theory of creation *simul*, both before the event and
in the event. At the same time, he seeks to connect this doctrine to
the theme of causation that bulks so large in his treatment of the
deity. Rejecting both the idea of exemplary causes, the idea of
preexistent matter or form of any kind, and the notion that there
are any creative intermediaries between God and the world, he
stresses that God is the first cause and the only cause of creation,
against both Plato and Aristotle.[87] The forms as well as the matter
are created, according to Robert. Instead of a threefold principle of
creation, he puts forward a single creator who creates everything all

---

[86] *Summa sent.* 3.3, *PL* 176: 93A–94B.
[87] Robert of Melun, *Sententie* 1.1.19, 1.1.20, 1.2.1, ed. Raymond-M. Martin in
Robert of Melun, *Oeuvres*, 4 vols. (Louvain: Spicilegium Sacrum Lovaniense,
1932–52), 3 part 1: 210–12, 223, 263. On this point, cf. Ulrich Horst, *Die Trinitäts-
und Gotteslehre des Robert von Melun* (Mainz: Matthias-Grünewald Verlag, 1964), pp.
84–85.

at once by a threefold operation, "in the creation of the unformed material substratum of material things, in the formation of creatures, and in the disposition of what has been formed" (*in omnium informi creatione, in creatorum formatione, in formatorum dispositione*).[88] As with Augustine, Robert emphasizes the point that God brought time itself into existence at the same moment in which He created everything else. This notion makes it impossible to hold that there is a sequence of any kind in creation. But it does not mean that God's manifestation of His simultaneous creation in time, or His own subsequent action in time or with time, refers to a creation that was initally imperfect and that was perfected later on. Here, Robert draws a useful distinction among things that are perfect according to their nature, such as a baby born with all his fingers and toes; things that are perfect according to time, such as the same baby grown to adulthood, having realized all his capacities as an adult; and things that are perfect universally. Only God, Who is not subject to development, is perfect in the third sense. But this does not detract from the perfection, in the first two senses, of creatures that can and do change.[89] This analysis deftly resolves the dilemmas in which Hugh embroils himself in the handling of exemplary causes and simultaneous creation.

On the other hand, Robert is less adept in dealing with the cosmological and physical problems in which the Genesis account of creation abounds. He expressly repudiates the natural philosophers (*physici*) but does not make effective use of the help available in the patristic tradition in sorting out these inconsistencies. In some cases where he has a clear preference for one opinion over another, as in the composition of the stars as fiery in makeup and as similar, in this respect, to the sun, where he follows Plato, he offers no reasons for preferring this view over its alternatives.[90] Most of the time, as with the question of why the waters above the firmament stay up there and do not fall down, he cites a range of opinions without indicating a need to choose among them.[91] Robert's disinterest in answering most of the cosmological questions which he raises makes the reader wonder why he raises them in the first place. Like Hugh, his main concern is to extract moral and spiritual significance from these natural phenomena; regardless of why the waters above the firmament stay there, they stand

---

[88] Robert of Melun, *Sent.* 1.1.19, *Oeuvres*, 3 part 1: 210. On God's creation of form as well as matter, see also 1.1.21–23, 3 part 1: 224–30.
[89] Ibid., 1.1.19–20, *Oeuvres*, 3 part 1: 213–21, 223.
[90] Ibid., 1.1.28, *Oeuvres*, 3 part 1: 245.
[91] Ibid., 1.1.25, *Oeuvres*, 3 part 1: 235–37.

for the higher forms of charity, he concludes.[92] And, in the case of
his other example, he takes up the nature of the stars primarily to
join Abelard in a long Augustinian attack against astral
determinism.[93] The detailed chapter headings which Robert supplies in his *Sentences* indicate that he planned to devote extensive
attention to the nature of man before the fall, concentrating on his
soul, and that he planned to offer a lengthy treatise on original sin,
and he does so. But his treatment of the creation of man is remarkably truncated. He reprises the position of the *Summa sententiarum*
and of Hugh in stating that man was created to know, serve, and
love God and hence to win beatitude. This point leads him into a
digression which in turn leads him to end his discussion of the
creation of man on a peculiar note. Having observed that man's
beatitude is God's objective in creating him, Robert acknowledges
that not all men attain beatitude. Does this mean that God's
intentions, with respect to those men who are not saved, are
fraudulent or frustrated? No, he answers, since beatitude can be
gained only with man's free will and cooperation.[94] This may be the
case, but his answer is not responsive to the question he has posed
and it does not address the vexing issue of what purpose is served
by the creation of those human beings who will not be saved. If his
account of creation is problematic when it comes to most of the
natural phenomena he discusses and when it comes to man, the
most serious deficiency in Robert's presentation of this subject is
his omission of angels. This is a decision on his part that reflects his
desire to follow the hexaemeral model strictly. But it leaves a gap in
his analysis of the created universe which mid-century theology
found unacceptable.

The theologians discussed above are the only ones worth treating
in detail as a backdrop for Peter Lombard on the creation, since
they are the ones who set the agenda in this period. None of the
other masters at work in his time offers any fresh or additional
insights or announces any new problems. Other than giving the
same reason as Hugh, Robert, and the author of the *Summa sententiarum* for the creation of man as an opportunity on his part to
know, love, and glorify God,[95] the only contribution made to this
subject by the author of the *Sententiae divinitatis* is to lay out and

---

[92] Ibid., 1.1.27–28, *Oeuvres*, 3 part 1: 239–43.
[93] Ibid., 1.1.28, *Oeuvres*, 3 part 1: 246–56.
[94] Ibid., 1.1.30, *Oeuvres*, 3 part 1: 259–62.
[95] Bernhard Geyer, ed., *Die Sententiae divinitatis: Ein Sentenzenbuch der Gilbertischen Schule* prologus, Beiträge, 7:2–3 (Münster: Aschendorff, 1909), p. 6*.

attribute clearly three of the four prevailing theories of creation *simul*. There is Augustine's view that all creatures were made simultaneously, Gregory's view that God made unformed matter all at once but that He formed it sequentially, and Isidore's view, which agrees with Gregory's, but which adds that the formation of matter took six days. The author omits Bede here while siding with Gregory, adding the Augustinian seminal reasons at the moment when creatures are formed and agreeing with Hugh that the hexaemeral account was written that way for man's instruction.[96] As for Robert Pullen, he is both extremely sketchy and unusually incoherent in handling the creation. He tries to combine the view of creation *simul* with creation in a six-day sequence in which it would make sense to ask when individual creatures came into being.[97] He is both vague and contradictory in treating man. Opposing the idea that man was created to make up the numbers of the fallen angels, he says that the reason was that the universe would have been less perfect without man, but does not explain why he thinks this is the case.[98] In addressing the question of the preexistence of the human soul he confuses it with the question of when the bodies of fetuses become ensouled. Here, he argues that the human soul is added to the body at the point when the body comes into existence. Presumably he means by this the moment of conception. At the same time, however, he supports the rule in Exodus on the penalty for causing a miscarriage, which regards the act as homicide only if the fetus is ensouled and has already moved in the womb, which would take place about five months into the pregnancy.[99] Robert Pullen is not at the top of his form on any of these subjects. Perhaps his most unusual contribution to contemporary discussions of creation is his treatment of Eden. He joins Honorius and the school of Laon in giving a description of it as a classical *locus amoenissimus*, going into far greater detail on this point than anyone else. Robert locates Eden with precision on the banks of the river Nile, commenting in depth on its climate and giving a full catalogue of its flora and fauna. He takes this geographical situation of Eden literally, adding a warning he is unique among his compeers for providing, while suggesting, possibly, that the quest for Eden may have been a motivation inspiring the pilgrims and crusaders now travelling to the east in large numbers. It is impossible, Robert stresses, to

---

[96] Ibid. 1.1.1–3, pp. 8*–12*.
[97] Robert Pullen, *Sententiarum libri octo* 2.1, *PL* 186: 717C–719A.
[98] Ibid., 2.16, *PL* 186: 741D–743B.
[99] Ibid., 2.7, 2.9, *PL* 186: 727B, 731A–733C.

recover Eden. However far and wide the traveller may search, however many seas and deserts he may cross, and with whatever *labor improbus* he may reconnoiter the territories watered by the Nile, he will never find it.[100]

The Lombard on Creation

We are now in a position to assess how Peter Lombard situates himself in the contemporary debates on creation. He certainly can be said to display no sympathy at all for the Chartrain project. He uses the resources of both philosophy and theology to show how and why he finds it misguided. In proposing an alternative approach, he relies heavily on the exegetical and patristic traditions. He shows himself to be thoroughly conversant with the recent treatments of the subject, with which he does not hesitate to agree, or disagree, selectively. There is one feature of Peter's treatment of creation that is, for him, unusual. As Ignatius Brady has pointed out very clearly in his annotations to this part of the *Sentences*, Peter reveals a dependence on intermediary sources, such as patristic *catenae*, that is quite atypical of his methodology more generally. This same fact can be detected from the form of his patristic citations on the subject of creation. While his normal standard is to name the author and the work and to quote or to paraphrase the text cited, exploring the reasoning that has brought the authority to his conclusion, here he merely mentions the authority's name and gives the nub of his opinion. It is certainly true that the authorities he presents in this fashion often have more to say on the questions at issue than Peter indicates. It is not clear why the Lombard departs from his usual working habits in treating the creation. At the same time, and despite the limits in his deployment of his materials in this context, he presents a streamlined and no-nonsense account of creation that is essentially hexaemeral in plan. He takes a firm stand on vexed questions such as exemplary causes and creation *simul* and does not hesitate to reject the Augustinian tradition on these points. Also thoroughly un-Augustinian is his position on why man was created, and his lack of interest in theodicy. In many other areas he uses Augustine, along with other patristic sources, constructively. His creation account shares many of the ideas found in Hugh of St. Victor, the *Summa*

---

[100] Ibid., 2.19, *PL* 186: 746B–747B. The allusion to Vergil's *Georgics* occurs at 747A. Cf. *Sent. Anselmi* 2, p. 58, whose author does not think that he can specify the location of Eden.

sententiarum, and Robert of Melun. But he manages to achieve something that is more than any of these masters accomplishes, an account of creation that fits angels coherently into the picture and that finds a way of combining the hexaemeral plan with both a modified version of creation *simul* and a sense that creatures should be discussed in an order that speaks to the order of their metaphysical constitution.

Peter begins by juxtaposing the idea, which he attributes to Bede and which he intends to support, that there is a single cause of creation, God, with the Platonic notion of three principles, "that is, God, and the exemplar, and matter, and the latter uncreated and without beginning, and God acting like an artisan, not as a creator" (*Deum scilicet, et exemplar, et materiam; et ipsa increata, sine principio, et Deum quasi artificem, non creatorem*).[101] In attacking this claim he plans to reject all three parts of it, starting with the notion of God as *artifex*. A creator is to be distinguished from an artisan in that a creator alone can make things out of nothing, while an artisan makes things out of existing matter. God can do both; but creatures can only do the latter. Aside from that, we can distinguish between creating and making in that human and other created makers must exercise motion, or heat, or some other change in the maker himself in the process, while God creates while remaining totally unchanged.[102] Next, Peter attacks another version of the Chartrain position, which he attributes to Aristotle, the idea that there are three principles of creation, seen as material, formal, and efficient causes, all eternal. It is this erroneous notion which has led some people to accept the eternity of both form and matter, an idea that Peter, along with Robert of Melun, rejects. This same idea, the Lombard observes, has led some people to equate the Holy Spirit with the efficient cause or with the cause that combines form and matter.[103] As the doctrine of God developed in Book 1 of the *Sentences* makes plain, for Peter it is totally unacceptable to divide up the work of creation among the Trinitarian persons since, in the act of creation, it is the divine nature common to the persons that is at work. It is also a divine nature that remains transcendent. It cannot be equated with the forces of nature which it brings into

---

[101] Peter Lombard, *Sententiae in IV libris distinctae* 2. d. 1. c. 1.2, 3rd ed. rev., ed. Ignatius C. Brady, 2 vols. (Grottaferrata: Collegii S. Bonaventurae ad Claras Aquas, 1971–81), 1: 330.

[102] Ibid., c. 2–c. 3.1–3, 1: 330–31. Noted by Newell, "Rationalism at the School of Chartres," p. 121 n. 49.

[103] Peter Lombard, *Sent.* 2. d. 1. c. 3.5, 1: 331. Noted by Bertola, "La dottrina della creazione," pp. 32–33.

being. Peter takes pains to remind his readers of these points, citing John Chrysostom and his own gloss on the Epistle to the Hebrews to undergird it still further.[104]

As he moves to the next item on his agenda, the question of why the creation was brought into being at all, Peter shows the influence of Hugh of St. Victor, and, even more so, of the *Summa sententiarum*, when it comes to the creation of spiritual beings and man, while at the same time he puts his own stamp on the subject. He agrees that God created rational beings so that they could come to a knowledge of the supreme good. In knowing God, they would love Him; in loving Him they would possess Him; and in possessing Him, they would enjoy Him. Praising and serving God would also lead to their enjoyment of Him. Everything else in the world, in turn, was made for man's sake, for man to use and enjoy with the ultimate enjoyment of God in view.[105] Agreeing with the Victorine notion of man's purpose, Peter adds to it a purpose for the other beings in the creation, whether material or spiritual, and connects the whole question to the Augustinian theme of use and enjoyment which he gives to the entire *Sentences*. This analysis also gives him more solid reasons than those supplied by the author of the *Summa sententiarum* for rejecting Hugh and Augustine on men making up the numbers of the fallen angels as the reason for their creation. Although he does not refer to the passages in Augustine's *Enchiridion* and *City of God* where this claim is defended, Peter indicates that he is aware of the Scriptural foundation on which Augustine sought to base it. He argues that Augustine has misconstrued the Bible in drawing this conclusion from the passages in question. So, man was not created to make up the numbers of the fallen angels both because the other positive reasons Peter has cited are the principal ones (*causae praeci-puae*) and because the alleged Scriptural basis of the Augustinian claim never existed (*nonnulla existit*).[106]

There is also another point where Peter corrects or expands on the Victorine legacy before moving on to the six days of creation, his handling of the question of why the human soul was joined to a body. He offers three reasons, the first and third stated straightfor-wardly and the second given more elaborate treatment. The first is that it is God's will, which we cannot question. The third is that, with the body and the mind both serving God, we may more greatly merit the crown of beatitude. The second is the man as

[104] Peter Lombard, *Sent.* 2. d. 13. c. 7.2–5, 1: 394–95.
[105] Ibid., d. 1. c. 4.1–7, 1: 322–33.
[106] Ibid., c. 5, 1: 334.

microcosm argument, although Peter does not use this term expressly. With Hugh and the *Summa sententiarum*, he agrees that, in uniting matter and spirit in man, God enables the whole creation to be glorified in the love of God which man displays. He adds another note to this argument. The intimate communion between mind and body in the human constitution helps man to see how he can commune with a higher spiritual being, and illustrates by analogy the future association of the human soul and God.[107]

Peter's assignment, following this discussion, moves from the why of creation to the when and the how. His chief guides at the outset are the authors of the *Summa sententiarum* and the *Sententiae divinitatis*. With the former, he yokes the creation of the angels to the creation of primordial matter at the beginning of the hexaemeral account. And, with the latter, he rejects Augustine's version of creation *simul* in favor of the principle that the angels and the elements were the only things created all at once. After that, he holds, God produced the other specific created beings in the course of six days. As he develops the second phase of this creation scenario, Peter shares with Robert of Melun the idea that the forms God used were created, no less than the matter, and reimports Augustine's seminal reasons into the story.[108]

In weaving the angels into the limited doctrine of creation *simul* that he defends, Peter introduces two related considerations. One is the felt need to refute the position of Origen, reported by Jerome, Augustine, and John Cassian, that angels existed before the creation of time. Peter's analysis appears to stem from a strong, and generic, desire to attack the more spiritualistic teachings of Origen, an attitude common in this period in itself and as an anti-Catharist tactic, for there was no contemporary *quidam* among the orthodox theologians who took this position. Another view he wants to repudiate is that the angels can be identified with the wisdom created before all creatures, referred to in Ecclesiastes 1:4 as distinct from the Son as the uncreated wisdom of God. Peter's combined strategy for disposing of these two positions at once is to use Genesis 1:1 as a countercitation to the Ecclesiastes text. He argues that the "heaven" in the heaven and earth created in the beginning refers to the angels while "earth" refers to the confused and unformed matter that was the first physical entity which God brought forth. He extends the principle of creation *simul* to the angels and to

---

[107] Ibid., c. 6.1–5, 1: 334–35.
[108] A good discussion is provided by Bertola, "La dottrina della creazione," pp. 35–40.

unformed matter and, after carefully considering the various versions of that doctrine, concludes that this is as far as it can be taken.
As with the author of the *Sententiae divinitatis*, his reason for rejecting
Augustine here is that the Gregorian or Isidorian accounts display
more conformity with the text of Genesis.[109]

Yet, Peter returns to Augustine's Genesis commentary for help
on how we can understand the unformed matter. He reflects his
awareness of an issue that Clarenbald of Arras had also found
problematic, the presumed difficulty of the human mind in grasping anything material that has no form. Here, he calls upon the
analysis of negative and privative terminology which Augustine
had developed to explain the meaning of darkness and the void
against the Manichees, who endowed them with real significance as
aspects of the evil material creation. With Augustine, he agrees that
these terms refer not to species but to the absence of species, the
absence of species of any kind, in the case of the void, or the
absence of the species of the reality to which it is correlative, that is,
light, in the case of darkness.[110] This is a topic which none of the
other current masters who discuss creation had thought of commenting on. Peter also reimports Augustine's seminal reasons into
the account, as created forms or causes. Using Alcuin to anchor his
sequential view of creation, once the angels and primordial matter
have come into being, he proposes four modes of divine operation
in the creation. First, God creates all things eternally in the Word.
Peter understands this to mean that God possesses the plan of the
creation in His mind from all time. When He chooses to manifest
this plan, God does so in stages. First, He creates the angels and the
unformed matter *simul* and *ex nihilo*. Then, in the work of the six
days, He produces individual creatures out of the unformed matter
and the forms which He creates for this purpose. Finally, he inserts
the seminal reasons He has prepared into these creatures to takes
care of future developments after the sixth day, both in the production of new kinds of beings and in the capacities of created beings to
carry out their natural functions.[111] As to the days of creation
themselves, Peter disagrees sharply with the position expressed by
Roland of Bologna. The days referred to in Genesis are to be
understood literally as lasting twenty-four hours. As to why the
days begin in the evening and not in the morning, he follows Hugh
of St. Victor in his one departure from literalism here, in saying

---

[109] Peter Lombard, *Sent.* 2. d. 2. c. 1–c. 3, d. 12. c. 1.2, 1: 336–39, 384–85.
[110] Ibid., d. 12 c. 3–c. 4, 1: 387–88.
[111] Ibid., c. 6, 1: 388–89.

that this notion stands, as a mystery (*pro mysterio*), for man's movement from the darkness of sin to the light of redemption.[112]

The passage just cited is the one and only occasion in which Peter treats the creation account in Genesis as a source of moral and spiritual edification. It is atypical of the straightforwardness with which he handles this subject in general. If he is not particularly concerned with ethics under this heading, neither is he drawn to cosmology or natural philosophy as such. He goes about his business with conscientiousness and also with brevity. He is not interested in whether the Genesis account has anything in common with philosophical accounts of creation and is far less intrigued by its physical problems and inconsistencies than Augustine is. There are only two issues he raises in discussing the work of the six days that could be described as remotely speculative. On the question of the waters above the firmament, and why they stay there, he opts for the explanation of Augustine, who says that these waters exist in the form of tiny droplets which can remain suspended in the air, on the grounds of common sense.[113] And, on the question of the creation of vermin and poisonous animals, he draws a distinction. Pestiferous creatures, now harmful to man, were not harmful in the original creation; the nuisance they now inflict is a punishment for sin. As for vermin such as maggots, which, following classical biology, Peter holds to be generated spontaneously out of carrion, they were indeed created during the six days, before the death of any animal whose carcass could engender them, but only potentially (*potentialiter*).[114] Consistent with the wish to draw brisk and down-to-earth conclusions and to curtail reflection on matters for which no answers are available is Peter's handling of Eden. What we can know about it, and all we need to know about it, is that Eden is meant to be understood both spiritually and materially, since man has both a spiritual and a physical nature, that it can be seen as a type of the church, that it was located in the east, and that it was a *locus amoenissimus* whose specific attributes we cannot describe. He pointedly refrains from further speculation on the subject.[115]

If Peter manifests a disinclination to wear the hat of the natural philosopher in his discussion of the work of the six days, he at least operates in a manner consistent with that intention, refusing to

---

[112] Ibid., d. 13. c. 4–c. 5, 1: 391–92.
[113] Ibid., d. 14. c. 4, 1. 396.
[114] Ibid., d. 15. c. 3–c. 4, 1: 401.
[115] Ibid., d. 17. c. 5.1–4. 5, 1: 413–14.

ventilate questions which he feels cannot be answered. He does
resolve the questions that he chooses to raise. On the other hand,
he is far more successful in handling the larger metaphysical issues
concerned with cosmogenesis, and this partly because of his elimination of issues, such as exemplary causes, which he finds unnecessary and fraught with confusion, and partly thanks to his
effective way of integrating angels into a creation account that
otherwise remains guided by Genesis and the exegetical tradition.
While in some respects Peter is less venturesome on creation than
on man and on many other topics that he takes up in Book 2 of the
Sentences, he none the less shows his ability to reflect independently
and selectively on that tradition. And, as a theologian, he is march-
ing to the beat of the contemporary drummer in being primarily
concerned, in this connection, not with the structure and function
of the physical universe but with angels and human beings.

ANGELS AMONG THE LOMBARD'S SCHOLASTIC PREDECESSORS AND CONTEMPORARIES

Angels were a subject on which there was a good deal of contemporary consensus among early and mid-twelfth-century theologians. To a striking degree they were in accord not only on what the
important questions were concerning angels, but also on the correct
answers to those questions. They occasionally differed on the best
way to defend the conclusions they drew. One topic on which there
was some disagreement, which we have considered above, was
when the angels were created. Wherever they came down on that
issue, most of the theologians were in agreement on their metaphysical constitution. Although Honorius compares their nature
with the element of fire, and one member of the school of Loan says
they have rarefied bodies, and while Roland of Bologna is inconclusive on whether they have a material constitution or not,[116] most
other theologians subscribe clearly to the idea that angels, created
ex nihilo, are purely spiritual beings, although Hugh of St. Victor
muddies the waters somewhat by calling them spiritual substances,
without indicating what he means by "substance" in this
context.[117] The only contemporary master to raise and to answer

---

[116] Honorius, *Eluc.* 1.27–31, p. 366, although he also asserts that they are
spiritual at 1.24, 1.26, p. 366; *Sentences of the School of Laon*, no. 305, 5: 243; Roland
of Bologna, *Sent.*, pp. 85–86.

[117] *Sent. Anselmi* 2, p. 50; Peter Abelard, *Hexaemeron*, p. 10; *Ysagoge in theologiam*,
ed. Artur Michael Landgraf in *Écrits théologiques de l'école d'Abélard* (Louvain:

the question of how these completely spiritual beings are different from God is the author of the *Summa sententiarum*, who, as we have seen, does a good job of it, locating the differences in the capacity of angels to change and to be conditioned by time, and to be subject to affections.[118] There is agreement on the idea that the angels are disposed in nine ranks, with the seraphim on top, following the angelic hierarchy of Dionysius the Areopagite, although Gregory the Great is sometimes brought in as well to support this point.[119] The author of the *Summa sententiarum* believes that only the good angels are graded but that there is no hierarchy among the fallen angels.[120] His view is atypical. One of the early Porretans notes that these spiritual beings can assume the bodies of men in carrying out their duties, and that, when they do so, they are capable of en-gendering children, acting as *incubi*. He rehearses the patristic debates on the metaphysical status of such children and whether they can be saved, declining to give an answer despite Augustine's assurances on this point.[121] But he appears to be alone among the mid-century masters in worrying about this issue.

Of greater interest in this period are the angels' possession of intelligence and free will and their moral exercise of these faculties in their fall, or in their decision not to fall, as the case may be. There is no dispute concerning the rationality and freedom of the angels as such. Nor is there dissent from the Augustinian opinion that they do not exercise these faculties in choosing the good without the assistance of divine grace.[122] Hugh of St. Victor distin-guishes between the spirituality and immortality which all angels possess equally and their reason and will, which he thinks they possess to different degrees.[123] All these ideas set the stage for the theme of the fall of the angels and its effects. Those masters who raise the question of when that fall took place agree that it occurred

---

Spicilegium Sacrum Lovaniense, 1934), p. 222; *Sent. mag. Gisleberti* I 13.15–16, p. 164; Hugh of St. Victor, *De sac.* 1.5.9, *PL* 176: 250D; *Summa sent.* 2.2–3, *PL* 176: 81D–83A; Robert Pullen, *Sent.* 2.2, *PL* 186: 719A.

[118] *Summa sent.* 1.5, 2.2–3, *PL* 176: 50C–51A, 81D–83A.

[119] Honorius, *Eluc.* 1.24, 1.26, p. 366; Roland of Bologna, *Sent.*, pp. 103–04, *Ysagoge in theologiam*, p. 230; *Sent. mag. Gisleberti* I 13.29, 13.37–47, pp. 166, 167–69; Hugh of St. Victor, *De sac.* 1.5.33, *PL* 176: 262B–D.

[120] *Summa sent.* 2.5, *PL* 176: 85C–87B.

[121] *Sent. mag. Gisleberti* I 13.31, p. 166.

[122] *Sent. Anselmi* 2, p. 50; Roland of Bologna, *Sent.*, pp. 85–104; *Ysagoge in theologiam*, p. 222; *Sent. mag. Gisleberti* I 13.15, 13.36, pp. 164, 167; Hugh of St. Victor, *De sac.* 1.5.9–14, 1.5.24–28, *PL* 176: 250D–252A, 257A–259B; *Summa sent.* 2.3.4, *PL* 176: 83A–85C.

[123] Hugh of St. Victor, *De sac.* 1.5.9–14, *PL* 176: 250D–252A.

immediately after the creation of the angels.[124] The concerns, and
the debates of the theologians, fall rather on three other matters:
What happened to the fallen angels? Are the good angels incapable
of sin? And, why is it that the fallen angels can never be saved?
Looming large on their agenda is the desire to refute Origen's
teaching that conversion and backsliding remain continuing possibilities for all spiritual beings, angels included.[125] While the theologians, to a man, oppose Origen, they differ as to the best argument
to bring to bear aginst his position. At the same time, they seek to
add to the dossier of patristic refutations from the work of more
recent masters.

Early in the century, Honorius gives a rather thorough review of
these problems. As he sees it, the fallen angels are confirmed in evil.
They have lost the capacity to will the good. Some of them are cast
into Hell, where they torment the damned; others inhabit the dark
air above it and are active on earth, seducing the weak and testing
the elect. After the last judgment, all the fallen angels will be
assigned to Hell. They are powerful, powerful enough to carry out
these nefarious roles, but not so powerful as the good angels. Their
major limitation after the fall lies in their will. Their inability to will
the good is one reason why they cannot be saved, in Honorius's
view. But another reason, and one he derives from Anselm of
Canterbury's *Cur deus homo*, is that, granted God's chosen method of
saving mankind, it could not have been extended to angels. Christ
could not have taken on an angelic nature, since each angel is the
object of a particular creation on God's part, a genus unto himself,
in effect. There is no generic angelic nature as such. Had Christ
taken on some one angel's nature, that angel would have been the
only one He could have redeemed. Further, Honorius adds, salvation means salvation from death and angels, whether fallen or not,
are immortal once created. The salvation of angels is thus a contradiction in terms. Likewise, for Honorius, the good angels are confirmed in good. They are free from evil desires.[126]

On the other hand, the members of the school of Laon, recognizing that, if God had willed to save the fallen angels, He would not
have been constrained to do so on the analogy of His chosen mode

---

[124] Honorius, *Eluc.* 1.32–37, p. 367; *Summa sent.* 2.3.4, *PL* 176: 83A–85C. The
author of the *Sent. Anselmi* 2, p. 53, does not think that the exact timing of the
angels' fall can be known.

[125] For the patristic background on this issue, see Jeffrey Burton Russell,
Lucifer: The Devil in the Middle Ages (Ithaca: Cornell University Press, 1984), p. 110.

[126] Honorius, *Eluc.* 1.38–41, 1.42–44, 1.48–49, 1.50–56, pp. 367–68, 368, 369–
70, 370.

of redemption for man, find this argument problematic and do not see the Anselmian and Honorian *Cur deus non angelus* position as convincing. Agreeing that the angels are confirmed in evil or good, as the case may be, they argue that the sin of the fallen angels is irremissible because their dignity was higher than that of man and they experienced no external temptation, as man did, and which can be seen as a mitigating factor, in man's case.[127] Given the general subscription of these masters to the principle that the essence of the moral act lies in inner intention, which they develop elsewhere, they make heavy weather of trying to explain why the lack of external temptation on the part of the angels should make such a critical difference in their case.

Both Honorius and the school of Laon received some support in the sequel. The author of the Abelardian *Ysagoge in theologiam* agrees with Honorius, arguing that the sacrifice of a God-angel would have been required for the salvation of the fallen angels, along the lines of the passion of Christ. This action would have been irrelevant since the angels are already immortal. Perhaps the most interesting feature of his argument is that, in order to make it, he departs from the Abelardian doctrine of man's redemption in stating his case.[128] Two of the early Porretans, on the other hand, follow the Laon masters, being equally unable to explain why the lack of external temptation should make any difference, for the angels.[129]

While picking up on the destination of the fallen angels as a fiery inferno or as a zone of dark and murky air, locations which he sees as alternatives between which he cannot choose, the author of the *Summa sententiarum* raises another problem flowing from the fate of angels after their fall or, alternatively, their decision not to fall. He asserts, against Origen, that the angels are confirmed in malice, or virtue, respectively. This being the case, he notes that both groups would appear to have undergone a serious limitation on their free will, because, in each case, an entire category of ethical action has now been closed to them. The author is sensitive to this problem. Following Hugh of St. Victor, however, he sees this as a real

---

[127] Anselm of Laon, *Sent. divine pagine* 4; *Sent. Anselmi* 2, pp. 15–18, 50–54; *Deus de cuius principio et fine tacetur*, pp. 256–57.
[128] *Ysagoge in theologiam*, pp. 227–28.
[129] *Sent. mag. Gisleberti* I 13.74, p. 174; Nikolaus M. Häring, ed., "Die *Sententie magistri Gisleberti Pictavensis episcopi* II. Die Version der florentiner Handschrift" 13.74, *AHDLMA* 46 (1979): 105. This dependence on the school of Laon at this point should be noted as a correction of Marcia L. Colish, "Early Porretan Theology," *RTAM* 56 (1989): 69.

limitation only on the free will of the fallen angels. He also reprises the Laon masters' critique of the *Cur deus non angelus* argument and gets hopelessly tangled up in it.[130] For his part, Robert Pullen, while he agrees that the angels are confirmed in evil or good, goes on to raise a question with respect to the good angels and their capacities. Should we think, following Augustine, that the good angels were given the incapacity to sin, the *non posse peccare*, of the saints in Heaven or, following Jerome, should we confine the state of *non posse peccare* to God alone? Robert sides with Jerome. He maintains that the good angels do retain some vestige of the capacity to sin although sinning is almost impossible for them, because they have become too habituated to virtue actually to do so. With regard to the parallel question of whether the fallen angels retain any vestige of the capacity to will the good, and why they cannot be saved, Robert airs it but does not answer it.[131]

A few other topics, of a lesser order of interest, arise under the heading of angels. Hugh of St. Victor, declining to speculate on how many angels there were and how many fell, does, however, suggest that there are the same number of good and bad angels at any given moment as there are human beings, since each man has his own personal guardian angel and tempter. Hugh asks, further, whether all the good angels act as messengers to and protectors of men, or only those in certain angelic ranks. He gives a thorough outline of the debate on this subject, although he does not take a stand on it.[132] This latter topic is also addressed by the author of the *Summa sententiarum*, who disagrees with those authorities who maintain that God uses only the lesser orders of angels as messengers. In his view, all the ranks of angels are sent. He agrees with Hugh, and ultimately with Gregory the Great, on the idea of personal guardian angels and demons but does not take up the matter of their number. Nor does he wish to return to the problem of *incubi* and their offspring.[133] He does, however, raise a question not tackled by many of his contemporaries, that of where the angels were created. Ignoring the fact that in his own teaching that angels and unformed matter were created *simul*, before the rest of the universe was given phenomenal form, he has a means of answering this question by

[130] Hugh of St. Victor, *De sac.* 1.5.31–32, *PL* 176: 261A–262B; *Summa sent.* 2.3.4, *PL* 176: 83A–85C.

[131] Robert Pullen, *Sent.* 2.2–6, *PL* 186: 719A–726A.

[132] Hugh of St. Victor, *De sac.* 1.5.31–33, *PL* 176: 261A–262D. This willingness at least to raise controversial questions on angels is ignored in the account of Hugh's angelology in Mignon, *Les origines*, 1: 339–73.

[133] *Summa sent.* 2.6, *PL* 176: 87C–88C.

noting that no "place" of any kind as yet existed, he wrestles with the question and then abandons it, unanswered.[134]

The Lombard on Angels

This was the contemporary state of play on angels when Peter Lombard composed the section of Book 2 of his *Sentences* dealing with this subject. With respect to his coevals and immediate predecessors, his angelology is richer and more ample, even as he corroborates the points on which consensus existed at this time. He draws together insights from a wider range of treatments of this topic than is true of any other mid-century master. He also shows a theoretical interest in the subject which reflects his use of the author of the *Summa sententiarum* as his major guide, while at the same time he goes more deeply into it than does this master or any of his other compeers. In terms of what he omits, Peter also indicates which questions concerning angels he regards as frivolous or unanswerable. Even when he is drawing the most closely on the work of other theologians, he frames his ideas in his own language and sometimes introduces distinctions of his own that enable him to pose and to resolve problems more clearly.[135]

Peter prefaces his account of angels with a crisp indication of what subjects he plans to take up and in what order. He proposes to treat when angels were created, where, their original nature, the effects on the angels of their fall or the lack of it, their ranks, gifts, duties, and names. The first two questions are correlatives. Taking a leaf from the book of the *Summa sententiarum*, and doing its author one better, he reviews his doctrine of the creation *simul* of angels and the elements, prior to the creation of the rest of the universe, and adds that the locus of the angels was the heaven or empyrean, which was the third and last item created *simul* along with the angels and primordial matter.[136] As for the created nature of angels, Peter supports while expanding on the consensus view, stating that they have a simple essence that is indivisible and immaterial, a status as persons, rationality including memory, intellect, and will, and free will, which he defines here as the freedom of the will to choose either good or evil on its own "without violence or

---

[134] Ibid., 2.1, *PL* 176: 81C–D.
[135] The best treatment of Peter Lombard on angels to date is Ermenegildo Bertola, "Il problema delle creature angeliche in Pier Lombardo," *Pier Lombardo* 1:2 (1957): 33–54.
[136] Peter Lombard, *Sent.* 2. d. 2. c. 1–c. 6, 1: 336–41.

constraint" (*sine violentia et coactione*).[137] But, going back to the issue
of whether there are respects in which all angels are the same and
respects in which they are different, aired by Hugh of St. Victor,
Peter puts the question in his own terms. Are angels all the same in
their essence, wisdom, and free will, that is, their substance, form,
and power? He answers that, with regard to their essence as rational beings, as persons, as immaterial, as simple, and as immortal,
they are all the same. Nevertheless, they exist in different grades of
tenuousness and different degrees of wisdom and will.[138] Peter has
added here the notion of gradations within the substance of the
angelic nature, as well as within their exercise of that nature, a
move that grounds the principle of angelic hierarchy metaphysically as well as psychologically. He indicates his view that the hierarchical principle is universal in creation, since it applies to spiritual
beings in both of these ways as well as to material beings.

While the ability to exercise free will in any direction, without
constraint, is a native endowment of the angels, some angels used it
to fall, which they could do on their own, and others used it
meritoriously, which they could not do unless grace were added.
The point that Peter wants to make here, agreeing with Augustine
on Genesis, is that nothing in the creation, including the angels
who fell, is intrinsically evil. In support of this principle he does not
hesitate to yoke Origen's *On Ezechiel* with Augustine as an authority
however much he may share in the contemporary antipathy to
Origen in other respects.[139] As for the natural rational capacity of
the angels before the fall, it was, according to Peter, threefold. The
angels knew that they were created, and by Whom, and for what
purpose. They also naturally shared a love of God and of each
other, although this was not yet a love that earned merit. They
were blessed in their innocence, rather than in the sense of the
blessedness enjoyed as a future state by those spiritual beings who
persevere in virtue. In this respect, and here Peter makes a distinction applied more generally to the creation by Robert of Melun, the
angels were perfect before the fall in that they had everything they
needed and that was appropriate to them at the time. But they were
not perfect in the sense that they had not yet actualized the potential capacity for glorification which they possessed. Nor were they
perfect in the absolute sense in which only God is perfect.[140]

---

[137] Ibid., d. 3. c. 1.2, 1: 342; repeated at d. 4. c. 2, 1: 252.
[138] Ibid., d. 3. c. 2.1–2, 1: 342.
[139] Ibid., c. 4.1–11, 1: 343–47.
[140] Ibid., c. 5–d. 4. c. 4, 1: 348–51.

Next comes the fall of the angels. Peter confirms the consensus position on its effects, but finds his own way of explaining why the good angels persevere in virtue and why the fallen angels cannot be saved, a position which avoids the problems of both the *Cur deus non angelus* argument of Anselm of Canterbury and the absence of external temptation argument of Anselm of Laon. The fall of the angels involves either conversion (*conversio*) or aversion (*aversio*). The converted angels, Peter argues, are confirmed in the love of God and are illuminated by Him so as to be granted a fuller wisdom, and are given the grace which now enables them to be just and to acquire merit. The averted, who fell through envy, are confirmed in that vice and also in hatred. Their minds are blinded, not just by their own malice but by the removal of grace. They are corrupted by guilt and made unjust. Now, both kinds of angels retain free will. But, Peter draws a distinction here that addresses some of the difficulties raised but not answered by both the author of the *Summa sententiarum* and Robert Pullen in this connection. The reason why the fallen angels cannot be saved is that, in order to exercise their will toward the good, they would need to have the gift of divine grace. And, grace has been removed from them as a consequence of their fall. So, since God does not choose to alter this state of affairs, they are incapable of improving. The good angels, on the other hand, are capable of improving, growing perfected in the love of God and in their obedience to Him; and this is possible because God grants them the cooperating grace without which no rational creature can improve and attain merit (*gratia cooperans, sine qua non potest proficere rationalis vel meritum vitae*). They also do so by using their free will to collaborate with God's grace. Grace is the key, in this analysis, for without it the angelic will cannot make those choices that contribute to merit. Peter agrees with those who say that the prize the converted angels win is itself the grace enabling them to enjoy the good.[141] But his real achievement here is to take the consensus view that merit-bearing choices, even for the angels, require the support of grace and to expand it into an argument that can refute the Origentist theory of openended conversion or aversion without undermining the free will of the angels. In the final accounting, it is the divine decision to extend grace, or to withhold it, that is the critical factor in an equation that leaves the fallen angels in a condition of permanent moral stasis while it extends to the good angels the capacity for glorification. Peter's earlier definition of angelic free will also enables him to resolve a

---

[141] Ibid., d. 5. c. 1–c. 5, 1: 351–53. The quotation is at c. 3. 1: 352.

problem raised by Robert Pullen under the heading of whether the good angels have the *non posse peccare*. He sides with Robert and Jerome in assigning this condition to God alone. He agrees that the angels after the fall have the capacity to will only good, or evil, and not their opposites. But, insofar as they now experience no conflicting desires, the angels' capacity to will good, or evil, as the case may be, with no violence or constraint, has been intensified, not limited; although, as he has argued, for the good angels the ability to translate good intentions into good, and meritorious, actions requires the collaboration of grace.[142]

The good angels continue to do just that, and to carry out the missions God assigns them. As for the fallen angels, who, Peter notes, are graded even as the good ones are, *pace* the author of the *Summa sententiarum*, they are thrown into the dark and murky air to consort with their depraved associates, or are sent to Hell to torment the damned. Peter does not specify where the dark and gloomy air is located, keeping an open mind on this question, but allowing that the demons dwelling there can return to earth to tempt mankind and to play the roles assigned to them in the time of Antichrist. The main point he wants to make about the work of the fallen angels is that, as devils, their powers as tempters will increase in the last days, in some cases, while in other cases, their powers will be diminished, the demons in the second group having been bested by the saints.[143] He adds that, if some demons will grow or diminish in their malicious powers, they will not lose their intelligence, just as they will not be deprived of free will.[144] Peter closes this section of his account by noting that the good angels can take on visible corporeal form in the conduct of their missions, and that the authorities do not resolve the question of what the metaphysical status of those bodies may be or what happens to them after the angels no longer need to use them.[145] He also observes that demons may enter into the bodies and minds of men in performing their nefarious work. When they do so, he maintains, they are present in human beings not substantially (*substantialiter*) but in their effects.[146] On the subject of *incubi*, Peter, along with most of his contemporaries, declines to comment.

Citing Dionysius, and bringing in Gregory as well, he also re-

---

[142] Ibid., d. 7. c. 1–c. 4, 1: 359–61.
[143] Ibid., d. 6. c. 1–c. 7, 1: 354–58.
[144] Ibid., d. 7. c. 5–c. 9, 1: 361–65.
[145] Ibid., d. 8. c. 1–c. 2, 1: 365–68.
[146] Ibid., c. 4. 1: 369–70.

ports the consensus position on the nine orders of angels, headed by the seraphim. But he expands on this common doctrine. The nine ranks of angels are led by the seraphim burning with love, outranking the cherubim, in order to point the lesson, for man's instruction, that love is greater than knowledge. Also, the angels are divided into three subsets of three, to reflect the Trinity. The virtues expressed by the angels in each rank are gifts common to all the angels, although they are manifested preeminently by the angels in each particular rank. The rank order itself, according to Peter, was established after the fall, although the metaphysical gradations of angelic substance for which he had argued earlier provide a philosophical rationale for this development. Sharply disagreeing with Honorius, who claims that each angel is *sui generis*, Peter thinks that there is more than one angel in each rank and that the angels in each order are graded, just as the ranks are.[147] Returning to a point that he had made under the heading of why man was created, he repeats the idea that men were not intended to form a tenth order of angels, or that they were created originally with such a status. Man would have been created and redeemed, he reiterates, even if the fallen angels had not fallen. The redeemed who win beatitude, further, receive it as human beings, not as angels.[148]

Turning from this critique of Augustine and of Hugh of St. Victor to another issue which Hugh had discussed inconclusively, the question of whether all ranks of angels or only some angels are sent on divine missions, Peter joins the author of the *Summa sententiarum* in supporting those authorities who state that all ranks of angels are sent. He offers his own amplification of this point. While all ranks are sent, the angels highest on the angelic hierarchy, especially archangels such as Raphael, Gabriel, and Michael, who are specifically named, receive the choicest assignments.[149] Aside from functioning as messengers, Peter agrees, angels are sent to guard individual human beings, just as demons are allowed to test and torment them. In addressing the claim made by Hugh that the number of angels and devils must therefore be the same as the number of human beings in existence at any given moment, he registers disagreement. We do not need to posit that hypothesis, he states, since individual angels and devils can perform their respective assignments for more than one person at the same time.[150]

---

[147] Ibid., d. 9, c. 1–c. 5, 1: 370–75.
[148] Ibid., c. 6–c. 7, 1: 375–76.
[149] Ibid., d. 10. c. 1–c. 2, 1: 377–79.
[150] Ibid., d. 11. c. 1, 1: 379–81.

Peter concludes his treatise on angels by considering the gifts of the good angels. The principal issue he takes up under this heading is whether the good angels continue to grow in love and knowledge, in merit and reward, from the time of their confirmation in the good up to the time of the last judgment. Or, are they perfected, with no subsequent change, at the moment of their confirmation? To be sure, he had already laid the foundation earlier on for the answer he provides here, in his contrast between the effects of their confirmation on the good and the fallen angels, respectively. But now Peter introduces a useful distinction, and one not found in any of his authorities, which permits him to support both af these alternatives at the same time. The same distinction also enables him to emphasize the point that angels can be differentiated from God despite their purely spiritual constitution. Since angels live in time, he observes, and since they do not have foreknowledge, they do grow in knowledge. They become informed of events that occur in time, as these events come to pass. In this kind of knowledge of external events, then, they can and do grow. On the other hand, in their contemplation of God they are confirmed, once and for all, and this knowledge does not change. With respect to their love and merit, the good angels are not enlarged as to its quality. But they can grow in their opportunities to exercise these virtues. In handling objections to this last point, Peter shows that it is fully compatible with the combination of the temporal development of angelic knowledge and the changeless state of divine contemplation that characterizes the epistemic modes of angelic activity.[151] While Peter has clearly profited from the distinction drawn between angels and God by the author of the *Summa sententiarum*, he puts his own stamp on this final topic concerning angels by differentiating among modes of angelic activity and by resting his case on the chief metaphysical attribute which created beings lack in comparison with the creator, a theme which he had earlier developed in his doctrine of God in Book 1 of the *Sentences* and had anchored there with an appeal to John Damascene: everything in the creation is changeable, in one way or another. Only God is immutable. This, more than the issue of substantial composition, is the basis on which he draws his final conclusions on what is specific and unique to the angels.

In sum, while raising a wider range of questions on angels than his contemporaries do and while providing more of the questions which he raises with lucid and defensible answers, Peter does far

---

[151] Ibid., c. 2, 1: 381–83.

more than to summarize the consensus view of angelology in his time. He takes a clear stand on disputed issues and finds fresh ways of posing and resolving many of them. His most important and characteristic contribution in this subdivision of his theology can be seen in his treatment of the gifts of the good angels and whether they change or not, and in his explanation of the irremissibility of the guilt of the fallen angels. In each case, he associates his solution with a more basic theme in his theology as such, in addition to developing a mode of attack different both from that of contemporaries and from the authorities on whom he and they rely. In the first mentioned case, the principle he invokes is the immutability of the divine nature and the mutability of created beings, as fundamental definitions of these two kinds of being. In the case of the fallen angels, and their differences from the good angels, the principle he invokes is the idea that all good actions require the assistance of grace, and that God grants, and subtracts, His grace according to His own will. This idea is also one that Peter will develop systematically in his handling of God's relationship with man, both before and after Adam's fall, and it is a signature of Peter's in the field of ethics more generally. In these ways, and in contrast to contemporaries who ignored angels, or who treated them in a sketchy, a hit-or-miss, a fanciful, an illogical, or an inconclusive manner, Peter presents a well organized, inclusive, and coherent angelology, which targets effectively the aspects of this subject most of interest to theologians in the middle of the twelfth century and which, at the same time, integrates angelology comprehensibly into the rest of his theology.

HUMAN NATURE BEFORE THE FALL: THE CONTEMPORARY DEBATES

In turning from angels to man before the fall, we move from an area in which there was a considerable degree of consensus among theologians in the first half of the twelfth century to one in which there was a good deal of disagreement. Not all scholastics regarded human nature as such as an issue of particular interest. Indeed, despite their renown, or notoriety, as speculative thinkers in other areas, the Abelardians and Porretans tend to give this subject extremely short shrift. Among those theologians who do devote extended attention to the subject, there is agreement that the main issues requiring investigation are the nature of man's physical and intellectual activities before the fall, the structure of the human soul, man's rationality, free will, and virtue, and, to a somewhat lesser degree, the question of whether female nature is equal to male nature or is its inferior. Within these areas, however, they disagree quite sharply, both in their substantive conclusions, the relative importance they grant to these topics, and the authorities and rational arguments on which they rely. In this connection, Peter Lombard offers a defense of the principle that human nature as such is an important issue, a defense stronger than that found in any other contemporary theologian. At the same time, his understanding of human nature offers a striking de-Platonizing of that subject, in comparison with some of the period's leading thinkers.[152] In this respect, while he draws heavily on Hugh of St. Victor for the formulation of the issues he wants to discuss and for a sense of where in the theological tradition to look for his sources, Hugh is also the contemporary theologian of whom he is the most critical.

Of all the topics pertinent to human nature before the fall, the one on which there is the most consensus, and the one that attracts the least speculative attention from the masters of his time up to Peter, is man's physical nature and life in Eden. The main point which, they agree, is the single most important one is man's sexuality before the fall. They also agree that the single most important authority on this subject is Augustine, Augustine, that is, in his anti-Manichean and pastoral incarnation and not Augustine the anti-Pelagian. In the works written to refute the Manichean conception of the human body, and procreative sexuality, as evil, and in works of his mid-career aimed at counseling married people or those preparing for marriage, Augustine stressed that marriage, and sexual reproduction, were an original part of God's plan. In these works, as well, Augustine had in mind the aim of refuting the position of Origen, who had taught that the body, and hence sexual differentiation itself no less than the sexual procreation of offspring, were consequences of original sin, ideas which, in one form or another, were finding a resonance in some of Augustine's more

---

[152] The best introduction to this object, at least for the Lombard's psychology, is Ermenegildo Bertola, "La dottrina lombardiana dell'anima nella storia delle dottrine psicologiche del XII secolo," *Pier Lombardo* 3:1 (1959): 3–18. See also Chenu, *La théologie au douzième siècle*, p. 295; Joseph de Ghellinck, "Pierre Lombard," in *DTC* (Paris: Letouzey et Ané, 1935), 12 part 2: 1194–96; Richard Heinzemann, *Die Unsterblichkeit der Seele und die Auferstehung des Leibes: Eine problemgeschichtliche Untersuchung der frühscholastischen Sentenzen- und Summenliteratur von Anselm von Laon bis Wilhelm von Auxerre*, Beiträge, 40:3 (Münster: Aschendorff, 1965), pp. 63–68; Giuseppi Lorenzi, "La filosofia di Pier Lombardo nei *Quattro libri delle Sentenze*," *Pier Lombardo* 4 (1960): 32–34, who follows Bertola closely: Johann Schupp, *Die Gnadenlehre des Petrus Lombardus* (Freiburg im Breisgau: Herder, 1932), pp. 15–23.

ascetic contemporaries. Twelfth-century scholastics follow Augustine's lead here, and on two related points. First, they agree that, before the fall, human sexuality would have lacked the attributes of desire and pleasure. It would have been exercised subject to the rational will of the partners, as devoid of lustful feeling or sensual gratification as a handshake. Secondly, they agree, before the fall, children would have been born to Eve without labor pains.[153] The only twelfth-century theologians to depart from this Augustinian position are Robert of Melun, who ignores the topic of sex altogether at the relevant location in his *Sentences*, and one of the early Porretans, who treats the question of whether sex would have been free of lust and childbirth free of pain, absent the fall, as an open one.[154]

There is a corollary of the Augustinian position on marriage in Eden which attracts less general interest and agreement, the nature of the children who would have been born to Adam and Eve. Would they, like their parents, have been engendered as adults, or as able to walk and talk already? Augustine himself airs the matter as a possibility but takes no definite stand. Undeterred, Honorius Augustodunensis treats the walking and talking as a certainty; Hugh of St. Victor thinks the children would have inherited all the perfections of their parents but would not have been born as adults; and the author of the *Summa sententiarum* more prudently retreats to the issue of walking and talking, and, less definite than Honorius and more definite than Augustine himself, thinks that these capacities in the newborn children of Adam and Eve would have been possible, and likely.[155]

Far less sustained attention was devoted to the other aspects of the physical life of man in Eden before the fall. It was agreed that Adam and Eve had the capacity not to die and that, before the fall,

---

[153] For the Augustinian background and a fine survey of twelfth-century opinions, the standard work is Michael Müller, *Die Lehre des hl. Augustinus von der Paradiesesehe und ihre Auswirkung in der Sexualethik des 12. und 13. Jahrhunderts bis Thomas von Aquin* (Regensburg: Friedrich Pustet, 1954), pp. 19–101. His analysis and conclusions are amply supported by our own investigations. See Anselm of Laon, *Sent. divine pagine* 4; *Sent. Anselmi* 2, pp. 22–23, 57; *Sentences of Anselm of Laon*, no. 24, 38–39; *Sentences of William of Champeaux*, no. 246, 254; *Sentences of the School of Laon*, no. 252, 5: 26, 36–37, 203, 207, 252; Honorius, *Eluc.* 1.74–76, pp. 374–75; Roland of Bologna, *Sent.*, pp. 121–22; Hugh of St. Victor, *De sac.* 1.6.18–27, *PL* 176: 275A–281A; *Summa sent.* 3.4, *PL* 176: 94D; Robert Pullen, *Sent.* 2.18, *PL* 186: 745D–746B.

[154] Robert of Melun, *Sent*, 1.1.8, *Oeuvres*, 3 part 1: 208; *Sent. mag. Gisleberti* I 13.61–62, p. 171.

[155] Honorius, *Eluc.* 1.74–76, pp. 374–75; Hugh of St. Victor, *De sac.* 1.6.18–27, *PL* 176: 275D–281A; *Summa sent.* 3.4, *PL* 176: 95A–B.

they were not afflicted with illness or physical suffering. But, what about their need to eat and their need to work? A number of theologians acknowledge the fact that the need to eat is a natural need. Before the fall, it would have been morally neutral and unproblematic, simply an indicator of the body's nutritional needs. Adam and Eve would have eaten out of natural need and with natural pleasure, but without experiencing the pain of hunger pangs.[156] But there was an alternative approach to this question, offered by two members of the school of Laon. They argue that Adam and Eve possessed the physical need for food and drink, before the fall, but only potentially, and not *in actu*, a view which presupposes that the fall occurred almost immediately after the creation of Adam and Eve.[157] There was also the opinion of Honorius, noted above under the heading of why animals were created, that vegetarianism alone was natural in Eden, and that the need to consume flesh was a consequence of the fall.[158] As for work, and whether it existed in Eden, or whether it was an affliction laid on Adam as a punishment for sin, this issue evokes interest only from Roland of Bologna and Robert of Melun, who have much the same thing to say although Roland is more specific. Adam, they both think, would have exercised his natural aptitude to work in Eden, plowing, sowing, and harvesting, raising his family and building a house for it, but out of pleasure in these activities in their own right, and without fatigue or heavy effort.[159] This view, if it failed to receive support from other masters in the mainstream, is interesting for its understanding that meaningful work is a natural need of humankind, and that performing it brings satisfaction.

In surveying man's natural endowments and functions before the fall, these physical attributes cede pride of place to man's soul. Indeed, it is primarily, and sometimes exclusively, the soul to which most mid-century theologians turn in discussing prelapsarian man. The fact that they devote so much space to this topic, treating it in much more detail than man's body, is indicative of their strongly hierarchical assumptions about the human constitu-

---

[156] *Sent. Anselmi* 2, pp. 66–67; Hugh of St. Victor, *De sac.* 1.6.18–29, *PL* 176: 275A–282D; *Summa sent.* 3.4, *PL* 176: 94D.
[157] *Potest queri, quid sit peccatum*, ed. Heinrich Weisweiler in *Das Schrifttum der Schule Anselms von Laon und Wilhelms von Champeaux in deutschen Bibliotheken*, Beiträge, 33:1–2 (Münster: Aschendorff, 1936), p. 263; *Deus de cuius principio et fine tacetur*, p. 263.
[158] Honorius, *Eluc.* 1.66–67, pp. 272–73.
[159] Roland of Bologna, *Sent.*, pp. 121–22; Robert of Melun, *Sent.* 1.1.8, *Oeuvres*, 3 part 1: 208.

tion. Here, they could and did draw on the philosophical tradition as well as on patristic writers who held, with the Platonists, that a human being was a soul using a body, or even a soul trapped in a body as its prison, or, with the Stoics, that the mind was the ruling principle of the entire human constitution. At the same time, the treatises on the human soul found in systematic theologies in this period vary quite widely in the ways their authors conceive of this subject. Sometimes they include the theme of the five senses, and sometimes not. Some of them look at the question from a primarily ethical, and others from a primarily epistemological, standpoint, while still others seek to combine these perspectives. And, the mental faculties that different masters accent are not always the same ones, although they sometimes use the same terms to describe mental faculties that they define differently.

The school of Laon, early in the century, is a good index of both the eclecticism and the lack of consensus on man's psychology visible in this period. William of Champeaux combines a more or less Aristotelian psychology with a conception of mental faculties more Neoplatonic in appearance and geared to sustain man's supernatural activities. His account of sense perception takes the Peripatetic line that the sense data impress themselves on the sense organs, which remain passive in the process. The sense organs then convey these data to the mind, which fabricates concepts, both individual and abstract, out of them. William is aware of the fact that this account makes problematic the senses of sight and hearing, since the eye and ear perceive their objects at a distance. He mentions the problem but offers no resolution of it.[160] As for man's mental faculties, he holds that they are threefold. There is soul (*anima*), which animates the body and supervises the physical senses, and spirit (*spiritus*), the rational faculty which frames concepts and grasps supra-sensible realities. It is in the sense of his *spiritus*, William thinks, that man was made in God's image. There is also a third faculty, intuition (*intuitus*), man's suprarational faculty, which enables him to contemplate God's essence directly. William is not clear on why this suprarational faculty, which would appear to resemble God's own mode of intellection more closely than the ratiocination performed by *spiritus*, would not provide a better locus for the image of God in man.[161] Other Laon masters take a different tack, locating the image of God, in a traditional

---

[160] *Sentences of William of Champeaux*, no. 242–43, 5: 200–01.
[161] Ibid., no. 244, 5: 201.

Augustinian manner, in man's memory, intellect, and will.[162] The author of the *Sententie Anselmi* offers his own faculty psychology, dividing the soul into two faculties, the rational soul focused on the knowledge of incorporeal truths, which he confusingly calls *anima*, and the sensual soul, in charge of the body and sensory knowledge.[163]

A much more elaborate and important account of human psychology, if one not entirely free from inconsistencies, is the one developed by Hugh of St. Victor. He presents man as a microcosm. Since he possesses both a body and a soul, man displays God's desire to glorify both the material and the spiritual creation through the redemption of man.[164] This being so, one might expect to find that Hugh gives equal time to the body and soul of man before the fall. But such is not the case. Hugh is equally supportive of the view that man's soul alone is the microcosm, in that it can grasp invisible causes and also gain a knowledge of the visible world with the aid of the senses.[165] The soul itself is seen by Hugh as a substance, capable of being modified by accidents, without taking the body into account. The soul is where the human personality resides. The body can be called a person only indirectly, thanks to its union with the soul. While Hugh agrees with Augustine that the soul is spread evenly throughout the body, a point also reprised by the early Porretans,[166] it is not the combination of body and soul that is the definition of the human person for him but the individual substance of a rational nature, à la Boethius, whose union with the body to which it is joined is by no means perfect. The soul, or human person, can, for Hugh, live without a body. As a number of scholars have aptly noted, Hugh's understanding of human nature is strongly tinctured by Neoplatonism.[167]

Hugh distinguishes three forms of agency in man, mental, that is, voluntary; physical; and sensory or pertaining to pleasure. He

---

[162] *Sentences of the School of Laon*, no. 312–13, 315, 5: 246–49, 251.

[163] *Sent. Anselmi* 2, pp. 55–57. Heinzemann, *Die Unsterblichkeit*, pp. 6–15 does not note these differences of opinion within the school.

[164] Hugh of St. Victor, *De sac.* 1.6.1, *PL* 176: 263A.

[165] Hugh of St. Victor, *Didascal.* 1.1, pp. 4–5.

[166] *Sent. mag. Gisleberti* I 13.56, p. 170.

[167] Barkholt, *Die Ontologie*, pp. 17–19, 20–21; Roger Baron, "La situation de l'homme d'après Hugues de Saint-Victor," in *L'Homme et son destin d'après les penseurs du moyen âge* (Louvain: Éditions Nauwelaerts, 1960), pp. 431–36; Heinzemann, *Die Unsterblichkeit*, pp. 75–82; Heinrich Ostler, *Die Psychologie des Hugo von St. Viktor*, Beiträge, 6:1 (Münster: Aschendorff, 1906), pp. 26–30, 39–43, 81, 86–87; Heinz Robert Schlette, "Das unterscheidliche Personenverständnis im theologischen Denken Hugos und Richards von St. Viktor," in *Miscellanea Martin Grabmann: Gedenkenblatt zum 10. Todestag* (Munich: Max Hueber Verlag, 1959), pp. 57–61; Schütz, *Deus absconditus*, pp. 99–102.

makes it clear that he views their operations as much from a moral as from an epistemological perspective, and that the sub-rational impulses are far from neutral, in his estimation. The will is free, he observes; and it moves the body as well as the mind. But the sensory faculty can take over the mind, when the mind issues its bodily directives. If this happens, incorrect moral judgments will be made. It is only when the mind masters the sensory faculty that correct moral decisions will ensue.[168] Despite the hazards which the sensory faculty presents, it is noteworthy that Hugh sees this faculty, and not physical activity itself, as the seat of the problem. Man requires both the mental and the sensory faculties in order to come to a knowledge of both the visible and invisible worlds. This knowledge is desirable and valuable not, for Hugh, because it is a natural function of man as such, but because it provides him with the knowledge of God required for his spiritual well-being and for his acquisition of merit. Hugh is insistent, and consistent, in viewing man's natural faculties of soul in this kind of moral and religious perspective, adding that, while man can know the visible universe by nature, his knowledge of those invisible things that have not left their traces in the visible world depends on grace, collaborating with man's natural mental faculties. Further, these same mental faculties enable man to grasp the precepts of nature and of discipline. By this, Hugh means moral principles, as rationally ascertainable and as revealed, not the natural law in the physical sense.[169] For Hugh, the natural knowledge possessed by man before the fall was not derived purely from man's mental, physical, and sensory faculties working without impediment. According to Hugh, Adam had a perfect knowledge of the truth, all at once, which was reflected in his self-knowledge, his intimacy with the creator, and his knowledge of how to name the animals. This perfect knowledge, which lacked only foreknowledge, was his by divine illumination.[170]

The most notable heir to Hugh's legacy in the area of man's psychological endowment before the fall is Robert Pullen. The subject of the human soul is one he discusses at considerable length. To the Hugonian legacy, and some of its complications, he adds a number of observations on his own. Man was greater before the fall than he is now, Robert begins, but his nature will be still greater in the future resurrection.[171] This condition applies in

---

[168] Hugh of St. Victor, *De sac.* 1.6.4, *PL* 176: 265C–266A.
[169] Ibid., 1.6.5–6, 1.6.8, *PL* 176: 266B–268B, 268D–269B.
[170] Ibid., 1.6.12–15, *PL* 176: 270C–272C.
[171] Robert Pullen, *Sent.* 2.16, *PL* 186: 741A–B.

particular to man's soul. With Hugh, Robert calls the soul a substance, and an indivisible one, spread evenly throughout the
human body. He emphasizes that the soul is not localized in any
one organ, that it is not reduced or divided if a person suffers the
loss of a part of his body, and that the soul is the same "size" in
people of all ages and statures.[172] Robert has a good deal to say
about what this indivisible substance is not, but he is far from clear
on what it is, and what its relationship to the body is. The soul is
not of the same substance as the *anima mundi*, he notes, in a jab at
some versions of contemporary Platonism. Nor is it of the same
substance as the spirit of life which God breathed into Adam's
body. Robert explains neither of these points. He also leaves dangling the question of whether the souls of other people are created by
God, or issue from God, in the same way as Adam's soul and whether
Adam's soul is consubstantial with the souls of other human beings.[173]
Robert is treading on very marshy ground at this point. He appears to
be drawing a distinction between *spiritus* and *anima*, but it is impossible
to tell whether he means this in the same sense as William of Champeaux, since he does not define either of these terms. He does,
however, argue that the parents supply the *spiritus* as well as the body
to their children, which makes him a traducianist in some sense of that
word.[174] Also, having stated that the soul is a substance, he also says
that the soul and body are not two substances that blend when they
are united to produce a third and compound substance. Rather, they
are two aspects that cohere to make a man who remains a composite
being so long as he is not dead and unresurrected.[175] But, then again,
in the next breath, Robert calls both man's soul, and man as a
composite of body and soul, substances.[176]

These confusions in the meaning of substance with respect to
anthropology and Robert's waverings on whether man is an integral unit of body and soul or a person defined as a spiritual substance, which he derives from Hugh, are left unresolved. Ignoring the
debris he has left in his wake, Robert plunges on to address another
topic, faculty psychology. Noting that he is focusing on the particular version of the doctrine that he gives because it frames the
subject in terms of moral discretion and judgment, and that it is in
this connection that God's image is found in man's soul, he gives a

---

[172] Ibid., 1.10, *PL* 186: 690A–693A. The quotation is at 692A.
[173] Ibid., 2.9, *PL* 186: 733A.
[174] Ibid., 2.7, *PL* 186: 726A–D.
[175] Ibid., 2.10, *PL* 186: 724D.
[176] Ibid., 2.12, *PL* 186: 736D–738A. Robert's inconsistency here has been noted
by Heinzemann, *Die Unsterblichkeit*, pp. 84–117.

reprise of the Aristotelian distinction among the concupiscible, the irascible, and the rational faculties, or, as he puts it, *ratio, ira*, and *concupiscentia*. Now, there is a potential difficulty here. It was a standard consensus position, to which we have adverted above and which we will consider more fully below, that concupiscence was a consequence of the fall. Robert turns a blind eye to this fact. He does not see any need to explain the difference between concupiscence as a punishment for sin and the concupiscible faculty, in Aristotle's psychology, as a natural attribute of human beings. Moving right along, he notes that the rational faculty distinguishes good from evil. The irascible faculty distinguishes what caution should endure and what excessive zeal should reject. The concupiscible faculty tells us what to desire and what pertains to the needs of the body and to duty. While these definitions are not entirely Aristotelian, Robert joins the Stagirite in affirming that the functions of the irascible and concupiscible faculties can be conducive to virtue when they are guided by reason, and that the ability of reason to govern the infrarational faculties is what separates man from the animals.[177]

Robert adds that men have five senses and, like Hugh, he observes that they can draw men away from virtue, if they are inordinate in their attachments and are not used under reason's guidance.[178] But he at once launches into an analysis of the physiology of sight that is interesting in its own right. Plato, he observes, using the sense of sight as a paradigm case for sensation in general, saw vision as a flow of light issuing from the eye, going out to the sense object, and bringing sense data back with it to the eye. On the other hand, Aristotle saw the process as occurring in reverse, with the sense object sending out data across some sort of material bridge, the data impressing themselves on an eye that receives them passively. Robert thinks that the active and passive theories of sensation, as presented by these two traditions, each tell only half of the story. Without being aware of the fact that it is the Stoic theory of sensation which tells the whole story to which he is adverting, and without referring to Augustine, who is its likeliest source for him, he argues for a combined theory of sensation in which both the sense organ and the sense object play an active role.[179]

---

[177] Robert Pullen *Sent.* 2.11, 2.12, *PL* 186: 734D–735A, 736D, 738D. Heinzemann, *Die Unsterblichkeit*, pp. 82–84, in stressing Robert's dependence on Hugh of St. Victor, ignores this point and the other non-Victorine elements in Robert's psychology.
[178] Robert Pullen, *Sent.* 2.11, *PL* 186: 736B–D.
[179] Ibid., 2.12, *PL* 186: 738C–739A.

Interesting as is his discussion of sensation, and informative as it is in conveying the three ancient philosophical accounts of that process to his readers, the passage just noted is, strictly speaking, a digression in Robert's treatise on the soul, which is geared to the faculties of the soul viewed from a moral perspective. He returns to this agenda by emphasizing that intellectual assent is of the essence in moral acts. Not only must the mind consent to a sin, for example, before the body can carry it out, but there are sins that are purely mental, like pride and envy.[180] Less intimately connected to Robert's theme, and problematic in its own right, is his discussion of another mental faculty, imagination. He defines imagination as the representation in the mind of some sensible thing that is currently absent. Ignoring the fact that this same definition would apply equally well to a concept, from which he does not differentiate imagination, Robert adds that man shares this faculty with animals, anchoring the claim with the point that both men and animals dream. He does not indicate how we can know that animals dream, but concludes his treatment of mental faculties by noting that men can bring their rational judgment to bear on the content of their dreams while animals cannot.

There was one other essay in faculty psychology in our period, that of Robert of Melun, who calls upon another Aristotelian distinction, the distinction among the vegetative, animate, and rational souls, each in charge of a particular subdivision of human activity. His main reason for appealing to this principle is not the desire to criticize Robert Pullen's model of the concupiscible, irascible, and rational faculties but to support Abelard's Trinitarian theology and to attack the Augustinian analogy of memory, intellect, and will. His chosen substitute does not involve faculties that work in and through each other.[181] Robert of Melun gives most of the attention he devotes to the human soul to the effort to prove its immortality, an unusual activity since this was not a debated question at the time. His dialogue is principally with Augustine and Cassiodorus here and not with any contemporary *quidam*.[182] He begins with moral arguments which suggest that the nature of creatures possessing moral ends must be compatible with those ends. Since the human soul was given an innate desire for the good,

---

[180] Ibid., 2.15, *PL* 186: 740C–741A.
[181] Robert of Melun, *Sent.* 1.6.44, *Oeuvres*, 3 part 2: 334–40.
[182] The text is printed in Raymond-M. Martin, "L'immortalité de l'âme d'après Robert de Melun (d. 1167)," *Revue néo-scolastique de philosophie* 36 (1934): 139–45.

a capacity to recognize it, the ability to attain virtue and to be rewarded for it, the soul must be able to enjoy these ends eternally. Robert then offers proofs based on the metaphysical structure of the soul which align him with those contemporaries who profess a Platonizing psychology. The soul is capable of living without the body, he urges, and is the principle of being of the person to whom it belongs, the essence of that person. It lacks the kinds of mutability that affect the essences of things that are mortal. He concludes that only the deity, Who created it, can annihilate the soul. Against the claim that, as the form of the body, the soul dies with the body, he offers not a refutation but the counterclaim that this is only one of the soul's functions. When the body dies, the soul is free to do other things. To those who say that the soul is mortal because, like the body, it can be afflicted by illness, he answers that spiritual sickness is not terminal or irreversible. This may well be the case, but it does not demonstrate that the soul is immortal. In any event, these concerns delimit, for the most part, the issues that Robert wants to discuss about the nature of the human soul.

A related issue on which we also find a range of opinions and which serves as a point of transition for the theologians from man's created nature before the fall to the fall itself is free will. Everyone agrees that man was endowed with free will in paradise. But there is some disagreement over how to define it and also over its scope and capacity to win virtue for prelapsarian man. The school of Laon offers a range of opinions in defining free will. Anselm of Laon and one of his followers align themselves with Anselm of Canterbury and state that free will is the power to serve rectitude for its own sake.[183] Anselm adds that free will has two parts, approving (*approbans*) and desiring (*appetens*). The first is rational and always good (*semper bona*); it reflects man's natural desire for the good. The second draws man into sensual pleasures which may be bad as well as good.[184] Another view of free will found in the school of Laon and also in Bernard of Clairvaux, and one that recurs in Hugh of St. Victor, the *Summa sententiarum*, the *Sententiae divinitas*, and also Peter Lombard, is the idea that free will is threefold. It involves freedom from necessity, freedom from sin, and freedom from misery (*a necessitate, a peccato, a miseria*).[185] Freedom from necessity is the

---

[183] Anselm of Laon, *Sent. divine pagine* 4, pp. 27–28; *Sentences of the School of Laon*, no. 322, 5: 253.

[184] Anselm of Laon, *Sent. divine pagine* 4, pp. 27–28.

[185] *Sentences of Probable Authenticity*, no. 108, 5: 87. Cf. Bernard of Clairvaux, *De gratia et libero arbitrio* 3.6–7, ed. J. Leclercq and H. M. Rochais in *Bernard of Clairvaux, Opera*, 8 vols. (Rome: Éditiones Cistercienses, 1955–77), 3: 170–71. The best analyses of Bernard's doctrine are Bernard McGinn, intro. to Bernard of

natural capacity of the will to choose, to be the cause of its own actions, without any external constraint or impediment. Freedom from sin is the effective choice of the good according to the counsel of right reason. Freedom from misery adds to this choice its fruition in good action. The first of these, freedom from necessity, is substantive of the will and is indestructible; it is a gift of nature. The second and third freedoms are accidental; they are gifts of grace.

Twelfth-century scholastics who follow this last definition of free will tend to bring it to bear on the question of whether man had virtue before the fall. A good case in point is Hugh of St. Victor. Repeating the threefold definition just noted, he adds that Adam needed grace in order to exercise free will for the good. Defining virtue as "nothing other than an affection of the mind ordered according to reason" (*virtus namque nihil aliud est quam affectus mentis secundum rationem ordinatus*), he observes that virtue may be by nature or grace. Grace is both the grace of creation and the grace of restoration. The first operates in man; the second cooperates with man. All virtue, Hugh continues, must involve grace in order to be meritorious. Thus, for Hugh, Adam possessed created grace before the fall, although after the fall, man needs both kinds. And so,

---

Clairvaux, *On Grace and Free Will*, trans. Daniel O'Donovan (Kalamazoo: Cistercian Publications, 1977), pp. 15–42 and Luigi Sartori, "Natura e grazia nella dottrina di S. Bernardo," *Studia patavina* 1 (1954): 41–64. See also Gillian R. Evans, *The Mind of Bernard of Clairvaux* (Oxford: Clarendon Press, 1983), pp. 51, 159–62; Emmanuel Kern, *Das Tugendsystem des heiligen Bernhard von Clairvaux* (Freiburg im Breisgau: Herder, 1934), pp. 5–9; Bernard Maréchaux, "L'Oeuvre doctrinale de Saint Bernard," *La Vie spirituelle* 17 (1927): 196–200; Armando Rigobello, *Linee per una antropologia prescolastica* (Padua: Antenore, 1972), pp. 48–61. Scholars who have seen Bernard as the source of this idea in Hugh of St. Victor, the *Summa sententiarum*, the *Sententiae divinitatis*, and Peter Lombard while discounting or ignoring the possible influence of the school of Laon include Jean Châtillon, "L'influence de S. Bernard sur la pensée scolastique au XIIᵉ et au XIIIᵉ siècle," in *D'Isidore de Séville à Saint Thomas d'Aquin: Études d'histoire et de théologie* (London: Variorum, 1985), pp. 268–88; Ulrich Faust, "Bernhards 'Liber de gratia et libero arbitrio': Bedeutung, Quellen und Einfluss," in *Analecta monastica: Textes et études sur la vie des moines*, 6th ser. (Rome: Herder, 1962), pp. 35–51; Erich Kleineidam, "De triplici libertate: Anselm von Laon oder Bernhard von Clairvaux?" *Cîteaux* 11 (1960): 55–62; "Wissen, Wissenschaft, Theologie bei Bernard von Clairvaux," in *Bernhard von Clairvaux. Mönch und Mystiker* (Wiesbaden: Franz Steiner Verlag GMBH, 1955), pp. 131–32; Artur Michael Landgraf, "Der heilige Bernhard in seinem Verhältnis zur Theologie des zwölften Jahrhunderts," in ibid., pp. 44–62; *Dogmengeschichte*, 1 part 1: 88–168; Jean Leclercq, "S. Bernard et la théologie monastique du XIIᵉ siècle," in *Saint Bernard théologien* (Rome: Tipografia Pio X, 1953), pp. 7–23; McGinn, intro. to O'Donovan trans. of *On Grace and Free Will*, pp. 39–42; John R. Sommerfeldt, "Bernard of Clairvaux and Scholasticism," *Papers of the Michigan Academy of Sciences, Arts, and Letters* 48 (1963): 265–77; Sofia Vanni Rovighi, "S. Bernardo e la filosofia," in *S. Bernardo: Pubblicazione commemorativa nell'VIII centenario della sua morte* (Milan: Vita e Pensiero, 1954), pp. 143–45.

Adam had meritorious virtue.[186] This analysis, while it begins by opening the possibility that there could be natural virtue through man's exercise of reason and free will, ends by closing the door firmly on that possibility. The author of the *Summa sententiarum* and Robert Pullen follow Hugh's line of reasoning and reach the same conclusion.[187] This was not, however, the only position taken in the period by masters who accepted the threefold definition of free will. Robert of Melun, for instance, emphasizes the point that man enjoyed full integrity of both body and soul before the fall and argues that he could know the truth without error and that he could do the good without difficulty (*sine difficultate*); he does not raise the question of whether Adam needed grace in order to do good. Rather, what Robert wants to stress is the point that free will enables man to resist grace.[188] And, Roland of Bologna, who does take up the question, asserts that Adam possessed the virtue of charity before the fall and that he could seek the good "without the assistance of grace" (*absque gratia adiutrice*). He does confuse matters, however, by stating in the same passage that Adam did enjoy prevenient grace before the fall, although it did not prevent him from sinning.[189]

A final issue, directly pertinent to the fall, on which we find a range of opinions in the first half of the twelfth century, is the nature of woman, and whether it is equal to the nature of man. Here, we encounter a striking lack of logic. Many theologians, following Augustine, emphasize the point that Eve was taken from Adam's side, and not from his head or his feet, to show that, as a wife and loving companion, she was his equal, not his superior or inferior. As with Hugh of St. Victor and Abelard, they tend to gloss the point with an eye to the sacrament of marriage.[190] Despite the consubstantiality of Adam and Eve, the theologians reflect an unexcogitated sexism in viewing Eve as a weaker vessel. Anselm of Laon holds that she is Adam's physical inferior, although his spiritual equal; other members of the school of Laon see Eve as less rational than Adam.[191] Abelard also regards Eve's inferiority as

---

[186] Hugh of St. Victor, *De sac.* 1.6.16–17, *PL* 176: 272C–275A. The quotation is at 1.6.17, 273C.

[187] *Summa sent.* 3.7, *PL* 176: 98D–100B; Robert Pullen, *Sent.* 2.20, *PL* 186: 747C.

[188] Robert of Melun, *Sent.* 1.1.8, *Oeuvres*, 3 part 1: 207–08. The quotation is on p. 208.

[189] Roland of Bologna, *Sent.*, pp. 119–20.

[190] Hugh of St. Victor, *De sac.* 1.6.35, *PL* 176: 284C; Peter Abelard, *Hex.*, pp. 78, 133–35.

[191] Anselm of Laon, *Sent. divine pagine* 1, p. 25, *Sent. Anselmi* 2, p. 60; *Deus du cuius principio et fine tacetur*, p. 262.

intellectual, not physical; he represents the tradition that Eve was made only in God's likeness, but not His image as well.[192] And, several members of the school of Laon as well as Roland of Bologna think that Eve was Adam's inferior both in body and soul, and that she would rightly have been subordinated to him even if there had been no fall.[193] Hugh as well as Robert Pullen think that Eve was weaker than Adam although without specifying where the weakness lies.[194] None of these masters sees this inconsistency as a problematic feature of his treatment of human nature before the fall or of human nature as such.

The Lombard on Prelapsarian Human Nature

As Peter Lombard tackles the subject of human nature before the fall, he makes it plain that he is going to propose a less subordinationist model, both with respect to man and woman and with respect to the relations between body and soul. Launching the topic with his own version of the theme that man is made in God's image and likeness, he orchestrates it in such a way as to make both attributes applicable to all human beings as such. This argument can be read as a critique of Abelard and the tradition of antifeminism in which he stands here,[195] although, as noted, Abelard was scarcely the only proponent of female inferiority in this period. First, and characteristically, Peter defines his terms. In using the word "image" we are speaking of a created similarity that is understood in a relative sense (*relative*) with respect to its prototype, as with an image of Caesar on one of his coins and Caesar himself. The human soul resembles God in five respects: its rationality; its possession of the Trinitarian analogy of memory, intellect, and will; its natural capacity to be innocent and just; its immortality; and its indivisibility. The image of God can be seen in the human soul's formal, essential, or structural resemblance to God, while its likeness to God can be seen in its functional similarities to Him.[196]

---

[192] Peter Abelard, *Hex.*, pp. 70–72, 77. On this point, see Mary M. McLaughlin, "Abelard and the Dignity of Women," in *Pierre Abélard, Pierre le Vénérable: Les courants philosophiques, littéraires et artistiques en occident au milieu du XII* siècle*, ed. René Louis, Jean Jolivet, and Jean Châtillon (Paris: CNRS, 1975), pp. 306–08.

[193] *Sent. Anselmi* 2, pp. 57, 60; *Voluntas Dei, relata ad ipsum Deum*, in *Sentences of the School of Laon*, no. 523, 5: 346; *Deus de cuius principio et fine tacetur*, p. 262; Roland of Bologna, *Sent.*, pp. 125–29.

[194] Hugh of St. Victor, *De sac.* 1.7.3, *PL* 176: 287D–288B; Robert Pullen, *Sent.* 2.21, *PL* 186: 248B.

[195] Stephan Otto, *Die Funktion des Bildbegriffes in der Theologie des 12. Jahrhunderts*, Beiträge, 40:1 (Münster: Aschendorff, 1963), pp. 200–06.

[196] Peter Lombard, *Sent.* 2. d. 16. c. 1–c. 4.1, 1: 406–09.

We may note here that this argument accomplishes two things at once. It makes it impossible to ascribe either image only or likeness only to any human soul, since the structure and function of the soul are interdependent. Peter also provides another foundation, in man's psychology, for the utility of the memory, intellect, and will analogy, which he also defends persuasively, on other grounds, in his Trinitarian theology. For it is in this attribute of the soul that structure and function coincide the most clearly. Admitting that he cannot resolve the question of whether there was a time lag between the creation of Adam's body and the creation of his soul, which should not be seen as consubstantial with God despite the language of Genesis, and noting that the creation of Adam and Eve as adults was a unique event, Peter holds that, for the rest of the human race, the parents make the body as inferior causes, and then God creates the soul, and that He creates it in the body after the body is formed.[197]

Like the creation of Adam, the creation of Eve was an exception to this rule. This being the case, it is of interest to see which aspects of that topic Peter accents and which he omits. Eve is created from Adam, he notes, so that all human beings will appreciate his common paternity of the whole human race and will love each other as blood relatives. Eve was taken from Adam's side, and here Peter follows Augustine, Hugh, and others, to indicate the particular bond of love (*consortium dilectionis*) uniting husband and wife. The relationship is one of affection and not one of superiority or inferiority as would be suggested had she been created from Adam's head or feet.[198] He poses another question, as to why God created Eve when Adam was asleep, answering it with the observation that this was done to avoid causing Adam any pain, before continuing with the widely held opinion that this mode of Eve's creation also signifies the birth of the church from the side of the crucified Christ. Peter concludes by rejecting the theory put forth by the author of the *Summa sententiarum* on the creation of Eve's body by the action of seminal causes, asserting that her creation was purely miraculous.[199] He does not describe Eve as weaker in mind or body than Adam. The subordination of wife to husband is not a theme he takes up here. It occurs primarily in his Pauline commentaries, as a pendant of the consequences of original sin, but does not appear in Peter's discussion of the original creation in the *Sentences*.

---

[197] Ibid., d. 17. c. 2–c. 3, d. 18. c. 7.1–4, 1: 410–13, 420–21.
[198] Ibid., d. 18. c. 1. c. 2, 1: 416–17. The quotation is at c. 2, p. 416.
[199] Ibid., c. 5, 1: 418–19.

Rather, the creation of Eve prompts him to make a brief excursus
on the subject of causation, in which he distinguishes among God's
direct causation in making things out of nothing, as is the case with
God's creation of Eve's soul; God's direct causation in turning one
thing into another thing miraculously, as is the case with the
formation of Eve's body out of Adam's rib; and the action of
inferior or secondary causes in created nature, such as the parents'
conception of the bodies of their children, into which the souls
created by God are infused.[200] In short, the topic of Eve's created
nature inspires in Peter reflections that are largely physical and
metaphysical, and to a lesser extent matrimonial and ecclesiological. They are not reflections designed to justify a vision of female
inferiority as a condition of the creation. In the rest of what he has
to say, then, he means both male and female nature when he speaks
of the nature of man before the fall.

In turning to that subject, Peter acknowledges freely that it
contains many points of interest in themselves "which it is not
useless to know, even if they are sometimes investigated merely out
of curiosity" (quae non inutiliter sciuntur, licet aliquando curiositate
quaeruntur).[201] He divides the topic into what we can know about
man's body and soul, beginning with mortality, because it applies
to both aspects of man's constitution. He agrees with the consensus
here, that Adam and Eve had the capacity to die and not to die; in
the fallen condition, man has the capacity to die and lacks the
capacity not to die, while in the next life he will have the non posse
mori, the incapacity to die, since death will no longer have dominion
over him.[202] Moving to man's natural physical aptitudes and conditions before the fall, Peter agrees with the standard Augustinian
view of human sexuality in Eden. Armed with this authority, he
raises, and rejects, Origen's claim that the procreation of offspring
would have been asexual had the fall not occurred, and agrees that,
according to God's plan, the use of sex would have been free from
lust and fully under the control of man's rational will. As for the
children born of a sinless Adam and Eve, he finds it hard to take
seriously the claim that they would have been born as adults or that
they would have been born with faculties not possessed by newborn
infants. Taking a less credulous line here than Honorius, Hugh,
and the Summa sententiarum, he argues on the basis of naturalism and

---

[200] Ibid., c. 5.4–c. 7.4, 1: 418–21.
[201] Ibid., d. 19, c. 1.1, 1: 421.
[202] Ibid., c. 1.3–d. 20. c. 3, 1: 422, with more on this subject at d. 20. c. 2–c. 6, 1:
422–27.

common sense. The frame of the womb, he observes, is too small to permit the delivery of adult-size people. If offspring of this sort were to be born, they would constitute a physical anomaly, having the size of infants and the configuration of adults. The authority who had raised this question, Augustine, had raised it as a mere possibility, by no means as a certainty, or even as a likelihood. Peter thinks it far more reasonable to suppose that the children of Adam and Eve, like other children, would have undergone gestation in the womb, and normal development from infancy to childhood to adulthood over the course of time. For, as he points out, it was mortality, not the exercise of man's natural physical functions, that was the consequence of sin. Here, he annexes gestation and growth, as natural processes, to eating, drinking, sexuality, and other natural functions that he sees as basic to human nature as such and as hence forming a normal part of life in paradise.[203] In his handling of this entire topic, Peter makes it clear that natural physical functions and processes are not a defect, just as the body itself is not a defect or a consequence of sin. He makes a more solidly naturalistic application of the anti-Origen agenda here than any theologian of his time, despite the fact that he may have derived his sense of how to pose these questions from authorities from masters with a more Platonic anthropology, such as Hugh of St. Victor.

Peter also shows a willingness to speculate on contrary-to-fact conditions that cannot be verified either by reason or authority. After having borne children, he asks, would the original parents have continued to enjoy their immortality in Eden, along with their children, and their other descendants, or would they have been transferred to a celestial life, transformed not by death but by some other means, and likewise their children? The inquiry arises from the presumption that the garden of Eden was of finite size. Peter notes that Augustine, the source of this question, gives an ambiguous answer to it. He himself is willing to entertain the possibility of the celestial transfer, although he thinks that we cannot establish with certitude when and how it might have taken place.[204] This passage is a nice index of Peter's combination of curiosity, caution, and common sense in addressing life in Eden.

Given the fact that the life of the body, in its sinless state, was "neither silly or inappropriate" (*non sit absurdum vel inconveniens*), Peter asks, by way of making a crisp transition to man's spiritual faculties before the fall, whether it would have been possible for

---

[203] Ibid., d. 20. c. 1–c. 2, c. 4, 1: 127–28, 429–31.
[204] Ibid., c. 3, 1: 428–29.

prelapsarian man, through his senses and intellect, to have known
the truth and to have come to a perfect knowledge, perfect, that is,
in the light of what a created intelligence can know. He raises an
objection to this formulation of the possibilities. If sinless man
underwent a learning process, this would mean that he started out
ignorant, and ignorance is a consequence of sin. So, the objection
continues, and it is the position of Hugh of St. Victor which Peter
presents in this way, before the fall Adam possessed perfect knowledge all at once. Peter rejects this argument, and draws a distinction in so doing. The ignorance that is a consequence of sin is
ignorance caused by the clouding of man's intellect so that he does
not know what he ought to know. The beginning point for sinless
man, on the other hand, is not a weakened intellect but one that is
not yet as fully knowledgeable as it later could have become. For, it
was the divine plan to translate man subsequently to an even
better and worthier state, where his knowledge could be fuller and
where he could enjoy a celestial and eternal good. Two levels of
wisdom and goodness were prepared for man by the creator, a
temporal and visible one in Eden and an eternal and invisible one
in Heaven. The fact that mental and moral development are part of
sinless man's natural capacities is not a defect, just as the physical
development of the children he would have engendered is not a
defect. As for the specific types of knowledge possessed by man
before the fall, he had, according to Peter, the rational capacity to
distinguish good from evil. With regard to creatures, he knew that
they were created, that they were created for man to rule and enjoy,
and that they yield a knowledge of the providence of God. These
forms of knowledge, he adds, man retained after the fall. But Adam
also had a more direct mode of knowing God, through an inner
aspiration which enabled him to perceive the presence of God. This
knowledge, Peter holds, is not as great as the face to face vision of
God enjoyed by the saints in the life to come, but it was a knowledge that was direct and immediate, not through a glass darkly, as
men currently know God in this life. Further, Adam had self-
knowledge. He knew who he was, his place in the scheme of things,
what his duties were, what to do and what to avoid, which, as Peter
observes, made him responsible for what he did in the fall. Adam,
however, did not have foreknowledge of the fall or of anything
else.[205]

If Peter departs from Hugh of St. Victor's analysis of man's
knowledge before the fall, he also departs from the tripartite analy-

---

[205] Ibid., c. 5–d. 23. c. 4, 1: 131–50.

sis of his faculties given by Hugh and, indeed, from the Platonized or Aristotelianized faculty psychology found in other scholastics of this period. According to Peter, the soul of man has two faculties. There is an inferior power in his soul (*vis animae inferior*), which man shares with the animals and which he uses to regulate the body and sensible matters and the disposition of temporal things. There is also reason (*ratio*), the superior mental faculty, which is the intelligence that enables us to grasp higher things, whether rational or contemplative. The first or sensual soul he calls *anima* and the intellectual soul he calls *ratio*.[206] Thus far, the twelfth-century thinker to whom he comes the closest is William of Champeaux, although William calls the latter faculty *spiritus*. But Peter does not add on a special suprarational faculty as William does. His handling of the structure of the soul appears to be all his own, in this period.

If critical of Hugh and of other contemporaries in this regard, Peter agrees substantially with Hugh and the author of the *Summa sententiarum* in handling the free will and moral capacities of prelapsarian man, and uses much the same language as they do. He maintains, as they do, that free will is the natural rational capacity to choose either good or evil without restraint, and that the choice of good is assisted by grace, in Adam before the fall, just as it is in the case of the angels. With these Victorine masters, he argues for a grace of creation, which enables Adam to resist evil but not to perfect himself in good. In order to win merit and to attain the fullest virtue of which he was capable, Adam needed cooperating grace as well. Peter draws a distinction in his discussion of Adam's need for both created and cooperating grace which amplifies on the Victorine account. The former mode of grace is not the same as the operating grace that liberates fallen man from slavery to sin. Rather, it prepares Adam to receive the cooperating grace which man needs, both before and after the fall, to develop virtue and merit. Thus, while Peter calls the virtues Adam possessed before the fall cardinal virtues, these are not understood as the cardinal virtues available to the virtuous pagans, an ethical category which neither Peter nor his Victorine sources here acknowledges to exist. For Peter, as for Hugh, the *Summa sententiarum*, and, ultimately, Augustine, man before the fall faced no impediment to the doing of the good, and nothing impelled him to do evil. The divine aid he needed in order to do good efficaciously and meritoriously was available to him. But, the only efficacious moral choice which man

---

[206] Ibid., d. 24. c. 4–c. 5, 1: 453–54.

could make purely on the basis of his natural rational endowment of free will was the choice of evil.[207]

THE FALL: CONTEMPORARY DEBATES

This brings us to the last major topic dealt with the Lombard in Book 2 of the *Sentences* which we plan to treat in this chapter and which we need to understand in the light of contemporary analyses, the fall itself and the effects and transmission of original sin. These issues elicited wide interest in the first half of the twelfth century and inspired a notable variety of answers.[208] In outlining the scenario of the fall, in describing the motivation of Adam and Eve, and in considering whether one of these offenders was a worse sinner than the other, there is, indeed, considerable disagreement. Some theologians, like the author of the *Sententie Anselmi*, Honorius, Hugh of St. Victor, and Roland of Bologna, begin the story with the motivation of the devil as an exterior source of temptation, seeing him as inspired by envy of man and malice toward man.[209] Roland observes that the devil assumes the form of a serpent because serpents inspire fear. He raises but fails to answer the question of why Eve was not afraid of the serpent or surprised to hear it speak.[210] Other masters begin with the internal temptations experienced by the first parents or by man generically, or treat them as simultaneous with the devil's external temptation. The authors of the *Sententiae divinitatis* and *Summa sententiarum* opt for disobedience here,[211] Honorius adding vainglory and Roland adding pride, and both treating the interior and exterior temptation as simultaneous.[212] Robert of Melun is unique in seeing original sin as inspired by concupiscence, although he, like everyone else in this period, holds that this failing is a consequence of original sin more generally.[213]

---

[207] Ibid., c. 1–c. 2, d. 25. c. 1–d. 29. c. 2, 1: 450–52, 461–93.

[208] Excellent surveys are provided by Robert Blomme, *La doctrine du péché dans les écoles théologiques de la première moitié du XIIe siècle* (Louvain: Publications Universitaires de Louvain, 1958); Odon Lottin, "Les théories du péché originel au XIIe siècle: I. L'école d'Anselme de Laon et de Guillaume de Champeaux," *RTAM* 11 (1939): 17–32; "Les théories du péché originel au XIIe siècle: II. La réaction abélardienne et porrétaine," *RTAM* 12 (1940): 78–103; "Les théories du péché originel au XIIe siècle: III. Tradition augustinienne," *RTAM* 12 (1940): 236–74. These three papers of Lottin are reworked in his *Psych. et morale*, 4 part 1: 13–170.

[209] *Sent. Anselmi* 2, p. 60; Honorius, *Eluc.* 1.83–84, p. 376; Hugh of St. Victor, *De sac.* 1.7.1–2, *PL* 176: 287B–D; Roland of Bologna, *Sent.*, pp. 116–18.

[210] Roland of Bologna, *Sent.*, p. 118.

[211] *Sent. div.* 3.1, p. 39*; *Summa sent.* 3.14, *PL* 176: 111A.

[212] Honorius, *Eluc.* 1.94, p. 377; Roland of Bologna, *Sent.*, p. 116.

[213] This position is found in a portion of Robert's treatise that remains un-

Most contemporary masters break down the internal motivations to sin, assigning different ones to Adam and to Eve. Anselm of Laon and William of Champeaux find Eve guilty of avarice, in the sense of the desire to know, and idolatry, in the sense of her seeking to be God's equal, the author of the *Sententie Anselmi* adding that she is culpable as well of gluttony and of tempting Adam.[214] Hugh of St. Victor sees her basic temptation as that of doubt. It is Eve's intellectual curiosity that leads in turn to her pride, avarice, and gluttony.[215] Robert Pullen has no comment on Eve's motivations, but has a clear if narrow and politically conceived theory of how Adam went wrong. Adam, according to Robert, was the ruler in Eden. As head of the household he was responsible for keeping his wife, as his subject, in line. His sin, then, was not preventing Eve from sinning and failing to use his authority appropriately.[216] To the sin of a ruler giving in to his subject the author of the *Sententie Anselmi* adds to the bill of attainder against Adam both love and the desire for knowledge. To this he attaches six other sins of which he holds Adam guilty, pride, sacrilege, homicide in the sense that his fall brought death to mankind, fornication in the sense of spiritual infidelity to God, theft, and avarice. He thereby blurs the distinction between the causes and consequences of original sin.[217] But love alone, and the placing of his love for Eve over his duty to God, is the most popular description of Adam's motivation, attracting the support of William of Champeaux, Honorius, and Hugh of St. Victor.[218]

Despite the detail into which they go in assigning these motivations, and despite their possession of a theory of the psychogenesis of moral decision-making, it is noteworthy how few of these theologians integrate their general psychology of sin with their analysis of the fall in any way. The school of Laon sets the tone for what would become a widely held view, derived from Jerome and Augustine, that distinguishes temptation (*suggestio*), whether inner or outer, from contemplation of the sin toward which the temptation points

---

edited. We are indebted to the information supplied from the study of the manuscripts by Raymond-M. Martin, "Les idées de Robert de Melun sur le péché originel," *RSPT* 7 (1913): 700–25; 8 (1914): 439–66; 9 (1920): 103–20; 11 (1922): 390–415.

[214] Anselm of Laon, *Sent. divine pagine* 4, pp. 25–26; *Sentences of William of Champeaux*, no. 246, 5: 203; *Sent. Anselmi* 2, pp. 60–66.

[215] Hugh of St. Victor, *De sac.* 1.7.10, *PL* 176: 290C–291B.

[216] Robert Pullen, *Sent.* 2.21–22, *PL* 186: 748B–750A.

[217] *Sent. Anselmi* 2, pp. 60–66.

[218] *Sentences of William of Champeaux*, no. 246, 5: 203; Honorius, *Eluc.* 1.91, p. 377; Hugh of St. Victor, *De sac.* 1.7.10, *PL* 176: 290C–291B.

(*delectatio*), and from the voluntary capitulation to the temptation (*consensus*), in which sin is seen to reside, whether or not the intention is expressed in external action.[219] But the masters of that school do not bring this doctrine to bear on their analysis of original sin. The only two contemporary theologians who do so, prior to Peter Lombard, are the authors of the *Sententiae divinitatis* and *Summa sententiarum*. The former master observes that sin can be viewed as consisting in will or consent, or in operation. He does not clarify which of these modes constitutes the essence of the moral act.[220] The author of the *Summa sententiarum* gives a clearer and more elaborate analysis. Sin, he observes, involves a failure to participate in good as well as a participation in evil. The evil involved can be of the body or of the soul, or both. In either case, both a bad intention and its translation into an evil action are required. Following Isidore of Seville, he holds that the bad will inspiring these intentions and actions can spring from either desire or fear. Sins, he continues, can be committed against oneself, one's neighbor, or God. He attaches to this point, by way of conclusion, the seven deadly sins or seven vicious intentionalities, following Gregory the Great's classification, and agrees with Gregory that pride is the worst of the lot.[221] This account, indeed, may even tell the reader more than he needs to know in order to understand the psychology of Adam and Eve in the fall.

Especially for those theologians who assign different motives to Adam and Eve, a related topic on which there was a wealth of patristic disagreement that is reflected in twelfth-century discussions was the question of which of the primal pair was the worse sinner. After ventilating both sides of the controversy, the author of the *Sententie Anselmi* names Adam as the greater sinner. Since Eve was less intelligent and more credulous than Adam, he holds that she was deceived, while Adam sinned deliberately, with his eyes wide open. This solution appeals, for the same reasons, to other masters such as Roland of Bologna, who also thinks that Eve is intellectually inferior to Adam.[222] Whether or not they see Eve's inferiority as mental, physical, or both, a larger number of masters subscribe to the view that she bore a heavier weight of responsibility in the fall. Neither Anselm of Laon, his followers, Abelard, nor Robert Pullen sees Eve's alleged credulity as an extenuating cir-

---

[219] *Sentences of Anselm of Laon*, no. 85–86; *Sentences of William of Champeaux*, no. 278; *Sentences of the School of Laon*, no. 454, 523, 5: 73–74, 222, 304–05, 346.

[220] *Sent. div.* 3.1, p. 39*.

[221] *Summa sent.* 3.14–16, *PL* 176: 111A–114C.

[222] *Sent. Anselmi* 2, pp. 60–66; Roland of Bologna, *Sent.*, pp. 125–29.

cumstance. Instead, they give her the full blame for seeking equality with God, which, in their view, was more serious than anything
Adam did in the fall.[223] Some of those who emphasize Eve's guilt
feel a need to address the question of why original sin is nevertheless called the sin of Adam. Robert Pullen invokes his political
understanding of the relationship of Adam and Eve here. Since
Adam is the authority in charge, he has to assume responsibility for
the crimes of his underlings; Eve, from Robert's perspective, has to
be seen as a minor or as a legal incompetent incapable of assuming
responsibility for her own actions.[224] William of Champeaux, for his
part, offers an explanation that draws on biology as well as law.
The male sex is superior (*dignior*) not only because filiation and
inheritance are determined by association with the male line, but
also because the male seed is the active principle in the conception
of offspring.[225]

There are three other position that seek to mediate between these
extremes. The Porretan view is that both sides of the debate have
merit. Eve can be seen as bearing a greater guilt in that she sinned
against both God and Adam, while Adam sinned only against God.
Adam can be seen as being more guilty because he sinned more
knowingly. Our author finds it possible to support both of these
analyses without choosing between them.[226] The author of the
Summa sententiarum is more decisive. After reviewing the two positions, framed in the same way as the Porretan master presents
them, he provides a solution based on an analogy. If a cleric and a
layman commit the same kind of crime, he notes, the cleric is
regarded as incurring a greater degree of guilt. In the case of Adam
and Eve, he thinks that their guilt in the fall was equal, but that we
can impute guilt to Adam more heavily. He argues for this conclusion not on the basis of sexism but on the basis of Isidore of Seville's
point that sins of deliberation are worse than sins of ignorance.[227]
This is an ingenious answer, and one not without influence. It is
also one that departs from Hugh of St. Victor's handling of the
problem. Harking back to the point that Eve's temptation was the
desire for knowledge and Adam's temptation was the love of his

[223] Anselm of Laon, *Sent. divine pagine* 4, pp. 25–26; *Deus de cuius principio et fine tacetur*, p. 262; Robert Pullen, *Sent.* 2.21–22, *PL* 186: 748A–750B; Peter Abelard, *Hex.*, pp. 70–72, 77. For Abelard's position, see McLaughlin, "Abelard and the Dignity of Women," pp. 306–08; Sikes, *Peter Abailard*, pp. 42–44.
[224] Robert Pullen, *Sent.* 2.21–22, *PL* 186: 748A–750B.
[225] *Sentences of William of Champeaux*, no. 252, 5: 205–06.
[226] *Sent. mag. Gisleberti* I 13.64–66, p. 172.
[227] *Summa sent.* 3.6, *PL* 176: 98B–C.

wife, Hugh states that it is impossible to say that either sin was worse than the other. Since we all possess both the intellectual and the affective faculties, we should view the fall of Adam and Eve not as two separate falls but as two facets of the same delict that occurs whenever any moral subject makes sinful use of free will.[228]

The nature of the forbidden fruit is also a subject exercising some early twelfth-century masters. Did God forbid the fruit because the fruit was itself noxious? And, why would He have wanted to bar Adam and Eve from the knowledge of good and evil? Both Anselm of Laon, the author of the *Sententie Anselmi* and Robert of Melun agree that the fruit was not intrinsically harmful. In their estimation, God forbade it to Adam and Eve not because the fruit, or the knowledge it stands for, would have been bad for them but rather as a test of obedience.[229] Honorius concurs with the idea that the fruit was not harmful but worries more about the knowledge of good and evil connected with it in the text of Genesis. Following Augustine, he argues that this knowledge lay not in the tree or its fruit but, in part, in the transgression of God's orders. Adam and Eve did have a knowledge of good before they sinned; but, in their fall, they acquired the knowledge of evil as well.[230]

Honorius also raises two other questions concerning the fall as an event, to which he gives elaborate answers. When, he asks, did the fall take place? In response, he offers a detailed timetable of events during the sixth day of creation. Adam was created in the third hour of that day, Eve in the sixth hour. She was tempted within sixty minutes of her creation and had accomplished the temptation of Adam by the end of the seventh hour. For reasons best known to Honorius, God waited until the ninth hour of the sixth day to eject them from Eden. As for the flaming sword wielded by the angel left on guard after that time, Honorius follows Augustine on Genesis in reading this passage allegorically. The angel's sword stands for the wall of fire with which God surrounded Eden, as well as for two ranks of angels, one deputed to block man's body and the other deputed to block man's soul from returning to paradise.[231] Judging from the lack of resonance of these two points later in the century, we can conclude that other theologians in this period found Honorius's specificity on the timing of the fall fanciful and unnecessary

---

[228] Hugh of St. Victor, *De sac.* 1.7.10, *PL* 176: 290C–291B.
[229] Anselm of Laon, *Sent. divine pagine* 4; *Sent. Anselmi* 2, pp. 25, 58; Robert Pullen, *Sent.* 2.19, *PL* 186: 746C–D.
[230] Honorius, *Eluc.* 1.87, p. 376.
[231] Ibid., 1.90–91, p. 377.

and his sources insufficiently trustworthy, and also that they preferred a literal reading of the angelic guardian despite the Augustinian foundation for Honorius's account.

The Lombard on the Fall

Peter Lombard's handling of the fall shows him at his most eclectic. He does not regard any theologian or group of theologians either as his chief inspiration or as presenting the doctrine most in need of refutation. His own answers to the questions he poses can be found in a range of current and recent masters, from whom he borrows freely and selectively. He is less likely to rephrase their ideas in his own vocabulary here than is true of the teachings he presents elsewhere in Book 2 of the *Sentences*. To this mix of opinions Peter adds some reflections of his own. He also adds, it must be said, two self-contradictions, to which we will call special attention since this is a phenomenon quite unusual in his work. Agreeing with Honorius, the author of the *Sententie Anselmi*, Roland of Bologna, and Hugh of St. Victor, Peter sees the events leading up to the fall as having been triggered by external temptation, in the form of the devil's envy. In explaining why the devil tempted Eve first, Peter introduces his first major inconsistency. Notwithstanding his account of the creation of all human beings in the image as well as the likeness of God, and despite his assertion, later in his discussion of the fall, that Adam and Eve are equal in nature, he states that Eve was approached first because she was less rational than Adam.[232] He does not appear to be aware of this discrepancy or of the need to justify this departure from what he says elsewhere on the same subject. In dealing with the devil's assumption of the body of a serpent, Peter is less interested in why this particular animal was chosen than in the observation that, since the devil is a spiritual being, he needed to take on physical form of some sort in order to make his appearance to Eve and that God permitted him to do so, although he concedes that the nature of serpents makes this decision appropriate.[233] Accenting the devil's duplicitous rhetoric, the Lombard notes that the devil appealed to the internal temptations of vainglory, gluttony, and avarice in Eve's case, agreeing here with the school of Laon. As with its earlier advocates in that school, he sees avarice as the greed for knowledge, beyond what was appropriate (*supra modum*). It is here, in the very context

---

[232] Peter Lombard, *Sent.* 2. d. 21. c. 1, 1· 433.
[233] Ibid., c. 2 -c. 4, 1: 433–35.

of describing the capitulation of Eve to these temptations, that he
joins the authors of the *Sententiae divinitatis* and *Summa sententiarum* in
offering a brief account of the psychogenesis of moral acts, agreeing
with the Laon masters that the *suggestio* may be internal or external
and that it is not temptation itself or contemplation of the temptation that constitutes the sin but *consensus*, a position which he
himself had developed earlier in his commentary on the Psalms.[234]
Before moving to the consideration of the mode of temptation
experienced by Adam, and of whether Adam or Eve sinned more
grievously, he reprises an issue which he had already addressed,
and in a far more persuasive way, under the heading of the fall of
the angels earlier in Book 2, thereby committing his second act of
inconsistency. The fact that the devil experienced no external
temptation in his own fall, unlike Adam and Eve, is why he cannot
be saved, Peter says here.[235] It is not at all clear why he feels a need
to reintroduce the fall of the angels at this point, and even less clear
why he contradicts the far better answer to the question of why the
fallen angels are unredeemable which he had given above.

Moving on to the different temptations of Adam and Eve and
whether their guilt in the fall is also differential, he begins by
agreeing with Hugh of St. Victor that the source of Eve's inner
temptation was pride manifesting itself in the lust for knowledge
that would make her the equal of God, and with Hugh, Honorius,
and William of Champeaux that Adam's temptation was love for
his wife, which caused him to depart from his obedience from God
in order to please her. On the question of whose guilt was weightier, Peter feels that there is something to be said on both sides of the
issue. He agrees with the author of the *Summa sententiarum* that
responsibility for the fall can be imputed more strongly to Adam.
But he does not think Adam and Eve were equally guilty. Rather,
he sides with the theologians who place heavier blame on Eve,
seeing the sin of presumption as more serious than anything Adam
did. But, Peter now states, Eve cannot be excused on grounds of
ignorance. She had the same nature as Adam and the same understanding of the rules which God had laid down. It would be correct
to say that sin was brought into the world by a single person, Eve,
even if Adam had not fallen.[236] How, then, can we combine this
belief that Eve was more blameworthy with the weightier imputation of sin to Adam? Peter's argument is grounded on the under-

---

[234] Ibid., c. 5–c. 6.3, 1: 436–37. See above, chapter 3, p. 214.
[235] Ibid., d. 22. c. 1, 1: 439–40.
[236] Ibid., c. 3–c. 4, 1: 441–45.

standing of ignorance, and of the faculties of the soul, which he next provides, arguments which are also unique to him, among contemporaries who take up this topic, and who also tend to bring it up in other contexts. First, Peter notes that we can distinguish between invincible ignorance, in a case where a person does not know the rules, and which excuses him from blame, and vincible ignorance, for which we are morally responsible. Vincible ignorance can be divided, in turn, into the failure to learn what we need to know when we are able to learn it, and the desire to know what we need to know when we are unable to do so. The latter is a punishment for sin. Now, neither Adam nor Eve displays invincible ignorance. Nor does either of them act in a state of vincible ignorance, of either of the two types just noted. Their sin was activated, rather, by their conscious consent, deriving from their created nature as beings possessing free will. Agreeing with the author of the *Summa sententiarum* that moral choices involve both consent and its expression in action, he departs from that master in giving both moral and psychological priority to intentionality: "It was the act of will itself that constituted the sin" (*et ipsa voluntas iniquitas fuit*).[237] As to why God created human beings capable of willing evil, this is ultimately a mystery, for Peter. He declines to speculate, stating that only God Himself knows His own reasons (*Ipse novit*), and that we cannot know them.[238]

Having eliminated any extenuating conditions in Eve's culpability for sin by this analysis of ignorance, Peter now goes on to explain that the imputation of greater guilt to Adam can be justified by a consideration of the faculties of the human soul. Earlier, as we have seen, he had stated that there are two faculties of the human soul, *anima* or the sensual faculty and *ratio* or the rational faculty. He now subdivides *ratio* into two functions, *scientia*, which seeks knowledge for its own sake, and *sapientia*, which seeks wisdom by placing knowledge in the perspective of man's ultimate destiny. We now have three terms; and the three characters in the story of the fall, Adam, Eve, and the serpent, each represent one of the terms. The serpent stands for the movement of the sensual soul, Eve for *scientia*, and Adam for *sapientia*. Further, the marriage of Adam and Eve signifies the principle that the higher form of reason should govern the lower. The severity of a sin, Peter explains, depends on which mental faculty is involved. If one consents to the promptings of the sensual soul, the sin is quite venial (*levissimum*). If

---

[237] Ibid., c. 5–c. 6, 1: 446–47. The quotation is at c. 6, p. 447.
[238] Ibid., d. 23. c. 1, 1: 447–48.

one consents with *scientia*, then the sin is more serious. If one consents with *sapientia*, one capitulates completely to an evil which one fully recognizes to be evil. This is a mortal and damnable sin. From this standpoint, Eve's sin is less serious than Adam's since it springs from *scientia* and reflects the desire to enjoy knowledge for its own sake. In failing to govern that desire with the faculty of *sapientia* on Eve's part, and on his own, Adam commits a sin that is mortal for both of them. Closing with a reprise of the psychogenesis of sin in *suggestio, cogitatio*, and *consensus*, Peter suggests, by means of this analysis of faculty psychology, that consent, while equally voluntary in each case, may occur at both the *scientia* or *sapientia* levels of man's reason, with differing ethical consequences.[239] And, he can argue that it is possible to combine the doctrine of Eve's greater culpability on account of her greater presumption with the doctrine that Adam bears the greater guilt, on the grounds that his consent was of a quality that took more things into account than Eve's did. Peter imputes greater guilt to Adam not because of Eve's ignorance, as does the author of the *Summa sententiarum*, for he denies that she possessed ignorance, whether vincible or invincible. Nor does Peter impute greater guilt to Adam because of his extrinsic status vis-à-vis Eve, as is the case with Robert Pullen, but because of what Adam actually did do. And, unlike Hugh of St. Victor, his citation of two mental faculties from which the sins of Adam and Eve derive is not designed to equalize their culpability but rather to find a basis for grading them hierarchically.[240]

If it is the Victorines who help Peter to frame the agenda which he then addresses in his own way in the foregoing part of his analysis, Honorius is the theologian who triggers his handling of the forbidden fruit and the knowledge of good and evil. Peter offers an explanation of this subject which goes beyond the biblical account in Genesis. There were really two trees at issue, he argues. One is the tree bearing the forbidden fruit, which, he agrees, was forbidden not because it was harmful but as a test of obedience. He cites the same Augustinian text as Honorius uses in arguing that the knowledge of evil lay in and flowed from original sin, while the knowledge of good was available to Adam and Eve before the fall, irrespective of what they ate.[241] In Peter's opinion, the tree of life

---

[239] Ibid., d. 24. c. 6–c. 12, 1: 455–60.
[240] Mignon, *Les origines*, 2: 33 takes up the relationship of the Lombard on original sin to both Hugh and the *Summa sententiarum* without noticing these differences.
[241] Peter Lombard, *Sent.* 2. d. 17. c. 7.1–2, d. 29. c. 4, 1: 415–16, 494.

was another tree in the garden of Eden. This tree was not forbidden. There is no reason to suppose that Adam and Eve could not have eaten of its fruit before the fall. If they did so, the reason why it did no render them immortal that Peter gives here is that they did not have the time to eat of it frequently enough for this effect to have taken hold.[242] Another answer which he could have given here, and which he does not give, is that the decision to eat the forbidden fruit which brought on the fall also brought on mortality as one of its consequences, a doctrine that serves to point us toward the last constellation of topics to be considered in relation to original sin, its effects and transmission.

THE EFFECTS OF ORIGINAL SIN: THE CONTEMPORARY DEBATES

In the first half of the twelfth century there were three main ways of viewing the effects of original sin. One, represented most strongly by Robert Pullen, emphasized the physical consequences of sin. It is true that Robert holds that the soul is affected as well, in that it knows that it has rejected the good and thereby suffers; this self-consciousness of its own fall constitutes its punishment. But the main way in which the soul suffers is that it is united to a body that is now much more limited than it was before the fall. Despite the lengthy analysis of sensation which he provides, Robert does not comment on if, or how, man's ability to obtain true knowledge by means of the senses is included in this limitation. Rather, he accents the physical ills and sufferings to which the flesh is now heir. Mortality, sickness, pain, sensitivity to cold and heat, and a host of bodily afflictions are catalogued. Robert includes sexual concupiscence on the list. Man is now subject to sexual desire and sexual pleasure. Also, and here Robert follows the extremely late and anti-Pelagian Augustine on sex, man's sexuality now involves physical corruption in that it works with vitiated seeds; the very genetic materials have been tainted.[243] Another theologian who accents the physical consequences of original sin, in this case so

---

[242] Ibid., d. 29. c. 6, 1: 495.

[243] Robert Pullen, *Sent.* 2.7–8, 2.25, 2.27–31, *PL* 186: 727D–731A, 752B–753C, 754A–764C. For the Augustinian background and its parallels with Manicheism, a charge that Augustine's Pelagian antagonists were all too ready to hurl against him in this connection, see Elizabeth A. Clark, "Vitiated Seeds and Holy Vessels: Augustine's Manichean Past," in *Ascetic Piety and Women's Faith: Essays on Late Ancient Christianity* (Lewiston, NY: Edwin Mellen Press, 1986), pp. 291–349.

strongly that he all but ignores the intellectual ones, is the author of
the *Sententiae divinitatis*.[244]

A second view, taught by the Porretans but more influentially by
Hugh of St. Victor and modified by Robert of Melun, emphasized
the idea that original sin afflicts the soul and body equally.[245] In
Hugh's formulation of this doctrine, the chief spiritual weakness
borne by fallen man is ignorance, while his body is afflicted by
concupiscence. Robert agrees, and nuances this position. Instead of
knowledge, there is ignorance. Instead of love of the good, there is
concupiscence, which, he explains, means inordinate and misdirected love of any kind. Instead of trouble-free physical activity,
there is illness, pain, and death, and the need for labor and effort.
Man also suffers from the weakening of his will. Robert sees concupiscence here as the inclination to sin, in general, not so much as
a result of the physical limitations under which fallen man labors
but because of the spiritual disorder he has now contracted, an
inclination of the will toward evil.

The members of the school of Laon also see man as afflicted
intellectually by the fall and as suffering the standard physical
sufferings; but they emphasize the depression of free will as the
primary consequence of original sin. Agreeing with the late Augustine here, they hold that free will has now been so diminished that
fallen man cannot will anything but evil without the help of divine
grace.[246] The author of the *Summa sententiarum* endorses this emphasis of the school of Laon on the depression of the will in fallen
man and its consequent inability to will the good without grace.
Following the definition of free will *a necessitate*, *a peccato*, and *a
miseria* found in the Laon masters and Bernard of Clairvaux, he
explains that the freedom from sin and from misery have now been
withdrawn. At the same time, he emphasizes the point that the
freedom of will *a necessitate* remains in fallen man, leaving him free
to reject God's grace. He stresses the depression of the will so
heavily that it becomes, for him, the single most important consequence of the fall, far outstripping the effects that original sin may
have on the body or on man's ability to know.[247] It is with this third

---

[244] *Sent. div.* 3.1, p. 42*.
[245] *Sent. mag. Gisleberti* I 13.55, p. 170; Hugh of St. Victor, *De sac.* 1.7.27, *PL* 176:
291A; Robert of Melun, *Sent.* 1.1.18, *Oeuvres*, 3 part 1: 208–09.
[246] Anselm of Laon, *Sent. divine pagine* 4; *Sent. Anselmi* 2, pp. 27–28, 66–67;
Sentences of Probable Authenticity, no. 114; *Sentences of William of Champeaux*, no. 245;
Sentences of the School of Laon, no. 322, 324, 335, 5: 93, 201–02, 253, 254, 260; *Deus
hominem fecit perfectum*, ed. Heinrich Weisweiler in *Das Schrifttum der Schule Anselms
von Laon und Wilhelms von Champeaux in deutschen Bibliotheken*, Beiträge, 33:1–2
(Münster: Aschendorff, 1936), p. 294.
[247] *Summa sent.* 3.7–9, *PL* 176: 99C–105A.

view, the virtually preclusive understanding of the effects of original sin as directed to man's soul and, *a fortiori*, to his free will, that Peter Lombard most closely aligns himself.

The Lombard's Position

So strongly does Peter accent the depression of free will that it is actually the only effect of original sin which he discusses in any detail. He places it above and beyond all other punishments fallen man may incur. Although fallen man retains a conscience (*scintilla rationis*) urging him to seek the good and avoid evil, free will is partly lost, in the fall, and what remains is weakened. Peter's treatment of this topic sharpens the late Augustinianism of its terms, in comparison with contemporaries, although, with the author of the *Summa sententiarum*, he staunchly resists the idea that the will cannot reject grace. Augustine's doctrine of irresistible grace finds no hearing in his theology.[248] Peter begins by reprising the distinction among *libertas a necessitate, a peccato,* and *a miseria* and indicates how much he thinks free will in any of these respects remains in fallen man. Freedom from any necessity at all was a feature of the human will before the fall. This mode of free will, Peter states, going farther on this point than is conceded by the author of the *Summa sententiarum* or the Laon masters, now applies to no one but God, Who has perfect freedom. Man no longer enjoys the capacity to exercise free will without any constraints or conditions. We retain only enough free will to be able to earn punishment or reward, for "where there is no liberty, or will, there is no merit" (*ubi non est libertas, nec voluntas, et ideo nec meritum*). Freedom from sin has been obliterated by the fall. This freedom from sin, Peter notes, is what is restored in the redemption of man by grace,

---

[248] Scholars who have noted both the influence and the criticism of Augustine here include Peter Iver Kaufman, "Charitas non est nisi a Spiritui Sancto': Augustine and Peter Lombard on Grace and Personal Righteousness," *Augustiniana* 30 (1980): 209–20; Schupp, *Die Gnadenlehre*, passim and esp. pp. 287–302; Pietro Vaccari," Rapporti della concezione teologica di Pier Lombardo col diritto canonico del XII secolo," in *Misc. Lomb.*, pp. 258–59; A. Vanneste, "Nature et grâce dans la théologie du douzième siècle," *ETL* 50 (1974): 184–214. Chenu, *La théologie au douzième siècle*, p. 225, has not noticed Peter's rejection of irresistible grace here. Other studies surveying the treatment of grace and free will in the twelfth century include Landgraf, *Dogmengeschichte*, 1 part 1: 51–140, 152–54, 189–96, 220–37; Lottin, *Psych. et morale*, 1: 12–31; Alister E. McGrath, *Iustitia dei: A History of the Christian Doctrine of Justification* (Cambridge: Cambridge University Press, 1987), 1: 43–76. On conscience, see Peter Lombard, *Sent.* 2, d. 39, c. 3.3, 1:556; Odon Lottin, "Les premiers linéaments du traité de la syndérèse au moyen âge," *Revue néo-scolastique de philosophie* 28 (1926): 422–59.

collaborating with the will. In the redeemed, this state coincides
with the freedom to will evil as well. Peter gives careful consideration to the point made by Augustine in his *Enchiridion*, that, when
man is redeemed, his free will is his will freed by grace to do the
good. He contradicts it, citing Augustine's *De gratia et libero arbitrio*,
where he finds a preferable solution: In redeemed man, he concludes, the will is always free but not always good. As for freedom
from misery, this freedom is also lost in the fall. Man possessed it
before the fall and he will possess it even more fully in the state of
future beatitude. But, in the present life, no one has it. In sum,
Peter argues that man retains free will only in part after the fall. It
is a will that is not equally free in willing good and evil. It is freer in
willing good when it has been aided by grace than it is in willing
evil when it has not been redeemed, and freer in willing evil on its
own account than in willing good, since it cannot will the good
unless grace assists it. The grace involved is both prevenient, or
operating grace, which empowers the will and prepares man to will
the good, and cooperating grace, which collaborates with the will in
so doing. Peter makes a full stop short of the late Augustinian
doctrine that prevenient grace cannot be refused and, despite the
wealth of Augustinian references with which he documents the
position he expounds, he never cites any of the Augustinian texts in
which irresistible grace is mentioned.[249]

As Peter continues to expand on this doctrine, he fleshes out the
position which he had first stated in his Romans commentary.
Another way to understand the subject, he observes, is to view
operating grace as the faith that works in love, without which no
one earns merit. Faith, from this perspective, is not merely intellectual assent to theological propositions or to the authority of the
person proposing them. It also involves both the gift of grace
enabling a person to commit himself and the desire to believe
stemming from his own good will. This good will, Peter emphasizes, is prevenient to faith not by time, but by nature, as its cause.
So, one has desire and good will, which are necessary components
of the positive reception of the operating grace that in turn enables
one to have the faith that justifies, that is, the faith working in love
with the continuing assistance of cooperating grace. Although nothing done before the reception of grace is meritorious with respect
to man's salvation, moral acts done with the assistance of grace do
add to man's merit. The only things that fallen man can do by free

---

[249] Peter Lombard, *Sent.* 2. d. 25. c. 7–c. 8.11, 1: 465–69. The quotation is at c.
8.2, p. 466. See also *Sermo* 4, *PL* 171: 357C–D. Good treatments of this doctrine are
found in Schupp, *Die Gnadenlehre*, pp. 37–40, 68–69, 90–105.

will alone are actions that, while they may be constructive, are ethically neutral, such as building a house or cultivating a field. In response to the theory that two different graces are at work in operating and cooperating grace, Peter argues that it is a single grace which has two different effects. This understanding of grace as an effect of God, or as an effect of the Holy Spirit in the distribution of His charisms, and not as an immanental participation of God in man or as a divinization of man, undergirds the analysis of grace and merit with which Peter concludes his discussion of free will in man as fallen and as justified. On the one hand, he sees grace as the initiation of any goodness and merit that man can acquire; and it comes from God alone. Grace is the principal cause of merit in that it excites the free will, healing and aiding it so that it becomes a good will. On the other hand, this generic grace as well as the specific gifts of the Holy Spirit are activated in us by our free will, which grace does not exclude but rather empowers. The virtues and merits which this collaboration makes possible thus become the personal moral attributes of the human being whose free will is their agency.[250] What the Lombard has done here, and this can be seen by a careful examination of the Augustinian texts which he cites so profusely on free will and grace, is to draw on the anti-Manichean Augustine on free will as well as the anti-Pelagian Augustine on grace. Peter adds to Augustine the testimony of the Pseudo-Chrysostom. He thus arrives at a more balanced position than Augustine had developed in either of these two subdivisions of his oeuvre. The tonality Peter gives to this topic, despite his heavy dependence on Augustine is, finally, less typical of Augustine than it is of the theandric, synergistic relationship of grace and free will found in the Greek patristic tradition.

THE TRANSMISSION OF ORIGINAL SIN: THE CONTEMPORARY DEBATES

Peter does a better job of resolving contradictions between the positions taken on grace and free will by Augustine at different points in his career than he, or anyone else in his day, could do in the case of the controverted question of the transmission of original sin. The form in which this topic was first put on the agenda of twelfth-century theology owes much to the school of Laon. The

---

[250] Peter Lombard, *Sent.* 2. d. 26. c. 3–c. 8, d. 27. c. 3–d. 28. c. 4, 1; 477–78, 482–91. Peter's use of the Pseudo-Chrysostom is noted by Brady, *Sent.* 1: 482 n. 2. The presence of this tonality in his treatment of grace is missed by Landgraf, *Dogmengeschichte*, 1 part 2: 44–51.

Laon masters take it up initially not in the context of original sin
itself but in the effort to exclude the idea that actual sins are passed
on from parent to child, in glossing Ezechiel. None the less, in so
doing, they articulate the range of problems attached to this question with which subsequent theologians wrestled manfully. They
also expose the contradictions between Augustine's very late anti-
Pelagian view of sexuality, his more moderate, pastoral line on this
subject dating to the middle of his career, and the intentionalist
understanding of ethical acts which he supports, as they do. Aside
from Abelard, who rejected the Augustinian understanding of the
transmission of original sin in any of its forms, the other theologians
of the first half of the twelfth century struggled to sort out the
difficulties in the Augustinian legacy from within the Augustinian
tradition. However problematic they found it, none of them, including the Lombard, was able to find a satisfactory substitute for
it.[251] In this respect, and while agreeing that it was necessary to
refute Abelard, the major motivation in Peter's handling of the
transmission of original sin was to try to make the best of an
argument that had its acknowledged weaknesses but which he did
not feel able to dismiss. Instead, he aims at clarifying it and shoring
it up as best he can.

As the Laon masters lay out the problem, parents convey to their
offspring the guilt (*reatus*) of original sin, the penalty (*poena*) of
mortality and affliction which sin brings upon mankind, and the
spark of future sin (*fomes peccati*) or inclination to sin that leads to
actual sin. Some members of the school adhere to the anti-Pelagian
argument of Augustine that the fall produced physical corruption
and that man now engenders progeny with vitiated seeds, on the
model of the inheritance of acquired characteristics. This corruption of the genetic materials is confined to the male seed by William
of Champeaux, who follows Aristotle in viewing the male seed as
the active principle in conception; other Laon masters regard the
female body as just as corrupted.[252] Still other members of the
school do not see the problem as lying in vitiated seeds, but rather
in the sexual desire and pleasure that accompany the conception of
offspring. But, this theory entails two problems. Augustine says, in
his later works, that the sexual relations between spouses are
always at least venially sinful; and some Laon masters agree with
this view. But others note that believing parents, whose own origi-

---

[251] A good overview is provided by Landgraf, *Dogmengeschichte*, 4 part 1: 155–85.
[252] *Sentences of William of Champeaux*, no. 251; *Antequam quicquam fieret Deus erat* 5,
in *Sentences of the School of Laon*, 5: 205, 336; *Deus hominem fecit perfectum*, pp. 295–96.

nal sin has been washed away by baptism, and who have been united in the sacrament of marriage, for the sake of whose goods, one of which is offspring, they are having sexual relations, do not sin thereby, even though these relations may, unavoidably, involve lust. Now, in the case of the first position, how can the lust experienced by the parents in the act of conception inhere in the body of the fetus conceived thereby, given that the fetus, at its current stage of development, is physically incapable of feeling lust? How can that fetus be taxed for the feelings that other people experience? The masters who argue that original sin is transmitted by the concupiscence of the parents offer no real answers to these questions.[253] As for those who think that the parents' sex life is not sinful, they, too, grapple with the question of how their upright moral activity in this respect can convey sin to their children. The response to this question is that the fetus is not married and therefore lacks the exemption with respect to sexual feelings that applies to its parents, an answer which still fails to acknowledge the fact that the fetus, in any case, is incapable of experiencing these sexual feelings and, *a fortiori*, is incapable of contracting a marriage.[254]

As a refinement on this last argument, some Laon masters add the Augustinian point that parents, even if purified by baptism and cleansed of their own original sin, none the less pass on corrupted flesh to their children, using such examples as the circumcised father who sires a son born with a foreskin, or a hulled grain of wheat engendering wheat that has a hull,[255] examples that have the effect of undercutting the vitiated seeds idea because in these cases an altered state of being is not passed on to the offspring. Despite all these problems, the Laon masters agree with Augustine that it is the bodies of children that are engendered with sinful characteristics because their parents necessarily engender those bodies sexually. But this brings another difficulty in its train. Rejecting

---

[253] *Potest queri, quid sit peccatum*; *Deus hominem fecit perfectum*, pp. 265–68, 295–96; Anselm of Laon, *Sent. divine pagine* 4; *Sent. Anselmi* 2, pp. 32–35, 71–78; *Sentences of Anselm of Laon*, no. 28; *Sentences of Anselm of Laon from the Liber Pancrisis*, no. 43–46, 5: 29–30, 38–43.

[254] Anselm of Laon, *Sent. divine pagine* 4; *Sent. Anselmi* 2, pp. 32–35, 71–78; *Sentences of Anselm of Laon*, no. 29–30; *Sentences of Anselm of Laon from the Liber Pancrisis*, no. 43–46; *Sentences of William of Champeaux*, no. 246–50; *Sentences of the School of Laon*, no. 521, 5: 29–30, 38, 43, 202–05, 336–37; *Deus de cuius principio et fine tacetur*, p. 259; *Dubitatur quibusdam*, ed. Heinrich Weisweiler in *Schrifttum der Schule Anselms von Laon und Wilhelms von Champeaux in deutschen Bibliotheken*, Beiträge, 33:1–2 (Münster: Aschendorff, 1936), pp. 323–24.

[255] *Deus cuius principio et fine tacetur*, pp. 263–64; *Sentences of Probable Authenticity*, no. 117; *Sentences of the School of Laon*, no. 335, 5: 95, 260.

traducianism, a conviction which implicitly reflects their belief that
sin lies not in the body as such but in the voluntary consent of the
will,[256] they now have to explain how the pure and divinely created
souls of infants, souls that are infused into the bodies engendered
by their parents, contract original sin. Augustine's answer, which
they find themselves perforce repeating, is that the corrupted body
taints the soul joined to it, just as vinegar ruins the good wine with
which it may be mixed.[257] How this serves as an analogy of a union
of two entities that are not both material substances and that retain
their own characteristics in that union is by no means entirely
clear.

It is no doubt the problems intrinsic to the Augustinian heritage,
which the school of Laon reports so faithfully, as well as his desire
to push the principle of intentionalism in ethics as far as he could,
that inspire Abelard to offer a counter-argument. He dispenses with
the need to explain the transmission of original sin by dropping the
idea of original sin itself, in effect reducing original sin to actual sin.
Infants, he argues, do not have the powers of judgment and deliberation needed to exercise free will in an informed manner, any
more than insane persons do. Only mentally competent persons
above the age of discretion are capable of sinning. Augustine was in
error here, Abelard asserts. Augustine also erred on the corrolary of
this point, the damnation of unbaptized infants. Despite this dis-
missal of original sin, and confusingly so, Abelard thinks that we
bear the punishment (poena) for Adam's fall, even though we do not
bear his guilt (culpa), and that children are prone to sin because
their parents conceive them in carnal lust. He also agrees that a
purified stock can bear tainted fruit.[258] Abelard's rejection of original sin proved to be too extreme a solution for all but his most
intransigent disciples to accept. He also turns out to be no better
than the school of Laon in explaining those vestiges of the Augustin-

---

[256] Sentences of the School of Laon, no. 309–10, 5: 244–45; Deus de cuius principio et fine
tacetur, p. 259.

[257] Anselm of Laon, Sent. divine pagine 4; Sent. Anselmi 2, pp. 32–35, 71–78;
Sentences of Anselm of Laon, no. 29–30; Sentences of Anselm of Laon from the Liber
Pancrisis, no. 43–46; Sentences of William of Champeaux, no. 246–50; Sentences of the
School of Laon, no. 521, 5: 29–30, 38–43, 202–05, 336–37; Deus de cuius principio et fine
tacetur, p. 259; Dubitatur quibusdam, pp. 323–24.

[258] Peter Abelard, Ethics, ed. and trans. David E. Luscombe (Oxford:
Clarendon Press, 1971), pp. 20–22, 58–64; In Epistolam Pauli ad Romanos 5:19, ed.
Eligius M. Buytaert, CCCM 11 (Turnhout: Brepols, 1969), pp. 164, 166, 170–72.
Good discussions of Abelard on original sin are found in Julius Gross, "Abälards
Umdeutung des Erbsündendogmas," Zeitschrift für Religions- und Geistesgeschichte 15
(1963): 14–33; Sikes, Peter Abailard, pp. 43–65, 200–02.

ian doctrine of the transmission of original sin that he retains.

A tendency to back away from Abelard and to try to resolve the problem in more Augustinian terms is found even in masters influenced by him in other respects. Roland of Bologna, for instance, does a fairly thorough job of listing the positions that have been taken on the transmission of original sin, and the objections that can be leveled against some of them, before giving his own opinion. He cites Abelard's position and offers no objection to it; but this is not the view to which Roland subscribes himself. Apart from the rejected notion that people cannot sin before the age of discretion and that, therefore, children do not inherit original sin, Roland mentions four other arguments. One is that the sin is transmitted because Adam committed it in Eden. To this, Roland says, no objection is needed because it is just plain silly. One may agree, but one may also observe that a more telling reason for dismissing this argument is that it offers no explanation on how the sin is transmitted. Nor does Roland cite an objection to the analysis by which the guilt (*reatus*) and punishment (*poena*) which Adam's sin incurred for him are extended, by imputation, to other people who have not committed any sin themselves. In the remaining two options Roland offers before presenting his own solution, he does give objections. To the claim that Adam transmitted his fallen nature to his descendants materially, he responds that sin pertains to the soul, and that the parents do not engender the souls of their children. To the claim that original sin is transmitted by the libidinous ardor of the parents, one may object again that the parents do not engender their children's souls and also that the fetus cannot experience carnal concupiscence in the womb. He adds that this theory also does not work because the fetus has no say in the mode by which it is engendered. Roland now moves to articulate his own position. Some say, he notes, that the *fomes peccati* is carnal concupiscence. He supports this idea. He then, however, goes on to define this *fomes* as located in the will and not in man's physical inclinations. Concupiscence, so understood, is the will's tendency to seek the wrong ends in matters pertaining to mind and body alike. This analysis locates original sin in the mind, although it sees original sin as having a different effect on mind and body. In the body, it leads to physical corruption and death. In the mind, it works by the consent it renders to the wrong moral use of both mind and body, and also in the fact that the soul is stained by the corrupt body with which it is now associated.[259] In the effort to stress the will as the

---

[259] Roland of Bologna, *Sent.*, pp. 128–36.

seat of sin, Roland has forgotten a point which he had raised earlier in his account, the idea that the parents engender only the bodies, and not the souls, of their children. Since he now argues that these pure souls are tainted by their union with corrupt bodies, it is not clear why he rejects the idea that men are all material descendants of Adam, or how that theory really differs from the solution that he adopts.

A similar modification of the Augustinian position in defense of the idea that virtue and vice are located in the mind, not the body, is found in Robert of Melun. He agrees that original sin is transmitted through the sexual concupiscence of the parents, and that its effects include the inclination toward concupiscence in their offspring. But this effect, he argues, derives not from physical corruption or weakness but from the nature of original sin as a spiritual disorder, a spiritual penchant toward evil in all areas. Here, Robert wants to criticize the vitiated seeds theory. He observes that the members of the human race are not contained seminally in Adam, although they are similar to him in soul. But, he cannot explain how the concupiscent spirit gets passed to infants, as a consequence of the sexual feelings which their parents experience physically. Robert's terminology is also a bit out of the ordinary. Most theologians of the day see concupiscence, whether in the narrow sexual sense or in the wider sense of the inclination toward wrong or immoderate desires which Robert gives to the term, as the *fomes peccati*. He, instead, sees it as the punishment for sin. He also raises a new complication, suggesting a greater sensitivity to the nature of human sexuality than most theologians of the time exhibit. Not all sexual acts leading to conception, he notes, are undertaken with the same degree of sexual desire; nor are they all accompanied by the same degree of sexual pleasure. Since he holds that parental ardor is the vehicle for the transmission of original sin, he finds that, if one applies the principle of differential ardor here, one has to conclude that people are afflicted with original sin to different degrees.[260] This is an alarming idea, and Robert does nothing to deal with its ethical or sacramental implications, at least not in the part of his *Sentences* which he completed.

If Robert of Melun wants to eliminate the vitiated seeds from the account, as too crypto-Manichean, Robert Pullen rests his case entirely on that very theory, although he grounds it rather narrowly. His argument is integrally related to the virtually preclusive

---

[260] Martin, "Les idées de Robert de Melun," *RSPT* 7: 700–25, 8: 439–66, 9: 103–20, 11: 390–415.

emphasis he places on the corruption of the physical seed as the major bodily consequence of original sin. So, for Robert as well, it is not so much the parents' experience of lust as their vitiated genetic materials which give the fetus a corrupt body, which in turn corrupts the soul attached to it. Thus, children bear the guilt (*reatus*), the punishment (*poena*), and the *fomes peccati* of concupiscence transmitted by the corruption of the flesh.[261] Here, Robert ignores the objections made in the light of the baptismal and marital grace of the parents and adheres to the hardest of hard line late Augustinianism. In Robert's psychology, it will be remembered, he argues that the parents create the *spiritus* of their offspring. But he does not integrate this traducianist belief into his understanding of the transmission of original sin.

Another mid-century theologian who defends the anti-Pelagian Augustine here is the author of the *Summa sententiarum*. He agrees that the bodies of children are derived substantially from the corrupted flesh of their parents. But he is more circumspect in his handling of this idea than is Robert Pullen. He acknowledges that, in believing parents, baptism has remitted their own guilt. This fact, however, does not alter the changes in their genetic materials that remain, as a consequence of sin. Nor does it alter the fact that their sexual relations are perforce accompanied by lust. The author does not deal with the inability of the fetus to experience sexual desire or sexual pleasure, but moves on to how the corrupt fetal body infects the child's soul. It does so, he says, thanks to its intimate union with the soul. Having raised the question of the baptism of the parents, he pertinently adds the Augustinian argument concerning the hulled wheat and the circumcised father to explain why their redeemed state makes no difference.[262]

A much softer line is taken by the author of the *Sententiae divinitatis*, drawing heavily on the more moderate position articulated by Augustine in pastoral works such as *De nuptiis et concupiscentia*. He argues that, for parents, their baptism remits any guilt they would otherwise bear for the carnal concupiscence involved in their sexual relations. It is not that the ardor accompanying sex is not a consequence of sin and it is not that they can avoid experiencing it. But it is not imputed to them as sinful (*non ut non sit, sed ut in peccatum non imputetur*). He also argues that the *reatus* of sin is transmitted from parent to child, here combining in this term the guilt and the

---

[261] Robert Pullen, *Sent.* 2.7–8, 2.25, 2.27–31, *PL* 186: 727D–731A, 752B–753C, 754A–764C.

[262] *Summa sent.* 3.10–12, *PL* 176: 105A–110A.

punishment, along with the *poena*, by which latter term he means what other masters mean by the *fomes peccati*. But, having defended the principle that the parents' sexual feelings are not counted as sinful, for them, the author offers no explanation of how that *reatus* and *poena* descend to the children. The closest he comes is to analogize it to a physical defect that can be inherited.[263]

Apart from treating the question of traducianism as an open one,[264] which Robert's Pullen's teaching has also suggested was actually the case in some quarters, the other Porretan witnesses in our period make no contribution to the debate on the transmission of original sin. But Hugh of St. Victor, who gives the same report on traducianism, provides an analysis which adds a genuinely fresh point to his largely mid-Augustinian handling of that question. Further, his argument connects his position on this subject to his account of the effects of the fall and to the epistemological concerns that inform his treatment of human nature more widely. Hugh is clear in his own mind on where the human soul comes from. It is spiritual not material and it is created by God *ex nihilo*. Hugh's main point here is to stress that God infuses the soul into the body of the fetus after the body has started to develop, anchoring this point with the Exodus rule on causing a miscarriage and when it is accounted homicide. This being the case, he asks, how does the flesh contract and transmit sin and how does the body transfer sin to the soul? Now concupiscence, he reminds the reader, is the chief effect of original sin upon the body just as ignorance it its chief effect upon the soul. For the body, this means a weakened existence, an inability to engage in sexual activity without lust, even as the body now is mortal. Hugh sees the parents as creating the same kind of body in their children as they now have. He avoids the vitiated seeds idea but suggests, rather, that it is the limited fleshly endowment they have to pass on, and not the fact that they have experienced sexual desire or pleasure in engendering children, that defines the parental role here. This analysis obviates, for Hugh, the need to cope with the problem of how fetuses, incapable of experiencing lust, should be taxed with other people's feelings. As for how this weakened flesh, weakened in the sense that it disallows sexuality without lust when that sexuality becomes operational in the children, transmits sin to the soul, the link, for Hugh, is in

---

[263] *Sent. div.* 3.2, 3.4–5, pp. 43*–45*, 47*–51*. The quotation is at 3.4, p. 47*. On this question, see Raymond-M. Martin, "La péché originel d'après Gilbert de la Porrée (d. 1154) et son école," *RHE* 13 (1912): 674–91.

[264] *Sent. mag. Gisleberti* I 13.55, p. 170.

man's epistemology. Our knowledge, as he has already explained, depends on sense data, in the external rational mode of knowledge. The physical senses have been corrupted by concupiscence. Thus, they do not function as well as they did before the fall; and this situation contributes to the ignorance which is the chief limit under which the mind labors after the fall. Hugh has produced the most intelligent solution invented in this period to the problem of how the sinful body could corrupt the mind that is its ruling principle and the seat of the intentionality that controls man's ethical life. Finally, in addressing the question of how the redeemed parents can engender children who are themselves in need of redemption, Hugh avoids the issues embedded in Augustine's examples of the hulled wheat or circumcised father. He settles for something simpler. While the grace of baptism removes the parents' guilt for their original sin, they still have to bear the punishment for sin, Hugh points out, and that punishment is concupiscence and ignorance, which they pass on to their children.[265]

The Lombard on the Transmission of Original Sin

The originality displayed by Hugh of St. Victor on the transmission of original sin did not find support in Peter Lombard. He is far more resolutely Augustinian on this subject. Indeed, he draws on some features of Augustine's early teachings in order to defend Augustine's anti-Pelagian position in this area. Peter also recognizes the need to attack Abelard and to find a way to combine the doctrine of the key role of intentionality in ethics, which he certainly supports, with the principle of the universality of original sin. He also wants to lay to rest the possibility of espousing traducianism in any form. And, he wants to coordinate his position on the transmission of original sin with the doctrine of human nature he has developed. He brings some additional authorities to bear on the large, and largely Augustinian, dossier of sources that he uses. If Peter does not succeed in ironing out all the problems in Augustine's treatment of the problem of the transmission of original sin, he makes a valiant effort to do so and he is less troubled by the implications of this topic than is true of many of his contemporaries.

There is no single recent or current theologian from whom Peter

---

[265] Hugh of St. Victor, *De sac.* 1.7.31–38, *PL* 176: 301B–306B. Julius Gross, "Ur- und Erbsünde bei Hugo von St. Viktor," *Zeitschrift für Kirchengeschichte* 73 (1962): 42–61 emphasizes Hugh's dependence on Augustine but not his originality.

takes all his cues on the transmission of original sin, but it is clear to him that Abelard needs to be shown conclusively to be wrong. His opening salvo makes this plain. Adam's sin was actual, Peter observes, because is was something he willed to do, as well as original, as the first sin and the origin of sin in mankind. In the rest of mankind, however, original sin cannot be reduced to actual sin. Under this heading, Peter attacks the "Pelagians" but the Abelardian reference is unmistakeable. One can, none the less, say that original sin springs from the will, even if this statement is true only in Adam's case. Here, Peter draws on the anti-Manichean Augustine in arguing that there is nothing evil in nature, since the whole creation is good. Everything in creation, however, can be used badly. This was the case with human free will, a created good, which was used badly in the fall.[266] This argument locates original sin in the will. But Adam is not a model for the rest of the human race in this respect. While it comes to afflict the soul in fallen man, original sin finds its way into the soul and imposes its limitations on the soul, in the form of a weakened will, and inclines the soul to commit actual sin by way of the body. Peter is a staunch defender of Augustine here, and on two counts. First, he maintains that original sin is transmitted physically because it has resulted in the vitiation of the flesh. And second, this vitiated flesh involves the reproduction of itself accompanied by carnal lust.[267]

Before going on to explain how, and why, this is the case, Peter crisply defines his terms. Does the essence of original sin lie in the guilt, the punishment, or the inclination to sin; and what is included in each of these terms? In Peter's view, original sin is defined as the guilt (culpa), the burden of responsibility for the fall. The punishment (poena), which is largely the depression of the will and the corruption of the body, is the consequence of that guilt. The fomes peccati is concupiscence, which Peter views broadly, as the inclination to sin in all areas. He agrees with Hugh of St. Victor that the concupiscence which is passed on to the offspring as a function of the punishment is not the lust attending the particular sexual act in which the offspring is engendered, but the general weakness of the body, and, through the body, the mind. This weakness will incline the offspring to commit actual sins when the circumstances make this possible. Thus, in Peter's view, it is unnecessary to address the objection that the fetus cannot experience

---

[266] Peter Lombard, *Sent.* 2. d. 30. c. 3–c. 4, c. 13, d. 34. c. 1–c. 5, 1: 496–97, 503, 525–29.
[267] Ibid., d. 30. c. 5, 1: 497.

sexual desire or pleasure.[268] This Victorine understanding of concupiscence also settles in advance the question of the degrees of
parental ardor and hence of inherited culpability raised by Robert
of Melun. Parents, Peter points out, replicate in their children the
same kind of bodies as they have themselves. Addressing a question
which Robert of Melun takes up and answers differently, Peter asks
in what sense we are all children of Adam. It is absurd, he agrees,
to think that everyone contains an actual atom of Adam's body. It
was a finite body; and this would be a physical impossibility. But,
we all share Adam's physical nature, in both body and mind. We
can think of the passing on of physical nature from parent to child
under the rubric of the seminal reasons, implanted in Adam as the
first parent, and understood as Peter has treated them above, as the
created causes that enable natural phenomena to perform their
natural functions, such as reproduction, in this case.[269]

Peter makes crystal clear that he sees no grounds for supporting
traducianism. The soul of each person, he maintains, is created,
innocent, by God. The parents produce the body of their children
and they do so by sexual reproduction, which is inevitably attended
by sexual desire and pleasure. On this point Peter takes a softer line
than the anti-Pelagian Augustine and than some of his contemporaries, and one that he associates with the sacrament of marriage as
much as with the sacrament of baptism. Peter agrees that it is not
possible, now, to engender children without lust, and that this lust
"is always a vice and also culpable, unless it is excused by the
goods of marriage" (*semper vitium est, et etiam culpa, nisi excusetur per
bona coniugii*). This exemption, in his eyes, is a real one. But, while
the goods of marriage exculpate the parents, the only flesh they
have to pass on is the corrupted flesh which they now possess as a
consequence of the fall. They pass it on to their children, perforce,
and this corrupted flesh then contaminates the innocent soul which
God infuses into the bodies of their children. Peter draws on
Ambrose to help explain that this physical corruption is like the
defects or privations which are inflicted on a person's body, changing it for the worse, which he then bequeathes to his children willy
nilly. It is true, he allows, that baptized parents are released from
their own original sin, but they still retain the *poena* and the *fomes
peccati*, which they physically transmit to their children.

In elaborating this doctrine, Peter takes a middle position between those theologians who see the concupiscence imparted by

---

[268] Ibid., c. 6–c. 13, 1: 500–03.
[269] Ibid., c. 14, 1: 503–04.

original sin as completely washed away by the parents' baptism
and those who do not see their baptism as having any effect on it at
all. In his view, the parents' concupiscence is mitigated, but
enough of it remains to inspire the sexual union that will transmit a
corrupted body to their children.[270] The soul, however, comes from
God. Citing both the *physici* as well as Exodus 21:22–23 to make the
point that the soul is infused into the body after the body has been
growing in the womb, and ignoring the discrepancies among these
authorities as to when, during the gestation process, the fetus is
ensouled, he notes that, since the baptized parents do not create the
souls of their children, they cannot transmit the spiritual cleansing
which they have received themselves. It is in this light that Peter
presents the Augustinian examples of the circumcised father and
the hulled wheat. At the same time, the corrupt body into which
the soul is infused contaminates it as well, and here Peter cites the
Augustinian analogy of the vinegar and wine, without noticing the
respects in which it may be a disanalogy for the union of body and
soul in man, and without referring to Hugh of St. Victor's epistemological account of that contamination.[271]

Original sin is thus universal, and necessary, after the fall, in that
no one can avoid it. It is also voluntary, Peter claims, in that it
arose from the voluntary choice of Adam.[272] Pausing to note that
Adam's sin was the worst sin ever committed, even though it can be
remitted by baptism, worse even than the sin against the Holy
Spirit, which is irremissible, because of its permanent and negative
effect on the entire human race and not just on Adam himself,[273] he
distinguishes once more between the original sin which parents
transmit and the actual sin which they do not transmit.[274] Peter
then raises one final substantive question concerning original sin
before concluding his discussion of this subject. Why, he asks,
would God join the innocent souls that He creates to bodies vitiated
by sin, knowing full well that this will corrupt the souls as well? His
answer to this question ties Peter's understanding of original sin to
the hylemorphic constitution of man as he had presented that
doctrine in his account of creation at the beginning of Book 2 of the
Sentences. Although the body is now weakened by sin, it was necessary to join it with the soul, he argues, even though the soul will

---

[270] Ibid., d. 31. c. 2–c. 6, d. 32. c. 1–c. 5, 1: 505–08, 511–15. The quotation is at
d. 31. c. 4, p. 506.
[271] Ibid., d. 31. c. 6–c. 7, 1: 508–10.
[272] Ibid., d. 32. c. 5, 1: 515–16.
[273] Ibid., d. 33. c. 3, 1: 521–22.
[274] Ibid., c. 1–c. 2, c. 5, 1: 517–20, 522–23.

thereby be weakened in turn, in order to retain the integral union of body and soul that is intrinsic to human nature. It is as a unit of body and soul that man was created. It is as a unit of body and soul that man fell. And, it is as a unit of body and soul that man will be redeemed and glorified; and, through him, the universe as a whole will be perfected.[275] And so, Peter finds something providential even in the grimmest reality in the Christian doctrine of man.

Peter's most signal achievement in treating the transmission of original sin is a twofold one. First of all, while he retains both the vitiated seeds doctrine of Augustine and the idea that it is the sexual feelings of the parents that are responsible for transmitting original sin to the bodies of their children, he makes this a two-step process. Sexual desire and pleasure, vicious under other circumstances but excused for spouses in the context of their marriage, are what impel the parents to the sexual relations that lead to the conception of corrupt bodies in their offspring. The parents have no choice here, since they can only reproduce the same kind of body that they now possess. Part of the burden which they place on their children in so doing is to give them bodies which will themselves be liable to concupiscence in their sexual functioning, when the time comes. This second point, inherited from Hugh of St. Victor, enables Peter, like Hugh, to view concupiscence as a generic physical weakness brought about by the fall, and to unhinge the issue of the sensory capacities of a fetus, as a fetus, from the feelings experienced by the parents in the particular sexual union that led to its conception. It is far more debatable whether Peter succeeds in addressing Abelard's objections to Augustine. His argument that original sin is voluntary because Adam willed it in his own case is not particularly responsive to Abelard. His yoking of the Augustinian examples of the circumcised father and the hulled wheat to the anti-traducianist position is an effective argument. Despite Peter's assertion that everything in creation is good and is evil only in the way men choose to use it, his strong appeal to the anti-Pelagian theory of the corruption of man's genetic materials does leave him open to the same charge of inconsistency here as is the case with Augustine himself. While he frequently cites Augustine against Augustine in this part of his theology and while he combines Augustine's milder with his harsher position, it cannot truly be said that the Lombard has either discovered a way of resolving Augustine's inconsistencies or that, in this subdivision of his theology, he has sought, or found, a viable alternative to them.

---

[275] Ibid., d. 32. c. 6, 1: 516.

CHAPTER SEVEN

CHRIST, HIS NATURE, AND HIS SAVING WORK

The nature of Christ and His saving work were topics inspiring many debates in the first half of the twelfth century, debates conducted at varying levels of intensity and sparked by the proposals of different theologians. The Christological controversies of the day ranged from the intensely speculative, as was the case with the hypostatic union, to the devotional, as was the case with whether the human Christ should receive worship (*latria*) or veneration (*dulia*). A keen interest in the humanity of Christ is typical of the theology of this period, and the related issues of His moral capacities, His knowledge, and His psychology received extended attention. Aside from reflecting religious tastes that are a hallmark of twelfth-century Christian thought, these concerns are also indicative of the felt need to defend Christian orthodoxy against contemporary heretics who held that Christ's incarnation was an illusion. If the Word had never taken on human flesh, then the redemptive suffering and death of Christ on the cross was an illusion as well. Hence, theologians had a mandate to explain the reality of the incarnation and the principle that Christ was truly God and truly man. This doctrine is central to Christianity at any time. But its explication in our period was complicated by the confusion surrounding the theological language in which it would have to be done.

Peter Lombard makes a different kind of contribution to the various aspects of Christology that attracted discussion during his time. With respect to the human Christ, he is alarmed by what he perceives to be a contemporary tendency to divinize Him. Peter seeks to nuance this topic and to set limits to this inclination, in the effort to stress Christ's full consubstantiality with the rest of the human race. His efforts to do so, however, meet with only partial success. Peter's achievement is more solid in reshaping the doctrine of Christ's saving work. In a period marked by extremes of objectivism and subjectivism in the treatment of soteriology, Peter strikes a new balance. More than simply mediating between extremes, he also adds his own personal stamp to this doctrine, and makes possible the dropping of purely externalist ways of viewing the redemption, in which man is seen as the passive object of the actions of powers outside of himself, from the agenda of mainstream theology. With respect to the hypostatic union and related issues, Peter's contribution is threefold. The clear definitions and consistent uses that he gives to the theological language needed in this area enable him to expose and dismiss what is problematic or inconsistent in the Christological lexicons of other theologians, ancient and modern. By the same token, he effectively salvages ideas of which he approves in this subdivision of theology by separating them from the confusing terminology in whose company they sometimes traveled. His third service is to lay out plainly the options existing in current theology for understanding the coinherence of the divine and human natures in the incarnate Christ. He indicates their strengths, and the support in the Christian tradition on which they can draw, and also their weaknesses, in his estimation. He does so without making a personal choice among them. This last fact is one that a few contemporaries had difficulty grasping and, with them, some modern scholars as well. Yet, on this critical doctrine of the Christian faith, Peter really does think that the three opinions he outlines can truly be maintained within the orthodox consensus. This attitude of his toward the hypostatic union is the most powerful and extended expression, in Peter's thought, of the principle, distinctive of twelfth-century theology, that the unity of the faith does not preclude diversity in the ways in which it may be explained or practiced: *diversi sed non adversi*.[1]

The Hypostatic Union: Ancient and Current Understandings

The hypostatic union was second only to the doctrine of the Trinity in this period in provoking debate under the heading of the problem of theological language. It was likewise catalyzed by the intense study which Boethius's *opuscula sacra* were receiving in the schools, and by the fact that his own vocabulary was polyvalent. Theologians in this period, consequently, lacked a common understanding of the meaning of key terms such as substance, person, and nature, all of which had to be used in discussing the nature of the incarnate Christ. Complicating matters still further was the fact that Gilbert of Poitiers had used his commentary on Boethius's theological treatises as a vehicle for framing his own personal

---

[1] Good discussions of this theme in the twelfth century include Henri DeLubac, "A propos de la formule: *diversi sed non adversi*," in *Mélanges Jules Lebreton = Recherches de science religieuse* 40 (1952): 2. 27–40; Hubert Silvestre, "'Diversi sed non adversi'," *RTAM* 31 (1964): 124–32.

semantic theory and his own idiosyncratic lexicon, which coined neologisms and which also used the standard terms in unique Gilbertian ways. The thorough study of John Damascene, as well as Boethius and the Latin fathers, which the Lombard puts to such effective use in his Trinitarian theology and in his doctrine of God more generally, also proved to be equally helpful in addressing Christology. While in the field of Trinitarian theology he regarded Peter Abelard as the thinker most in need of refutation, with Gilbert second on the list, in the field of Christology Abelard offered no more, or less, of a challenge than did other theologians to whose teachings Peter took exception. On the other hand, here Gilbert was the master who set the agenda. And, Gilbert and the early Porretans set that agenda for the Lombard in two ways. First, they offered some trenchant criticisms of positions which Peter joined them in opposing. And, second, they offered some positive ideas which he was ready to accept, subject to the purgation from them of the rebarbative language in which Gilbert had originally framed them. Armed with the weapons derived from his Greek and Latin patristic sources, from the discussions surrounding the ideas of Gilbert, and from some insights of his own, Peter was able to set forth, with great terminological precision, for the day, the three major explanations of the hypostatic union, the *assumptus homo* theory, the subsistence theory, and the *habitus* theory. He was also able to equip himself with a vocabulary helpful in handling the other topics pertaining to the incarnation on which he took a personal stand.

The *assumptus homo* theory had a long history, going back to the patristic period and also undergoing change with respect to the positions it was formulated in order to refute. Many of the church fathers, east and west, supported the idea that the Word had assumed a human nature, that He had become man, a man fully united with the Word from the first moment of His conception, and not a man already in existence, the latter view being the heresy of Adoptionism. Later, in order to counter the threat of Nestorianism, proponents of this doctrine emphasized the intimacy of the union between the two natures in the incarnate Christ and their inseparability once united in a single person.[2]

---

[2] The patristic background and history of this doctrine up through the time of the Lombard are given by Auguste Gaudel, "La théologie de L'Assumptus Homo': Histoire et valeur doctrinale," *RSR* 17 (1937): 64–90; 18 (1938): 45–71, 201–17. For a good description of the three opinions as taught in the mid-twelfth century, see Jean Bresch, *Essai sur les Sentences de Pierre Lombard considérées sous le point de vue historico-dogmatique* (Strasbourg: Imprimerie de Veuve Berger-Levrault,

The subsistence theory accented, against what its proponents saw as an interpenetration of the divine and human natures of Christ in the *assumptus homo* theory so as to divinize His human nature, the idea that, in the union of the Word with a human body and soul, none of the constituents had lost its intrinsic nature substantially. The ingredients, they argued, had not merged to form a new semi-divine, semi-human *tertium quid*. Rather, in the incarnation, the Word, Who had been a simple person, now became a composite individual, with three substances joined together, divinity, body, and soul. Another version of this notion of a composite person, seen as a twin substance, found support in Augustine.

The partisans of the *habitus* theory, so called because they viewed the humanity of the incarnate Christ as a habit or garment which He puts on, could trace this theory back to biblical, patristic, and more recent authorities. The language itself occurs in the Vulgate account of Christ's emptying of Himself and taking on the form of a man, *et habitus inventus ut homo*, in Philippians 2:7. The fullest patristic discussion of this phrase is Augustine's analysis in his *Eighty-Three Diverse Questions*. There, he notes that *habitus* can be understood in several senses. There is a habit of mind, such as the mind's grasp of intellectual subject matter, which is strengthened by use. There is a habit of body, such as the strength acquired through physical exercise. *Habitus* also refers to things attached to people externally, such as clothing, weapons, or shoes. In each of these cases, the *habitus* is applied accidentally to the person in question, who might just as well not possess it. Moving on, he adds that in some cases a *habitus* changes the person who has it, as is the case with wisdom or physical strength. In other cases, what the person takes on is itself changed, while simultaneously changing him, as is true of food which, when eaten and assimilated into someone's body, becomes his bodily tissue as well as giving him energy. There is also the *habitus* which is changed while not changing the person to whom it is attached. Such is the case with a garment that assumes the shape of the person wearing it. There is a fourth case, in which neither the person nor the *habitus* is changed when the *habitus* is

---

1857), pp. 39–43; Walter H. Principe, *William of Auxerre's Theology of the Hypostatic Union* (Toronto: Pontifical Institute of Mediaeval Studies, 1963), 1: 9–12, 68–70; Horacio Santiago-Otero, "El 'nihilianismo cristológico' y las tres opiniones," *Burgense* 10 (1969): 431–43. This last cited essay also gives a thorough review of the scholarship on this question and on the attribution of the three positions to contemporary theologians. See also Landgraf, *Dogmengeschichte*, 2 part 1: 71–104, which is weak on the Porretans; Ludwig Ott, *Untersuchung zur theologischen Briefliteratura der Frühscholastik*, Beiträge, 34 (Münster: Aschendorff, 1937), pp. 164–87.

taken on. The placing of a ring on a person's finger is an example. With all this in mind, Augustine asks, in what sense is *habitus* involved in Christ's incarnation? In the sense of the garment that takes on the shape of the person wearing it, he answers. With this, Augustine also argues that the human nature taken on by the Word was affected, and for the better, by its association with the divine nature. And so, in Philippians, the apostle means that, when Christ clothed Himself with humanity He did not transform it, but He conformed it to Himself, associating it with His own immortality, without changing it into His own divinity.[3]

As the editor of this Augustinian text and others have confirmed, the *Eighty-Three Questions* was known and cited up through the Carolingian period.[4] Up until that time, the other major interpretation of the *habitus* theory was the one provided by Boethius, who gives it a different sense than Augustine does, the sense in which it was appropriated by John Scottus Eriugena and many of its twelfth-century supporters and detractors. In his *Contra Eutychen et Nestorium*, Boethius attacks the argument by which each of these heretics would reduce Christ's humanity to nothing at all (*omnino nihil*). The theology of Nestorius, he says, leads to this conclusion by making the union of divinity with humanity so adventitious that they exist side by side, and are not truly united. On the other hand, Eutyches absorbs Christ's humanity into His divinity to such a degree that there is no real human nature left in Him. Now, Boethius adds that one can say that Christ's divinity became humanity, that His humanity became divinity, or that each was modified to such an extent that neither retained its original nature, but a new *tertium quid* resulted. The first is impossible since the divine nature is immutable. The second is impossible because human nature involves a body. Just as one body cannot change into another body, so, *a fortiori*, a body cannot change into an incorporeal entity. The third is impossible since it can take place only in the merging of beings that possess a common nature, a common material substratum that serves as a bridge between them. Boethius's own solution is to compare the union of man and God in the incarnate Christ with that of the gold and gems that

---

[3] Augustine, *De diversis quaestionibus octoginta tribus* q. 73. ed. Almut Mutzenbecher, CCSL 44A (Turnhout: Brepols, 1975), pp. 209–12. On this doctrine, see Tarsicius J. van Bavel, *Recherches sur la christologie de Saint Augustine: L'humain et le divin dans le Christ d'après Saint Augustin* (Fribourg, Suisse: Éditions Universitaires, 1954), pp. 34–37.

[4] Mutzenbecher, intro. to his ed., pp. l–lix, lxxv; John Marenbon, *From the Circle of Alcuin to the School of Auxerre: Logic, Theology and Philosophy in the Early Middle Ages* (Cambridge: Cambridge University Press, 1981), pp. 37, 42–45, 53, 56.

combine to form a crown, or the vesting of a man with a garment, examples in which, is his view, neither element is changed.[5] And, although he cites Augustine's *Eighty-Three Questions*, John Scottus clearly intends the same thing as Boethius on the incarnation in describing Christ's human nature as a sandal which He puts on. His choice of this particular article of clothing is made to reflect Christ's retention of His humanity unchanged in the incarnation as well as it allegorical significance in relation to John the Baptist as His forerunner.[6] The twelfth-century theologians who support the *habitus* theory invoke it in order to stress the point made by Boethius and Eriugena: neither the divinity nor the humanity of Christ was changed in their union. Both they and their critics also notice that another feature of the *habitus* doctrine in both its Augustinian and Boethian forms is that the union is adventitious and accidental; the two natures of Christ are partible.

As the Lombard reads these three position, they all have problems. The chief difficulty to be alleged against the *assumptus homo* theory is that it falls into Boethius's second impossibility, and even conceivably into the danger of Eutychianism, by assimilating Christ's humanity into His divinity in the bestowing on that humanity of the blessings and exemptions that elevate the human Christ so far above other human beings that His consubstantiality with them is put at risk, a consubstantiality necessary if His life and death are to have their intended soteriological effects. Peter also sees a real problem in calling the person of the incarnate Christ a mixed one. In the *Sentences*, he regards the idea of three substances as unacceptable, although he had entertained that idea earlier in his career in one of his sermons. He had also, in his earlier Pauline exegesis, made use of the Augustinian twin substance language, although he viewed it in such as way as to avoid the confusion between the two substances. With respect to the *habitus* theory, if one follows the Augustinian explanation of it, which Peter cites in full, there is a problem in it analogous to the problem affecting the *assumptus homo* position, as he analyzes it, the change in Christ's human nature. Even in his commentary on Philippians, where he had indicated acceptance of the *habitus* theory earlier, he had never

---

[5] Boethius, *Contra Eutychen et Nestorium* 4–7, ed. and trans. H. F. Stewart, E. K. Rand, and S. J. Tester in Boethius, *The Theological Tractates* (Cambridge, MA: Harvard University Press, 1973), pp. 92–94, 104–16, 120. The quotation is at 4, p. 94.

[6] John Scottus Eriugena, *Commentaire sur l'Évangile de Jean* 1.29, ed. Édouard Jeauneau, Sources chrétiennes, 180 (Paris: Les Éditions du Cerf, 1972), pp. 150, 152.

understood it in that sense himself. But the larger problem Peter sees with the *habitus* position it that it makes Christ's manhood accidental. Instead of a hypostatic union, there is the adventitious human garb, which the Word can put on and take off, and which is not really united to the person Who wears it. This being the case, an adherant of the *habitus* theory would not really be able to endorse the scriptural principle that the Word became flesh, or that God became man in the incarnation.[7]

In coming to the conclusion that all three positions, despite their biblical and patristic warrants, were problematic, Peter had before him the arguments of contemporaries who espoused one or another of the positions and whose terminology was so unclear or inconsistent that they did not, in his estimation, succeed in making their case. He also had before him Gilbert and the Porretans, whose language was not only indiosyncratic but was also an impediment in conveying their ideas. While Peter certainly repudiates the Porretan lexicon, taking a leaf from the book of some of Gilbert's earliest followers in this respect, he shares many of Gilbert's Christological positions. Indeed, he comes closer to Gilbert, substantively, than to any other contemporary theologian on the hypostatic union. And, it is both the agenda he shares with Gilbert and his criticism of Gilbert that enable him to pinpoint what he finds unacceptable in the views of other masters, whichever of the three opinions they held.

This being the case, it will be useful to reprise briefly the account of Gilbert's treatment of the hypostatic union and of the language in which he expresses it given above in chapter 3.[8] To begin with, in his use of the term "substance," Gilbert largely seeks to apply it to the level of being on which beings are concrete and are subject to modification by accidents, or *subsistens*, in his vocabulary. He also wants to use the term "nature" to refer to beings at this level. Sometimes, however, he refers to the deity as such as a substance, using this term to refer to what would be equivalent, in the deity, to

---

[7] Peter Lombard, *Sententiae in IV libris distinctae* 3. d. 6–d. 7. c. 3.3, 3rd ed. rev., ed. Ignatius C. Brady, 2 vols. (Grottaferrata: Collegii S. Bonaventurae ad Claras Aquas, 1971–81), 2: 49–66. For his earlier use of the *gemina substantia* language, see the second redaction of Peter's *In Epistolam Pauli ad Romanos* 1:3, *PL* 191: 1307C. This same language occurs in *Sermo* 7, 9, 55, 99, *PL* 171: 371C, 382A, 396A, 605D–606B, 806B. He refers to Christ as having three substances in *Sermo* 43, *PL* 171: 559B–C. On this point, see above, chapter 4, p. 216 and n. 157. For Peter's earlier alignment with a Boethian or Eriugenian version of the *habitus* theory, see *In Epistolam ad Philippenses* 2:1–8, *PL* 192: 235A–D. See above, chapter 4, p. 223.

[8] See above, pp. 132–48.

the level of being he calls *subsistentia* in created beings, which refers to their formal properties. Since Gilbert holds that everything that is in God is God, that the perfectly simple deity is His own qualities perfectly, there really is no distinction that can be made between *subsistentia* and *subsistens* in God's case. Even for creatures, Gilbert holds that the *subsistentia* inheres in the being in a radically individual way and that it cannot be abstracted from that being. He also rejects the Boethian definition of a person as the individual substance of a rational nature. He does so because, in Trinitarian theology, he recognizes that this definition of person would yield three substances, that is, three Gods. In the case of human beings, he rejects Boethius on *persona* because he is a strong proponent of the view, against more Platonizing anthropologies, that the human person is not the soul alone but the integral union of body and soul, not a casual or separable combination or a new *tertium quid* but a union whose constituent ingredients retain their own distinctive characteristics. With respect to *persona* in the deity, Gilbert provides only a numerical distinction among the Father, Son, and Holy Spirit. He accents the unity of the deity so strongly that it is not at all clear how, or if, these persons are really different from each other and why one of them, and not the others or the whole Trinity, was incarnated. Given Gilbert's view of human nature as the concrete *subsistens* of each individual man, it is also hard to see how he can distinguish between nature and person in the case of human beings. It is likewise hard to see how individual human beings can be part of a wider human community, since, even at the level of *subsistentia*, each man's formal aspect inheres in him in a completely individual way. In any event, whether a *persona* is divine and simple, or human and a composite of body and soul, a person is a *res per se una*, a single individual being, for Gilbert.

While they may create problems in Gilbert's Trinitarian theology, this assortment of principles engenders even greater difficulties in his Christology. His chief target is the *habitus* theory and the anthropology undergirding it. Gilbert disagrees with the idea that the humanity and divinity of the incarnate Christ are partible and that their relationship is accidental. He sees this claim as modeled on a notion of the union of body and soul in man as divisible, which he also rejects. Gilbert also wants to attack the view that the *homo* assumed by the Word was a man already in existence, a position that had gotten attached to the *homo assumptus* theory despite the fact that it had originally been formulated with the express purpose of excluding Adoptionism. He sees the Word, in the hypostatic union, as both a divine person and as the divine substance. His vocabulary does not make it possible for him to distinguish between these aspects of a Trinitarian person. This divine component unites with a concrete human *subsistens*. Gilbert insists on this latter point in order to emphasize that it was the historical man Jesus Who was involved. And so, Gilbert says that the Word united with *homo*, the concrete noun standing for this concrete *subsistens*, in contrast with the *humanitas*, the abstract noun standing for his *subsistentia*. There is, to be sure, a problem here, in that Gilbert's language, and his metaphysics, weaken the connection between the human Christ and other human beings. This tends to circumscribe the impact of Christ's saving work. In order to rule out Adoptionism, Gilbert argues that the *homo* assumed by the Word was not a subsistent man already in existence. Rather, He took on the body and soul of a man, neither of which existed before their union with each other and their simultaneous union with the Word. Once that union has taken place, one can call the ingredients that make up the human Christ a human substance composed of body and soul. While Gilbert cannot distinguish person from substance in the deity, he tries vigorously to do so in the case of the man Jesus. What Jesus contributes to the incarnation are the components of a human substance. But, while in other human beings, the combination of body and soul produces a *subsistens* that is also a person, with Jesus this is not the case. There is, to be sure, a person in the incarnate Christ, but it is the divine person of the Word. This divine person does not change when the incarnation takes place. It remains one and simple. By definition, for Gilbert, no person can be duplex, so there cannot be more than one person in the incarnate Christ. Further, for Gilbert, in the hypostatic union, both the divine and human natures remain unconfused. Neither assimilates the other, and no new *tertium quid* is produced. Thus far, the contemporary position to which Gilbert comes the closest is the subsistence theory, but with two important qualifications. For Gilbert, the person of the incarnate Christ does not become a composite *persona* at the time of the incarnation. Rather, Christ retains the same fully divine *persona* that He has always had. Secondly, Gilbert's lexicon permits him to speak of the human contribution to the incarnation as a substance. It also allows him, confusingly, to speak of the divine contribution as a substance as well, although, as noted, without being able to clarify the difference between nature and person in God. He therefore does not use the language of three substances in God, divinity, body, and soul. And, while he is firm in ruling out the idea that there is a human person in the incarnate Christ, his anthropology makes it difficult to see why the man Jesus is not a human person after His body and soul have been united with each other and with the Word.

As Gilbert summarizes his findings, they take the form of the dictum *non persona personam, nec natura personam, nec natura naturam, sed persona naturam assumpsit*. A person cannot assume a person, since no person can be duplex. The divine nature does not assume a human person, and this for two reasons. It was a single member of the Trinity and not the divine nature as a whole Who was incarnated. Also, if He assumed a human person, one would be teaching Adoptionism. A nature does not take on a nature. Here, once again, the first part of the statement is designed to rule out the idea that the Godhead as such, and not the Word, was incarnated. The second part of the statement is designed to reinforce the point that the Word was joined to a particular human being and not to mankind in general. And so, in Gilbert's preferred formula, a divine person takes on a human nature in the incarnation. This conclusion raises as many problems as it resolves; for, given Gilbert's terminology, the difference between a human nature and a human person is all but invisible, or, at any rate, it is inexplicable. Also, it is hard to see why, if human nature is ruled out in the *nec natura naturam* part of the formula, as standing for the human race and not one historic member of it, the term *natura* should suddenly acquire the latter denotation in the *persona naturam assumpsit* part of the formula which he supports. Further, in his effort to rule out Adoptionism, or any Adoptionist leanings as he may find in contemporary proponents of the *assumptus homo* theory, Gilbert fails to see that what he really needs to say is that what the Word assumed is neither *natura* nor *homo*, but the infra-subsistent human body and soul, as yet not joined.

The early Porretans, particularly the authors of the two sentence collections written in Paris in the early 1140s, make some notable modifications in Gilbert's language in the effort to disembarrass his Christology of it. At the same time, they backpedal with respect to some of Gilbert's most useful ideas. Avoiding the language of *subsistens* and *subsistentia*, they observe the distinction drawn by the Greeks and assign *substantia* in principle to the task of denoting the divine essence common to the Trinitarian persons. While they reimport into their discussion of the Trinity the idea that the Trinitarian persons are one in essence and three in operation, they proceed to confuse matters by applying *substantia* both to the divine unity and to the divine plurality, thereby undermining their ability to distinguish meaningfully between substance and person in the deity. They do not have as clearly developed an anthropology as

Gilbert but agree with him that man is an integral unit of body and soul. They also endorse his idea that what the Word took on was not a man already in existence but the body and soul out of which man is made, *ex quibus fit homo*, that once united with the Word, the human component remained attached to Him, and that neither the divinity nor the humanity of Christ was changed by their union or merged to form a *tertium quid*. They follow as well Gilbert's summary formula and assent to the principle that a divine person assumed a human nature in the incarnation.

There are, however, two signal respects in which the early Porretan sentence collectors depart from Gilbert. As to why a person cannot assume a person, they drop Gilbert's elegant and simple answer based on the definition of a person as a *res per se una* and substitute a less responsive one, the argument that, were it possible for a person to take on a person, Christ's divinity would have been diminished in the incarnation. What they seem to have in mind here is the subsistence theory notion that the incarnate Christ has a composite *persona*. They also disagree with themselves, and with Gilbert, in endorsing the three-substance model of the subsistence theory along with the *gemina substantia* of Augustine. Having made this move, they find themselves hard pressed to explain in what sense an unattached human body, or an unattached human soul, can both be called substances, or why either of them can be called a substance in its own right after they have been united. One of the authors calls these substances, indifferently, natures, which is equally difficult to explain. It is true that Boethius, and assorted twelfth-century theologians with Platonizing anthropologies, could define the soul as a substance or as a person. But the Porretans join Gilbert in rejecting Boethius on this score. Still, in supporting the idea that a person assumes a nature, they do not clarify whether they mean by "nature" here these two aspects of the human constitution viewed one by one, or human nature in its more general acceptation. At the same time the early Porretans use two other formulae, describing the hypostatic union as the conjunction of divinity and humanity and also under the statement that, in the incarnation, God became man. The first of these seems to support Gilbert's idea that, in addition to being impartible after they were joined, these natures were not confused when they were united. On the other hand, the notion that God became man makes quite different claims, whether in Gilbertian terms or in ordinary Latin, a point which the authors ignore.

One did not have to be a supporter of the subsistence theory to make use of the three-substance or two-substance language found in the Porretans. This vocabulary can also be found in a number of other theologians in the first half of the twelfth century who associate it with one or more of the other two positions on the hypostatic union. And, while they do not use *substantia*, in Gilbert's sense of the word, with respect either to God or to man, their own theological terminology in this connection is capable of being equally inconsistent or problematic. A good case in point is Abelard, Gilbert's major target, who has been linked, and with excellent reason, to the *habitus* theory, a theory firmly connected in his own mind with a Platonizing view of human nature, which he analogizes to the hypostatic union. Just as he sees the human soul as the essence of human nature, so he accents the divine over the human natures in the incarnate Christ.[9] Abelard's earliest treatments of the hypostatic union occur in sermons dating from his period as abbot of St. Gildas in the 1130s. In them, he demonstrates a view of the union of idioms in the incarnate Christ in which both the divinity and the humanity of Christ preexist their amalgamation, and the notion that the human component is accidental. He expresses both of these ideas in formulating one of his most deplorable analogies. The incarnate Christ, he states, can be compared with an *electrum* or alloy of two metals, in this case gold and silver representing His divinity and humanity respectively. They are fused in the incarnation, and neither ingredient changes in the process. Nor is a new *tertium quid* produced. And, they are partible. The humanity is separated from the divinity when Christ dies on the cross, just as the silver is rendered out of the alloy with the application of heat to the *electrum*.[10]

Later in the same period Abelard wrote commentaries on the Apostles' Creed and the Athanasian Creed in which he compares the union of idioms in the incarnate Christ with the union of body and soul in man, a body and soul which are also separable. These

---

[9] The best treatments of Abelard's Christology are Richard E. Weingart, *The Logic of Divine Love: A Critical Analysis of the Soteriology of Peter Abailard* (Oxford: Clarendon Press, 1970), pp. 102–03, 119; J. G. Sikes, *Peter Abailard* (Cambridge: Cambridge University Press, 1932), pp. 167–68; Paul L. Williams, *The Moral Philosophy of Peter Abelard* (Lanham, MD: University Press of America, 1980), pp. 105–10. Lauge Olaf Nielsen, *Theology and Philosophy in the Twelfth Century: A Study of Gilbert Porreta's Thinking and the Theological Expositions of the Doctrine of the Incarnation during the Period 1130–1180*, Acta theologica danica, 15 (Leiden: E. J. Brill, 1982), pp. 214–23 accents Abelard's differences from Gilbert and gives a truncated account. Edward Filene Little, "The Heresies of Peter Abelard," University of Montreal Ph.D. diss., 1969, pp. 231–33, 239–312 thinks that the charge of Nestorianism made against Abelard was unfounded and merely reflects the ignorance of his monastic critics.

[10] Peter Abelard, *Sermo* 1, 2, *PL* 178: 385D–386A, 396A.

two natures are united—and Abelard uses the same language in
both commentaries—in one person, "a person that is said to be
almost unitary" (*persona quippe quasi per se una*) and which can be
defined as the individual substance of a rational nature. This
rational substance, in the case of both the incarnate Christ and
human beings, is then joined to something else with which it makes
another substance.[11] Abelard comes back to this point in the *Theologia "scholarium"*, where he also raises, without answering, the question of how Christ's substance is different from His person and
whether it is just the human soul, and not the body and soul as
united, that is a substance. Here, he observes that the ingredients
do not change in the union. Nor does the person of Christ, which is
a single, divine *persona* and now, presumably, entirely and not *quasi*
simple.[12] The one other question Abelard raises and which he has
predictable difficulty in answering given his identification of the
Trinitarian persons with the attributes of power, wisdom, and
goodness, all of which he thinks were involved in the incarnation, is
why it was the Son Who was incarnated rather than the Father or
the Holy Spirit, or all three.[13] More than merely reflecting problems which opponents of the *habitus* theory might ascribe to it, as
involving a relationship between divinity and humanity where the
two natures are partible and the humanity is adventitious, Abelard's
account of the hypostatic union reveals difficulties stemming from
his own terminological imprecision, especially with respect to the
terms "substance" and "person," and from the connection between
Christology and other controversial areas of his theology. As for his
followers, they do no better. We find the same equivocal use of
substantia in Hermannus. And Roland of Bologna, agreeing with the
idea that the divine and human natures in the incarnate Christ are
partible and with the idea that the soul of man is the essence of
human nature, argues that, during Christ's three days in the tomb,
His divinity remained united with His soul only.[14]

---

[11] Peter Abelard, *Expositio in symbolum apostolorum; Expositio in symbolum Athanasii*,
PL 178: 624A, 631A.
[12] Peter Abelard, *Theologia "scholarium"* 3.74–82, ed. Constant J. Mews in Peter
Abelard, *Opera theologica*, CCCM 11–13 (Turnhout: Brepols, 1969–87), 13: 531–35.
[13] Peter Abelard, *Theologia christiana* 4.68, ed. Eligius M. Buytaert, CCCM 12:
296.
[14] Hermannus, *Sententie magistri Petri Abaelardi (Sententie Hermanni)*, ed. Sandro
Buzzetti, Pubblicazioni della Facoltà di lettere e filosofia dell'Università di Milano, 101, sezione a cura di storia di filosofia, 31 (Florence: La Nuova Italia, 1983),
p. 109; Roland of Bologna, *Die Sentenzen Rolands*, ed. Ambrosius M. Gietl (Amsterdam: Editions Rodopi, 1969 [repr. of Freiburg im Breisgau: Herder, 1891 ed.]),
pp. 164–65. 172–74, 191. On these figures, see Nielsen, *Theology and Philosophy*,

One did not have to be a defender of either the *habitus* theory or the subsistence theory to talk, with equally confusing results, about the incarnate Christ as having three substances, or, for that matter, to be able to insist, as both Abelard and the Porretans do, that the humanity and divinity in Christ remained distinct substantially. The three-substance position is found as well in the school of Laon.[15] And, while a number of masters in this group, espousing the *habitus* theory, state that the Word assumed humanity like a garment (*ex vestimento*) but without His divine nature increasing or decreasing thereby,[16] the school as a whole is more usually associated with the *assumptus homo* theory. This is the language which William of Champeaux uses, while also insisting that the two natures unite but without either nature changing or being involved in a substantial participation in the other. He adds, here making the point also made by Gilbert and his followers, that once the two natures were united, they remained united; Christ's divinity stayed with His body in the tomb as well as accompanying His soul in the harrowing of Hell.[17] Most of all, the school's handling of the incarnation is obscured by their insensitivity to the debates on theological language that raged in this period and their disinclination to define any of the key terms they use. They are basically less interested in questions of this order than with other matters pertaining to the incarnation. They want to discuss why it was the second person of the Trinity Who was incarnated, and respond that the Son is the appropriate person for the job because He is already a manifestation of the Father.[18] They also want to consider why the incarnation took place at the particular moment in history when it occurred. To this question they give a response that became standard in the period. God, they state, waited until men had the chance to internalize the fact that they could not free themselves from sin by themselves, whether through the moral law of the Old

---

pp. 222–28, 235–42, although he errs in thinking that Roland did not regard the divinity and humanity of Christ as partible. This judgment may result from the idea that Roland equated Christ's humanity entirely with His human soul. For a survey of contemporary discussions of the partibility of Christ's divinity and humanity in the tomb, see Landgraf, *Dogmengeschichte*, 2 part 1: 274–88.

[15] *Sentences of Plausible Authenticity*, no. 182, ed. Odon Lottin in *Psychologie et morale aux XIIᵉ et XIIIᵉ siècle*, vols. 1–5 (Louvain: Abbaye de Mont-César, 1948–59), 5: 128.

[16] *Sentences of the School of Laon*, no. 343, 346, 349, ed. Lottin in *Psych. et morale*, 5: 263–64, 265, 266. The quotation is at no. 343, p. 264.

[17] *Sentences of William of Champeaux*, no. 262–63, 265–66, 268, ed. Lottin in *Psych. et morale*, 5: 213, 214–215, 216.

[18] Anselm of Laon, *Sententie divine pagine*, ed. Franz P. Bliemetzrieder in *Anselms von Laon systematische Sentenzen*, Beiträge, 18: 2–3 (Münster: Aschendorff, 1919), pp. 39–40.

Testament or through the natural moral law.[19] And, raising one
more question which they leave open and whose implications they
do not notice, they wonder whether the human soul of Christ was
infused into His body at the moment when the body was conceived
or, as the *physici* teach, at some point later, as is the case with
everyone else.[20] Other theologians of the time who take up this
question are more definite, and agree that Christ's body and soul
were created and joined together simultaneously in a miraculous
event, *pace* the *physici*.[21]

Another theologian who adopts the three-substance position, in
the effort to oppose Adoptionism, is the author of the *Summa sententiarum*. He is an exponent of the *assumptus homo* theory,[22] much more
strictly than Hugh of St. Victor, the master whom he follows in
most other areas of his Christology and whose confusions and
inconsistencies on the hypostatic union he perpetuates. At the same
time, he joins Hugh in commenting on the Mariological dimensions
of the incarnation. Hugh's own handling of this subject is bedeviled
by a lack of clarity.[23] In discussing the hypostatic union, Hugh uses
assumptus homo language in stating that Christ, Who was God from
the beginning, also became man, taking on a human body and soul
at the same time. Neither nature was altered in the process. Yet,
Hugh also uses *habitus* theory language that makes this human

[19] *Sentences of the School of Laon*, no. 283, 5: 232.
[20] *Deus de cuius principio et fine tacetur*, ed. Heinrich Weisweiler in "Le recueil des
sentences 'Deus de cuius principio et fine tacetur' et son remaniement," *RTAM* 5
(1933): 267–68. Others who adopt the same argument are Honorius Augustodunensis, *Elucidarium* 1.121–24 in *L'Elucidarium et les lucidaires: Contribution, par
l'histoire d'un texte, à l'histoire des croyances religieuses en France au moyen âge*, ed. Yves
Lefèvre (Paris: É. de Boccard, 1954), pp. 383–84; Hugh of St. Victor, *De sacramentis
fidei christianae* 1.8.2–3, *PL* 176: 306C–307D. For the range of views inherited from
ancient science on the ensoulment of embryos available in this period, see John T.
Noonan, *Contraception: A History of Its Treatment by the Catholic Theologians and
Canonists*, enlarged ed. (Cambridge, MA: Harvard University Press, 1986), pp.
86–90.
[21] *Sentences of Plausible Authenticity*, no. 184, 5: 129. See, on the other hand, the
solutions of Hugh of St. Victor, *De sac.* 2.1.5, *PL* 176: 381C; Bernhard Geyer, ed.,
Die Sententiae divinitatis: Ein Sentenzenbuch der Gilbertischen Schule 4.3.8, Beiträge,
7:2–3 (Münster: Aschendorff, 1909), pp. 90*–91*; *Summa sententiarum* 1.16, *PL* 176:
72B–D; F. Anders, *Die Christologie des Robert von Melun* (Paderborn: Ferdinand
Schöningh, 1927), pp. xvi–xvii.
[22] *Summa sent.* 1.15–16, *PL* 176: 70C–72D. The reference to the three-substance
idea is at 1.16, 72B.
[23] Good accounts are found in Nielsen, *Theology and Philosophy*, pp. 193–213;
Everhard Poppenberg, *Die Christologie des Hugo von St. Viktor* (Herz: Jesu-
Missionshaus Hiltrup, 1937), pp. 48–87; A. Mignon, *Les origines de la scolastique et
Hugues de Saint-Victor*, 2 vols. (Paris: P. Lethielleux, 1895), 2: 68–69, although the
latter fails to note that, for Hugh, the divinity of Christ remains attached only to
His human soul during the *triduum*.

nature look accidental in the incarnate Christ. He quotes Philippians and Augustine's analysis of *habitus* and agrees with him that
Christ's humanity can be compared to a garment which a man may
put on (*quam vestis ab homine cum induitur*).[24] Hugh is not clear on
whether he follows the Boethian interpretation of *habitus*, in which
neither what is taken on nor the person who takes it on is changed,
which he claims he is supporting, or the Augustinian view that the
manhood conforms to the divinity as the garment takes on the
shape of the wearer, which his own treatment of Christ's humanity
would suggest. Hugh is also unclear on whether these components,
once united, are impartable or not. It is not appropriate, he states,
and this against Abelard and other holders of the *habitus* theory, to
think of the incarnate Christ as a being Who had parts. Yet, in the
three days between His death and resurrection, Christ's divinity,
according to Hugh, remained united only with his human soul, not
his body. Hugh emphasizes the importance of Christ's retention of
a human soul at all times, for soteriological reasons, so that Christ
can be united with all men and extend his saving work to them.[25]
But here, he seems to forget the point he makes about man's
possession of a body as well as a soul, its necessity in man's
knowledge, and its function as a link between the physical creation
and man's redemption, which he offers in his analysis of human
nature. The single biggest contradiction in Hugh's account sur-
rounds his discussion of *persona*. He complains at length that there
is too much confusing debate on the definition of this term. Yet, he
offers no real understanding of his own use of it. On the one hand,
he sees *persona* as the union of body and soul in man, and argues
that there was no such human *persona* in the incarnate Christ
because His human body and soul were not already joined to each
other before they were united with the Word. He does not succeed
in explaining why they do not form a human person when they do
get joined together in the incarnate Christ, not only with each other
but also with the divine nature. Here, Hugh's inability to differentiate adequately between person and nature in the deity, a problem
which also haunts his Trinitarian theology, takes its toll. On the
other hand, and here Hugh's Platonizing anthropology comes to
the fore, he sees the soul of man alone as his *persona*, meaning that
there would be a human person in the incarnate Christ from the

---

[24] Hugh of St. Victor, MS. Douai 365, fol. 74^v–75^r; MS. Douai 366, fol.
102^v–102^r, ed. Roger Baron in "Textes spirituels inédits de Hugues de Saint-
Victor," *Mélanges de science religieuse* 13 (1956): 168; *De sac.* 2.1.5, *PL* 176: 381C.
[25] Hugh of St. Victor, *De sac.* 2.1.1, 2.1.12, *PL* 176: 401B–404C, 412A–413A.

moment when He assumed the soul, irrespective of whether He assumed, or retained His connection with, a body.[26]

Hugh adds a number of other points to this analysis of the incarnation that are less confusing. On the question of why the Son was incarnated and not the Father or the Holy Spirit, he follows the tradition set forth by the Laon masters, but adds his own twist. It is true, he observes, that power, wisdom, and goodness are all involved in the incarnation. Further, we cannot say that the other two persons of the Trinity lacked the ability to take on human flesh. But, he adds, it was more fitting for the Son to take up this assignment. If the Father or the Holy Spirit had done so, there would have been two Sons. Now, the Son already was a Son, with respect to the Father, from all eternity. He comes to men as a brother, enabling them to become sons of God as well and co-heirs of the kingdom of God.[27] Another point Hugh develops in his own way is the Mariology required by the incarnation. He shares the consensus view, derived from Augustine, and particularly from Augustine's doctrine of the transmission of original sin by means of the lust accompanying sexual relations and/or the vitiated seeds with which such relations must operate, which says that the Virgin Mary was cleansed of her own original sin at the moment of Christ's conception. She did not experience lust and she did not possess vitiated genetic materials. Thus, she did not pass original sin on to her child. Hugh adds to this a description of conception itself which looks to be a corruption of the opinion of Galen. Without citing his source, he states that, in normal human situations, conception occurs only when the sexual partners unite willingly, through love, and not just when sexual congress occurs devoid of love. This account of conception does carry over to the Virgin Mary, in his estimation. In her case, there was mutual love between Mary and the Holy Spirit. Also, His work in her enabled her miraculously to produce the male seed required as well as the female contribution, out of her own body alone. There was no original sin in the conception of Christ, therefore, because no relations between a man and a woman took place.[28] This analysis, consistent with Hugh's treatment of the transmission of original sin, puts the emphasis on Mary's lack of sexual feelings in the event.

Despite the conceptual and terminological problems it leaves

---

[26] Ibid., 2.1.9, 2.1.11, *PL* 176: 393D–399B, 401B–412A.
[27] Ibid., 2.1.2–4, *PL* 176: 371D–381D.
[28] Ibid., 2.1.5–7, *PL* 176: 381C–393B.

unsolved, Hugh of St. Victor's treatment of the incarnation was surprisingly influential. Aside from his jettisoning of the *habitus* theory language and his insistence on three substances as well as two natures in the incarnate Christ, a point that departs from his tendency to equate substance and nature when speaking about the deity, the author of the *Summa Sententiarum* follows Hugh's lead. He adds to the confusion on *persona* by reimporting the Boethian definition of person as the individual substance of a rational nature into his analysis of Christ's human nature, even though he had redefined this phrase in his Trinitarian theology. He is aware of the fact that, if this definition is accepted, one has to grant the incarnate Christ a human person, whenever His human soul was assumed, and whether with a body or not. The author sees the problem, wrestles with it manfully, and fails to solve it. He agrees that Christ's human body and soul were assumed simultaneously. But, even if one sees the *persona* as lying in the union of body and soul, the theory the author prefers, and even if one argues, against the Adoptionists, that they were not united with each other before their union with the Word, the human person still cannot effectively be eliminated. The author comes no closer than Hugh does to solving this problem. The root cause, for him as well as for Hugh, is a vocabulary whose terms he does not clearly define.[29] Omitting Hugh's theory that mutual love is required for conception, the author follows the rest of his analysis of the conception of Christ, adding that He was truly sinless although truly consubstantial with the rest of the human race.[30] Yet, despite the reminder that Christ came to redeem both the body and the soul of man, he endorses Hugh's position on the union of Christ's human soul alone with His divinity during the *triduum*.[31] He also follows Hugh on why it was the Son Who was incarnated.[32]

Less full, but equally Victorine, is Robert of Melun.[33] He returns to a positive acceptance of the Boethian definition of person, for the human Christ, despite his clear-eyed grasp of its inappositeness when applied to the Trinity. He agrees that Christ's body and soul

---

[29] *Summa sent.* 1.19, *PL* 176: 70D–71D.
[30] Ibid., 1.16, *PL* 176: 73A–C.
[31] Ibid., 1.19, *PL* 176: 78D–80B.
[32] Ibid., 1.15, *PL* 176: 70B.
[33] Raymond-M. Martin, ed. of Robert of Melun, *Oeuvres*, 4 vols. (Louvain: Spicilegium Sacrum Lovaniense, 1932–52), 3 part 2: 55–58 n.; Martin, ed., "Un texte intéressant de Robert de Melun (*Sententiae*, libr. II, part 2, cap. cxcvii–ccxiii)." *RHE* 28 (1932): 316–17, 320–22; Anders, *Die Christologie*, pp. xxx–xxxvii, xliv–lxxxv; A. L. Lilly, "A Christological Controversy of the Twelfth Century," *Journal of Theological Studies* 39 (1938): 225–35.

were joined to the Word at the same time, regardless of what the *physici* say about human conception. His lack of a clear distinction between person and substance in God leads him to state, confusingly, that the divine substance is incarnated in the person of the Son. He argues, also confusingly, that the humanity taken on by the Son is not a substance or a person, despite the language of Boethius on person, which he accepts. His effort to mediate between nihilianism and Adoptionism, predictably, is a failure. He says that the incarnate Christ has no parts. Yet, he agrees with Hugh that Christ's divinity remains united with His soul alone while His body is in the tomb. Robert adds a question to this topic, whether that body underwent decay in the tomb or, as with the bodies of some of the saints, it was preserved from decay miraculously. He can find no authoritative answer, but is sympathetic to the idea that Christ's human body suffered no corruption, since it was a more glorious body than that possessed by any saint.[34] He takes the same position as Hugh on the virgin birth and, like the author of the *Summa Sententiarum*, locates the issue in the absence of concupiscence on the part of the Virgin without speculating on the nature of normal conception.

The author of the *Sententiae divinitatis* associates himself with Hugh of St. Victor on the mode of Christ's conception and on the moment at which Mary was exempted from concupiscence.[35] He also agrees with Hugh that there were no parts in the incarnate Christ but that He still was partible, with His divinity remaining joined to His soul alone while His body lay in the tomb.[36] But, this author is distressingly vague on the actual character of the hypostatic union itself. He contents himself with quoting the line that is standard in the accounts of twelfth-century theologians in their discussions of Christ's human nature more generally, "whatever the Son of God had by nature, the man had by grace" (*Quicquid habuit Filius Dei per naturam, habuit homo ille per gratiam*),[37] and lets it go at that.

To complete the survey of contemporary opinions which Peter Lombard had before him, there was the treatment of the incarnation by Robert Pullen. This is an area where he is at his most self-contradictory, and where the total absence of any definitions of his terms wreaks the most havoc. Robert omits certain issues which his contemporaries avidly debated, such as whether Christ's body

---

[34] Martin, "Un texte intéressant," pp. 317–19.
[35] *Sent. div.* 4.5.5, pp. 103*–04*.
[36] Ibid., 4.4.1–4. pp. 94*–99*.
[37] Ibid., 4.1.5, p. 75*.

and soul preexisted their union with the Word. On the hypostatic
union, he offers a smorgasbord of views without indicating a preference. He states that the union is one in which the divinity and
humanity are not confused in substance with each other. There are
two substances, or essences, in the incarnate Christ, bound in a
unity of person. Robert inappositely cites Augustine's *gemina substantia* on this point. While he does not clarify the difference between substance and person in the Word, he asserts that, in the
incarnation, this *persona* was not composite. Christ had both a
human and a divine will. Consistent with the notion of an integral
union of Christ's two natures, Robert rejects the Victorine view and
agrees with William of Champeaux and the Porretans that Christ's
divinity remained united with both His body and His soul during
the *triduum*.[38] At the same time. Robert presents as equally viable
the idea that the incarnate Christ had three substances, divinity,
body, and soul. He adds that the Word took on this body and soul
essentially (*essentialiter*) and not in name only, attacking as heretical
those who disagree. None the less, he is vague on why it was the
Son Who was incarnated. He does not really notice the debate on
this question. All of the persons of the Trinity are ubiquitous, he
observes. As is the case with the creation more generally, They are
all present in the man Jesus as well. We recall, from Robert's
account of the divine ubiquity in his doctrine of God, that he holds
God to be present in the creation *essentialiter*, a view he maintains
without seeing that it leads down the garden path to pantheism.
With respect to the Word, He is present in the man Jesus *personali-
ter*. But, Robert never succeeds in explaining the difference between
essence and person, or between substance and person, in the Word.
At some points, he treats Christ's divine *persona* as identical with
the divine substance and essence. At other times, however, he
treats the *persona* as the mode by which Christ's human body and
soul were united with the Word, which would preclude its existence
prior to the moment of the incarnation.[39] On this problematic note,
Robert not so much concludes as ends his report on the doctrine of
the incarnation.

The Lombard on the Hypostatic Union

In positioning himself in the contemporary debates on the in-

---

[38] Robert Pullen, *Sententiarum libri octo* 3.16–18, 3.19, *PL* 186: 782D–788D, 789C.
[39] Ibid., 2.10, 3.15, 3.16–18, 3.20, *PL* 186: 734B–C, 780D–782B, 782D–788D, 791C–D, 792C–793D.

carnation, Peter Lombard dissociates himself pointedly from theologians who fail to clarify their terms, or who use their terminology inconsistently, whether the language is of their own devising or is traditional. His own crisp distinctions between substance, essence, and nature, on the one hand, as denoting the divinity as such, and person, on the other, as denoting the properties and relations that distinguish one Trinitarian person from the other two persons, vis-à-vis each other, provides him with a useful and economical means of explaining the divine contribution to the hypostatic union. His stress on human nature as an integral union of body and soul and his strong disagreement with the Platonizing accounts of human nature professed in his day help him as well to deal effectively with Christ's humanity, not just in the constitution of Christ, as incarnated, but in His subsequent behavior. Peter is firm in rejecting the Boethian definition of person as appropriate either for divine or human persons. He is also unhesitating in his rejection of the three-substance analysis of the hypostatic union, since it conflicts with his understanding of human beings as substances whose ingredients have to be seen metaphysically as infrasubstantial. Likewise, and even though he had earlier subscribed to this doctrine as well, he dismisses Augustine's *gemina substantia* doctrine because he sees it as standing for a conflation or combination of two kinds of person in Christ, which he sees as utterly unacceptable.

In arriving at a positive position on all of these matters, and at a statement about what he thinks the incarnation is, as well as what it is not, Peter was inspired by Gilbert of Poitiers and the Porretans, both positively and negatively. Negatively, he finds Gilbert's lexicon obstructive; and he also finds some of the language which his earliest disciples substitute for it unclear. Positively, he agrees with many of Gilbert's specific Christological ideas, and disagrees with the early Porretans when they depart from their master. On the hypostatic union, Gilbert and the Porretans serve as his principal stimulus. On other matters relating to the incarnation, he takes his cue largely from Hugh of St. Victor, whether directly or indirectly. Sometimes he agrees with the Victorine position, restating it while adding his own elaborations on it. At other times, he takes sharp exception to it. In relation to all the theologians of his time, Peter's approach to Christology stands out for his frequent appeal to John Damascene. This is as true in this area of his theology as it is true of his treatment of the Trinity. From Damascene Peter draws three principal doctrines. One has to do with Christ's characteristic moral stance toward God the Father, and it will be taken up in the second section of this chapter. A second has to do with the soteriological reasons for the incarnation, which certainly affects the way in which Peter views the hypostatic union. The third is Damascene's doctrine of *enhypostasis*, which likewise is central to Peter's understanding of that union, in combination with what he derives from the Porretans.[40]

Peter begins his account with the question of why the Son was incarnated and not the Father or the Holy Spirit. His treatment of this issue is Victorine, most clearly resembling that of the *Summa sententiarum*, although he adds his own touch. Since Christ is the wisdom of God, he observes, thereby pointing ahead to an important aspect of the doctrine of the atonement which he plans to discuss later in Book 3 of the *Sentences*, it is appropriate that He be sent to enlighten fallen man. From the very beginning, we see Peter framing the doctrine of the incarnation in soteriological terms, as Damascene had suggested to him. The Lombard then adds that it was also more suitable to send the Trinitarian person Who is Himself engendered than the Father, Who is *a nullo*. To be sure, the Holy Spirit is sent as well, and, indeed, Peter has much to say about His missions elsewhere in the *Sentences*. In explaining why the Holy Spirit was not incarnated, he follows Hugh's argument that, since the Word is already a Son, it is more suitable for Him to be the Trinitarian person Who extends to mankind the capacity to become children of God.[41] He also endorses the point made by the author of the *Summa sententiarum* that the Father and the Holy Spirit are in no sense incapable of incarnation. Since God is omnipotent, this would have been possible. Without invoking the power, wisdom, and goodness language of Hugh, which, we recall, Hugh had applied inconsistently to the divine nature and to the Trinitarian persons as persons, Peter contents himself with reminding the reader that, since the work of the Trinity is one work, and since the Son is the one sent, the divinity He joins with humanity is the single divinity inhering equally in all the Trinitarian persons. This common divine action, however, can be delegated; redemption is delegated to the Son just as the task of incarnating Him is delegated to the Holy Spirit.[42]

Moving next to the issue of what Christ took on in the incarnation, Peter reveals his sensitivity to the problems surrounding the abstract and concrete nouns raised by Gilbert of Poitiers. We recall

---

[40] Excellent background here is supplied by Keetje Rozemond, *La christologie de Saint Jean Damascène* (Ettal: Buch-Kunstverlag, 1959), ch. 1–2.
[41] Peter Lombard, *Sent.* 3. d. 1. c. 1, 2: 24–26.
[42] Ibid., c. 2–c. 3, d. 4, 2: 26–27, 37–41.

that Gilbert has insisted on the point that the Word took on *homo*, to designate a human nature at the concrete level of *subsistens* where it could be modified by accidents. *Homo*, in this context, also designates for Gilbert a specific, historical human being, the man Jesus. Peter appreciates this point, and also its problems. His own claim is that the Word took on both *homo* and *humanitas vel humana natura*. The point he wants to establish by this formulation is a double one. In the first place, the noun "man," as the grammarians point out, and as the early Porretans had suggested, is itself capable of referring to an individual human being and to mankind in general. The second of these acceptations is, of course, also indicated by the terms humanity and human nature. Peter wants thereby to accent both the historicity of Christ's incarnation in the man Jesus and also the consubstantiality of that man with the rest of the human race. And, just as substance and nature refer to the same aspect of divinity, so human nature can be called a substance. Peter stresses that all features of human nature, that is, body and soul, and the capacity of both to be modified by accidents, are involved here. And his reason, which he defends more consistently than the Victorines, is anchored by a citation from Damascene: "For what is not assumable is not curable" (*Quod enim inassumptibile est, incurabile est*). Christ must have a fully human body and a fully human soul in order to redeem both body and soul. And, agreeing with Gilbert, the Porretans, William of Champeaux, and Robert Pullen here, he holds that the union of Christ's human nature with His divine nature was integral, and permanent, once it was achieved.[43]

Peter goes into more detail than do many masters of the day in describing the manner in which this union occurred. Once again, his reading of Damascene gives him a fuller range of options for understanding this event. God the Son took on a body and a soul, he states, "but the body through the mediation of the soul" (*sed carnem mediante anima*). Damascene is the authority He cites for the idea that a material entity, such as the human body of Christ, could not with congruity unite with a purely spiritual entity, such as the deity, without the mediation of an entity, such as the human soul of Christ, which shares both a spiritual nature with the deity and the capacity to unite intimately with the body. Here, Peter takes exception to the scenario that Augustine had developed for the incarnation, in which Christ takes on a human soul, and then the body through the soul, in supporting the contemporary anti-Adoptionist

---

[43] Ibid., d. 2. c. 1.1–4, 2: 27–29. The quotation is at c. 1.4, p. 29.

position that the body and soul were created and assumed by Christ in the same instant, in a manner departing from the embryology of the *physici*.[44]

In line with the anti-traducianist view that parents engender the bodies of their children while God creates their souls, Peter next turns to the virgin birth of Christ. Here, he goes beyond the views of the school of Laon and of Hugh of St. Victor, as well as his own earlier position as expressed in his sermons, where he states that Mary was exempted from the capacity to feel carnal concupiscence, as a special dispensation of the Holy Spirit, at the moment of Christ's conception. It was not merely her virginity that was retained *ante partum, in partu,* and *post partum* in this respect. In the *Sentences,* Peter amplifies on this doctrine in two ways. First, he maintains that Mary's exemption from the effects of original sin occurred not at the moment of Christ's conception but before that moment. In his view, the Holy Spirit prepared Mary for Christ's conception by coming to her beforehand, cleansing her both of original sin and its consequences, including the inclination to sin (*Mariam quoque totam Spiritus Sanctus in eam praeveniens a peccato prorsus purgavit, et a fomite peccati etiam liberavit*).[45] Thus, for Peter, there was a certain amount of time prior to the incarnation when Mary was unique among human beings, in gaining, ahead of time, what would later be available to mankind in baptism. But, in being freed from the *fomes peccati* as well, she enjoys a privilege that no one else is granted except the human Christ. Peter does not state how far ahead of time this dispensation was granted. But it is clear that, in comparison with other contemporary masters, even the Victorines, who thought deeply and wrote extensively on Mariology, he has extended the range of possible speculation on Mary's moral condition prior to the annunciation. Peter's amplification of this topic has another dimension as well, a rationale that accounts for his development of it in the first place. As we have seen above, in his treatment of the transmission of original sin, Peter takes a harder line than some of his contemporaries, in combining the vitiated seeds theory with the notion that the sexual feelings of the parents are the vehicle of original sin. Now, if one views the vehicle as the sexual feelings, it is clear why Mary would have to have been

---

[44] Ibid., c. 2.1–3, d. 3. c. 3.2–3, 2: 29–31; 36–37. On this issue, see Landgraf, *Dogmengeschichte,* 2 part 1: 150–71.

[45] Peter Lombard, *Sent.* 3. d. 3. c. 1.2–c. 3, 2: 32–35. The quotation is at c. 1.2, p. 32. For Peter's earlier position, see *Sermo* 12, 55, *PL* 171: 395D, 608A, *Sermo de adventu Domini,* ed. Damien Van den Eynde in "Deux sermons inédits de Pierre Lombard," in *Misc. Lomb.,* p. 76.

released from this consequence of original sin at the moment of Christ's conception. But, if one adheres to the vitiated seeds theory, then presumably some back-up time would be required to enable Mary to produce genetic materials, under her new dispensation, that would be as uncorrupted as those of the prelapsarian parents. The line of argument developed by the Lombard on this issue reminds us forcibly of the fact that Mariology in the twelfth century was fueled not only by the new winds of devotion blowing through western Christendom at this time but also by technical speculations in dogmatic theology.

Stressing the importance of the Virgin Mary's exemptions, because they are required in her engendering a human Christ free from original sin and its effects, but otherwise the same, physically, as other mortals, and rejecting Robert Pullen's idea that the presence of the Word in the Virgin's womb was just another instance of the divine ubiquity,[46] Peter moves on to the far more controversial issue of the coinherence of divinity and humanity in the incarnate Christ. Peter formulates this whole issue in Porretan terms, and agrees with much of the substance of Porretan teaching. The Word having assumed a human body and soul at the same time, in union with His divine person, Peter observes, it remains to ask whether *persona personam, vel natura naturam, vel persona naturam, vel natura naturam assumpserit*. He agrees with Gilbert of Poitiers that a nature cannot take on a person in the incarnation since there is no human person in Christ. To admit that He had a human person would be to teach Adoptionism. For the same reason, a person cannot take on a person in the incarnation. In addition to sharing Gilbert's anti-Adoptionist agenda, Peter agrees with him that no person can be mixed or duplex, although he does not advert to the specific Porretan definition of a person as a *res per se una*. It is also clear to Peter that Gilbert is correct in arguing that a person takes on a nature in the incarnation. As we will see shortly, what he accomplishes here is to unhinge these terms from their association with *subsistens* and *subsistentia*, which had made it so hard for Gilbert to show that a person is different from a nature both in God and in man. This step will simplify Peter's handling of this Porretan argument considerably.

Where Peter disagrees with Gilbert is on the question of whether a nature takes on a nature in the incarnation. Gilbert's objections to the affirmative on that point had been twofold. If a nature takes on a nature, he held, then it would not be possible to explain why it was the

---

[46] Peter Lombard, *Sent.* 3. d. 3. c. 3.1, c. 3.5, 2: 35–36, 37.

Son, and not the deity in general, Who was incarnated. At the same time, it would deny the individuality and historicity of the incarnation of the Word in the man Jesus. In addition to citing a number of early church councils on this subject, which Gilbert had ignored, Peter tackles the first objection by recalling his own analysis of how terms denoting the perfections of the deity as such can be applied with propriety to the Trinitarian persons, an analysis which he develops in Book 1 of the *Sentences*. There, he had observed that this language is acceptable when one is referring to the divine essence which the Trinitarian persons share equally. It is in this sense that Christ's *divinitas* or divine nature was brought by Him into the incarnation, just as the *humanitas* which He brought into it was not different from that of His mother. At the same time, as in making the point above that the Word was united both with *homo* and with *humanitas* or *humana natura*, Peter wishes to stress here the consubstantiality of Christ with other human beings, in that they all possess a human nature that is a combination of body and soul. Once again yoking nature to the hylemorphic unit that man is, Peter concludes that we must say both that the person of the Son assumed human nature, and that the divine and human natures were united in the Son (*dicentes et personam Filii assumpsisse naturam humanam, et naturam divinam humanae naturae in Filii unitam*). When we say that the incarnation took place in the person of the Son, we are also saying that the divine nature He shares with the Father and the Holy Spirit was acting in the *hypostasis* of the Son. Peter cites Damascene here to support this analysis. As for the biblical statement that the Word became flesh, Peter does not think it can be read literally, as if to signify the convertibility of one nature into another. Rather, what it means is that the Word assumed human nature, that is, a human body and a human soul, but not a human *persona* (*hominis naturam, scilicet carnem et animam assumpsit, sed non personam hominis*).[47]

This brings Peter to the task of explaining how an individual who is fully man can lack a human *persona*, a reef on which so many contemporary theologians foundered, especially if they held the Boethian definition of a human person as the individual substance of a rational nature. It is here that Peter's debt to Gilbert's Christology is perhaps the heaviest. He endorses the point that there was no preexisting human person in the incarnate Christ because His body and soul had not yet been joined to each other prior to the incarnation. What the Word took on, thus, was not a human

---

[47] Ibid., d. 5. c. 1.1–c. 2.1, 2: 41–46. The the quotations are at c. 1.10, p. 45, and c. 2.1, p. 46, respectively.

person but the human components, body and soul, out of which a human nature would arise when they were joined to each other and, simultaneously, to the Word. Adding to this Gilbert's idea that no person can be duplex, and that no divine person can be composite, he observes that there was only one person in the incarnate Christ, His simple, eternal, divine person, which was not altered in its constitution when it accepted a human body and soul. Here, he notes, the Boethian definition of person must simply be jettisoned. It reduces the human being to his soul; and it would be descriptive only of beings like angels, who have a spiritual nature only. It also confuses substance and person. For Peter, the incarnate Christ can have a fully human nature without having a human *persona*. The lack of a human *persona* does not compromise the full humanity of Christ, since, in His humanity, He is a single, unique individual and, in possessing a human body and soul, He possesses all the faculties of a man. Once again warning that, if you look for a human person as what Christ assumed, you are succumbing to Adoptionism, he concludes by saying that, if you ask whether the manhood of Christ is a human person, the answer is "no." But if you ask whether the manhood of Christ is a human nature, the answer is "yes."[48] Thus, in responding to the question which was to engender such debate in the sequel, "whether Christ, insofar as He was a man, was a person, or, likewise, if He was anything" (*utrum Christus secundum quod homo sit persona vel etiam sit aliquid*), Peter points out that it is only the proponents of the Boethian definition of *persona*, who conflate person and substance in the human Christ, who are constrained to answer that one has denied to Christ a human substance if one denies to Him a human person. It is they who are forced to make of His humanity a *non-aliquid*. According to his own solution, on the other hand, this answer is not required. We distinguish between person and substance in the human Christ, he observes. Thus, in stating that He did not have a human person, we are in no sense asserting that, as a man, He was not *aliquid*. For He was *aliquid*: *aliquid natura*, an individual made up of body and soul.[49]

---

[48] Ibid., c. 3.1–4, 2: 47–48.

[49] Ibid., d. 10. c. 1, 2: 72–74: This point is confirmed literally by the Lombard's students Peter Comestor and Odo of Ourscamp. Comestor is cited from an unpublished manuscript reporting his views by Ignatius C. Brady, "Peter Manducator and the Oral Teachings of Peter Lombard," *Antonianum* 41 (1966): 473. Odo is cited, from two unpublished manuscripts of his *Quaestiones*, by Artur Michael Landgraf, "Der Magister Petrus episcopus," *RTAM* 8 (1936): 201 n. 14; "Der Einfluss des mündlichen Unterrichts auf theologische Werke der Frühscholastik," *Collectanea Franciscana* 23 (1953): 286.

Among other things, it is precisely to obviate the possibility of Christological nihilianism no less than Adoptionism that Peter joins Gilbert of Poitiers in rejecting Boethius. But he is able to show, much more convincingly than Gilbert, why adherents of Boethius's definition of *persona* are the theologians most vulnerable to the charge of Christological nihilianism.

It is with these clarification of terminology in place and it is with the Christology he largely shares with Gilbert in hand that Peter turns to the analysis of the three opinions on the hypostatic union. We have introduced them briefly above. It will now become clear that, underlying the objections that the Lombard has to all of them is the view that they either obscure the distinction between the divine and human natures of Christ, as is true for him of the *assumptus homo* and subsistence theories, or that they deemphasize the humanity of Christ, as is the case for him of both the *assumptus homo* and the *habitus* theories. As Peter sees it, the *assumptus homo* theory and the subsistence theory both involve a blurring of the two natures. Proponents of the first theory, in analogizing the union of the two natures in Christ with the union of the body and soul in man, produce thereby an human individual who has, as well, the divine knowledge and power. Hence, they divinize the humanity of Christ even while claiming that the two natures remain distinct in Him. In effect, however, a new *tertium quid* has been produced, according to the *assumptus homo* theory, that draws upon both the divine and human natures of Christ.

The problem that Peter sees with the subsistence theory is similar, although it lies in the composite *persona* given to the incarnate Christ by defenders of this position. This kind of *persona* cannot truly be equated with the divine person which the Word has possessed from all eternity. It must, now, contain some human aspects, meaning that the divinity of Christ's *persona* has been diluted in the incarnation. How an immutable being, such as a divine person, can be altered in any way is itself deeply problematic. Equally so is the fact that, as a composite person, the Word incarnate introduces a fourth member into the Trinity. This is why the Augustinian language on the person of Christ as a *gemina substantia* must be rejected. At the same time, the three-substance language used by proponents of this position gives a false, and incomprehensible, understanding of *substantia* as it applies to Christ's human nature. True, a human being is a composite of body and soul. But, once they have been joined, they make a single substance. The infrasubstantial components that go to make up a human being cannot be called substances individually, either before or after they have been joined together. Nor can the union of divine and human natures in the incarnation be understood as the union of parts that together make up a whole. No person is made up of parts. *A fortiori*, this is true of the Word, Who was "whole" from all eternity and did not require the incarnation for His completion. Altogether, Peter finds the subsistence theory more rife with difficulties, both conceptual and terminological, than he finds the other two theories.

The *habitus* theory, in his estimation, emphasizes the divinity of Christ at the expense of His humanity, but in a manner different from the *assumptus homo* theory. Where the *assumptus homo* theory threatens to absorb Christ's humanity into His divinity, the *habitus* theory threatens to treat Christ's humanity as accidental, and as not integral to the hypostatic union. The two natures are regarded as partible once joined, by defenders of this theory. At the same time, if one accepts the Augustinian interpretation of *habitus*, which Peter presents in full, the human nature of Christ does not retain its integrity. While, in the case of the *assumptus homo* theory, the divinization of the humanity of Christ is seen as more substantial, and in the *habitus* theory, it is seen as more spatial and adventitious, in both cases the human Christ becomes more than human. Both of these theories, in Peter's eyes, are hence vulnerable to the charge of Christological nihilianism, the *assumptus homo* theory by absorbing the humanity of Christ and changing it into something else, and the *habitus* theory by making it hard to see how the Word truly became man, or truly took on human nature, in such a way that the two natures were, and remained, truly united while at the same time each nature retained its own characteristics.[50]

What Peter thinks he can say positively here is that the incarnate Word, as a divine person, is not made lower than the Father by the fact that a human nature was predestined to be joined to Him at a particular point in time. Likewise, we cannot say that, in the incarnation, Christ's human nature was deified, a problem which, in one form or another, he sees in all three opinions. Both natures, he insists, retain their own character in the incarnation.[51] And so, notwithstanding the detailed support of the authorities which, as Peter shows, can be brought forward to bolster each of these positions, he recommends none of them. As he puts it at the conclusion of this segment of Book 3 of the *Sentences*: "What has been said above is not sufficient for the determination of this

---

[50] Peter Lombard, *Sent.* 3. d. 6. c. 2.1–d. 7. c. 3.3, 2: 50–66.
[51] Ibid., d. 7. c. 2, 2: 65.

question" (*Quod predicta non sufficiunt ad cognoscendam hanc quaestionem*). Advising that the matter should not be foreclosed prematurely, or with prejudice, he urges further research and reflection.[52]

The Debates over the Lombard's Christology

The vast majority of modern commentators have been able to take Peter at his word here, accepting the fact that he was not a Christological nihilianist and that he was not a proponent of the *habitus* theory or, indeed, of any of the three opinions which he outlines and criticizes.[53] There are, however, a few who make the mistake of believing the twelfth-century opponents of the Lombard who erroneously imputed these views to him.[54] The most typical claim of contemporaries who misconstrued the Lombard's Christology was to associate him with the *habitus* theory, seen, in turn, as the theory of the hypostatic union that leads most easily to nihilianism. The earliest of these critics, Gerhoch of Reichersberg, on the other hand, sometimes treats him as an adherent of the *habitus* theory[55] and sometimes as an Adoptionist.[56] Gerhoch's criticism

---

[52] Ibid., c. 3, 2: 66.

[53] An excellent survey of these debates is provided by Joseph de Ghellinck, *Le mouvement théologique du XII*ᵉ *siècle*, 2nd ed. (Bruges: De Tempel, 1948), pp. 250–76; *L'Essor de la littérature latine au XII*ᵉ *siècle*, 2 vols. (Brussels: L'Édition Universelle, 1946), 1: 73–76; Ludwig Hödl, "Logische Übungen zum christologischen Satz in der frühscholastischen Theologie des 12. Jahrhunderts," *Zeitschrift für Kirchengeschichte* 89 (1978): 291–94, 296–300, 302; Jean Longère, *Oeuvres oratoires des maîtres parisiens au XII*ᵉ *siècle: Étude historique et doctrinale*, 2 vols. (Paris: Études Augustiniennes, 1975), 1: 83–85; Landgraf, *Dogmengeschichte*, 2 part 1: 116–37; P. Glorieux, "L'orthodoxie de III Sent. d. 6, 7 et 10," in *Misc. Lomb.*, pp. 137–47; Mignon, *Les origines*, 2: 53–56; Horacio Santiago-Otero, *El conocimiento de Cristo en cuanto hombre en la teología de la primera mitad del siglo XII* (Pamplona: Universidad de Navarra, S.A., 1970), pp. 125–26 n. 1; "El 'nihilianismo cristológico' y las tres opiniones," *Burgense* 10 (1969): 431–43; Robert F. Studeny, *John of Cornwall, an Opponent of Nihilianism: A Study in the Christological Controversies of the Twelfth Century* (Vienna: St. Gabriel's Mission Press, 1939), pp. 104–16, 145.

[54] Jean Châtillon, "Achard de Saint-Victor et les controverses christologiques du XIIᵉ siècle," in *Mélanges offerts au R. P. Ferdinand Cavallera* (Toulouse: Bibliothèque de l'Institut Catholique, 1948), pp. 117–37; "Latran III et l'enseignement christologique de Pierre Lombard," in *Le troisième concile de Latran (1179): Sa place dans l'histoire*, ed. Jean Longère (Paris: Études Augustiniennes, 1982), pp. 79–81; Philip S. Moore and Marthe Dulong, intro. to their ed. of Peter of Poitiers, *Sententiae*, Bk. 1 (Notre Dame: University of Notre Dame Press, 1961), pp. xlii, xliv; Nielsen, *Theology and Philosophy*, pp. 243–64, 279–361.

[55] Gerhoch of Reichersberg, *De gloria et honore Filii hominis* 7.3, PL 194: 1097B.

[56] Gerhoch of Reichersberg, *Libellus de ordine donorum Sancti Spiritus* in *Opera inedita*, ed. Damien and Odulph Van den Eynde, Angelinus Rijmensdael, and Peter Classen, 2 vols. in 3 (Rome: Antonianum, 1955–56), 1: 71.

began in the 1140s, and reflects a familiarity with the earlier works
of the Lombard and not the most recent version of the *Sentences*, in
which Peter was able to profit from the ideas of John Damascene.
Gerhoch's concern is less to enter into the debates on dogmatic
theology than to defend the *assumptus homo* theory, complete with a
divinized human Christ, in a battle with the Greek church in which
he yokes that theory to the argument that the human Christ deserves *latria* and not just *dulia*. This was a point on which the
Lombard changed the position he had articulated early in his
career in his Psalms commentary, under the influence of Damascene. In the *Sentences* he actually endorses the *latria* position. This
change was unknown to Gerhoch, who had failed to keep up with
the Lombard's more recent teachings. Gerhoch thus keeps belabor-
ing the point, well on into the mid-1160s, that Peter is wrong on
dulia and *latria* here, in treatises and letters addressed to his bishop
and to the pope.[57] The bishop in question, Eberhard of Bamberg,
was clearly better informed than Gerhoch and points out to him
that he has mistaken what Peter actually says in the *Sentences*.[58]
Following this well-documented reproof, Gerhoch's attacks on the
Lombard subsided.

Gerhoch's letters were written in 1164, well after the final edition
of the *Sentences* had become available in Germany. Conceivably, it
was Gerhoch's preoccupation with the impact of the Gregorian
reform movement in Germany and his own east-west polemics that
account for his failure to inform himself about what was up-to-date
in Parisian scholasticism. But no such extenuating circumstances
excuse the garbling of the Lombard's Christology on the part of
John of Cornwall and Walter of St. Victor, thinkers whose work
and study in Paris put them in a position to have understood what
Peter had actually taught.

John of Cornwall had himself been a student of the Lombard's in
the 1150s, before Peter became bishop of Paris and gave up

---

[57] Gerhoch of Reichersberg, *De gloria* 7.2–3, 19.2, *PL* 194: 1097A–1111A,
1143C–1144A; *Utrum Christus homo sit filius dei naturalis et deus*, ed. Van den Eynde et
al., 1: 284–87; *Epistola* 15, to Eberhard, bishop of Bamberg, *PL* 194: 547A–548C;
Epistola 17, to Pope Alexander III, *PL* 194: 565B–566A. Good treatments can be
found in Damien Van den Eynde, "De nouveau sur deux maîtres lombards
contemporains du Maître des Sentences," *Pier Lombardo* 1 (1955): 6–7; *L'Oeuvre
littéraire de Géroch de Reichersberg* (Rome: Antonianum, 1957), pp. 6, 49–66, 78–85,
107, 157–63, 265, 274; Peter Classen, *Gerhoch von Reichersberg: Eine Biographie*
(Wiesbaden: Franz Steiner Verlag GMBH, 1960), pp. 89–97, 162–73, 248–72,
318–19.
[58] Eberhard of Bamberg, *Epistola* 16, to Gerhoch of Reichersberg, *PL* 193;
555B–556C, 561D–564A. On Eberhard, see Van den Eynde, *L'Oeuvre*, pp. 279–80.

teaching. The early 1170s find John back in his native England, where he taught theology, perhaps at Oxford. He composed his *Eulogium*, in which he accuses Peter of Christological nihilianism, in two redactions between 1177 and 1179. The first of these was written with an eye to the Third Lateran council, convened by Pope Alexander III in the latter year.[59] In this work, John associates nihilianism with the *habitus* theory. He was aware of the fact that Alexander was interested in repressing nihilianism, as the matter had come up at a synod convened by the pope at Tours in 1163, although no particular theologians were named in this connection. It was no secret that the pope planned to put the matter on the agenda of Lateran III. He had suggested as much in a letter written to William of the White Hands, archbishop of Sens, in 1170. At the Lateran council itself, however, no formal determination concerning the views, or alleged views, of Peter Lombard was made. John then drafted the second version of the *Eulogium*, after Lateran III had risen, in a last-ditch effort to persuade Alexander not to let the matter drop.

Despite the fact that he had frequented the Lombard's lecture-room in the 1150s and was thus in a position to know that he had abandoned the support which he had given to the *habitus* theory in his Philippians gloss, John gives an account of the *habitus* doctrine and of Peter's own position that leave much to be desired from the standpoint of accuracy. John has been characterized by his editor, Nikolaus M. Häring, as conscientious but as a thinker who did not understand the problems surrounding Boethius's polyvalent use of the terms *substantia*, *natura*, and *persona*, on which, as we have seen, so much of the debate centered. Consequently, John's description and critique of the positions he presents "frequently results in a fog of 'double talk'."[60] As John outlines the three opinions, the subsistence theory, which he attributes to Gilbert of Poitiers, and the *habitus* theory, which he attributes to Abelard, are the sources for the Christological nihilianism which he attributes to Peter. In

---

[59] For John of Cornwall's biography and the dating on the work, see Nikolaus M. Häring, ed., "The *Eulogium ad Alexandrum Papam tertium* of John of Cornwall," *MS* 13 (1951): 254; Eleanor Rathbone, "John of Cornwall: A Brief Biography," *RTAM* 17 (1950): 46–60; Studeny, *John of Cornwall*, pp. 1–4. The evidence is reprised by Châtillon, "Latran III," pp. 79–65. I. S. Robinson, *The Papacy, 1073–1198: Continuity and Innovation* (Cambridge: Cambridge University Press, 1990), pp. 142–44, offers the shaky opinion that John was commissioned by Pope Alexander III to prepare a dossier on Peter's Christology in preparation for Lateran III.

[60] Häring, "The *Eulogium*," p. 255.

support of this charge, he refers to Maurice of Sully, Peter's successor as bishop of Paris, and Robert of Melun, who had taught at
Paris two decades earlier, and who had opposed the Lombard.
Robert's works were not available to John; and there is no evidence
to show that Maurice wrote anything except the sermons that made
him a favored preacher at the French royal court.[61] The oddest
feature of John's attack is that, although he depends on the Lombard for his reprise of the three opinions, the formula for Christological nihilianism which he uses to frame the charge against Peter,
Christus secundum quod homo non est aliquid, does not appear in the
Sentences. This technique of interpolating lines into Peter's work, or
of misreading the lines that are there and that say something
different, along with his appeal to the views of masters whose
writings he had not and could not have read, scarcely inspires
confidence in John's reliability.[62]

John gets off on the wrong foot at once in his prologue, by conflating
the claim that Christ is not any man (*Christus non est aliquis homo*) with
the claim that, insofar as He is a man, Christ is not anything (*Christus
secundum quod homo non est aliquid*).[63] In his summary of the three
positions that follows, he puts an extremely Porretan construction on
the subsistence theory, complete with three substances and a per-
mixed *persona*, precisely the features of this position which Peter
criticizes, making it extremely difficult to see how John thinks he can
assimilate Peter's teaching to this one. In his account of the *habitus*
theory, John presents it as saying that Christ's human nature was
apparent, not real, which is not what its proponents taught, according
to the Lombard. John also states that this position excludes the idea
that the Word took on a human body and soul which then, as
combined, had reality as a substance. This latter doctrine was one
that Peter taught, although he took pains to describe the combination
of body and soul in the human Christ as a human nature and not as a
substance. Still, this again makes it difficult to see how the *habitus*
theory as John gives it can be ascribed to Peter.[64] It must be said that
John's attribution of the subsistence theory to Gilbert, as he reports it,
is just as incorrect. For, unlike some of the early Porretans, Gilbert
himself did not adhere to the three-substance view and he stressed the
principle that a *persona* is a *res per se una*. But, no doubt strangest of all,

---

[61] C. A. Robson, *Maurice of Sully and the Medieval Vernacular Homily* (Oxford:
Blackwell, 1952).
[62] Häring, "The *Eulogium*," pp. 255–56.
[63] Ibid., p. 257.
[64] John of Cornwall, *Eulogium* 1, pp. 259–61.

considering the great lengths to which the Lombard went to refute Abelard as a dogmatic theologian, John states that he inherited the *habitus* theory, and with it, nihilianism, from his master, Peter Abelard (*a magistro Petro Abailardo hanc opinionem suam magister Petrus Lumbardus accepit*). John also claims that he had heard the Lombard expound this view before he became bishop, although he admits, ingenuously, that Peter advised his hearers that "this was not his own position but only an opinion" (*non esset assertio sua sed opinione sola*). And, he wraps up this decidedly weak case by observing that he has heard, through heresay evidence, that other masters continue to endorse Christological nihilianism. He supplies no information on who these masters may be.[65] This is a spectacularly poor performance for a person who had actually studied with Peter Lombard, reminding us that even the best of instruction sometimes falls on stony ground.

The second and final contemporary who sought to tar the Lombard with the brush of Christological nihilianism and to bring the charge expressly to the attention of Alexander III is a rather different kettle of fish. He is Walter, prior of St. Victor, whose *Four Labyrinths of France*, like the first redaction of John's *Eulogium*, was written in 1177 or 1178, before the Lateran council, in the effort to influence its doctrinal outcome. Where John was a scholastic, if not a very alert one, Walter was an arch-conservative, representing a St. Victor that had decidedly fallen away from the academic distinction which it had enjoyed under Hugh and Richard of St. Victor. The abbey itself was in a parlous state in the 1160s.[66] The abbot, Ernis, had become a tyrant by 1163, setting aside the rule of the abbey in that year. By 1169 he had stopped consulting the brethren. He neglected their and his own religious life and did not even maintain a regular residence at St. Victor. Things had come to such a pass that in September of 1169, Alexander III ordered a reform of St. Victor, charging William, archbishop of Sens, and Odo, abbot of Ourscamp, with carrying it out. The desired results did not eventuate. The pope again ordered William to spearhead a reform of the abbey in February of 1172, writing as well to King

---

[65] Ibid., 3, p. 265.
[66] This account is based on the excellent contributions of Jean Châtillon, "De Guillaume de Champeaux à Thomas Gallus: Chronique d'histoire littéraire et doctrinale de l'école de Saint-Victor," *Revue du moyen âge latin* 8 (1952): 139–62, 245–72; Saralyn R. Daly, "Peter Comestor: Master of Histories," *Speculum* 32 (1957): 69–70; Dietrich Lohrmann, "Ernis, abbé de Saint-Victor (1161–1172): Rapports avec Rome, affaires financières," in *L'Abbaye parisienne de Saint-Victor au moyen âge*, ed. Jean Longère (Paris: Brepols, 1991), pp. 186–93.

Louis VII to inform him of the problem. The result was the
resignation of Ernis and the election of a new abbot, Guérin, in
1172. Discord, however, continued. Although he had been
banished to a country priory, Ernis returned to Paris and created
both a disturbance and a scandal by robbing the treasury of St.
Victor, seizing funds that had been left there in trust by Eskyl,
archbishop of Lund. Eskyl complained to Maurice, bishop of Paris,
who, with the assistance of William of Sens, managed to get the
property restored to St. Victor. By May of 1173 peace had
apparently returned to the abbey, because when the pope wrote to
St. Victor at that point, he referred to its religious calm.

While this series of conflicts did not force anyone to leave St.
Victor except Ernis, and he appears to have been no loss, it was not
calculated to attract scholars to join the community. After his
installation, Guérin wrote to the pope complaining about the
wretched state of intellectual life at the abbey, compared with the
glory days of the earlier twelfth century. He suggests that Ernis was
to blame for a policy of discouraging the admission of learned men
who could add luster to the school. While this complaint may well
have been a canard aimed at his predecessor, it is certainly true
that, with the death of Richard of St. Victor in 1173, we find the
school of St. Victor increasingly in a state of eclipse. It remained a
center known for its preaching. But it did not produce or draw to it
great works or great thinkers. Under the pretext of remaining loyal
to its past, St. Victor sank into a narrow traditionalism, unresponsive to the intellectual currents of its time. The one Victorine in this
period who tried to keep alive the optimism about human reason,
the intellectual breadth, and the vision of Hugh of St. Victor was
Godfrey, author of the *Microcosmus* and the *Fons philosophiae*. He was
the exception who proved the rule. More typical of St. Victor in the
last quarter of the twelfth century was its prior, Walter, known for
his sermons and his pessimistic and hostile outlook on innovation of
any kind. He was the author of the garbled, intemperate, misinformed, and largely plagiarized work in which he attacked Peter
Lombard, along with Peter of Poitiers, Gilbert of Poitiers, and
Peter Abelard, as profane innovators who had brought ruination
upon theology in his time. Even Walter's editor cannot repress his
distaste for the man and his work, describing is as a "mauvaise
action et mauvais travail," as ineptly written, inspired by ignorance and prejudice, in a style that is "brutale, grossière."[67]

---

[67] P. Glorieux, "Mauvaise action et mauvias travail: Le 'Contra quatuor laby-

Walter is such a confused writer that, in his introduction, he tells a tale, meant to criticize the cardinals helping Alexander III to prepare for the Third Lateran council at a consistory in Rome prior to that council, which instead redounds to his own discredit. Alexander, he observes, was considering whether to put Peter Lombard's alleged Christological nihilianism on the agenda of the council. But, some of the cardinals, who, in Walter's estimation, were "not responding rightly" (*non recte respondentes*), dissuaded him from doing so. A key figure in shaping their opinion was bishop Adam of Wales, by whom Walter means Adam of St. Asaph. According to Walter, Adam spoke up in opposition to the idea that Peter had taught nihilianism. As Walter reports the event, Adam said, "Lord pope, I, as a clerk and as a former moniter over his pupils, will defend the opinions of the master" (*Domine papa, ego et clericus et prepositus olim scholarum eius defendam sententias magistri*). He proceeded to do so, and carried the day, much to Walter's disgust.[68]

Now, this Adam of St. Asaph has traditionally been identified as Adam of Balsham, better known as Adam du Petit-Pont, the distinguished logician who taught in that location for many years and who would certainly have been well acquainted with the Lombard.[69] But Lorenzo Minio-Paluello has offered a persuasive corrective to that view. Noting that Adam of Balsham wrote his major work, the *Ars disserendi*, in 1132, that he taught John of Salisbury before 1148, that he became a canon of Notre Dame, and that in this capacity, he testified against Gilbert of Poitiers at the consistory of Paris in 1147 and the council of Rheims in 1148, and that the fragments of some theological *quaestiones* which he left indicate his qualifications as a *peritus* in that connection, Minio-Paluello also points out that he died before 1159. In any event, given the fact that the regnal years of Adam of St. Asaph were 1175 to 1181, it is difficult to imagine that the king of England would have viewed as a likely candidate for the bishopric a man of the age Adam of Balsham would have been had he still been alive at the time. In the opinion of Minio-Paluello, the Adam who did actually

---

rinthos Franciae'," *RTAM* 21 (1954): 179–93. The quotation is at p. 180. Glorieux repeats this judgment in the intro. to his ed. of the text, "*Contra quatuor labyrinthos Franciae,*" *AHDLMA* 19 (1952): 192–94.

[68] Walter of St. Victor, *Contra quatuor labyrinthos*, p. 201.

[69] See, for example, Glorieux, intro. to his ed., p. 194; Daniel D. McGarry, intro. to his trans. of John of Salisbury, *Metalogicon* (Berkeley· University of California Press, 1955), p. 98 n. 181. This opinion is repeated by Robinson, *The Papacy*, p. 143.

occupy the see of St. Asaph during these years was a Welshman who had, indeed, studied with Peter Lombard in Paris and who had become a canon of Notre Dame. This is the Adam to whom Walter refers in the *Four Labyrinths*. This same Adam of St. Asaph is also known to have attended the Third Lateran council.[70]

While it would no doubt add piquancy to the story if Walter's Adam of Wales had, in fact, been the famous master with whom Adam of St. Asaph has been confused, the key point, which Walter evidently has not grasped, is that the Adam who spoke at the consistory in Rome was a man fully qualified to give an accurate and well-informed report of the Lombard's teaching, one better informed than Walter's own. Adam did so; and the members of the papal court were intelligent enough to recognize the fact that he knew whereof he spoke. As for Alexander, he contented himself with writing to William of the White Hands, now archbishop of Rheims, adjuring him to be on the lookout for Christological nihilianism within his jurisdiction, but naming no names. At the Lateran council itself, the detractors of the Lombard behaved in so obnoxious and so underhanded a manner, not scrupling even to charge that he had obtained the bishopric of Paris through simony, that his supporters could ride the wave of revulsion they inspired to persuade the council fathers to drop the whole matter. It was the later objections to another aspect of the Lombard's Christology on the part of Joachim of Fiore and others at the turn of the thirteenth century that prompted the reinvestigation of the matter and that led the fathers of the Fourth Lateran council to open the third book of Peter's *Sentences*, which no one in authority had apparently thought of doing before this time, there to discover that he had taught Christological nihilianism no more than he had taught that there was a quaternity in the Trinity. As a result, they dismissed Joachim's charge, affirmed Peter's orthodoxy by name and declared the case closed.[71] And, in 1215, the same year in which the fathers of Lateran IV arrived at this judgment, the Lombard's *Sentences* were mandated as required reading for doctoral candidates in theology in the statutes legislated by the University of Paris.

But we have anticipated ourselves, and must return to Walter of St. Victor's argument, if such it may be called. To begin with, he plagiarizes John of Cornwall almost verbatim in the section of the

[70] Lorenzo Minio-Paluello, "The 'Ars disserendi' of Adam of Balsham 'Parvipontanus'," *Mediaeval and Renaissance Studies* 3 (1954): 116–69.
[71] Châtillon, "Latran III," pp. 85–90.

Four Labyrinths where he reprises the three opinions about the hypostatic union,[72] in itself no recommendation. To this he adds his own lucubrations. Walter treats both the *assumptus homo* and the *habitus* theories as heretical and claims that Peter had espoused both of them, although he thinks that Peter supported the *habitus* theory more strongly.[73] He objects to the fact that Peter aired the problems connected with Boethius's definition of *persona* as the individual substance of a rational nature, without noting the fact that, among other things, Peter's reason for doing so was to avoid an incarnate Christ with two persons. As Walter sees it, the only way in which the human Christ can be an *aliquid* is if He has a human person. Here, he treats a position to which the Lombard had objected as one to which he adhered, even though he acknowledges Peter's point that the Word took on a human body and a human soul, and, therefore, a human nature.[74] But, why go on? Having reviewed and criticized Peter's Christology, to his own satisfaction at least, Walter moves on to the real source of the problem as he sees it. Peter, like the other three labyrinths of France, has gone astray because he is too addicted to the *artes*. He has tried to understand transcendent theological mysteries as if they could be reduced to grammatical and logical rules. He is sophist, a partisan of frivolous dialectical arguments.[75] That onslaught delivered, Walter adds, as a throwaway line before going on to the next labyrinth, that Peter also espoused many other heretical opinions about the Eucharist, which he declines to relate.[76]

It would seem that Christological nihilianism, as a teaching of the Lombard, was, to some extent, a product of the overheated imaginations of men such as John of Cornwall and Walter of St. Victor, and a product of the tendency, even on the part of such members of the literate elite as these men, to rely on word-of-mouth reports rather than textual evidence. Yet, before leaving this topic, it is worth noting that it does have some basis, or at least possible basis, in the teachings of some of the Lombard's followers, notably Gandulph of Bologna and, even more importantly, Peter of Poitiers, since the latter held the chair of theology at Notre Dame from 1167 to 1193, when he became chancellor of the school. While

---

[72] Robert Studeny, "Walter of St. Victor and the 'Apologia de Verbo Incarnato'," *Gregorianum* 18 (1937): 579–85.

[73] Walter of St. Victor, *Contra quatuor labyrinthos* 3.1–2, pp. 246–49.

[74] Ibid., 3.3–6, 4, pp. 250–56, 328–30.

[75] Ibid., 3.7–8, pp. 256–57.

[76] Ibid., 3.11, p. 260.

one can no more find the claim that Christ, insofar as He was a man, was not anything, in the writings of either of these masters than one can in the Lombard's, it is the case that they accent more strongly than he does the *habitus* theory, seen at the time as the likeliest connecting link with nihilianism, especially if one stresses, as they do, the accidental character of the manhood of the incarnate Christ.[77] In this sense there was a real theological basis for the debate in the 1170s. But it is one that post-dates the Lombard's teaching and writing by two decades. And, it was a debate that could scarcely be entered into effectively by thinkers like Walter and John, who were insensitive to the problems in Boethius's lexicon that had bedeviled the mid-century discussions, just as they were unfamiliar with the more integrally Aristotelian language that informed the treatments of Christology of the mainstream theologians later in the century. In the sequel, it would be by the appropriation and use of the newly received Aristotle, and not through the tactics of a John or a Walter, that a consensus could emerge, in the early thirteenth century. This newly developed consensus was to make a reformulated version of the subsistence theory, and one embodying many of the features of the doctrine of the hypostatic union that the Lombard did endorse, the theory of choice.[78]

The position held by a mid-twelfth-century theologian on the hypostatic union was important not only in and of itself but also for its influence on his other Christological teachings. There are two major indices of this fact. The first can be found in contemporary treatments of the question of whether Christ's human and divine natures, once joined, were partible and, as a corollary of that question, whether Christ's divinity remained attached to His humanity during the three days when His body lay in the tomb, separated from His soul, between His death and His resurrection. As we have seen above, it was not only proponents of the *habitus* theory but also thinkers associated with the *assumptus homo* theory who felt perfectly comfortable with the idea that Christ's divinity could not remain attached to His human body in the tomb. They accented, instead, the idea that His divinity remained attached to His soul alone during the *triduum*.[79] This position reflects, as well,

---

[77] Peter of Poitiers, *Sententiae* 4.10, *PL* 211: 1176B–C. On this point, see Moore and Dulong, intro. to their ed. of Peter's *Sentences*, Bk. 1, pp. xliii–xliv; Nielsen, *Theology and Philosophy*, pp. 279–361.

[78] This development has been traced magisterially by Principe, *William of Auxerre's Theology of the Hypostatic Union.*

[79] Landgraf, *Dogmengeschichte*, 2 part 1: 273–318, although his survey omits the Porretans.

the Platonizing anthropologies found in the Abelardian and Victorine traditions alike. Among theologians prior to Peter Lombard,
the only ones to insist forcibly on the point that, once Christ's
divinity and humanity were united, they remained united, were
William of Champeaux, Gilbert of Poitiers and the early Porretans,
and Robert Pullen. Peter certainly draws on their arguments in
making his own case against what he calls the "desertion of divinity" in the incarnate Christ during the *triduum*. At the same time,
since he himself endorses the idea that Christ's divinity is united to
His body through the mediation of His soul, he needs to develop a
more finely nuanced defense of the claim that this desertion did not
occur either in His soul or in His body.

Acknowledging that the soul of Christ, which mediates the
hypostatic union, was indeed separated from His body in the tomb,
Peter argues that, with respect to His body, Christ's divinity sub-
tracted its protection, but did not dissolve their union, so that His
dead body did not exhibit the effects of Christ's divine power
during the *triduum* (*separavit se divinitas quia subtraxit protectionem, sed
non solvit unionem . . . Mortuus est Christus divinitate recedente, id est
effectum potentiae defendendo non exhibente*).[80] Peter then turns to attack
those who say that Christ's divinity was not united to His body in
the tomb, although without the manifestation of His divine power
in it, as being forced to accept the conclusion that Christ thus
underwent incarnation twice, once when He took on human nature
from the Virgin Mary, and then when He took on a glorified human
nature in the resurrection. This conclusion is not only pernicious
but perfidious, since it casts doubt on the doctrine of the resurrection. Peter himself concludes that, although Christ truly died as a
man, His divinity was never divided from His humanity either in
body or soul.[81] And, introducing a distinction derived from Damascene, he concludes further that Christ's ubiquity, during the *triduum*, depends on whether He is seen as being where He is *totus* or
totum. *Totus* refers to Christ's divinity as a member of the Trinity, in
which sense He is fully God and shares the divine ubiquity in the
same way as the Father or the Holy Spirit. But, God is not all
Christ is; He is also fully man. We cannot ascribe ubiquity to
Christ's human nature, although He possesses fully both the divine
and the human natures that He has.[82]

---

[80] Peter Lombard, *Sent.* 3. d. 21. c. 1.4, 2: 131.
[81] Ibid., c. 1.5–c. 2, 2: 132–35.
[82] Ibid., d. 22. c. 2–c. 4, 2: 137–40.

The Lombard is quite consistent in defending this consequence of the doctrine that Christ's divinity and humanity were integrally united, that the union was not accidental, or one leading either to the lowering of His divinity or the divinization of His humanity. At the same time, in turning to the range of issues associated with Christ's human nature, the second test case for a theologian's application of his position on the hypostatic union, it must be said that he does not carry this principle to its ultimate logical conclusions. To be sure, Peter offers a vigorous and forthright defense of the idea that, as a human being, the man Jesus was a created being and no more. While Jesus was unique in His manner of birth and in His sharing, by grace, in a union with the Word, He also shares, by nature, the fact of being human, being born at a particular time, being capable of being predestined, and of having free will with other human beings. This individual human being, Peter stresses, had no claim on the fact that God chose to assume His body and soul; God could have chosen to assume a different human body and soul, making that other individual exactly the same kind of being as the incarnate Christ was and giving that individual the same sort of redemptive role. Further, and this point is argued against Abelard, God could have assumed the body and soul of a woman instead of a man, although, Peter notes, God's actual choice made sense since, given the morés of His time and place, Christ's mission was facilitated by His incarnation in masculine form.[83] All these assertions are made by Peter against theologians, whether on the Abelardian or the Victorine side of the debate, who see Christ's human nature as assimilated by or conformed to His divinity, in such a way that it stops being purely human. Yet, in treating Christ's human aptitudes, especially His human knowledge and His capacity to sin, Peter does not succeed entirely in pressing the logic of this position. Rather, he tends to align himself, to a greater of lesser degree, with a quasidivinized view of Christ's human nature that is more compatible with views of the hypostatic union that he does not support than with those which he defends.

CHRIST'S HUMAN KNOWLEGE: ANCIENT AND CURRENT DEBATES

Such is particularly the case with Christ's human knowledge, a topic receiving considerable attention in the first half of the twelfth

---

[83] Ibid., d. 10. c. 2–d. 12. c. 4, 2: 74–83.

century.[84] The debate itself goes back to the time of Augustine and Bede. Augustine had argued that the human Christ possessed perfect knowledge, from the earliest moment of His life. Confronted by the statement in the Gospel of Luke, that, as a boy, Jesus grew in grace and wisdom, he states that this means that the omniscient Jesus merely manifested His perfect knowledge gradually, in accordance with the stages of human development through which He passed as a child and a youth. Bede rejects Augustine's argument and sees the text of Luke as one that should be read literally. For his part, there is no problem in accepting the idea that Jesus underwent the intellectual development normal to childhood, just as He underwent a standard physiological development. The particular theologian who sparked the debate in the early twelfth century was Walter of Mortagne. While there were some monastic defenders of Bede, particularly in the Cistercian tradition, who endorsed this position for devotional reasons,[85] Walter was the first scholastic to support Bede against Augustine, and on dogmatic grounds. If the human Christ were omniscient, he argues, then His humanity would be placed in jeopardy and a creature would be made the equal of the creator.[86] This claim provoked an outburst of opposition from other scholastic theologians, an outburst that also inspired them to make some distinctions not drawn by Walter. The members of the school of Laon, following the *Glossa ordinaria*, side forcefully with Augustine, adding, in a formula destined to be repeated widely, that, while the human Christ knew as much as the Word knew, His mode of knowing was different; the human Christ knew by an infusion of grace, not by nature. The Laon masters are followed on this point by the *Sententiae divinitatis*, Roland of Bologna, and Robert of Melun.[87] In essence, this position denies to the

---

[84] The most important survey of this subject is Santiago-Otero, *El conocimiento de Cristo*, which has superseded earlier studies such as William J. Forster, *The Beatific Knowledge of Christ in the Theology of the 12th and 13th Centuries* (Rome: Pontificium Athenaeum Internationale "Angelicum," 1958), pp. 1–25; Landgraf, *Dogmengeschichte*, 2 part 2: 47–78; John C. Murray, *The Infused Knowledge of Christ in the Theology of the 12th and 13th Centuries* (Windsor, Ontario, 1963), pp. 7–19; Ott, *Die Briefliteratur*, pp. 32–47, 354–76, 379–80; Laurence S. Vaughan, *The Acquired Knowledge of Christ according to the Theologians of the 12th and 13th Centuries* (Rome: Pontificium Athenaeum Internationale "Angelicum," 1957), pp. 5–16.

[85] Santiago-Otero, *El conocimiento*, pp. 229–43.

[86] Walter of Mortagne, *Epistola ad Hugonem prioris Sancti Victoris*, PL 186: 1052B–1054B. On Walter, see Horacio Santiago-Otero, "Gualterio de Mortagne (d. 1174) y las controversias cristológicas del siglo XII," *Revista española de teología* 27 (1967): 271–83; *El concimiento*, pp. 18–19, 58–70.

[87] *Biblia latina cum Glossa ordinaria*, 3. *In Isaiam* 7:5, editio princeps (Strassburg: Adoph Rusch?, c. 1481); repr. with intro. by Karlfried Froelich and Margaret T.

human Christ a truly human psychology. It is in reaction to this idea, as well as to Walter of Mortagne's position, that the Abelardians come up with another distinction. On the one hand, they cede to the human Christ even more, the vision of God during His lifetime. But, on the other, they argue, He did not possess the full understanding of God, which cannot be communicated perfectly to any created intelligence. Thus, the Abelardians conclude, while the human Christ could contemplate the divine essence, He could not do so, during His lifetime, in an exhaustive manner; and God thus retains, for the human Christ, a measure of His unknowability.[88]

A still stronger effort to refute Walter, and by extension Bede, and to amplify on the teaching of the school of Laon, can be found in the position of Hugh of St. Victor. In its extremity it can be called the "maximalist" view in this debate, in the words of Horacio Santiago-Otero, who also finds not a little Apollinarianism in Hugh's doctrine. Hugh agrees with the school of Laon and Augustine that Christ's human knowledge was exhaustive, and that He possessed it from the moment when the human Christ came into being. Hugh also agrees that the human Christ has a mode of knowing different from that of the Word. The Word is wisdom; the human Christ possesses wisdom. And, the human Christ obtains this wisdom by a participation of the divine wisdom in His mind. From Hugh's point of view, this participated knowledge is not identical with the knowledge enjoyed eternally by the Word, in that a process must occur in order for the human Christ to acquire it, even if that process is an instantaneous one. Equally, however, this theory, much as it may seek to preserve the distinction between creature and creator, goes even farther than the school of Laon in obliterating a human psychology in Christ and in overtaking His humanity by His divinity. The author of the *Summa sententiarum* follows Hugh in this teaching, although he is somewhat less participationist than Hugh.[89]

Judging from the position they take on the *gemina substantia* in the

---

Gibson (Turnhout: Brepols, 1992); also *PL* 113: 1246A; Anselm of Laon, *Sent. divine pagine*, p. 40; *Sentences of Probable Authenticity*, no. 150, 5: 114–16; *Sent. div.* 4.3.3–4, pp. 82*–86*; Roland of Bologna, *Sent.*, pp. 166–70; Anders, *Die Christologie*, pp. xxxviii–xliv; Horacio Santiago-Otero, "El conocimiento del alma de Cristo según las enseñanzas de Anselmo de Laon y de su escuela," *Salmanticenses* 13 (1966): 61–79; *El conocimiento*, pp. 33–56. Jean Châtillon, "Quidquid convenit filio dei per naturam convenit filio hominis per gratiam: A propos de Jean de Ripa, *Determinationes* I, 4, 4," *Divinitas* 11 (1967): 715–28, has tracked the fortunes of this formula in this period.

[88] Santiago-Otero, *El conocimiento*, pp. 18–19, 138–77.

[89] Hugh of St. Victor, *De sac.* 2.1.6, *PL* 176: 283C–284B; *Summa sent.* 1.16, *PL*

person of the incarnate Christ, departing thereby from Gilbert of Poitiers, it may not be very much of a surprise to find that the early Porretans, in their effort to moderate Hugh's position and to strike a balance between it and that of Walter of Mortagne, do not prove to be very successful. They accord to Christ's human intelligence a knowledge of its own, distinguishable from the divine wisdom possessed by the Word. At the same time, they argue that Christ's human knowledge was infinite, perfect, and thus the equivalent of what the Word knows. The way they try to frame this distinction is to say that, although created, the mind of the human Christ possesses a representative, adequate understanding corresponding to the divine knowledge, which enables it to function as omniscient, even though it is not divine. As an effort at compromise, this account clearly cedes the ground to the maximalists.[90]

Equally unsurprising is the fact that the knowledge of the human Christ is a subject on which Robert Pullen has a hard time making up his mind. His handling of this topic is an acute example of his tendency to lay out all the alternatives and to make heavy weather out of taking a stand. The result is extreme inconsistency. To be sure, he says, Christ took on humanity and He was like us in all but sin. Yet, Robert finds it incredible (*incredibile*) that the human Christ should have had to undergo a learning process, over the course of time, the way that other human beings do. But, equally, he sees it as *incredibile* that the human Christ should have had a fullness of divine knowledge, beyond what other men have and beyond what human beings need. Robert feels that the safest course is to go back to the position of the school of Laon, thus, in effect, cancelling out the last few decades of discussion. He agrees that the human Christ knew everything, from the moment of the incarnation, although He displayed that knowledge gradually. Robert distinguishes here between His physical growth and development over time and the instantaneous nature of His acquisition of knowledge. Since Christ lacked original sin, He lacked ignorance, Robert notes, while also failing to observe that this would have given the human Christ the mental aptitudes of prelapsarian man, and no

---

176: 72C–75A; Horacio Santiago-Otero, "La actividad sapiencial de Cristo en cuanto hombre en la 'Suma de las sentencias'," *Revista española de teología* 28 (1968): 77–91; "La sabiduría del alma de Cristo según Hugo de San Víctor," *RTAM* 34 (1967): 131–58; *El conocimiento*, pp. 81–99, 102–15, 118–21; "'Esse est habere' en Hugo de San Víctor," in *L'Homme et son univers au moyen âge*, ed. Christian Wenin (Louvain-la-Neuve: Institut d'Études Médiévales, 1986), 1: 426–31.

[90] *Sent. mag. Gisleherti* I 3.31 35, pp. 129–30; this text is not cited by Santiago-Otero, *El conocimiento*, pp. 19, 183–99, in his treatment of the Porretans.

more. Christ received a plenary infusion of divine knowledge, which, for Robert, can be compared with the capacity to perform miracles, which He also received. This knowledge does not make the human Christ divine, he asserts, since it was received by grace, not possessed by nature. Here, in making this comparison, Robert does not indicate whether he thinks that Christ's miracles stem from the exercise of His divine nature or from a special gift granted to His human nature. None the less, while advancing this claim, Robert also states that Christ did not know everything. He was, to be sure, full of grace and truth, but in the sense that, what He knew, He knew exhaustively, not in the sense of omniscience.[91]

The Lombard on Christ's Human Knowledge

In relation to these debates, and for all his insistence on the full humanity and creaturely status of the human Christ, Peter Lombard also ends by aligning himself with an only slightly modified version of the Laon masters' treatment of Christ's human knowledge. The participationist aspect of Hugh of St. Victor's position clearly does not appeal to him. Peter agrees that the human Christ enjoys a fullness of grace and wisdom from the moment of His conception. This created wisdom never grows, just as the uncreated wisdom of the Word never grows. Peter subscribes to the distinction between grace and nature as modes of knowledge in the human and divine natures of Christ, respectively, and also to the idea that the created wisdom possessed by the human Christ as a gift of grace transcends what other human beings can know. The human Christ, for him, did know everything that God knows. But, and here is Peter's one concession to the minimalist position, not with the same clarity and precision. The human Christ knows the same things, but less exhaustively and with less penetration than God knows them. And, He did not have all of God's power, so that He could have not have translated all that He knew into fact. For example, the human Christ knew how the world was created, but He could not have created it Himself. As to why the human Christ received more knowledge than power, Peter replies, somewhat unsatisfactorily, that He was naturally capable (*naturaliter capax*) of the knowledge, but not of the power.[92] In any event, and notwithstanding

---

[91] Robert Pullen, *Sent.* 3.21–24, 3.27–30, 4.5, *PL* 186: 793A–797C, 800C–806A, 810C–811A; Santiago-Otero, *El conocimiento*, pp. 204–26.
[92] Peter Lombard, *Sent.* 3. d. 13. c. 2–d. 14. c. 2, 2: 84–91; the quotation is at d.

other aspects of his Christology, Peter is thus willing to deny to the human Christ a fully human psychology of knowledge.

OTHER ATTRIBUTES OF CHRIST'S HUMANITY

This unsymmetrical distinction between the human Christ's fullness of knowledge and the limits of His power, or His human weaknesses, is one that Peter joins other theologians of the day in following. There is general agreement, in this period, that Christ took on some of the consequences of original sin, such as mortality, the capacity to suffer hunger and thirst, to feel affection, and to feel fear, especially the filial fear of God that is a virtue. Contemporaries likewise agreed that Christ underwent a normal gestation in the womb and a normal physical development from infancy to childhood. In these areas, the Lombard shares the current consensus and adds only a few touches of his own to it.[93] He supports the position that Christ suffered weaknesses of both body and soul, voluntarily and not by nature or as a consequence of sin. At the same time, in handling this topic, he makes the point, inherited from Augustine, that sensation derives not from the body but from the mind, and also that the mind uses the body as an instrument (*Omnis autem sensus animae est: non enim caro sentit, sed anima utens corpore velut instrumento*).[94] This observation is not entirely of a piece with Peter's treatment of human nature as an integral unit of body and soul in Book 2 of the *Sentences*. Here, in the effort to root the essence of moral choice in the mind, he imports a Stoic-Platonic view of man's nature into the account, which is quite atypical of his anthropology. In any event, Peter adds that, while Christ took on some human weaknesses that were expedient for Him to have and that did not derogate from His dignity or the efficacy of His mission, He did not take on all the human weaknesses that fall to mankind as a consequence of sin. This is the reason why Christ did not take on ignorance or concupiscence, both of which, Peter argues, would have impeded His mission. In these two respects, as well as with respect to His knowledge, Christ was not

---

14. c. 2.1, p. 91; Horacio Santiago-Otero, "Pedro Lombardo: Su tesis, acerca del saber de Cristo hombre," in *Miscelánea José Zunzunegui (1911–1974)* (Vitoria: Editorial Eset, 1975), 1: 115–25.

[93] Landgraf, *Dogmengeschichte*, 2 part 2: 266 ff.; Ott, *Die theologische Briefliteratur*, pp. 218–34, 400–01.

[94] Peter Lombard, *Sent.* 3. d. 15. c. 1.1–c. 2, d. 16. c. 1, 2· 93 ·100, 103–04. The quotation is at c. 1.2, p. 93.

like us in all but sin. As for those weaknesses which Christ did accept as critical to His mission, such as the capacity to suffer and the capacity to experience temptation so that He would be able to empathize with men, Peter thinks that He did not feel these things in the same way that men do, in that He lacked the weakened will and clouded knowledge with which men have to come to grips with their afflictions and temptations. In this respect, while men undergo temptation (*passio*) and contemplation of the temptation (*propassio*) prior to the consent (*consensus*) which is of the essence in their moral decisions, Christ only experienced the *propassio* and the *consensus.* He was not subject to *passio* as a necessity of His nature, as men are. In these respects, as well, Christ is not like us in all but sin: His moral psychology no less than His psychology of knowledge differs from that of other human beings.[95] While, in this section of his Christology, Peter feels impelled to reject flat out the claim of Hilary of Poitiers that Christ was incapable of suffering,[96] his own handling of Christ's human weaknesses does exempt Him from full participation in the human condition. As Peter sums up this point, because Christ came to save all mankind, He accepted something from all phases of human experience, before sin and after sin, before grace and under grace, as well as in glory. From prelapsarian man he took the lack of human weakness that inclines man more to evil than to good. From man in his fallen state, Christ took on the punishment for sin and those other weaknesses of fallen humanity not demeaning to Him or obstructive in His mission. From man in the state of grace, He took on a fullness of grace. And, from man in the state of glory, He took on, in His resurrection, the *non posse peccare* and the perfect contemplation of God that characterize the saints in the life to come. Thus, the human Christ possesses both the goods of the *patria* and the goods and evils of the *via.*[97]

This last point reflects another current debate, the question of whether the human Christ during His earthly life had the *non posse peccare* or, alternatively, the *posse peccare et non peccare* of prelapsarian man, or some other range of moral possibilities.[98] Some thinkers during this period extended to the human Christ during His earthly life the *non posse peccare* which, more typically, was granted by the theologians only to the deity, or to the saints in Heaven. The

[95] Ibid., c. 2.1–2, 2: 98–99.
[96] Ibid., c. 3, 2: 100–02.
[97] Ibid., d. 16. c. 2, 2: 105.
[98] See Landgraf, *Dogmengeschichte*, 2 part 1: 320–53.

masters taking the most extreme line on this question are the Porretans and Robert Pullen, who agree that Christ had the incapacity to sin. He had, to be sure, free will. Yet, on the analogy of the angels confirmed in the good by grace, He had the *non posse peccare*.[99] As we have seen above,[100] not all theologians thought it was appropriate to attribute the state of *non posse peccare* to the angels, Peter Lombard included. That problem aside, it was more usual, in this period, to grant, at least potentially, a greater capacity to sin to the human Christ than that accorded by the Porretans and Robert Pullen. William of Champeaux and other members of the school of Laon offer a formula here that many found persuasive. According to them, Christ in His human nature had the capacity to sin. But, the presence of the divine nature in Him conformed the human to the divine will, confirmed Him in virtue, and assured that He would not sin, by grace, to be sure, not by nature.[101] The author of the *Sententiae divinitatis* agrees with this view, although he nuances it. In his estimation, Christ accepted the possibility of sin by will, not by nature. In practice, Christ's human and divine wills were functionally joined "by habit and participation" (*per habitum et participationum*), so that, in the event, He did not sin.[102] These formulations suggest how easily a support for the *assumptus homo* and subsistence theories of the hypostatic union could inform a view of Christ's free will in action that is functionally Monothelite.

On the other side of the debate stood Peter Abelard. Abelard begins by arguing strongly for the principle of Christ's free will as a man. He objects to the idea that Christ possessed this faculty but never exercised it, out of a gift of grace. For, if such were the case, a divine psychology would have replaced a human psychology in the incarnate Christ. Abelard thinks that Christ did indeed have a fully human psychology. He hopes to shed light on this point by recasting it in terms of the distinction between possibility and necessity. From this perspective, the human Christ had the capacity to sin and not to sin. But this capacity was suspended after He was united and while He remained united with the Word (*non tamen postquam unitus vel unitum est*). Just as when a natural necessity follows from a contingent action which sets a chain of cause and effect in motion, so, once the human Christ has been united with the Word, it is

---

[99] *Sent. mag. Gisleberti* I 3.22–23, p. 127.

[100] See above, chapter 6, pp. 344–46.

[101] *Sentences of Plausible Authenticity*, no. 185–87; *Sentences of William of Champeaux*, no. 363–64, 5: 129–30, 213–14.

[102] *Sent. div*, 4 3.9, pp. 91*–94*. The quotation is on p. 94*.

impossible for the divine-human Christ to sin in any way (*modibus omnibus impossibile peccans*).[103] This pretended solution is actually no solution at all. While ostensibly trying to defend the free will of the human Christ, Abelard ends by denying it functionally in just as strong a sense as William of Champeaux, the author of the *Sententiae divinitatis*, the Porretans, and Robert Pullen. Further, by claiming that this free will was an option prior to the incarnation but not afterwards, he opens himself to the charge of Adoptionism.

Hugh of St. Victor takes another line of attack, and one equally problematic. On the one hand, he urges that the human Christ had the same capacity to sin, or not to sin, as Adam enjoyed before the fall. On the other hand, Hugh says that Christ was morally unlike prelapsarian man, in that He possessed no vices and experienced no inordinate inclinations or temptations. As Hugh sees it, Christ's possession of all the virtues, all at once, on the model of His possession of all knowledge, precludes any moral decision-making on His part. It is difficult to see how this conclusion squares with Hugh's premise that He had the *posse peccare et non peccare* of Adam before the fall.[104]

The master who comes the closest to the position which the Lombard espouses, even though he follows Hugh with a good deal of fidelity on Christ's human knowledge, is the author of the *Summa sententiarum*. He accents, it must be said, even more thoroughly than Peter does, the creaturely status of the human Christ, and, with greater consistency, argues that He took on all our infirmities, ignorance excepted, apart from sin. This author does not make the distinction between expedient and demeaning infirmities. As he sees it, the human Christ had the *posse peccare*. He was capable of experiencing temptation. But, having the freedom to resist temptation, He did so. Thus, by His own act of will, assisted by grace, He brought His human will into perfect alignment with the will of God. This He could do without losing His status as a creature.[105]

Peter, in effect, seeks to split the difference between the *Summa sententiarum* and Hugh of St. Victor. With the former, he agrees that Christ had two wills, a human and a divine. Also, with the former and against thinkers seeking to assimilate the human to the divine

---

[103] Peter Abelard, *Commentaria in Epistolam Pauli ad Romanos* 3:4, ed. Eligius M. Buytaert, CCCM 11: 98–99; the quotations are on p. 99. Hermannus follows suit and does not resolve the problem either; see Neilsen, *Theology and Philosophy*, pp. 223–28.

[104] Hugh of St. Victor, *De sac.* 1.2.6, 2.1.7, *PL* 176: 383C, 389B–391C.

[105] *Summa sent.* 1.17–18, *PL* 176: 75A–78D.

will, he argues that the human will of Christ functions in the same
way as the wills of other human beings. At the same time, and here
he supports Hugh, he sees the human Christ as having been freed
from those consequences of original sin that impede or limit the free
exercise of the will in fallen man, adding, as we have seen, concupiscence to ignorance as consequences of sin that He does not
take on, and which therefore do not limit His use of free will.
Further, as we have noted above, he grants to the human Christ a
fullness of knowledge that has the effect of exempting Him from the
false judgments that might otherwise incline Him to consent to
inappropriate or false goods; and he exempts the human Christ
from *passio* in the psychogenesis of His moral choices. In this sense,
for Peter the human Christ does not suffer the experience of the
divided self. His will is not weakened; His flesh does not lust
against His spirit; and the eye of His intellect is not clouded.
According to Peter, the human Christ had the full power to choose
evils or lesser goods. Indeed, He did not shrink from accepting the
evils of physical suffering and death, because He judged them to be
compatible with rational goods. Thus, Christ always exercised His
human free will in perfect conformity with His divine will. He could
be tempted to do otherwise, *pace* Hugh; if not, His temptation by
the devil would have been meaningless. And, if not, it is impossible
to take seriously His prayer that the chalice might pass from Him,
along with His submission to the will of the Father. Peter concludes
his discussion of this point by citing a barrage of witnesses against
the heresies of Monophysitism and Monothelitism, to which his
reading of Damascene has sensitized him[106] and which he clearly
sees as a problem in the teaching of many of his own contemporaries on this subject. We can say here that, if Peter does not endow
the human Christ with a moral psychology that is entirely isometric
with that of other human beings, whether before or after the fall, he
comes a tiny bit closer to humanizing that psychology than is true
for most of the theologians of his time, even though he joins the
consensus, to a very great extent, in denying to the human Christ a
human epistemology. At the same time, it cannot be said that he
coordinates these two dimensions of his doctrine of Christ's human
nature very smoothly. For his human Christ has more than a lack of
ignorance induced by original sin; He has virtual omniscience.
How that latter state actually impinges on Christ's ethical decision-

---

[106] Peter Lombard, *Sent.* 3. d. 17, 2: 105–11. See also the references cited above,
nn. 94, 97.

making in practice is a topic which Peter does not address.

It is this impulse to dignify the human Christ, to endow Him with qualities not enjoyed by other men, to stress the exemptions from the consequences of original sin which He chose not to take on, so visible in mid-century treatments of Christ's human knowledge, His free will, and His capacity to sin, that serves as the backdrop for the change of mind Peter undergoes on the theme of *dulia* and *latria* as applied to the human Christ. On this question, early twelfth-century theologians were evenly divided, although, curiously enough, their breakdown on this subject has little to do with their position on omniscience or freedom from sin in the human Christ.[107] Peter gives a thorough review of the debate and the authorities who can be cited on both sides of it. In the *Sentences*, it is no longer just a question for him of whether the humanity of Christ, as such, deserves veneration or worship. While he retains a clear distinction between the creature and the creator here, he observes, on the *dulia* side of the question, that there are physical objects to which Christians rightly pay reverence, for their use in divine worship. He comes down on the side of *latria* for the human Christ, but not in an undifferentiated way. The contemporary theologian to whom he comes the closest here is Gilbert of Poitiers, in Gilbert's gloss on the Psalms. With Gilbert, he agrees that the human Christ deserves worship, but not the human Christ understood as separate from the Word or as assimilated by the Word. It is, rather, the human Christ, as human, and as united with the Word, Who should receive *latria*.[108] This formula seeks to strike a balance between the doctrine that the two natures of Christ are inseparable yet not to be confused, which Peter maintains in his treatment of the hypostatic union, on the one side, and his glorification of the human Christ during His human lifetime, on the other. This view he joins his contemporaries in supporting, although with more circumspection and with somewhat less unmodified enthusiasm than is the case with many other masters.

THE ATONEMENT: CONTEMPORARY DEBATES

If Peter's role in the discussion of the hypostatic union was to provide clarification, which most scholastics were able to put to use

---

[107] Landgraf, *Dogmengeschichte*, 2 part 2: 132–46, although he does not note the shift in the Lombard's position or his differences from the Porretans.

[108] Peter Lombard, *Sent.* 3. d. 9, 2: 68–71. Brady has tracked the reference to Gilbert's unpublished gloss in his note *ad loc.*, 2: 69.

as research on the subject continued, and if his role in the development of the doctrine of the human Christ was to support, without a
great deal of resistance, a consensus more impressed by His functional differences from than by His similarities with the rest of
mankind, his role in the debates surrounding the doctrine of the
atonement was to moderate the extreme positions taken on this
subject during his time and to offer an understanding of Christ's
saving work that is very much His own. The outlines of this
controversy, as they had been posed by other theologians when the
Lombard entered the field, had been laid down, initially, by proponents of the traditional view that Christ's saving work was to
liberate man from the devil, who had gained power over man with
the fall. The first major reaction against the "rights of the devil"
theory had come from Anselm of Canterbury, who offered an
alternative in his *Cur deus homo* which left the devil entirely out of
the account, in explaining how Christ had paid the debt owed by
man to God and how Christ had communicated the redemptive
effects of His action to man. Another alternative to the "rights of
the devil" theory which placed much more emphasis on the role of
Christ in altering man's attitudes and moral capacities was offered
by Peter Abelard. Abelard's view has much in common with the
doctrine of the redemption taught by Bernard of Clairvaux,
although neither of these thinkers appears to have been aware of
that fact. The range of opinions provided by theologians in the first
half of the twelfth century extended from the frank espousal of one
or another of these positions to a selective combination of ideas
taken from a number of them.[109] In this spectrum of views, Peter
can be classed as one of the eclectics, yet as one who adds a decisive
and original note to the mix of ideas on which he draws.

The "rights of the devil" position had the longest genealogy of
any of the views of the redemption taught in the twelfth century,
going back to the writings of Gregory the Great for its classic

---

[109] Good surveys are provided by J. Patout Burns, "The Concept of Satisfaction
in Medieval Redemption Theory," *Theological Studies* 36 (1975): 285–304; D. E. de
Clerck, "Droits du démon et nécessité de la rédemption: Les écoles d'Abélard et
de Pierre Lombard," *RTAM* 14 (1947): 132–64; "Le dogme de la rédemption de
Robert de Melun à Guillaume d'Auxerre," *RTAM* 14 (1947): 253–86; "Questions
de sotériologie médiévale," *RTAM* 13 (1946): 150–84; Landgraf, *Dogmengeschichte*,
2 part 2: 170–253; Jean Rivière, "Le dogme de la rédemption au XIIe siècle
d'après les dernières publications," *Revue du moyen âge latin* 2 (1946): 102–12,
219–30; "Le mérite du Christ d'après le magistère ordinaire de l'église, II: Époque
médiévale," *RSR* 22 (1948): 213–39; Jeffrey Burton Russell, *Lucifer: The Devil in the
Middle Ages* (Ithaca: Cornell University Press, 1984), pp. 104–06, 161–72, 176–91;
Sikes, *Peter Abailard*, pp. 82–94.

formulation. It had received considerable support in the interven-
ing centuries. At the beginning of the twelfth century, it found
defenders in the school of Laon, whose members are also a good
source for the differences of opinion among its supporters. The
basic scenario as envisioned by proponents of the "rights of the
devil" theory was that man, in succumbing to the external temptation of the devil in the fall, had voluntarily placed himself under the
devil's sway, withdrawing allegiance from God and granting it
instead to the devil. Having done so, man was no longer free. He
lacked the ability to override the devil's power. Hence, Christ, a
Christ possessing divine power, had to be sent, since no other man,
nor even an angel, would be strong enough to overcome the devil.
The way in which the situation of man, and Christ's rectification of
it, was envisioned by supporters of the "rights of the devil" theory
was in an entirely external, objectivist sense. Christ is not seen as
changing either God's attitude or man's. What He changes is the
outward circumstances in which man has placed himself through
sin by defeating the devil, understood as an external power extrinsic to man. Christ battles against the devil, wins, and liberates man
from the devil's political control, restoring man to his proper allegiance to God. The language typically used in the "rights of the
devil" scenario is that of political jurisdiction and military force.
The main difference of opinion found among supporters of this
theory has to do with whether the devil's power over fallen man,
which God tolerates, is just. Some hold that the devil's sway is
exercised justly (*recte*). Not only does he hold dominion over man,
he also holds a right (*ius*), owing to the fact that man gave himself
over to the devil freely.[110] Other members of the school of Laon who
adhere to the "rights of the devil" position, on the other hand,
maintain that the devil has no true rights. Vis-à-vis God, his rule
over man is not just because it is a usurpation of God's rights over
man. And, vis-à-vis man, the devil's rule is not just either because it
is grounded in fraud and deception. Thus, while the devil holds
power, he does so without rights.[111] Some authors in the school
nuance this point still farther, in arguing that the devil's rule is just
with respect to man but unjust with respect to God,[112] or that, while

---

[110] Anselm of Laon, *Sent. divine pagine*, pp. 41–42; *Sentences of Anselm of Laon*, no.
47–48, 54, 5: 44–47, 50–51.
[111] *Deus de cuius principio et fine tacetur*, pp. 266–68.
[112] *Sentences of William of Champeaux*, no. 253–58, *Sentences of the School of Laon*, no.
353–55, 5: 206–07, 209, 269–70.

it has been seized in an unjust manner, it is wielded justly over man because of man's consent to the devil's temptation in the fall.[113]

Although there are some Laon masters who give Anselm of Canterbury's doctrine of the atonement a hearing,[114] their basic stance is to defend one variant or another of the "rights of the devil" position against his vigorous criticism of it. Anselm begins his *Cur deus homo* by clearing the deck of objections, before developing his own theory.[115] He argues that God could not have sent an angel or a newly created sinless man to do the job, although he offers his own reasons for this claim. Man, he says, would naturally be inclined to worship and serve whoever redeemed him; and it would not be fitting for him to accord to a creature an honor belonging to God alone. Another objection he presents is the claim that, since God is omnipotent, He could have redeemed man purely out of His mercy, without requiring Christ's sacrifice on the cross. While acknowledging that God operates under no constraints, Anselm rejects this position as well on grounds of theological appropriateness. The argument from God's mercy, he says, is not fitting. For, in his estimation, it is fitting that satisfaction be made for man's sin. Some kind of *quid pro quo* for the offense to God's honor which sin represents is only fair, just, and reasonable, as he sees it. Anselm also offers a series of objections which he attacks as reflecting the Nestorian belief that Christ was not fully man, and that God would not lower Himself by taking on the weaknesses of human nature. Against these objections, he insists that Christ was fully human. The fall, he notes, occurred through an act of human free will; so must the redemption. Thus, Christ must be a man possessing free will. Further, redemption by a God-man does not lower God's divinity since it was accomplished by the human Christ. It is not unfitting for the Son of God to suffer, he adds, for Christ accepted His sufferings voluntarily. In any event, His consent to His sufferings is appropriate, given the fact that the mode of redemption selected by God was the most congruous way to achieve man's redemption. Anselm, finally, turns his fire against the "rights of the devil" theory. After outlining it and indicating his awareness of the fact that its proponents differ on the degree to

---

[113] *Sentences of the School of Laon*, no. 342, 5: 263.

[114] *Sentences of the School of Laon*, no. 343, 346, 349, 358, 5: 263–64, 265, 266, 271.

[115] Anselm of Canterbury, *Cur deus homo* 1.3–10 in *Opera*, ed. Franciscus Salesius Schmitt, 2 vols. (Stuttgart: F. Fromann, 1968), 1: 50–67. On the *Cur deus homo*, see Gillian R. Evans, *Anselm and Talking about God* (Oxford: Clarendon Press, 1978), pp. 126–71.

which the devil's sway can be seen as just, he observes that they all
concur in viewing the redemption in military and political terms:
Christ's role is to besiege and take the fort in which the devil keeps
man imprisoned, and to restore man to God's rightful authority.
Anselm's response to this theory is simply to reject it as irrelevant.
He agrees that God allows the devil to tempt man, a permission
that does not grant the devil any rights. For, in Anselm's view, to
assent that there can be any justice at all in the devil's actions
would be to imply that God has somehow entered into a compact
with the devil, which is an utterly unseemly idea to hold about the
deity.

Now, in turning to the exposition of his own positive substitute
for the positions he rejects, we should note that Anselm in no sense
plans to dispense with the idea of justice, or with a view of the
atonement that could be described as externalist or objective.
Rather, he changes the way in which he handles these principles.
Having shown that man needs redemption, since he cannot obtain
happiness, the end for which he was created, in the state of sin, and,
having shown that man cannot achieve this redemption on his own,
since nothing in his finite resources offers sufficient recompense to
God for the infinite offense of man's disobedience, infinite because
it was an offense against an infinite being, Anselm concludes that
the atonement requires a God-man, Who is the only kind of being
capable of supplying both a satisfaction acceptable to God and of
communicating the effects of that satisfaction to man. Sin, in itself,
consists in not rendering to God His due, a formula invoking the
legal maxim *suum quique tribuere* as the definition of justice.[116] For
Anselm, justice must be served; and Christ can serve it in offering
to God His voluntary and unmerited death on the cross. God is
repaid in accepting this offering, not on the analogy with a mone-
tary composition, but in terms of His honor. Anselm is sensitive to
the point that nothing man does can actually increase or diminish
God's honor, God being infinite. But the rendering of proper honor
to Him expresses a proper attitude in creatures, which contributes
to the wholeness and order of the universe.[117] This is the level on
which Anselm analyzes the objective side of the transaction, the
restoration of honor to God as the service of justice, which therefore
requires satisfaction as essential. Here, Christ mediates between

---

[116] Anselm, *Cur deus homo* 1.11, 1: 68–69. For the whole argument, see ibid.,
1.11–2.20, 1: 68–133.
[117] Ibid., 1.15, 1: 72–74.

man and God and rectifies man's position in God's eyes, now making man acceptable to God again.

Anselm is equally an objectivist when it comes to the transmission of the effects of Christ's saving work to mankind. As with other Christian theologians, he holds that Christ's passion was efficacious in that it was a punishment He accepted although it was unmerited, since Christ was exempted from original sin. In all other respects, Christ is like other men, a point which Anselm had emphasized against Nestorian-type accounts of the atonement. But, in his own account, he describes what is an external transaction, based on Christ's nature, both between Christ and God and between Christ and mankind. When Christ offers His unmerited sacrifice to God, He thereby earns a reward from God. But, being perfectly sinless Himself, He does not need this reward. So, He transfers it to mankind. The model Anselm invokes in describing this transfer is the giving or bequeathing of a gift or an inheritance to a kinsman. The beneficiary has done nothing to earn it. It is like a windfall, which alters his credit with God by canceling a debt which man hitherto had lacked the wherewithal to pay.[118] The key point to note here is that, for Anselm, the beneficiary has not himself been changed by the gift, existentially. He receives a good that is imputed to him as if he were better than he actually is. In this respect, Christ's redemption changes man's standing with God; it does not change man's inner life itself.

It is precisely this last point that provoked a reaction, which can be seen as much as a critique of the *Cur deus homo* as it is of the "rights of the devil" position, on the part of Abelard.[119] Abelard develops his doctrine of the atonement in his commentary on Romans. He offers a forthright attack on the "rights of the devil" theory. The devil, he asserts, has no rights. Further, and this

---

[118] Ibid., 2.19, 1: 130–31.

[119] Good accounts of Abelard's doctrine of the atonement, which correctly see it as more than merely exemplaristic but as also efficacious, include A. Victor Murray, *Abelard and St. Bernard: A Study in Twelfth-Century "Modernism"* (Manchester: Manchester University Press, 1967), pp. 117–39, who also notes the parallels between Abelard and Bernard here; Philip L. Quinn, "Abelard on Atonement: 'Nothing Unintelligible, Arbitrary, Illogical, or Immoral about It'," In *Reasoned Faith*, ed. Eleonore Stump (Ithaca: Cornell University Press, 1993), pp. 281–300; Sikes, *Peter Abailard*, pp. 69–99; Weingart, *The Logic of Divine Love*, passim and esp. pp. 121–40, 149–50, 164–65. Briefer but also useful accounts are found in Gillian R. Evans, *Anselm and a New Generation* (Oxford: Clarendon Press, 1980), pp. 164–65; Robert S. Franks, *The Work of Christ: A Historical Study of Christian Doctrine*, 2nd ed. (London: Thomas Nelson and Sons Ltd. 1962), pp. 142–49. David E. Luscombe, "St. Anselm and Abelard," *Anselm Studies* 1 (1983): 213–18 sees Abelard as closer to Anselm here than most scholars do.

against Anselm, Abelard states that God indeed does have the
power, and mercy, to forgive man's sin without sacrificing His Son
and killing an innocent person. The reason why God chose the
mode of redemption that He did choose, in Abelard's view, was not
because God needed to have His attitude toward man changed.
God's love for man is unfailing. What was needed was the alteration of man's attitude toward God. Christ accomplishes this
change, and He does so in two ways, according to Abelard. By his
condescension and by His teaching, in word and example, Christ
gives man a model to follow. And, secondly, by displaying the
depths of His love for man, Christ gives man the moral power to
turn around his own heart and to respond to the love which God
has given to him. Through His own love for man, Christ inspires
man's love for Him, and man's yearning for the divine grace He
proffers, which man now gratefully receives and with which he can
now collaborate, in the moral reclamation of himself in charity.
The love that man is now capable of receiving and giving exceeds
the wildest dreams of fallen man. Christ's loving sacrifice of Himself on the cross, which caps this teaching and example during His
lifetime, in this sense was just, for Abelard, "because, in inflaming
man's love for God He grants a gift greater than man had hoped
for" (*quia amplius in amorem accendit completum beneficium quam
sperandum*).[120] It is clear that in raising the issue of justice here,
Abelard is advocating a stress on intentionality designed to replace
legalism. There is no trace in his theory of the atonement of
satisfaction, God's honor, or His rightful jurisdiction, of the type
found both in the "rights of the devil" position and in Anselm's
argument. The conversion of man's heart away from the bad
intention of the sinner into the good intention required of the saved
is the work of Christ in the redemption. The devil, for Abelard,
never had any power over God's elect; but the elect still need to be
converted. And, by both Who He is and by what He does, Christ
makes effectual their salvation by energizing men morally and
psychologically, by liberating their power to love.

---

[120] Peter Abelard, *In Ep. ad Romanos* 3:26, CCCM 11: 114–18. The quotation is
on pp. 117–18. Abelard's position is reiterated by his disciples. See Hermannus,
Sent., pp. 102–5; *Ysagoge in theologiam*, ed. Artur Michael Landgraf in *Écrits théolo-
giques de l'école d'Abélard* (Louvain: Spicilegium Sacrum Lovaniense, 1934), pp.
158–61. For the school of Abelard on this doctrine, see David E. Luscombe, *The
School of Peter Abelard: The Influence of Abelard's Thought in the Early Scholastic Period*
(Cambridge: Cambridge University Press, 1969), pp. 158–64, 236–40; Neilsen,
Theology and Philosophy, pp. 231–34.

Although Abelard was his bête noire, Bernard of Clairvaux develops a doctrine of Christ's saving work that is extremely close to his, marked by a similar disinterest in the criteria of theological seemliness that govern Anselm's reasoning in the *Cur deus homo*. Bernard is likewise disinclined to view the redemption in political or military terms along the lines of the "rights of the devil" theory. Like Abelard, Bernard accents the efficacy of Christ's action in changing man's attitude and in releasing his capacity to love God.[121] At the same time, he retains the idea of the rights of the devil, while radically reinterpreting this notion. Bernard's position on the atonement has to be gathered from a number of his works, where it is brought in by way of advancing some other argument. These include his *De consideratione*, his writings promoting the new religious order of the Knights Templars, and his sermons on the Song of Songs. For Bernard, Christ does triumph over the devil. But He does so emotionally, not politically, militarily, or juridically, by emptying Himself, taking on human nature and human suffering. For Bernard, the most painful aspect of human suffering that Christ endured was not His physical agony on the cross, but the experience of rejection. By His willingness to accept these trials, which He undertakes in order to heighten His empathy with other men, Christ inspires man's love, exacting in return from man a debt which only love can repay (*Sane multam fatigationis assumpsit, quo multae dilectionis hominem debitorem tenerit*).[122] This love, which Christ makes possible for man, enables man to turn away from the attraction of sin. It is this internal proclivity toward sin and man's bondage to it that Bernard understands as the devil's sway. He internalizes completely his interpretation of the devil in this connection. As he sees it, man is liberated not from an external power but from slavery to his own vice and ignorance. And, it is the superior attractiveness of the loving and suffering Christ that serves as the corrective, in turning around man's heart. As Bernard

---

[121] For Bernard on the redemption, see Gillian R. Evans, "*Cur Deus Homo*: St. Bernard's Theology of the Redemption. A Contribution to the Contemporary Debate," *Studia Theologica* 36 (1982): 27–36; *The Mind of St. Bernard of Clairvaux* (Oxford: Clarendon Press, 1983), pp. 152–59; Franks, *The Work of Christ*, pp. 149–55, who note the similarities with Abelard. Jean-Marie Déchanet, "La christologie de S. Bernard," in *Saint Bernard théologien* (Rome: Tipografia Pio X, 1953), pp. 78–91, notes the parallels and yet treats Abelard as a pure exemplarist. J. Gottschick, "Studien zur Versöhnungslehre des Mittelalters," *Zeitschrift für Kirchengeschichte* 22 (1901): 384–429, sees Bernard's view as opposed to Abelard's.

[122] Bernard of Clairvaux, *Sermones super Cantica canticorum* 11.7, ed. J. Leclercq and H. M. Rochais in Bernard of Clairvaux *Opera*, vols. 1–2 (Roma: Editiones Cistercienses, 1957–58), 2: 58–59.

instructs his brethren in his Song of Songs allocutions, "Your affection for your Lord Jesus should be both tender and intimate, to oppose the sweet enticements of sensual life. Sweetness drives out sweetness as one nail drives out another."[123] This sweetness Bernard analogizes to a pleasing fragrance that is multiform, addressed to the psychological needs and responses of different sorts of men. Some are drawn by the memory of Christ's passion, some by the example of His virtue, some by His wisdom; each man receives the sweetness that will energize him.[124]

The framework in which Bernard sets this doctrine in his sermons on the Song of Songs is particularly well adapted to display his understanding of the subjective efficacy of Christ's saving work and its continuation in the inner life of the Christian, since the Song of Songs is a nuptial poem which he reads as a figurative statement about the relation of the soul with Christ. The text, for him, is an itinerary of the inner life, in which Christ is the bridegroom whose kiss, given to the bride in the opening passage, awakens the soul's love and helps the hearer to activate the redemptive love which Christ bestows, enabling the soul to move through the steps of conversion and penance to the stage of growing intimacy with God. It is not just the fact of His incarnation and suffering, but also the emotional initiative which He takes, that gives man the assurance he needs to make a loving response. Further, as the example of Christ as a sweet fragrance drawing each man according to his own spiritual disposition suggests, Bernard combines an objective as well as subjective view of Christ's saving work with the understanding that Christ operates in and through each man's emotions. Christ comes to man where and how man is, and loves each person according to his own longings and needs. This theory of the atonement is not only generic, it is also individualized. As with Abelard, Bernard clearly has no interest in satisfaction, the weighing of accounts, or God's honor. These categories are utterly irrelevant to his view of Christ's saving work. His closest bond with Abelard is the fact that each combines an objective and exemplary understanding of the redemption with a highly subjective mode of its

---

[123] Ibid., 20.3–4, trans. Kilian Walsh and Irene Edmonds, *On the Song of Songs*, 4 vols. (Spenser, MA/Kalamazoo, MI: Cistercian Publications, 1971–80), 1: 150. The Latin text at 1: 117, reads: "Sit suavis et dulcis affectui tuo Domino Jesus, contra male utique dulces vitae carnalis illecebras, et vincat dulcedo dulc linum, quemadmodum clavum clavis expellit."

[124] Bernard of Clairvaux, *Sermones super Cantica* 2.6, 2.9, 6.3–4, 11.7.20, 20.2.3–4.5, 22.3.3–4.9, 1: 11–12, 13–14, 33–34, 58–59, 115–18, 133–36.

transferral to man, in which Christ efficaciously inflames the human heart and empowers it to love, and to love the good. It may be no accident that Bernard's image of sweetness driving out sweetness as one nail drives out another is an unacknowledged allusion to Cicero's *Tusculan Disputations*, where it speaks to erotic love, the context in which Abelard refers to the same citation in his fifth letter to Heloise, exhorting her to replace himself in her affections with the members of her monastic community.[125] The chief difference between Bernard and Abelard is Bernard's retention, if in drastically modified form, of the idea that Christ liberates man from the devil. But, as has been shown, for him this notion is purged of all externalism and militarism and it refers to man's internal, self-inflicted sin. The terrain where this liberation is effected is the inner life of man; and Bernard understands it primarily in terms of Christ's unshackling of man's affective faculty.

Faced with the alternatives presented by the "rights of the devil" theory, the *Cur deus homo*, and the sweeping rejection of both of these approaches to the redemption found in Bernard of Clairvaux and Abelard, the majority of theologians in the first half of the twelfth century responded not by aligning themselves with one or another of these positions exclusively but by effecting a combination of two of them. Exceptions to the rule are the author of the *Summa sententiarum*, who supports the "rights of the devil" argument without indicating that there is a debate, and the author of the *Sententiae divinitatis*, who follows Anselm in the same vein.[126] The more typical tendency toward a combination of theories cuts across the allegiances which a theologian might otherwise have felt to the master or masters whom he follows in other areas. For instance, despite his up-to-the-minute familiarity with the *Cur deus homo* argument, early in the century Honorius Augustodunensis freely combines it with the "rights of the devil" position. Declining to comment on whether the devil's power over man is just, he agrees that it exists, and argues that Christ's nature as a God-man and His unmerited suffering as a man are both required to enable Him to win victory over the devil as well as to offer a worthy satisfaction to God for man's sin.[127] The only point of his own that he adds to this combination is that both Jews and gentiles were involved in Christ's

---

[125] Cicero, *Tusc. disp.* 4.35.75. Cf. Peter Abelard, *Epistola* 5; the Ciceronian connection is noted by Betty Radice in her trans. of *The Letters of Abelard and Heloise* (Harmondsworth: Penguin Books, 1974), p. 159.

[126] *Summa sent.* 1.15, *PL* 176: 70B; *Sent. div.* 4.1.2, p. 72*.

[127] Honorius Augustodunensis, *Eluc.* 1.104–18, 1.141–53, pp. 380–82, 387–89.

death, because He died to redeem both groups of people.[128] A more influential exponent of the mixture between the Anselmian and the "rights of the devil" theories is Hugh of St. Victor. For Hugh, Christ's work of redemption is to make an adequate satisfaction for man's sin, and thereby to change God's attitude by calming His anger toward man. At the same time, Christ liberates man from the devil's unjust and usurped power.[129] Hugh stages the anti-devil scenario in two ways. In the prologue to Book 2 of *De sacramentis*, he uses the military language traditional to this position. He envisions Christ as a princely commander, going forth into battle with His saints arrayed in His host and fighting under His banner, and the sacraments of the church as His weapons.[130] In the body of Book 1, Hugh agrees that the devil's power is unjust vis-à-vis God, since it is a usurpation. From the devil's point of view, his power over man is just since man ceded to him voluntarily; from man's point of view it is unjust, since the devil defrauded man. In any event, man cannot terminate this situation by himself and needs an advocate (*patronus*). Shifting from military to forensic language here, Hugh portrays Christ as pleading man's case with God, persuading God to turn aside His wrath and to entertain the idea of man's redemption. Having succeeded in that plea, Christ next functions as the unmerited sacrifice that is fully compensatory in repaying God for the injustice done to Him. The one new twist added by Hugh is this: once God welcomes man back, man can simply pick up and leave the devil behind. The devil's power, as Hugh sees it, is exercised by default. Once the divine alternative is made available to man again, the devil's power evaporates on the spot.[131]

Another possible combination was to mix the "rights of the devil" position with an Abelardian or Bernardine doctrine of the atonement. Roland of Bologna and Robert of Melun take this tack. They agree that the devil holds sway over man, although unjustly, internalizing the character of that power. And, they also agree that

---

[128] Ibid., 1.158, p. 389.
[129] Good accounts which, however, do not note the modes in which Hugh presents the "rights of the devil" argument, are Franks, *The Work of Christ*, pp. 159–67; and Gottschick, "Versöhnungslehre," pp. 429–36. See also Roger Baron, ed., "*Tractatus de trinitate et de reparationis hominis* du MS. Douai 365," *Mélanges de science religieuse* 18 (1961): 111–12, 115–16; Poppenberg, *Die Christologie*, pp. 7–19.
[130] Hugh of St. Victor, *On the Sacraments of the Christian Faith* prologue 2, trans. Roy J. Deferrari (Cambridge, MA: Medieval Academy of America, 1951), p. 3. This passage is drawn from the edition on which Deferrari bases his translation, which does not occur in the Migne ed.
[131] Hugh of St. Victor, *De sac.* 1.8.4, 1.8.6–10, *PL* 176: 307D–309C, 310D–312A. The quotation of at 1.8.4, 308B.

Christ's role is to activate man's power to love, changing man's mind so that he looks in the right direction for the good and empowering his heart so that he desires it.[132] Easily the most eclectic of the mid-century theologians on this subject is Robert Pullen, who draws on both the mixture of Anselm and the "rights of the devil" view as found in Hugh and on the Abelardian or Bernardine argument. Agreeing with Hugh, he sees Christ both as a mediator, engaged in changing God's mind, and as the giver of an acceptable gift, in His own obedience, which satisfies God. Robert likewise sees man as a captive held unjustly. His new angle on the theme of the liberation of man from the devil is that it is God the Father Who performs this function; the Father and Son agree to a division of labor here. Robert adds that, although God is in no sense constrained in so doing, He effects this liberation by the sacrifice of His Son, reverting here to the more standard assignment of duties. This mode of redemption was chosen by God, according to Robert, in order to stimulate man's love and to instruct man. As for the transmission of Christ's saving work, Robert departs from the Anselmian idea of imputation. Just as Christ changes God's mind in the initial phase of the story, so He changes man's mind and heart. Christ enables man to win redemption, by giving him the faith that works in love, and by enabling him to love, and thus to collaborate with God's grace and to earn merit.[133]

The Lombard's Doctrine of the Atonement

Peter Lombard's treatment of Christ's saving work is even more broad-gauged than that of Robert Pullen. Like Bernard of Clairvaux, to whom he is deeply indebted, he retains the notion of the rights of the devil while radically internalizing his understanding of that doctrine. He agrees with Bernard, Abelard, Roland, and Robert of Melun in seeing the subjective change brought about by Christ in man's mind and heart as the manner in which His redemptive work is communicated to man and made efficacious in man. While Peter certainly can be positioned clearly in relation to these contemporary thinkers, he also draws heavily on his own

---

[132] Roland of Bologna, *Sent.*, pp. 157–62; Anders, *Die Christologie*, pp. xx–xxxv; Clerck, "Le dogme de la rédemption," pp. 253–67.
[133] Robert Pullen, *Sent.* 4.13–15. *PL* 186: 820B–822D. Gottschick, "Versöhnungslehre," pp. 436–38 sees Robert's position as primarily Abelardian.

commentary on the Pauline epistles, notably his gloss on Hebrews 1:11–18 but even more on his gloss on Romans 8:10. Indeed, this segment of Peter's Christology offers an extended example of the creative interplay between his exegesis and his systematic theology, as we have also noted in chapter 4 above, for we see both a carryover of ideas found in his Pauline commentaries and a departure from them as well. The departures are most noticeable in Peter's treatment of the devil, in his understanding of the theme of justice, and in his increasingly critical stance toward Anselm of Canterbury in his most mature work.

It will be recalled that, as an exegete of Paul, Peter had been both a supporter of the "rights of the devil" theory and of some features of Anselm's doctrine.[134] As he explains in his Romans gloss, God could have saved man some other way, since He is omnipotent; but He ordained the incarnation and passion of Christ as the most suitable way. This is because one of the effects of the fall is that man can grasp both the hopelessness of his situation and the fact that he is fully responsible for it. He has lost the eternal life he desires and he is frustrated by his futile attempts to possess it. This, according to Peter, is why Christ must be a God-man. Since He is the Son of God, He is immortal. He can therefore free man from mortality and hence from his frustration and despair. Christ's saving work thus has a subjective dimension, in Peter's Romans gloss, as well as an objective one. This is true of the effects of Christ's actions in the hearts of men. It is also true of Christ's liberation of man from the devil, whom Peter still sees here as an external power. He agrees with those who hold that the devil's power is an unjust usurpation of God's legitimate authority. The devil himself rules man by brute force. If He had so wished, God could have overcome the devil by an act of violence of His own, since He is more powerful than the devil. But God does not want to counter violence with violence. Rather, He wants to oppose the injustice of the devil with divine justice. At this juncture, Peter incorporates Anselm's analysis into his gloss. Since Christ is wholly blameless as a man, His unmerited death on the cross is a just recompense to God for man's sin. At the same time, Christ's justice in this connection plays an exemplary role for man. He serves as a

---

[134] See above, chapter 4, pp. 217–20. The rights of the devil, in this case seen as the "princeps regionis illius dissimilitudinis," are also noted by Peter in *Sermo de adventu domini*, ed. Damien Van den Eynde, "Deux sermons inédits de Pierre Lombard," in *Misc. Lomb.*, p. 78.

moral example for man, offering a behavioral model that God wants man to imitate, by following the path of justice, not violence, in his own moral life. In this connection, as well, Christ must be both God and man. His divinity is the guarantee of His ability to offer an infinitely worthy gift to God, a gift certain of acceptance by the Father, Who is already bound to the Son in love. Christ must also be a man, otherwise he could not have been put to death. As with Anselm, in the Romans gloss Peter views Christ as transferring to man the immortality that He has won for man by imputation. Eternal life is His objective gift to man, and it is the meaning of His liberation of man from the devil, while His subjective gift is the substitution of hope for fallen man's despair and frustration.

In Peter's reworking of his doctrine of Christ's saving work in the *Sentences*, he continues to regard the atonement as having both an objective and a subjective dimension. At the same time, in the manner of Bernard of Clairvaux, he assimilates the externalist understanding of the rights of the devil into a thoroughly internalist account of the redemption as occurring entirely within man's soul.[135] He now grounds his doctrine of the redemption in his doctrine of Christ's human nature, and, in particular, in the principle that Christ possessed all the virtues. Christ had complete ethical merit because, in the exercise of His faculty of free will, and despite His capacity to be tempted, He brought His will into perfect conformity with the will of God at all times. This total obedience to the Father made the human Christ perfectly virtuous. Since He did not need anything for Himself, His merit allows Him to win redemption for mankind from the devil, from sin, and from punishment for sin. Christ's redemption means as well the opening of God's kingdom to man, the glorification of the body and the impassibility of the soul which He earned for Himself and made possible for man in the resurrection.[136] Here Peter emphasizes that the obedience and hence the merit of the human Christ was so exhaustive that it was fully present at all points during His earthly life. Christ was obedient to the Father not only in submitting to death on the cross but also in submitting to His conception and

---

[135] The appreciation of both of these dimensions is found in the balanced commentaries of Franks, *The Work of Christ*, pp. 167–76; Rivière, "Le mérite du Christ," pp. 234–35; Gottschick, "Versöhnungslehre," pp. 35–36. On the other hand, Landgraf, *Dogmengeschichte*, 2 part 2: 338 overemphasizes the objective aspect, while Fritz Bünger, "Darstellung und Würdigung der Lehre des Petrus Lombardus vom Werke Christus (Sentent. 1. III, dist. 18–20)," *Zeitschrift für wissenschaftliche Theologie* 45 (1902): 92–126 overemphasizes the subjective side.
[136] Peter Lombard, *Sent.* 3. d. 18. c. 1, 2: 111–12.

birth and throughout all the stages of His life on earth. In the
behavior He manifested at all times, the virtues and charisms were
perfect in Him to the full limits of the human condition; they could
not, at any time, have been improved on. This view is one that
Peter holds so strongly that it moves him to conclude that the
passion of Christ was not, for Him, a critical event in His relationship with God the Father. The passion simply afforded Him
another opportunity to display the perfect obedience that He had
always possessed. Qualitatively, the passion did not enlarge
Christ's merit. He may have merited more, in a quantitative sense,
because of His passion and crucifixion, but not better.[137]

Given this startling claim that Christ's crucifixion was not greater
in merit than the virtue He possessed throughout His life, Peter
has to address the question of why the passion was ordained, given
the fact that God could have effected man's redemption in some
other way. Here, he begins by making the point that Christ underwent the passion not for Himself but for mankind. His suffering and
death were meant to be a form and a cause, a form of virtue in man,
especially in the imitation of His paramount virtues of obedience
and humility, and a cause of liberty, beatitude, and glory. In a very
objectivist description of the redemption here, Peter states that
Christ earned paradise for man, in freeing him from sin, from
punishment, and from the devil, and in a more positive sense, in
creating the opportunity for men to become adopted sons of glory.
For this, is was necessary for Christ to be a man of the line of
Judah, consubstantial both with Adam and with the rest of the
human race. And, He must be the possessor of the most consummate humility, in order to counteract the consummate pride that
led to Adam's fall. Perfect humility cannot be shown more fully
than in the voluntary acceptance of undeserved suffering and
death. Here, Peter departs from Bernard's view that personal rejection was the most grievous suffering that Christ endured, adhering
to the more standard notion of the passion and crucifixion and
anchoring the point with Ambrosiaster, the author who, like everyone else at the time, he takes to be Ambrose. Still, like Bernard, he
sees pride as the quintessential sin and humility as its necessary
antidote, although in more specifically dogmatic terms.[138]

---

[137] Ibid., c. 2, c. 4, 2: 113–114, 115–116. This point is misinterpreted by
Gottschick, "Versöhnungslehre," p. 35, who overemphasizes the function of
Christ's death in Peter's soteriology.
[138] Peter Lombard, *Sent.* 3. d. 18. c. 5, 2: 116.

But how, then, do Christ's suffering and death, which He accepts thanks to His perfect humility, redeem mankind from sin, from punishment, and from the devil? It is instructive to note that, in addressing this question, Peter begins with man's subjective appropriation of the redemption. It is, indeed, the very conditions of man's subjective appropriation of the redemption that set the terms for Peter's description of Christ's objective nature and actions. By displaying His humility up to His death on the cross, Christ, although He does not enlarge His own merit thereby, shows forth His love for man in a manner so full of drama and pathos that He revolutionizes the human heart, inflaming in it a responding love of God, the God Who has offered this electrifying sacrifice for man's sake. As with Bernard of Clairvaux, Abelard, Roland, and Robert of Melun, Peter sees this love, both as extended to man and as responded to by man, as a force that changes man from within, energizing him and enabling him to reorder his own loves, to accept the grace of God, and to reorient himself, as justified, in charity to his fellow man: "Having shown, with regard to us, such an earnest of His own love, He both inflames us and moves us to the love of God, Who has done so such for us, and by this we are justified, that is, released from our sins; we are made just. The death of Christ thus justifies us, since through it charity is excited in our hearts" (*Exhibita autem tantae erga nos dilectionis arrha, et nos movemur accendimurque ad diligendum Deum, cui pro nobis tantum fecit; et per hoc iustificamur, id est soluti a peccati, iusti efficamur. Mors igitur Christi nos iustificat, dum per eam caritas excitatur in cordibus nostris*).[139] While the word *arrha* is evocative of Hugh of St. Victor in another context, we see Peter decisively departing from the Anselmian doctrine of imputation in favor of the more subjective understanding of Christ's effecting a change within man's soul itself, thanks to which man can now set foot on the positive path of moral growth that leads to glory.

It is with this interpretation of the redemption in mind that Peter addresses, and internalizes, the idea that Christ's passion liberates man from the devil. In agreement with Bernard of Clairvaux, he now sees the sway of the devil not as an external, political constraint but as nothing else than man's self-inflicted bondage to his own sin. The love that Christ inspires in the human heart enables man to turn away from sin, to resist temptation. Unlike Hugh of St. Victor, who holds that, once the divine alternative is tendered, the devil's power self-destructs, Peter argues that the devil will still be

---

[139] Ibid., d. 19, c. 1.2, 2: 118.

able to tempt redeemed and justified mankind. But, he stresses, it is the unimpeded and unopposed failure to love within the human heart that must be understood as the devil's power. The love that man now feels empowers him to shed the devil who resides within his own heart. The appropriation of Christ's saving work frees man from the pressure to consent to evil under which he suffered as fallen and unredeemed. Peter points out that this continuing ability to be tempted is a function of the *fomes peccati* which remains in man after the redemption, if in a milder form than before. He uses this analysis against authorities who support the idea that the devil is totally vanquished by the cross, such as Augustine with his pungent phrase about the cross as the devil's mousetrap, because he sees it as too external an understanding of the redemption, and also one that denies the continuing reality of temptation and backsliding in the moral lives of justified Christians.[140]

It is as a corollary of this account of man's subjective appropriation of redemption as the liberation from his own internal bondage to sin that Peter introduces the all-important point that Christ had to be a God-man in order to accomplish His saving work. Here, he brings in some of the argumentation of his *Collectanea* while handling the subject in a different way. Unless Christ were a man, Peter observes, He would not have been able to inspire the love that enables other men to overcome voluntarily the devil within their own psychology of sin. Anselm of Canterbury had made the point that, since the fall was voluntary, on man's part, Christ's acceptance of the suffering and death that corrects for it had to be voluntary as well. Peter turns this argument around. Because the fall was voluntary, on man's part, so his turning away from the devil within must also be voluntary, on man's part. God wants man to respond to the violence of the devil with justice, and this is what Christ's empowering love enables man to do. Peter resists any interpretation of this liberation that treats man as passive in the process, acted on by forces outside himself. Just as Christ must be a man in order to inspire the change of heart that makes possible the virtuous use of man's free will, so He must be God, in order that He Himself may be rendered free from sin. For Peter, Christ's sinlessness is important in this connection not because it enables Him to offer an acceptable gift, payment, or propitiatory sacrifice to the Father, sufficient to assuage God's wounded dignity. It is not necessary, in Peter's view, for Christ to change God's mind.

---

[140] Ibid., c. 1.3–4, 2: 119–20.

Rather, Christ's sinlessness is important because it is what enables Him to possess the perfect humility that is sufficient to overcome the pride causing man's fall and keeping man enslaved to the sins from which Christ's activating love redeems him.[141] For Peter, the redemption is as little a transaction between Christ and God the Father as it is a battle between Christ and the devil, seen as external forces. It is, instead, an interaction between Christ and mankind, which takes place entirely within the ground of the individual human soul.

Having explained the sense in which he holds that Christ redeems man from sin and the devil, Peter turns to the question of how Christ redeems man from the punishment and guilt which original sin incurred. There are two kinds of punishment involved, he observes, eternal and temporal. We are released from eternal punishment and from guilt absolutely, and are granted immortality, he states. But we are released from temporal punishment only partially, for the physical and spiritual weaknesses deriving from original sin remain part of the human condition. At the same time, he argues, there is a real if not a total release here in that these weaknesses no longer have to dominate man's moral life as they do before the redemption. In explaining how Christ achieves these forms of release, Peter again offers a balance between the objective and subjective approaches to the atonement. Christ releases us by meriting, for man, the lifting of punishment and guilt, through His own acceptance of a punishment which He did not deserve. At the same time, Christ makes this release efficacious in the human soul. Our punishment abates when we feel, in an operational sense, the love of Christ that leads to our conversion, baptism, and penance. Christ is thus properly called the redeemer, Peter observes, both in His exercise of the divine power and in the subjective effects which His humility produces in man, as well as through the efficacy which He grants to His sacraments, which in turn are causes of man's redemption in the Christian life.[142] For Peter, the accent is as much on Christ's operations as on His nature, and His operations are seen as both exemplary and efficacious in man. This whole section of his account of the redemption can be read as an extended critique of Anselm's view of Christ's merits being imputed to men,

---

[141] Ibid., c. 2, 2: 120–21. This stress on Christ's humility is also found in the Lombard's sermons. See, for instance, *Sermo de Ascensione*, ed. Damien Van den Eynde, "Deux sermons inédits de Pierre Lombard," in *Misc. Lomb.*, p. 83. This point is also noted by Longère, *Oeuvres oratoires*, 1: 85–86.

[142] Peter Lombard, *Sent.* 3. d. 19. c. 3–c. 5, 2: 121–22.

who are thereby given a status they have not earned but without
being changed in the process. Instead, with Bernard and Abelard
and the theologians whom they influenced, he holds that Christ's
merits accomplish a psychic and moral change in man, a change
that now enables him to earn his own merit, in collaboration with
God's grace.

Peter rings yet another change on a standard description of the
work of Christ as interpreted by Anselm. Christ can, he agrees, be
regarded as a mediator between God and man, but not in the sense
of an advocate or negotiator arguing man's case with a God whose
mind Christ wants to change. Rather, Christ mediates in the sense
that He acts as a catalyst or facilitator, removing the obstacles
between man and God that have made man an enemy of God, so
that man can now return to God in loving friendship. God has no
need of this mediation, for His love is constant. It is man who
stands in need of the unblocking of his power to love which the
work of Christ achieves.[143]

Like other contemporary theologians, Peter raises the question of
whether there could have been another mode of redemption; and,
like them, he holds that one must answer in the affirmative, since
God is omnipotent, but also that the mode He did choose was the
most suitable. His own handling of this question makes use of some
of the reasoning in his Romans gloss, in responding to the point
that the chosen mode was the most suitable one. The union of God
and man in Christ, His combination of divine immortality and
heart-wrenching humanity, cures mankind of desperation, substituting hope for sinful man's frustrated yearning for eternal life.
Peter is well aware of the extensive tradition supporting the exter-
nalistic "rights of the devil" position and outlines it *in extenso* here,
insisting that the authorities have to be read in the internalist and
nonlegalistic manner in which he interprets the redemption. It is
the justice of Christ's humility that liberates man, he stresses, and
not justice in the sense invoked either by the partisans of the "rights
of the devil" or by Anselm.[144] This being the case, and along with
the sharply restricted understanding of what "the devil" means in
this context, he agrees that there are three parties in the scenario,
God, man, and the devil. The devil is convicted of injury against
God, because he fraudulently abducted man, God's servant, and
violently held him. Man is convicted of injury against God because

---

[143] Ibid., c. 6–c. 7, 2: 122–24.
[144] Ibid., d. 20. c. 2.2–c. 3.2, 2: 125–27.

he repudiated God and gave himself over to another lord. This human injury can also be charged to the devil's account since it was he who deceived man with fallacious promises, and afterwards, afflicted man. With respect to himself, the devil holds man unjustly; with respect to man, his sway is just, because man, through his own fault, deserves the sufferings he receives at the devil's hands. Now, God, had He willed it, could have resolved this situation by fiat. But, for the reason given above, He wished to use the justice of humility instead.[145] This passage is a reminder of how important it is to read the Lombard on the devil in context. If one were not aware of His radical internalizing and psychologizing of the devil along Bernardine lines, one might think that the analysis just given places Peter in alignment with the school of Laon and with the traditional authorities whom he subjects to such forcible reinterpretation on that point. For, given the way in which he does understand the devil, not to mention the psychogenesis of sin, the three parties in the scenario he describes can actually be reduced to two, God and two dimensions or consequences of the divided self in man.

There are two other topics which Peter takes up in his consideration of Christ's saving work. One is a subject to which other theologians of the time advert, the question of who bears the responsibility for Christ's passion and crucifixion.[146] The position Peter takes, while aimed largely against Abelard's claim that the people who crucified Christ were not culpable because they did not regard the deed as the contravention of God's will, has a wider interest for its analysis of causation, no less than of intentionality. Who was responsible, Peter asks, God the Father? the whole Trinity? Judas? the Jews? Curiously, he omits the Romans, although the analysis he is about to offer would cover their case as well. In any event, he responds by distinguishing the senses in which we can talk about responsibility, in maintaining that all the parties he names are responsible in some way. Christ is responsible, in that He gave Himself up to suffering and death freely. The Father and, indeed, the whole Trinity, is also responsible, for ordaining this mode of redemption and for predestining the human Christ to be joined to the Word in order to carry it out. Judas brought about Christ's death by his betrayal, and so did the Jews, by instigating it. Had Peter included the Romans, he could have added that they

---

[145] Ibid., c. 4.1–2, 2: 127.
[146] On this subject, see the survey by Landgraf, *Dogmengeschichte*, 2 part 2: 329–58.

gave the order for the crucifixion and executed it. In discriminating among the roles and responsibilities of the persons he does include, Peter observes that Christ's own act was a good one, as were the acts of the other persons of the Trinity, for they were undertaken for the salvation of man. On the other hand, the acts of Judas and the Jews were evil, because they sprang from malicious intentions. Thus, although the same event is at issue, these different actions are really quite distinct with respect to it, because of the difference in intentionally which the persons in question brought to it. And, in the case of Christ and the Trinity, the persons involved functioned as a sufficient cause, while in the case of Judas and the Jews they functioned as an efficient cause, forms of causation which, as Peter notes, are not the same thing.[147]

Peter also brings up another question which is not found in many of the scholastic theologians of his time, under the heading of the merits of Christ. Christ merited, he states, the name above all names, the honorific title "God." This topic derives not from the controversies carried on by the summists and sentence collectors, but from Peter's own exegesis of Philippians 2:9 and that of Gilbert of Poitiers.[148] This is another good example of the positive interaction between Peter's Pauline commentaries and his systematic theology, not only as an index of what to say and which authorities to call upon but also of what questions to put into his doctrinal schema in the first place. The question is also a good example of the way Peter reconciles conflicting authorities, at least in cases where he thinks that it is possible to do so. The two competing authorities at issue here, Augustine and Ambrose, apparently disagree. Augustine says that the appropriate title to be given to the human Christ, by grace, is "Son of God." Ambrose says that the appropriate title to be given is "God." The two positions, Peter observes, are not incompatible. Ambrose was referring not to the humanity of Christ but to the divinity of Christ, which certainly merits the term "God" quite literally. For his part, Augustine was referring to the trope by which a thing is said to exist when it becomes known, as the resurrected Christ came to be known both by men and by other spiritual beings. Thus, the terms "God" and "Son of God" are both applied appositely, and honorifically, to the resurrected human Christ.[149]

---

[147] Peter Lombard, *Sent.* 3. d. 20. c. 5–c. 6, 2: 128–29.
[148] Noted by Brady *ad loc.*, 2: 114.
[149] Peter Lombard, *Sent.* 3. d. 18. c. 3, 2: 114–15.

Interesting as these last two points may be, it is not so much from the introduction of new questions or new distinctions that the Lombard's soteriology acquires its own personal character. Rather, what gives it its distinctiveness is his ability to bring together an objective understanding of the atonement based on Christ's nature and action with a subjective understanding of the atonement based on a psychological account of the existential change that Christ's actions, and the humility inspiring them, provoke in man. Just as the human Christ has to attain His own merit by the consistent, obedient functioning of a will that remains free, so human beings are made capable of liberation from their lesser selves by an enabling act on Christ's part that unleashes their love for the good and their capacity to exercise their own free will in pursuit of it in conjunction with God's grace, despite the remaining, if partial, weakness under which the human will must labor. Peter places the redemption of mankind by Christ on a trajectory that includes their justification, their sanctification, and their glorification. No doubt the single most striking feature of this Lombardian doctrine is his emphasis on Christ's perfect humility, as the sufficient corrective to the perfect pride that brought about the fall, a humility expressive of the consummate obedience manifested at all times during the earthly life of Christ, so that His crucifixion is rendered unnecessary, except for its unique power to provoke an emotional response from man. With Bernard of Clairvaux, Peter emphasizes the suffering of Christ more than His other deeds and experiences, and he does so more restrictively. On the other hand, the systematic account he takes of the "rights of the devil" theory, which we do not find in Bernard, has the effect of enabling Peter to marginalize that theory in scholastic theology after his time, in favor of a more internalist understanding of sin and redemption, and one that squares more neatly with the intentionalism of twelfth-century theology than its alternatives. If the "rights of the devil" model continued to appeal to the popular imagination and to medieval artists, being easier to visualize than the turning around of man's heart, the Lombard succeeded in bringing the latter view, which he shares with Bernard and Abelard, fully into the mainstream of scholastic analyses of Christ's saving work.

Peter's success in attaining his objectives in the other areas of Christology which he takes up in Book 3 of the *Sentences* is not always as striking. As the debates of his contemporaries and immediate successors indicate, it took some time for the lexical clarifications he imposed on terms such as substance, nature, and person, essential in the consideration of the hypostatic union, to sink in, and there remained thinkers who failed to take his point and who garbled what he had said, thanks to their own insensitivity to his terminology. And, no sooner had they been dismissed, when the reception of Aristotle provided theologians in the sequel with a larger and less ambiguous vocabulary of terms which they could apply to the understanding of that doctrine. Peter's account of the three opinions, and their problems, became a classic one, wherever these later theologians decided to plant their own standards. Peter's willingness to leave the question open and to admit the orthodoxy of the three opinions, despite their difficulties, stands as an object lesson of the advantages of viewing the orthodox consensus as a non-monolithic one. Peter's handling of the human Christ, reflective as it is of the growing interest which this subject was attracting in devotion and dogmatic theology alike, suffers from the twelfth century's unwillingness, and ultimately, the Lombard's own, to grant a truly human psychology to the human Christ. This problem emerges with particular acuteness in his discussions surrounding Christ's human knowledge, and it can also be seen in his consideration of His free will and His nature and functions as a moral agent. In part, the hard line that Peter takes on the transmission of original sin and Christ's exemption from it inclines him to agree with the picture of a quasi-superhuman Christ favored by his contemporaries. In part, he seems to be as inspired as they are by the devotional attractiveness of the humanity of Christ. While he does try to take a minimalist line in these debates, and to hedge his description of the honors, dignities, and exemptions of the human Christ with qualifications, in the end Peter's human Christ is no more a man like us in all but sin than theirs is. This conclusion is one that Peter does not avoid drawing despite the fact that it is at odds with the doctrine that neither of the two natures of the incarnate Christ was altered by their union, so central to his treatment of the communication of idioms in the incarnate Christ, and with the doctrine of the full consubstantiality of Christ with the rest of mankind, so central to his soteriology.